PATH THROUGH SCRIPTURE

NEW INTERACTIVE EDITION

RESOURCE MANUAL

MARK LINK, S.J.

Allen, Texas

IMPRIMI POTEST
Bradley M. Schaeffer, S.J.

NIHIL OBSTAT
Rev. Glenn D. Gardner, J.C.D.
Censor Librorum

IMPRIMATUR
† Most Rev. Charles V. Grahmann
Bishop of Dallas

August 8, 1995

The Nihil Obstat and Imprimatur are official declarations that the material reviewed is free of doctrinal or moral error. No implication is contained therein that those granting the Nihil Obstat and Imprimatur agree with the contents, opinions, or statements expressed.

ACKNOWLEDGMENTS

Unless otherwise noted, all Scripture quotations are from Today's English Version text. Copyright © American Bible Society 1966, 1971, 1976, 1992. Used by permission.

"Lincoln's Dream" from *The Day Lincoln Was Shot* by Jim Bishop. Copyright © 1955 by Jim Bishop. Copyright renewed 1983 by Jim Bishop. New York: HarperCollins Publishers, Inc.

Excerpts from "Peter, Me, and Mary" by Bob Combs and Scott Ross, *Campus Life* (May 1972). Reprinted by permission of Pearl Combs.

Excerpts from "Reflections from Prison" by John Dear, S.J., *National Jesuit News* (February 1944). Reprinted by permission of U.S. Jesuit Conference.

Letter to the students of a Catholic high school regarding their son's suicide, reprinted by permission of Mr. and Mrs. John Monlezun.

Send all inquiries to:
Tabor Publishing
200 East Bethany Drive
Allen, Texas 75002–3804

Toll free 800-822-6701
Fax 800-688-8356

Printed in the United States of America

ISBN 0–7829–0471–8 (Resource Manual)

ISBN 0–7829–0470–X (Student Text)

2 3 4 5 6 00 99 98 97 96

ABOUT THIS MANUAL

This resource manual has a complete lesson plan for each of the 115 lessons in the textbook. Each plan contains five parts:

1. LESSON BACKGROUND

This section gives references to the *Catechism of the Catholic Church* that relate to the lesson.

2. LESSON QUIZ

This section provides teachers with three questions for evaluating the students' grasp of the informational content of the lesson. Each quiz follows the same threefold format:

Question 1 *reviews* some point from the content of the previous lesson.

Question 2 *reviews* some notebook entry that students were instructed to make during the presentation of the previous lesson.

Question 3 *previews* (tests) whether the students read and understood the content of the reading assignment covering the new lesson.

Teachers should consider having the students exchange quizzes and grade them immediately. This gives them the correct answers while the questions are still fresh in their minds.

Keep a record of the points each student earns in each quiz and total them into a single grade at the end of each chapter. This motivates the students to keep up with the material and to improve their point total as the chapter progresses.

3. LESSON HOMEWORK

This section provides teachers with practical reminders concerning student homework.

Return	previous homework.
Collect	current homework.
Read	upcoming lesson.
Write	answers to review questions for upcoming lesson (lower corner of right-hand page).
Appoint	individual students to prepare readings of Bible passages referred to in interactive section, as needed.

N.B.: The author did not grade the written homework assignments. He merely indicated with a check in his gradebook that the student had done the assignment satisfactorily.

The author did, however, write notes on many of the homework papers: for example, "Good!" "Not quite right!" "Keep up the good work!" It is amazing how the practice of putting notes on the homework improves the quality of subsequent written homework.

4. LESSON PRESENTATION

This section presents points that develop the informational (mind) level of the lesson.

5. LESSON INTERACTION

This section contains exercises that develop (a) the formational (value) level and (b) the transformational (faith) level of the lesson.

STUDENT MATERIALS

1. *Path through Scripture: New Interactive Edition*
2. Notebook (standard three-ring binder) so that students can reinsert homework and quizzes for future reference.

CLASSROOM MATERIALS

1. Six hardcover copies of the *Good News Bible: Today's English Version for Catholics*, Second Edition, 1992. It has an imprimatur, "Study Notes," and "Study Aids" and is published by Catholic Bible Press, a division of Thomas Nelson Publishers, Nashville, Tennessee.
2. *Catechism of the Catholic Church,* 1994, published by Thomas More, a division of Tabor Publishing, Allen, Texas.

CONTENTS

Three Stages

LESSON 1

1. LESSON BACKGROUND

▶ *Catechism of the Catholic Church,* 121–126.

2. LESSON QUIZ

In subsequent lesson plans a three-question quiz will appear in this section.

3. LESSON HOMEWORK

▶ **Read** Lesson 2 ("Ancient Scrolls," pages 4–5).

▶ **Write** Lesson 2 review questions (lower right-hand corner of page 5).

▶ **Appoint** Two students to prepare class readings from Luke 4:16–21 (relating to exercise 1 of lesson 2) and Isaiah 2:1–5 (relating to exercise 2).

4. LESSON PRESENTATION

Point ❶ **Read** Begin by having student volunteers alternate reading aloud the core content of lesson 1.

▶ **Clarify** *Grimm's Fairy Tales* has been translated into over fifty languages. It has sold over a billion copies.

Stress that stories like "Snow White" and "Cinderella" were not written down right away because few people could read or write.

The African version of "Cinderella" was modified to have Cinderella go to the ball in a canoe. Similarly, the witch's house in another story, "Hanzel and Gretel," was made out of salt instead of what? (Gingerbread) Finally, Snow White's name was changed to Flower White.

▶ **Discuss** Ask: Why did the African version change these details?

Ask: Why do you think this did/didn't change the lesson of each story?

Ask: What is the lesson of the story of Rapunzel?

Point ❷ **Clarify** Scribes have existed since the dawn of writing. This is because the earliest systems of writing were too complex for the average person to master. In some third-world countries, scribes still flourish because literacy is still a problem.

Most Israelite kings, officers, nobles, and merchants were illiterate. They depended on scribes for all the vital information they needed. This catapulted scribes into a position of power.

▶ **Discuss** Ask: With whom did scribes associate in Jesus' time, and what was their attitude toward Jesus?

The Gospels link the scribes (translated "teachers of the Law" in some Bibles) with the Pharisees. Both groups saw Jesus as a threat to their leadership and power. Consider two examples of the hostility between "teachers of the Law" and Jesus:

1. *Some teachers of the Law and some Pharisees wanted a reason to accuse Jesus of doing wrong, so they watched him closely to see if he would heal on the Sabbath.* Luke 6:7
2. *Jesus said to his disciples, "Be on your guard against the teachers of the Law, who like to walk around in their long robes and love to be greeted with respect in the marketplace; who choose the reserved seats in the synagogues."* Luke 20:45–46

▶ **Notebook** Have the students enter the following summary of the core matter into their notebooks.

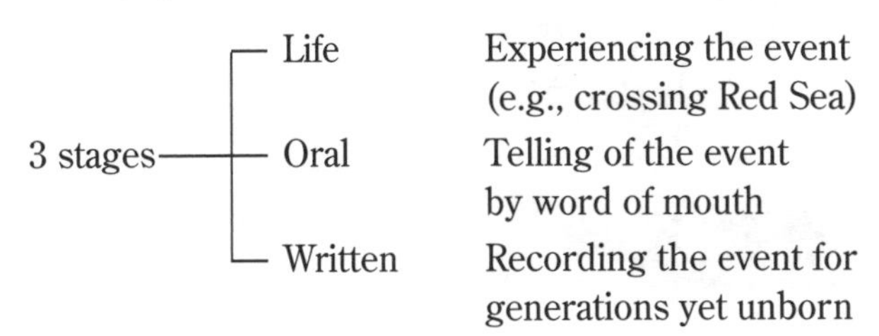

5. LESSON INTERACTION

Exercise ❶ **Clarify** Fahrenheit 451 is the temperature at which a book catches fire and burns.

Bradbury's story concerns a future society where all people are brainwashed to think alike. Since books make people think differently, they are banned. In this future society where everything is fireproofed, the firefighters' job has evolved into one of hunting down books, burning them, and arresting their owners. Bradbury's book, among other things, is a comment on censorship.

▶ **Discuss** Violence on TV has been linked to violence in society. This is why many people seek to censor TV.

Ask: Why do/don't you think this kind of censorship differs from the kind Bradbury writes about?

Ask: Why do you think censorship is/isn't an effective way to promote a better society?

Ask: Why do/don't you think censorship is the answer to violence and pornography (readily available on TV and the "information highway")? If you don't think it is the answer, what do you think the answer is?

▶ **Discuss** Copy this sentence on the chalkboard: "Internal conviction is the best way to counter external pressure."

Ask: How does this sentence suggest a better way to improve society without resorting to censorship? (The only effective way to protect people, especially the young, from violence and pornography is not *external* censorship, but *internal* censorship, building within them a strong internal conviction that will offset the external pressures created by the irresponsible media.)

▶ **Discuss** Ask: How do you build internal conviction? "Building an internal conviction" is one of the goals of this course. That particular goal is to show that Jesus and his teaching can change our modern world. The first step, however, is to change ourselves.

▶ **Notebook** Have the students take a few minutes to record their response to parts *a, b, c,* and *d* of exercise 1. Students enjoy answering these questions.

It was "memories" of God's action in their lives that led the Israelites to "write down for the coming generation what the LORD has done, so that people not yet born will praise [the LORD]" (Psalm 102:18).

Exercise ❷ **Clarify** Consider three of the passages cited in this exercise:

1. *An angel of the Lord said to Philip, "Get ready and go south to the road that goes from Jerusalem to Gaza." (This road is not used nowadays.)* Acts 8:26
2. *That field is called "Field of Blood" to this very day.* Matthew 27:8
3. *The guards took the money and did what they were told to do. And so that is the report spread around by the Jews to this very day.* Matthew 28:15

All three passages make it clear that the events they describe happened quite a while ago (for example, "to this very day"). This indicates that they were passed on orally for an extended period before being recorded.

▶ **Notebook** Have students make this entry in their notebooks indicating evidence from Scripture itself that parts of it went through an *oral stage,* that is, they were passed on orally for years before being recorded.

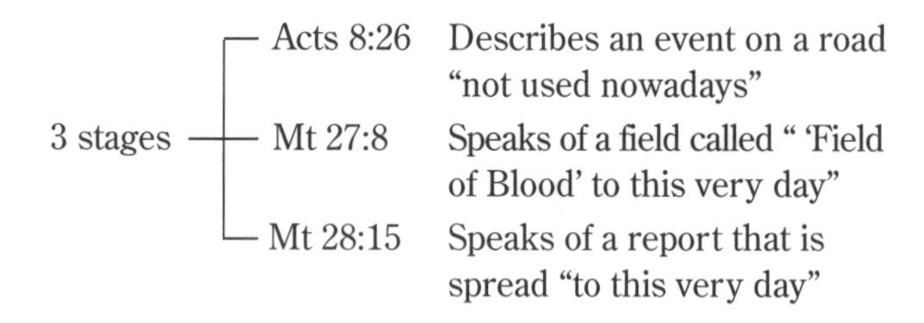

Exercises ❸ & ❹ **Activity** Exercise 3 sets up exercise 4 (which is designed to evaluate the biblical literacy of your students).

Responses to the questions in exercise 4 are: **(a)** Old Testament and New Testament, **(b)** Genesis, **(c)** twenty-seven, **(d)** four (Matthew, Mark, Luke, and John), **(e)** Revelation.

Exercise ❺ **Clarify** Psalm 78:1–4 reads as follows:

Listen, my people, to my teaching,
and pay attention to what I say.
I am going to . . . explain mysteries
from the past, . . .
things that our ancestors told us.
We will not keep them from our children;
we will tell the next generation
about the LORD's power and his great deeds
and the wonderful things he has done.

The passage makes it clear that ancient peoples communicated their history (God's "great deeds") orally ("Listen"). Psalm 78:13–29 lists these "great deeds."

Exercise ❻ **Discuss** List the questions of the students on a chalkboard, and have the students respond to as many as they can. This exercise provides you with a helpful insight into the biblical literacy of your students.

Ancient Scrolls

LESSON 2

1. LESSON BACKGROUND

▶ *Catechism of the Catholic Church,* 105–108.

2. LESSON QUIZ

Begin each new lesson with a *three-question* quiz. The thinking behind the lesson quiz is explained more fully in "About This Manual," page iii.

Perfect score = 10 points

1. What do stories like Rapunzel and Snow White have in common with Scripture? *(Lesson 1 review—1 point)*
2. List and briefly describe the three stages by which Scripture reached the form it now has in the Bible. *(Lesson 1 notebook review—6 points)*
3. When, where, and by whom were the first Dead Sea Scrolls found? *(Lesson 2 preview—3 points)*

3. LESSON HOMEWORK

▶ **Collect** Lesson 2 review questions (page 5).

The author did not grade the homework with a letter or numerical grade. He merely indicated with a check in his grade book that the student had done the assignment satisfactorily.

The author did, however, write notes on many of the student papers: for example, "Good!" "Not quite right!" "Keep up the good work!" It is amazing how the practice of putting notes on the homework improves the quality of subsequent homework.

▶ **Read** Lesson 3 ("Inspired by God," pages 6–7).

▶ **Write** Lesson 3 review questions (page 7).

▶ **Appoint** Two students to prepare readings from 1 Samuel 31:1–6 (Saul killed himself) and 2 Samuel 1:1–10 (an Amalekite killed him).

4. LESSON PRESENTATION

Point ❶ **Read** Begin by having student volunteers alternate reading aloud the core content of lesson 2.

▶ **Notebook** Think of the Bible as being a bookcase (draw one on the chalkboard and have the students copy it in their notebooks). Ask: What would the top shelf stand for? (New Testament) The bottom shelf? (Old Testament)

NT
OT

Next, divide the New Testament into four sections. Ask: What do the sections stand for? (NT divisions: Gospels, Acts, Letters, Revelation) Have the students list the number of books in each section.

Gospels (4)	Acts (1) NT	Letters (21) (27)	Revelation (1)
		OT	

Next, divide the Old Testament into four sections. Ask: What do the sections stand for? (OT divisions: Torah, Historical books, Prophetic books, Wisdom books) List the number of books in each section.

Gospels (4)	Acts (1) NT	Letters (21) (27)	Revelation (1)
Torah (5)	Historical (18) OT	Prophetic (16) (46)	Wisdom (7)

Point ❷ **Clarify** We might compare the Old Testament to a literary time capsule buried 2,500 years ago. And we may think of the New Testament as a time capsule buried 2,000 years ago.

▶ **Discuss** Ask: What is a literary time capsule, and what is its purpose? (A sampling of the literature of our time that reflects our beliefs and values as a people)

Notebook Have the students answer this question in their notebooks: If we buried a literary time capsule to give future generations an idea of the beliefs and values of our generation, what five magazines might we choose as being typical of our beliefs and values?

Discuss Have a "class secretary" list responses on the chalkboard. Then have the students vote on the five top magazines, giving their reason for each selection.

Point 3 **Clarify** The first section of the Old Testament is called the *Torah.* This Hebrew word is usually translated into English as "law," or "instruction."

Early Greek Christians called the Torah the *Pentateuch* ("five scrolls"). Point out that the prefix *penta* means "five." (The Pentagon in Washington is so called because it is five-sided.)

The Bible sometimes refers to the Torah as the "Book of Moses," because it contains the teachings of Moses (2 Chronicles 25:4, Mark 12:26).

Notebook Have students summarize the following in their notebooks.

Five books		
	Torah	Hebrew word meaning "law," or "instruction"
	Pentateuch	Greek word meaning "five scrolls"

Clarify The Torah is housed in a place of honor in synagogues and is the foundation for all Scripture.

The five books contained in the Torah are Genesis, Exodus, Leviticus, Numbers, Deuteronomy.

Genesis The name means "origins" (universe, human beings, sin, suffering, and the like). The book begins with creation and ends with the death of Joseph (he was sold into slavery by his brothers).
Exodus The name means "departure" and refers to Israel's flight from Egypt (where they had been enslaved for centuries). The book describes the journey from Egypt to Mount Sinai, and God's covenant with the Israelites at Mount Sinai.
Leviticus The name is derived from the name *Levi.* The book is made up largely of instructions for the priests of the tribe of Levi.
Numbers The name is derived from two censuses of the Israelites: one taken at Mount Sinai and the other taken about a generation later, at Moab, just before the Israelites entered the Promised Land (Canaan).
Deuteronomy The name means "second law." This book is a repetition, expansion, and completion of the "first law," given at Mount Sinai. It takes the form of a series of instructions and exhortations by Moses to the Israelites at Moab, before entering the Promised Land.

Point 4 **Clarify** Point out the three photographs relating to the Dead Sea Scrolls. Ancient peoples put scrolls and important documents in jars and then sealed the jars. Jeremiah refers to this practice, saying, "Take these deeds . . . and . . . place them in a clay jar, so that they may be preserved for years to come" (32:14).

Cave 4 is visible in the front center portion of the "cloverleaf" (left side of the photograph on page 4). The ruins shown on page 5 are adjacent to the cloverleaf.

Point 5 **Notebook** Develop interactively with the students the following diagram. Have them enter it in their notebooks.

Dead Sea Scrolls	
What was found	800 documents (mostly fragments; 200 biblical)
When found	Between 1947 and 1956
Where	Eleven caves at Qumran near the Dead Sea
Why important	They are closer to originals by 1,000 years and thus give us a clearer picture of biblical times.

5. LESSON INTERACTION

Exercise 1 **Clarify** Explain to the students that during its lifetime, a living substance absorbs radioactive carbon. When it dies, it releases the carbon 14 back into the atmosphere at a constant rate. This allows scientists to determine when the substance died.

Dr. Willard Libby fixed the date of the scroll of the Book of Isaiah by reducing its linen wrappings to pure carbon. His conclusion? The flax used to make the linen was alive and growing long before the time of Jesus.

Discuss Before discussing the three questions at the end of exercise 1, have the student who prepared Luke 4:16–21 read the passage to the class.

Exercise 2 **Read** Before discussing what *Popular Science* had in mind, have the student assigned to prepare Isaiah 2:1–5 read the passage aloud to the class.

Exercise 3 This exercise is self-explanatory.

Exercise 4 Equivalents are *synagogue* (church), *scroll* (lectionary or book of readings), *ark* (somewhat akin to our tabernacle), *Torah* (Gospels), *rabbi* (priest).

Inspired by God

LESSON 3

1. LESSON BACKGROUND

▶ *Catechism of the Catholic Church,* 105–108.

2. LESSON QUIZ

Perfect score = 13 points

1. When, by whom, and from whom were the Dead Sea Scrolls probably hidden? *(Lesson 2 review—3 points)*
2. List the four main sections into which the Old Testament divides and the number of books in each. *(Lesson 2 notebook review—8 points)*
3. List two extremes that need to be avoided in the way we understand *inspiration. (Lesson 3 preview—2 points)*

3. LESSON HOMEWORK

▶ **Return** Lesson 2 review questions (page 5).

▶ **Collect** Lesson 3 review questions (page 7).

▶ **Read** Lesson 4 ("Guided by God," pages 8–9).

▶ **Write** Lesson 4 review questions (page 9).

▶ **Assign** Remind the students to pray nightly the prayer they composed (exercise 3).

4. LESSON PRESENTATION

Point ❶ **Read** Begin by having student volunteers alternate reading aloud the core content of lesson 3.

▶ **Discuss** Monks in Thailand were transporting a clay Buddha to a new location because their ancient temple was being torn down to make way for a modern freeway.

Suddenly, the clay Buddha cracked under the stress of being transported. The huge crack revealed something shiny just below the surface of the clay. It turned out to be a solid gold Buddha.

The gold Buddha had apparently been coated with clay centuries before to keep invading Burmese armies from carrying it off. The monks were massacred and the gold Buddha remained hidden beneath the clay for all these years.

Had the ancient temple not been torn down, and had the clay not cracked open while being transported, the gold Buddha (valued at $200 million) would still be lost to the world. The two events that the monks thought were catastrophes (losing their temple and having the Buddha crack open) turned out to be an immense blessing to them.

Ask: What lesson for life may we draw from this? (God often uses what we think to be catastrophes to bless us immensely.)

Ask: How is the story of the gold Buddha similar to the story of the Dead Sea Scrolls? (Both were hidden from invading armies. Both stayed hidden for the same reason. [Modern scholars think that the Dead Sea Scrolls remained hidden in the caves because all the Essene monks were massacred by the invading Roman army.] Finally, both were rediscovered by accident.)

Ask: How is the clay coating, concealing the gold Buddha, an image of the human words of Scripture and the divine message of God that they contain? (The human ["clay"] words of the human writers conceal the divine ["gold"] message of God. The "clay" words must be broken open to discover the "gold" message that they conceal.)

Point ❷ **Clarify** There are three theories about what we mean by *inspiration.*

The *first* theory is that the Holy Spirit dictated to the human writers, much as an executive dictates to a secretary. This theory is sometimes called the "Divine Dictation" theory. It treats the human writers as robots and fails to explain stylistic differences (for example, the elegant style of Isaiah and the crude style of Amos).

The *second* theory is that the human writers were inspired in a "religious" way, much as poets are inspired in a "poetic" way. According to this theory, the Holy Spirit simply intervenes when the human writer is on the verge of making an error. This theory is sometimes called the "Negative Assistance" theory. It reduces the Holy Spirit to a "divine watchdog" who keeps the human writers from making any mistakes.

The Church rejects both of these extreme theories. It holds that the first theory goes too far and that the second theory doesn't go far enough. In other words, in the first theory the Holy Spirit does too much; and in the second theory, the Holy Spirit doesn't do enough.

This brings us to the *third* theory. It is the theory the Catholic Church espouses and is sometimes called the "Positive Assistance" theory. It holds that:

The Holy Spirit worked
in *and* through *the human writers*
in such a way
that they were empowered
to use their own talents and words
to communicate
what God wanted them
to communicate. (Text, page 7)

In conclusion, then, whatever the Holy Spirit's "positive assistance" was (and this remains a mystery), it left the human writers free to use their own talents and resources.

Because of this, we can truly say that the Bible is the "word of God in the words of men" (Alexander Jones). In other words, God's "gold" message is encased in a layer of "clay" words.

▶ **Notebook** With the interactive help of the students, develop the following diagram on the chalkboard for entry in the students' notebooks.

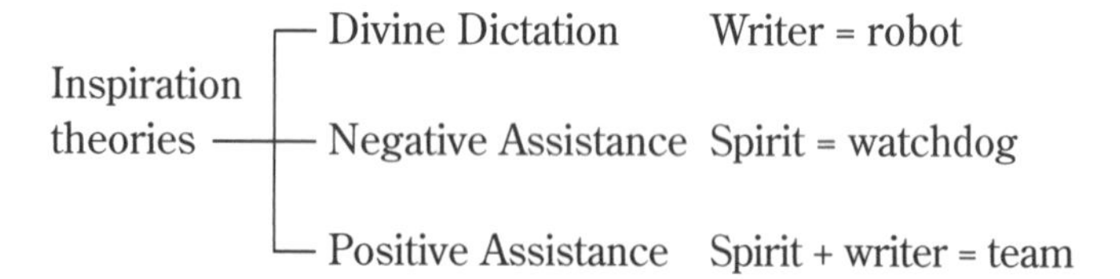

▶ **Clarify** The human writer is sometimes called the "instrumental," or "secondary," author of Scripture and God the "primary" author. In other words, God communicates the divine message through the human author much as a musician communicates through a musical instrument.

The important point to keep in mind in all of this is *that* the human author was inspired, and not *how* the human author was inspired.

▶ **Clarify** Three biblical passages, especially, refer to the fact of inspiration:

Mark 12:36	David was inspired by the Spirit.
2 Peter 1:21	Prophets were impelled by the Spirit.
2 Timothy 3:16	All Scripture is inspired by God.

▶ **Clarify** Stress the idea that because Scripture is inspired, it is free from *religious* error, that is, *errors in matters related to salvation.*

This does not mean Scripture is free from scientific or historical errors. God did not intend to write a scientific or historical treatise.

Have the two students who prepared the readings from 1 and 2 Samuel read the passages that clearly contradict each other from a *historical* viewpoint.

Point ❸ **Notebook** The photo in the upper left corner of page 6 introduces us to the development of writing materials and the form these materials have taken in history. Have the students summarize the materials and forms by entering these diagrams in their notebooks.

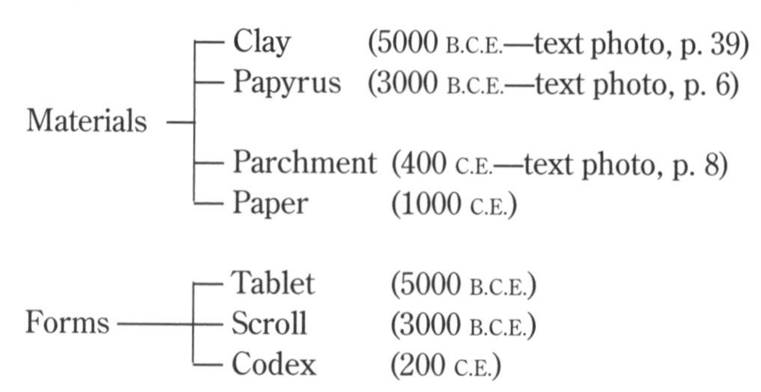

5. LESSON INTERACTION

Exercise ❶ **Clarify** **(a)** Pronouncing "each individual word" reduces the possibility of error. **(b)** Pronouncing the "sacred formula" stresses the fact that copying God's word is different from all other scribal tasks. It must be done more reverently.

▶ **Activity** **(c)** The logical place where students will err is in pronouncing the "sacred formula" before the words *Father, Son,* and *Holy Spirit.*

Exercise ❷ **Activity** Don't feel compelled to respond immediately to the "questions" a student may pose concerning this or that passage in the Bible. Three responses you may make are:

- Ask for volunteers to respond to the question.
- Compliment the student and say, "That's one of the questions we'll be taking up during the course of our study."
- Compliment the student and say, "I'd like to think about that and get back to you on it."

Exercise ❸ **Activity** Have volunteers share with the class the prayers they wrote. Instruct the students to pray their prayer daily for the next week. At the end of the week, have the students respond to questions *a* and *b*.

Guided by God

LESSON 4

1. LESSON BACKGROUND

▶ *Catechism of the Catholic Church,* 109–114.

2. LESSON QUIZ

Perfect score = 10 points

1. Explain what we mean when we say that the Bible is free from *religious* error, and give one example of scientific error in the Bible and one example of historical error in the Bible. *(Lesson 3 review—3 points)*
2. List and briefly explain the three theories of inspiration. *(Lesson 3 notebook review—6 points)*
3. What name do we give to the first translation of the Bible into Greek? *(Lesson 4 preview—1 point)*

3. LESSON HOMEWORK

▶ **Return** Lesson 3 review questions (page 7).

▶ **Collect** Lesson 4 review questions (page 9).

▶ **Read** Lesson 5 ("Interpreting Scripture," pages 10–11).

▶ **Write** Lesson 5 review questions (page 11).

4. LESSON PRESENTATION

Point 1 **Read** Begin by having volunteers alternate reading aloud the core content of lesson 4.

▶ **Clarify** The Gospel of James elaborates on Jesus' infancy. It is the source that tells us that the names of Mary's parents were Anna and Joachim.

The Gospel of Thomas elaborates on the boyhood of Jesus and narrates some "far-out" miracles that the young Jesus supposedly performed.

Point 2 **Clarify** Scholar Louis F. Hartman describes the story behind the Septuagint in these words:

At first the LXX [Septuagint] was highly regarded by all Jews; it spread from Egypt to the whole Jewish Diaspora and became the official Bible of Greek-speaking Judaism.

The NT writers, writing in Greek for Greek-speaking people, usually quoted from the OT according to the LXX. Naturally, therefore, the LXX became the official OT of the early Church. . . .

However, after the destruction of Jerusalem in A.D. 70, when Jewish opposition to Christianity became pronounced . . . the LXX, though originally made by Jews for Jews, was frowned upon by the Jews as a quasi-Christian book.

Hence, for the benefit of the Greek-speaking Jews of early Christian centuries, new Greek translations of the Hebrew Scriptures were made.

▶ **Notebook** Have the students make the following entry in their notebooks concerning the translations of the Old Testament.

Bible translations		
	Into Greek	200 B.C.E.
	Into Latin	400 C.E.
	Into English	1400 C.E.

Point 3 **Clarify** The study of translations is fascinating. Take the word *father.* Here is how it appears in six different languages:

English	*father*	Swedish	*fader*
Dutch	*vader*	German	*vater*
Latin	*pater*	Persian	*pidar*

▶ **Discuss** Ask: What do you notice immediately about this list? (The words are somewhat similar.) What might this suggest? (Perhaps at one time there was a common language that evolved into many languages over the years.)

Point 4 **Clarify** If Moses walked up to a Jewish girl at a bus stop in New York's Jewish district and asked directions, would she understand him?

The answer is no. Most modern Jews speak Yiddish, which is not the same as biblical Hebrew, even though it is written in Hebrew letters. Yiddish is a European tongue akin to German.

Modern Israelis, however, have embarked upon a return to biblical Hebrew. This trend was begun by Eliezer Ben Yehuda, a medical student who returned to Palestine in 1880. He startled his bride by telling her that from then on he would speak only in Hebrew.

Eliezer's crusade caught fire. Eventually, Jewish scholars systematized the language and created modern equivalents for words like *radar* and *electricity.*

Originally, the Old Testament contained 8,000 different Hebrew words. Modern Hebrew dictionaries now list over 50,000 words. Almost all young people in Israel now read Hebrew fluently.

Point 5 **Discuss** To help students appreciate the growth of languages in modern times, ask: If Shakespeare picked up the morning paper, why would he have difficulty understanding it? (Words like *parking meter, bus, car,* and *pizza* would baffle him.)

Activity Have the students volunteer other words that Shakespeare would not understand. List them on the chalkboard.

5. LESSON INTERACTION

Exercise 1 **Discuss** Four items from the *New American Bible* translation of the passage from the Book of Ecclesiastes need interpretation. List them on the chalkboard and have the students interpret (explain) each one.

- *guardians of the house tremble* (arms fail)
- *grinders are idle because they are few* (teeth fail)
- *windows grow blind* (eyes fail)
- *doors to the street are shut* (ears fail)

Exercise 2 **Discuss** **(a)** The *Good News Bible* translation of the passage from the Book of Ecclesiastes focuses more on the translation of the meaning of the idea. The *New American Bible* translation focuses more on the meaning of the words.

Ask: What is the difference between translating the idea and translating the words?

(b) A big "pro" for the *Good News Bible* translation is that it is clear what the passage is talking about. A big "con" is that the translator is involved in interpreting the meaning of the phrases. Scholars say this is going beyond what a translator should do.

Ask: What is meant in saying "the translator is involved in interpreting the meaning . . . [which is] going beyond what a translator should do"?

Ask: What danger is involved in letting the translator be involved in interpretation?

(c) You might give the students time to think about this question and have them record their response in their notebooks before sharing it with the group.

Discuss Read three other phrases from the *New American Bible* translation of this particular passage in the Book of Ecclesiastes and have the students explain what they refer to.

- *when the almond tree blooms* (hair turns white)
- *before the silver cord is snapped* (death)
- *and the dust returns to the earth as it once was* (our bodies decay)

Clarify Have the students read the caption for the photograph of the two elderly people on page 9.

Point out that early Jews had little or no idea of an afterlife. They believed in a nether world, *Sheol,* but thought it was just a place where the dead (good and bad) went. What happened there they did not know. They were waiting for further revelation from God.

Exercise 3 **Clarify** The girl's point is a good one. Obviously, not every book of the Bible is of equal importance.

For example, there's no comparison between the importance of the prophetic Book of Isaiah (which both Protestants and Catholics accept as canonical) and the prophetic Book of Baruch (which only Catholics accept as canonical).

In any event, most Protestants include books like Baruch in their Bibles under the title of Apocrypha (worthy of reading but not inspired).

Exercise 4 **Activity** Have several volunteers give their responses to the three quotations.

Interpreting Scripture

LESSON 5

1. LESSON BACKGROUND

▶ *Catechism of the Catholic Church,* 109–114.

2. LESSON QUIZ

Perfect score = 7 points

1. What is the list of inspired books of the Bible called, and how is it discerned or determined? *(Lesson 4 review—2 points)*
2. List the approximate dates of the initial translation of the Bible into Greek, Latin, and English. *(Lesson 4 notebook review—3 points)*
3. What verdict did the Dayton jury render, and how did the Tennessee Supreme Court react to it? *(Lesson 5 preview—2 points)*

3. LESSON HOMEWORK

▶ **Return** Lesson 4 review questions (page 9).

▶ **Collect** Lesson 5 review questions (page 11).

▶ **Read** Lesson 6 ("First Creation Story," pages 12–13).

▶ **Write** Lesson 6 review questions (page 13).

▶ **Appoint** Three students to prepare readings from (1) Genesis 1:1–13, (2) Genesis 1:14–25, and (3) Genesis 1:26–2:4a (lesson 6, exercise 4).

4. LESSON PRESENTATION

Point 1 **Read** Begin by having student volunteers read aloud the core content of lesson 5.

▶ **Discuss** Ask: What did the new Tennessee law forbid public schools in the state to do?

Ask: What is meant by the "theory of evolution"?

Ask: What is the ACLU, and why would it want to challenge the law?

(The theory of evolution holds that the more complex forms of life, like humans, evolved from lower forms of life in a process that involved millions of years. The American Civil Liberties Union is one of the guardians for civil rights. As such, it opposes any state legislation that relates to religious matters. For example, the new Tennessee law was trying to impose a fundamentalist view of the Bible on state schools.)

▶ **Clarify** An insight into the Tennessee trial and the fundamentalist mentality that brought it on appears in *Time-Capsule/1925,* pages 205–18. (Many libraries have the *Time-Capsule Series: A History of the Year.* It is a fascinating condensation of events from the pages of *Time* magazine.) One excerpt reads:

A man beats his wife in any one of the 47 states. He is sent to jail. There he loafs. The maltreated wife is without support. He comes back, beats her again. In the 48th state, Delaware, the wife-beater . . . is lashed with a tough-thonged whip once, twice—30 stinging times. . . . Last week, a bill to abolish the whipping-post came up to a vote in the Delaware legislature. It was defeated, 31–1.

▶ **Discuss** Ask: Why have laws such as the 1925 Delaware law on whipping been repealed for the most part? Some people think they should be brought back. Do you? Why?

▶ **Clarify** Chicago's Clarence Darrow was an interesting lawyer of the time. He took many "unpopular" cases like the Scopes defense. For example, he defended Loeb and Leopold, two University of Chicago students who kidnapped and murdered a schoolboy. He also represented Pennsylvania coal miners in their battle against mine owners for better working conditions.

▶ **Clarify** Darrow's tactics were often tricky or resourceful, depending on your viewpoint. Once, when the opposition lawyer was summing up his case before the jury, Darrow sat puffing vigorously on a rather long and thin cigar. The cigar had been rigged with a wire to keep the ash from falling. The jury took the bait and watched breathlessly for the hot ash to topple onto Darrow's shirt, oblivious of the opposing lawyer's words.

▶ **Clarify** Finally, *Time-Capsule/1925* reports on Bryan's sudden death in Dayton a few days after the trial. One sentence from the report deserves special mention. It reads, "Mocking mouths were shut . . . and the snarling armies stood silent."

▶ **Notebook** Summarize the following on the chalkboard for entry in student notebooks.

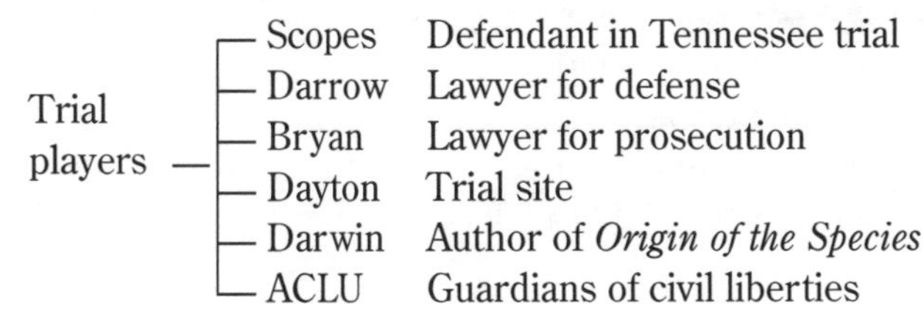

5. LESSON INTERACTION

Exercise ➊ **Discuss** (a) *Time-Capsule/1925* reported that when someone asked Lady Darwin, the daughter-in-law of evolutionist Charles Darwin, what she thought about the Tennessee trial, she said, "I think men are beginning to make monkeys of themselves."

▶ **Discuss** (b) Have the students write out their response to this question before sharing it with the class. Hold off any serious discussion of evolution until lesson 9.

Exercise ➋ **Discuss** Once again, have the students write out their response to this question before sharing it with the class. The responses will give you a good sense of where your students are when it comes to biblical literacy. They will also set the stage for subsequent lessons.

Exercise ➌ **Clarify** *Time-Capsule/1925* compared John Scopes to Socrates. Recall that Socrates was one of history's greatest thinkers. He left no writings. His philosophy is preserved in the writings of Plato, who was one of his students.

About 400 B.C.E. Socrates was accused of corrupting youth. (His teachings downplayed worship of Greek gods and goddesses.)

Brought to trial, he acted as his own lawyer. He was convicted and executed by being given hemlock to drink. (Hemlock is made of one of several poisonous herbs related to the carrot.)

▶ **Discuss** (a) Scopes (Cates) implies that fundamentalists have distorted the true image of God to fit their own ideas—rather than what the Bible says.

▶ **Discuss** (b) Drummond (Darrow) implies that the theory of evolution is compatible with what the Bible says. This is one of the topics that will be taken up in lesson 9. Again, hold off a serious discussion of the question of evolution until then.

Note that *Inherit the Wind* is available on videocassette. If you have time and equipment, you might rent the video and show segments to the class.

Exercise ➍ **Discuss** Be sure to have the students record their responses privately in writing before sharing them. It might be good to collect the responses and review them. Again, this will help you get a better idea of where your students are when it comes to biblical literacy.

Miniposter **Discuss** This remarkable painting was done by high school students in Brussels, Belgium. It covers an entire wall of their cafeteria. Unfortunately, only a portion of it could be shown here. A more complete view appears on page 234 in connection with the battle in heaven (before the creation of the humans) between Michael and the dragon (Satan). Hold off having the students look at that painting for the time being.

Have the class compile a list (on the chalkboard) of the various elements (not their symbolic meaning) that make up the painting. Have a class secretary list them in a single column. Begin on the right side and proceed to the left side, going from the bottom to the top. The list should look something like this:

Right side: several dragons.

Left side: (1) two people, (2) round object, (3) seated person, (4) person slaying a dragon, (5) two people holding up a lamb, (6) a bright light, looking like the sun.

Next, have the students identify the elements. The identification list should look something like this:

Right side: Satan and his cohorts.

Left side: (1) Adam and Eve right after creation, (2) apple, symbolizing Satan's temptation of Adam and Eve (human race), (3) Adam (human race) after being defeated, (4) Jesus (representative of the human race) defeating Satan.

Recall God's words to the snake (Satan) after he successfully tempts the woman (Eve): "I will make you and the woman hate each other. . . . Her offspring [Jesus] will crush your head, and you will bite her offspring's heel" (Genesis 3:15). (Jesus will defeat Satan but will be wounded in the process.)

(5) Adam and Eve offering Jesus ("the Lamb of God").

Recall John the Baptist's identification of Jesus as "the Lamb of God" (John 1:29). Recall also the words of the priest as he holds up the sacred host at Mass just before communion:

"This is the Lamb of God
who takes away the sins of the world."

(6) God poised to accept humanity's offering to God (sacrificial death of Jesus on the cross).

First Creation Story

LESSON 6

1. LESSON BACKGROUND

▶ *Catechism of the Catholic Church*, 282–289.

2. LESSON QUIZ

Perfect score = 15 points

1. Identify (a) Scopes, (b) Dayton, (c) Bryan. *(Lesson 5 review—3 points)*
2. Identify (a) Darrow, (b) Darwin. *(Lesson 5 notebook review—2 points)*
3. List and explain the fivefold poetic pattern the biblical writer uses to describe each day of creation. *(Lesson 6 preview—10 points)*

3. LESSON HOMEWORK

▶ **Return** Lesson 5 review questions (page 11).

▶ **Collect** Lesson 6 review questions (page 13).

▶ **Read** Lesson 7 ("Literal Interpreters," pages 14–15).

▶ **Write** Lesson 7 review questions (page 15).

▶ **Appoint** Two students to prepare readings from (1) Matthew 18:16–20 and (2) Acts 15:1–11, 22–29 (lesson 7, exercise 2).

4. LESSON PRESENTATION

Point ① **Read** Have volunteers read aloud the core content of lesson 6.

▶ **Clarify** The second day of creation portrays God making a dome (to separate the "water above it" from the "water below it"). Three things need clarification to understand this description.

First, ancient Hebrews viewed the universe as having three tiers (see miniposter on page 12):

- the world of the dead (nether world),
- the world of the living (our world), and
- the world of God (God's home).

Second, ancients Hebrews viewed water as being located in two different places: below the sky (stored in oceans) and above the sky (stored in clouds [Job 26:8]).

Separating the "waters above" from the "waters below" was a glasslike dome. Through holes in the dome, God occasionally let rain fall.

Psalm 104:2–3 reflects the three-tiered universe, saying of God, "You have . . . built your home on the waters above." And Psalm 104:5–6 says, "You have set the earth firmly on its foundations. . . . You placed the ocean over it like a robe."

Finally the world of the dead (nether world) was located below the world of the living. Early Hebrews had no concept of life after death until the second century B.C.E. (as we shall see later). All the dead went to the nether world.

Point ② **Clarify** A study of the creation story portrays God creating the universe in six days and then resting on the seventh day.

A closer study shows that the "week of creation" follows a highly stylized, poetic pattern.

Three Days of Separation

Day 1 God created light
and separated it from the darkness.

Day 2 God separated the water above (rain)
from the water below (ocean).

Day 3 God separated the water below (ocean)
from the dry land.

Three Days of Population

Day 4 God populated the sky
with sun, moon, and stars.

Day 5 God populated the air
with birds and the ocean with fish.

Day 6 God populated the land.

One Day of Celebration

Day 7 God celebrated, resting from work,
blessing creation, and setting the day apart
from the other day (Sabbath).

▶ **Notebook** These important conclusions should be summarized for entry in student notebooks.

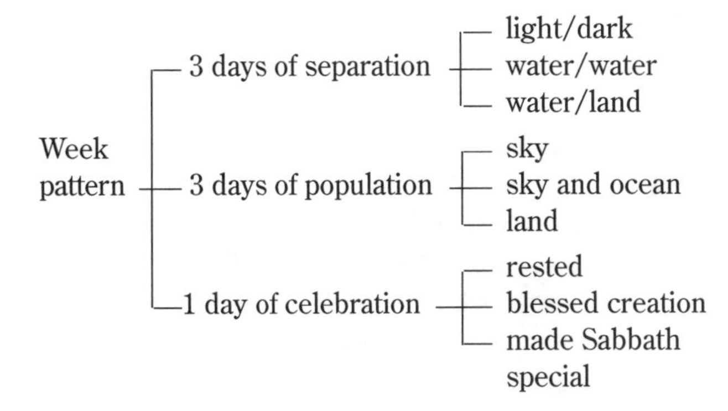

▶ **Clarify** This highly stylized, poetic pattern suggests that we are dealing with a special kind of writing. It is not the kind found in eyewitness accounts or in science books.

Rather, it is the kind found in children's books. For like small children, most ancient people could not read or write.

▶ **Notebook** Have students copy in their notebooks the following three reasons why highly stylized, poetic stories were ideal for teaching illiterate audiences.

	Entertaining to listen to
Stylized stories were	Easy to remember
	Simple to repeat to others

▶ **Clarify** Ask students: Why does the biblical writer end each day with the words "Evening passed and morning came"? Why not the other way around, which would be more logical?

(Hebrews considered sunset to be the end of a day. Thus Sabbath observance begins at sunset on Friday.)

Early Christians observed this practice with regard to Mass. Modern Catholics continue it, allowing Saturday evening Masses to satisfy the Sunday requirement.

Point ❸ **Clarify** The creation story describes God beginning the "sixth day" with these words: "And now we will make human beings; they will be like us and resemble us" (Genesis 1:26).

The words "we will" should not be interpreted as a revelation of God as "three persons" or Trinity. Important persons frequently used the so-called editorial we to refer to themselves. Thus Daniel says to the king:

"This was the dream; now we will tell the king its interpretation." Daniel 2:36 (RSV)

5. LESSON INTERACTION

Exercise ❶ Each day of creation follows a highly stylized, poetic pattern, just as the week of creation does.

▶ **Notebook** We may summarize the general pattern of each day of creation for entry in student notebooks.

	Introduction	"God commanded"
	Command	"Let there be"
Day structure	Execution	"It was done"
	Reaction	"God was pleased"
	Conclusion	"Evening passed"

The stylized poetic pattern suggests that we should not interpret the creation story in a strict, literal way.

Exercise ❷ **Review** This exercise acts as a review of the week of creation and the Hebrew view of the universe.

▶ **Notebook** As part of the above review, have the "class artist" construct on the chalkboard the following diagram (Hebrew view of the universe) for entry in student notebooks.

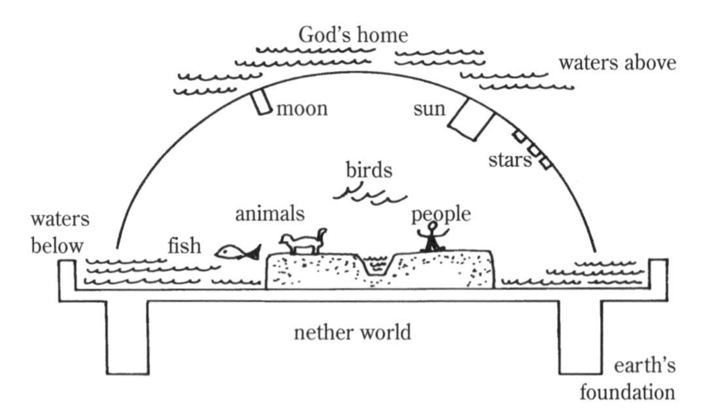

Exercise ❸ **Discuss** **(a)** The description of the creation of the bear is written in the same highly stylized way. The overall story has a highly structured sequence of events. And each event follows a similar poetic structure.

(b) The stylized, poetic structure of the creation of the bear story is intended to entertain children, to help them remember, and to help them repeat the story to others.

(c) One obvious lesson of the story of the creation of the bear is that beauty comes at a price. There is no such thing as "cheap grace" or success without great effort—and often great suffering.

(d) Give the students time to reflect on this part of the exercise. Then have them record it before sharing it with others. You might want to collect the student responses, screen them, and share them with the students at the next class.

Exercise ❹ **Discuss** If time permits, have the appointed students read the passage from Genesis. Allow time for students to record and share their responses.

Photo **Clarify** Refer the students to the photo of the clay tablet on page 13. Remarkably, the biblical account of creation has parallels in many other cultures. Sometimes these parallels have striking similarities. More often, however, they exhibit striking differences.

For example, the Babylonian creation story on this clay tablet (and its companion tablets) portrays the world coming about as a kind of by-product of a bloody battle between two rival gods: Marduk and Tiamat. From the lacerated and slain body of Tiamat, Marduk fashions the world.

Thus the Babylonian story portrays the world being created by whim or accident, whereas the Hebrew story portrays it being created by design and out of love.

CHAPTER TWO: Creation (pages 14–15)

Literal Interpreters

LESSON 7

1. LESSON BACKGROUND

▶ *Catechism of the Catholic Church,* 85–87.

2. LESSON QUIZ

Perfect score = 10 points

1. List three reasons why the repetitive, stylized, poetic stories were ideal for teaching illiterate audiences. *(Lesson 6 review—3 points)*
2. List the threefold pattern or structure that the Genesis writer uses in describing the week of creation. *(Lesson 6 notebook review—3 points)*
3. List and briefly describe the two main groups into which Bible readers fall. *(Lesson 7 preview—4 points)*

3. LESSON HOMEWORK

▶ **Return** Lesson 6 review questions (page 13).

▶ **Collect** Lesson 7 review questions (page 15).

▶ **Read** Lesson 8 ("Contextual Interpreters," pages 16–17).

▶ **Write** Lesson 8 review questions (page 17).

4. LESSON PRESENTATION

Point ① **Read** Have volunteers read aloud the core content of lesson 7.

▶ **Clarify** Stress that Bible readers, for the most part, fall into two main groups: *literalist* (fundamentalist) and *contextualist.*

Literalists hold that the Bible means exactly what it says. You need only its *text* to determine its meaning.

Nevertheless, literalists split into two groups ("strict" and "less strict") when it comes to interpreting certain words in the Bible. Take the word *day.* Strict literalists, like the Church of God, hold that it must be interpreted to mean "twenty-four hours." Less strict literalists, like Jehovah's Witnesses, hold that you may interpret it to mean "an era." For example, we may say "in Moses' day" (meaning when he lived).

Contextualists hold that you must consider both the *text* and the *context* of the Bible. For example, you must consider what the biblical writer intended. Pope Pius XII put it this way for Catholic biblical scholars over fifty years ago:

You must go back, as it were,
in spirit to those remote centuries of the East.
With the aid of history, archaeology, ethnology,
and the other sciences,
you must determine accurately what modes of writing
the ancient writers would likely use, and in fact did use.

In other words, the pope told them that they must approach the Bible from the viewpoint of the ancient writers and not impose their own twentieth-century viewpoint on it. For example, as we shall see, the Genesis writer clearly did not intend his story of creation to be taken literally. He intended us to interpret it much as we do Jesus' parables. Thus, the word *day* was intended symbolically, not literally.

▶ **Notebook** Develop interactively the following diagram on the chalkboard for entry in student notebooks. It sums up the difference between the two groups of literalists and the contextualists in terms of how they interpret the word *day* in the creation story.

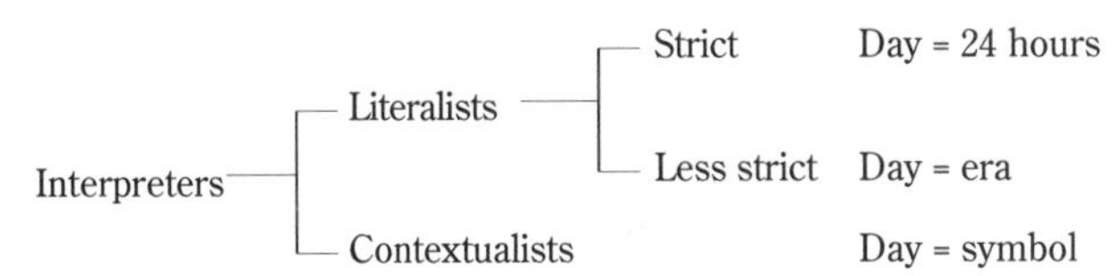

Point ② **Clarify** The dispute over the Bible is far from over. It leaped back into the news in the mid-1970s when Missouri Synod Lutherans voted to adopt a stricter interpretation of the Bible. The vote received a great deal of coverage in the news.

It is now absolute dogma within the sect that a man named Jonah was swallowed by a whale and lived to tell the tale. . . . And Adam and Eve were real people created by God, which means that the theory of evolution is fantasy. . . .

For the moment, the future is uncertain for at least one million Missouri Synod Lutherans whose ideas of Christian orthodoxy do not include Biblical literalism.

"The Lutheran Pope," *Newsweek* (July 23, 1973)

▶ **Activity** Have the students take a piece of scrap paper (unsigned) and answer the following questions.

1. Do you believe there was a real man named Jonah who was swallowed by a real whale and lived to tell the tale?
2. Do you believe there was a real man who had the name Adam and a real woman who answered to the name Eve?
3. Do you believe the theory of evolution is pure fantasy, that is, totally out of the question because of what the Bible says about the origin of each species?

Collect the answers and tally the results on the chalkboard. You are merely interested in dramatizing a point and getting a "preview" of the stance of the class on biblical interpretation. The questions will be discussed as the course unfolds; don't enter into a definitive discussion of them at this point.

Clarify Stress the following reasons that militate against having church members vote to settle doctrinal disputes. Allowing church members to vote presumes they are (1) equally informed, (2) free from external pressure and internal bias, (3) totally open to the Holy Spirit.

5. LESSON INTERACTION

Exercise ➊ **Discuss** Have the students record their responses before sharing them.

Most assuredly the biblical editor was aware of the contradictory nature of the two back-to-back creation stories. As we saw earlier—and will see again in lesson 9 ("Second Creation Story")—large sections of the Bible were passed on orally for long periods before being written down. Two complementary creation traditions were among these sections. The biblical writer simply recorded both traditions side by side.

Exercise ➋ **Notebook** The following diagram might be copied on the chalkboard to dramatize Morrison's point. It gives a rough idea of the origin and flow of Protestantism since the Reformation. (The diagram is incomplete and dates are approximate.)

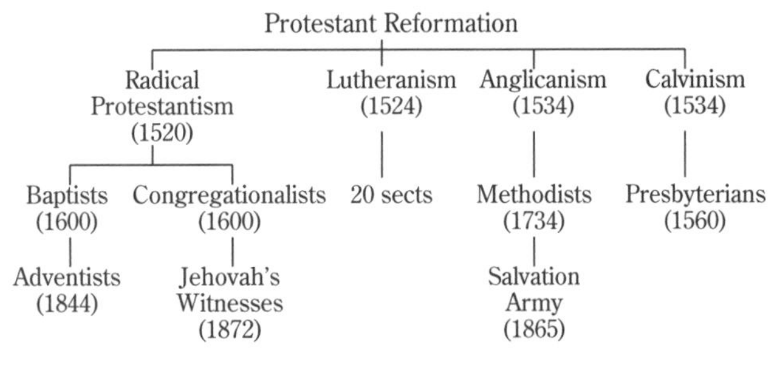

Clarify An illustration of how Protestantism split into so many different sects is the Salvation Army. It was organized in 1865 in England by William Booth, an ordained Methodist minister.

Booth left the pulpit to preach to people . . . on street corners in the slum district of East End, London. His original plan was to supplement the work of the churches. But when the latter refused to accept his converts into active membership, Booth established a religious society of his own. John A. Hardon, *The Protestant Churches of America*

Notebook Since the Salvation Army is quite visible in the United States, it might be helpful to give the students some idea of its structure and beliefs.

Booth saw life as a war between good and evil, so he renamed original Methodist structures to give them a quasi-military orientation. Have students copy the following in their notebooks.

Soon the Army fanned out to other countries. It came to the United States in 1880.

Discuss **(a)** It is unreasonable to think that Jesus would give us an invitation to enter with him into eternal life but leave us in the dark about how to go about accepting that invitation.

Discuss **(b)** Have the student appointed to prepare Matthew 18:16–20 read this passage to the class.

Ask: How does this passage suggest the procedure early Christians used to settle disputes?

Clarify Acts 15 describes how early Christians (following Jesus' teaching in Matthew) did, in fact, settle disputes relating to faith and morals. Have the student appointed to prepare Acts 15:1–11, 22–29 read the passage to the class.

Clarify Acts 15 describes the first ecumenical council in the history of the Church. The problem it took up was the question of whether converts from paganism had to become Jews (be circumcised) before they became Christians. Acts says, "The apostles and the elders met together to consider this question" (15:6).

Announcing their decision later, they said, "The Holy Spirit and we have agreed . . . " (15:28). In other words, they believed their deliberation to be guided by the Holy Spirit and in accord with God's will.

Clarify The early Christians recalled Jesus' words about "prohibiting" and "permitting" within the context of gathering in Jesus' name and being guided by discussion and prayer. See also Matthew 16:19, where Jesus says to Peter, the leader of the young Church:

"I will give you the keys of the Kingdom of heaven;
what you prohibit on earth
will be prohibited in heaven, and
what you permit on earth
will be permitted in heaven."

Exercise ➌ **Write** This is an important assignment. Encourage the students to illustrate their prayers in whatever way they see fit. For example, they may want to use several illustrations.

Consider having a committee of students screen out the better response (five or six) and have the class vote in a secret ballot on the top three.

CHAPTER TWO: Creation (pages 16–17)

Contextual Interpreters

LESSON

1. LESSON BACKGROUND

▶ *Catechism of the Catholic Church*, 296–301.

2. LESSON QUIZ

Perfect score = 10 points

1. If taken literally, how do the two creation stories contradict themselves concerning the creation of people? *(Lesson 7 review—2 points)*
2. Using the word *day*, explain how literalists disagree among themselves on interpreting certain words of the Bible. *(Lesson 7 notebook review—4 points)*
3. List the four truths the creation story teaches us. *(Lesson 8 preview—4 points)*

3. LESSON HOMEWORK

▶ **Return** Lesson 7 review questions (page 15).

▶ **Collect** Lesson 8 review questions (page 17).

▶ **Read** Lesson 9 ("Second Creation Story," pages 18–19).

▶ **Write** Lesson 9 review questions (page 19).

▶ **Appoint** Two students to prepare (1) Genesis 1:1–2:4a and (2) Genesis 2:4b–25 (lesson 9, core content).

4. LESSON PRESENTATION

Point 1 **Read** Have volunteers read aloud the core content of lesson 8.

▶ **Clarify** Recall the similar tragedy of Dennis Byrd, rising New York Jets star. Paralyzed in a collision with a teammate in the early 1990s, he was told by doctors that he would never walk again.

Yet about a year later, audiences thrilled to the TV documentary *Rise and Walk: The Dennis Byrd Story.* It credited Byrd's tremendous Christian faith and the support of his wife and teammates for the miracle (mixed in with his own personal determination and painful, unrelenting effort) of being able to walk again.

▶ **Clarify** You might also want to recall the case of Darryl Stingley of the New England Patriots. In the late 1970s everything was going his way in his football career. Then, as he dove for a pass, he was hit with bone-crunching force by Oakland's Jack Tatum.

The injury left Stingley able to move only one arm, but his spirit was incredible. In an interview with the *Chicago Tribune* (7/27/79) he said, "I've come to accept myself as I am. . . . This is rebirth for me. . . . I really have a lot more meaning and purpose to live for now."

Stingley spelled out his thoughts more in detail in an interview with *Newsweek* (12/21/81). "I had tunnel vision," he said of his football days. "All I wanted was to be the best athlete I could, and a lot of other things were overlooked. Now I've come back to them."

▶ **Notebook** The key ideas of this lesson may be summarized this way for entry in student notebooks.

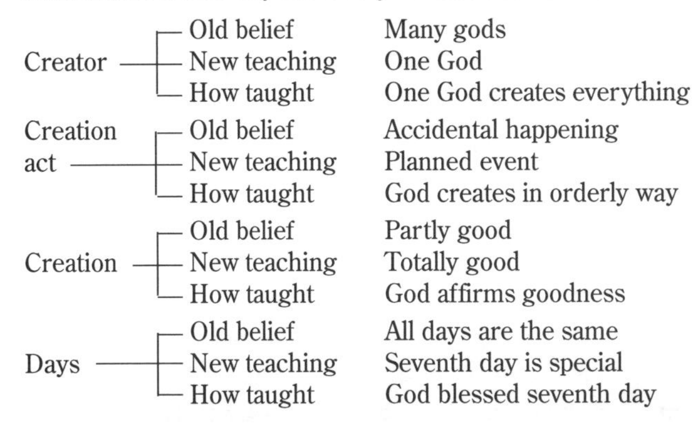

▶ **Discuss** Ask students: What is the worship of one god called? (Monotheism) Many gods? (Polytheism)

The prefixes *mono*(theism) and *poly*(theism) derive from the Greek, meaning "one" and "many." Students will recognize how the prefixes combine to form the word *monopoly*.

▶ **Notebook** Develop the following "God views" on the chalkboard for entry in students notebooks.

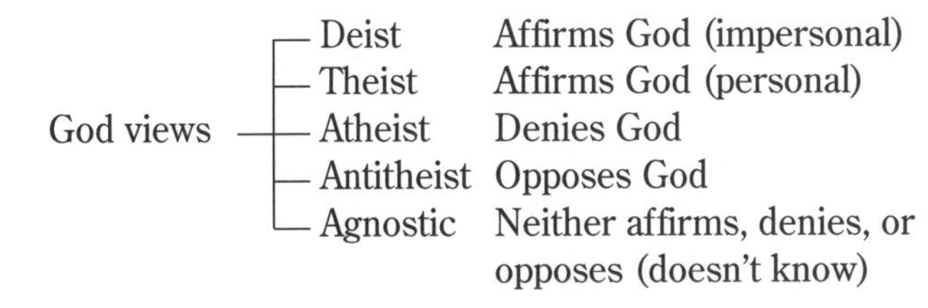

▶ **Clarify** The deist views God impersonally. In other words, God created the universe, but in such a way that leaves God free from personal concern about what happens to it. God lives in a detached state from the world.

Karl Marx seems to fit the category of an antitheist. He opposed the idea of God, because he felt religionists were "using" the idea of God to maintain an unjust status quo. They promised exploited workers reward ("pie in the sky, by and by") instead of justice on earth right now.

Review Have students recall the difference between the way literalists (fundamentalists) and contextualists interpret the Bible.

Interpreters	Literal	Consult text only
	Contextual	Consult text and context

Clarify A way to view the first creation story is to think of it in terms of being an "overture" to the Torah. Just as the overture of a symphony previews key themes to be developed in the symphony, so the first creation story does something similar for the Torah (first five books of the Old Testament).

5. LESSON INTERACTION

Exercise 1 **Activity** **(a)** CB (citizens-band radio) is a good example of metaphorical language, as opposed to literal language.

The answers to the matching exercise are:

3	Drop the hammer	1. Gasoline
5	Portable parking lot	2. Passengers
4	Pregnant roller skate	3. Accelerate
6	Window washer	4. Volkswagen
7	Nap trap	5. Auto carrier
1	Motion lotion	6. Rainstorm
2	Seat covers	7. Motel

Have the students sleuth out these additional expressions: Fly in the night (police aircraft overhead), Smokey's got ears (police car with CB), Texas Chevy (Cadillac), Tijuana taxi (police car with lights), Harvey Wallbanger (reckless driver).

(b) The above examples illustrate the importance of context in determining the meaning of a word or expression. Stress the point that the contextual interpreter believes the Bible to be "God's word in the words of man" (Alexander Jones). Ask: What does that expression mean?

Exercise 2 **Discuss** Caution: Be prepared for the infamous, single-finger sign—one of our culture's most vulgar hand signs. The less said about it, the better.

TV's Gene Siskel (*Chicago Tribune*) and Roger Ebert (*Chicago Sun Times*) popularized the thumbs-up sign to recommend a movie. They also used a thumbs-down sign to pan a movie.

Exercise 3 **Discuss** These three quotes fit together. You might wish to treat them that way. Ask: What is Browning referring to when she says that those who see "take off their shoes"? (Recall that God told Moses to take off his shoes as he approached the "burning bush" [Exodus 3:5].)

Exercise 4 **Clarify** In "Man into Superman," *Time* magazine says, "Human cloning, the asexual reproduction of genetic carbon copies, raises questions." For example, who shall be cloned and why? The article goes on to suggest possible answers: "Great scientists? Composers? . . . a breed of superwarriors?"

Clarify Cloning introduces us to the little-noticed revolution in reproductive biology that is going on today. We may outline it this way.

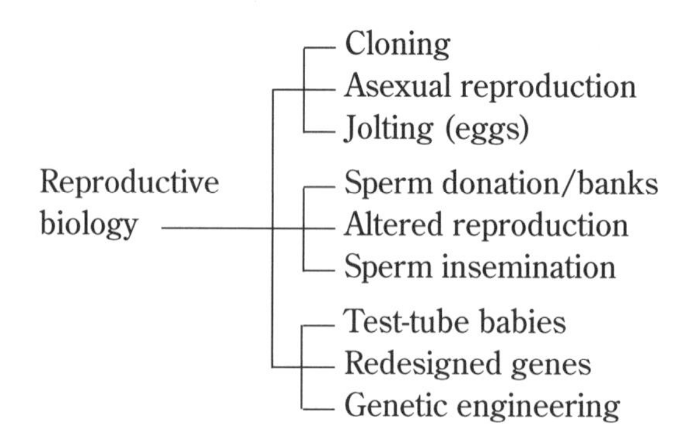

Clarify Asexual reproduction is also called parthenogenesis, after the Greek *parthenos* ("virgin"). It refers to generating birth by a single parent only. For example, numerous plants reproduce themselves from a single parent. Some insects like the honeybee and wasp give birth asexually.

Clarify Another facet of the reproductive revolution is the redesigning of genes (genetic engineering).

In Cambridge, England, in 1953, James Watson and Francis Crick decoded the structure of the DNA (salt of deoxyribonucleic acid), the fundamental molecule of life.

Conceptually, DNA is a tiny computer, miniaturized beyond Sony's wildest dream. . . . A single thread of DNA located in just one human cell may house as much information as one thousand books, each six hundred pages thick.

Ted Howard and Jeremy Rifkin, *Who Should Play God?*

In 1973, the first human gene was isolated for study. Scientists now have information on many of the twenty thousand pairs of genes in a human.

This information opens up a whole new world of possibilities. Alvin Toffler gives examples in his book *Future Shock:* "The ability to preset the sex of one's baby, or even to 'program' its IQ, looks, and personality traits, must be regarded as a real possibility."

Photo **Discuss** Direct the students to the de Mello quote in the photo caption on page 17. It makes an important point. God not only created the world but holds it in being.

We might compare creation to the images on a movie screen and God to the projector that holds them there. Without the projector the images wouldn't be there. Nor would they remain there. De Mello makes this same important point in a more poetic, striking way.

CHAPTER TWO: creation (pages 18–19)

Second Creation Story

LESSON **9**

1. LESSON BACKGROUND

▶ *Catechism of the Catholic Church,* 80–84.

2. LESSON QUIZ

Perfect score = 10 points

1. Explain why the following truths, taught in the first creation story, were revolutionary: (a) God is one, (b) God created the universe according to a plan, (c) God created everything good. *(Lesson 8 review—3 points)*
2. What view or attitude do the following have toward God: (a) deist, (b) theist, (c) atheist, (d) antitheist, (e) agnostic? *(Lesson 8 notebook review—5 points)*
3. List the two ways that the second creation story complements the first. *(Lesson 9 preview—2 points)*

3. LESSON HOMEWORK

▶ **Return** Lesson 8 review questions (page 17).

▶ **Collect** Lesson 9 review questions (page 19).

▶ **Read** Lesson 10 ("Creation of Woman," pages 20–21).

▶ **Write** Lesson 10 review questions (page 21).

▶ **Appoint** Student to prepare reading from Genesis 2:4b–25 (lesson 10, exercise 4).

4. LESSON PRESENTATION

Point ① **Read** Have volunteers read aloud the core content of lesson 9.

▶ **Clarify** Acquaint the students with some of the differences between the first and the second creation stories.

Have the students appointed to prepare Genesis 1:1–2:4a and Genesis 2:4b–25 read aloud to the class. Have them include the verse numbers in their reading.

▶ **Notebook** After each reading, have the students record in their notebooks how the two stories differ concerning (1) what was present *before* God began creation, (2) the order in which God created, (3) the amount of time God spent in the creation process. (There are many other significant differences between the two stories. These are listed only for the sake of illustration, simplicity, and clarity.)

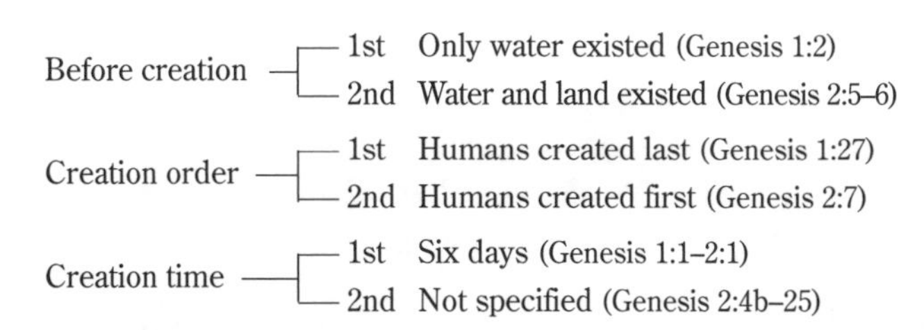

Point ② **Clarify** Some experts suggest the breath imagery was inspired by mouth-to-mouth resuscitation, with which ancients seem to have been familiar. For example, 2 Kings 4:32–34 reads:

When Elisha arrived, he . . . lay down on the boy,
placing his mouth, eyes, and hands
on the boy's mouth, eyes, and hands.
As he lay stretched out over the boy,
the boy's body started to get warm.
[The boy was restored to life.]

▶ **Clarify** God is portrayed in the second story of creation in a similar manner: breathing life into the nostrils of the clay figure that God fashioned from the soil.

Point ③ **Discuss** Have the reader appointed to prepare the second creation story reread Genesis 2:19–20.

Stress the point made in the core content: "Naming something is a symbolic way of showing that the person naming it has power or dominion over it."

Ask: What point (first story) does this reinforce? ("We will make human beings. . . . They will have power over the fish, the birds, and all animals" (Genesis 1:26).

▶ **Clarify** This ancient idea (naming something gives you control over it) is used extensively today. For example, psychologists and psychiatrists try to get people to "name" their problems and fears. This is the first step in controlling them.

▶ **Notebook** We may sum up the two key images in the second creation story for entry in student notebooks:

Second story
- Breath — Symbolizes the intimacy between God and people
- Name — Symbolizes authority of people over animals

5. LESSON INTERACTION

Exercise ① **Clarify** Because literalists believe that creation took place as the Bible describes it, they reject the theory of evolution. They hold that the kinds of life on earth came directly from God's hand.

Literalists do stress, however, the importance of the word *kind.* They do not rule out the possibility of variations within a specific "kind."

For example, they point out that there are many varieties of dogs, horses, cats. Yet, each is still a member of the same original "kind." (See William E. Dankenbring, "Why the New Evolution Creation Controversy?" *Plain Truth* magazine (June 1973).

Clarify Contextual Bible readers have no problem with evolution. They hold that the biblical writer did not intend his account to be a blow-by-blow account of how creation took place. That is not its purpose.

Christian evolutionists, like Augustine, theorize that God could have created a "seed" of matter, which contained the ingredients for every created thing that now is. The original seed then evolved into our present world.

Notebook We may summarize the creationist/evolutionist theories of the origin of things this way:

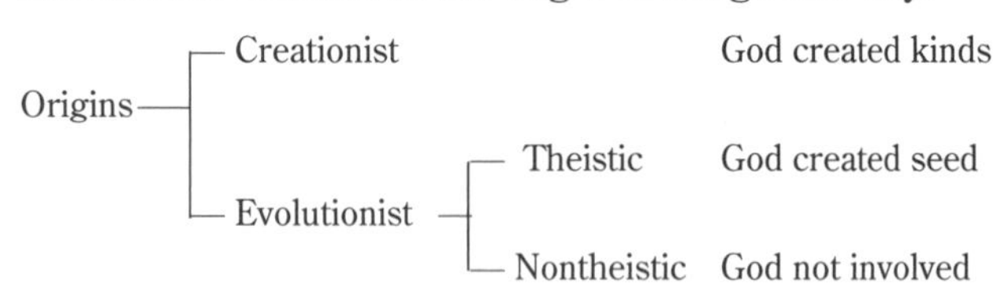

Clarify Christian evolutionist theories do not contradict the biblical story of creation. It was never intended to be a literal description of the way God created the universe.

Christian evolutionists theorize that the "seed matter" developed by a series of "quantum leaps"

- from nonlife to vegetative life,
- from vegetative life to sense life,
- from sense life to conscious life.

With the final "quantum leap," the evolutionary process became conscious of itself. And for the first time, it could ask itself: Is this the final "leap" in the evolutionary process, or is there another?

Christian evolutionists say there is "another." Jesus himself revealed this when he said, "I have come in order that you might have life—life in all its fullness" (John 10:10). But Jesus went an important step further, saying, "I am the way, the truth, and the life" (John 14:6).

Clarify And so the next "quantum leap" in life is the leap from *human* life to *divine* life. And that leap occurred in Jesus, who wishes to communicate it to us.

Previous to the leap to conscious life, the evolutionary process was "blind" and proceeded without the subjects of the process involved in a conscious way. Now all that is changed. We have the power and the free will to decide whether or not we will take the next "quantum leap."

Notebook We may summarize Jesus' role in the Christian evolutionists' view this way:

Jesus	Truth	Teaches about divine life
	Life	Has divine life
	Way	Gives divine life to his followers

Exercise 2 **Clarify** **(a, b)** If students show an interest in the "big bang" theory, you might pursue the subject. For example, how long ago did the "big bang" occur?

Estimates range from 10 to 20 billion years. Space-age expert Dr. Carl Sagan suggests an interesting illustration. Suppose it occurred 15 billion years ago. Here is what the "creation" timetable would look like if telescoped into one year.

January 1	Big Bang takes place
May 1	Milky Way galaxy appears
September 1	Earth appears
December 1	Animals appear
December 31	Humans appear
January 1	Space age begins

Commenting on the "big bang" theory, the British astronomer Sir Bernard Lovell says that one second after the explosion came the "critical period," when the amounts of helium and hydrogen were established.

Had the forces of attraction between protons been minutely stronger, Lovell says, "then all the hydrogen in the primeval condensate would have turned to helium." Had this happened, no stars or life would have emerged.

The automatic conclusion that flows from the "big bang" theory delights theologians. It points to a beginning (creation) of the universe. Where did the original fireball come from?

Robert Jastrow, former director of NASA's Goddard Institute for Space Study, says that the idea of an "abrupt beginning" of the universe caught the scientific community by surprise. In his book *God and the Astronomers,* Jastrow sums it all up with this colorful image:

The story ends like a bad dream. The scientist has scaled the mountains of ignorance; he is about to conquer the highest peak; as he pulls himself over the final rock, he is greeted by a band of theologians who have been sitting there for centuries.

(c) The "big bang" backers might say that the "light" that God created first was that created by the "big bang." From then on, the rest of the universe came into being.

Exercise 3 **Activity** This can be a fun exercise for students. Have them share their findings with the rest of the class.

Exercise 4 **Discuss** This exercise sets up the question that will be taken up in lesson 11. Merely raise the question here.

Creation of Woman

LESSON **10**

1. LESSON BACKGROUND

▶ *Catechism of the Catholic Church*, 337–349, 369–376.

2. LESSON QUIZ

Perfect score = 7 points

1. Explain the difference between theistic and non-theistic evolutionists. *(Lesson 9 review—2 points)*
2. In what sense is Jesus (a) the "truth," (b) the "life," and (c) the "way"? *(Lesson 9 notebook review—3 points)*
3. Explain the twofold interpretation (teaching) that contextualists give to the story of God's creation of woman. *(Lesson 10 preview—2 points)*

3. LESSON HOMEWORK

▶ **Return** Lesson 9 review questions (page 19).

▶ **Collect** Lesson 10 review questions (page 21).

▶ **Read** Lesson 11 ("Problem of Evil," pages 22–23).

▶ **Write** Lesson 11 review questions (page 23).

▶ **Appoint** Two students to prepare the "Dark Willard" TV report (lesson 11, exercise 5).

4. LESSON PRESENTATION

Point ❶ **Read** Have volunteers read aloud the core content of lesson 10.

▶ **Discuss** Tom Anderson of Bernardsville, New Jersey, rented an ocean cottage for a two-week vacation. Before driving to the beach with his wife, he resolved that for two weeks he would be the ideal husband.

So he began. For two weeks he made no phone calls to the office. For two weeks he held his tongue when tempted to say something unkind. For two week he was caring and thoughtful. Everything went great until the last night, when Tom caught his wife staring at him with a deeply concerned look on her face. He said to her, "Honey, what's wrong?"

Tears rolled down her cheeks and she said, "Tom, do you know something I don't know?"

"What do you mean?" he replied.

"Well," she said, "just before our vacation, I went to the doctor for a checkup. Did he tell you something about me? Do you know something I don't know? Do I have cancer? Is that why you've been so kind to me?"

It took a full minute for her words to sink in. Then Tom broke into a laugh. Throwing his arms around her, he said, "No, Honey, you're not going to die. I'm just starting to live."

After reading the above story in *Guideposts* magazine, someone said, "If people worked at their marriages as hard as they do at their jobs, the world would be transformed overnight."

Ask: Why don't people work as hard at their marriages as they do at their jobs?

Point ❷ **Clarify** In *Dictionary of the Bible*, scholar John L. McKenzie points out that in the ancient Near East, women were always subject to a man (husband or father). In general, she had no rights as a free person.

In contrast to this situation, the Genesis story of God's creation of woman presents her as

- a "companion" to man (2: 2:18),
- flesh from his flesh (2:23), and
- one who becomes "one" with her mate (2:24).

McKenzie concludes that the Genesis story implies equality between the sexes. He says, "The implication is made clear in Genesis 3:16, where the existing inferiority of woman is . . . presented as a deterioration from the primitive, unspoiled condition of man."

▶ **Notebook** Develop these two diagrams on the chalkboard for entry in student notebooks.

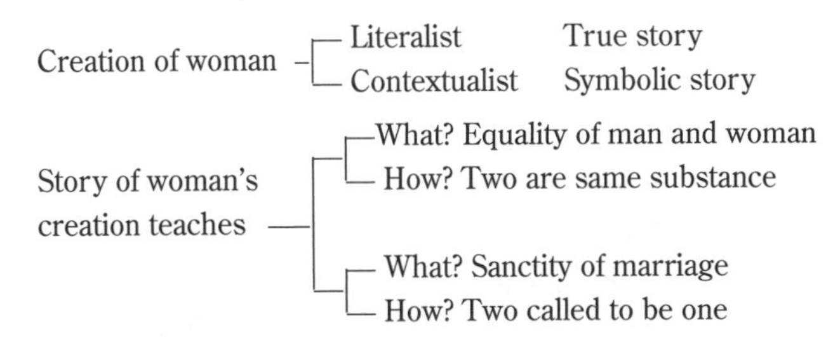

▶ **Clarify** Jehovah's Witnesses use the story of woman's creation (from a rib) to argue the credibility of their "literal" approach to the story, saying, "You accept the scientist's word that we may soon clone from a cell, so why do you reject God's word that he made woman from a rib?"

Contextualists interpret the Genesis story symbolically: teaching the equality of man and woman.

Clarify In his book *Catholicism,* Richard P. McBrien says that of all the possible love relationships (friend-to-friend, mother-to-son, etc.), the only one Jesus raised to the level of a sacrament was the love relationship of wife and husband.

McBrien adds that the "linchpin" of Jesus' teaching concerning this love relationship "was his concern for the dignity of woman, which went far beyond contemporary Jesus attitudes and customs."

Clarify Some students protest the idea of "equal dignity," because Adam "named his wife Eve, because she was the mother of all human beings" (Genesis 3:20). They say, "Doesn't naming someone or something symbolize control over the person or object?"

The answer is normally "yes." But the reason for the name ("because she was the mother of all human beings") takes it out of the normal context of intending to show Adam's "dominion" over Eve. The naming here falls into the category of receiving a name consonant with one's future vocation.

Point ❸ **Activity** The love relationship between man and woman raises the question of love relationships in general. Have the students list the various types of love relationships that can exist between people.

Next, dictate these three questions to the students. Have them respond in writing and in private.

1. List three qualities (in the order of their importance) that you look for in a friend.
2. When should you try to save a friendship that is breaking up, and how would you go about doing it?
3. What should/can you do when your parents strongly disapprove of one of your friends?

Finally, have the students share and discuss their response to each question.

Point ❹ **Discuss** Dr. Lee Salk was the brother of Jonas Salk, who developed the first polio vaccine in the 1950s. Lee, a practicing psychologist, wrote *My Father, My Son.* In this book, Lee quotes Mark Chapman, convicted slayer of Beatle John Lennon, as saying:

"I don't think I ever hugged my father. He never told me he loved me. . . . I needed emotional love and support. I never ever got that."

Have the students answer this question anonymously on a small sheet of paper: When was the last time your father kissed you? Collect the sheets and tally the results on the chalkboard.

Activity It is against the background of modern parent-child relationships that the Mormon Church ran an ad in the *Reader's Digest* some years ago.

The ad consisted of a series of questions. Here are three of them. Before reading the questions, ask the students: How do you think your parents would answer them? Then read the questions one by one, pausing after each one to allow time for the students to respond in writing—and anonymously. Also have them explain why they answered as they did.

1. If your children saw a teenage boy on television kiss both of his parents good night, would they consider this to be normal?
2. If you had guests for dinner, would you be comfortable asking *any* of your children to say grace?
3. If your child asked you, "Why did God let Grandpa die?" would you be able to give the child an answer that would reassure him or her?

Now have the students go back and give the answer that they hope their own children would give to these questions—and explain why.

Collect the responses, screen out the best four or five, and comment on them in the next class.

5. LESSON INTERACTION

Exercise ❶ **Discuss** **(a, b)** The students should be able to understand and respond to these two questions without difficulty.

Exercise ❷ **Activity** **(a)** This question could be done in writing and discussed right in class.

(b, c, d) These questions might be a written assignment. They could be highly instructive.

Exercise ❸ **Activity** This exercise is self-explanatory.

Exercise ❹ **Discuss** Again, this exercise is self-explanatory. Have the appointed student read Genesis 2:4b–25.

Photo **Clarify** Direct the students' attention to the photo caption on page 20. It is a reading that couples sometimes choose to have read as part of the Liturgy of the Word at their wedding Mass.

Photo **Discuss** Direct the students' attention to the photo caption on page 21 and ask them to explain it.

Miniposter **Discuss** Ask the students: What is the point of the quote on the miniposter on page 20? Why do/don't you think this quote would make an appropriate toast at your brother's or sister's wedding banquet?

CHAPTER THREE: De-creation (pages 22–23)

Problem of Evil

LESSON 11

1. LESSON BACKGROUND

▶ *Catechism of the Catholic Church*, 386–387.

2. LESSON QUIZ

Perfect score = 6 points

1. What was the status of women in many ancient societies? *(Lesson 10 review—1 point)*
2. List and explain the two things the story of woman's creation teaches about men and women and their marriage. *(Lesson 10 notebook review—4 points)*
3. What do we mean by "de-creation" stories, and how should they be interpreted: literally or symbolically? *(Lesson 11 preview—1 point)*

3. LESSON HOMEWORK

▶ **Return** Lesson 10 review questions (page 21).

▶ **Collect** Lesson 11 review questions (page 23).

▶ **Read** Lesson 12 ("Self Alienation," pages 24–25).

▶ **Write** Lesson 12 review questions (page 25).

4. LESSON PRESENTATION

Point ❶ **Read** Have volunteers read aloud the core content of lesson 11.

▶ **Clarify** Call students' attention to the photo and caption on page 22. The stone mural was part of a series of murals found while excavating the palace of Assyrian King Ashurnasirpal II (883–859 B.C.E.) at Nimrud.

Two inscriptions on these murals testify vividly to the brutality of the ancient Assyrians. Ashurnasirpal boasts how he treated a certain conquered nation.

The first inscription is quoted in the photo caption on page 22. The second inscription reads, "Their young men and their maidens, I burned in fire."

Photos of other discoveries at the Nimrud palace are found on page 24 (next lesson) and page 80.

Have the students locate Nimrud (also called Calah) on the minimap on page 24. Nimrud was in what is now Iraq.

Point ❷ **Notebook** Develop the following diagram on the chalkboard. It summarizes the key ideas concerning the de-creation stories for entry in student notebooks.

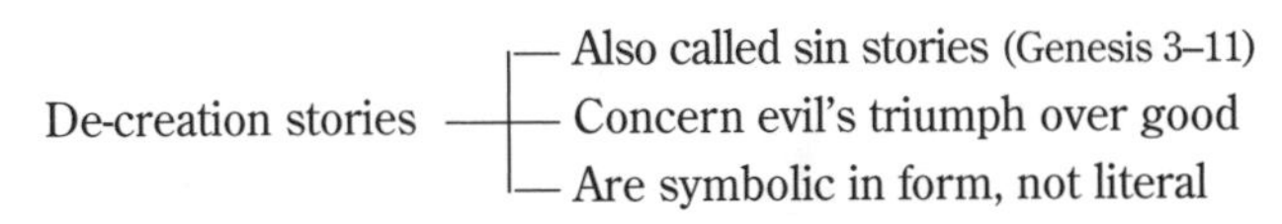

▶ **Notebook** Develop the following diagram on the chalkboard for entry in student notebooks. It summarizes the key ideas concerning the first sin story.

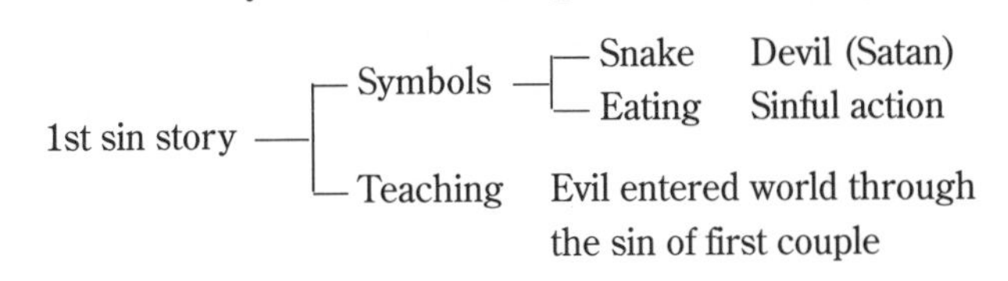

Point ❸ **Discuss** Ask the students: How did ancient Greeks explain the presence of evil in the world?

Recall the story of "Pandora's Box." There are many versions of it. Here is one:

> Prometheus steals fire from the gods to improve the lot of humans. This angers the gods, because it moves humans a step closer to being like gods. In retaliation, the chief god, Zeus, has Prometheus chained to a mountain.
>
> For a thousand years, Prometheus remains bound and is attacked nightly by vultures. Finally, Hercules frees Prometheus. Now the gods really get mad.
>
> Zeus has Pandora created from earth and water. All the other gods bring "gifts" (*pan-dora* means "all gifts") and put them in a box to be carried down to earth by Pandora.
>
> Once on earth, Pandora opens the box. From it fly all the evils that now plague the human race. When Pandora sees what happens, she closes the box, accidentally trapping the last gift—"hope"—from flying out.

Ask students: What is the major difference between the Bible story of how sin entered the world and the Greek story?

▶ **Notebook** Summarize the conclusions on the chalkboard for entry in student notebooks.

Origin of evil
- Bible story — People responsible
- Greek story — Gods responsible

5. LESSON INTERACTION

Exercise 1 **Activity** Consider dramatizing this exercise by having a student come to the front of the room and hold a book (representing the hot shell casing). Then have volunteers come up and demonstrate the three ways of learning whether the shell casing is hot.

First, the volunteer might touch the metal. That is, the student could experience the heat firsthand.

Second, the volunteer could reason it. For example, the student might put something on it, like water or cheese. If it sizzled or melted, the student could reason that the casing is hot.

Third, the volunteer could ask the person, who would presumably tell the truth. In other words, the student could take the word of (believe) another.

▶ **Discuss** Ask: By which of these three ways did the first couple learned about evil? (Clearly, they learned about it by experiencing evil firsthand—becoming evil. They both shared some evil act.)

▶ **Notebook** Summarize the three ways of learning for entry in student notebooks.

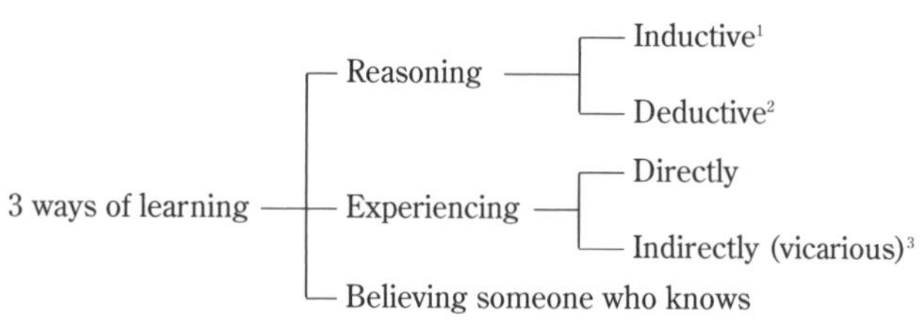

[1] Inductive reasoning goes from the particular to the general. I meet five people from Yale. All are smart. I conclude that everybody who goes to Yale is smart.

[2] Deductive reasoning is just the opposite. It goes from the general to the particular. Such reasoning is syllogistic.

[3] An indirect (vicarious) experience substitutes for a direct one. I can have a vicarious experience by reading a report of another's direct experience.

Obviously, reasoning is subject to error. Stuart Chase gives a fascinating example.

Years ago, New Hebrides inhabitants once believed lice contributed to health. They drew this conclusion because their sick people rarely had lice. Their reasoning went like this:

Syllogism	Major	All healthy people have lice.
	Minor	Sick people rarely have lice.
	Conclusion	Lice contribute to health.

The real explanation was quite different. Sick people usually run a fever. The added body heat makes the lice uncomfortable and causes them to switch bodies for a while.

▶ **Clarify** Review the purpose of this chapter. It seeks to answer this important question: If *moral* evil (sin) is our fault, whom do we blame for *physical* evil (pain)?

Exercise 2 **Discuss** This exercise makes for good discussion and sets up exercise 3.

Exercise 3 **Discuss** **(a, b)** Corman's point is this: God gave us a free will, which we can use for good or ill. God also gave us the intelligence and the necessary grace to defeat evil (misuse of free will). It is up to us to use our intelligence and to open our hearts to God's grace and destroy the evil in our world.

▶ **Discuss** George Burns played God in the film version of Corman's book. Burns wore thick glasses and a funny little hat. Ask: Why dress God this way?

John Denver played a supermarket employee. One day God appeared to Denver with a message for the people of the world.

Getting people to take the message seriously, however, turned out to be harder than Denver anticipated. Soon he found himself on the verge of losing his job.

Frustrated, he turned to God and complained bitterly, "Preaching your word is costing me my job."

God replied, "'That's not a bad trade, is it? Lose your job in exchange for saving the world?"

This bit of dialogue illustrates the point God makes in the passage quoted in the exercise. God has given us all we need to bring about God's kingdom on earth. The problem is that we aren't willing to make the sacrifices necessary to bring it about.

Exercise 4 **Activity** This exercise can be extremely valuable for both the students and the people interviewed. Sift through the responses and share the better ones (or excerpts from them) with the class.

Exercise 5 **Activity** Have the appointed students present their skit to the class. It can be a real fun affair.

Miniposter **Discuss** Direct students' attention to the miniposter on page 22. Ask: What point is Shakespeare making by his statement?

Photo **Discuss** Direct students' attention to the photo caption on page 23. Ask: What point does it make?

Self Alienation

LESSON 12

1. LESSON BACKGROUND

▶ *Catechism of the Catholic Church*, 390–398.

2. LESSON QUIZ

Perfect score = 7 points

1. What is the Bible's answer to the question: If God created everything good, where did evil come from? *(Lesson 11 review—1 point)*
2. List and explain the two main symbols of the first sin story in the Bible. *(Lesson 11 notebook review—4 points)*
3. What did nakedness symbolize in many ancient cultures, and how does the Genesis writer use it in the second sin story? *(Lesson 12 preview—2 points)*

3. LESSON HOMEWORK

▶ **Return** Lesson 11 review questions (page 23).

▶ **Collect** Lesson 12 review questions (page 25).

▶ **Read** Lesson 13 ("God Alienation," pages 26–27).

▶ **Write** Lesson 13 review questions (page 27).

4. LESSON PRESENTATION

Point ❶ **Read** Have volunteers read aloud the core content of lesson 12 .

▶ **Discuss** Again, call attention to the photo and caption on page 24. Recall that the stone mural was one of several excavated by archaeologists at an ancient palace at Nimrud.

Ask: Why do you think Assyrians treated conquered people as brutally as this and other murals depict? (They wanted the reputation of being brutal. This induced enemies to negotiate with them to surrender rather than fight.) Again, locate Nimrud (also called Calah) on the minimap on page 24.

Point ❷ **Clarify** Isaiah used the image of nakedness to prophesy defeat and disgrace for Egypt and Ethiopia, saying:

The emperor of Assyria
will lead away naked the prisoners
he captures from those two countries.
Young and old,
they will walk barefoot and naked,
with their buttocks exposed. Isaiah 20:4

Summarize the key symbol for entry in student notebooks.

First couple's nakedness symbolizes —
- Defeat and disgrace
- Alienation (from self)

5. LESSON INTERACTION

Exercise ❶ **Discuss** **(a)** Ask: If you agree with Paul Horn that most people today are uptight, what is causing this unrest?

Ask: How does Maharishi's metaphor of the trees and forest apply to society today?

▶ **Discuss** **(b, c)** How does the ancient Chinese proverb, quoted below, suggest a link between "the way people feel today and the way the first couple felt after the first sin"?

If there is right in the soul,
There will be beauty in the person;
If there is beauty in the person,
There will be harmony in the home;
If there is harmony in the home,
There will be order in the nation;
If there is order in the nation,
There will be peace in the world.

▶ **Discuss** Maharishi agrees with the Chinese proverb and insists that the first step in changing the world is changing individuals. In other words, by bringing peace to individuals you bring peace to the world.

He maintains that changing the world is not as impossible as you think. He says that if just 1 percent of the world's population changes, significant changes will begin to take place in the world. And if 5 percent of the world's population changes, you will see dramatic changes take place in the world.

Ask: Why should such small changes impact our world so dramatically?

▶ **Clarify** In the 1970s Maharishi launched a massive TM meditation movement. It spread rapidly to twenty-three countries.

In the United States alone, he established four hundred centers out of which six thousand meditation teachers operated.

The TM program involved two twenty-minute sessions daily, using a "mantra form" of meditation.

That is, the meditation procedure involved the repetition of a word or phrase with each breath you took.

Interest in TM boomed when scientific testing by Harvard's Dr. Hubert Benson and R. Keith Wallace demonstrated dramatic stress reduction in meditators.

The TM movement also involved controversy. Many religious groups, especially fundamentalists, charged that Maharishi was exporting (in a subtle way) his own brand of Eastern religion. Others maintained that TM lacked an "ethical stance." In other words, a bank robber might use it before a heist to lessen tension.

Dr. Benson went on to adapt TM so that it was completely separated from any hint of religion. He demonstrated that one meditation period (fifteen to twenty minutes daily) would produce similar results (dramatic stress reduction).

Benson proposed these five simple guidelines for those who wanted to experiment.

1. Meditate before eating (or at least two hours after eating), because digestion interferes with the meditation process.
2. Meditate in a quiet spot, sitting straight up (don't slouch) in a comfortable chair.
3. Begin meditation by closing your eyes and relaxing your body, beginning with your toes and moving upward to the crown of your head.
4. Pick a word or phrase of your choice and repeat it in rhythm with your breathing. (If your mind wanders during meditation, simply return your focus, gently, to your chosen word or phrase.)
5. When you finish, open your eyes and sit quietly for a few minutes before going about your business.

▶ **Activity** If the mood in class is right, have the students experiment with meditation, using Benson's five guidelines.

▶ **Activity** Ask for volunteers to meditate each day for a week for at least four minutes. If they wish, they may meditate longer, but not longer than fifteen minutes.

At the end of the week have them report to the class about how the meditation affected them. (It might be helpful for them to jot down a few lines in a journal after each meditation: Did you find it hard to do this for four minutes? Did you feel more relaxed? Did any thoughts occur to you during the meditation? If so, what?)

Exercise 2 **Discuss** Begin by clarifying what is meant by "group," or "social," sin.

We may think of sin as falling into two categories: personal sin and social sin.

Personal sin involves the free act of a single individual and takes two forms: commission and omission.

A sin of *commission* is doing something we should not do, for example, lying or stealing.

A sin of *omission,* on the other hand, is failing to do something we should do. For example, we see people in need but look the other way to avoid the inconvenience of helping them.

That brings us to group, or *social,* sin. This sin concerns the actions or behavior of a group of which we are a part. For example, some friends in my school or neighborhood group are beginning to steal or experiment with drugs. I may not approve of what they are doing, but I accept it passively without opposing it.

But as Martin Luther King Jr. warned, whoever passively accepts evil is as much involved in it as someone who helps to perpetrate it. And whoever accepts evil without protesting against it is really cooperating with it.

Ask: Why do we accept evil passively, without opposing it? What is the best way to oppose evil in a group?

▶ **Clarify** Regardless of our reasons or excuses, the bottom line on social (group) evil is this: The responsibility to oppose it rests on individuals. It rests on us. To shirk that responsibility is to be guilty of the personal sin of omission.

▶ **Notebook** Develop the following summary on the chalkboard for entry in student notebooks.

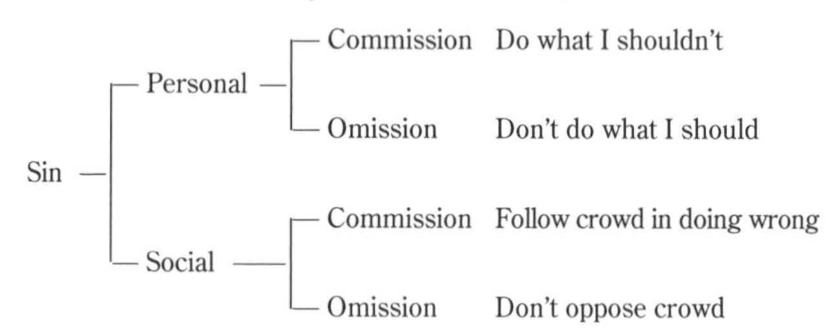

Exercise 3 **Discuss** If the atmosphere is right in class, this can be a tremendous exercise. If there is any doubt about the atmosphere, have the students write out their responses. Then you can collect them, select the best responses (or excerpts), and share them with the class.

Exercise 4 **Activity** You might read this sample prayer by a student. It will help "prime the pump" for your students in creating their own prayers.

Father, the evil in the world today makes me angry.
For example, it seems everybody is greedy.
Even funeral homes cash in on people's tragedies. . . .
Father, it's hard to be a Christian in a greedy world like that!

Jesus, when I am about to give up, remind me of your teachings. Otherwise, I'm going to end up like everyone else.

Holy Spirit, without your help, I can't live as I should. When I'm about to give in or give up, help me.

CHAPTER THREE: De-creation (pages 26–27)

God Alienation

LESSON 13

1. LESSON BACKGROUND

 *Catechism of the Catholic Church*, 399.

2. LESSON QUIZ

Perfect score = 10 points

1. What is the first effect of the first sin on the first couple, and how does the biblical writer teach it? *(Lesson 12 review—2 points)*
2. Explain what is meant by (a) personal sin of commission, (b) personal sin of omission, (c) social sin of commission, (d) social sin of omission. *(Lesson 12 notebook review—4 points)*
3. List and explain the two points (teachings) that emerge from the conversation between God and the first couple. *(Lesson 13 preview—4 points)*

3. LESSON HOMEWORK

Return Lesson 12 review questions (page 25).

Collect Lesson 13 review questions (page 27).

Read Lesson 14 ("Nature Alienation," pages 28–29).

Write Lesson 14 review questions (page 29).

4. LESSON PRESENTATION

Point 1 **Read** Have volunteers read aloud the core content of lesson 13.

Discuss The dialogue between the knight and Death in Ingmar Bergman's play *The Seventh Seal* points up a problem experienced by a lot of people. It is this: Why is God so silent in modern times?

Ask students: How would you answer that question?

One answer is given by the sixteenth-century British poet John Donne. He dramatizes it in one of his poems.

The poem concerns a person who is told that God lives atop a mountain at the end of the earth. The person travels to the mountain and sets out on the long journey up the mountain.

At the moment that the person begins the journey up the mountain, God thinks, "What can I do to show my people how much I love them?"

After thinking about the question, God gets the idea to journey down the mountain and take up residence among the people he loves so much. So he sets out on the long journey down the other side of the mountain.

Thus it happens that when the person (climbing the mountain in search of God) reaches the top, God is nowhere to be found.

The person is crestfallen and thinks, "God doesn't live here! Perhaps God doesn't even exist."

Ask: What point is Donne making in his poem? (Donne implies that God is silent because we are looking for God in the wrong place. We are looking for God in all kinds of faraway, esoteric places. We should be looking for God dwelling in our midst in these places, especially:

- Dwelling in God's least

  "Whenever you did this for one
  of the least important
  of these followers of mine,
  you did it for me!" Matthew 25:40

- Knocking at our hearts

  "Listen! I stand at the door and knock;
  if any hear my voice and open the door,
  I will come into their house and eat with them,
  and they will eat with me." Revelation 3:20

- At the Lord's Supper

  The cup we use in the Lord's Supper
  and for which we give thanks to God:
  when we drink from it,
  we are sharing in the blood of Christ.
  And the bread we break: when we eat it,
  we are sharing in the body of Christ.
  Because there is the one loaf of bread,
  all of us, though many, are one body,
  for we all share the same loaf. 1 Corinthians 10:16–17

- At Christian gatherings

  "Where two or three come together in my name,
  I am there with them." Matthew 18:20

Notebook Develop for entry in student notebooks this summary on God's presence in today's world.

God's presence
- Dwelling in God's least
- Knocking at our hearts
- At the Lord's Supper
- At Christian gatherings

Miniposter **Discuss** Direct the students' attention to the miniposter on page 26.

Ask: Why did one disciple kneel down, while the other disciple wept? (Each read the handwriting in the sand in a different way. The first disciple read it "God is NoW here!" The second disciple read it "God is No Where!")

The way we look at something makes all the difference in the world. For example, a professor lecturing on creativity asked his students to come up with two perfectly correct—but totally unconventional—answers to these two questions:

1. How many seconds are in a year?
2. What are two days that begin with the letter "T"?

Ask: Can you come up with two "creative" answers to those two questions? (1: There are twelve seconds in a year: second of January, second of February, and so on. 2: Today and tomorrow)

Point ❷ **Notebook** The key idea of this section may be summed up this way for entry in student notebooks.

Literary symbols	Hiding	God alienation
	Shifting blame	Self alienation[1]

[1] Shows the unwillingness or inability to accept responsibility for what one has done. The five key symbols of the chapter may also be summarized for entry in student notebooks.

Key symbols	Snake	Evil tempter
	Eating	Evil act
	Hiding	God alienation
	Nakedness	Self alienation
	Shifting blame	Further self alienation

Point ❸ **Discuss** Ask students: What do these two quotations have in common? (1) "The greatest of all faults is to be conscious of none" (Thomas Carlyle). (2) "If we say that we have not sinned, we make a liar out of God" (1 John 1:10).

Both questions relate to what might be called a "sense of sin." John R. Connery describes a sense of sin in "Sin, Sickness and Psychiatry."

The sense of sin is linked to the sense of God. As a man comes into more intimate contact with infinite sanctity and goodness, his awareness of his own defects is sharpened. Remoteness from God, on the contrary, removes the contrast necessary for the sinner to recognize his true condition.

5. LESSON INTERACTION

Exercise ❶ **Clarify** Merton went on to become a priest. His decision to do so came after a night on the town with two friends. They returned to his flat about 4 A.M. They awoke around noon the next day.

While they were sitting on the floor listening to music and eating breakfast, the conviction that he should become a priest came unexpectedly out of nowhere. He said later that it came not as a whim or as a fancy, but as a deep, spiritual longing that suddenly made itself felt.

That Sunday night, Tom got something to eat at a little German bakery and then headed for St. Francis Xavier Church on New York's Sixteenth Street. The Catholic community was gathered in what was known in those days as Benediction (Prayer before the Blessed Sacrament). Tom wrote later in *The Seven Storey Mountain:*

I looked straight at the Host, and I knew, now, Who it was that I was looking at, and I said: "Yes, I want to be a priest, with all my heart I want it. If it is Your will, make me a priest, make me a priest."

It was God's will, and Merton went on to become one of the best known and most respected priests of the twentieth century.

Ask students: Have you ever felt God's presence or a "spiritual longing" in a nonreligious setting, as Merton did? If so, describe the setting and what you felt or thought at the time.

Ask: Have you ever seriously felt called to a religious or priestly ministry? Explain.

Here is what one student wrote in response to those questions. Share it with the students to get them thinking.

I was lying on some grass, fishing near a lake.
I had picked a secluded spot, so I was all alone.
Suddenly, I found myself listening to sounds
and looking at nature around me. I felt so good. . . .
I sat up and felt happy just to be alive.
Then I hooked a fish.
It was the biggest one I had caught all day.
But because of the way I felt,
I put the fish back in the lake and let it swim away.
When I returned to where my friends were,
I didn't mention the fish I caught.

Exercise ❷ **Discuss** **(a)** Be sure to have the students explain each of the four terms before illustrating them. Here is an example: *Self-sufficiency* means I can handle everything on my own. I don't need God.

Commenting on insufficiency, Jesus said:

"I am the vine, and you are the branches. . . .
You can do nothing without me." John 15:5

► **Discuss** **(b)** This question never fails to get a good response from students. Be sure to take it up.

Exercise ❸ **Activity** This exercise requires a certain level of skill that some students may not possess. Ask for volunteers.

Exercise ❹ **Activity** Have students devote the first paragraph to the first question, the second paragraph to the second question, and the third paragraph to the third question.

Nature Alienation

LESSON 14

1. LESSON BACKGROUND

▶ *Catechism of the Catholic Church*, 400.

2. LESSON QUIZ

Perfect score = 9 points

1. Explain how the Genesis writer teaches that the second effect of Adam and Eve's sin is to alienate the couple from God. *(Lesson 13 review—1 point)*
2. List four places where the Bible tells us we can find God, in a special way, in today's world. *(Lesson 13 notebook review—4 points)*
3. Explain the meaning of (a) moral evil, (b) physical evil, (c) tree of life, (d) cherubim. *(Lesson 14 preview—4 points)*

3. LESSON HOMEWORK

▶ **Return** Lesson 13 review questions (page 27).

▶ **Collect** Lesson 14 review questions (page 29).

▶ **Read** Lesson 15 ("People Alienation," pages 30–31).

▶ **Write** Lesson 15 review questions (page 31).

4. LESSON PRESENTATION

Point 1 **Read** Have volunteers read aloud the core content of lesson 14.

▶ **Clarify** The conversation between God and the first couple dramatizes the third effect of sin: alienation from nature. The earth now resists the domination of human beings as they attempt to cultivate it and make it produce food. Human beings will lose domination even over their own bodies, which will now be subject to suffering and death.

And so, the Genesis writer answers the big question: If God created everything good, how did *physical* evil (suffering and death) enter the world? They entered it through *moral* evil (the first sin of the first couple).

▶ **Notebook** Develop the following diagrams on the chalkboard for entry in student notebooks. The first diagram lists the two evils of the world that entered the world through the first sin.

Two evils
- Moral (sin)
- Physical (suffering and death)

The second diagram extends the series of alienations that resulted from the first sin.

Sin alienates		
	Person/self	Shame
	Person/God	Hiding
	Person/nature	Loss of harmony

Point 2 **Discuss** Ask: Does the Genesis writer imply that suffering and death are punishment for sin? (Some would say this, but many others would say that they were *products of* sin, not *punishments for* sin.)

In other words, suffering and death are the result of sin, just as hunger is the result of our refusing to eat or suffocation is the result of our refusing to breathe. Thus, God's words to Adam and Eve need not be interpreted as "inflicting" punishment. They can also be interpreted as "explaining" punishment. (It is the natural consequence of human sin.)

▶ **Notebook** Develop the following diagram on the chalkboard. It points up the distinction between sin as punishment and sin as product (a natural consequence of sin brought on by people themselves).

Suffering and death
- Not a *punishment* from God
- But a *product* of sin itself

Point 3 **Discuss** Recall the point made in this manual (lesson 11, exercise 3), namely, that thanks to God's grace and goodness, we can transform suffering (the cross) into something good (a blessing). An example of what we mean by this is found in Edna Ferber's novel *So Big*.

In the story, Dallas O'Meara (a young artist) tells Dirk DeJong (a young architect who has fallen in love with her), "You're all smooth; I like 'em bumpy!" She says that the man she marries will have to be someone who has struggled and suffered.

Dallas goes on to explain that struggle and suffering give a person a special kind of beauty and a special kind of strength. This beauty and strength shine in the person's eyes, radiate from his face, and even make themselves felt in the touch of his hand.

Ask students: How do struggle and suffering, when accepted and dealt with positively, give someone a special strength and a special beauty?

Notebook Summarize these symbols on the chalkboard for entry in student notebooks.

Two symbols		
	Tree of life	Source of immortality
	Cherubim	Stumbling block to immortality

Photo **Discuss** Direct attention to the photo at the bottom of page 28. Before having a student read the caption, ask: Besides the humanoid head, what else is unusual about the cherubim? (It has five legs. The caption explains the reason for this.)

Photo **Clarify** To get a better idea of the enormous size of the cherubim sculptures, direct students' attention to the cherubim pictured in the upper left-hand corner of page 28.

Point ❹ **Clarify** Conclude by reading to the students this passage from Genesis 3:14–15:

Then the LORD God said to the snake . . .
"From now on you will crawl on your belly,
and you will have to eat dust as long as you live.
I will make you and the woman hate each other. . . .
Her offspring will crush your head."

Clarify New Testament writers showed special interest in God's remarks to the snake. They interpreted them as the first indication of a savior:

The Son of God appeared for this very reason,
to destroy what the Devil had done. 1 John 3:8

In other words, the enmity or hostility between the Devil and people has existed from the beginning.

But people (in the offspring of Jesus) will eventually crush evil and destroy it forever.

Notebook Summarize the gist of God's remarks to the snake for entry in student notebooks.

God reveals		
	Hostility	People and the Devil will fight
	Victory	People (led by Jesus) will win

Clarify Unlike today's popular, modern savior-heroes, Jesus paid a high price for his saving activity. Today's savior-heroes are "all smooth." After a few setbacks they win, reinforcing the lie that saving people can be done at no personal cost to oneself.

5. LESSON INTERACTION

Exercise ❶ **Clarify** Pollution occurs when more wastes are dumped into the environment than it can handle or recycle.

Notebook Summarize the forms of pollution for entry in student notebooks.

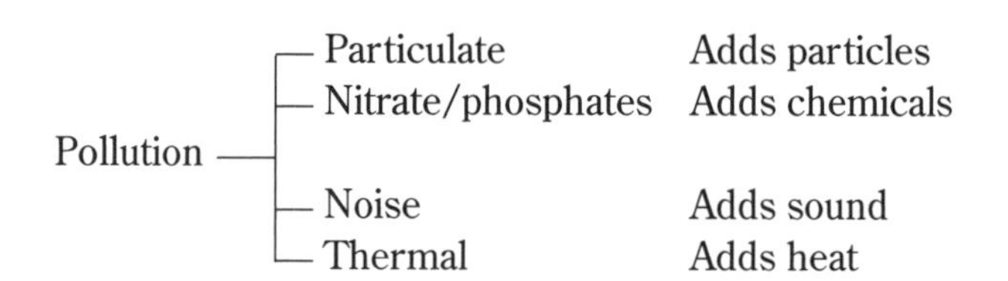

Clarify There are three basic approaches to preserving our environment:

1. Antipollution: We don't add undesirable things to it.
2. Conservation: We don't subtract desirable things from it.
3. Ecological: We respect life and life cycles

Notebook Develop the three approaches to our environment on the chalkboard for entry in student notebooks.

3 approaches		
	Antipollution	Nothing undesirable added
	Conservation	Nothing desirable subtracted
	Ecological	Respecting life and life cycles

Clarify Point out these indications of how badly we had let our environment deteriorate.

1. Breathing the polluted air of some major cities is equivalent to smoking two packs of cigarettes daily.
2. For a while Cleveland's Cuyahoga River got so polluted with chemicals and oil slicks that it caught fire periodically.
3. Power plants and dams shoot hot water into lakes and rivers. Water temperatures rise, disrupting spawning and migration cycles of fish.

Exercise ❷ **Discuss** "Dear Abby," a column by Abigail Van Buren, cites these facts from the publication *50 Simple Things You Can Do to Save the Earth.*

1. If we recycled our Sunday newspapers, we'd save half a million trees a week.
2. If every driver carried one or more passengers to and from work instead of driving alone, we'd save over half a million gallons of gas and keep over ten million pounds of "greenhouse gases" from polluting the atmosphere each day.
3. The U.S. throws away 2.5 million plastic bottles every hour; only a small percentage of these is recycled.

Exercise ❸ **Activity** Encourage the students to be creative. If they wish, they may work in teams.

Photo **Activity** Direct attention to the photo and the photo caption on page 29. You might get the students started by reading these captions turned in by a Dallas class.

1. There's your lost homework—by that inner tube!
2. How would you like to be called the Statue of Litter?

People Alienation

LESSON 15

1. LESSON BACKGROUND

▶ *Catechism of the Catholic Church,* 401, 54–58.

2. LESSON QUIZ

Perfect score = 10 points

1. Briefly describe tree of life and cherubim, and describe what function each played in ancient society. *(Lesson 14 review—4 points)*
2. List and briefly describe the two things God reveals through God's conversation with the snake. *(Lesson 14 notebook review—4 points)*
3. Explain how literalists and contextualists differ on how they interpret the flood story described in the Book of Genesis. *(Lesson 15 preview—2 points)*

3. LESSON HOMEWORK

▶ **Return** Lesson 14 review questions (page 29).

▶ **Collect** Lesson 15 review questions (page 31).

▶ **Read** Lesson 16 ("Alienation Spiral," pages 32–33).

▶ **Write** Lesson 16 review questions (page 33).

▶ **Appoint** Three students to prepare readings of (1) Genesis 7, (2) Genesis 8 (lesson 16, exercise 4), and (3) Matthew 24:37–39 (lesson 16, exercise 5).

4. LESSON PRESENTATION

Point ❶ **Read** Have volunteers read aloud the core content of lesson 15.

▶ **Discuss** Direct students' attention to the photo of Marvin Gaye on page 30, taken at the start of his brilliant twenty-five-year career. Marvin's friend David Ritz entitled his biography of Marvin *Divided Soul.* He explained Marvin's "dividedness" by saying that he was

- part sinner and part saint,
- part artist and part entertainer,
- part macho man and part gentleman.

Now direct the students' attention to the miniposter on page 30. Ask: How does the quote apply to Marvin Gaye?

Biographer David Ritz answers this question, saying of Marvin:

He really believed in Jesus a lot,
but he could not apply the teaching
of Jesus on forgiveness to his own father.
In the end it destroyed them both.

In other words, because Gaye didn't have *within* him that which was *above* him (God's grace to forgive—which he refused), he yielded to that which was *about* him (the way of the world: not to forgive).

▶ **Discuss** Ask: What connection do you see between the quote on the miniposter and Jesus' words:

"I am the vine, and you are the branches. . . .
You can do nothing without me." John 15:5

Point ❷ **Discuss** Contrast Marvin's inability to forgive his father with the following story by Doris Donnelly in her book *Putting Forgiveness into Practice.* Read the story to the class.

Thirty years ago, a seven-year-old boy
was riding between his two older brothers
in the backseat of the family car.
Suddenly, their mother,
drained and distraught from the experience
of her husband's abandonment and a recent divorce,
reached over the front seat
and slammed the seven-year-old across the face. . . .
"You! The only reason I had you," she screamed,
"was to keep your father. I never wanted you!
I hate you!"

The scene was indelibly engraved
in the child's memory. Over the years,
the mother reinforced the sincerity of those remarks
by praising the older sons
and by unnecessarily and continually
finding fault and blame in the youngest one. . . .

I saw the son
many months after he made his decision to forgive.
"I can't tell you
how many times in the last twenty-three years
I relived the scene as a boy in the car," he told me.
"Thousands, probably. But recently . . .
I put myself in my mother's place for a change.
Here she was, a high school graduate
with no money, no job and a family of four to support.
I realized how powerless, lonely, hurt, and depressed
she must have felt.

I thought of the anger, the fear, the pain
that must have been there.
And I thought of how much I must have reminded her
of the failure of all her young hopes.
It was the beginning of my forgiveness of her. . . .
I told her that I understood and that I loved her.
We wept in each other's arms. . . .
It was the beginning of a new life for me. For us."

Ask: What do you think is the main reason why the boy arrived at the point where he could forgive his mother, while Marvin never reached that point? (One thing that the boy seems to have done that Marvin didn't do was to meditate on the situation and put himself prayerfully in his mother's shoes.)

▶ **Discuss** Stress that Marvin's inability to forgive his father was *death-dealing* to both, while the boy's forgiveness of his mother was *life-giving* to both.

Ask: Who should take the initiative when it comes to forgiveness and the reconciliation of two people?

In a *TV Guide* article, Jane Fonda described her movie-star father, Henry, as being a "shy, somewhat troubled and distant parent," who "didn't know how to reach out" to his children. She added that now that she has experienced being a parent herself, she realizes that "blame and judgment are no way to go through life. Forgiveness is important." Then Jane addresses the question of who should take the initiative, saying, "It's the child who must usually make the first move."

Ask: Why must a child usually do this?

Point ❸ **Discuss** Cain's motive for murdering his brother is that God looked with favor on Abel's sacrifice, but not on Cain's. Thus jealousy prompted the act.

Ask: How prevalent is jealously among children in families that you are aware of? What is usually the source of the jealousy among children?

▶ **Discuss** The Bible says, "Abel became a shepherd, but Cain was a farmer" (Genesis 4:2).

The modern musical *Oklahoma* recalls the age-old antipathy between the farmer and the cowman, who should "sing together rather than feud."

Ask: Why should these two be age-old enemies? (One reason was their ongoing dispute concerning what land should be farmed and what land should be left for grazing.)

▶ **Discuss** After slaying Abel, Cain was condemned to wander as a nomad (Genesis 4:12).

Cain complained to God, saying, "Anyone who finds me will kill me" (Genesis 4:14). Nomads had no fortresses for protection. They were targets of armies and roving tribes.

The Genesis writer says that because of Cain's complaint, "the LORD put a mark on Cain to warn anyone who met him not to kill him" (Genesis 4:15).

Some scholars think the "mark" was a tattoo or brand, since these were in common use among Near Eastern nomads. These "marks" identified the tribe to which the nomad belonged and served as protection.

Ask: Why would these marks serve as protection? (For the same reason that having a modern-day gang tattoo or brand affords protection. Harm the gang member, and you have to deal with the gang's retaliation.)

▶ **Clarify** Saint Paul alludes to the idea of a "protective mark" in his letter to the Galatians, saying:

From now on, let no one make trouble for me;
for I carry the marks of Jesus branded on my body.

Galatians 6:17 (NRSV)

Revelation 7:4 describes four angels putting a "mark" on the foreheads of the "servants of our God" to protect them from the punishment that will visit the people of the world.

▶ **Notebook** Develop the following diagram for entry in student notebooks. It extends the series of alienations produced by the first sin of the first couple.

Sin alienates	Person/self	Shame
	Person/God	Hiding
	Person/nature	Suffering and death
	Person/person	Murder

5. LESSON INTERACTION

Exercise ❶ **Discuss** Ask: How is Dr. Norman MacDonald's pessimistic view of our world's future related to the miniposter quote on page 30? (Unless we open our hearts to Jesus *above* us—knocking at the door of our hearts to enter *within* us—we will yield to that which is *about* us, which is precisely what MacDonald is concerned about.)

Exercise ❷ **Discuss** The importance of exercises like this cannot be stressed enough. They make the difference between "head" learning and "heart" learning.

Exercise ❸ **Discuss** **(a)** Henry's point is that one sin produces another, usually larger than the first, just as ripples in water produce more ripples.

▶ **Discuss** **(b)** Gaye could not apply Jesus' teaching on forgiveness to his own father. He had the head knowledge of what he should do, but not the heart knowledge that would enable him to do it.

▶ **Discuss** **(c)** This question should be written out *anonymously.* Collect the responses, screen them, and share the better ones with the group.

Alienation Spiral

LESSON 16

1. LESSON BACKGROUND

2. LESSON QUIZ

Perfect score = 17 points

1. List the four effects of sin that we have seen so far, and tell how the Genesis writer teaches them. *(Lesson 15 review—8 points)*
2. List four ways that sin alienates us, and tell how each is a result of the first sin. *(Lesson 15 notebook review—8 points)*
3. Identify Mount Ararat. *(Lesson 16 preview—1 point)*

3. LESSON HOMEWORK

Return Lesson 15 review questions (page 31).

Collect Lesson 16 review questions (page 33).

Read Lesson 17 ("Alienation Climax, pages 34–35).

Write Lesson 17 review questions (page 35).

4. LESSON PRESENTATION

Point 1 **Read** Have volunteers read aloud the core content of lesson 16.

Notebook Genesis lists two family trees. Both deal with biblical prehistory (pre-Abraham). The first deals with the preflood era (Adam to Noah); the second, with the postflood era (Adam's son to Abraham's father).

The age spans in the family trees decline dramatically, from Adam (930 years) to Terah (70 years).

The purpose of the family trees is to let the Genesis writer (1) leapfrog over centuries of time and (2) show the impact of sin on the human race, evident from the fact that age spans are decreasing.

We may summarize all this on the chalkboard for entry in student notebooks.

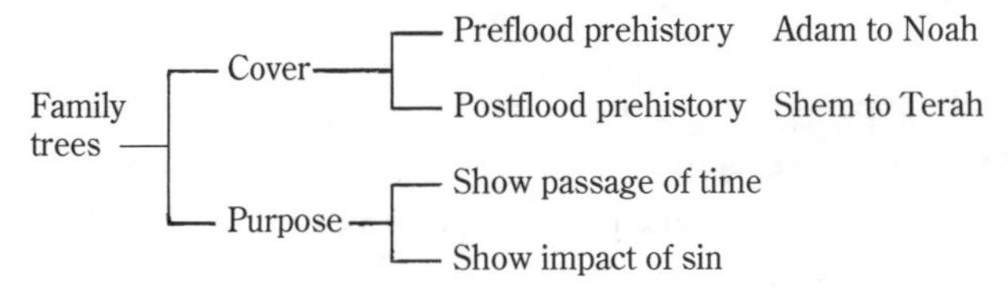

Discuss A good example to illustrate the biblical writer's conviction that sin impacts people not only spiritually but also physically is Oscar Wilde's novel *The Picture of Dorian Gray.* Because it was made into a movie, many students are familiar with the story.

> Dorian Gray was a young man of extraordinary charm and good looks. An artist was so captivated by Dorian's appearance that he produced a striking full-length painting of him. When Dorian saw the painting, he exclaimed, "I'd give my soul to the devil if I could remain young all my life on earth, and have my body in the painting grow old in my stead."
>
> This happens. Soon Dorian gets caught up in a life of sin. He is astounded how his sinful life begins to etch itself into the face on the painting. He becomes so shocked at what he sees that he hides the painting. As Dorian's body in the painting grows more ugly, his physical body is the envy of everyone, because it retains its youthful charm and beauty.
>
> As the years pass, Dorian steals occasional looks at the body in the painting and is horror-stricken at what he sees. One day when he can't stand to look at it anymore, he takes a knife and plunges it into the painting. A bloodcurdling scream echoes throughout the house. Dorian's servants come running. On the wall they see the painting of beautiful Dorian. On the floor, with a knife in his heart, they see a hideously ugly old man. Only when the servants examine the rings on the old man's fingers do they realize who he is.

Ask: How does this story relate to one of the points made by the two family trees? (Sin impacts people not only spiritually but also physically.)

Ask: What are some examples from everyday life that illustrate this point? (The effect of drugs or alcohol on the body)

Point 2 **Clarify** Literalists interpret the flood story in the Bible as describing an actual worldwide flood. They interpret it literally.

In an attempt to document their literal position, Jehovah's Witnesses point out that 70 percent of our planet is covered by water. They point out further that the average land height is one-half mile while the average ocean depth is two and one-half miles.

As a result, if planet Earth were perfectly round and smooth, it would be buried under a layer of water eight thousand feet deep.

Jehovah's Witnesses ask, "Was the earth once smoother than it is now?" They cite *The Scientific Monthly,* which says that "once there were no high mountains forming physical and climatic barriers." Indeed, Psalm 104:9 seems to describe such an event:

You set a boundary they can never pass,
to keep them from covering the earth again.

▶ **Clarify** Contextualists hold the flood story to be prehistory. Since prehistory (before written records were kept) is narrated in symbol stories, they hold the flood story to be a symbol story. Most contextualists, however, think that it is based on a flood tradition, but it was in no way intended to be a literal account.

▶ **Clarify** Genesis says the flood lasted forty days and nights. The number *40* is used symbolically to designate an event that acts as a bridge between two significant eras in salvation history.

▶ **Notebook** Develop this partial list of such events for entry in student notebooks.

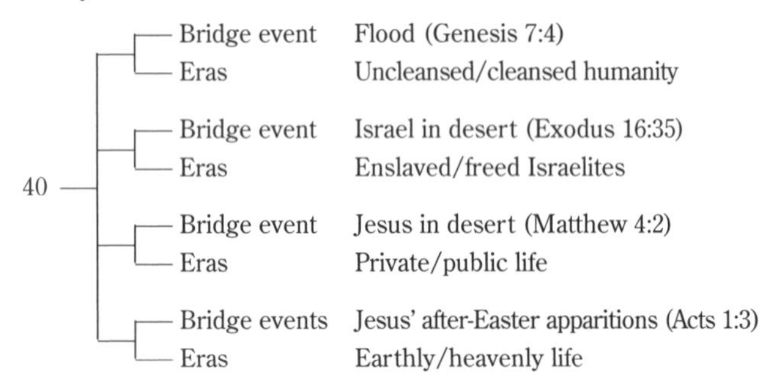

▶ **Notebook** The positions of literalists and contextualists concerning the flood story may be summarized for entry in student notebooks.

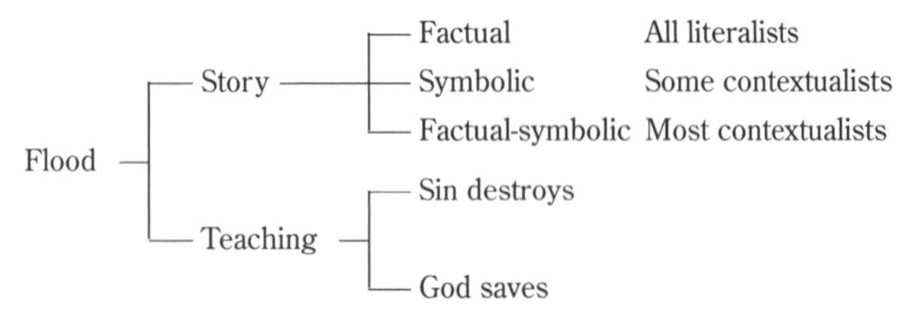

▶ **Clarify** Regardless of how we interpret the flood story (factual, symbolic, or factual-symbolic), the flood teaching is the same.

5. LESSON INTERACTION

Exercise ❶ **Discuss** Literalists (fundamentalists) are eager to find the ark for one big reason: If they do, then this would prove that the prehistory section of the Bible includes not just symbol stories but also historical stories.

Exercise ❷ **Clarify** News of the possible discovery of the ark on Mount Ararat (modern Armenia) made headlines in 1955. An L-shaped wood beam was found in an icy crevice 13,500 feet up Ararat.

Excitement died, however, when UCLA archaeologist Rainer Berger dated it. Using the carbon-14 method, he found "that the timber came from a tree that was chopped down around A.D. 700." One theory about the L-shaped wood beam is that it may have been part of the remains of a shrine built there by early monks in honor of the biblical event.

▶ **Clarify** Despite ark stories like the ones above, there are reliable scholars who question whether Mount Ararat is the same site mentioned in Genesis 8:4. The present Mount Ararat may have been named after the biblical event, not the other way around.

Exercise ❸ **Discuss** Like so many people, the woman mentioned in this exercise thought that she would find happiness in doing whatever she wished. Like the prodigal son (Luke 15:1–24), she discovered this was not true. In that sense "the experience of sin often results in the discovery of the path to light."

Exercise ❹ **Activity** Have the appointed students read Genesis 7 and Genesis 8. Pause after each reading to permit students to enter their reflections in their notebooks, as a prelude to sharing them with the class.

Exercise ❺ **Discuss** Have the appointed student read Matthew 24:37–39. The context of Jesus' words makes it clear that Jesus did not intend to teach that the flood actually happened. Rather, his intention is to use the story (factual or symbolic) to illustrate how the unexpected coming of the flood caught people totally unprepared. So it will be at the end of time. Jesus' second coming will come unexpected and catch many people totally unprepared. This point is stressed by the two parables that follow immediately after Jesus' remarks.

Exercise ❻ **Activity** This exercise is often illuminating and instrumental in helping the students get to know and appreciate one another better.

Alienation Climax

LESSON 17

1. LESSON BACKGROUND

► *Catechism of the Catholic Church*, 406–409.

2. LESSON QUIZ

Perfect score =10 points

1. Identify (a) Mount Ararat, (b) clay tablets, (c) Epic of Gilgamesh. *(Lesson 16 review—3 points)*
2. Genesis lists two family trees. What two periods of time does each deal with, and what twofold purpose do these family trees serve? *(Lesson 16 notebook review—4 points)*
3. List the threefold way we can sum up the state of original sin, created by the first sin of the first couple. *(Lesson 17 preview—3 points)*

3. LESSON HOMEWORK

► **Return** Lesson 16 review questions (page 33).

► **Collect** Lesson 17 review questions (page 35).

► **Read** Lesson 18 ("Call of Abraham," pages 36–37).

► **Write** Lesson 18 review questions (page 37).

► **Appoint** Three students to prepare readings from (1) Genesis 12:1–7, (2) Genesis 12:8–13, (3) Genesis 12:14–20 (lesson 18, exercise 5).

Two students to prepare lesson 18, exercise 1. Suggest they use props.

4. LESSON PRESENTATION

Point ① **Read** Have volunteers read aloud the core content of lesson 17.

► **Clarify** The sin stories of the Book of Genesis end with the Tower of Babel story. Its primary purpose is to introduce us to the fifth and final effect of sin: *alienation of people* (groups and nations) from other people. Sin is the root of divisions, prejudices, and wars.

► **Notebook** Develop the final summary of the five effects of the first sin of the first couple.

Sin alienates
- Person/self — Shame
- Person/God — Hiding
- Person/nature — Disharmony
- Person/person — Murder
- Nation/nation — Pride

Point ② **Clarify** The story behind the ziggurat is interesting. It dates back to the Sumerians, who worshiped on hilltops in their native highland country. When they came to flat Mesopotamia, they built artificial hills called *ziggurats* (literally "mountain peaks") for their worship purposes.

Point ③ **Clarify** Stress the bleak impression that the sin stories leave us with (textbook page 34).

► **Notebook** The impact of the first sin of the first couple may be summarized in this threefold way for entry in student notebooks.

Original sin
- Opens door to evil
- Flaws human race (sin-prone)
- Dooms all to destruction

► **Clarify** When Christians say, "We have found Jesus and accepted him as our savior," they mean that they are no longer doomed. They have been saved, or redeemed, from the situation of original sin.

Faith and baptism into Jesus give Christians a power that will allow them to enter the world and bring themselves and the world to a new level of fulfillment.

► **Notebook** Sketch the following drawings on the chalkboard for entry in student notebooks.

Only Jesus Christ can save me. This is what I mean when I say "Jesus is my savior." When I am baptized into Christ, I am empowered to overcome sin and bring myself and my world to the ultimate fulfillment God intended me to have.

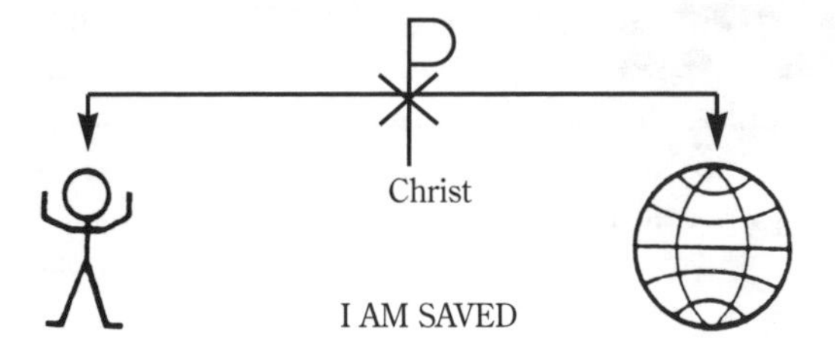

Point ❹ **Discuss** Read the following poem by an anonymous author. As the students listen, have them ask themselves, "Why is/isn't the poem a fair expression of the creation and de-creation of our world?"

In the beginning was the earth.
And it was beautiful.
And people lived upon the earth. And they said:
"Let us build skyscrapers and expressways."
And they covered the earth with steel and concrete.
And the people said: "It is good."

On the second day,
the people looked upon the clear blue waters of the earth.
And they said: "Let us dump
our sewage and wastes into the waters."
And they did. The waters became dark and murky.
And the people said: "It is good."

On the third day, the people gazed at the forests on the earth.
The trees were tall and green.
And the people said: "Let us cut the trees
and build things for our enjoyment."
And they did. The forests grew thin.
And the people said: "It is good."

On the fourth day, the people saw the animals
leaping in the fields and playing in the sun.
And they said: "Let us trap the animals for money
and shoot them for sport."
And they did. And the animals became scarce.
And the people said: "It is good."

On the fifth day, the people felt a cool breeze in their nostrils.
And they said: "Let us burn our refuse
and let the wind blow away the smoke and debris."
And they did. The air became dense with smoke and carbon.
And the people said: "It is good."

On the sixth day, the people saw the many kinds of people
on the earth— different in race, color, and creed.
And they grew fearful and said: "Let us make bombs
and missiles in case misunderstandings arise."
And they did. Missile silos checkered the landscape.
And the people said: "It is good."

On the seventh day, the earth was quiet and deathly still.
For there were no more people. And it was good!

5. LESSON INTERACTION

Exercise ❶ **Discuss** Dorothy Thompson's observation confirms that even the best people—doctors (healers of humanity), statesmen (leaders of humanity), and soldiers (defenders of humanity)—all behaved the same under pressure. They caved in. In other words, given our human vulnerability and the world's corruptibility, we are doomed to capitulate to evil, just as the prison camp victims did. Had God not intervened in human history in the person of Jesus, we would be without hope.

In brief, just as many concentration camp victims were trapped in a situation that doomed them to be corrupted by it, so Genesis 3–11 portrays people trapped in a giant whirlpool of sin that dooms them to be corrupted by it.

Exercise ❷ **Discuss** **(a)** "Deep down people are basically evil" is the thesis of Golding's *Lord of the Flies.* He says of his book, "The theme is an attempt to trace the defects of society back to the defects of human nature."

In other words, the fourteen-year-olds (removed from civilized society) revert back to their basically evil nature.

► **Discuss** **(b)** "Deep down people are basically good" is the thesis of *Catcher in the Rye.* Holden Caulfield is corrupted by evil society.

Have the students write out in private which of the above theses coincides with their view and why. Share their conclusions with the class.

Exercise ❸ **Discuss** William Golding ends his book with an officer from a British cruiser spotting the boys on the island. He arrives just in time to stop the boys from a manhunt for the only boy who has not turned savage. Golding concludes:

The officer having interrupted a manhunt prepares to take the children off the island in a cruiser which will presently be hunting its enemy in the same implacable way. And who will rescue the adult and his cruiser?

Ask students: How would you answer Golding's question? (The Christian's answer, of course, is Jesus Christ. If he had not come into the world, we would be doomed with no hope of salvation.)

► **Discuss** Ask: Assuming your class was marooned on a desert island on which there was just enough food and fresh water to survive, provided a strict ration was maintained, what should be done to a classmate who was caught stealing food or water? What if the person continued to steal in spite of everything?

Ask: What might our class do to guard against a breakdown of morale and morality? For example, would daily or weekly meetings or prayer sessions help?

Exercise ❹ **Discuss** The students should be able to handle the quotations without too much difficulty.

CHAPTER FOUR: Re-creation (pages 36–37)

Call of Abraham

LESSON **18**

1. LESSON BACKGROUND

▶ *Catechism of the Catholic Church,* 59–61.

2. LESSON QUIZ

Perfect score = 10 points

1. With what bleak impression do the sin stories of Genesis 3–11 leave us? *(Lesson 17 review—1 point)*
2. List the threefold way that the first sin of the first couple impacts the human race. *(Lesson 17 notebook review—3 points)*
3. List and briefly explain the ways in which the Book of Genesis may be thought of as being like a stage play in three acts. *(Lesson 18 preview—6 points)*

3. LESSON HOMEWORK

▶ **Return** Lesson 17 review questions (page 35).

▶ **Collect** Lesson 18 review questions (page 37).

▶ **Read** Lesson 19 ("Covenant with Abraham," pages 38–39).

▶ **Write** Lesson 19 review questions (page 39).

4. LESSON PRESENTATION

Point 1 **Read** Have volunteers read aloud the core content of lesson 18.

▶ **Notebook** The fifty chapters of Genesis may be divided as follows: Chapters 1–2 deal with creation; chapters 3–11 deal with de-creation; chapters 12–50 deal with re-creation.

These three divisions may be compared to a three-act play. Summarize them for entry in student notebooks.

Three-act play
- Act 1 Creation — God creates
- Act 2 De-creation — Sin destroys
- Act 3 Re-creation — God saves

▶ **Notebook** The above three acts may be described in fuller detail for entry in student notebooks.

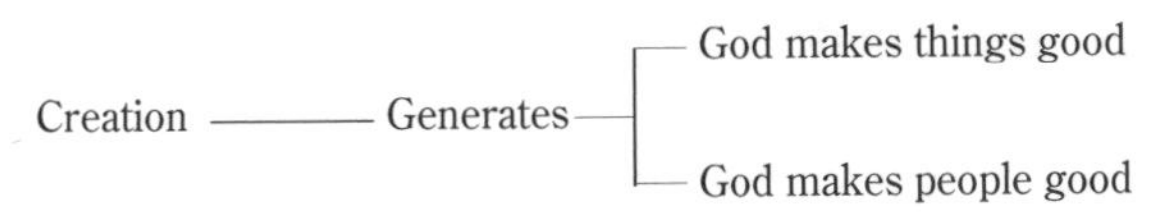

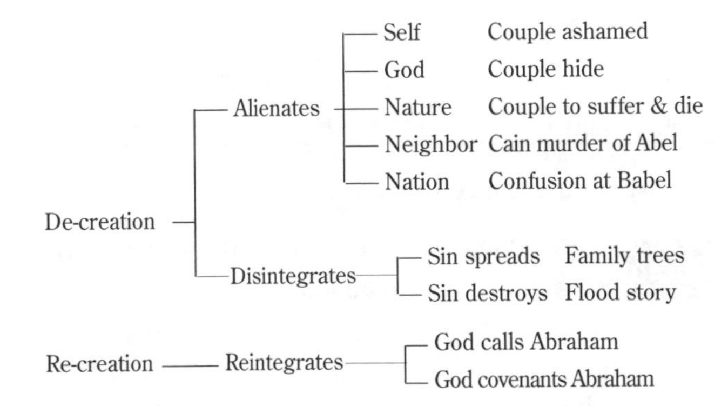

Point 2 **Clarify** An attempt to formulate how God intended us to "use" creation is found in one of the exercises in *The Spiritual Exercises of Saint Ignatius.* Called "Principle and Foundation," it is freely translated below.

Before reading it slowly to the students, instruct them to write the numbers *1* to *4* vertically in their notebooks, leaving four lines after each number.

Next, read the four statements below. Pause after each statement to give the students time to write one of the following three letters after the appropriate number.

A—if they *agree* totally with the statement
D—if they *disagree* totally with the statement
P—if they *partially* disagree with the statement

If they write *P* or *D,* they should explain briefly their reason for doing so.

Now read "Principle and Foundation" slowly, pausing after each statement.

1. I believe that I was created to share my life and love with God and other people, forever. *[Pause]*
2. I believe that God created all other things
   to help me achieve this goal. *[Pause]*
3. I believe, therefore,
   that I should use the other things God created
   insofar as they help me attain my goal and
   that I should abstain from them
   insofar as they hinder me. *[Pause]*
4. It follows, therefore,
   that I should not prefer certain things to others.
   That is, I should not value, automatically,
   health over sickness, wealth over poverty,
   honor over dishonor, or a long life over a short one.
   I believe my sole norm
   for valuing and preferring a thing should be this:
   How well does it help me attain the end
   for which I was created? *[Pause]*

Discuss Tabulate on the chalkboard the number of students who wrote *A, D,* or *P* after each number. The tabulation chart might look something like this:

	A	D	P
Statement 1	33	0	3
Statement 2	26	5	5
Statement 3	24	10	2
Statement 4	20	10	6

Finally, discuss the conclusions.

Point ❸ **Clarify** Stress that three kinds of history are found in the Book of Genesis.

Prehistory — Communicated in *symbol* stories
Folk history — Communicated in *folk* stories
Recorded history — Communicated in *documentary* stories (a clay table or artifact = document)

Clarify Stress that prehistory deals with the origin of the world, humanity, nations, good, evil, and so forth. Folk (oral) history (starting with Abram) deals with the origin of the Jewish people, customs, and so forth.

Point ❹ **Notebook** Summarize Abram's first encounter with God as follows:

1st God-encounter —
- Leave present surroundings
- Listen for future instructions

Ask: Why do you think God's first instruction to Abram is to leave his present surroundings? (Perhaps the seed of his faith is too fragile to grow in his present surroundings. God wanted to transplant him to better soil—away from present distractions and temptations.)

Clarify The "leave/listen" pattern is a familiar one. Someone says, "I must get away [leave] to sort things out [listen]." A retreat is a good example of a "leave/listen" pattern.

Notebook Develop the following graphic on the chalkboard for entry in student notebooks. It contrasts Adam's "no" (to God), igniting the de-creation cycle, with Abram's "yes" (to God), igniting the re-creation cycle.

ADAM'S "NO"

DE-CREATION
Sin: People break off communication with God.

ABRAM'S "YES"

RE-CREATION
Revelation: God reopens communication with people.

5. LESSON INTERACTION

Exercise ❶ **Activity** Have the two students who prepared this exercise present it to the class. After the presentation have the class evaluate how credible or believable they were.

Exercise ❷ **Discuss** Have the students record their responses in private and in writing before sharing them with the class.

Exercise ❸ **Discuss** The boy's conclusion was probably wrong. He did not psyche himself.

Explain that when we commit ourselves to God, we commit only that part of ourselves that we are aware of at the moment. That is all any person can do.

Psychology tells us that the greater part of ourselves lies below our consciousness. It surfaces only gradually with each new experience. This means that people are constantly evolving and changing as persons.

A commitment of faith is never achieved by one decision. It is an ongoing, never-ending process.

Exercise ❹ **Discuss** Folk history is told in a human, anecdotal style, whereas recorded history is told in a more scientific way. Obviously, folk history should not be interpreted as strictly and literally as recorded or eyewitness history.

Exercise ❺ **Activity** **(a, b)** Have the assigned students present their reading of "The Call." After the reading, have the students record their responses before sharing them with the class.

Minimap **Activity** Direct attention to the minimap on page 36. Ask the students to trace Abram's journey. He was born in Ur, migrated to Haran, and eventually ended up in Canaan (modern Holy Land).

Photo **Discuss** Direct attention to the photo caption on page 36 and have the students respond to the question that concludes it.

Photo **Discuss** Direct attention to the photo caption on page 37 and ask the students to explain it.

Covenant with Abraham

LESSON 19

1. LESSON BACKGROUND

▶ *Catechism of the Catholic Church*, 144–147.

2. LESSON QUIZ

Perfect score = 6 points

1. What kind of stories are used to narrate prehistory? *(Lesson 18 review—1 point)*
2. List the two ways de-creation disintegrates, and explain how Genesis teaches them. *(Lesson 18 notebook review—4 points)*
3. Explain how archaeologists have shed light on why Sarai told Abram to have a child by Hagar. *(Lesson 19 preview—1 point)*

3. LESSON HOMEWORK

▶ **Return** Lesson 18 review questions (page 37).

▶ **Collect** Lesson 19 review questions (page 39).

▶ **Read** Lesson 20 ("Mission of Abraham," pages 40–41).

▶ **Write** Lesson 20 review questions (page 41).

4. LESSON PRESENTATION

Point ➊ **Read** Have volunteers read aloud the core content of lesson 19.

▶ **Clarify** Abram's world is no longer a faceless world buried under the debris of history. Archaeologists have exhumed the cities of Abram's time and made them retell their stories and well-kept secrets. Among these cities is Ur, Abram's birthplace.

Ur was the center of a moon cult. And since Abram's father's name, *Terah*, means "moon," his ancestors were probably moon worshipers.

Archaeologists began digging at Ur around 1845. Not until the 1920s, however, did Ur come alive under the excavations of Sir Leonard Woolley, the British archaeologist. Among his discoveries was a tomb chamber dating from 2500 B.C.E. It contained seventy-four skeletons (still ornately clothed), teams of oxen (still in harness), tableware, and musical instruments. Apparently, the whole group was buried alive to join their nobleman master in death.

▶ **Clarify** When Abram arrived in Canaan (modern Holy Land), which God promised to show him, it was under Egyptian control. A portrait of daily life at that time is preserved not only in Scripture but also in Egyptian documents. One such record is the "Story of Sinhue."

The story concerns a man who is traveling from Egypt to Canaan. He runs out of water and his throat is dry with the "taste of death." At the last minute he is found and saved by a Bedouin chief.

The "Story of Sinhue" goes on to confirm existing biblical details about daily life in Canaan. Sinhue says:

It was a good land. . . . Figs grew and so did grapes. Wine was more available than water. We had plenty of honey and olives. There was every kind of fruit tree.

It is this land "flowing with milk and honey" that God promises to Abram and his descendants.

Point ➋ **Clarify** Abram's second encounter with God takes the form of a covenant.

Ask: What does the flaming torch symbolize in the description of the covenant in the textbook? (It symbolizes God's presence.)

Ask: Where else in the Bible is fire used to symbolize God's presence? (*Burning bush,* out of which God speaks to Moses; *pillar of fire* that guides the Israelites through the desert; the *fiery cap* over Mount Sinai at the giving of the Ten Commandments; the *fiery tongues* that appear above each disciple on Pentecost)

Ask: What two things does God promise? (*Descendants* as countless as the stars and the *land* to which God has led Abram. These two promises give rise to two important Old Testament concepts: the Promised Land and the Chosen People.)

▶ **Notebook** Develop these two important Old Testament concepts for entry in student notebooks.

Concepts
- Descendants — Chosen People (Jewish people)
- Land — Promised Land (Holy Land)

▶ **Clarify** A covenant is a solemn promise, sealed with a solemn ritual. Somewhat the way we "seal" a promise with a ritual (handshake), Jews "sealed" a covenant promise with a covenant ritual. The ritual was called "cutting a covenant." Ask: Why this name? (Probably because of the cutting up of the animals)

▶ **Notebook** Develop the following diagram on the chalkboard for entry in student notebooks.

Covenant
- Solemn promise
- Sealed with a solemn ritual

Notebook Review and update the key points of Abram's two God-encounters for entry in student notebooks.

1st God-encounter (instructs Abram)	Leave present surroundings Listen for future instructions
2nd God-encounter (promises Abram)	Descendants (Chosen People) Land (Promised Land)

Point ❸ **Discuss** *Letters from the Desert,* by Carlo Carretto, is exactly what the title says it is: a book of reflections by a person who went into the desert to learn to pray.

Like Abraham, Carlo felt an "inner call" to leave behind his old life and to set out on a new one. He says that God led him by three stages, each one taking him a step further, much as God seems to have led Abraham.

The first stage was his conversion when Carlo was a teenager. He attended a retreat given by an old missionary, explaining:

What I remember most of all
was how boring and outdated the sermons were.
It certainly wasn't the words
which shook my state of apathy and sin. . . .
From that day on I knew I was a Christian,
and was aware that a completely new life
had been opened up for me.

Ask: If it wasn't the missionary's words that inspired Carlo, what was it? (It was God, using the "boring and outdated" words of the missionary. It was Carlo opening his heart to grace, even though he was getting no help from the missionary's preaching.)

Discuss The second stage occurred when Carlo was twenty-three years old and thinking about marriage. He said, "It never occurred to me that I should do anything else." But then it hit him. He felt called to serve God as a single person, free from the responsibilities of a family.

The final stage came when, eventually, Carlo experienced a call to join an order called the Little Brothers of Jesus, who devoted their life to prayer and meditation in the Arabian desert.

Carlo says the thing he loved most about the desert was the stars at night. He writes:

I had come to know them by their names. . . .
I could distinguish their colour, their size,
their position, their beauty.

Summing up his reflections on the starry nights, Carlo writes:

Night is an image of faith. . . . Faith is a gift of God
but it needs effort on our part if it is to bear fruit.

Ask: Explain Carlo's point when he says that "night is an image of faith." (Most people fear going out into the night, partly because they are not familiar with the stars and the peace and beauty of the night. Actually, the night is a gift from God. But to appreciate the gift takes study and effort, as Carlo discovered.)

Ask: Do you think God calls all of us gradually, by degrees? Why might God call us this way? (Probably! Most important things in life unfold gradually, by degrees.)

Activity You might have a student do "extra-credit" research on the Little Brothers of Jesus. Who are they? What do they do?

5. LESSON INTERACTION

Exercise ❶ **Discuss** The cellar-wall inscription speaks eloquently to the question of faith. Faith is not a feeling; it is trusting in God or another, because something deep down inside us (not a feeling, but a conviction) invites us to do this.

Exercise ❷ **Discuss** Be sure to have the students write this exercise out before sharing it. You might collect the responses, screen them later, and share the three or four better responses with the class.

Exercise ❸ **Discuss** Except for the first quote, students should have no trouble handling this exercise. An illustration of what is at issue in *a* is two people who commit themselves in marriage. Their commitment derives partially from *reason* (they have experienced each other's concern and love) and partially from *faith* (they trust they will both continue to show love and concern for each other).

Exercise ❹ **Discuss** Concretize the questions by asking questions such as these: Why have a prom before graduation? Why give a person a ring?

Photo **Clarify** Direct students' attention to the photos on page 39. Wedge-shaped writing dates from about 3500 B.C.E. (some fifteen hundred years before Abraham was born). It began as a pictorial language of about six hundred different characters. It evolved into a more abstract script of about thirty characters. Below are some of the early pictorial symbols.

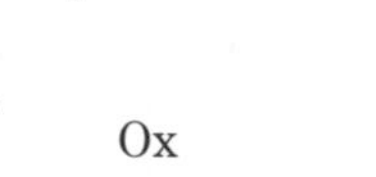
Ox Grain

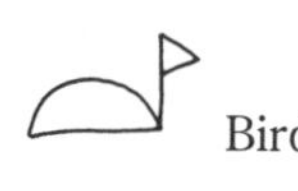
Bird

Fish

CHAPTER FOUR: Re-creation (pages 40–41)

Mission of Abraham

LESSON 20

1. LESSON BACKGROUND

▶ *Catechism of the Catholic Church*, 839–846.

2. LESSON QUIZ

Perfect score = 10 points

1. What twofold promise did God make to Abram in the context of "cutting a covenant," and what did the ritual of passing between two animal halves signify? *(Lesson 19 review—3 points)*
2. Identify and briefly explain the two key Old Testament concepts that result from Abram's second encounter with God. *(Lesson 19 notebook review—4 points)*
3. List the names of Abram's two sons, and tell to which of these sons Arab nations trace their ancestry. *(Lesson 20 review—3 points)*

3. LESSON HOMEWORK

▶ **Return** Lesson 19 review questions (page 39).

▶ **Collect** Lesson 20 review questions (page 41).

▶ **Read** Lesson 21 ("Schooling of Abraham," pages 42–43).

▶ **Write** Lesson 21 review questions (page 43).

▶ **Assign** Student to prepare Genesis 22:1–8 (lesson 21, exercise 7).

4. LESSON PRESENTATION

Point ❶ **Read** Have volunteers read aloud the core content of lesson 20.

▶ **Clarify** Abram's third God-encounter results in Abram receiving a mark (circumcision) and a new name (Abraham). The mark of circumcision becomes a sign of God's covenant with Abraham. The new name becomes a sign of his calling. *Abraham* means "father of many."

▶ **Clarify** Ancients often used names to say something about people. Native Americans did the same thing. For example, they called Annie Oakley, the sharpshooter, Little Miss Sure-shot.

Ask: What name changes still take place from time to time and for what reason? (One example is African-Americans who feel their change in thinking has transformed them into a new person requiring a new name.)

▶ **Notebook** Review and extend Abram's three God-encounters for entry in student notebooks.

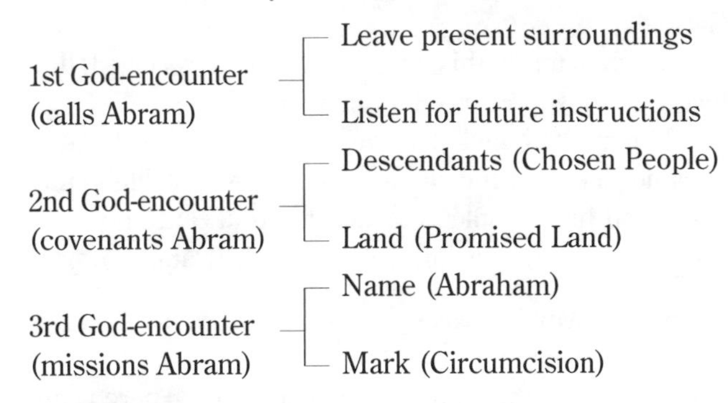

Point ❷ **Clarify** A motivation for Sarah's negative attitude toward Hagar is hinted at in Genesis 16:4, which reads:

When [Hagar] found out that she was pregnant,
she became proud and despised Sarai.

Proverbs refers to such a situation when it says:

There are four things that the earth itself cannot tolerate:
a slave who becomes a king,
a fool who has all he wants to eat,
a hateful woman who gets married,
and a servant woman who takes the place of her mistress.
Proverbs 30:21–23

▶ **Clarify** Nuzi documents specified that an adopted son must yield to a true son, should one be born at a later date. Ishmael yields to Isaac.

Point ❸ **Clarify** Modern Muslims claim direct descent from Ishmael, Abram's son by Hagar. Use Ishmael as an opportunity to introduce students to Islam. Many know little about it.

Visitors to Saudi Arabia are surprised to find that even TV programs come to a halt when the "Call to Prayer" (Azam) sounds. They are surprised to find, also, that the weekly holy day for Muslims is Friday, not Sunday (Christians) or Saturday (Jews).

The Azam is sounded five times daily: before sunrise, shortly after midday, late afternoon, after sunset, after nightfall.

Inside the mosque, the men (women do not usually attend) stand in rows facing a niche that indicates the direction of Mecca. The imam, or prayer leader, begins the prayer. All follow his words and movements exactly.

During the service a passage from the Qur'an (Koran) may be read and a short address may be given. The Qur'an (Muslim "Bible") consists of 114 chapters in the Arabic language. Children in school repeat it continually until some can recite the whole book.

▶ **Clarify** Muhammad was born in Mecca about 570 C.E. At age forty he became disturbed about his religious life. One day in a cave he had a terrifying experience. First he saw the eyes, then the face of an unearthly being whom he later identified as the angel Gabriel.

Much later in his life, Muhammad received the teachings now preserved in the Qur'an.

Muhammad died of a fever in 632. After his death it became clear that the Qur'an did not cover all life's situations, so his disciples recalled his oral teaching and. recorded it in what is known as Sunnah (tradition).

▶ **Clarify** Muslims accept what are known as the Five Pillars of the Faith.

The first is the faith simply expressed: "There is no god but Allah and Muhammad is his prophet."

The second is the practice of daily prayer.

The third is almsgiving to the poor.

The fourth is fasting. For a whole month during the famous Fast of Ramadan, Muslims must not eat or drink between sunrise and sunset. In hot climates this can be a great hardship.

The fifth is pilgrimage to Mecca, the holiest city on earth for Muslims. It houses the sacred Kaaba, a small cube-shaped shrine, which Muslims believe was originally built for worship of God by Abraham and Ishmael.

Before Muhammad took control of Mecca, the Kaaba was full of idols. He destroyed them, leaving only one picture there: Mary and Jesus. He did so because he looked on his religion as a fulfillment of Christianity and Judaism.

Muhammad viewed the Bible as an earlier revelation of Allah and called Abraham the first Muslim. He also regarded Moses, David, and Jesus as great prophets.

In his last sermon, Muhammad said, "Know ye that every Muslim is a brother to every other Muslim and that ye are now one great brotherhood." This spirit of unity continues and grows.

▶ **Clarify** Researchers Dr. Martin Marty of the University of Chicago and Dr. Yvonne Haddad of the University of Massachusetts predict that Islam will be the second-largest religion in America shortly after the turn of the century.

The spectacular growth of Muslims stems from many factors: immigration, conversion, and birth. Large increases in immigration took place in the late 1970s and early 1980s as students and professionals came to the United States seeking education and opportunity.

It is estimated that one-third of all Muslims in America are American converts, and about two-thirds are immigrants or children of immigrants. Of the American converts, the vast majority (possibly 95 percent) are African-American.

▶ **Notebook** Develop the following summary on the chalkboard for entry in student notebooks.

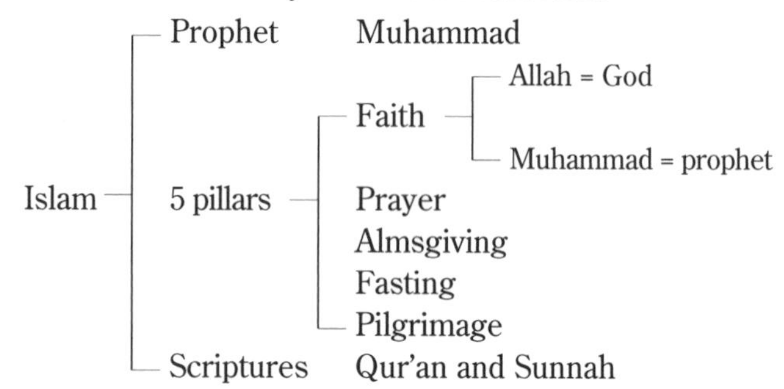

5. LESSON INTERACTION

Exercise ① **Clarify** *Time* magazine (November 28, 1977) reported that Sadat began his day with prayer in A1 Aqsa mosque in Jerusalem's Old City. Have students locate this mosque in the photo on page 41.

▶ **Clarify** *Time* noted that Sadat's "forehead bears a mark from touching it so often to the ground in prayer." Review what was said above about Muslim prayer practices.

▶ **Discuss** (a, b, c, d) The students should have plenty of opinions about each of these questions, especially the final one.

Exercise ② **Clarify** (a, b) On October 6, 1981, Sadat paid the supreme price for his willingness to be sacrificed. He was assassinated at a military parade in Cairo. Ten other people were killed in the hail of gunfire and forty were injured, including three U.S. military officers.

Exercise ③ **Discuss** This could be a fascinating exercise. Would it be possible for your school to do something along these lines, for example, invite guest speakers or panelists?

Exercise ④ **Discuss** Paton's point seems to be that by the time white South Africans turn to loving, black South Africans may be completely discouraged and turn to hating.

Schooling of Abraham

LESSON 21

1. LESSON BACKGROUND

▶ *Catechism of the Catholic Church*, 128–130.

2. LESSON QUIZ

Perfect score = 7 points

1. Through whom do Arab nations trace their ancestry back to Abraham, and what do Muslims celebrate on Id al-Adha? *(Lesson 20 review—2 points)*
2. List the mark and the new name Abram received in his third God-encounter. *(Lesson 20 notebook review—2 points)*
3. List the names of the two sons of Isaac and Rebecca, and explain how the younger son acquired the firstborn rights. *(Lesson 22 preview—3 points)*

3. LESSON HOMEWORK

▶ **Return** Lesson 20 review questions (page 41).

▶ **Collect** Lesson 21 review questions (page 43).

▶ **Read** Lesson 22 ("Isaac to Jacob," pages 46–47).

▶ **Write** Lesson 22 review questions (page 47).

▶ **Appoint** Four students to prepare readings from (1) Genesis 25:27–34, (2) Genesis 27:1–17, (3) Genesis 27:18–29, (4) Genesis 27:30–45 (lesson 22, exercise 4).

4. LESSON PRESENTATION

Point ❶ **Read** Have volunteers read aloud the core content of lesson 21.

▶ **Discuss** A young working mother used to hurry home to spend her lunch hour with her six-year-old handicapped son, Robbie, who was staying next door. But when she left after lunch, Robbie would grow hysterical. One day the mother stopped coming. Robbie wondered if his mother had grown cool in her love for him, just because he was handicapped.

Years later, Robbie learned that his mother never missed a lunch period. She would eat at the window, watch Robbie struggle to walk, and long to hold him close—especially when he fell. But for Robbie's own good, she didn't spend her lunch hour with him.

Ask: How do you explain the last sentence?

Ask: Which of the three things about faith (great trust, constant struggle, times of darkness) does this story illustrate? (Great trust on Robbie's part that his mother still loves him, in spite of the fact that she no longer joins him for lunch.)

▶ **Clarify** Obviously, great trust involves great risk. To illustrate this point, consider a parable by the nineteenth-century Danish philosopher Soren Kierkegaard. It goes something like this.

> A certain king fell in love with a girl who was a subject and commoner in his kingdom. This created a problem. If he married her, she would be ecstatic. But could she really love him? Wasn't the inequality between them too great?
>
> The king decided on another approach. He could give up his throne, become a commoner, and then propose to her. But this approach involved great trust on his part. His subjects might think him foolish and lose their respect for him. And the girl might be disappointed and reject him.
>
> But the king decided to trust and take the great risk. It was better to risk all to make love possible.

Faith is a lot like that. If I want to make God's love possible in my life, I must take the risk of faith.

Ask: In what sense is this parable a parable of what Jesus did for us? (He gave up his throne, lived among us, and invited us to take him into our hearts.)

Point ❷ **Discuss** An anonymous young person wrote the following. Read it to the class.

One day I decided to make Jesus the center of my life. This decision gave me unbelievable peace and joy. But two days later, I found myself doing something that no true follower of Jesus should do. I concluded that I had not really committed my life to Jesus at all. I had only psyched myself into thinking I had. But then I realized something important. I realized that when we commit our lives to Jesus, we commit only that part of ourselves that we are conscious of at the moment. That's all we can do.

This young person's experience illustrates something important about growing up, namely, that we are continually learning about ourselves. The greater part of ourselves lies below our consciousness. It surfaces only gradually with each new experience.

Ask: Which of the three things about faith (great trust, constant struggle, times of darkness) does this story illustrate? (Faith involves struggle. This is because we are constantly evolving and changing as persons. As a result, we must constantly recommit ourselves to God as we change and evolve. Our faith can never be a one-time decision to believe. It must always remain an ongoing decision, a lifelong struggle.

Point ❸ **Discuss** Finally, faith involves times of darkness. Faith has a way of going in and out of focus. What was once clear to us becomes fuzzy for a while. Worse yet, our faith sometimes seems to go behind a cloud and disappear in darkness.

▶ **Clarify** Dark periods are often caused by neglecting our faith. That is, we let our faith grow weak from lack of spiritual nourishment—or even sin. In other words, just as our body grows weak from lack of physical nourishment or abuse, so our soul grows weak from lack of spiritual nourishment or abuse.

God allows periods of darkness to happen in order to strengthen and deepen our faith. For example, adversity and sickness end up making us stronger in our faith than we were before they occurred.

Dark periods	Ourselves	Neglect of faith
	God	Permits for our good

▶ **Clarify** One final point. In adolescent years, the young person cuts the "spiritual" umbilical cord. This is akin to cutting the "physical" umbilical cord. Just as a baby must begin to live its physical life on its own, so we must begin to live our spiritual life on our own and not because of our parents or another person. (See John 4:30–42 for a good example of this.)

Questioning one's faith (times of darkness) is a part of moving from childhood to adulthood faith, from being Christian by culture to being Christian by conviction.

▶ **Notebook** We may summarize the three things faith involves for entry in student notebooks.

Faith involves
- Great trust
- Constant struggle
- Times of darkness

5. LESSON INTERACTION

Exercise ❶ **Discuss** God did not play games with Abraham by testing him. To illustrate what God had in mind, consider the following example. You might read it to the students.

An early TV star, Arthur Godfrey, framed this saying and hung it in his office: "The fire, Lord, not the scrap heap.""I hung it there," he told someone, "to remind me of a story. There was once a blacksmith who had great faith in God in spite of a lot of sickness in life. An unbeliever asked him one day how he could go on trusting in a God who let him suffer.

"The blacksmith responded, 'When I want to make a tool, I take a piece of iron and put it in a fire. Then I take it out, place it on an anvil, and strike it to see if it will take temper. If it does, I can make a useful article out of it. If not, I toss it on the scrap heap.' "

Exercises ❷ & ❸ **Discuss** These exercises might be taken together. The best approach would be to have students write out their responses. When they finish, collect the responses and go through them at your leisure. They will give you valuable information about your students and their faith status. You might then spend some time in the following class commenting on the responses.

Exercise ❹ **Discuss** One student responded this way to this question: "If you had a coach that let you do anything you wanted and would never demand discipline from you or the team, you'd lose all respect for him. It's kind of like that if your idea of God is someone who lets you do anything you want."

Exercise 4 is designed to set up the next exercise.

Exercise ❺ **Discuss** This exercise builds on exercise 4 and sets up exercise 6.

Exercise ❻ **Discuss** Some students see no value in "turning the other cheek." The story of Jackie Robinson, the first black athlete to play in the majors, helps to dramatize this value.

Before Branch Rickey of the Brooklyn Dodgers invited Jackie to ink his major league contract on October 23, 1945, he told Jackie, "Don't sign it if you can't turn the other cheek. For that's what you will have to do." Rickey was right. Pitchers brushed Jackie back with blazing fastballs; opposing players and fans taunted him; in certain cities he could not eat in the same restaurants or stay at the same hotels where his teammates did.

Ask: Where would black athletes be today had Jackie *not* learn to turn the other cheek?

Recall, also, Plato's famous words: "The wise person will always suffer evil rather than do evil."

Exercise ❼ **Discuss** Recall that Isaac (1) was his father's only son, (2) carried the wood of sacrifice on his shoulder, (3) was to be sacrificed on a hill, like Calvary, (4) was not defeated by death.

Photo **Clarify** Direct students' attention to the photo caption on page 43. It is an excellent statement of what many saints have experienced as they matured in their own faith.

Isaac to Jacob

LESSON 22

1. LESSON BACKGROUND

▶ *Catechism of the Catholic Church*, 410–412.

2. LESSON QUIZ

Perfect score = 9 points

1. What is a "type," and how did early Christians use it? *(Lesson 21 review—2 points)*
2. List and briefly explain the two reasons why we sometimes experience periods of darkness in our faith. *(Lesson 21 notebook review—6 points)*
3. To whom did Isaac give the "firstborn" blessing, and why didn't he retract it when he learned that he had given it to the younger son? *(Lesson 22 preview—2 points)*

3. LESSON HOMEWORK

▶ **Return** Lesson 21 review questions (page 43).

▶ **Collect** Lesson 22 review questions (page 47).

▶ **Read** Lesson 23 ("Israelite Forerunners," pages 48–49).

▶ **Write** Lesson 23 review questions (page 49).

▶ **Appoint** Three students to prepare readings from (1) Genesis 37:1–11, (2) Genesis 37:12–36, (3) Genesis 39:1–6, (4) Genesis 39:7–23 (lesson 23, exercise 3).

4. LESSON PRESENTATION

Point ➊ **Read** Have volunteers read aloud the core content of lesson 22.

▶ **Discuss** Ask: What does Esau's trading away his firstborn birthright illustrate about the way God treated biblical people? (God did not program them to be saints, but gave them a free will, just as God gave us a free will.)

Ask: How does the story of Isaac's blessing of Jacob illustrate how Iranian teachers of rug weaving handled the mistakes of their students? (God did not remove Esau's mistake, but found a way to weave it into the divine plan.)

▶ **Discuss** When Isaac learned that he had given the "firstborn" blessing to Jacob rather than to Esau, he "began to tremble and shake." And when Esau learned of it, "he cried out loudly and bitterly" (Genesis 27:33–34).

Ask: What does this show concerning Jewish belief in the spoken word? (Once uttered, it is like an arrow shot from a bow. You can't unshoot it. It goes on to do what the archer intended. Or it is like a siren that has been sounded; it cannot be unsounded. It goes on to deliver the message to its hearers.)

▶ **Clarify** A clay tablet found at Nuzi (see minimap on page 38 for the location of Nuzi) states that the oral statement of a dying father to a son had the force of law. Thus archaeology confirms the binding force of the Isaac-Jacob episode.

Point ➋ **Clarify** The spoken word has an irreversibility, even in modern times, and not only in a religious way but also in a perfectly natural way.

For example, a young person, in a burst of anger, says to a parent, "Damn you!" The moment those two words are uttered, the young person wishes he or she could recall them. But it can't be done. All the apologies in the world will not fully erase or reverse the remark and its impact on the parent.

▶ **Clarify** Our generation has lost a great deal of respect for the spoken word. To us goes the infamous credit for coining the phrase "credibility gap."

Ask: What is meant by this phrase?

▶ **Clarify** Students sometimes ask, "What is wrong with a lie?" Multiply lies ten million times and it is clear what is wrong with it. The people in an entire culture grow suspicious, skeptical, and distrustful of one another and of people in authority.

Point ➌ **Clarify** Jews believed the spoken word had a unique power, especially when uttered in the form of a blessing or a curse.

▶ **Notebook** Develop the following summary on the chalkboard for entry in student notebooks. It illustrates two important points that grow out of the Isaac story, involving his twin sons, Esau and Jacob

Isaac story illustrates
- God's way of dealing with Bible people (Respects their free will and weaves their sinfulness into plan of salvation)
- Jewish belief in power of spoken word (Once uttered, words can't be revoked; like a shot arrow, they can't be unshot.)

5. LESSON INTERACTION

Exercise 1 **Discuss** There is no pat answer for this question. It depends a lot on what the friend did, her faith in God, and her motivation for wanting to put God back in her life. Answers could range from speaking to a parent, friend, or school counselor, to celebrating the sacrament of Reconciliation, to beginning a serious program of daily prayer, to breaking with "friends" who are a bad influence on her.

Exercise 2 **Discuss** Children have a wisdom that comes from innocence. Film director Michael Lessac alluded to this innocence and the wisdom that comes from it in an interview.

Lessac tells an old anecdote about a young family into which a baby has just been born. The elder child, about four years old, keeps asking the mother to be left alone with the new baby. The mother doesn't understand but finally consents. To her amazement, the mother overhears the elder child ask the baby, "Tell me about God. I think I'm forgetting."

Exercise 3 **Discuss** One reason for the high "turn-on" power of words is that they not only denote but also connote. Moreover, it is often a word's connotation that accounts for its "turn-on" power.

Ask: What is the difference between *connote* and *denote?* (*Denote* refers to the "meaning" of a word; *connote* refers to "associations" linked to the word.

Ask: Explain how the following three pairs of words or phrases have the same denotation but a very different connotation.

1. Home/House
2. Father/Old Man
3. Son of God/Son of Man

(*Home* connotes something "warm and personal";
house connotes something "cold and impersonal."

Father connotes someone "who gave me birth";
Old Man connotes someone "who gives me trouble."

Son of God connotes someone "divine in origin";
Son of Man connotes someone "human in origin," though having a special, mysterious quality.)

The "turn-on" power of the three groups listed in this exercise is listed below. The first figure indicates the relative ranking of the three items: 1 (lowest) to 3 (highest). The second figure is the actual psychogalvanometer measurement.

Group A	*Group B*	*Group C*
3/37.4 dance	3/48.7 your name	1/17.8 white
1/72.8 kiss	1/32.2 friend	2/20.6 blue
2/59.3 love	2/35.6 money	3/30.4 green

Exercise 4 **Read** Have the student appointed to prepare Genesis 25:27–34 ("The Trade") read it to the class.

▶ **Clarify** As the "firstborn," Esau automatically became head of the family at his father's death. He also received double the inheritance of the other family members (Deuteronomy 21:17).

Stress that the term *firstborn* was a legal title given to the first male to open the womb (Exodus 13:13).

The title was retained whether the child was an only child or not. An Egyptian inscription on a funeral stele, contemporary with Jesus, tells of a Jewish mother who died while giving birth to her "firstborn." Clearly, there is no question of further children here. Recall that Luke identifies Jesus as Mary's "firstborn" (Luke 2:7).

▶ **Clarify** At one point in our space program, thirty-one of the thirty-two astronauts were "firstborn" or only children.

A survey of National Merit Finalists shows that all other things being equal, the greatest number of finalists, by far, fall into the same category.

Ask: How might we account for these statistics? (Some suggest that the greater responsibility and attention shown them by parents made the difference.)

▶ **Discuss** (a, b) Have the students record their responses before sharing them.

▶ **Discuss** Have the three students appointed to prepare the lengthy but captivating reading of Genesis 27:1–45. Have the other students record their responses before sharing them.

Photo **Clarify** Direct the students to the photo and photo caption on page 46. The young man (center and facing us) has just celebrated his Bar Mitzvah, which means "Son of the Law." He proudly displays his skull cap *(yarmulke)*, a reminder of God's presence in his life. He also wears about his shoulders a prayer shawl *(tallith)*. It is somewhat like the priest's stole, which is worn whenever he functions in a liturgical, priestly capacity.

Finally, the boy wears leather wrappings *(tefillin)* wound around his left arm and forehead. These are donned by all Jewish men during weekly prayer.

Attached to the *tefillin* are tiny pouches containing passages from Exodus and Deuteronomy. Wearing the pouches this way reminds the worshiper that his mind (pouch about forehead) and his heart (pouch about his left arm—closest arm to his heart) should be united with God, in a special way during the time of prayer (Deuteronomy 6:8).

▶ **Clarify** Abraham, Isaac, and Jacob are called patriarchs. This word derives from a Greek word that means "chief fathers."

CHAPTER FIVE: Peoplehood (pages 48–49)

Israelite Forerunners

LESSON 23

1. LESSON BACKGROUND

▶ *Catechism of the Catholic Church*, 74–83.

2. LESSON QUIZ

Perfect score = 7 points

1. Who were the two sons of Rebecca and Isaac, and how did their younger son happen to receive the blessing of the "firstborn"? *(Lesson 22 review—3 points)*
2. What two points did the Isaac story illustrate about God's dealings with biblical people and Jewish belief in the power of the spoken word? *(Lesson 22 notebook review—2 points)*
3. Why was Joseph his father's favorite son, and how did Joseph become an Egyptian slave? *(Lesson 23 review—2 points)*

3. LESSON HOMEWORK

▶ **Return** Lesson 22 review questions (page 47).

▶ **Collect** Lesson 23 review questions (page 49).

▶ **Read** Lesson 24 ("Israelites to Egypt," pages 50–51).

▶ **Write** Lesson 24 review questions (page 51).

▶ **Appoint** Six students to prepare readings from (1) Genesis 40:1–23, (2) Genesis 41:1–36, (3) Genesis 41:37–57 (lesson 24 core content); (4) Exodus 2:1–10 (lesson 24, exercise 3); (5) Genesis 44:1–17, (6) Genesis 44:18–34 (lesson 24, exercise 4).

4. LESSON PRESENTATION

Point ① **Read** Begin by having volunteers read aloud the core content of lesson 23.

▶ **Clarify** A key point in Jacob's dream is the passing on of God's promise of descendants and land. The promise was made first to Abraham (Genesis 13:15), next to Isaac (Genesis 17:19), and finally to Jacob (Genesis 28:13).

▶ **Notebook** Develop on the chalkboard the following summary of the passing on of God promise of land and descendants.

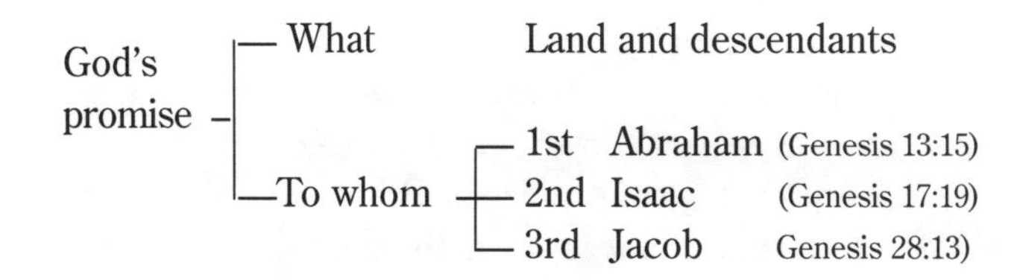

▶ **Clarify** Jacob's name change highlights his new vocation. Recall that a new name was a "sign" of a new vocation. Thus Abram's name was changed from *Abram* ("exalted father") to *Abraham* ("father of many").

Recall what was said earlier about name changes—prevalent even in our modern times. For example, when a person becomes a pope or a king, that person takes a new name. Catholics take new names upon baptism, upon confirmation, and sometimes upon entrance into religious life. Ask: Why? (By faith, they become new persons.)

Point ② **Clarify** Introduce the subject of dreams as a medium of God's revelation. Besides the remarkable dream of Jacob in Genesis 28, consider such other examples as Joseph's dream about Mary's pregnancy (Matthew 1:20) and his dream to flee to Egypt with Jesus and Mary (Matthew 2:19). Merely introduce the subject now. It will be discussed more fully in lesson 24.

A provocative opener is Abraham Lincoln's famous dream, which occurred days before his assassination on Good Friday, April 14, 1865. The following excerpts from Jim Bishop's *The Day Lincoln Was Shot* tell how Lincoln described his dream to a few friends.

"There seemed to be a deathlike stillness about me.
Then I heard subdued sobs,
as if a number of people were weeping.
I thought I left my bed and wandered downstairs. . . .

"I arrived in the East Room, which I entered. . . .
Before me was a catafalque,
on which rested a corpse in funeral vestments.
Around it were stationed soldiers
who were acting as guards;
and there was a throng of people,
some gazing mournfully upon the corpse,
whose face was covered, others weeping pitifully.

" 'Who is dead in the White House?'
I demanded of one of the soldiers.

" 'The President,' was his answer.
'He was killed by an assassin.' . . .

"I slept no more that night."

Clarify In *Myth, History, and Faith,* Morton Kelsey notes that Lincoln's assassination carries some striking parallels to John F. Kennedy's assassination.

Both presidents had been urged by their personal secretary not to go to the place where they were assassinated. (Amazingly, Kennedy's secretary was named Lincoln and Lincoln's secretary was named Kennedy.)

The assassins in each case were born in the same year a century apart (Booth, 1839; Oswald, 1939).

Each president was succeeded by a vice president named Johnson, who was a senator from the south and was born in the same year of his century (1808 and 1908).

And each president, during his term of office, had lost a son. Finally, both presidents were part of a series of seven who were elected in a multiple-of-twenty year and died in office: Harrison (1840), Lincoln (1860), Garfield (1880), McKinley (1900), Wilson (1920), Roosevelt (1940), Kennedy (1960).

Point 3 **Notebook** Develop the following diagrams concerning the type of origins that are treated in prehistory and in folk history.

History —
- Pre- Deals with *human* origins (how evil began)
- Folk Deals with *tribal* origins (how Bethel began)

Rudyard Kipling's *Jungle Book* and *Just So Stories* make use of fictional origin stories: "How Fear Came," "How the Camel Got His Hump," "How the Leopard Got His Spots," and others.

Point 4 **Notebook** The following family tree that emerged from Abraham may be outlined on the chalkboard for entry in student notebooks.

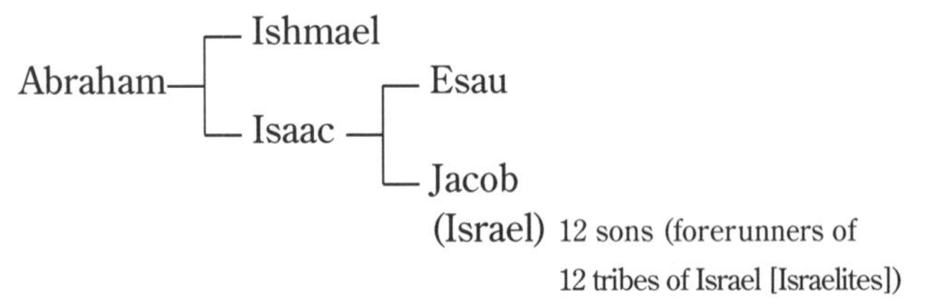

5. LESSON INTERACTION

Exercise 1 **Discuss** **(a)** Origin stories were important in giving the Israelites a sense of their common roots and identity.

(b) Have students check with the school librarian about books that deal with origins of customs, such as toasting and the seventh-inning stretch.

Surprisingly, some things that are regarded as the origin of something really aren't. For example, many people think the Baby Ruth candy bar was named after the "Sultan of Swap" (Babe Ruth). Wrong! It was named after President Grover Cleveland's daughter.

Another example. Referring to the South as "Dixie" did not come from the famous North-South dividing line, surveyed by Mr. Mason and Mr. Dixon. Rather, it came from a denomination of currency called "dix" that circulated in nineteenth-century New Orleans.

Exercise 2 **Discuss** The story of Jacob's dream concludes with the Genesis writer saying of Jacob, "He named the place Bethel" ("House of God"). *Beth* in Hebrew means "house" and *El* means "God."

Notebook Develop a list of other names that begin with the prefix *Beth.*

Beth —
- *Bethsaida* "House of fishing"
- *Bethpage* "House of unripe figs"
- *Bethlehem* "House of bread"

Clarify The name *Bethlehem* ("house of bread") takes on almost a mystical significance when we recall that Jesus called himself the "bread of life" (John 6:35).

Exercise 3 **Read** The good news/bad news jokes assembled by Pat Williams in *The Power within You* recall the good news/bad news story popular in the Chinese culture. Read it to the students.

An old wise man in ancient China
had one son and one horse.
One day the horse escaped its corral
and fled into the hills.
"Bad news," said the neighbors.
"How can you be so sure?"
said the old wise man.
Next day the horse returned home,
leading back ten wild horses.
"Good news," said the neighbors.
"How can you be so sure?" said the man.
Next day the man's son was thrown
by a wild horse and broke his leg.
"Bad news," said the neighbors.
"How can you be so sure?" said the man.
Next day an enemy invaded the village
and led off all able-bodied young men.
The man's injured son was left behind.
This time the neighbors said nothing.

Ask: What point does this good news/bad news story (like story of Joseph) make?

Exercises 4 & 5 **Discuss** The students should be able to handle both of these discussions without too much trouble. Both of them could be handled without being written out.

Israelites to Egypt

LESSON 24

1. LESSON BACKGROUND

▶ *Catechism of the Catholic Church*, 203–221.

2. LESSON QUIZ

Perfect score = 8 points

1. How many sons did Jacob have, and to what are they the forerunners? *(Lesson 23 review—2 points)*
2. List the origins that prehistory and folk history deal with, and give one example of each origin. *(Lesson 23 notebook review—4 points)*
3. How did Joseph end up in prison in Egypt, and how did he win the attention of the king while he was in prison? *(Lesson 24 preview—2 points)*

3. LESSON HOMEWORK

▶ **Return** Lesson 23 review questions (page 49).

▶ **Collect** Lesson 24 review questions (page 51).

▶ **Read** Lesson 25 ("Leadership of Moses," pages 52–53).

▶ **Write** Lesson 25 review questions (page 53).

4. LESSON PRESENTATION

Point ❶ **Read** Have volunteers read aloud the core content of lesson 24.

▶ **Clarify** Give the students some background on Egypt. Begin by referring them to the photo of the Great Pyramid and the Sphinx on page 50.

When Joseph walked into Egypt, he must have stared in disbelief at the Great Pyramid, the tomb of Pharaoh Cheops (Khufu). (It was already over a thousand years old in his time.)

Each side of its square base measured two and a half football fields. Its peak soared 480 feet into the air, the height of a 40-story building.

Medieval pilgrims, en route to the Holy Land, called the pyramids (there were several) "Joseph barns."

Ask: Why this name?

▶ **Clarify** The Great Sphinx would also have amazed Joseph. Built around five hundred years after Cheops, it stands 66 feet tall and has a body almost the length of a football field.

Its purpose, like that of the cherubim, was to keep unworthy intruders from disturbing the tombs of the pharaohs (kings) in the area of the pyramids.

Point ❷ **Clarify** Potiphar bought Joseph. Potiphar's wife caused him to be unjustly imprisoned. You might read this intriguing story (Genesis 39:6b–23) to the class.

Ask: Why do you think the biblical writer preserved this story?

▶ **Clarify** Have the appointed student read Genesis 40:1–23. This passage describes how Joseph won fame interpreting dreams while in prison.

Have the two appointed students read Genesis 41:1–57. Genesis 41:1–36 describes how Joseph came to the attention of the king. Genesis 41:37–57 describes how Joseph became the vizier, or seal-bearer, of Egypt. Pharaoh give him a gold chain and a signet ring.

The signet ring entitled the wearer to act and do business in the name of the seal it bore. (See Esther 3:10 where the infamous Haman wrote a decree against the Jews "in the name of King Xerxes and stamped with his ring.")

▶ **Clarify** Genesis 50:2 says that Joseph ordered the physicians in his service to embalm his father, Jacob. Genesis 50:26 says Joseph was embalmed.

Herodotus, a fifth-century Greek historian, describes the embalming process at great length in Book II of his *Histories* (Penguin Books, pp. 133–34). He describes three procedures, each taking seventy days.

Egyptians mummified the body so that its departed spirit, *ka*, could return to it when the time came for the person's rebirth into eternal life. If the body decayed, the spirit that departed from it at death would not be able to find it. Thus there could be no rebirth into eternal life. The spirit would search ceaselessly for a body that no longer existed.

▶ **Clarify** Be sure the students get the key idea behind Joseph's "test" of his brothers (Genesis 44:1–34). Ask: How have they changed?

After the test Joseph reveals his identity (Genesis 45:1–5). His concluding remark is important. It is quoted and presented for discussion in exercise 1 (page 51).

Clarify The ending of lesson 24 is important. It returns the focus to Moses and sets up lesson 25.

Notebook Develop on the chalkboard the following summary of two important biblical details that Egyptian records confirm and help to clarify.

Egyptian records confirm —
- dream interpretation
- severe famines

5. LESSON INTERACTION

Exercise ❶

Discuss **(a)** God "weaves" human sinfulness into the overall plan of salvation.

Discuss **(b)** One of the author's students gave this example of "bad news" becoming "good news." Read it to the students to stimulate their own ideas. Be sure to have them write out their response. You may then screen the responses and share the better ones with the class.

My baby brother was born with cerebral palsy, which causes muscular-coordination and speech problems. When we first learned of the sickness, we thought only of the sorrow and difficulty it would bring into our lives. For example, he never learned to walk until he was three. And almost immediately my parents had to send him to a special school.

Through the years our family made many sacrifices for my brother. We had to be patient with him and just hope.

As I look back now, I can see that his cerebral palsy brought our family together. Because of our sacrifices as a family, we became more close and more loving.

Today my brother is in the sixth grade. He has been in a regular school now for three years. We are all proud of his achievements and we are thankful to God for the blessing he gave us through what began as "bad news."

Exercise ❷

Discuss **(a)** The Talmud, an ancient Jewish commentary on the Torah, says, "A dream uninterpreted is like a letter unopened."

Sigmund Freud repeated the same idea. And this idea still persists in modern times. An example is John A. Sanford's book *Dreams: God's Forgotten Language.*

The book's thesis is that dreams are to be taken seriously as a medium by which God sometimes communicates with people. Sanford says we have forgotten that God comes to us in our sleep on occasions.

Regardless of how seriously you take Sanford's thesis, there is no question that the dream is presented in the Bible, on a number of occasions, as being a medium of revelation.

Clarify Dreams have also been a source of revelation outside the Bible, as mentioned in this exercise.

The case of Nobel prize winner Niels Bohr is especially interesting. Erich Von Daniken describes the experience in his controversial and popular book *Gods from Outer Space.* He says that Bohr saw planets rushing by him. They were connected by fine threads to the sun about which they were spinning. Suddenly, the gas solidified and the sun and the planets shriveled up and became motionless.

Niels Bohr said that he woke up at this moment. He realized at once that what he had seen in his dream was the atom model.

Notebook Researchers can detect dreams taking place in sleeping people in three ways. Summarize them on the chalkboard for entry in student notebooks.

Dream clues
- Using an EEG (electroencephalograph)
- REM (rapid eye movement)
- Rapid breathing, heartbeat, body movement

Clarify The average person dreams one to four hours nightly. People blind from birth dream in audible images (not visual). Though people rarely remember their dreams, researchers say that the dreams do affect people's moods during the day.

Discuss **(b)** When you think about it, God could speak more subtly—even more tellingly—through dreams.

Activity **(c)** Again, have students record their dreams, allowing for screening and sharing later.

Exercise ❸

Discuss Have the appointed student read Exodus 2:1–10.

Some examples of "warmth and naturalness" in the story of Moses' birth are (1) the baby's sister watching to see what would happen, (2) the crying of the baby, (3) the pity of the princess for the baby, (4) the sister's offer to get a Hebrew mother to nurse the baby, (5) the bringing of the baby's own mother to do the nursing.

Exercise ❹

Have the two appointed students read the passages in preparation for the discussion. You might read Genesis 45:1–28 to complete this beautiful story.

Photo

Clarify Direct students' attention to the photo of Rameses II on page 51. Rameses II continues to grab headlines in the modern world. His mummified body was taken to Paris in 1976 to stop the spread of decay.

Leadership of Moses

LESSON 25

1. LESSON BACKGROUND

▶ *Catechism of the Catholic Church* (see lesson 24).

2. LESSON QUIZ

Perfect score = 7 points

1. How did Joseph end up in an Egyptian prison, and what was there about Joseph that brought him to the king's attention? *(Lesson 24 review—2 points)*
2. List two significant points in the biblical story of Joseph that are confirmed by Egyptian records. *(Lesson 24 notebook review—2 points)*
3. How is God's name spelled in Hebrew, translated into English, and pronounced today? *(Lesson 25 preview—3 points)*

3. LESSON HOMEWORK

▶ **Return** Lesson 24 review questions (page 51).

▶ **Collect** Lesson 25 review questions (page 53).

▶ **Read** Lesson 26 ("Exodus from Egypt," pages 54–55).

▶ **Write** Lesson 26 review questions (page 55).

4. LESSON PRESENTATION

Point ❶ **Read** Have volunteers read aloud the core content of lesson 25.

Miniposter **Discuss** Have a student read the quotation on the miniposter on page 52.

Ask: How does the quotation relate to this lesson, and what point does it make? (It recalls the "burning bush" episode).

Point ❷ **Clarify** Few Old Testament events have caused more discussion than the ten plagues. Interestingly, the Bible does not refer to the plagues as "miracles," but as "signs" (*'ot* in Hebrew).

Somewhat like the creation story, the plague story follows a general pattern.

In the first three plagues, Pharaoh's magicians and Aaron play major roles. The magicians duplicate Aaron's two plagues (blood and frogs), but they fail to duplicate the third (gnats). The last seven plagues spotlight Moses and Pharaoh, as Aaron and the magicians fade into the background.

▶ **Notebook** Each individual plague also follows a general pattern, just as each individual day of creation followed a general pattern. Develop a diagram of this pattern for entry in student notebooks.

Fourfold pattern —
- God gives a command.
- Moses obeys.
- The plague occurs.
- Pharaoh remains obstinate.

You may wish to read the first three plagues to illustrate the above points (Exodus 7:19–8:19).

▶ **Notebook** Develop the following summaries on the chalkboard for entry in student notebooks.

Story pattern —
- First three: Aaron/magicians featured
- Last seven: Moses/Pharaoh featured

Plague pattern —
- God commands.
- Moses obeys.
- Plague occurs.
- Pharaoh remains obstinate.

Plague explanation —
- Completely supernatural
- Completely natural
- Combination of the above

▶ **Clarify** The key point to keep in mind about the plagues is this: No matter how you interpret them, the biblical writer presents them as signs of God's action in behalf of the Israelites.

Point ❸ **Clarify** The word *passover* derives from the tenth plague. The Israelites slay a lamb and mark the doorposts of their houses with it. Exodus 12:13 has the LORD explain:

"The [lamb's] blood on the doorposts will be a sign
to mark the houses in which you live.
When I see the blood,
I will pass over you and will not harm you
when I punish the Egyptians."

Paul likened Jesus to the sacrificial lamb, saying, "Christ, our Passover lamb, has been sacrificed" (1 Corinthians 5:7).

As the Hebrews are saved from physical death by the blood of the lamb, so all believers are saved from spiritual death by the blood of the lamb (John 1:29).

Similarly, as the Hebrews are nourished for their journey by eating the lamb's body, so too Christians are nourished on their journey to the "promised land" (heaven) by the body of the lamb of God (Eucharist).

Notebook The parallel between the two passovers may be summed up for entry in student notebooks.

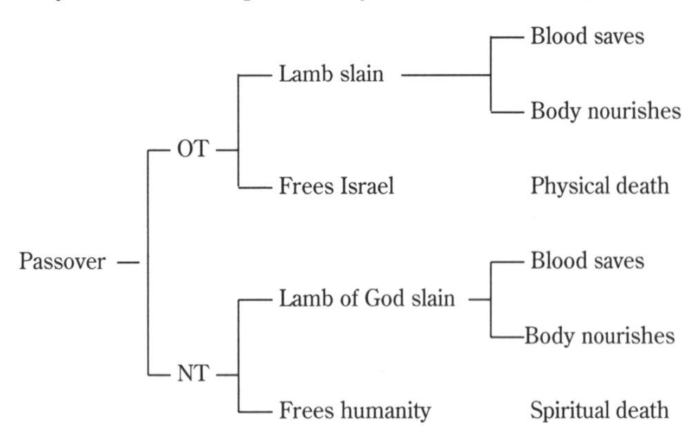

5. LESSON INTERACTION

Exercise 1 **Discuss** Moody makes a point that God made though the prophet Isaiah centuries before Jesus:

"My thoughts," says the Lord, "are not like yours,
and my ways are different from yours.
As high as the heavens are above the earth,
so high are my ways and thoughts above yours."

Isaiah 55:8–9

Suppose that you had to select a person to be president of the United States in the most critical moment of American history. You are handed the resumés of ten people that you might consider. One of the resumés includes these items:

1832—was defeated for the legislature
1833—failed in business
1836—suffered a nervous breakdown

Ask: Would you send for this person as someone you might think qualified to be president in the most critical moment in American history? Explain. (That person, as some of the students may have guessed, was Lincoln. Later on in his presidency, Lincoln said, almost jokingly:

"God selects his own instruments,
and sometimes they are queer ones;
for instance, he chose me to steer the ship
through a great crisis.")

Ask: Why would God select such an apparently unqualified person to lead the country in such a critical period of history? (Lincoln was eminently prepared for the ordeal of the Civil War years. He was used to setbacks and difficulties. More importantly, he knew that God—not he—was the only one who could save the union from splitting apart.)

Exercise 2 **Clarify** The Hebrew name for *God,* translated "I AM" in the text, is designated by the consonants *YHWH* (the Hebrew alphabet has no vowels).

At first students may not understand how an alphabet could have no vowels. It is really not as difficult as it would seem. For example, most students (after a little thought) would be able to figure out this phrase: GD LVS Y. You might have the students list some other examples.

At one point in their history, Jews, out of reverence, stopped pronouncing God's name. Instead, they substituted the word *Adonai,* which means "my Lord." An example might help. Suppose that out of reverence for the pope, Catholics would never use his name. Rather, they would substitute instead "His Holiness." It is the same idea.

Clarify Because Jews did not pronounce God's name for centuries, the correct pronunciation for *YHWH* was lost. In medieval times, scholars conjectured that it was pronounced *YaHoWaH,* or *Jehovah.* Thus we get the name Jehovah's Witnesses. Now, with far better resources at our disposal, scholars agree that *YHWH* should be pronounced *JaHWeH.*

Notebook Develop the following summary on the chalkboard for entry in student notebooks.

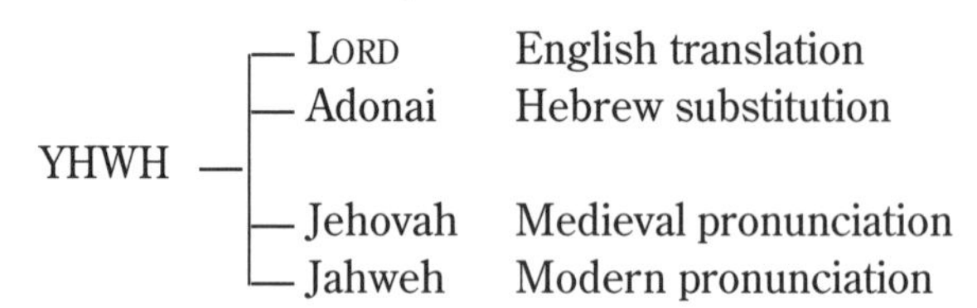

Exercise 3 **Discuss** The commentary in exercise 1 (above) applies to this exercise as well. Stress the sentence following God's promise: "If Moses thought he would have smooth sailing with God on his side, he had another thing coming."

More often than not, God does not remove burdens from the backs of those called to be God's instruments. Rather, God strengthens their backs to be able to carry the burden.

Exercise 4 **Discuss** The comments in the core content apply here. Why shouldn't God use ordinary events in an extraordinary way to accomplish God's works?

Rather than undermine the biblical account of the plagues, this suggestion opens up a whole new way of looking at them.

Exodus from Egypt

LESSON 26

1. LESSON BACKGROUND

▶ *Catechism of the Catholic Church* (see lesson 24).

2. LESSON QUIZ

Perfect score = 8 points

1. What was the tenth and final plague, and what joyful celebration grew out of the way the Israelites prepared for it? *(Lesson 25 review—2 points)*
2. List the fourfold pattern that the narration of each plague followed. *(Lesson 25 notebook review—4 points)*
3. Regardless of how you interpret the ten plagues, what is the important thing to keep in mind, and what conclusion did the Israelites draw from it? *(Lesson 26 preview—2 points)*

3. LESSON HOMEWORK

▶ **Return** Lesson 25 review questions (page 53).

▶ **Collect** Lesson 26 review question (page 55).

▶ **Read** Lesson 27 ("Journey to Sinai," pages 56–57).

▶ **Write** Lesson 27 review questions (page 57).

▶ **Appoint** Two teams (each made up of two or three musically inclined students) to prepare exercise 2 of lesson 27.

4. LESSON PRESENTATION

Point ❶ **Read** Have volunteers read aloud the core content of lesson 26.

Minimap **Clarify** Have students study the map on page 54 to get a general idea of the route followed by the Israelites out of Egypt. They crossed the Red (Reed) Sea in the area south of Pithom. Recall Pithom's mention in Exodus 1:11:

The Israelites built the cities of Pithom and Rameses
to serve as supply centers for the king.

Recall that the left finger of the Red Sea is better known today as the Gulf of Suez. The Suez Canal now creates a water route joining the Red Sea finger and the Mediterranean Sea.

▶ **Notebook** Develop the following diagram on the chalkboard for entry in student notebooks. It reviews the three ways people interpret the plagues and Israel's crossing of the Red (Reed) Sea. It also underscores the important thing about the crossing: not *how* the event took place, but *why* it took place. In other words, what teaching is the biblical writer making through his account?

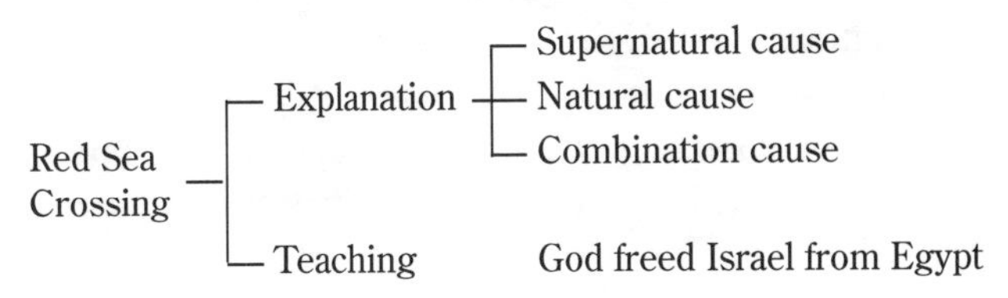

5. LESSON INTERACTION

Exercise ❶ **Discuss** The story of the six-year-old points up the need to reconstruct the context of the times in which the biblical events took place.

An example of how children transpose our own culture into ancient cultures is the story of a kindergarten teacher of affluent children who asked her students to retell the story of the flood. One five-year-old said:

"God told Noah that he was going to make a lot of rain fall. So much that it would make the whole earth like the ocean. So he told Noah to build the biggest 'yacht' he could, so that he and his family would be safe."

The same teacher asked the same students to tell a story about what it would be like to be poor. One child began:

"This is the story of a very poor family. The father was poor. The mother was poor. The children were poor. But poorest of all was the chauffeur, the cook, and the maid."

Exercise ❷ **Discuss** This story makes an important point: Israel's faith in God. Recall the passage from the Gospel according to Mark, where Jesus makes it clear that miracles do not create faith. It is the other way around: Faith creates miracles. Mark writes about Jesus' visit to Nazareth during his ministry:

He was not able to perform any miracles there,
except that he placed his hands on a few sick people
and healed them.
He was greatly surprised,
because the people did not have faith. Mark 6:5–6

Exercise ③ **Activity** This could be presented as an "extra-credit" research activity. Certain students could be helped by this kind of an opportunity.

Exercise ④ **Activity** Again, collect these, screen them, and present the better ones to the class.

Photo **Clarify** Direct students' attention to the photo of the large wooden chest on page 55. The painting on the side of the chest portrays the young King Tutankhamen ("Tut") pursuing enemy warriors. He reigned at the start of the final century of the Hebrews' slavery in Egypt.

The wooden chest was part of a spectacular treasury of ancient royal objects found in the burial chamber of Tut. It was dug up by British archaeologist Howard Carter on November 26, 1922. Read the following summary of the discovery. (It is written in sense lines to facilitate reading.) Students find it interesting. It also helps them put the events of the Exodus into a context that brings them alive.

Carter and his team had been digging for six years
in the Valley of the Kings, some miles from the Nile.
He was bankrolled by Lord Carnarvon,
a rich Englishman.
At the end of the sixth season of digging,
Carnarvon had decided that enough was enough.

Carter, however, was determined to keep going.
He was certain that Tut's tomb was somewhere,
because every tomb of Egypt's kings
had been accounted for except Tut's.
Since all the tombs had been rifled by tomb robbers,
Carter was painfully aware
that if they did find Tut's tomb,
it could well be empty too.
Carter prevailed on Carnarvon
to bankroll one more attempt.

This time the team hit pay dirt.
They found an underground stairway cut in rock.
They followed its sixteen steps to a sealed doorway,
which bore the name "Tutankhamen."
That door led through a thirty-foot passageway
to another sealed passageway.

Carter cut a hole in it, lit a candle, and peered inside.
Everyone stood breathless, awaiting Carter's report.
He described it later, in these dramatic words:

As my eyes grew accustomed to the light,
details of the room within emerged slowly . . .
strange animals, statues, and gold. . . .
I was struck dumb with amazement,
and when Lord Carnarvon,
unable to stand the suspense any longer,
inquired anxiously, "Can you see anything?"
it was all I could do to get out the words,
"Yes, wonderful things." John A. Wilson, "The World of Moses"

Carter was looking into the largest of four rooms.
Three were packed with fabulous treasures.
They included the king's gold-covered throne,
beautiful jewelry and gold pieces,
four dismantled chariots, and the chest (photo)
containing things for the king's use in the afterlife.

The fourth room contained
the most important find of all: a great stone coffin.
When it was opened, it was found to contain
a large mummy-shaped coffin
made of wood and covered with gold leaf.
Inside it was yet another mummy-shaped coffin,
also covered with gold leaf.

Finally came the last coffin, which was solid gold.
When it was opened, it revealed the king's body.
Some 143 jeweled objects adorned it.
And over the king's face and shoulders
laid an extraordinary gold mask
that had been undisturbed for thirty-three centuries.

The discovery was the most spectacular
of all archaeological discoveries.

▶ **Clarify** From a biblical point of view, this report gives us an insight into

- the nation that enslaved the Hebrews,
- the opulence of the Egyptian court life in which Moses was reared as the son of Pharaoh's daughter, and
- the life and time of the Israelite exodus from Egypt.

▶ **Clarify** Students may ask about the "curse of the pharaohs" that has been linked with King Tut's tomb. In *Gods, Graves, and Scholars,* C. W. Ceram writes:

If any single circumstance started the "curse of the Pharaohs" legend, very probably it was the sudden death of Lord Carnarvon. When he died, on April 6, 1923, after a three-week losing battle with the effects of a mosquito bite, people began to talk about punishments visited from the spirit realm on blasphemers.

Such headlines as "Revenge of the Pharaohs" began to appear . . . "Second Victim" . . . "Third Victim" . . . Nineteenth Victim," and so on. . . . Carter himself tried to quell the tide of rumor [calling it] . . . a "form of literary amusement" . . . [pointing out that] "curses of this nature have no place in the Egyptian ritual."

The news media was no different in those days than it is today: always searching for a story.

Journey to Sinai

LESSON 27

1. LESSON BACKGROUND

▶ *Catechism of the Catholic Church*, 751, 762.

2. LESSON QUIZ

Perfect score = 9 points

1. How else may we translate the Hebrew term *Red Sea*, and how does this translation fit better with what the Bible says? *(Lesson 26 review—2 points)*
2. What are three ways people interpret the crossing of the Red Sea; and, regardless of the interpretation, what point does the biblical writer want to make by the narration of these events? *(Lesson 26 notebook review—4 points)*
3. What three events took place to help the Israelites as they journeyed through the desert after leaving Egypt? *(Lesson 28 preview—3 points)*

3. LESSON HOMEWORK

▶ **Return** Lesson 26 review questions (page 55).

▶ **Collect** Lesson 27 review questions (page 57).

▶ **Read** Lesson 28 ("Encounter with God," pages 58–59).

▶ **Write** Lesson 28 review questions (page 59).

4. LESSON PRESENTATION

Point ① **Read** Have volunteers read aloud the core content of lesson 27.

▶ **Discuss** Ask: How is the situation of the Israelites (described in the lesson's opening paragraph) applicable in a special way to youth, especially after graduation from high school? (With the advent of adulthood, youth enter an unknown world. What life holds for them lies hidden. What direction they should take is not all that clear.)

▶ **Discuss** The Israelites experienced three amazing events as they fled into the desert. The first of these events consisted of pillars of cloud and of fire.

During the day
the Lord went in front of them in a pillar of cloud
to show them the way,
and during the night
he went in front of them in a pillar of fire. Exodus 13:21

This is the third time in the Old Testament narrative, thus far, that fire has been used as a symbol of God's presence.

Ask: What were the other two times? (The first was in Genesis 15:17—the "flaming torch" passing through halves of animals in the Abraham covenant. The second was in Exodus 3:3—the "burning bush" that Moses saw.)

▶ **Clarify** Some scholars have tried to explain these phenomena as signs of an active volcano that led the Israelites toward Mount Sinai. J. Edgar Park treats the volcano thesis in *The Interpreter's Bible* (vol. I, p. 931 [Nashville: Abingdon Press]).

There is no question that the biblical writers were familiar with volcanic behavior (see photo caption on page 56). A fuller description of volcanic behavior appears in Psalm 18:7–8:

The earth trembled and shook;
the foundations of the mountains rocked and quivered,
because God was angry.
Smoke poured out of his nostrils,
a consuming flame and burning coals from his mouth.

▶ **Clarify** The second amazing event that the Israelites experienced was a "rain" of quail in a time of hunger.

Suddenly the Lord sent a wind
that brought quails from the sea,
flying three feet above the ground.
They settled on the camp and all around it
for miles and miles in every direction.
So all that day, all night, and all the next day,
the people worked catching quails. Numbers 11:31–32

The ancient historian Josephus describes a similar "quail phenomenon" in *Jewish Antiquities* (vol. III, p. 5). More recently, *National Geographic Magazine* (December 1958, p. 852) cited a similar phenomenon that saved Mormon pioneers in 1846. It quotes the *History of Brigham Young* as saying:

The Lord sent flocks of quail, which lit . . .
upon the ground within their reach,
which the saints, and even the sick caught with their hands
until they were satisfied.

▶ **Clarify** The third amazing event that Israel experienced was manna, which appeared in the morning (in contrast to the quail, which appeared in the evening).

When the dew evaporated, there was something
thin and flaky on the surface of the desert.
It was as delicate as frost. . . .
It was like a small white seed,
and tasted like thin cakes made of honey. Exodus 16:14, 31

Some scholars suggest that manna might have been a substance secreted by plant parasites as they nourished themselves on tamarisk trees (found in the Sinai peninsula).

Jesus referred to manna, saying to the people:

"Your ancestors ate manna in the desert,
but they died. . . .
I am the living bread that came down from heaven.
If you eat this bread, you will live forever." John 6:49, 51

Clarify In addition, a fourth amazing event that Israel experienced while crossing the desert was getting water from a rock.

Clarify Ask: What conclusion do we draw from the three amazing events (pillars, quail, manna) that Israel experienced in crossing the desert? Were they miraculous, ordinary, or literary symbols (symbolic stories) intended to teach that God aided Israel in their journey across the desert?

You will find Bible readers on all sides. One thing is for certain. As the Israelites looked back on their crossing of the desert, they were sure that God was aiding them. Without this aid, they would never have made it.

Notebook Develop on the chalkboard for entry in student notebooks the three ways people interpret the events that Israel experienced while crossing the desert.

Interpretations		
	Miraculous events	Worked by God to aid Israel
	Ordinary events	Used by God to aid Israel
	Symbolic stories	Used to express Israel's faith that God aided them

Notebook Some Bible readers suggest that the three events that Israel experienced while crossing the desert were *ordinary* events that God used in an *extraordinary* way to aid Israel. Develop this idea on the chalkboard for entry in student notebooks.

Ordinary events		
	Pillars	Volcanic activity
	Quail	Migration victims
	Manna	Insect secretions

5. LESSON INTERACTION

Exercise ❶ **Discuss** Be sure to have the students write out their responses in private, right in class. Then, volunteers can read aloud their responses as a prelude to discussing the questions.

Exercise ❷ **Activity** The "rap-style" rhythm of this hymn makes it easy to render. If it is performed slowly enough, the class can "drum" it out with the team. Have fun!

Discuss Ask: How do you interpret the last phrase of the first verse: "Who fashioned and made us, protected and stayed us"?

We might liken ourselves and our world to a movie on a movie screen. And we might liken the movie projector to God. Just as the movie owes its presence on the screen to the projector, so we and our world owe our existence to God ("Who fashioned and made us").

Moreover, just as the projector keeps the images on the movie screen once it puts them there, so, too, God keeps us and the world in existence once we have been put there. In other words, if the projector withheld its light, the movie would cease ("protected and stayed us"). This is also true of ourselves and the world.

Lastly, as the projector becomes present on the movie screen through the images it creates, so God becomes present in our world through the things God creates.

Discuss Ask: How does this hymn make reference to Israel's desert journey? ("pillar of fire shining forth in the night")

Ask: How might we say that God leads people today by a "pillar of fire"? (This sets up the example in exercise 3.)

Exercise ❸ **Clarify** John Henry Newman (1801–1890) was thirty-two when he composed the lyrics to "Lead, Kindly Light." At the time, he was a distinguished member of the Church of England and was tormented by a growing attraction to the Roman Catholic Church.

To resolve the situation, he took a boat trip to Rome to consult and pray. His boat was detained at Sicily (on the return trip), where he fell ill and almost died. During his convalescence, he wrote the lyrics to "Lead, Kindly Light."

Newman converted to Roman Catholicism, had a brilliant ministry, and ended up as a cardinal.

Discuss **(a)** Be sure the students grasp the following images in the hymn: "kindly Light" = God; "encircling gloom" = darkness and confusion that we all feel at times; "distant scene" = where I am headed (or should be headed); "one step" = next best thing.

(b) Newman is simply saying that he wasn't always so ready and willing to seek and do God's will.

Encounter with God

LESSON 28

1. LESSON BACKGROUND

▶ *Catechism of the Catholic Church*, 2052–2082.

2. LESSON QUIZ

Perfect score = 10 points

1. What is one thing the Israelites realized for sure as they reflected on their safe journey across the desert? *(Lesson 27 review—1 point)*
2. List four amazing things the Israelites experienced while crossing the desert, and explain how some Bible readers interpret them in an ordinary or natural way. *(Lesson 27 notebook review—8 points)*
3. What new identity did the covenant and the Ten Commandments give the Israelites? *(Lesson 28 preview—1 point)*

3. LESSON HOMEWORK

▶ **Return** Lesson 27 review questions (page 57).

▶ **Collect** Lesson 28 review questions (page 59).

▶ **Read** Lesson 29 ("New Life & Worship," pages 60–61).

▶ **Write** Lesson 29 review questions (page 61).

4. LESSON PRESENTATION

Point 1 **Read** Have volunteers read aloud the core content of lesson 28.

Minimap **Clarify** Have students identify Egypt, the Red Sea, and Mount Sinai.

Technically, the left finger of the Red Sea is called the Gulf of Suez. The right finger, the Gulf of Aqaba.

The Israelites crossed at the northern tip of the Gulf of Suez. Mount Sinai is located in the Sinai peninsula (Sinai desert).

▶ **Discuss** A covenant is a solemn or sacred pact between two parties. God's covenant with the Israelites on Mount Sinai followed the pattern of ancient suzerainty treaties (pacts between a powerful king and a weak king). The weak king pledged loyalty to the powerful king in exchange for favors or protection.

Israel's pledge is to keep the commandments. God's pledge is to make the Israelites God's "chosen people" (new identity) and God's "priestly people," the instrument by which God will re-create the world (new destiny).

▶ **Notebook** Develop the following diagram on the chalkboard for entry in student notebooks.

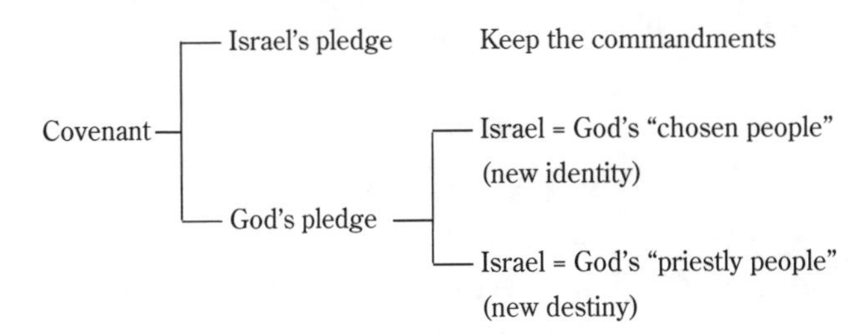

▶ **Notebook** Develop on the chalkboard this summary of the Ten Commandments for entry in student notebooks.

Respect God	1	Worship God only
	2	Respect God's name
	3	Observe God's day (Sabbath)
Respect neighbor	4	Respect parents
	5	No killing
	6	No adultery
	7	No stealing
	8	No false testimony
	9	No coveting (other's wife)
	10	No coveting (other's property)

Ask: How do the first eight commandments differ somewhat markedly from the final two? (The first eight refer to actions; the last two refer to desires.)

Recall that Mark 7:21–22 warned that evil desire is the seed of evil action: "For from the inside, from your heart, come the evil ideas which lead you to do immoral things, to rob, kill, commit adultery, be greedy, and do all sorts of evil things."

Point 2 **Clarify** The Old Testament covenant rituals took different forms at different times and in different circumstances. For example, in the Abraham covenant, animals are halved and laid apart, while in the Sinai covenant, animals are sacrificed.

Ask: Why the differences? (For one thing, religious expression had undergone a certain sophistication or refinement since Abraham's time.)

▶ **Notebook** Develop on the chalkboard for entry in student notebooks an outline of the Sinai covenant ritual that Moses (who acted as the mediator between God and the Israelites) followed.

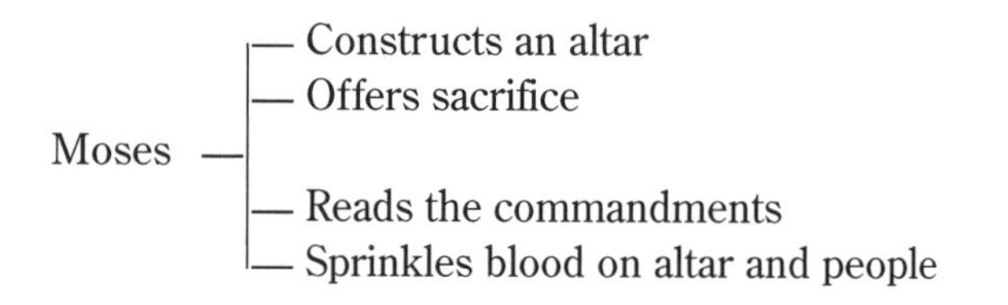

▶ Discuss Why pour (sprinkle) blood on both the altar and on the people? (The altar stood for God. The blood makes God and the Israelites "blood brothers and sisters," as it were.)

Recall that Tom Sawyer and Huck Finn pledged eternal friendship by cutting their fingers and sharing each other's blood.

5. LESSON INTERACTION

Exercise 1 **Notebook** Stress Herberg's point about the difference between the origin of Israel and the origin of all other nations. Summarize it this way for entry in student notebooks

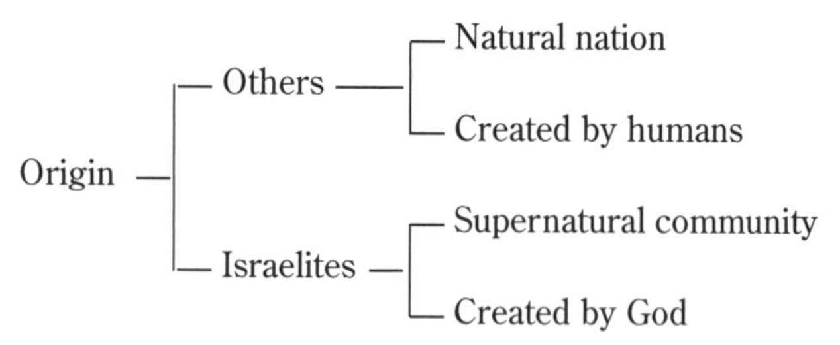

▶ Discuss The encounter the Israelites had with God was a turning point in their lives. It transformed them from a mob of fleeing slaves into a powerful people.

Individuals have similar turning points in their lives. Recall that getting polio was the turning point in Franklin Roosevelt's life.

Ask: Why do you think this event was the turning point in Roosevelt's life? (It forced him to channel his many talents in one direction. It gave him a focus that he never had previously. Focus gave him power.)

Recall that playwright Eugene O'Neill had a similar turning point. At twenty-five he was a drifter. Then a serious illness made him evaluate the direction his life was heading. Result? He changed and went on to revolutionize American theater.

Ask: Why is adversity often a turning point in life?

Exercise 2 **Clarify** Born in Mecca around 570 C.E., Muhammad felt called to continue the prophetic work of Jesus. He regarded himself as God's last prophet.

Muhammad's revelation (reputedly from the angel Gabriel) was written in the Qur'an ("reading"). A book of 114 suras, or chapters, it is regarded as an incarnation of God's voice. *Islam* means "to surrender" to Allah (Arabic for "the god").

Exercise 3 **Discuss** Ask: To whom is the fourth commandment directed, primarily?

▶ Clarify Scholars say it is to adults, not children. Ancient societies abandoned old people when they ceased to be productive and became a burden. God forbids Israel to follow this practice.

A vivid example of the primary intent of this commandment is this true story reported in *Time* magazine (April 6, 1992, p. 24).

"An old man in a wheelchair with a bag of diapers dangling at his side" was left outside a racetrack in Idaho.

All labels had been cut from the man's clothing and all identifying marks "scoured from his wheelchair." A typewritten note taped to his chair identified him as "John King," an Alzheimer's patient. It was an example of "grandpa dumping," something that occurs routinely but usually outside of public hospitals.

Currently about five million people suffer from Alzheimer's disease. The figure will triple by 2050. Medicare will not pay for maintaining an Alzheimer patient in a nursing home.

▶ Discuss Ask: Why does God permit things like Alzheimer's disease and "grandpa dumping"?

▶ Clarify One country that has experimented with physician-aided suicide (for patients requesting it) is Holland. The *Chicago Tribune* (February 13, 1993) reported on the results of the experiment, calling them "not reassuring."

The Dutch parliament found some 1,000 cases of euthanasia performed without the explicit request of the patient. In about half of these, the patient was fully conscious. . . . The fear of opponents—that voluntary euthanasia seriously erodes respect for individual life—has been realized.

Ask: What is the point of the final sentence?

(a, b, c, d) Before listing the commandment under which each quote falls, discuss its meaning. Then decide what commandment it falls under.

Quote	Commandment
a. Capital punishment	Fifth
b. Respect parents	Fourth
c. Pornography	Sixth
d. Deception	Eighth

Exercise 4 **Discuss** Jesus summed up the Ten Commandments under two headings: God (first three) and neighbor (last seven).

CHAPTER SIX: Covenant (pages 60–61)

LESSON 29

1. LESSON BACKGROUND

▶ *Catechism of the Catholic Church,* 2056–2074.

2. LESSON QUIZ

Perfect score = 15 points

1. List the Ten Commandments. *(Lesson 28 review—10 points)*
2. What pledge did Israel make to God, and what twofold pledge did God make to Israel? *(Lesson 28 notebook review—3 points)*
3. List the two revolutionary changes that the Mount Sinai covenant introduced into Israel. *(Lesson 29 preview—2 points)*

3. LESSON HOMEWORK

▶ **Return** Lesson 28 review questions (page 59).

▶ **Collect** Lesson 29 review questions (page 61).

▶ **Read** Lesson 30 ("Teaching & Testing," pages 62–63).

▶ **Write** Lesson 30 review questions (page 63).

▶ **Appoint** Two students to prepare readings from Numbers 21:4–9 and John 3:14–17 (lesson 30, exercises 5 and 6).

4. LESSON PRESENTATION

Point ❶ **Read** Have volunteers read aloud the core content of lesson 29.

▶ **Clarify** The birth of a nation usually begins on a *battlefield,* but it must always end at a *conference table.*

We have something similar in the case of the Israelites. Their escape from the Egyptian army was their *battlefield* victory. But this did not make them a *people.* They were only a mob of ex-slaves with no education, no organization, and no apparent way to survive.

It was the Sinai covenant, spelled out in the commandments, that transformed them into God's "Chosen People." It is against this background that we must view the Ten Commandments.

▶ **Discuss** Different people understand the words *commandment* and *law* in different ways. For example, one person understands them as being *restrictions* to freedom. They cramp our lifestyle and keep us from doing what we would like to do.

A second person understands them as being a *guide* to growth. They free us *from* evil *for* good.

Ask: *From* what and *for* what do traffic laws free us? (They free us *from* dangerous travel *for* safe travel.) Thus they are a guide for personal and social growth.

▶ **Notebook** Develop the following summary on the chalkboard for entry in student notebooks.

Law frees us
- *From* evil
- *For* good

Point ❷ **Discuss** When we talk about laws, we must keep in mind that some laws are bad.

Ask: Give an example of a bad law. (In the early days of the South, bad laws abounded: poll tax laws designed to deny the vote to blacks, and segregation laws forcing blacks to sit in rear seats of buses and forbidding blacks to drink from certain public fountains, use certain public rest rooms, and eat in certain public restaurants.)

Point ❸ **Clarify** Jesus added a third understanding or interpretation of laws and commandments. He presented them as an *invitation to love,* saying:

"If you love me, you will obey my commandments."
John 14:15

Thus Jesus brings our understanding and interpretation of love into the realm of being an opportunity to express love. In other words, I may not see how a law is a *guide* to growth, but I obey it because of what Jesus said: "If you love me, you will obey my commandments." I accept it as an *invitation* to express my love for Jesus himself.

▶ **Notebook** Develop the following diagram on the chalkboard for entry in student notebooks.

Law (3 interpretations)

Restriction	To freedom
Guide	To growth
Invitation	To love

Point ❹ **Discuss** Israel's laws showed a deep sensitivity and humanity. Consider an example. After a priest had admonished Israelite soldiers to trust in Yahweh, an officer was instructed to make this announcement before battle:

"Is there any man here
who has lost his nerve and is afraid?
If so, he is to go home.
Otherwise, he will destroy the morale of the others."
Deuteronomy 20:8

Ask: What are some of the pros and cons of such a law?

Ask: What kind of courage is being referred to in this example of Israel's law: moral or physical? (Moral = capacity to endure mental pain; physical = capacity to endure physical pain.)

► **Notebook** Develop the following summary of courage on the chalkboard for entry in student notebooks.

Courage—
- Moral — Capacity to endure mental pain
- Physical — Capacity to endure physical pain

► **Discuss** Ask: Is courage (moral or physical) like brains and strength? Is it a gift, or is it acquired?

(Some people have a high threshold of pain. By nature they don't feel pain as keenly as others.

Similarly, by nature some people seem to have a high threshold of fear. By nature they don't feel fear as keenly as others.

From this viewpoint, moral and physical courage may be considered a gift. On the other hand, a certain degree of both can probably be acquired.)

► **Notebook** Develop the following summary of the key ideas of this chapter for entry in student notebooks.

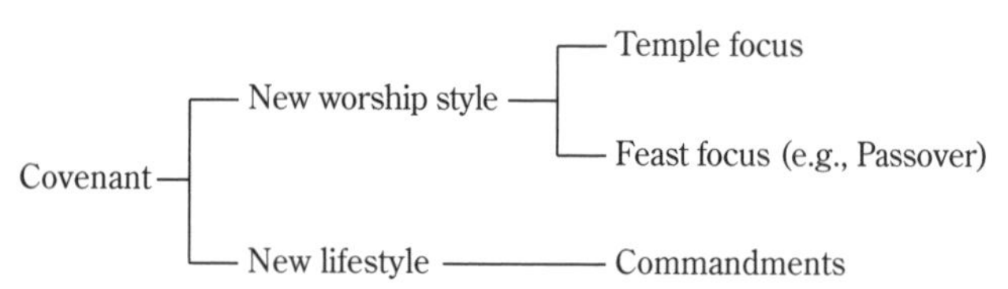

5. LESSON INTERACTION

Exercise ❶ **Discuss** Ritual appeals not just to the intellect (as a verbal statement does) but to the total person (heart and soul).

Exercise ❷ **Discuss** **(a)** The symbolic imposition of hands (on a goat's head) is a gesture of "corporate" involvement. It signifies the community's involvement in the ritual through its representative. (Our term *scapegoat* derives from this Yom Kippur ritual.)

(b, c) The acts of confessing the people's sins over the goat and driving it into the desert represent an effort to symbolize the meaning of forgiveness of sins.

This ritual of having the goat take on the sins of the community paved the way for an understanding of how Jesus would and could "take upon himself" the sins of the world.

"The Son of Man . . .
came to serve and to give his life
to redeem many people." Mark 10:45

Exercise ❸ **Discuss** This raises an important question: To what extent can or should a political leader be a leader of spiritual or moral inspiration as well?

Exercise ❹ **Discuss** The students should have no difficulty explaining the point of these quotes.

Exercise ❺ **Activity** Have students do this as a written assignment right in class. Collect the responses, sift through them, and share the better ones in the next class. One student combined the three elements into a single prayer (a good approach). You might read it to the students to "prime the pump" for them.

Jesus, recently someone I used to think was neat
ridiculed me at the lunch table for wearing clothes
that she said she wouldn't even give to the Salvation Army.
I laughed with everybody else,
but down deep I began to feel a hatred welling up for her.
Just because her family can afford designer clothes
does not give her the right to make fun of those who can't.

That night, while walking home from school all alone,
I passed a church with a crucifix on the outside wall.
As I passed it, I prayed for the girl.
I asked Jesus to bless her and help me to forgive her,
the way he blessed and forgave people
who made fun of him.

Then an amazing thing happened.
My hatred dissolved and seemed to float away,
and I felt more at peace with the world and myself
than I have for years.

Miniposter **Discuss** Direct students to the quotation on the miniposter on page 60. Break the quotation down into two questions: (1) How did the Sabbath keep Israel? (2) How did Israel keep the Sabbath?

Ask: What might be a parallel today, and why?

Teaching & Testing

LESSON 30

1. LESSON BACKGROUND

▶ *Catechism of the Catholic Church*, 128–130.

2. LESSON QUIZ

Perfect score = 10 points

1. What was placed in the Ark of the Covenant, and where was the Ark placed within the sacred Tent? *(Lesson 29 review—2 points)*
2. *From* what and *for* what do the commandments (laws) free us? *(Lesson 29 notebook review—2 points)*
3. List and explain the three regions that made up the desert into which the Israelites went after leaving Mount Sinai. *(Lesson 30 preview—6 points)*

3. LESSON HOMEWORK

▶ **Return** Lesson 29 review questions (page 61).

▶ **Collect** Lesson 30 review questions (page 63).

▶ **Read** Lesson 31 ("Journey's End," pages 64–65).

▶ **Write** Lesson 31 review questions (page 65).

4. LESSON PRESENTATION

Point ❶ **Read** Have volunteers read aloud the core content of lesson 30.

▶ **Clarify** The material for this lesson is drawn from the Book of Numbers. It gets this name from two censuses described in the book.

The first census opens the book and takes place before the Israelites depart from Mount Sinai (1:1–46).

The second census takes place toward the end of the book, about a generation later on the heights of Moab, before the Israelites enter the Promised Land (26:1–51).

▶ **Clarify** The Book of Numbers divides into three sections: (1) preparing to depart Mount Sinai (1:1–10:10), (2) journeying to Moab, east of the Jordan River (10:11–21:35), (3) preparing to enter the Promised Land (22:1–36:13). The time span of the Book of Numbers is about a generation.

▶ **Notebook** Develop on the chalkboard the following summary of the Book of Numbers for entry in student notebooks.

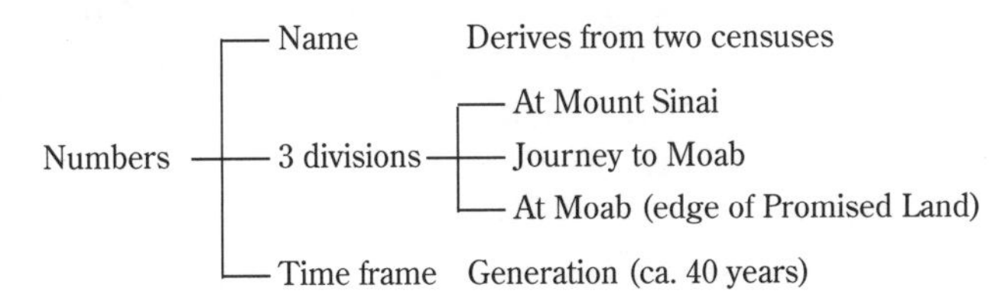

▶ **Notebook** Develop for entry in student notebooks the following summary of the three regions of the desert across which the Israelites journeyed.

Desert
- Sandy land — Little water and vegetation
- Rocky land — Minimal water and vegetation
- Semiarid land — Some water and vegetation

Point ❷ **Notebook** Develop for entry in student notebooks the following summary of how the existence of the Israelites was threatened from within and from without during their journey into the desert.

Threat
- Within — Rebels challenged Moses and his leadership
- Without — Edomites prepared to attack the Israelites

▶ **Clarify** After the threat by the Edomites, Aaron dies. Moses is left alone in his difficult task of leadership (Numbers 20:22–29).

▶ **Notebook** Develop on the chalkboard the following diagram of the story of the Bible up to this point. It traces the journey of humanity from the garden of Eden to the heights of Moab, where the people are encamped, poised to enter the Promised Land. The biblical books that treat the five phases of the journey are listed at the bottom of the diagram.

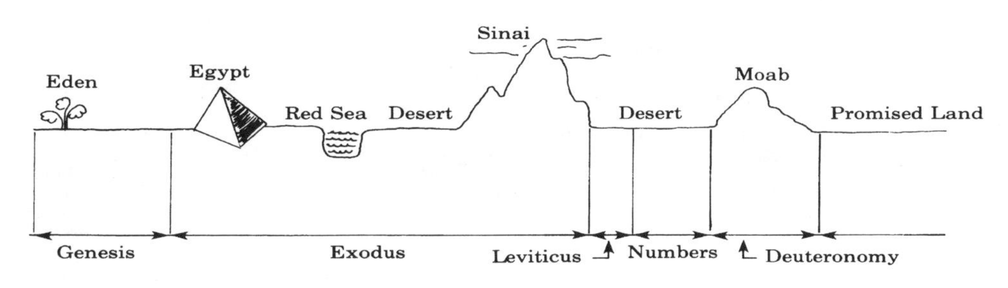

5. LESSON INTERACTION

Exercise 1 **Discuss** If the discussion is not as fruitful as you would like, you might rephrase the question this way: When should/shouldn't the principal of a school be influenced by the opinions of the student body?

Exercise 2 **Discuss** **(a)** This is an application of the above exercise to the political situation. In other words, if a politician is simply reading the polls and letting them dictate policy, that politician is not leading, but following.

Dr. Martin Luther King Jr.'s comment about the Church has relevance here. He said it must be a "thermostat," not a "thermometer."

Ask: What did Dr. King mean? (The Church should not *reflect* what people say is right or wrong; it should *guide* them. Gilbert Keith Chesterton put it something like this: "I don't need the Church to be right when I'm right. I need the Church to be right when I'm wrong."

(b) When leaders do not care about people, you end up with a situation like Israel's. God said of Israel's noncaring leaders:

"You are doomed, you shepherds of Israel!
You take care of yourselves, but never tend the sheep. . . .
You have not taken care of the weak ones,
healed the ones that are sick,
bandaged the ones that are hurt,
brought back the ones that wandered off,
or looked for the ones that were lost. . . .
I will take my sheep away from you and
never again let you be their shepherds." Ezekiel 34:2, 4, 10

(c) Ask: How do the following words of Victoria Farnsworth relate to the quote in question?

Not until I became a mother did I understand how much my mother sacrificed for me; . . . not until I became a mother did I understand how proud my mother was when I achieved; not until I became a mother did I understand how much my mother loved me.

Exercise 3 **Discuss** You might relate this quote to the Dolly Parton quote in the miniposter on page 116 ("If you want the rainbow, you gotta put up with the rain") and to the William Penn quote in the miniposter on page 222 ("No pain, no palm; No thorns, no glory; No cross, no crown").

Ask: How do these quotes relate to the one in question?

Exercise 4 **Discuss** The third quote is really a powerful one. What does Eliot mean when he says "the greatest treason"?

Exercise 5 **Discuss** The purpose of this exercise is to set up the next exercise. Begin by having the appointed student read aloud Numbers 21:4–9. (Clearly "The Pole" recalls "The Cross.")

Exercise 6 **Discuss** Have the appointed student read aloud John 3:14–17.

Ask: How does the Old Testament event ("The Pole") point to the New Testament event ("The Cross")?

1. A snake wounded humanity spiritually (Genesis 3).
2. Humanity was doomed to die.
3. Jesus was raised on the cross.
4. Those who looked upon the crucified Jesus with faith were healed spiritually.

Review Recall that a type is an Old Testament person or event that points to a New Testament person or event. Early Christians used types to show that Jesus was the one toward whom the Old Testament pointed. Thus, they saw Isaac as pointing to Jesus. Isaac, like Jesus,

1. was his father's only son,
2. carried the wood of sacrifice on his shoulder,
3. was to be sacrificed on a hill, like Calvary,
4. was not defeated by death.

Photo **Clarify** Direct students' attention to the minimap and to the photo and photo caption on page 62.

The Sea of Galilee is a fisherman's paradise; the Dead Sea, a fisherman's nightmare. They are both fed by the same source: Mount Hermon to the north of the Sea of Galilee (not shown on map). The difference is that the Sea of Galilee gives up all the water that flows into it. On the other hand, the Dead Sea keeps all the water that flows into it. This is why no fish can live in it.

Commenting on these two seas, someone said, "They are images of the two kinds of people in the world."

Ask: What did the person mean? (The world is made up of "givers" and "takers." Givers generate life; takers destroy life.)

Notebook The following diagram is vastly telescoped to fit the page and to show the contrast in terrain in the Holy Land. Note that the Dead Sea is 1,300 below sea level (bsl) and Moab (where the Israelites were poised to cross the Jordan into the Promised Land) is 3,000 feet above sea level (asl). The Mediterranean Sea is at sea level. Develop the diagram on the chalkboard for entry in student notebooks.

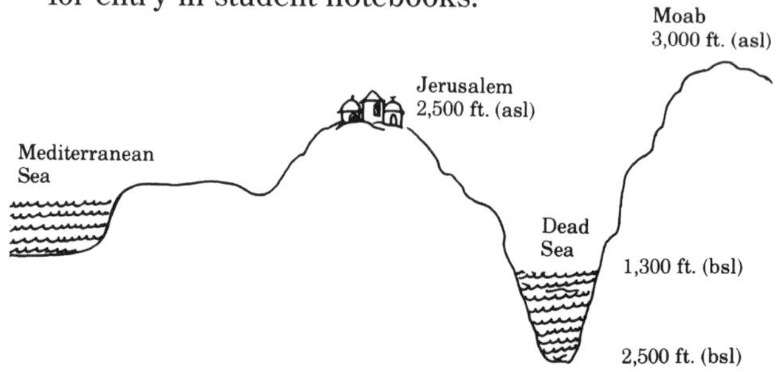

Journey's End

1. LESSON BACKGROUND

► *Catechism of the Catholic Church*, 2574–2577.

2. LESSON QUIZ

Perfect score = 10 points

1. Explain what threatened Israel's existence—from *within* and from *without*—during their journey in the desert. *(Lesson 30 review—2 points)*
2. Where did the Book of Numbers get its name, and at what site does the book (a) begin its narrative and (b) end it? *(Lesson 30 notebook review—3 points)*
3. List the five books of the Torah. *(Lesson 31 preview—5 points)*

3. LESSON HOMEWORK

► **Return** Lesson 30 review questions (page 63).

► **Collect** Lesson 31 review questions (page 65).

► **Read** Lesson 32 ("Into the Land," pages 68–69).

► **Write** Lesson 32 review questions (page 69).

► **Appoint** Three students to prepare readings from Joshua 9:1–8, 9–15, 16–27 (lesson 32, exercise 5).

4. LESSON PRESENTATION

Point 1 **Discuss** Moses prepared the Israelites for entry into the Promised Land by rehearsing how God had schooled and tested them—as an eagle schools and tests its young to fly.

An eagle takes its young into the air and lets them fall. If they fail to fly (pass the test), it catches them and repeats the process.

God taught the Israelites the same way. Eventually they learned that without God they could do nothing. With God they could do all things.

Recall Jesus' words: "I am the vine, and you are the branches. . . . You can do nothing without me" (John 15:5).

► **Clarify** God still teaches people (individually and collectively) the same lesson that was taught the Israelites. Recall the example of John Newton.

John Newton was a slave trader and a sinner in the late 1700s. One night a storm threatened to sink his slave ship. John cried out to God, "Save us, and I'll quit this business and be your slave forever." The ship survived, and John quit the slave trade and became a minister.

To celebrate his conversion, John wrote "Amazing Grace." A portion of it reads: " 'Tis grace hath brought me safe thus far, / And grace will lead me home."

Moses makes the same point with the Israelites before their entry into the Promised Land. God led them safely for "forty years," and God will continue to do so.

► **Notebook** Have the students copy the following in their notebooks. Ask them to match the right-hand column with the left-hand column. (They may use each response only once.) This exercise summarizes Israel's spiritual journey.

ISRAEL'S SPIRITUAL JOURNEY

Event	Experience
1. __ creation	*a.* victory in God
2. __ fall	*b.* need for God's help
3. __ flood	*c.* alienation from God
4. __ exodus	*d.* recommitment to God
5. __ Mount Sinai	*e.* doomed without God
6. __ desert	*f.* experience of God's help
7. __ land	*g.* innocence before God

(Answers: 1. *g*, 2. *c*, 3. *e*, 4. *f*, 5. *d*, 6. *b*, 7. *a*)

► **Notebook** Repeat the above exercise to show how our human spiritual journey parallels Israel's.

MY SPIRITUAL JOURNEY

Event	Experience
1. __ creation	*a.* I begin life in innocence.
2. __ fall	*b.* God continues to guide me.
3. __ flood	*c.* I fall into sin.
4. __ exodus	*d.* I recommit to God.
5. __ Mount Sinai	*e.* I learn of sin's destructive power.
6. __ desert	*f.* I falter but don't abandon God.
7. __ land	*g.* God does not abandon me.

(Answers: 1. *a*, 2. *c*, 3. *e*, 4. *g*, 5. *d*, 6. *f*, 7. *b*)

► **Activity** Have the students follow up this exercise by:

1. discussing their responses,
2. listing on an unsigned sheet of paper where they think they are in their faith journey,
3. tallying the results of 2 on the chalkboard to determine where the class, as a whole, is on its spiritual journey.

Point 2 **Discuss** Ask: Who were some great leaders who, like Moses, fought valiantly for causes but died before seeing the fruits of their struggle? (A sampling, in alphabetical order, reads:

Susan B. Anthony	Women's rights
Mahatma Gandhi	India's freedom
Jesus	God's kingdom on earth
Helen Keller	Education for the handicapped
Martin Luther King Jr.	Racial equality in America
Abraham Lincoln	Unity between the states)

Clarify Why was Moses denied the pleasure of enjoying the fruits of his struggle? The Book of Numbers links the answer to an episode in the desert when Moses lost his cool with the Israelites, who were complaining about the lack of water at a place called Meribah. Standing with Aaron before a huge rock, he shouted:

"Listen, you rebels!
Do we have to get water out of this rock for you?"
Numbers 20:10

Commenting on this episode, Psalm 106:32–33 says:

Moses was in trouble on their [Israelites'] account.
They made him so bitter
that he spoke without stopping to think.

Point 3 **Notebook** The first five books of the Bible are called by various names. Develop this diagram for entry in student notebooks.

Five books	Torah	Hebrew word meaning "law," or "instruction"
	Pentateuch	Greek word meaning "five scrolls"
	Book of Moses	Bible writers occasionally referred to Torah this way (e.g., 2 Chronicles 25:4, Ezra 6:18, Mark 12:26)

Clarify Literalists hold that Moses himself wrote the Torah. But the last chapter of Deuteronomy describes Moses' death. Clearly, he did not write it. Contextualists hold that the Book of Moses is given this name because it contains Moses' teachings.

Notebook The Torah describes the following stages in the journey of God's people to the Promised Land.

Torah	Genesis	Eden to Egypt
	Exodus	Egypt to Mount Sinai
	Leviticus	Mount Sinai
	Numbers	Mount Sinai to Moab
	Deuteronomy	Moab

5. LESSON INTERACTION

Exercise 1 **Discuss** **(a)** Have the group check the photo and caption on page 65. Note the mountains that are slightly visible (upper right) in background. Irwin said, "I was taken aback . . . that the mountains were not gray or brown, as I expected. They were golden."

Each night before falling asleep in the lunar module, Irwin reflected on the mountains "to etch in my mind a lasting impression" of them. He said Psalm 121 kept coming to mind:

I look to the mountains; where will my help come from?
My help will come from the LORD,
who made heaven and earth. Psalm 121:1–2

(b) Mental preparation focuses our attention, much as a lens focuses ordinary sun rays to the point where they can burn a hole into wood. Pro football coach George Allen said preparation was the key to success: "Winning is the science of being totally prepared."

A Chinese proverb makes the same point with this concrete image: "Dig the well before you are thirsty."

(c, d, e) Have the group take a few minutes to think out their responses to these three questions.

Next, have them record their responses in their notebooks. Finally, have volunteers read and explain their responses to the group.

Exercise 2 **Discuss** Ask: Who are Calvin and Hobbes? (A boy and a tiger in a popular cartoon) Recall how one strip shows Calvin reflecting on the same three questions posed by Sandburg.

Ask: Do you recall how Calvin responded? ("Well, I'm a kid with big plans. I just came from my room and I'm going outside!") Calvin's lightweight response to this heavyweight question is how many people respond to these same questions.

Notebook Have the students take a few minutes to think out their responses to the same three questions and record them in their notebooks. Finally, have volunteers read and explain their responses.

Exercise 3 **Discuss** Keith Miller survived. Slowly the memory of the accident faded, and Miller experienced a deep void in his life. It got so bad one day that he got into his car and started driving.

Coming to a secluded spot he stopped and shouted, "God, if there is anything you want from me, take it!" Then it dawned on him what God wants from us. Miller wrote later:

God wants our will. If we give God our will, God will begin to show us life as we've never seen it before. It is like being born again.

This experience changed Miller in a way similar to how the Israelites' desert experience changed them. Eventually Miller gave up his job with a Texas oil company and became a successful spiritual writer and national lecturer.

Ask: On a scale of 1 (not very) to 10 (very), how ready are you to give your will to God? Explain.

Into the Land

LESSON **32**

1. LESSON BACKGROUND

▶ *Catechism of the Catholic Church*, 707–708.

2. LESSON QUIZ

Perfect score = 10 points

1. With what event does the Torah end? *(Lesson 31 review—1 point)*
2. Match the following events in Israel's spiritual journey to show how they parallel your own journey. *(Lesson 31 notebook review—7 points)*

Event	*My own spiritual journey*
1. __ creation	*a.* I begin life in innocence.
2. __ fall	*b.* God continues to guide me.
3. __ flood	*c.* I fall into sin.
4. __ exodus	*d.* I recommit to God.
5. __ Sinai	*e.* I learn of sin's destructive power.
6. __ desert	*f.* I falter but don't abandon God.
7. __ land	*g.* God does not abandon me.

3. What is a tell, and why is pottery (found in a tell) valuable? *(Lesson 32 preview—2 points)*

3. LESSON HOMEWORK

▶ **Return** Lesson 31 review questions (page 65).

▶ **Collect** Lesson 32 review questions (page 69).

▶ **Read** Lesson 33 ("Era of the Judges," pages 70–71).

▶ **Write** Lesson 33 review questions (page 71).

▶ **Appoint** Three students to prepare readings from (1) Judges 10:6–17, (2) Judges 11:1–6, (3) Judges 11:29–40 (lesson 33, exercise 3). (Note: The reading from Judges 10 is somewhat tedious and contains several names that are difficult to pronounce. You might have the student summarize the main idea of the passage, avoiding the difficult names.)

4. LESSON PRESENTATION

Point ❶ **Read** Have volunteers read aloud the core content of lesson 32.

▶ **Clarify** Joshua took command of the Israelites. Appointed by Moses before he died, Joshua fired the desert-hardened Hebrews with his own deep faith.

When preparations were complete, horns sounded everywhere. As the great wave of Israelites thundered downhill to cross the Jordan, the entire valley echoed with shouts. Yahweh's ancient promise was being fulfilled:

- To Abraham

  I am going to give you
  and your descendants
  all the land that you see, and
  it will be yours forever. Genesis 13:15

- To Isaac

  I am going to give
  all this territory to you. . . .
  I will keep the promise I made
  to your father Abraham. Genesis 26:3

- To Jacob

  I am the LORD*,*
  the God of Abraham and Isaac.
  I will give to you and
  to your descendants this land
  on which you are lying. Genesis 28:13

- To Israelites

  I will make you my own people, and . . .
  bring you to the land
  that I solemnly promised
  to give to Abraham, Isaac, and Jacob. Exodus 6:7–8

Point ❷ **Discuss** Ask: To what earlier event in Israel's history does the crossing of the Jordan remind you? (Red Sea crossing)

The Red Sea looked and ran away;
the Jordan River stopped flowing.
The mountains skipped like goats;
the hills jumped around like lambs.
What happened, Sea, to make you run away?
And you, O Jordan, why did you stop flowing?
You mountains, why did you skip like goats?
You hills, why did you jump around like lambs? Psalm 114:3–6

▶ **Discuss** Ask: How do you interpret the last two sentences of this psalm excerpt?

You mountains, why did you skip like goats?
You hills, why did you jump around like lambs?

(They seem to describe an earthquake, not in a terrifying sense, but in a joyful sense. Nature is jubilant in being able to participate in the event. The Bible refers to earthquakes in a number of places. A few are Zechariah 14:5, Matthew 24:7, and Matthew 27:51.)

Notebook Develop the following diagram for entry in student notebooks. It summarizes the psalmist's view of the two crossings. They are two sides of the same coin.

Twin events	Red Sea	Exit (land of slavery)
	Jordan River	Entry (land of freedom)

Point ❸ **Clarify** Excavations of the destroyed city of Jericho suggest that its walls collapsed suddenly. (They didn't show the effects of a battering ram.) Moreover, a thick blanket of soot covering the ancient remains of the city was carbon dated to 1400 B.C.E.

These facts suggest that an earthquake may have figured in Jericho's destruction and are consistent with the Bible's assertion that Joshua destroyed (burned) the city under "the ban."

Time magazine comments on all this in an article entitled "Score One for the Bible" (March 5, 1990).

5. LESSON INTERACTION

Exercise ❶ **Discuss** Recall that the classic example of this is Jesus' visit to Nazareth at the beginning of his ministry:

[Jesus] was not able to perform any miracles there,
except that he placed his hands on a few sick people
and healed them.
He was greatly surprised,
because the people did not have faith. Mark 6:5–6

Exercise ❷ **Discuss** **(a)** We constantly simplify and telescope in our oral communication with others. For example, we say, "To make a long story short."

Discuss **(b)** Nothing is worse than somebody who rambles on and on in telling a story. It is not uncommon for someone to say, "Skip all the details and get to the point." This is what the Book of Joshua does. It skips a lot of the detail and gets to the point.

Notebook Develop the following summary of the Book of Joshua on the chalkboard for entry in notebooks.

Book of Joshua	Not historical in our sense, since it telescopes time and simplifies events
	Handed down orally for generations
	Point: God's power, not Israel's might, brought Israel's victory

Exercise ❸ **Discuss** Point out that the concept of reward and punishment in an afterlife did not emerge fully until the second century B.C.E. Even then it was vague. Not until Jesus did it come into clearer focus. This helps explain the Israelites' attitude toward people who worshiped idols. The Israelites regarded themselves as instruments by which God punished these people.

Exercise ❹ **Discuss** An example of what Augustine is saying is found in the words we use to describe God. Our point of reference is humans. For example, humans are knowing, powerful, and finite. So we describe God is being all-knowing, all-powerful, and infinite (that is, not finite). In other words, we describe God by simply removing human limitations of God.

Discuss **(a)** Recall the example of the college girl who said to her professor, "I can no longer believe in God." The professor responded, "Congratulations!" Shocked at the professor's remark, the girl said, "What do you mean?" The professor responded, "The God image you have in mind probably ought to be rejected. It's to your credit that you reject that image. That doesn't mean there is no God. It simply means that the God image you have in mind needs correction."

Discuss **(b)** How is Martin Buber's point similar to Tolstoy's point in the previous quotation?

Exercise ❺ **Discuss** **(a)** Have the three appointed students read Joshua 9 ("The Deception"). It is a great story. The author of Joshua ends the story of the Gibeonites, saying, "To this day they have continued to do this work." The key is "to this day," indicating a substantial lapse of time between the event and the recording of it. In other words, the story was passed on orally for a substantial period of time.

Discuss **(b)** Verse 18 reads: "But the Israelites could not kill them, because their leaders had made a solemn promise to them in the name of the LORD, Israel's God."

Miniposter Direct students' attention to the ostracon in the small photo on page 68. People recycled everything in Joshua's time, even broken pottery, using it as a writing surface for contracts, bills of sale, and so forth.

Photos Direct students' attention to the photos on pages 68 and 69. Point out that a number of college students studying archaeology spend their summers on "digs" in Israel, as the girl in the photo on page 68 is doing.

CHAPTER SEVEN: Nationhood (pages 70–71)

Era of the Judges

LESSON 33

1. LESSON BACKGROUND

► *Catechism of the Catholic Church,* 94–95.

2. LESSON QUIZ

Perfect score = 8 points

1. What is meant by "the ban," and what does it reveal to us about Israel's understanding of God? *(Lesson 32 review—2 points)*
2. Explain how the crossings of the Red (Reed) Sea and the Jordan River are interrelated so that we may refer to them as "twin events." *(Lesson 32 notebook review—2 points)*
3. Describe the fourfold pattern that the Israelites followed in the Book of Judges. *(Lesson 33 preview—4 points)*

3. LESSON HOMEWORK

► **Return** Lesson 32 review questions (page 69).

► **Collect** Lesson 33 review questions (page 71).

► **Read** Lesson 34 ("Era of the Kings," pages 72–73).

► **Write** Lesson 34 review questions (page 73).

► **Appoint** Four students to prepare readings from 1 Samuel: (1) 17:41–58, (2) 18:1–16, (3) 26:1–12, (4) 26:13–25 (lesson 34, exercises 1, 2, 5).

4. LESSON PRESENTATION

Point 1 **Read** Have volunteers read aloud the core content of lesson 33.

► **Clarify** The Book of Joshua ends on a deeply religious note: Joshua assembled all the people at Shechem and led them in a renewal of the covenant. "After that, the LORD's servant Joshua son of Nun died" (Joshua 24:29).

Point 2 **Notebook** Develop on the chalkboard the contrast between the portrayal of the Israelites in the Book of Joshua and that in the Book of Judges.

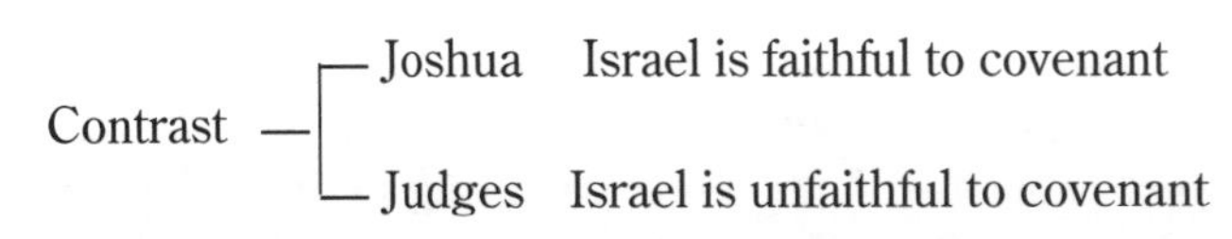

► **Notebook** Develop on the chalkboard the fourfold pattern that we see repeated over and over in the major events of the Book of Judges. We might compare it to a play in four acts.

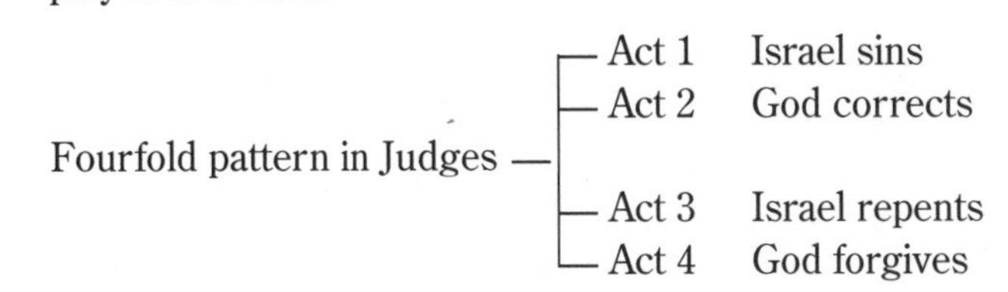

► **Clarify** Some scholars divide the judges into "major" judges (Deborah, Gideon, Jephthah, and Samson) and "minor" judges (like Tola, Jair, and Elon). The number of judges is usually set at twelve.

► **Notebook** Develop the following summary of the judges on the chalkboard for entry in student notebooks.

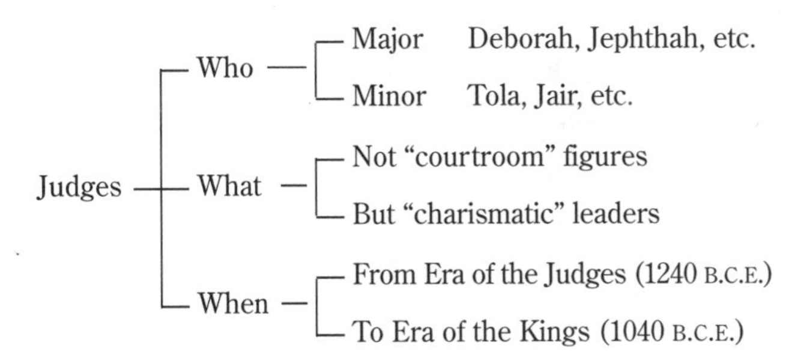

Point 3 **Clarify** A fascinating judge is Samson (Judges 13–16). It seems that he did not lead armies but worked as a loner, living at times in a cave in a cliff (Judges 15:8).

The Samson stories give us a fairly accurate picture of the twelfth-century B.C.E. relationship between Israel and the Philistines. They lived in adjoining towns along the frontier border. They had free access through one another's territory. Sometimes their dealings were friendly; sometimes they were brutally hostile.

On one occasion Samson caught a number of foxes, tied them tail to tail, attached a torch to each pair, and sent them off through the Philistine grain fields. Soon the whole countryside was ablaze with fire (Judges 15:4–8).

► **Clarify** Rounding out the two-hundred-year Era of the Judges is the Book of Ruth. This brief book opens in the midst of a great famine that struck Israel. The book's heroine, Naomi, sets out with her husband and their two sons to Moab. (Recall that Moses and the Israelites camped in this region before entering the Promised Land.) There her husband dies. Her two sons marry Moabite women (non-Jews). Soon tragedy strikes and both sons die.

Naomi decides to return home. Ruth, the wife of one of her dead sons, goes with Naomi. They arrive back at harvesttime. While gathering grain in a field, Ruth meets Boaz, the wealthy owner of the field. When Boaz learns he is a relative of Ruth's dead husband, he marries her. Thus he honors the ancient custom that a kinsman is responsible for a widow's care. Ruth bears him a son.

[They] named the boy Obed. . . .
Obed became the father of Jesse,
who was the father of David. Ruth 4:17

▶ **Discuss** And so the Book of Ruth acts as a bridge book between the Era of the Judges and the Era of the Kings.

Ask: How does it do this? (By presenting the family tree that leads to David, Israel's greatest king)

▶ **Discuss** In addition, the book challenges over-nationalistic Jews to widen their vision about God's concern for non-Jewish people.

Ask: How does it do this? (It presents Ruth, a non-Jew, as a direct ancestor of David.) New Testament writers used the line of descendancy in the Book of Ruth to indicate Jesus' descendancy from David:

This is the list of the ancestors
of Jesus Christ, a descendant of David. . . .
Boaz . . . Obed (his mother was Ruth),
Jesse, and King David. Matthew 1:1–6a

5. LESSON INTERACTION

Exercise ① **Discuss** The spiritual journey of ballerina Gelsey Kirkland comes close to the fourfold pattern that repeats itself over and over in the Book of Judges.

Exercise ② **Discuss** The students should have no difficulty discussing and understanding the three quotes. After discussing the first quote (Thomas Carlyle), have the students explain the caption on page 71.

Exercise ③ **Read** Have the assigned students read the assigned passages. The first reading is somewhat tedious and contains several names that are difficult to pronounce. You might have the student summarize the idea rather than stumble through the reading.

▶ **Discuss** Jephthah was born of a prostitute. His father had other sons. When they found out about Jephthah's background, they drove him out of town, saying, "You will not inherit anything from our father" (Judges 11:2).

Jephthah became an outlaw, heading up a gang of raiders. His reputation as a skilled fighter and leader spread. When the Israelites needed a leader, they turned to Jephthah. The Spirit came upon Jephthah, and he led them to victory. Before going into battle, Jephthah followed a practice of Israel's enemy nations (2 Kings 3:27). He vowed that if he were successful, he would sacrifice the first living thing to greet him upon his return home (Judges 11:30–31). It was his daughter. He cried out in anguish: "I have made a solemn promise to the LORD, and I cannot take it back!" (Judges 11:35).

Ask: What earlier incident does this recall? (Isaac's inability to take back his blessing of Jacob)

▶ **Discuss** Jephthah's daughter understood her father's vow. She had only one request: to be left alone for two months so she could "wander in the mountains and grieve that I must die a virgin" (Judges 11:37).

Ask: Why does the daughter "grieve" that she must die a virgin? (To die childless was a grave misfortune.)

Exercise ④ **Activity** This exercise should be done privately in the students' notebooks. It sets up exercise 5.

Exercise ⑤ **Activity** Here is one girl's reflection on her present relationship with God. Read it to your students to get them started.

Lord, I used to be able to talk to you just as I talked to my best friend. But something happened to change that relationship. Like Adam and Eve in the garden, I found myself hiding from you. I no longer felt comfortable in your presence.

All of a sudden my carefreeness and fun disappeared.

At first I thought it was you punishing me. I no longer think that. I think you let me have my way, knowing that it would eventually bring me to my senses.

Recently I've begun thinking more about my relationship—or lack of it—with you. I'm not sure why, but it has made me want to be friends with you again.

Lord, thank you for putting this desire back in my heart. Help me to use it as a stepping-stone to a renewed friendship between us.

Era of the Kings

LESSON 34

1. LESSON BACKGROUND

▶ *Catechism of the Catholic Church*, 2578–2580.

2. LESSON QUIZ

Perfect score = 10 points

1. Give the approximate dates of the Era of the Judges. *(Lesson 33 review—2 points)*
2. Briefly describe what a "judge" was and into what two groups judges are sometimes divided. *(Lesson 33 notebook review—3 points)*
3. Briefly identify (a) Samuel, (b) Saul, (c) David, (d) Solomon, (e) Jerusalem. *(Lesson 34 preview—5 points)*

3. LESSON HOMEWORK

▶ **Return** Lesson 33 review questions (page 71).

▶ **Collect** Lesson 34 review questions (page 73).

▶ **Read** Lesson 35 ("Israel's Soul Book," pages 74–75).

▶ **Write** Lesson 35 review questions (page 75).

▶ **Appoint** Two students to prepare excerpts of lyrics (6–8 lines) from two songs that they think qualify as modern psalms. A modern psalm gives us a glimpse into the soul of the song-writer in a time of doubt, sorrow, or joy (lesson 35, exercise 1).

4. LESSON PRESENTATION

Point 1 **Read** Have volunteers read aloud the core content of lesson 34.

▶ **Clarify** Although the details of Samuel's life are wrapped in obscurity, his role in history is as bright as the noonday sun. For this reason alone, he deserves to have two books of the Bible bear his name.

Some scholars label Samuel the "last judge" and the "first prophet" (1 Samuel 3:20). But Samuel does not fit either description in a strict sense. Perhaps Samuel is best described as a "bridge man" between the Era of the Judges and the Era of the Kings. He anoints Saul to be the first king of Israel.

In a similar way the Book of Ruth may be described as a "bridge book" between the Era of the Judges and the Era of the Kings, because it introduces us to the genealogy of King David, Israel's greatest king.

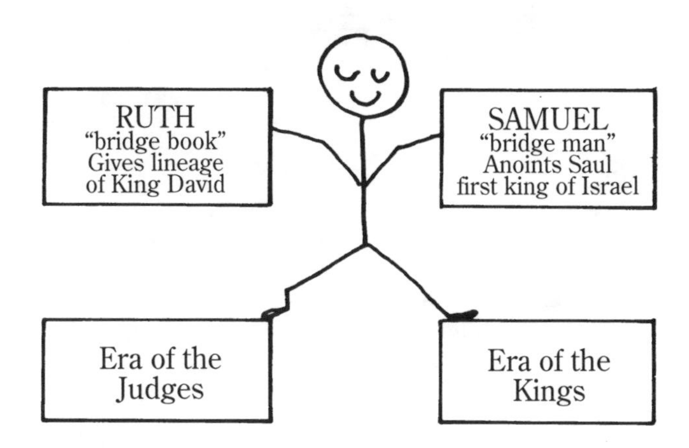

▶ **Notebook** Develop the following summary on the chalkboard for entry in student notebooks.

Saul
- Anointed Israel's first king
- Began well
- Ended badly

Point 2 **Discuss** David had a remarkable charism for leadership. Commenting on it, Robert Wallace wrote:

David's ability to inspire love and loyalty
was remarkable; no other biblical figure,
until the appearance of Christ, approaches it.
During one battle in which he was severely pressed,
David expressed a longing
for a drink of cool water from a well in Bethlehem,
apparently several miles distant.
Without hesitation three of his men
broke through the enemy lines to gratify the whim.

Ask: What do you think David did when the three men returned with the water? (David poured it on the ground, saying he could not drink the blood of the men who risked their lives for the water [2 Samuel 23:14–17].)

Ask: Was that an appropriate response? Why or why not?

After David made Jerusalem his political and religious capital, there came a remarkable moment. God instructed the prophet Nathan to tell David:

"You will always have descendants,
and I will make your kingdom last forever. . . ."
Nathan told David everything. . . . Then King David
went into the Tent of the LORD's presence,
sat down and prayed. 2 Samuel 7:16–18

Notebook Develop the following diagram on the chalkboard. It sums up how the covenants with Abraham, Israel, and David impact their identity and destiny.

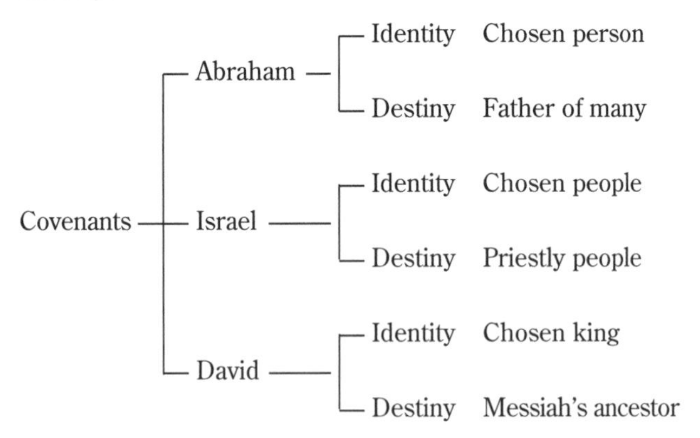

Notebook Develop the following diagram. It sums up two key points of God's "messianic promises" to David and shows how the Hebrew word *Messiah* translates into Greek *(Christos)* and into English *(Anointed)*. English tradition, however, chose to modify the Greek translation and use *Christ* rather than *Anointed*.

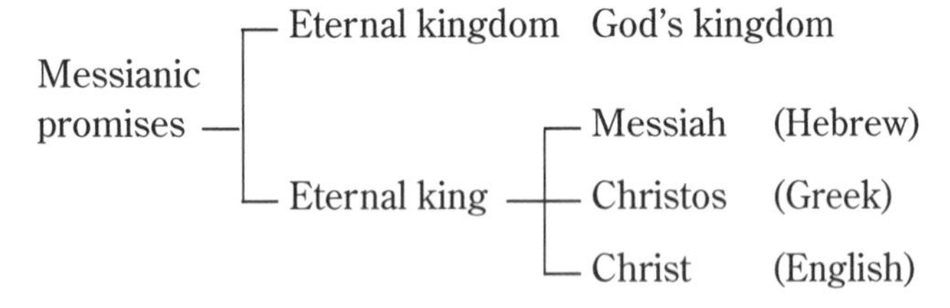

5. LESSON INTERACTION

Exercise 1 **Discuss** Have the appointed students read 1 Samuel 17:41–18:16. The reactions to David are:

a. Goliath—Scorned David (1 Samuel 17:42)
b. Philistines—Ran away (1 Samuel 17:51)
c. Jonathan—Became great friends (1 Samuel 18:3)
d. Saul's officers and men—Admired David (1 Samuel 18:5)
e. Women—Preferred David to Saul (1 Samuel 18:7)
f. Saul—Grew jealous of David (1 Samuel 18:9)

Exercise 2 **Discuss** Have the appointed students read 1 Samuel 26. Many responses are possible.

Exercise 3 **Discuss** Sometimes we do not like the personnel of a certain church. We need to learn to distinguish between the church and its personnel. We shouldn't sink the ship just because we don't like the captain or its crew.

Exercise 4 **Discuss** You might want to read the following actual statement of a poor person.

It's really funny. Some liberals want to take from us poor the only nice thing we have: our church. We don't mind giving for it. It's the only decent thing a lot of us have. . . . Let the liberals sell their extra car or boat if they want to help the poor. But don't take away the one thing we can be proud of: a beautiful place for worship.

Exercise 5 **Discuss** This exercise is self-explanatory.

Photo **Discuss** Direct attention to the photo on page 72. Ask: Can you spot and explain the three clues that identify the man and the boy on the left? (*knife* in man's right hand, *rope* binding the boy's hand and foot, *ram* on which man and boy stand. Explanation: "Abraham . . . tied up his son and . . . picked up the knife to kill him. But the angel of the LORD called to him from heaven. . . . 'Don't hurt the boy. . . .' Abraham . . . saw a ram caught in a bush . . . and offered it . . . instead of his son [Isaac]" [Genesis 22:9–13].)

Ask: Can you spot and explain the three clues that identify the next man? (*pole* in the man's hand, *snake* entwined around the top of the pole, *sheep* on which the man stands. Explanation: "Moses was taking care of the sheep. . . . Many Israelites were bitten and died. . . . Then the LORD told Moses to make a metal snake and put it on a pole, so that anyone who was bitten could look at it and be healed" [Exodus 3:1, Numbers 21:6, 8].)

Ask: What are the three clues that identify the man on Moses' left? (*knife* in the man's right hand, *lamb* tied up and held by man's left hand, *angel* catching the lamb's blood in a chalice. Explanation: "Samuel [sacrificed] . . . a young lamb . . . to the LORD. . . . While Samuel was offering the sacrifice, the Philistines . . . became completely confused and fled" [1 Samuel 7:9–10].)

Ask: Can you spot and explain the three clues that identify the final man? (*crown* on the man's head, *scepter* in the man's left hand, *lion* on which the man stands. Explanation: David convinced Saul that he was qualified to fight Goliath, saying, " 'I have killed lions . . . and I will do the same to this heathen Philistine.' . . . They anointed him, and he became king" [1 Samuel 17:36, 2 Samuel 5:3].)

Clarify It is not clear what David holds in his right hand. Some say it is a crown of thorns and three large nails, symbolizing Jesus, who will come from David's line.

CHAPTER SEVEN: Nationhood (pages 74–75)

Israel's Soul Book

LESSON **35**

1. LESSON BACKGROUND

▶ *Catechism of the Catholic Church*, 2585–2589.

2. LESSON QUIZ

Perfect score = 10 points

1. List and explain the new identities and destinies that God gave Abraham, Israel, and David through covenants. *(Lesson 34 review—6 points)*
2. Explain how Ruth serves as a "bridge book" and Samuel as a "bridge person" between the Era of the Judges and the Era of the Kings. *(Lesson 34 notebook review—2 points)*
3. Who is credited with authoring the Book of Psalms and why? *(Lesson 35 preview—2 points)*

3. LESSON HOMEWORK

▶ **Return** Lesson 34 review questions (page 73).

▶ **Collect** Lesson 35 review questions (page 75).

▶ **Read** Lesson 36 ("Israel's Wisdom Books," pages 76–77).

▶ **Write** Lesson 36 review questions (page 77).

4. LESSON PRESENTATION

Point ❶ **Read** Have volunteers read aloud the core content of lesson 35.

▶ **Clarify** The 150 books in the Book of Psalms are not listed according to theme. They were simply collected and arranged without any order in mind.

Someone compared the 150 psalms to 150 poems found in the home of a poet who had just died. His heirs simply published them in the order in which they were found. Later, editors divided the Book of Psalms into five divisions (probably in imitation of the Torah's five books): (1) Psalms 1–41, (2) 42–72, (3) 73–89, (4) 90–106, (5) 107–150.

▶ **Notebook** Develop the following diagram interactively for entry in student notebooks.

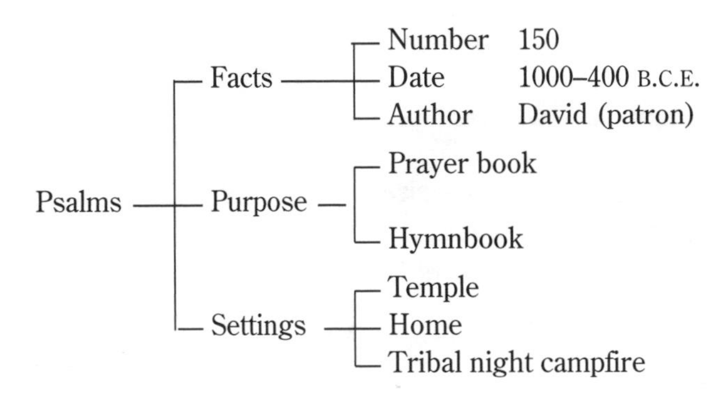

Point ❷ **Discuss** Unlike English poets, Hebrew poets used "thought" rhyme, not "sound" rhyme. That is, they connected and related lines by *repeating, contrasting,* or *completing* a thought.

1. Repeating: (Psalm 144:4)	*We are like a puff of wind; our days are like a passing shadow.*
2. Contrasting: (Psalm 30:5)	*Tears may flow in the night, but joy comes in the morning.*
3. Completing: (Psalm 127:1)	*If the LORD does not build the house, the work of the builders is useless.*

▶ **Clarify** In 1787 the Constitutional Convention was teetering on the brink of failure because the thirteen colonies could not agree on a form of national government.

Benjamin Franklin stood up and quoted the above passage from Psalm 127. Then he moved that the delegates begin the next day's session with a prayer led by a clergyman. The delegates passed the motion. The current practice of beginning sessions of Congress with a prayer dates from Franklin's motion.

Point ❸ **Clarify** On May 18, 1980, Mount Saint Helens exploded. Everything for miles around was destroyed. Caught in the suffocating, falling ash was photographer David Crockett of Seattle's KOMO TV News. Nearly buried alive and barely able to breathe (the falling ash was so thick), he was trapped for ten hours before being spotted and rescued by a helicopter. He wrote later: "During those ten hours, I saw a mountain fall apart. I saw a forest disappear. I saw that God was the only one who was immovable."

Shortly afterward, Crockett read Psalm 46 and put an excerpt from it in the corner of a photograph of Mount Saint Helens on his wall.

Discuss: Instruct the students to listen to this excerpt from the King James Version of Psalm 46 and to explain how it relates to the photographer's experience.

1 *God is our refuge and strength,*
a very present help in trouble.
2 *Therefore will not we fear,*
though the earth be removed,
and though the mountains be carried
into the midst of the sea;
3 *Though the waters thereof roar*
and be troubled,
though the mountains ***shake*** *. . .*
7 The LORD of hosts is with us. . . .
9 He maketh wars to cease . . .
and cutteth the ***spear*** in sunder;
he burneth the chariot in the fire.
10 *Be still, and know that I am God:*
I will be exalted among the heathen,
I will be exalted in the earth.
11 *The LORD of hosts is with us;*
the God of Jacob is our refuge.

If we take Psalm 45 (KJV) and count down, the 46th word from the top is *shake.* And if we count up from the bottom, the 46th word is *spear.*

Ask: What famous name do these two words form? (They form the name *Shakespeare.*)

Ask: Is this a mere coincidence? (Shakespeare was born in 1564, making him 46 when the King James Version was completed in 1610. Since fifty-four translators worked on the KJV translation, he may have been among them and saw the chance to leave his "signature" in Psalm 46.)

5. LESSON INTERACTION

Exercise ❶ **Discuss** Have the two students appointed to prepare excerpts of song lyrics explain and discuss why they think the songs qualify as modern psalms. (The lyrics give us a glimpse into a person's soul in an emotional time: doubt, sorrow, joy.)

Exercise ❷ **Discuss** The students should have no trouble with these quotations. The first quote is especially important: "Give me the making of the songs of a nation, and I care not who makes its laws."

Exercise ❸ **Notebook** Develop the following diagram on the chalkboard for entry in student notebooks.

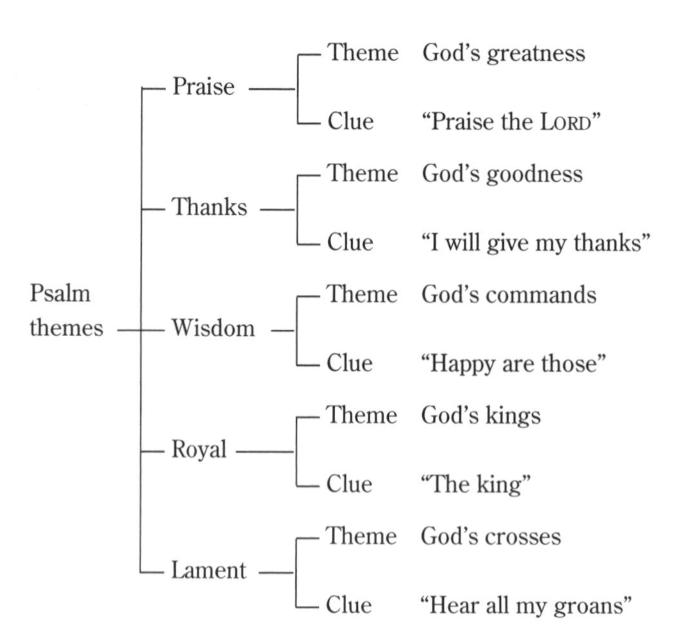

Here is the list of excerpts from the psalm passages cited in this exercise.

a. Psalm 30:11–12:
You have taken away my sorrow
and surrounded me with joy. . . .
LORD, you are my God;
I will give you thanks forever.
(Type: thanksgiving; clue: "I will give you thanks")

b. Psalm 32:1–2
Happy are those whose sins are forgiven,
whose wrongs are pardoned.
(Type: wisdom; clue: "Happy are those")

c. Psalm 38:9–11
O Lord . . . you hear all my groans. . . .
My friends and neighbors will not come near me
because of my sores;
even my family keeps away from me.
(Type: lament; clue: "You hear all my groans")

d. Psalm 45:1–3
Beautiful words fill my mind,
as I compose this song for the king. . . .
God has always blessed you.
(Type: royal; clue: "I compose . . . for the king")

e. Psalm 103:1–2
Praise the LORD, my soul!
All my being, praise his holy name!
Praise the LORD, my soul,
and do not forget how kind he is.
(Type: praise; clue: "Praise the LORD")

Exercise ❹ **Activity** Encourage the students to illustrate their psalms. Read and display the better ones.

CHAPTER SEVEN: Nationhood (pages 76–77)

Israel's Wisdom Books

LESSON **36**

1. LESSON BACKGROUND

▶ *Catechism of the Catholic Church,* 1830–1832.

2. LESSON QUIZ

Perfect score =10 points

1. Who is credited with authoring the Book of Psalms and why? *(Lesson 35 review—2 points)*
2. List the five categories into which tradition divides the 150 psalms. *(Lesson 35 notebook review—5 points)*
3. List the three biblical books credited to Solomon. *(Lesson 36 preview—3 points)*

3. LESSON HOMEWORK

▶ **Return** Lesson 35 review questions (page 75).

▶ **Collect** Lesson 36 review questions (page 77).

▶ **Read** Lesson 37 ("Two Nations," pages 78–79).

▶ **Write** Lesson 37 review questions (page 79).

4. LESSON PRESENTATION

Point ❶ **Read** Have volunteers read aloud the core content of lesson 36.

▶ **Notebook** Develop the following diagram on the chalkboard for entry in student notebooks. It compares the contributions and the personality differences of David and his son Solomon.

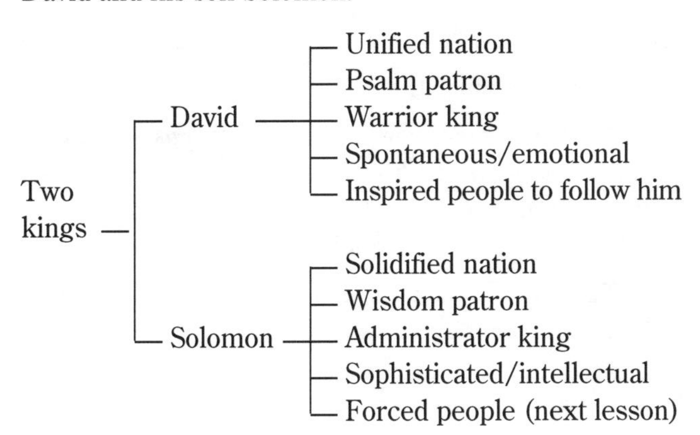

▶ **Notebook** Develop the following diagram on the chalkboard for entry in student notebooks. It summarizes King Solomon's contributions to Israel.

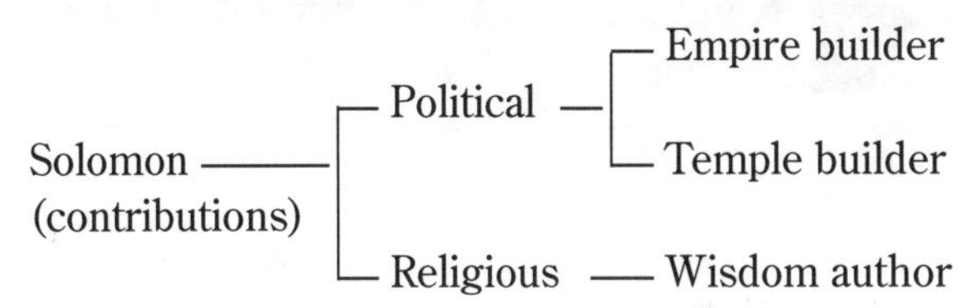

Point ❷ **Discuss** The Book of Proverbs was a kind of "textbook" to teach people "how to live intelligently," especially Israel's young people.

Ask: Why would proverbs be ideal for teaching young people who could not read or write? (Proverbs taught by the "discovery" method. They afforded a kind of "puzzle" that involved the young people creatively. Moreover, Proverbs were easily communicated orally and easily committed to memory.)

▶ **Discuss** Missionary Joseph Healey lists several African proverbs in his article "Africa's Fifth Gospel" (*Maryknoll* magazine, February 1981, pages 19–22).

Read the following proverbs (left column) and have the students "discover" what Africans meant by them. (If you think they are beyond your students' ability, put the two columns on the chalkboard and have the students match them.)

	African Proverb		Proverb's Meaning
1. ___	He points to the moon; we see only his finger.	*a.*	We need others.
2. ___	When elephants fight, the grass gets hurt.	*b.*	Perseverance wins.
3. ___	You can't play a drum with one finger.	*c.*	We miss the point.
4. ___	A steady walk goes far.	*d.*	Helpless people suffer when powerful people clash.

(1. *c*, 2. *d*, 3. *a*, 4. *b*)

Point ❸ **Discuss** African missionaries soon discovered that Christian teachings were more readily accepted if they could be shown to be consistent with African proverbs.

Ask: How does the miniposter on page 76 point to the reason for this? (A proverb is a capsule summary of some truth that has been distilled from centuries of human experience.)

▶ **Discuss** Healey notes that some proverbs are common to all cultures, for example, "Blood is thicker than water." Ask: What does this mean? (Blood relationships run deep.)

Clarify An example of how African proverbs can help to teach Christian truths is cited by Healey. African friends sometimes cut their arms and let the blood drip into a drink. Then they share the drink to symbolize that their friendship is as deep as a blood relationship.

Healey uses this proverb and the custom to teach Africans about the Eucharist (drinking Jesus' blood).

Point 4 **Notebook** Develop the following on the chalkboard for entry in student notebooks. It summarizes the two levels of meaning of the Song of Songs.

Song of Songs (2 levels)	Surface	Groom's love for bride
	Deeper	God's love for Israel

5. LESSON INTERACTION

Exercise 1 **Discuss** The Greek proverb derives from *Aesop's Fables,* a collection of stories by a Greek slave-teacher who lived seven centuries before Jesus. Each story in Aesop's collection ends with the words, "The moral of the story is . . ." One story concerns a hungry fox who can't reach the grapes. But because he doesn't want to admit defeat, he says, "I really don't want the grapes anyway; they're sour."

Exercise 2 **Discuss** Have the students take out a dollar bill (bring a few extra bills to class).

Ask: Who is responsible for the U.S. use of paper money? (Benjamin Franklin designed the first bill, using an involved leaf pattern to discourage counterfeiters.)

Ask: Can you locate and translate the Latin words *E Pluribus Unum?* (Back: banner in eagle's mouth. Translation: "From many, one.") Ask: Why this motto?

Ask: What does the eye over the pyramid stand for? (God. *Annuit Coeptis, Novus Ordo Seclorum* means "He looked with favor on our beginnings, the new order of the century.")

Ask: What is the eagle holding in its talons, and what do they symbolize? (Olive branch and arrows. The arrows were originally in the eagle's right talon. President Truman ordered them switched to symbolize that we seek peace before we seek war. We are ready for both.)

Ask: What do the leaves on the olive branch, the arrows, and the stars above the eagle's head have in common? (Each numbers thirteen.) Ask: Why? (Thirteen colonies)

Clarify Franklin was immensely creative. He designed

- the first bifocals for himself, at age seventy-seven,
- the arm-writing chairs, still used in classrooms,
- the first odometer—attached to a wheel axle,
- the first lightning rod.

Discuss Some points to clarify are:

a. Visitors outlive their welcome.
b. Ask: What are examples of pride and folly? (Pride: I buy designer clothes to impress others. Folly: I buy lottery tickets I can't afford.)
c. We are so busy excusing our failures that we don't learn from them.
d. Have the students give examples of something they wished for, but after they had it for a while, they wished they hadn't gotten it.
e. A similar saying is "You're never taller than when you stoop to help a child."

Exercise 3 **Discuss** Alcoholics Anonymous is the "best therapy" ever devised to help alcoholics. The heart of the program is its "Twelve Steps." Check the A.A. listing in the phone book and inquire about the availability of speakers (free of charge?) to address youth groups. Share the first five steps of the A.A. program with your students. They show how spiritual the program is.

1. *We admitted we were powerless over alcohol—that our lives had become unmanageable.*
2. *Came to believe that a Power greater than ourselves could restore us to sanity.*
3. *Made a decision to turn our will and our lives over to the care of God* as we understood Him.
4. *Made a searching and fearless moral inventory of ourselves.*
5. *Admitted to God, to ourselves and to another human being the exact nature of our wrongs.*

Concerning step five, the A.A. manual says:

Many an A.A., once agnostic or atheist, tells us that it was during this step that he first felt the presence of God. And even those who had faith already often became conscious of God as they never were before. *

Ask: How do you explain why A.A.'s feel God's presence so powerfully in step five?

* *Twelve Steps and Twelve Traditions* (Alcoholics Anonymous, 1952), p. 63. Reprinted with permission.

CHAPTER EIGHT: Division (pages 78–79)

Two Nations

LESSON **37**

1. LESSON BACKGROUND

▶ *Catechism of the Catholic Church*, 82.

2. LESSON QUIZ

Perfect score = 10 points

1. List and explain the two levels of meaning in the Song of Songs. *(Lesson 36 review—4 points)*
2. List and explain King Solomon's two great contributions to Israel. *(Lesson 36 notebook review—4 points)*
3. What happened to Israel after Solomon died and why? *(Lesson 37 preview—2 points)*

3. LESSON HOMEWORK

▶ **Return** Lesson 36 review questions (page 77).

▶ **Collect** Lesson 37 review questions (page 79).

▶ **Read** Lesson 38 ("Era of the Prophets," pages 80–81).

▶ **Write** Lesson 38 review questions (page 81).

▶ **Appoint** Two students to prepare readings from (1) Malachi 4:1–5 and Matthew 17:12–13 (lesson 38, exercise 1) and (2) Matthew 6:24–34 (lesson 38, exercise 2).

4. LESSON PRESENTATION

Point ❶ **Read** Have volunteers read aloud the core content of lesson 37.

▶ **Notebook** Some years ago, a survey (*Commonweal* magazine, March 3, 1979) shocked the public. It showed that among Native Americans the following situations prevailed relative to the national average:

Areas		
	Suicide	Double the average
	Infant mortality	Double the average
	Unemployment	Seven times the average
	Family income	One-half the average
	College students	One-third the average

▶ **Clarify** In the light of situations like these, it was not surprising that some Native Americans responded with violence to dramatize their plight. Concerning this kind of violence, historian Arnold Toynbee said:

Human beings are committing acts of violence
because they feel that they are being treated
not as persons but as things . . .
and in many cases
they have found by infuriating experience
that recourse to violence is the only means
by which they can exhort attention
to legitimate claims and genuine grievance.

Toynbee's remarks help us understand the violence that erupted in Israel after Solomon's death. An example of King Solomon's treatment of the people is preserved for us in 1 Kings 5:13–16:

King Solomon drafted 30,000 men
as forced labor from all over Israel. . . .
He divided them into three groups of 10,000 men,
and each group spent one month in Lebanon. . . .
Solomon also had 80,000 stone cutters in hill country,
with 70,000 men to carry the stones,
and he placed 3,300 foremen in charge of them.

Point ❷ **Discuss** The German poet and philosopher Johann Wolfgang von Goethe (1749–1832) said, "Treat people the way they ought to be and you help them become what they are capable of being."

Ask: Do you think parents—or teachers—can hurt young people by having too high of an expectation of them? (Expectation needs to be realistic. When another's expectation of me exceeds my capability, it results in frustration for me. When it is in harmony with my capability, it results in progress.)

Point ❸ **Clarify** David had made Jerusalem his political and religious capital. Joining these two stressed the fact that the nation owed its origin to God. It was "religious" in origin.

Having only one Temple stressed that there was only one God. Polytheism was as widespread in David's time as the worship of one God (monotheism) is today.

And so when the North split off from the Jerusalem Temple and set up two rival religious centers, it did something David would never have dreamed of doing.

Just as incredibly, when the North split its political capital (Samaria) from its religious centers (Dan and Bethel), it did something David would never have dreamed of doing.

▶ **Notebook** Develop the following diagram on the chalkboard for entry in student notebooks. It sums up the significant details that resulted from the North's revolt from the South after Solomon's death.

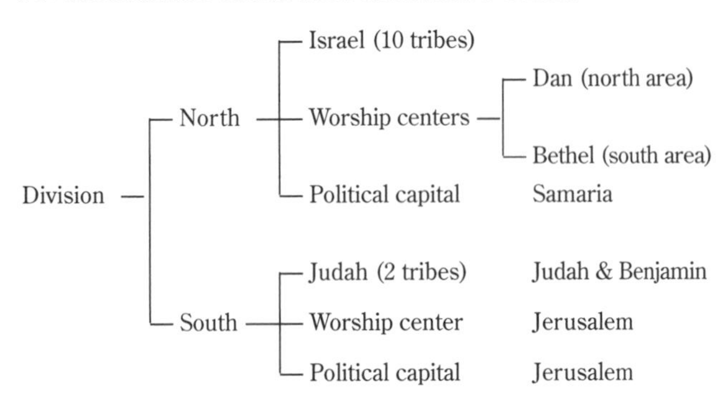

Point ❹ **Clarify** The North's split from the South sowed the seeds of religious disunity and idolatry.

These seeds germinated and sprouted into a full-blown crisis when Ahab became king of the northern kingdom (Israel) and married a foreign princess (Jezebel) who imported her religion (Baalism) and its prophets into Israel.

▶ **Clarify** Stress the reason for Baalism's appeal to Israel's uneducated herdsmen and farmers, especially when God (Yahweh) seemed to turn a deaf ear to their prayers in time of famine.

Baal prophets were quick to capitalize on the situation by pointing out that Yahweh was a "desert god" who knew nothing about agriculture, while Baal was a "farm god" who knew everything about agriculture.

▶ **Notebook** Develop the following diagram on the chalkboard for entry in student notebooks. It spotlights the situation that developed in the North (Israel) after its revolt from the South (Judah).

Result
- Religious idolatry
- Religious disunity
- New era (appearance of prophets)

5. LESSON INTERACTION

Exercise ❶ **Discuss** Perhaps the younger "hard-liners" thought that a "soft-line" policy would be interpreted as weakness on Rehoboam's part.

Perhaps the older "soft-liners" knew that Solomon was in the wrong and figured the North would interpret Rehoboam's gesture as a sign of weakness.

Exercise ❷ **Discuss** **(a)** Have a class secretary compile on the chalkboard (with the help of the students) a list of the major evils that threaten today's society.

Next have the students vote (by secret ballot) on the five *concrete* evils they consider to be the greatest threats to society.

Then have the students suggest ways that people like themselves might register some form of protest (do something positive) about these five evils.

Finally, select one evil for some kind of class "protest." The chalkboard compilation might look like this:

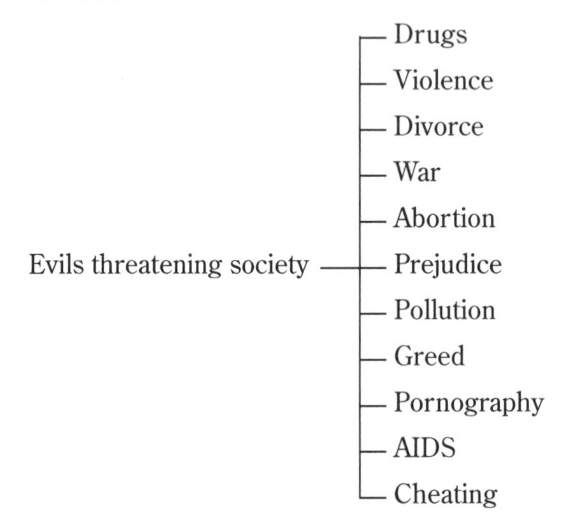

5 Major Evils	5 Protests (positive strategies)
Drugs	
Pollution	
Abortion	
Violence	
Pornography	

▶ **Discuss** **(b, c, d)** One way to handle these three quotations is to have the students explain how each one relates to the first quotation: "Who accepts evil without protesting against it is really cooperating with it."

Exercise ❸ **Discuss** **(a)** Relate this quotation to Jesus' words: "Love your enemies, do good to those who hate you, bless those who curse you, and pray for those who mistreat you" (Luke 6:27–28).

(b) Have the students discuss how their "protests" or "positive strategies" in exercise 2a might be done with "humor" and without "harshness." (A button campaign against apathy might do it with humor: "I'm neither for nor against apathy." Or a button campaign against pollution might do it without harshness: "Good planets are hard to find.")

CHAPTER EIGHT: Division (pages 80–81)

Era of the Prophets

LESSON **38**

1. LESSON BACKGROUND

▶ *Catechism of the Catholic Church*, 2581–2584.

2. LESSON QUIZ

Perfect score = 10 points

1. What new era in history dawned for God's people as a result of the religious chaos in the North? *(Lesson 37 review—1 point)*
2. After Solomon's death, God's people split into two nations. List (a) the name of the northern nation, (b) its political capital, (c) the two worship centers it set up, (d) the name of the southern kingdom, (e) its political capital, (f) its religious center. *(Lesson 37 notebook review—7 points)*
3. What event gave rise to the belief that Elijah would return, and what prophet succeeded him? *(Lesson 38 preview—2 points)*

3. LESSON HOMEWORK

▶ **Return** Lesson 37 review questions (page 79).

▶ **Collect** Lesson 38 review questions (page 81).

▶ **Read** Lesson 39 ("Writing Prophets," pages 82–83).

▶ **Write** Lesson 39 review questions (page 83).

4. LESSON PRESENTATION

Point ❶ **Read** Have volunteers read aloud the core content of lesson 38.

▶ **Discuss** As many biblical names end with *el* ("God"), so many names begin with it. Two examples are *Elijah* ("God is Yahweh") and *Elisha* ("God has saved").

Ask: Can you name any other biblical names that begin with the letters *el* ("God")? (Elizabeth, Eli, Eliezer, Eliphaz, Elihu)

▶ **Discuss** Jesus mentioned both Elijah and Elisha (Luke 4:26–30). Elijah is portrayed as appearing with Moses and speaking to Jesus.

Ask: When is this portrayed as taking place? (Jesus' transfiguration on the mountain [Luke 9:30–31])

Point ❷ **Notebook** Develop the following diagram on the chalkboard for entry in student notebooks. It summarizes two teachings of the Elijah stories: (1) have faith in Yahweh (God) and (2) worship only Yahweh.

Elijah stories taught —
- Have faith in God, as Elijah did
- Worship God alone, as Elijah did

Point ❸ **Discuss** Elijah's prophetic ministry ended abruptly. The Second Book of Kings 2:11 describes it this way:

A chariot of fire pulled by horses of fire came . . .
and Elijah was taken up to heaven by a whirlwind.

Ask: What Negro spiritual takes its name from this event? ("Swing Low, Sweet Chariot," which puts the description of this event to music)

5. LESSON INTERACTION

Exercise ❶ **Discuss** The Second Book of Kings 1:8 describes Elijah "wearing a cloak made of animal skins, tied with a leather belt." This is practically identical with the description of John the Baptist in Matthew 3:4:

John's clothes were made of camel's hair;
he wore a leather belt around his waist.

Ask: What conclusion do you draw from these two descriptions? (John is depicted as Elijah come back to earth.)

Point out that an angel instructed Zechariah concerning the son to be born to his wife, Elizabeth:

"You are to name him John. . . .
He will bring back many of the people of Israel
to the Lord their God.
He will go ahead of the Lord,
strong and mighty like the prophet Elijah. . . .
He will get the Lord's people ready for him." Luke 1:13, 16–17

And when Jesus' disciples asked him about the prophecy that Elijah would return, Jesus answered:

"I tell you that Elijah has already come
and people did not recognize him,
but treated him just as they pleased.
In the same way they will also mistreat
the Son of Man."

Then the disciples understood that he was
talking to them about John the Baptist. Matthew 17:12–13

Clarify Orthodox Jews still place an empty chair for Elijah at each seder (Passover) meal. When Reform Jews updated their seder celebration, they gave new prominence to the "cup of Elijah," also called "the fifth cup," "because the future may well be the greatest period of Jewish spirituality" (Rabbi Bronstein, quoted by Roy Larson in the *Chicago Sun-Times*, April 21, 1973).

Unlike *Orthodox* Jews, *Conservative* Jews and *Reform* Jews do not await the coming of a personal Messiah. Rabbi Stuart E. Rosenberg says in his book *Judaism:*

Conservative and Reform Jews, by and large,
do not accept the idea of a personal Messiah. . . .
Rather, they . . . see Jewish messianism
as . . . a Golden Age yet to come. . . .
God is going to be the winner, because man,
whom he created in his image,
can learn to repent his evil ways and do good.

Clarify Reform Jews include a "collection of supplementary resources" for reading at the seder meal. Some of them are not biblical. For example, one is a passage from *The Diary of Anne Frank.* Ask: Who was Anne Frank?

During World War II, Anne Frank's family and four other people (nine in all) hid from the Nazis for two years in a small attic in Amsterdam. The group was finally discovered and sent to concentration camps. Anne and her sister Margot died in one camp. Anne's father, Otto, survived. It was in his briefcase that the original manuscript was preserved.

When the Nazis broke into the Frank hideout, they took everything of value. Needing a container for confiscated jewelry, the Nazis grabbed the briefcase, dumped its contents on the floor, and stuffed jewels inside.

After the Nazis had gone, a friend of the Frank family found the diary on the floor. Today, it has been translated into more than twenty languages and sold millions of copies. It has also been made into a movie and a play.

Anne's diary recounts not only the horror of being hunted but also the dreams and doubts of a teenager confronted with the horror of humanity gone berserk. Yet, she was not defeated by it, saying, "In spite of everything, I still believe that people are really good at heart." Here is a sample entry:

Why do we trust one another so little?
I know there must be a reason, but still
I sometimes think it's horrible
that you find you can never really confide in people,
even those who are nearest you.

Activity Have the students answer the following question (anonymously) on a half sheet of paper: To what extent do you confide in the following people? (Check appropriate column.)

	Never	Rarely	Usually
Father			
Mother			
Brother/sister			
Friend			
Other (e.g., counselor)			

Collect the responses, tabulate them on the chalkboard, and discuss the results.

Exercise ❷ **Discuss** **(a)** Like many other Elijah stories, this story is a call *to have faith in God.*

(b) Jesus makes the same point in Matthew 6:24–34. Have the appointed student read it aloud.

(c) Jesus spoke these words to his disciples about worrying about the necessities of life:

"Your Father in heaven knows
that you need all these things.
Instead, be concerned above everything else
with the Kingdom of God
and with what he requires of you,
and he will provide you with all these other things.
So do not worry about tomorrow." Matthew 6:32–34

Ask: How do Jesus' words square with the following:

1. "Before God can do his thing, we must do our thing." Saint Augustine (free translation)
2. "Work as though all depends on you; pray as though all depends on God." Saint Ignatius of Loyola
3. "Don't tell me worry doesn't do any good. I know better. The things I worry about never happen." Anonymous

Exercise ❸ **Discuss** This Elijah story makes an important point: We often look for God in the sensational and miss God in the ordinary, everyday things.

Exercise ❹ **Discuss** **(a)** Jesus said, "A tree is known by the kind of fruit it bears" (Matthew 12:33).

Ask: What fruit did the girl's experience bear? (She refers to it in the final sentence of the description of the "Elijah experience" that she shared with those around her: "The effect of this experience was to deepen our faith in God and in our ability to change our world."

Writing Prophets

LESSON 39

1. LESSON BACKGROUND

▶ *Catechism of the Catholic Church,* 61–64.

2. LESSON QUIZ

Perfect score = 13 points

1. How are Elisha and Jehu linked? *(Lesson 38 review—1 point)*
2. What two things did the Elijah stories teach the Israelites? *(Lesson 38 notebook review—2 points)*
3. List the two groups into which the writing prophets divide, and list four prophets who fall into the first group and four who fall into the second group. *(Lesson 39 preview—10 points)*

3. LESSON HOMEWORK

▶ **Return** Lesson 38 review questions (page 81).

▶ **Collect** Lesson 39 review questions (page 83).

▶ **Read** Lesson 40 ("Israel Says 'No,'" pages 84–85).

▶ **Write** Lesson 40 review questions (page 85).

4. LESSON PRESENTATION

Point 1 **Read** Have volunteers read aloud the core content of lesson 39.

▶ **Notebook** Develop the following diagram on the chalkboard for entry in student notebooks. It lists (1) the two kinds of prophets, (2) the two groups into which the writing prophets divided, and (3) representatives of each kind and division.

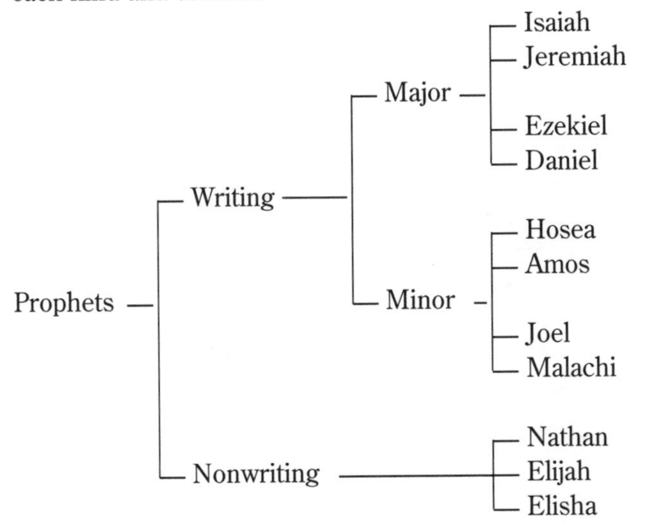

Point 2 **Clarify** Prophets and kings are like the two rails of a train track. Where you find one, you usually find the other. Prophets served as spokespersons for God, counseling and confronting Israel's kings and leaders.

Nathan is a good example. Acting as God's spokesperson, he counseled David (messianic promise) and confronted David (sinfulness).

▶ **Discuss** David was a noble person. But he also had his moments of weakness, as every human being does.

On one occasion, when one of David's soldiers (Uriah) was far away in battle, David was overwhelmed by a passion for Uriah's beautiful wife. He had an affair with her, and she became pregnant.

Then David did something even more sinful. To cover up his sin, he sent a note to Uriah's commanding officer, instructing him to put Uriah on the front lines, that he might be killed. The officer obeyed and Uriah was killed. This brought Nathan into the picture.

The LORD sent the prophet Nathan to David.
Nathan went to him and said,
"There were two men who lived in the same town;
one was rich and the other poor.
The rich man had many cattle and sheep,
while the poor man had only one lamb. . . .
He took care of it, and it grew up in his home
with his children. . . .
One day a visitor arrived at the rich man's home.
The rich man didn't want to kill one of his own animals
to fix a meal for him;
instead, he took the poor man's lamb
and prepared a meal for his guest."
David became very angry at the rich man
and said, ". . . The man who did this ought to die! . . ."
"You are that man," Nathan said to David. . . .
"I have sinned against the LORD," David said.

2 Samuel 12:1–7, 13

Ask: Why did Nathan confront David by drawing this comparison? (It allowed David to discover on his own how terrible his crime against Uriah was. Nathan used this parable as a kind of "mirror" into which David looked and indirectly passed judgment on himself.)

▶ **Notebook** Develop the following diagram for entry in student notebooks. It sums up the key points about the prophets: (1) whose spokesmen they were, (2) their twofold role, and (3) how Nathan exemplifies this role.

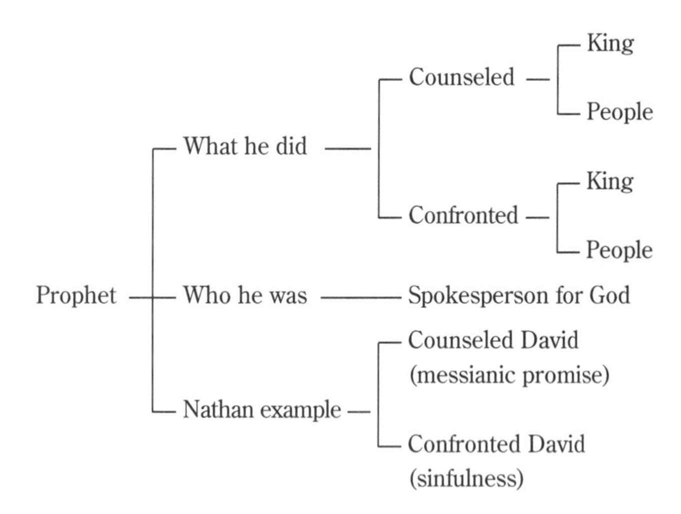

5. LESSON INTERACTION

Exercise ① **Discuss** Make sure the students understand Martin Buber's remark.

Ask: What does it mean to "oppose history," and who is an example of someone who did this? (Lincoln opposed slavery, which had been a part of history in countless nations from almost the beginning of history itself. In a similar way, Martin Luther King Jr. opposed the curtailment of civil rights for African-Americans. This denial of civil rights had been a part of southern history for decades.)

▶ **Discuss** **(a)** Kennedy's point is that there should be a built-in government to make peaceful revolution possible. For example, a democracy, such as we have in the United States, provides a way for people to change things that they do not like.

▶ **Discuss** **(b)** Omar Bradley was one of the top U.S. generals in World War I. Bradley's full quote (below) explains the quote in the text:

Ours is a world of nuclear giants and ethical infants. We know more about war than we know about peace, more about killing than we know about living. We have grasped the mystery of the atom and rejected the Sermon on the Mount.

▶ **Discuss** **(c)** A good explanation or commentary on this statement is this quotation from Theodore Roosevelt:

Far better it is to dare mighty things, to win glorious triumphs even though checkered by failure than to rank with those poor spirits who neither enjoy nor suffer much because they live in the gray twilight that knows neither victory nor defeat.

Exercise ② **Discuss** **(a, b)** At the outset of his ministry, Jesus stood up in the synagogue at Nazareth and said to his hometown relatives and friends: "Prophets are never welcomed in their hometown" (Luke 4:24).

In line with Moche's experience and Jesus' words, the great Russian novelist Feodor Dostoevski said, "Men reject their prophets and slay them, but they love their martyrs and honor those they have slain."

Again, we are reminded of people like Jesus, Ghandi, and King. We are also reminded of people like Susan B. Anthony, who was not slain but imprisoned for her pioneer work in women's rights.

Exercise ③ **Discuss** **(a)** Thomas Edison was left partially deaf from scarlet fever at age seven. His teacher gave up trying to teach him. The problem was bigger than his teacher. Edison's mother was "bigger than the problem." She took him out of school and educated him herself. Result?

When Edison died decades later in October 1931, he had over a thousand patents to his credit. Today, the lights we study by, the motion pictures we watch, and the record players we listen to—all are trophies to a mother who was bigger than the problem that threatened her son's education.

▶ **Discuss** **(b)** We can't change the course of our past, but we can change the course of our future.

▶ **Discuss** **(c)** An anonymous poet said something similar: "Go not where a path happens to be. Go rather where a path ought to be." If you follow the crowd, you will never know anything more than it does.

Photo **Discuss** Direct the students' attention to the "page" from the thirty-six foot Isaiah scroll found at Qumran (page 82). Use the photo to review some key facts about the Dead Sea Scrolls.

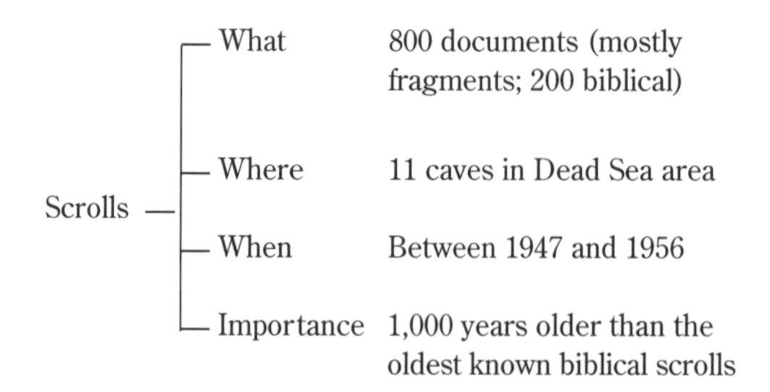

Israel Says "No"

LESSON 40

1. LESSON BACKGROUND

▶ *Catechism of the Catholic Church*, 222–227.

2. LESSON QUIZ

Perfect score = 6 points

1. How may we describe the twofold role of the prophets? (Lesson 39 review—2 points)
2. Briefly describe how Nathan lived out this twofold role, concretely, in his relationship with David. (Lesson 39 notebook review—2 points)
3. What was one abuse Amos addressed, and how did the leaders of Israel react to it? *(Lesson 40 preview—2 points)*

3. LESSON HOMEWORK

▶ **Return** Lesson 39 review questions (page 83).

▶ **Collect** Lesson 40 review questions (page 85).

▶ **Read** Lesson 41 ("Day without Brightness," pages 86–87).

▶ **Write** Lesson 41 review questions (page 87).

▶ **Appoint** Three students to prepare readings from (1) John 6:48 and Luke 9:51–56, (2) Luke 10:25–37, Luke 17:11–19, and John 4:1–10, 39–41, (3) Amos 2:6–3:2 (lesson 41, exercises 1 and 3).

4. LESSON PRESENTATION

Point ❶ **Read** Have volunteers read aloud the core content of lesson 40.

▶ **Discuss** Ask: What is the point of the cartoon of the bearded old man and his sign? (We have the power to destroy ourselves, and some fear that we will if we don't start living in peace and love.)

Ask: To what extent do you agree/disagree with the cartoon's caption: "Have you noticed? No one's laughing at him anymore!"

Point ❷ **Discuss** Recall that the North and the South were enemies at this period in history. Recall, also, that Amos was not only from the South but also a poor farmer, sent by God to confront wealthy northerners.

Ask: Why did God complicate Amos's job with these obstacles? Seems like poor judgment on God's part. (The prophet's power lay not in his human skill so much as in God's power working through him.) Recall Paul's words to the Corinthians:

My teaching and message were not delivered
with skillful words of human wisdom, but with convincing
proof of the power of God's Spirit. 1 Corinthians 2:4
What seems to be God's foolishness
is wiser than human wisdom. 1 Corinthians 1:25

Point ❸ **Notebook** Have the students list and briefly describe in their notebooks the two abuses of the northern kingdom that Amos addressed:

Two abuses —
- Social injustice (trampling down the weak, pushing away the poor)
- Religious formalism (singing on the Sabbath, oppressing the poor the rest of the week)

▶ **Discuss** Share the following story with the students. Lawrence LeShan tells it in his book *How to Meditate*. It goes something like this:

A monk prayed many years for a vision from God.
One day it came. The monk's soul leaped for joy.

Suddenly the monastery bell rang, indicating
it was time to feed the poor at the monastery gate.
It was the old monk's turn to share with them
whatever food was on hand for that day.
The monk was torn between his heavenly vision
and his earthly duties.

Before the echo of the bell faded,
the monk made the difficult choice.
He left the vision to feed the beggars.

Nearly an hour later, he returned to his room.
As he opened the door, he fell on his knees.
The vision was still there.
As the monk bowed his head, the vision said,
"Had you not gone, I wouldn't have stayed."

Ask: How does this story relate to Amos's mission to the North?

Notebook Develop the following diagram to illustrate the different approaches of Amos and Hosea.

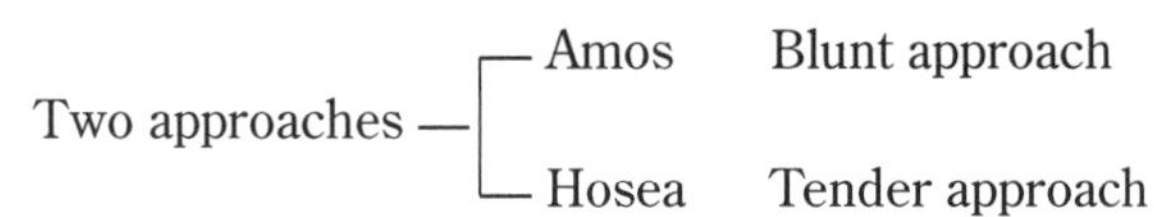

Discuss Have the students give pros and cons for each approach. Relate them to dealing with discipline problems in the school.

5. LESSON INTERACTION

Exercise 1 **Discuss** In preparation for discussing this situation, divide the students into three groups.

Group 1: Write out an American teenager's response to this situation.
Group 2: Write out a third-world teenager's response.
Group 3: List some things that might be done to reverse this "unjust" situation.

Ask for volunteers to share their written responses.

Exercise 2 **Notebook** Students often do not understand poverty and its complex network of causes. Begin by distinguishing individual poverty from poverty affecting large groups. Develop the following on the chalkboard.

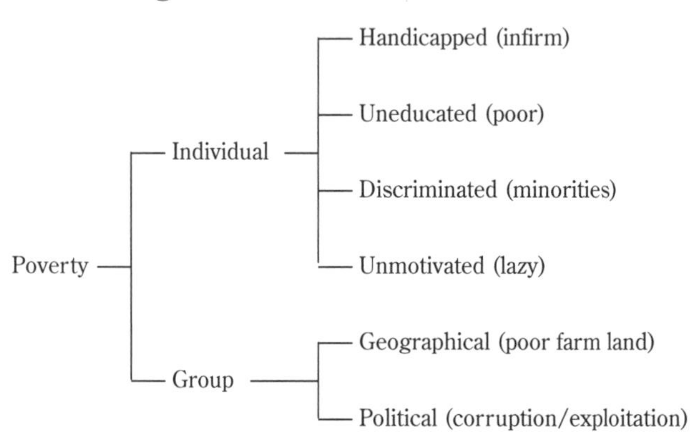

Discuss Narrow the focus to individual poverty. There are many reasons for it. The diagram lists just a few. Ask: What are some reasons that employers might be reluctant to hire the following?

1. Handicapped (Problem of fitting their handicap to a job they can do, safety problems, trained supervisors to deal with special problems that might arise)
2. Uneducated (Good paying jobs often require a good education—even a college education. The poor can't afford a college education [about $25,000 a year].)
3. Discriminated (Women and minorities still suffer from hiring discrimination. A recent TV program documented another, surprising hiring discrimination. It documented—with hidden cameras—that "physically attractive" people were hired after "ordinary-looking people"—with greater skills for the same job—were turned away.)
4. Unmotivated (Some people are surprised to learn that documentation shows clearly that this is not nearly as big a problem as they think. In other words, it is way down on the list of reasons for poverty.)

Exercise 3 **Discuss** **(a)** Lisa has "depersonalized" poverty. Because she does not see it or experience it herself, it has no practical meaning for her.

(b) Ask: After Pat shouts, "Lord, how can you stand by and let such injustice exist? Why don't you do something?" what do you think the Lord says to her? ("I did do something. I made you." God intends for us to get involved and not sit back and complain that God is doing nothing.)

(c) People often treat their pets with more concern than they do the poor. Recall the old priest who got up in the pulpit and said:

"My sermon today will be the shortest and one of the most important that I have ever preached. It has just three points.

"First, tens of thousands of people are starving and homeless right now. Second, most people don't give a damn about them. Third, you are probably more shocked that I said damn *than that there are tens of thousands of starving and homeless people."*

Then the old priest made the sign of the cross and sat down.

Exercise 4 **Discuss** **(a, b, c)** Be sure to take these questions in sequence. You might list the questions on the chalkboard to insure a logical, orderly discussion of the problem. Have students list (1) three reactions, (2) the reasons for these reactions, (3) positive actions to create better reactions.

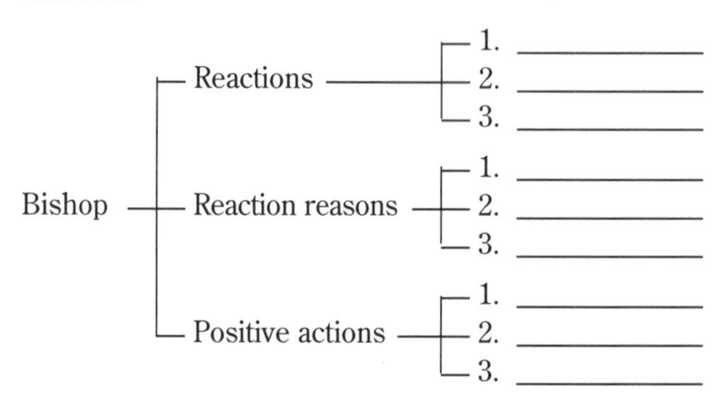

Day without Brightness

LESSON **41**

1. LESSON BACKGROUND

► *Catechism of the Catholic Church,* 2443–2449.

2. LESSON QUIZ

Perfect score = 10 points

1. What prophet followed Amos in preaching to the North, and how did their two approaches differ? *(Lesson 40 review—3 points)*
2. List and briefly describe the two abuses in the northern kingdom that Amos addressed. *(Lesson 40 notebook review—4 points)*
3. List the three evils into which Judah (the South) drifted in the years ahead. *(Lesson 41 review—3 points)*

3. LESSON HOMEWORK

► **Return** Lesson 40 review questions (page 85).

► **Collect** Lesson 41 review questions (page 87).

► **Read** Lesson 42 ("Day of Warning," pages 88–89).

► **Write** Lesson 42 review questions (page 89).

4. LESSON PRESENTATION

Point ❶ **Read** Have volunteers read aloud the core content of lesson 41.

► **Discuss** Someone said that "hell begins the day we see what we could have done but failed to do."

Ask: How does that statement apply to the alcoholic priest described in Greene's novel?

Ask: Why do/don't you think the priest was correct in evaluating himself as having "to go to God empty-handed"? (At the very least, the priest's admission of his sins and his tears of repentance were something of great value. Note that young people especially put themselves down too much. They do many good things.)

Point ❷ **Clarify** The Assyrian defeat of Israel in 722 B.C.E. is recorded not only in the Bible but also in ancient Assyrian records. In the 1840s Paul-Emile Botta, a French diplomat, bartered with a one-eyed pasha for an excavating permit in modern Iraq. He got it, and the "dig" turned out to be a bonanza. It unearthed the palace of Sargon II (see photos on page 28 of the textbook).

Apart from this discovery and a brief reference in Isaiah 20:1, Sargon is virtually unknown to history. Thanks to archaeology, it is almost possible to construct a biography of this Assyrian king.

Among the ruins of Sargon's palace were records of his victory over the North. One entry reads:

I attacked and conquered Samaria,
and led away as booty 27,290 inhabitants. . . .
And I installed over them one of my officers.

Point ❸ **Clarify** Some years ago, Janice Rothschild wrote a popular article on the current situation of Samaritans. She writes:

The Samaritans . . . are neither Arabs nor Jews, although in some respects they resemble both.

They have kept to themselves, married only among their own. . . .

Their number dwindled from an estimated 40,000 at the time of Jesus to a mere 152 at the beginning of the twentieth century. Today improved economy and hygiene have helped increase their population to 400.

The South's reaction to the North's fall may be summarized on the chalkboard for entry in student notebooks.

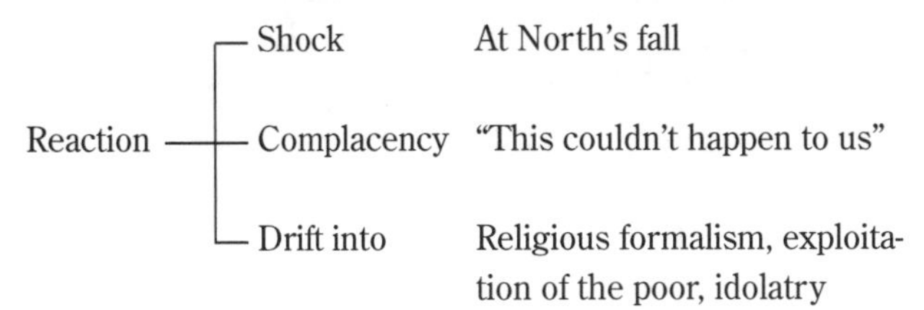

5. LESSON INTERACTION

Exercise ❶ **Discuss** **(a)** The Assyrian strategy behind uprooting large portions of a conquered nation and replacing them with peoples from another conquered nation was to keep the conquered nations from regrouping and causing problems for the Assyrians.

► **Discuss** **(b)** Have the appointed student read the two passages that reflect Jewish-Samaritan hostilities.

In John 8:48, Jewish leaders accuse Jesus of being a Samaritan and having a demon.

In Luke 9:51–56, Samaritan villagers refuse to let Jesus and his disciples pass through their village on their way to Jerusalem.

When the disciples James and John saw this,
they said, "Lord, do you want us
to call fire down from heaven to destroy them?"
Jesus turned and rebuked them.
Then Jesus and his disciples went on to another village.
Luke 9:54–56

Discuss **(c)** Have the appointed student read the three passages as each is discussed.

The first is Luke 10:25–37, the parable of the Good Samaritan. Recall the parable.

A Jewish traveler lay on the side of a road. First a Jewish priest and then a Jewish Levite (going to Jerusalem to the Temple) saw him and "walked on by on the other side of the road." Why?

Maybe they thought the man was dead. A Jewish priest who touched a corpse became unclean and was banned temporarily from Temple worship. The priest's priority, therefore, would have been *worship* before *charity.* (Recall the monk who turned his back on a vision to feed the poor in lesson 40 of the Resource Manual. The monk's priority was just the opposite: *charity* before *worship.*)

A Levite was somewhat like a modern deacon. He was assigned to work in the Temple. (1 Chronicles 23:3–5 lists some of his duties.) When it came to touching a corpse, some Levites followed a cleanliness code similar to that of priests (Numbers 6:6).

Another reason why the priest and the Levite did not stop could have been safety. Ancient outlaws used "setups" in their trade. One outlaw played the victim while others waited for an innocent passerby to put down his baggage and help the victim. Then both pounced on him. If this was their concern, their priority was *safety* before *charity.*

Finally, a Samaritan traveler saw the Jewish victim, stopped, and ministered to him.

Jesus ends his parable, saying to his Jewish audience, "In your opinion, which one of these three acted like a neighbor toward the man?"

Ask: Some people say that Jesus could have made the same point by choosing another person (rather than an arch enemy of Jews) to make his point. Why antagonize them? How would you respond to their observation?

The second example of Jesus' attitude toward Samaritans is the story of the ten lepers whom Jesus cured (Luke 17:11–19).

Jesus told the lepers to show themselves to a priest to have their cure confirmed, so that they could return to the community. (Lepers had to live in a leper camp apart from the community, lest they infect others.) Only one leper returned to thank Jesus. "The man was a Samaritan" (Luke 17:16).

A final example is described in John 4:1–10, 39–41. There Jesus befriends a Samaritan woman and makes her the first missionary to non-Jews.

So when the Samaritans came to him,
they begged him to stay with them,
and Jesus stayed there two days.
Many more believed because of his message,
and they told the woman,
"We believe now, not because of what you said,
but because we ourselves have heard him,
and we know that he really is the Savior of the world."
John 4:40–42

Exercise ❷ **Discuss** **(a, b)** The angel responds bluntly, "Because there is nothing to hear."

Ask: What is the point of this story, and how does it relate to this lesson? (Religious formalism)

(c) A variety of responses is possible.

Exercise ❸ **Discuss** Have the appointed student read the prepared passage from Amos 2:6–3:2. A portion reads:

"They sell into slavery honest people
who cannot pay their debts, the poor who
cannot repay even the price of a pair of sandals.
They trample down the weak and helpless
and push the poor out of the way." Amos 2:6–7

Clarify The passage speaks of "nazirites." For an explanation of these young men, see "The Nazirite Vow" in the Good News Bible, Today's English Version, second edition, page 132.

Exercise ❹ **Discuss** This could be an interesting exercise for a "day of recollection." You might even present a modification of it during class time. But the mood and rapport with the class would have to be right before trying it.

Day of Warning

LESSON 42

1. LESSON BACKGROUND

▶ *Catechism of the Catholic Church,* 2419–2425.

2. LESSON QUIZ

Perfect score = 10 points

1. What happened in 722 B.C.E., and what happened to the citizens of Israel who were left behind? *(Lesson 41 review—2 points)*
2. List and briefly describe the threefold reaction of Judah (South) to the events of 722 B.C.E. *(Lesson 41 notebook review—6 points)*
3. The armies of what nation under what king (leader) threatened to destroy Judah in 701 B.C.E. *(Lesson 42 preview—2 points)*

3. LESSON HOMEWORK

▶ **Return** Lesson 41 review questions (page 87).

▶ **Collect** Lesson 42 review questions (page 89).

▶ **Read** Lesson 43 ("Day of Decline," pages 90–91).

▶ **Write** Lesson 43 review questions (page 91).

▶ **Appoint** Two students to prepare exercise 1 of lesson 43. Have them begin their enactment by reading Jeremiah 20:7–18 to the group.

4. LESSON PRESENTATION

Point 1 **Read** Have volunteers read aloud the core content of lesson 42.

▶ **Clarify** Isaiah's experience of God's "holiness" affected his entire prophetic ministry. He referred to God as the "Holy One of Israel" no less than twenty-nine times. And it is to "holiness" that God called Israel, saying, "You shall be . . . a holy nation" (Exodus 19:6 [NAB]).

The idea of biblical "holiness" is not well understood by modern Christians. It is not reserved for saints. Holiness is best understood in terms of its opposite—sinfulness. Sin alienated (divided) people from God, neighbor, and nature. Holiness is reconciliation (oneness) with God, neighbor, and all of creation. Jesus prays at the Last Supper, "May all be one. Father! . . . I in them and you in me" (John 17:21, 23).

▶ **Notebook** Develop the following diagram, which sums up the relationship between sin and holiness.

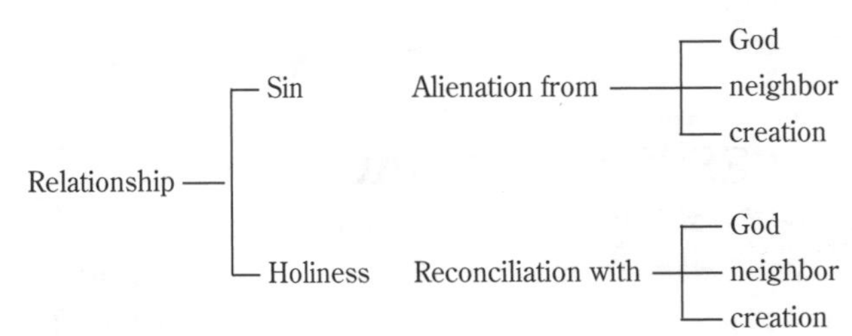

Point 2 **Clarify** Because of his keen sense of holiness, Isaiah spoke out repeatedly against Judah's sinfulness. He called Judah to conversion, warning that if they did not reform, they were "doomed to die" (Isaiah 1:20).

Normally, conversion (reform) takes place by degrees or levels. Cardinal Newman said there is no such thing as a "sudden conversion." What is "sudden" is the realization that we have gone through a conversion.

▶ **Notebook** We may sum up the degrees (levels) of conversion for entry in student notebooks.

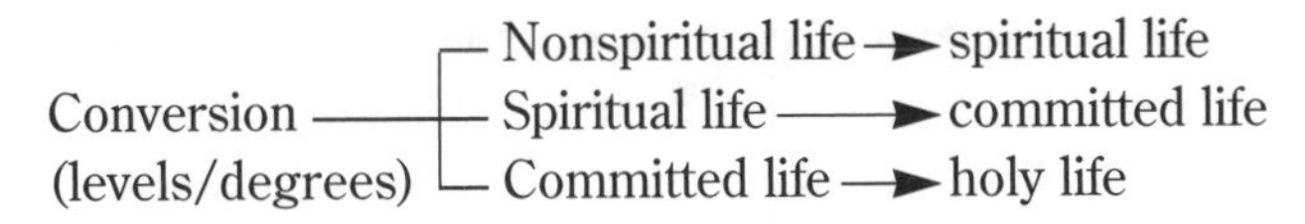

▶ **Activity** Have the students respond to the following questions on an unsigned sheet of paper.

1. At what degree of conversion would you say you are at this point in your life?
2. What is the main thing that keeps you from moving to the next degree or level? Explain.
3. What might you do to overcome this obstacle and move to the next degree or level? Explain.

Collect the papers, screen them, and report the results at the next class. Feel free to comment on the responses of the students. Have volunteers comment on them as well.

Point 3 **Discuss** In regard to what happened in the Assyrian camp, compare 2 Kings 19:35–36 and Sirach 48:21.

An angel of the LORD went to the Assyrian camp
and killed 185,000 soldiers.
At dawn the next day there they lay, all dead!
Then the Assyrian emperor Sennacherib withdrew
and returned to Nineveh. 2 Kings 19:35–36

God struck the camp of the Assyrians
and routed them with a plague. Sirach 48:21 (NAB)

Ask: What is the difference between these two descriptions, and how do you explain it? (The first gives the impression that "an angel of the LORD" acted in some direct way. The second gives the impression that God acted in an indirect way— through a natural event, that is, a plague.)

5. LESSON INTERACTION

Exercise ① **Discuss** Point out the trinitarian structure (Father, Son, and Spirit) of the prayer model. Each person of the Trinity is addressed, followed by a conclusion. A structure like this helps students organize their thoughts and put them down on paper in an orderly way.

Exercise ② **Discuss** **(a)** Saint Cyprian, bishop and martyr (ca. 250 C.E.), sums up the heart's role in prayer this way: "God hears our heart, not our voice."

Ask: What is Saint Cyprian's point? (It is the love of the heart, not the eloquence of the words, that makes for prayer.)

In most cases there is an element of the heart or love in every prayer. It is a question of how much: lots or a little.

Make sure the students know the difference between "heart" and "feeling." "Feeling" may be present, but it need not be. Prayer is a lot like love. Love is not always measured by a "warm glow." If we pray to get a "warm glow," then prayer can become just another form of self-indulgence. Love is doing what is right, even though we may not "feel loving" at the time.

Ask: What is an example of this? (Helping someone who needs my help, when I would rather be doing something else) Thomas Merton summed up this idea with a surprising (but true) statement:

Pure love and prayer are learned in the hour
when prayer has become impossible
and your heart has turned to stone.

Ask: What is Merton's point? (We prove the sincerity of our love and our prayer by doing them when we least feel like doing them.)

► **Discuss** **(b)** We often think of prayer as "speaking" to God. This is correct, but it is not complete. Prayer is also listening to God speak to us in the depths of our heart.

Andrew Murray put it this way: "Prayer is not a monologue, but a dialogue; God's voice in response to mine is its most essential part." Someone else said, "If you want God to listen to you when you pray, shouldn't you listen to God when God speaks to you?"

Ask: How does God speak to us? (Through Scripture, through other people, in the depths of our heart)

Exercise ③ **Discuss** **(a, b, c)** Isaiah's *friend* is "God." The *vineyard* is "God's people." Isaiah's *point* is that God did everything possible for the Chosen People, but they did little or nothing in return.

► **Discuss** **(d)** Isaiah confronted the people in parable for the same reason that Nathan confronted David in parable. A parable is a kind of "word mirror" into which people can look and see themselves as they really are.

► **Notebook** Perhaps Isaiah "sang" the parable to dramatize his sorrow over what happened. Jews showed sorrow at three levels: tears, silence, and song. (Recall that the slaves did not sing in the cotton fields because they were happy. Rather, it was to express a deep sorrow within their hearts over their tragic plight.) We may summarize the three levels this way:

Sorrow	Tears	deep pain
	Silence	deeper pain
	Song	deepest pain

Exercise ④ **Activity** The rap-style rhythm of this hymn makes it easy to render. If it is performed slowly enough, the class can "drum" it out with the team. Have fun!

► **Discuss** **(b)** Lord Byron describes the coming and the leaving of the Assyrians, using the imagery of the four seasons: spring, summer, autumn, winter. It is a familiar one for most people and gives unity and color to his poem.

The same imagery might be applied to human beings. Human growth follows a pattern similar to the four seasons of the year.

Ask: How is this so? (Spring is a time of beginning, much like childhood. Summer and fall are adolescence and adulthood. Winter is like the culmination of life.)

Miniposter Direct attention to the miniposter on page 88. Ask the students to identify and correct the three bloopers that the kids made.

1. "playing the liar"—lyre, or harp (1 Samuel 18:10)
2. "the Finkelsteins"—Philistines (2 Samuel 5:24)
3. "700 porcupines"—300 concubines (1 Kings 11:3)

Photo Refer the students to the photo of the Sennacherib prism on page 88. It is a remarkable example of how archaeology is confirming and clarifying what the Bible says.

Day of Decline

1. LESSON BACKGROUND

▶ *Catechism of the Catholic Church*, 1830–1832.

2. LESSON QUIZ

Perfect score = 10 points

1. How was Judah saved from the Assryian armies, and what effect did this have on them? *(Lesson 42 review—2 points)*
2. Explain the relationship between sin and holiness. *(Lesson 42 notebook review—6 points)*
3. What "spiritual giant" worked with Josiah to reform Judah, and how was the "call" of each somewhat similar? *(Lesson 43 preview—2 points)*

3. LESSON HOMEWORK

▶ **Return** Lesson 42 review questions (page 89).

▶ **Collect** Lesson 43 review questions (page 91).

▶ **Read** Lesson 44 ("Day of Drums," pages 92–93).

▶ **Write** Lesson 44 review questions (page 93).

4. LESSON PRESENTATION

Point 1 **Read** Have volunteers read aloud the core content of lesson 43.

▶ **Discuss** Compare Jeremiah's protest to God's call to the following protests of other biblical figures:

Moses: *"I am a poor speaker"* (Exodus 4:10).
Gideon: *"I am the least important member of my family"* (Judges 6:15).
Amos: *"I am not . . . [a] prophet . . . [but] a herdsman"* (Amos 7:14).

Ask: Why didn't God choose more qualified people to preach God's word if people were to listen to it and follow it? (Recall that the power of God's word comes not from the eloquence of the preacher but from God's power, which uses the preacher as an instrument.)

Point 2 **Discuss** Jeremiah 5:1 presents a disturbing picture of the spiritual health of people:

People of Jerusalem, run through your streets!
Look around! See for yourselves!
Search the marketplaces! Can you find one person
who does what is right and tries to be faithful to God?

Jeremiah's words remind us of Psalm 14:2–3:

The LORD looks down from heaven at us humans
to see if there are any who are wise,
any who worship him.
But they have all gone wrong; they are all equally bad.
Not one of them does what is right, not a single one.

Ask: Why do/don't you think this is a fair description of our world today? How do you explain this situation, and what do you think is the reason for it? What do you think is the answer to turning this situation around?

Point 3 **Discuss** Ask: Isn't Jeremiah's prayer (bottom of page 90) disrespectful? (Jeremiah's prayer may seem disrespectful to modern Christians. It was not to ancient Jews. Recall the "lament" psalms and their blunt honesty.)

Jeremiah's prayer was "telling it like it is." It was being "honest to God." The first principle of prayer is to be honest to God. Practically, this means that I present myself to God as I am: angry, tired, bitter, brokenhearted.

I place myself before God, letting it all "hang out." I tell God where I hurt and how much I hurt. I ask God either to strengthen me to bear the hurt or to heal it. A splendid example of this kind of prayer is the prayer of Tevye, the father of a poor Jewish family in *Fiddler on the Roof.* In a memorable scene, he looks skyward and says to God:

"Sometimes I think when things get too quiet up there,
you say to yourself, 'Lets see, what kind of mischief
can I play on my friend Tevye?' . . .
I'm not complaining—after all, with your help,
I'm starving to death."

You might invite the students to take five minutes and write an "honest-to-God" prayer similar to that of Jeremiah or Tevye. Tell it "like it is." Let it all "hang out."

Collect the prayers, screen them, and share them with the students at the next class.

5. LESSON INTERACTION

Exercise ❶ **Activity** Have the two students appointed to reenact this scene begin by reading Jeremiah 20:7–18.

Exercise ❷ **Activity** This exercise builds on exercise 2b of lesson 42 (page 89). You might give the students five or ten minutes to compose their prayer right in class. Volunteers could then share their prayer with the rest of the class.

Exercise ❸ **Discuss** **(a)** The point is that God "teams up" with us much as the Holy Spirit "teamed up" with the biblical writers:

The Holy Spirit worked
in *and* through *the human writers*
in such a way that they were empowered
to use their own talents and words
to communicate
what God wanted them to communicate.
(Textbook, page 7)

Recall that for this reason, we can truly say that the Bible is the "word of God in the words of men" (Alexander Jones). Review the three theories on how the biblical writers were inspired:

Inspiration theories		
	Divine dictation	Writer = robot
	Negative assistance	Spirit = watchdog
	Positive assistance	Spirit + writer = team

The Catholic Church and most mainline Protestant churches opt for the "positive assistance" theory.

► **Discuss** **(b)** When we are too busy to pray, we are too busy. To illustrate the truth of this statement, consider this comparison: When we are working so hard *physically* that we do not have time to nourish our bodies *physically*, we will become *physically weak and ill.* The same is true if we are so busy that we do not have time to nourish our bodies *spiritually*. We will become *spiritually weak and ill.*

Exercise ❹ **Discuss** To protect a priest, brother, sister, or deacon from being avalanched by the students, you might do one of three things:

1. Have the students interview members of the parish staff: DRE, youth minister, R.C.I.A. director, CCD teacher, and so on.
2. Have the students, working in teams of three or four, call for an appointment with someone holding a leadership role in the parish and interview that person as a team.
3. Have a committee of students invite one or two people in parish leadership roles to come and field the four questions listed in the exercise. They might also compile their own interview questions.

Photo **Clarify** Direct students' attention to the secret tunnel of Hezekiah on page 90. For centuries, its location was unknown. Then one day in 1880, a schoolboy rediscovered the tunnel while playing in an old section of Jerusalem. Entering it he slipped and fell.

When he got up, he noticed strange writing on the wall. It turned out to be an inscription in eighth-century B.C.E. Hebrew script, telling how Hezekiah built the tunnel hastily to insure a water supply for the city. Part of the inscription reads:

Quarry men cut through the rock,
each man toward his fellow, axe against axe.

Water still flows in the tunnel and venturesome tourists still explore its near-1,800-foot length. Sirach 48:17 says of it:

[Hezekiah] had a tunnel built through solid rock
with iron tools and had cisterns built to hold the water.

Miniposter **Discuss** Direct attention to the miniposter on page 90. Ask: Can you identify and correct the three "bloopers" cited?

1. "Bake bread without straw" should read "make bricks without straw."
2. "Mount Cyanide" should read "Mount Sinai."
3. "Canada" should read "Canaan" (Promised Land).

Day of Drums

LESSON **44**

1. LESSON BACKGROUND

2. LESSON QUIZ

Perfect score =10 points

1. Against what nation did Jeremiah warn the people, and how did the people respond to Jeremiah? *(Lesson 43 review—2 points)*
2. List and explain the three inspiration theories. *(Lesson 43 notebook review—6 points)*
3. List two ways in which Jews responded to their exile in Babylon. *(Lesson 44 preview—2 points)*

3. LESSON HOMEWORK

Return Lesson 43 review questions (page 91).

Collect Lesson 44 review questions (page 93).

Read Lesson 45 ("Years of Waiting," pages 94–95).

Write Lesson 45 review questions (page 95).

4. LESSON PRESENTATION

Point ❶ **Read** Have volunteers read aloud the core content of lesson 44.

Notebook Develop the following diagram on the chalkboard for entry in student notebooks. It sums up Babylon's two military operations against Judah.

Babylonians	597 B.C.E.	Conquered Judah, carrying off key officials and skilled workers
	587 B.C.E.	Torched Jerusalem and Temple, destroying both

Point ❷ **Notebook** Develop the following diagram on the chalkboard. It summarizes the fates of three groups of Jews after the fall of Jerusalem.

Three groups	Poor and aged	Left behind
	Prisoners	Deported to Babylon
	Escapees	Fled to Egypt

Clarify Many escapees settled at Alexandria in Egypt. Two hundred years later, their ancestors translated the Old Testament into Greek. This translation, called the Septuagint, became the official Old Testament for Greek-speaking Christians. Matthew, Mark, Luke, and John all quoted from it.

Notebook Develop the following diagram on the chalkboard. It summarizes the two ways in which Jews reacted to their exile in Babylon.

Jews in Babylon	Some	Compromise (faith)
	Others	Convert (deepen faith)

Point ❸ **Notebook** Develop the following diagram on the chalkboard. It summarizes the two unexpected blessings that resulted from Judah's exile in Babylon.

Two blessings	Synagogue	New worship place (Temple lay destroyed thousands of miles away)
	Written word	Scribes begin to record God's word, which had been passed on orally.

Notebook The following diagram sums up the two worship places of the Jews.

Two places	Temple	Place of instruction (mainly)
	Synagogue	Place of sacrifice (mainly)

Point ❹ **Clarify** Synagogue services were held every Sabbath and on feast days. They were conducted by members of the congregation or by invited guests (Acts 13:13–16).

Synagogue services began with the congregation facing Jerusalem and reciting the Shema Israel. It reads:

"Israel, remember this!
The LORD—and the LORD alone—
is our God.
Love the LORD your God
with all your heart,
with all your soul, and
with all your strength." Deuteronomy 6:4–5

The Shema Israel was the first prayer a Jewish child learned and the last prayer a dying Jew uttered.

Clarify The recitation of the Shema Israel was followed by prayer, readings, a homily, and a blessing.

To hold a synagogue service, the Law requires ten men to be present. *The Tenth Man,* a play by Paddy Chayefsky, takes its name from the Law.

The play focuses on the "tenth man," whom the sexton of a Long Island synagogue coaxes from the streets on a bitterly cold morning to complete the *minyan* (quorum).

Luke 12:11 alludes to the fact that the local synagogue served as a kind of local courtroom as well. Apparently, even punishments were administered in it (Matthew 10:17). Finally, to be expelled from the synagogue was a grave punishment (John 9:22).

Clarify Today a rabbi, assisted by a cantor, usually delivers the sermons and leads the service.

In ancient times, the rabbi was merely a highly respected scholar in the community to whom people turned for religious guidance. He worked in the fields like everyone else.

Today, the title *rabbi* is reserved for those educated in rabbinical schools and seminaries.

Discuss An old Jewish story concerns a woman who stopped going to the synagogue. One day the rabbi went to her house and asked to come in and sit with her by the fireplace. For a long time, neither spoke. Then the rabbi picked up a tongs, took a glowing coal from the fireplace, and set it on the hearth. As the two watched, the coal lost its glow and died A few minutes later, the old woman said, "I understand. I'll return to the synagogue."

Ask: What is the point of the story? (Just as a glowing coal dies if separated from the other glowing coals in the fireplace, so the woman's faith will die if she continues to separate herself from the synagogue congregation.)

5. LESSON INTERACTION

Exercise 1 **Clarify** The months after the diving accident were a nightmare for Joni. The girl who enjoyed travel and excited horse-show audiences with her riding ability lay encased in a Stryker frame. Much of the time she lay face to the floor. Her appearance went from a beautiful girl to that of a grotesque shell. She wrote later in *Joni:*

As I stared at my own reflection,
I saw two eyes, darkened and sunk into sockets,
bloodshot and glassy.
My weight had dropped from 125 to 80. . . .
[My teeth were] black from the effect of medication.

In desperation for something to hang on to, Joni turned, reluctantly at first, to the Bible. Gradually, a remarkable change took place. She explains it this way in her talks to thousands of young people across the country:

If my body were suddenly and miraculously healed,
I'd be on my feet another thirty or forty years. . . .
[But my soul] lives for eternity.
From the standpoint of eternity, my body
is only a flicker in the time-span of forever.

Discuss **(a, b, c)** Two things that strike you about Joni's story are (1) the impact the Bible had on her and (2) the impact she has had on other people as a result of her tragedy.

Ultimately, faith is usually the deciding factor in whether tragedy makes a person bitter or better. One student's story illustrates the power of faith in helping a person accept tragedy. The student told a counselor, "Were it not for this poem, I could not have accepted my mother's death." The poem, which appears on page 101 of the student text, reads:

For ev'ry pain we must bear,
For ev'ry burden, ev'ry care,
There's a reason.

For ev'ry grief that bows the head,
For ev'ry teardrop that is shed,
There's a reason.

For ev'ry hurt, for ev'ry plight,
For ev'ry lonely, pain-racked night,
There's a reason.

But if we trust God, as we should,
It will work out for our good.
He knows the reason. Author unknown

Exercise 2 **Discuss** Golda Meir said of her lack of beauty: "It forced me to develop my inner resources. I came to understand that women who can't lean on their beauty [have to work hard and, therefore,] . . . have the advantage."

Exercise 3 **Discuss** The students should be able to handle these quotes adequately.

CHAPTER NINE: Rebirth (pages 94–95)

Years of Waiting

LESSON **45**

1. LESSON BACKGROUND

▶ *Catechism of the Catholic Church*, 711.

2. LESSON QUIZ

Perfect score = 10 points

1. When and by whom was Jerusalem eventually destroyed? *(Lesson 44 review—2 points)*
2. List and describe the fate of the three groups of Jews who survived the fall of Jerusalem. *(Lesson 44 notebook review—6 points)*
3. Into what two periods did the ministry of the prophet Ezekiel fall? *(Lesson 45 preview—2 points)*

3. LESSON HOMEWORK

▶ **Return** Lesson 44 review questions (page 93).

▶ **Collect** Lesson 45 review questions (page 95).

▶ **Read** Lesson 46 ("Day of Joy," pages 96–97).

▶ **Write** Lesson 46 review questions (page 97).

▶ **Appoint** Student to prepare Acts 8:26–38 (lesson 46, exercise 2).

4. LESSON PRESENTATION

Point 1 **Read** Have volunteers read aloud the core content of lesson 45.

▶ **Clarify** Stress the two military operations of Babylon against Judah: (1) before destruction of Jerusalem (597 B.C.E.) and (2) after destruction (587 B.C.E.).

Stress that Ezekiel was among the Jews exported to Babylon after the first military operation.

▶ **Notebook** Develop the following diagram on the chalkboard for entry in student notebooks. It sums up the two periods of Ezekiel's prophetic ministry.

Ezekiel	First period	Before 597 B.C.E.
	His ministry	Disturber (warns people)
	Second period	After 587 B.C.E.
	His ministry	Comforter (lifts people)

▶ **Clarify** Emphasize Ezekiel's three main prophecies and their ultimate New Testament fulfillment.

1. King's restoration ("Shepherd-King" prophecy):

   "I will give them a king like my servant David
   to be their one shepherd,
   and he will take care of them." Ezekiel 34:23

   New Testament fulfillment:

   [Jesus said,] "I am the good shepherd." John 10:14
   "My kingdom does not belong to this world." John 18:36

2. Nation's restoration ("Dry Bones" prophecy):

   "I will put my breath in them,
   bring them back to life." Ezekiel 37:14

   New Testament fulfillment:

   [Jesus] breathed on them. John 20:22
   They were all filled with the Holy Spirit. Acts 2:4

3. Temple's restoration ("Glory Vision" prophecy):

   The Temple was filled with the glory of the LORD. . . .
   [The LORD said,] "I will live here . . .
   and rule them forever." Ezekiel 43:5–7

   New Testament fulfillment:

   God's Spirit lives in you! . . .
   You yourselves are his temple. 1 Corinthians 3:16–17

▶ **Notebook** Develop the following diagrams on the chalkboard for entry in student notebooks. They summarize the prophecies and their fulfillment.

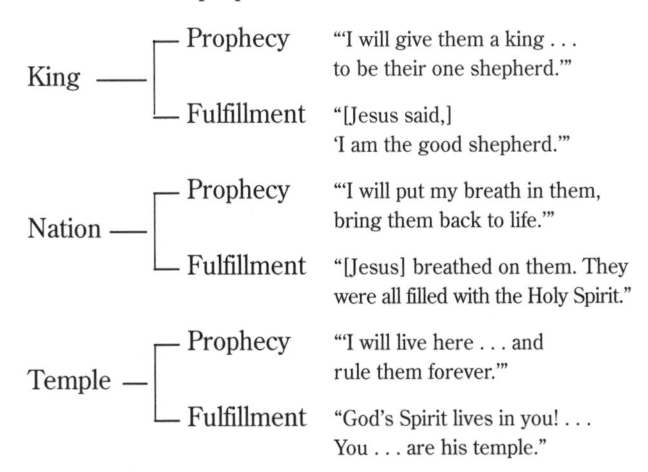

▶ **Clarify** Second Isaiah is so called because he prophesied in the spirit of Great Isaiah. His writings are appended to Great Isaiah's and are called the Book of Consolation (chapters 40–55).

Clarify How do we know these chapters were written by a different prophet?

A number of reasons. For example, their *content* reflects the historical situation of the exile (vs. the preexilic situation of Great Isaiah).

Moreover, his *writing style* differs decidedly (original Hebrew) from the other chapters of the Book of Isaiah.

Notebook Develop the following diagram on the chalkboard for entry in student notebooks.

2nd Isaiah
- Prophesies — Radiate "spirit" of Great Isaiah
- Writings — Chapters 40–55, joined to writings of Great Isaiah

5. LESSON INTERACTION

Exercise 1 **Discuss** Scripture was written not just for people of ancient times but for people of all time.

Jesus himself applied passages written for people of ancient times to his own personal experience. Take his temptations in the desert. Matthew 4:3–4 reads:

The Devil came to him and said,
"If you are God's Son,
order these stones to turn into bread."
But Jesus answered, "The scripture says,
'Human beings cannot live on bread alone,
but need every word that God speaks.'"

Exercise 2 **Notebook** Develop the following chart on the chalkboard. It sums up (1) the Old Testament prophecy (image), (2) an explanation, and (3) the New Testament fulfillment.

OT Prophecy	Explanation	NT Fulfillment
Shepherd-King	Restored king	Jesus = king
Dry Bones	Restored nation	Church = nation
Glory Vision	Restored Temple	Church = Temple

Exercise 3 **Discuss** In a similar way, people wonder if perhaps the finding of the Dead Sea Scrolls (in modern times) could be part of God's plan for people whose faith needs extra support in our day.

Interestingly, had the Dead Sea Scrolls been found fifty years earlier, we would have lacked the technology (infrared photography, etc.) to unroll the brittle hides and restore them sufficiently to read them.

Photo **Clarify** Direct students' attention to the photos on page 94.

A fascinating report of Robert Koldewey's dig at Babylon is found in Chapter 23, "The Tower of Babel," of *Gods, Graves, and Scholars* by C. W. Ceram.

Begun in 1989, Koldewey's work showed that Herodotus (fifth-century B.C.E. Greek historian) was right when he said that the tops of strategic sections of the walls of Babylon could accommodate two chariots passing in opposite directions.

Clarify Walls were normal protection for ancient cities—even whole countries. Recall the Great Wall of China (said to be the only structure visible from the moon).

Begun in the second century B.C.E., the Great Wall of China took generations to complete. It twists over 1,500 miles (several hundred miles longer than the distance from Chicago to New York) over deserts and mountains. It has been called the longest graveyard on earth, because nearly half a million workmen died from the heat of the desert and cold of the mountain regions as they labored on the wall.

The wall ranges from fifteen to fifty feet in height and from fifteen to thirty feet in width. A roadway runs along the top of the wall. Thousands of watchtowers give it added protection against would-be invaders.

Day of Joy

LESSON 46

1. LESSON BACKGROUND

▶ *Catechism of the Catholic Church*, 712.

2. LESSON QUIZ

Perfect score = 10 points

1. List the three pillars of Judaism that Ezekiel foretold would be restored. *(Lesson 45 review—3 points)*
2. List the New Testament fulfillment of Ezekiel's three prophesies. *(Lesson 45 notebook review—3 points)*
3. What *prophet* foretold what *leader* of what *people* would free the Jews from what *country? (Lesson 46 preview—4 points)*

3. LESSON HOMEWORK

▶ **Return** Lesson 45 review questions (page 95).

▶ **Collect** Lesson 46 review questions (page 97).

▶ **Read** Lesson 47 ("Call to Refocus," pages 98–99).

▶ **Write** Lesson 48 review questions (page 99).

▶ **Appoint** Four students to prepare a reading of the brief Book of Jonah. Have each student read one chapter. The reading time of this great story is about ten minutes.

4. LESSON PRESENTATION

Point 1 **Read** Have volunteers read aloud the core content of lesson 46.

▶ **Clarify** As rumors of the victories of Cyrus's armies circulated through the streets and alleys of Babylon, the hope of the exiled Jews began to mount.

To raise their hopes even more, Babylon's King Nabonidus was losing popularity among his own people.

Then came news that Cyrus and his armies were headed for Babylon. The excitement of the Jewish exiles reached fever pitch.

Unlike conquerors before him, Cyrus did not deport defeated people for slave labor. Nor did he suppress the religious traditions of the people he conquered. Rather, he allowed them to remain in their homeland, and Cyrus himself honored their gods.

Ask: How was Cyrus's approach to people totally different from the approach of King Rehoboam (who followed Solomon to the throne), which led to the revolt of Israel (North) from Judah (South)? Have the students refresh their memories by reading the description of Rehoboam's approach in exercise 1 of lesson 37 (page 79 of the student text).

▶ **Discuss** The Book of Ezra preserves this decree issued by Cyrus to all the Jews in Babylon:

"This is the command of Cyrus, Emperor of Persia.
The LORD, the God of Heaven, . . . has given me
the responsibility of building a temple for him
in Jerusalem in Judah.
May God be with all of you who are his people.
You are to go to Jerusalem and rebuild
the Temple of the LORD, the God of Israel." Ezra 1:2–3

The news of the decree was carried by runners throughout Babylon.

Ask: If you were a Jew who had given up your Jewish faith and taken on Babylonian beliefs and ways, how would you feel as you listened to a Babylonian official read this decree?

▶ **Clarify** You might draw a parallel between how these Jews felt and how Christians who have given up their faith will feel at the Second Coming of Jesus.

▶ **Clarify** Even the former captors of the Jews got caught up in the spirit of Cyrus's decree. The Book of Ezra says they came forth to help in every way.

Cyrus himself returned to the Jewish exiles "the bowls and cups that King Nebuchadnezzar had taken from the Temple in Jerusalem" (Ezra 1:7).

▶ **Notebook** Develop the following summary of Cyrus on the chalkboard for entry in student notebooks.

Cyrus	King	Instrument of God (Isaiah 45:4)
	Cylinder	Record of victory (Babylon)
	Proclamation	Release of Jews

5. LESSON INTERACTION

Exercise ① **Discuss** Read the full account of Augustine's conversion in *The Confessions of Saint Augustine* (VIII, 12). It took place in the summer of 386 at Milan, Italy, when Augustine was about thirty-two years old. He was doing well in his professional career and should have been happy. But he wasn't. He was downright unhappy. Here is a free translation of his writing about this experience:

I threw myself on the ground
under a nearby fig tree and began to weep bitterly.
I cried out to God in words like this:
"And you, Lord! How long? How long will you
keep on being angry with me—forever?
How long will it be—tomorrow and tomorrow?
Why not now? Why not at this very hour
put an end to my evil life?"

I was crying out like this when, suddenly,
I heard the voice of a little boy or a little girl—
I couldn't tell which.
In sing-song fashion the voice said,
"Take and read! Take and read!"

Immediately, my whole mood changed.
I asked myself if children at play
normally used such words.
I couldn't remember them ever doing so.

I stood up. For now the voice sounded
like a divine command to open the Bible
and read the first passage
that my eyes would fall upon. . . .
I got a Bible, opened it, and read:

"Let us conduct ourselves . . .
as people who live in the light of day—
no orgies or drunkenness. . . .
But take up the weapons of the Lord Jesus Christ,
and stop paying attention to your sinful nature
and satisfying its desires." Romans 13:13–14

Then I stopped. There was no need to go on.
My heart suddenly became flooded with light,
vanishing the dark doubts
and leaving me with a profound peace.

▶ **Discuss** **(a)** Recall these words of poet Robert Browning Hamilton:

I walked a mile with sorrow,
And ne'er a word said she;
But, oh, the things I learned from her
When Sorrow walked with me.

(b) Imagine that a distraught person played Bible roulette and opened to these words: "Away from me! . . . Away to the eternal fire which has been prepared for the Devil and his angels!" (Matthew 25:41). The mental disturbance it might cause the average person could be incalculable.

Exercise ② **Discuss** Have the appointed student read Acts 8:26–38. Philip, a deacon (Acts 6:5), refers to the "Suffering Servant" quoted at the beginning of this exercise.

For a brief, clear explanation of why the Ethiopian official was reading from Hebrew Scriptures, see page 184 of the student text. This event took place roughly seven hundred years after the prophecy was spoken by Isaiah. Recall that his ministry took place about seven centuries before Jesus.

Exercise ③ **Discuss** One reason why the disciples failed to link Jesus to the "Suffering Servant" prophecies was that the Spirit had not yet come. They were still in the dark about many things Jesus had said and done. Recall that Jesus said:

"When . . . the Spirit comes, who reveals the truth
about God, he will lead you into all the truth." John 16:13

Ultimately, the Suffering Servant songs refer to Jesus. Hold off a detailed discussion of the Holy Spirit's role in clarifying Jesus' words and mission until lesson 52.

Exercise ④ **Activity** Apart from "nonwriting prophets" like Elijah, Elisha, and Nathan, lists of major and minor "writing prophets" appear on page 82 of the student text.

Photo **Discuss** Direct students' attention to the photo of the Cyrus Cylinder on page 96. The writing on the cylinder appears more like decoration. When the code of the unusual script was broken, it was found to agree with 2 Chronicles 36:22, which reads:

In the first year that Cyrus of Persia was emperor,
the Lord *made what he had said*
through the prophet Jeremiah come true.
He prompted Cyrus to issue
the following command and send it out in writing
to be read aloud everywhere in his empire.

Photo **Discuss** Direct students' attention to the photo of the ruins of Persepolis shown on page 97. They are located in modern Iran. Also in modern Iran is the tomb of Cyrus.

The Roman historian Plutarch says that Alexander the Great's joy of victory over Persepolis was sobered when he read the inscription on Cyrus's tomb. Refer the students to the photo caption on page 100, in which this inscription is quoted.

Call to Refocus

LESSON 47

1. LESSON BACKGROUND

▶ *Catechism of the Catholic Church,* 713.

2. LESSON QUIZ

Perfect score =10 points

1. How long did the Jews sit in darkness in faraway Babylon? *(Lesson 46 review—1 point)*
2. Identify (a) King Cyrus of Persia, (b) the Cyrus Cylinder, (c) the Cyrus proclamation. *(Lesson 46 notebook review—3 points)*
3. Name two leaders and two prophets who guided the Jewish exiles upon their return to Jerusalem, and list two problems the returned exiles encountered. *(Lesson 47 preview—6 points)*

3. LESSON HOMEWORK

▶ **Return** Lesson 46 review questions (page 97).

▶ **Collect** Lesson 47 review questions (page 99).

▶ **Read** Lesson 48 ("Shattered Dreams," pages 100–101).

▶ **Write** Lesson 48 review questions (page 101).

4. LESSON PRESENTATION

Point ❶ **Read** Have volunteers read aloud the core content of lesson 47.

▶ **Clarify** The sight that greeted the exiles as they walked into Jerusalem was that of a desolate, destroyed city. Two problems emerged immediately.

First, neighbors offered to help rebuild the city, but the exiles refused their offer. The resulting rift between the exiles and their neighbors exploded into hostility. Nehemiah 4:17–18 describes the situation:

Those who carried building materials
worked with one hand and kept a weapon in the other,
and everyone who was building
kept a sword strapped to their waist.

The second problem was the failure of crops. Enthusiasm turned to deep discouragement.

▶ **Notebook** Summarize the two problems (external and internal) for entry in student notebooks.

Two problems
- External — Hostility from neighbors
- Internal — Crop failure

Point ❷ **Clarify** Into this situation stepped the prophets Haggai and Zechariah. Haggai "disturbed" the people; Zechariah "comforted" them.

Haggai told the people that they themselves were to blame. For one thing, they were focusing on building homes for themselves rather than on rebuilding the Temple for God.

Zechariah "comforted" the people, lest they become totally discouraged. He shared with them a vision he had:

People of Zion! Shout for joy. . . .
Look, your king is coming to you . . .
humble and riding on a donkey. Zechariah 9:9

New Testament writers cited this prophecy when Jesus rode into Jerusalem on a donkey on Palm Sunday. Matthew says:

This happened in order to make come true
what the prophet had said:

"Tell the city of Zion,
Look, your king is coming to you!
He is humble and rides on a donkey." Matthew 21:4–5

▶ **Notebook** Summarize the messages of the two prophets for entry in student notebooks.

Two prophets
- Haggai — Disturbed the people ("Reverse your priorities! Rebuild the Temple!")
- Zechariah — Comforted the people ("Hang in there! Days of glory lie ahead!")

Point ❸ **Clarify** Soon, more exiles returned from Babylon. Among them were Nehemiah and Ezra. These two leaders worked in tandem.

Nehemiah addressed the *material* needs of the people (rebuilding the city and the Temple).

Ezra addressed the *spiritual* needs of the people (renewing the covenant).

By 450 B.C.E. both needs were met.

▶ **Notebook** Summarize the contributions of the two leaders for entry in student notebooks.

Two leaders	Nehemiah	Addressed material needs (rebuilding of Jerusalem)
	Ezra	Addressed spiritual needs (renewal of covenant)

Point ❹ **Discuss** Have the appointed students read the Book of Jonah. Preface their reading with these remarks:

> People preoccupied with their own problems tend to forget there are other people in the world. Something like this happened to the Jews. They turned in on themselves and temporarily forgot that they were "God's chosen instrument" for re-creating the world. This led to a forceful challenge from the prophetic Book of Jonah.
>
> Let us now listen to a reading of the story.

Ask: How did the Book of Jonah challenge Jews to take a more universalistic view of God? (It shows God's concern for the salvation of all, even Jewish enemies.)

Ask: Do you think Jonah's heart was in his preaching? If not, how do you account for its success? (Recall that the power of a prophet's words comes not from the prophet's human eloquence but from the "word" itself, which is from God. Only the hearer's openness to the word and faith in the word can release its power.)

Ask: What reason (start of chapter 4) does Jonah give for not wanting to preach in Nineveh? (Jonah knew that God would forgive the Ninevites, and he didn't want this to happen to Judah's arch enemy.)

Ask: Does this tell us anything about the kind of man Jonah was? (He was not a forgiving person. He reminds us of the elder son in the parable of the prodigal son. He resents the fact that God is so forgiving.)

5. LESSON INTERACTION

Exercise ❶ **Discuss** **(a)** This first question could be explosive. Be careful not to let it get out of hand.

(b) Have students answer this question in writing and anonymously. Collect the responses, screen them, and share the better responses at the next class.

(c) Have students write out their response privately before sharing it with the group.

Exercise ❷ **Discuss** **(a)** Jonah was a "warning sign" to the people. Unless they repented, Nineveh would be destroyed.

(b) Jesus is a similar "warning sign." He too called the people to repentance. Jesus adds:

"On the Judgment Day
the people of Nineveh will stand up and accuse you,
because they turned from their sins . . . and . . .
there is something here greater than Jonah!" Luke 11:32

The terrifying implication is that Jesus' hearers will *not* turn from their sins as the Ninevites did—even with Jesus doing the preaching.

(c) Jesus' reference is not "proof" that he regarded the Jonah story as "historical." He simply uses this well-known story to make a point. For example, a homilist might say, "Parents, forgive your children as the father of the prodigal son forgave his son." He does not intend to affirm the "historical reality" of the story. He simply uses the story to make a point.

Exercise ❸ **Discuss** **(b)** Give the students time to collect their thoughts and write out their responses before sharing them with the group.

Exercise ❹ **Activity** Screen the letters and share the better ones with the group at the next class.

Miniposter **Discuss** Direct students' attention to the miniposter on page 98.

Ask: To what do the words "big ten" refer? (Ten Commandments)

Ask: How can you remove six of the fifteen sticks and still have ten remain on the table?

(Begin with the box on the left and remove the extreme left stick, extreme right stick, and bottom stick. This leaves you with "T." Next, go to the middle box and remove the extreme right stick. This leaves you with "E." Finally, remove the top stick and the bottom stick of the third box. This leaves you with "N." And so you have "T E N" remaining on the table.)

Shattered Dreams

LESSON 48

1. LESSON BACKGROUND

▶ *Catechism of the Catholic Church*, 714.

2. LESSON QUIZ

Perfect score = 6 points

1. List the names of the two men who acted as leaders of the exiles upon their return to Jerusalem. *(Lesson 47 review—2 points)*
2. How did the messages of the prophets Haggai and Zechariah differ in the approach they took with the exiles who returned to Jerusalem? *(Lesson 47 notebook review—2 points)*
3. What question does the Book of Job raise, and what answer does it give to the question? *(Lesson 48 preview—2 points)*

3. LESSON HOMEWORK

▶ **Return** Lesson 47 review questions (page 99).

▶ **Collect** Lesson 48 review questions (page 101).

▶ **Read** Lesson 49 ("Call to Trust," pages 102–3).

▶ **Write** Lesson 49 review questions (page 103).

▶ **Appoint** Two students to prepare Amos 5:11–24 and Daniel 7:9–18 (lesson 49, exercise 3a).

4. LESSON PRESENTATION

Point ① **Read** Have volunteers read aloud the core content of lesson 48.

▶ **Clarify** The word *Ecclesiastes* is derived from the Greek word *Ekklesia*, meaning "church." The book takes the form of a series of random reflections about life and its ultimate meaning.

Sensing that Judah has reached it "day of drums," the author writes:

Fast runners do not always win the races,
and the brave do not always win the battles. 9:11

Repeatedly, the author raises the question: What is the meaning of life? His inability to answer that question gives Ecclesiastes a tinge of sadness—the kind of sadness that trademarks so many great works.

Classic writers see moments of human joy and peaks of human glory, but deep in their hearts they see that these things are like the dawn dew—doomed to disappear. It is this affirmation of people's fragility that gives great literature its timeless appeal.

Occasionally Ecclesiastes counterpoints its tone of sadness with flights of advice to enjoy life.

Go ahead—eat your food and be happy;
drink your wine and be cheerful. 9:7

But in the end, "everything . . . is all useless. It is like chasing the wind" (1:8, 14). Human life moves in a monotonous, tragic cycle. Television viewers caught this feeling as they listened to the reading from Ecclesiastes during the funeral services for President John F. Kennedy on November 25, 1963:

[God] sets the time for birth and the time for death . . .
the time for sorrow and the time for joy,
the time for mourning and the time for dancing . . .
the time for silence and the time for talk. 3:2, 4, 7

The Book of Ecclesiastes helps us enter into the heart of a Jew waiting for more revelation from God on the meaning of life.

Point ② **Clarify** The Book of Ecclesiastes leads naturally to the Book of Job. It, too, is a book struggling for answers.

For example, Jews had little or no idea of an afterlife. True, they believed in a nether world, called *Sheol.* But they thought it was just a place for the dead, good and bad alike. What happened there, they did not know. They did not think of it as a place of reward or punishment for the sins of this life. They thought that God rewarded and punished in this life.

This raised a big question. If God is so good, and if this is our only home, why do so many good people go unrewarded. Worse yet, why do so many good people suffer. This is the question raised in the Book of Job.

▶ **Clarify** American poet Archibald MacLeish put the Book of Job into a play set in modern times. The play, called *J.B.,* was a Broadway hit. J.B. is an upright businessman in his late thirties. His five children meet with violent deaths. For example, his daughter is raped and murdered by a nineteen-year-old, high on drugs. Finally, J.B. contracts a horrible skin disease.

In spite of these monstrous tragedies, J.B. retains faith in God. This "passivity" angers his wife and she deserts him.

Next, three friends come to console J.B. Each one represents an area of modern thought: psychiatry, political science, and religion. None of them really succeeds in helping J.B. to understand his plight. The play ends with J.B. being rewarded by a return to good health, the return of his wife, and the possibility of future wealth and children.

Ask: Why do/don't you like the ending?

Notebook Sum up the question raised in the Book of Job and its response for entry in student notebooks.

Book of Job
- Question: Why do good people suffer?
- Response: God alone knows. Trust!

5. LESSON INTERACTION

Exercise 1 **Discuss** **(a, b)** The angel's point is that people are motivated more by reward and punishment than by love of God.

Ask: To what extent do you agree/disagree with the angel's point? (Stress that motivation is like a cable made up of many strands of wire. Perhaps 30 percent of the reason why a person keeps God's law is fear of punishment. Perhaps another 30 percent is hope of reward. Perhaps another 40 percent is pure love of God.)

Exercise 2 **Discuss** **(a)** Children born of parents who are alcoholics or drug addicts do, indeed, often suffer for the sins of their parents.

Ask: How fair is this? Why does God permit what seems to be such an "injustice"? This is precisely the question that the Book of Job raises.

Refer the students to exercise 4 and ask: How does this exercise provide some insight into the "mystery of suffering"?

(The point of the poem that the student found under the glass top on his dresser is a poetic expression of the response that the Book of Job gives to this vexing question.)

The poem does not answer Job's question directly, but it does suggest a new line of thought. It is this: If Job admits that God's wisdom greatly surpasses his, why does he question God's fairness to him? If he cannot understand other things, why does he expect to understand this?

Job's experience of God toward the end of the Book of Job changes him from a sage (a person of wisdom) to a saint (a person of faith). It transforms him from a person who walked by the "light of reason" to a person who now walks by the "light of faith."

Notebook **(b)** Ancient Jews came up with three reasons why a good person may suffer. They may be summarized as follows:

Why good suffer
- Secret sins of the person
- Members of sinful community[1]
- Sins of parents/children

[1] This is equivalent to punishing an entire class because of one or two members who have misbehaved.

Exercise 3 **Discuss** Ezekiel 18:20 reads:

"A son is not to suffer because of his father's sins,
nor a father because of the sins of his son.
Good people will be rewarded for doing good,
and evil people will suffer for the evil they do."

Jesus responded to the question about whose sin caused the blind man to be born blind by saying:

"His blindness has nothing to do
with his sins or his parents' sins.
He is blind so that God's power
might be seen at work in him." John 9:3

Exercise 4 **Discuss** **(a)** See exercise 2a above for an explanation of how the student's point illustrates the point of the Book of Job.

Photo **Discuss** Direct students' attention to the mosaic of Alexander the Great on page 100.

Stress the point that Alexander was not a power-mad egotist, at least in the beginning of his career. A student of the great Aristotle, he saw himself as a disciple of Hellenic (Greek) culture. He wanted to share its blessings with the rest of the world.

Alexander marched his armies all the way to India before he stopped to solidify his gains.

But death, the ultimate tyrant, closed the door on his brilliant career. He died at about the same age as Jesus.

Ask: What similarities do you see between Alexander and Jesus, apart from their age at death? (Both set out to conquer the world: one physically, the other spiritually. Both wanted to give a gift to the human race: cultural enrichment (Alexander), eternal life (Jesus).

Miniposter **Discuss** Direct students' attention to the miniposter on page 100. Ask: How does it relate to the Books of Ecclesiastes and Job? (Only faith can provide the "light" to see.)

Call to Trust

LESSON 49

1. LESSON BACKGROUND

▶ *Catechism of the Catholic Church,* 715.

2. LESSON QUIZ

Perfect score = 8 points

1. What Greek general ruled the largest empire ever headed by one person, and who divided up this great empire when he died an early death? *(Lesson 48 review—2 points)*
2. What question does the Book of Job ask, and what response does it make to this question? *(Lesson 48 notebook review—2 points)*
3. List and briefly describe the two major sections into which the Book of Daniel divides. *(Lesson 49 preview—4 points)*

3. LESSON HOMEWORK

▶ **Return** Lesson 48 review questions (page 101).

▶ **Collect** Lesson 49 review questions (page 103).

▶ **Read** Lesson 50 ("Unfinished Story," pages 104–5).

▶ **Write** Lesson 50 review questions (page 105).

4. LESSON PRESENTATION

Point 1 **Read** Have volunteers read aloud the core content of lesson 49.

▶ **Clarify** American archaeologists found coins bearing the name of Antiochus IV while digging at a site west of the Dead Sea in the 1930s. Antiochus was the king who tried to make Greeks out of his Jewish subjects in 167 B.C.E.

The First Book of Maccabees describes how Antiochus went about doing this:

The king . . . sent messengers with a decree
to Jerusalem and all the towns of Judea,
ordering the people to follow customs
that were foreign to the country. . . .
They were commanded to build pagan altars,
temples, and shrines. . . .
Any books of the Law which were found
were torn up and burned. 1:44, 47, 56

This decree created an impossible situation. Those who disobeyed it were persecuted brutally. Typical was the martyrdom of seven brothers, which their mother was forced to witness (2 Maccabees 7).

This reign of terror shook Judah's faith to the roots. Devout Jews cried out to God:

How long will your anger burn like fire? . . .
Lord, where are the former proofs of your love?
Where are the promises you made to David?
Psalm 89:46, 49

Point 2 **Clarify** Into this crisis stepped the unknown prophet of the Book of Daniel. Like prophets before him, he faced the problem of communicating a profound religious message to simple, uneducated people. He did this by telling the story of a young Jewish hero, named Daniel. The prophet makes use of two literary devices in telling the story: (1) folktales of how Daniel remains faithful to God, and (2) visions granted to Daniel by God.

▶ **Notebook** Develop the following summary on the chalkboard for entry in student notebooks.

Daniel	Folktales	Daniel's fidelity to God
	Visions	God's revelation to Daniel

Point 3 **Discuss** Daniel came to the attention of King Nebuchadnezzar of Babylonia when the king had a dream that no one else could interpret. After he interpreted the dream, Daniel rose to national prominence in Babylonia. Then followed a series of folktales and visions.

Ask: What other young Jewish hero does Daniel remind you of? (Joseph in Egypt. Like Joseph, Daniel

- was taken captive to a foreign country,
- remained faithful to his religious heritage,
- was wrongly imprisoned,
- was expert in interpreting dreams,
- rose to prominence by interpreting the king's dream.)

Point 4 **Clarify** You may want to read aloud the story of how Daniel violated the king's decree on prayer and ended up in the lions' den (Daniel 6).

Daniel prayed three times daily (Daniel 6:10). Early Christians continued this Jewish practice, praying at the third hour (morning), the sixth hour (noon), and the ninth hour (evening).

Acts 2:15 has the Holy Spirit descend upon the apostles at prayer at the *third* hour (9 A.M.).

Acts 10:9 says Peter was praying at the *sixth* hour (noon) when a vision came to him.

Acts 3:1 says Peter and John went to the Temple to pray at the *ninth* hour (3 P.M.).

▶ **Clarify** Later Christians continued the practice of praying three times daily. For example, up until the 1960s in the United States, the bells of Catholic churches were sounded at 6 A.M., noon, and 6 P.M. Catholics were taught to stop whatever they were doing at these times and pray the Angelus.

Ask the students to listen closely as you read the Angelus so that they can identify the three great Christian mysteries it refers to. (Jesus' birth, death, and resurrection)

The angel of the Lord declared to Mary,
and she conceived of the Holy Spirit.

[First Hail Mary recited.]

Behold the handmaid of the Lord.
Be it done to me according to your word.

[Second Hail Mary recited.]

And the Word was made flesh
and dwelt among us.

[Third Hail Mary recited.]

Pour forth, we ask you, O Lord,
your grace into our hearts,
that we, to whom the Incarnation of your Son
was made known by the message of an angel,
may by his passion and cross
be brought to the glory of his resurrection
through the same Christ our Lord. Amen.

▶ **Clarify** Muslims follow a similar practice of regular daily prayer. The *Azam* (call to prayer) sounds five times a day: (1) before sunrise, (2) shortly after midday, (3) late afternoon, (4) after sunset, (5) after nightfall.

In countries like Saudi Arabia, the *Azam* sounds over national television, interrupting all programming.

Ask: Why do/don't you think daily prayer of this kind is important?

Point ❺ **Clarify** The most striking reference to Jesus as the Son of Man came when Jesus was standing trial for his life. Jesus himself makes the reference by alluding directly to the vision of Daniel given in the text.

HIGH PRIEST *Are you the Messiah,*
the Son of the Blessed God?
JESUS *I am, and you will all see the Son of Man*
seated at the right side of the Almighty
and coming with the clouds of heaven!
HIGH PRIEST *We don't need any more witnesses!*
You heard his blasphemy. Mark 14:61–64

For New Testament writers, the image of "the Son of Man seated at the right side of the Almighty" captured the mysteriousness of Jesus' personality: God and man.

▶ **Notebook** Develop the following diagram on the chalkboard for entry in student notebooks. It sums up the mysterious identity of Jesus.

Jesus —
- Son of God Begotten of God
- Son of Man Born of Mary

5. LESSON INTERACTION

Exercise ❶ **Discuss** **(a, b)** Have the students write their responses to the first two questions of this exercise before sharing them with the rest of the class.

(c) Have the students write their responses on a separate sheet of paper. Collect the responses, screen them, and share the better responses, anonymously, with the group at the next class meeting.

Exercise ❷ **Discuss** **(a)** Stories appeal to the total person: senses, mind, heart, and soul.

(b, c) Have the students answer these two questions privately and in writing. After they have finished, have them share their conclusions.

Exercise ❸ **Notebook** Summarize the main differences between prophetic and apocalyptic writing for entry in student notebooks.

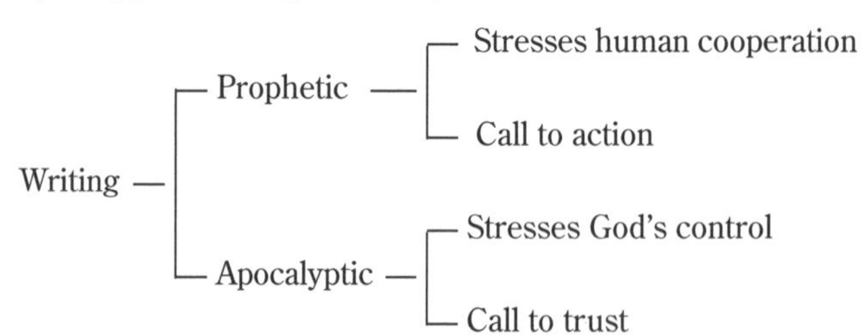

▶ **Discuss** **(a, b)** Have the appointed students read the passages before discussing them. Amos illustrates prophetic writing and is a "call to action" (Reform your ways!). Daniel illustrates apocalyptic writing and is a "call to trust" (Have faith! God's in control!).

Unfinished Story

LESSON **50**

1. LESSON BACKGROUND

▶ *Catechism of the Catholic Church,* 716.

2. LESSON QUIZ

Perfect score = 9 points

1. What vision in the Book of Daniel did Jesus apply to himself? *(Lesson 49 review—1 point)*
2. List and briefly describe the two major divisions into which the Book of Daniel divides. *(Lesson 49 notebook review—4 points)*
3. Briefly identify (a) Maccabees, (b) Hasmoneans, (c) Herod the Great, (d) Augustus Caesar. *(Lesson 50 preview—4 points)*

3. LESSON HOMEWORK

▶ **Return** Lesson 49 review questions (page 103).

▶ **Collect** Lesson 50 review questions (page 105).

▶ **Read** Lesson 51 ("Gospels," pages 108–9).

▶ **Write** Lesson 51 review questions (page 109).

4. LESSON PRESENTATION

Point ① **Read** Have volunteers read aloud the core content of lesson 50.

▶ **Clarify** Fired by the spirit of the Book of Daniel, loyal Jews came alive. Soon a resistance movement against the Syrians was mounted under the leadership of the Maccabees (three brothers), especially Judas. Their story is contained in the two Books of Maccabees. The First Book of Maccabees says of Judas:

He advanced the cause of freedom by what he did.
He made life miserable for many kings,
but brought joy to the people of Israel.
We will praise him forever for what he did. 3:6–7

The Second Book of Maccabees says:

Judas would make sudden attacks
on towns and villages and burn them.
He captured strategic positions
and routed many enemy troops. . . .
People everywhere spoke of his bravery. 8:6–7

Under Judas's leadership, the "freedom fighters" recaptured the Temple, which had been desecrated. They lit the Temple lights and reconsecrated the Temple to God. Modern Jews still celebrate this great event with Hanukkah (the Feast of Lights).

The tide finally turned in complete favor of the "freedom fighters" when Antiochus overtaxed his army on all fronts and ran into serious financial problems.

Typical of so many leaders, Judas and Jonathan were killed in the process of bringing victory to their people; and it fell to their brother Simon to bring the revolt to a successful conclusion around 142 B.C.E.

Point ② **Clarify** During the Maccabean Era a new attitude concerning the afterlife began to spread in the popular mind.

We see this change in attitude reflected in the martyrdom stories of the seven brothers in 2 Maccabees 7. The first brother says to his tormentors:

"You may kill us, but the King of the universe
will raise us from the dead
and give us eternal life." 2 Maccabees 7:9

The fourth brother echoes the same idea, saying:

"I am glad to die at your hands,
because we have the assurance
that God will raise us from death." 2 Maccabees 7:14

Similarly, a new attitude toward the relationship between the living and the dead began to spread in the popular mind. For example, on one occasion Judas and his men prayed for the dead and took up a collection to offer sacrifice for them. We read:

Judas did this noble thing because he believed
in the resurrection of the dead.
If he had not believed that the dead would be raised,
it would have been foolish and useless
to pray for them.
In his firm and devout conviction
that all of God's faithful people
would receive a wonderful reward,
Judas made provision for a sin offering
to set free from their sin those who had died.
2 Maccabees 12:43–45

Point ③ **Clarify** An example of Judas's military genius is given in 1 Maccabees 4. Judas heard that the enemy was advancing for a night attack on the Jewish camp. In total silence, his soldiers evacuated the camp. As a result the enemy attacked an empty camp. Worse yet, the next morning the enemy woke up to the sight of Judas's army drawn up for battle.

It is said that George Washington, who knew the Book of Maccabees well, employed a similar strategy on one occasion to trick and defeat the British.

▶ **Clarify** Judas is still a favorite with poets. Longfellow celebrated his exploits in poetry. The great composer Handel wrote his oratorio *Judas Maccabeus* to commemorate England's victory over the Scots.

Point ④ **Clarify** The Maccabean Era was followed by the Hasmonean Era.

If Jewish existence was threatened from *without* during the Maccabean Era, it was threatened from *within* during the Hasmonean Era. How so?

The Hasmoneans used the office of high priest for political purposes. Furthermore, under the Hasmoneans, Greek culture tore at the fabric of Jewish religious society. Even Temple priests got caught up in the "modern" movement.

2 Maccabees 4:9–12 tells how the high priest, Jason, built a gymnasium right next to the Jerusalem Temple. 2 Maccabees 4:14 tells how Temple priests neglected their duties "to take part in the games that were forbidden by our Law."

Orthodox Jews were appalled at having a gymnasium next to the Temple, because all the athletes competed in the nude. (The word *gymnasium* comes from the Greek word *gymnos,* meaning "naked.")

Jews abhorred nudity on several counts. One was that it played a prominent part in the pagan fertility rites of their ancient enemy, the Canaanites.

▶ **Notebook** Develop the following diagram on the chalkboard for entry in student notebooks.

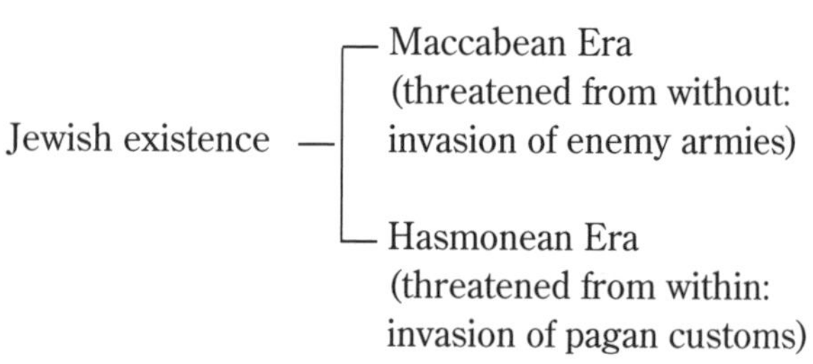

5. LESSON INTERACTION

Exercise ① **Notebook** Develop on the chalkboard the following "ballpark" summary of the five major groups in Judah as the Old Testament era ended.

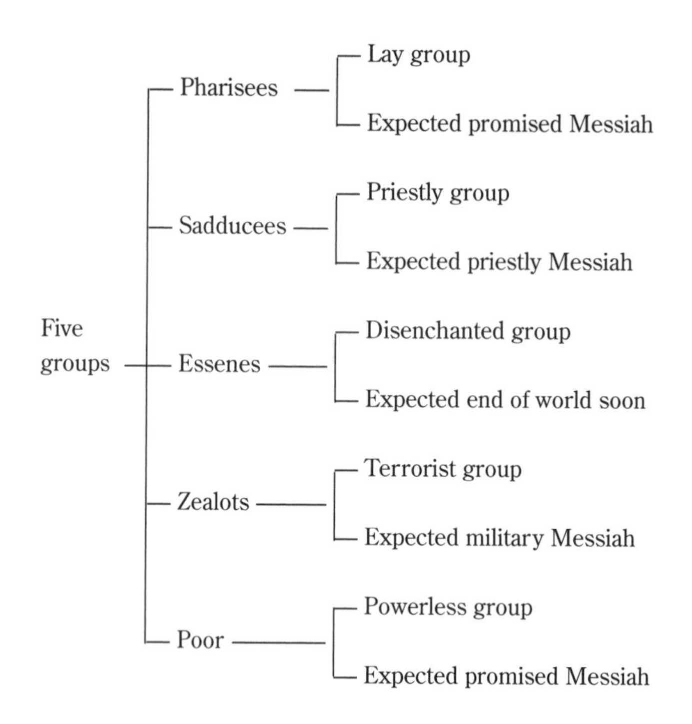

▶ **Discuss** **(a, b)** Allow the students to interject their own personal questions about angels, afterlife, final judgment, and messiah.

Exercise ② **Discuss** The key idea is this: The olive tree had much of its trunk rotted away. But there was still enough of the tree's trunk and root system left that it could produce fruit.

Judah was very much like this. There was still enough of its "trunk" and its "root system" that it could bear the fruit God had chosen it to produce. It could still bring forth the promised Messiah, who would effect the "re-creation" of the world.

Miniposter **Discuss** Direct attention to the miniposter on page 104. Ask the students how it applies not only to Israel's situation at the end of the Old Testament era but also to our situation at the end of the twentieth century.

CHAPTER TEN: Good News (pages 108–9)

Gospels

LESSON 51

1. LESSON BACKGROUND

▶ *Catechism of the Catholic Church,* 121–125.

2. LESSON QUIZ

Perfect score = 15 points

1. Identify the following: (a) Maccabees, (b) Hasmoneans, (c) Augustus Caesar. *(Lesson 50 review—3 points)*
2. How did the "poor" people in Judah feel about the following: (a) Pharisees, (b) Sadducees, (c) Essenes, (d) Zealots? *(Lesson 50 notebook review—4 points)*
3. List and describe the four categories of books into which the New Testament divides. *(Lesson 51 preview—8 points)*

3. LESSON HOMEWORK

▶ **Return** Lesson 50 review questions (page 105).

▶ **Collect** Lesson 51 review questions (page 109).

▶ **Read** Lesson 52 ("Birth of Gospels," pages 110–11).

▶ **Write** Lesson 52 review questions (page 111).

▶ **Appoint** Two students to prepare Bible readings from Jude 3–4 and 1 John 4:1–3 (lesson 52, exercise 2).

4. LESSON PRESENTATION

Point ➀ **Read** Have student volunteers alternate reading aloud the core content of lesson 51.

▶ **Clarify** Nathaniel Hawthorne (1804–1864) was an American author. His novels include *The House of the Seven Gables* and *The Scarlet Letter* (regarded by many critics as the greatest American novel ever written).

▶ **Discuss** Ask: How is Hawthorne's unfinished story a story about every person? (The "real you" and the "real me"—the main characters in our lives—rarely appear. Instead, all kinds of minor characters do: the sinner in me, the skeptic, the coward. These minor characters steal the show. Meanwhile, the "real you" and the "real me" never appear.)

Ask: Why do the "real you" and the "real me" never—or rarely—appear?

Point ➁ **Clarify** A Peanuts cartoon illustrates the hopeless situation of humanity before Jesus entered the world.

The first frame shows Charlie Brown staring at a toolbox, saying something like this: "I can't do it! I can't do it!" The second frame shows Lucy entering and saying, "What's wrong, Charlie? You seem unhappy." The final frame has Charlie answer Lucy, saying, "I am unhappy! I want to build a workbench, but I don't have a workbench to build it on."

Ask: How might we relate the cartoon to the situation of humanity before Jesus entered our world? (Before Jesus entered the world, people were like Charlie Brown. They had no "workbench" on which to rebuild their lives. Jesus gave them that "workbench"—by his teachings and his death and resurrection.)

Point ➂ **Notebook** Develop the following diagram for entry in student notebooks.

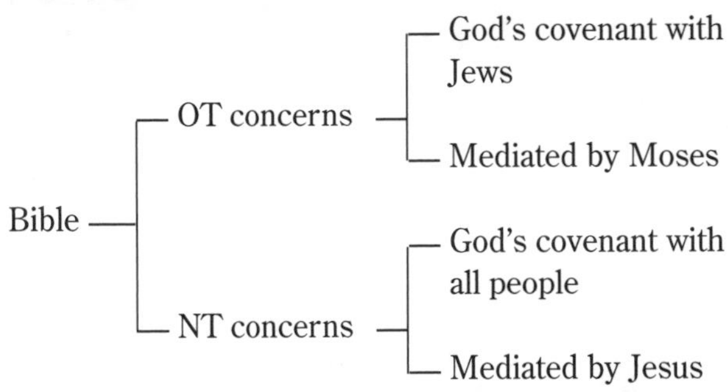

▶ **Clarify** The New Testament does not replace the Old Testament, but brings it to fulfillment. Jesus said:

"Do not think that I have come to do away with
the Law of Moses and the teachings of the prophets.
I have not come to do away with them,
but to make their teachings come true." Matthew 5:17

Notebook Develop on the chalkboard the following bird's-eye view of the Bible.

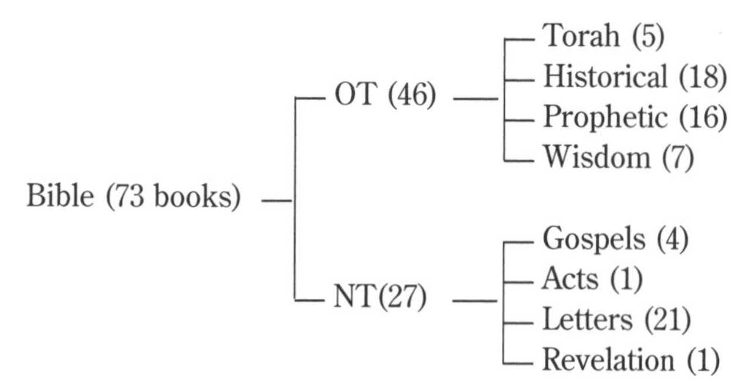

Notebook Develop on the chalkboard the four categories into which the New Testament divides.

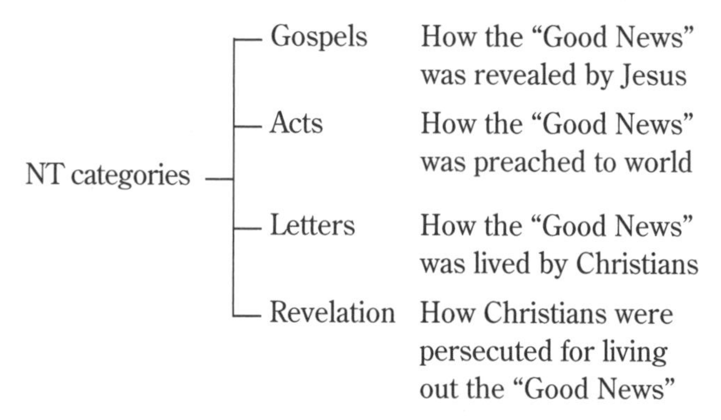

5. LESSON INTERACTION

Exercise ❶ **Discuss** **(a)** Ask: How could you get around Liz's two objections?

Ask: What would be your response to Kevin's point that "seeing is believing"?

Discuss **(b)** After giving the students time to think and record their responses to this question on a piece of paper, have volunteers read and discuss their responses. Meanwhile, have a "class secretary" keep a running score of their responses (*gospel version* or *video version*) on the chalkboard.

Exercise ❷ **Clarify** **(a)** The disciples were enlightened by the coming of the Holy Spirit on Pentecost, just as Jesus had foretold earlier in his ministry:

"The Helper, the Holy Spirit,
whom the Father will send in my name,
will teach you everything and make you remember
all that I have told you." John 14:25

The impact of the Holy Spirit's coming will be discussed more fully in the next lesson.

Clarify Two other examples that dramatize how the disciples did not understand something Jesus said or did during his lifetime are the following:

Example 1: One day, Jesus expelled money changers from the Temple. The Jewish authorities challenged Jesus, saying to him:

"What miracle can you perform
to show us that you have the right to do this?"

Jesus answered, "Tear down this Temple,
and in three days I will build it again."

"Are you going to build it again in three days?"
they asked him. "It has taken forty-six years
to build this Temple!"

But the temple Jesus was speaking about
was his body. So when he was raised from death,
his disciples remembered that he had said this,
and they believed the scripture
and what Jesus had said. John 2:18–22

To help the students better understand this episode, refer them to the model of the Temple on page 155 of the textbook. Also refer them to the artist's aerial view of the Temple on page 178 of the textbook.

The money changers were located in the "Court of Gentiles," the outermost court of the Temple.

Example 2: One day, Jesus told his disciples:

"The Son of Man will be handed over
to those who will kill him.
Three days later, however, he will rise to life."
But they did not understand
what this teaching meant,
and they were afraid to ask him. Mark 9:31–32

Discuss **(b, c)** Have students respond to these two questions in writing before discussing them.

Miniposter **Clarify** Ask: What is the point of the miniposter on page 108?

Ask: What do you fear most about life? In other words, in what sense is your life "dark and steep"?

CHAPTER TEN: Good News (pages 110–11)

Birth of Gospels

LESSON **52**

1. LESSON BACKGROUND

► *Catechism of the Catholic Church,* 109–114.

2. LESSON QUIZ

Perfect score = 11 points

1. How is Hawthorne's unfinished story similar to the Old Testament story? *(Lesson 51 review—1 point)*
2. List and briefly explain the four categories of New Testament books. *(Lesson 51 notebook review—8 points)*
3. Who foretold the coming of the Holy Spirit, and what did he say about it? *(Lesson 52 preview—2 points)*

3. LESSON HOMEWORK

► **Return** Lesson 51 review questions (page 109).

► **Collect** Lesson 52 review questions (page 111).

► **Read** Lesson 53 ("Three Gospel Stages," pages 112–13).

► **Write** Lesson 53 review questions (page 113).

4. LESSON PRESENTATION

Point ❶ **Read** Have student volunteers alternate reading aloud the core content of lesson 52.

► **Clarify** Ask: In what sense are certain events in Jesus' life like an undeveloped negative? (An undeveloped negative appears meaningless. That is, it seems to be blank. Only when exposed to the "light of the sun" does the meaning appear. Certain events in Jesus' life are like that. At first the disciples didn't see any meaning in them. Only when exposed to the "light of the Spirit" on Pentecost did the meaning appear.)

Ask: Can you recall one event from Jesus' life that seemed meaningless to his disciples until it was exposed to the "light of the Spirit"? (Refer students to the previous lesson [Jesus' entry into Jerusalem on Palm Sunday]. Also remind them of Jesus' expulsion of the money changers from the Temple [example 1 in manual].)

► **Discuss** Ask: How are biblical writers like X-ray photographers, while history writers are more like regular photographers? (History writers are mainly concerned with the "outer" dimension of events [what happened]. Biblical writers are mainly concerned with the events' "inner" dimension [deeper meaning].) Historian H. G. Wells refers to this difference in "The Three Greatest Men in History" (*Reader's Digest,* May 1935). He writes:

The historian must treat Jesus as a man just as a painter must paint him as a man. . . . Of course the reader and I live in countries where to millions of persons, Jesus is more than a man. But the historian must disregard that fact. He must adhere to the evidence that would pass unchallenged if his book were to be read in every nation under the sun.

► **Notebook** We may summarize the above discussion for entry in student notebooks.

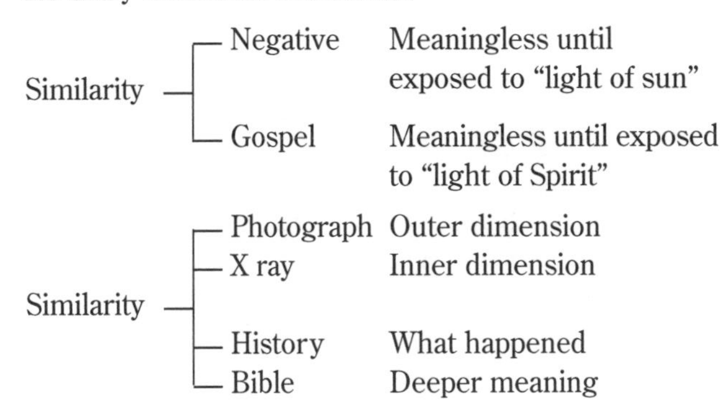

Point ❷ **Notebook** We may list the "three key results" of Pentecost this way:

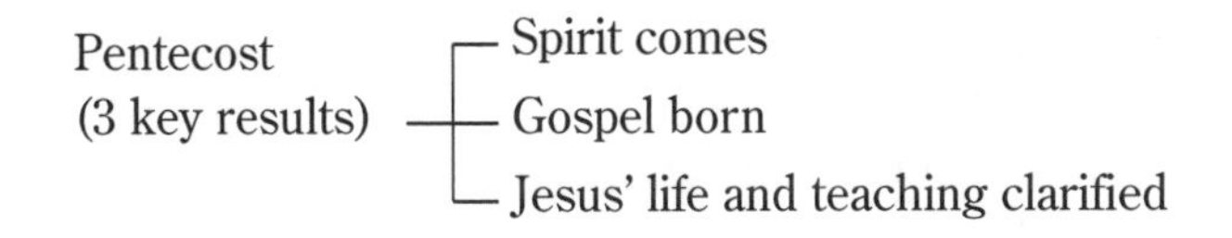

► **Notebook** Sum up the initial reaction to Pentecost:

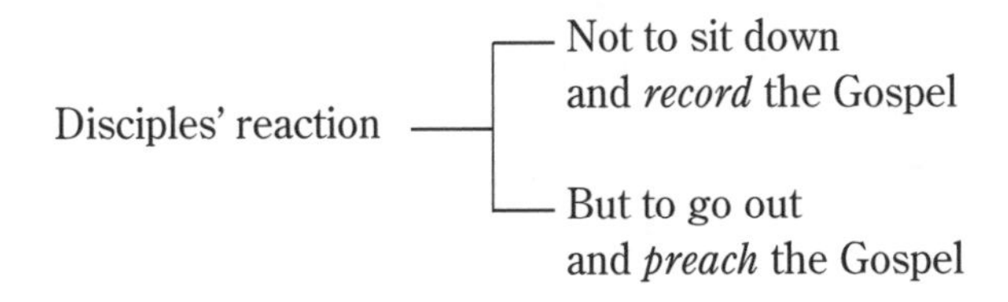

Notebook Sum up the reason for the urgency to "preach" the Gospel for entry in notebooks.

Preaching "urgency"
- Believed Jesus would return when Gospel was preached to all nations
- Believed Gospel could be preached to all nations within their own lifetime

5. LESSON INTERACTION

Exercise ❶ **Clarify** **(a, b)** Several years ago, the *Chicago Sun-Times* carried an article by columnist Bob Greene. It concerned the publication of a book by Arthur R. Butz called *The Hoax of the Twentieth Century* (Torrance, Calif.: Noontide Press, 1977).

The book argues that no extermination of Jews took place in Nazi concentration camps. Butz says that camps, like Auschwitz, merely "happened to have a high death rate." Understandably, the book outraged many, especially those who had lost family members in such camps. Greene writes:

In response . . . the Anti-Defamation League in Chicago said . . . "It is a documented fact. Millions of people were exterminated by the Nazis in death camps. American soldiers went into Auschwitz and found the bodies and the bones piled high. There is no debate over what happened. It is like saying atomic bombs were not dropped on Hiroshima and Nagasaki. We are simply talking about a part of history that everyone knows happened."

Butz's book would appeal to people more interested in "advancing a prejudice" than in "advancing the truth." It would also appeal to TV shows more interested in "sensationalism" than "professionalism."

Exercise ❷ **Clarify** Something like the Butz situation took place in the early Christian community. Some people began to distort the truth about Jesus and his teaching. Have the two assigned students read the passages cited in this exercise. Jude 4 reads:

Some godless people have slipped in unnoticed
among us, persons who distort the message
about the grace of our God
in order to excuse their immoral ways,
and who reject Jesus Christ,
our only Master and Lord.

In a similar vein, 1 John 4:1–2 reads:

Do not believe all who claim to have the Spirit,
but test them to find out if the spirit they have
comes from God.
For many false prophets have gone out everywhere.
This is how you will be able to know
whether it is God's Spirit:
anyone who acknowledges
that Jesus Christ came as a human being
has the Spirit who comes from God.

In other words, people begin to distort the truth about Jesus in *two ways:* (1) denying he was truly God and (2) denying he was truly human.

Jude says that *one reason* why people denied that Jesus was true God was "to excuse their immoral ways."

Exercise ❸ **Clarify** **(a, b)** Price entitled this droodle "Man in a Tuxedo Who Got Too Close to the Elevator Doors."

Another example of a droodle is the drawing below. Price entitled it "Fat Man Smoking Pipe in Soft Bed."

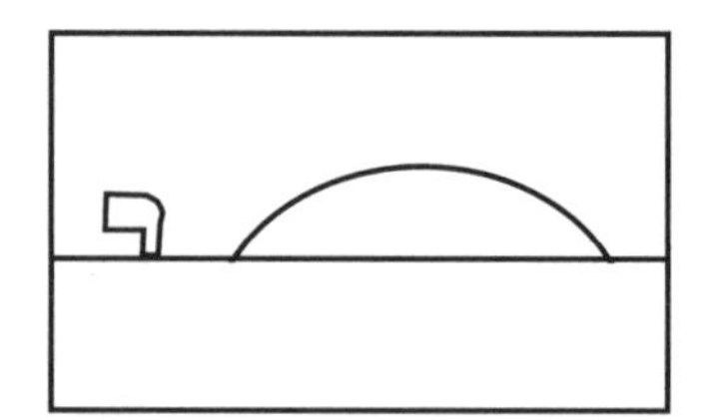

Exercise ❹ **Clarify** The Chicago student entitled the droodle in this exercise "Boy with Too Many Balloons."

Exercise ❺ **Activity** Have students create droodles of their own. Here are some examples of creativity by the author's students.

B.A.
M.A.
Ph.D.
———
0

The student called it "Three Degrees above Zero."

PAS

The student entitled it "Incomplete Pass."

The student entitled it "Hole in One."

Miniposter **Clarify** Ask: How is the miniposter on page 110 related to the content of this lesson? (The coming of the Spirit on Pentecost brought not only "light to the world" but also "joy to the world.")

Three Gospel Stages

LESSON 53

1. LESSON BACKGROUND

▶ *Catechism of the Catholic Church*, 126.

2. LESSON QUIZ

Perfect score = 10 points

1. Why was the first reaction of the disciples to go out and preach the Gospel rather than to record it for future generations? *(Lesson 52 review—1 point)*
2. List "three key results" of Pentecost. *(Lesson 52 notebook review—3 points)*
3. List and briefly describe the three stages the Gospels went through in reaching their final form. *(Lesson 53 preview—6 points)*

3. LESSON HOMEWORK

▶ **Return** Lesson 52 review questions (page 111).

▶ **Collect** Lesson 53 review questions (page 113).

▶ **Read** Lesson 54 ("Four Gospel Perspectives," pages 114–15).

▶ **Write** Lesson 54 review questions (page 115).

4. LESSON PRESENTATION

Point 1 **Read** Have student volunteers alternate reading aloud the core content of lesson 53.

▶ **Notebook** Develop the following diagram interactively with the students.

Stages	Life	What disciples experienced (what Jesus said and did)
	Oral	What apostles preached
	Written	What evangelists recorded

▶ **Clarify** Of special significance is the oral stage. It lasted about thirty years. During this period, parts of the Gospel began to take the shape they now have.

For example, the Eucharist, or Lord's Supper (1 Corinthians 11:20), was celebrated in memory of Jesus, as Jesus requested (Luke 22:17).

A part of each meal, therefore, was to recall a particular event or teaching of Jesus' life (much as we do in our modern Liturgy of the Word). Events related to the Eucharist, or Lord's Supper, were recalled in a special way.

▶ **Notebook** List four of these special events on the chalkboard for entry in student notebooks.

1. The wine miracle at Cana — John 2:1–10
2. The bread miracle by the sea — John 6:1–13
3. The Last Supper — Luke 22:17–20
4. The Emmaus Supper — Luke 24:13–35

Refer students to the photo on page 157 and have them identify each of these events on the tabernacle door shown there. Ask: How are these events related to the Lord's Supper in a special way?

▶ **Clarify** Christians also recalled Jesus' words and works on other special occasions. One was when they gathered to anoint and pray for the community's sick members. A first-century plate, unearthed in Palestine, recalls the instruction of James:

Are any among you sick?
They should send for the church elders,
who will pray for them and rub olive oil on them
in the name of the Lord. James 5:14

Archaeologists believe the plate was designed specifically for use in this sacramental ceremony.

▶ **Clarify** Christians recalled Jesus' teaching, also, when they met to discuss problems related to daily life in the world in which they lived.

For example, Jesus' followers were criticized for showing concern for sinners, for ignoring certain Sabbath observances, and for paying taxes to Rome. The community answered these criticisms by recalling what Jesus taught concerning these three things: sinners, the Sabbath, and taxes.

- Sinners: *"I have not come to call respectable people, but outcasts."* Mark 2:17
- Sabbath *"The Sabbath was made for the good of human beings; they were not made for the Sabbath."* Mark 2:27
- Taxes *"Pay to the Emperor what belongs to the Emperor, and pay to God what belongs to God."* Mark 12:17

Point ❷ **Clarify** It is hard for us in this age of the "printed word" to appreciate the role that the "oral word" played in certain civilizations. Alex Haley can be a help here.

As a boy, Haley used to sit on the front porch of his grandmother's house in Tennessee and listen to his grandmother tell stories about his ancestors. The stories went all the way back to Kinte ("Kin-tay"), who had been kidnapped into slavery while chopping wood near "Kambay Bolongo."

Fifty years later, Haley went to Africa to try to learn his ancestry. He talked with villagers in the back-country. He writes in his book *Roots:*

They told me something of which I never dreamed, of very old men, called griots *[who could recite from memory] . . . African history literally for as long as three days without ever repeating themselves. [Haley eventually found his ancestral village and its griot.]*

The old man . . . began to recite . . . the ancestral history of the Kinte clan. . . .

Two hours later Haley heard the name he was listening for: "Omorro Kinte begat Kunta." More amazing was the detail that followed: "Kunta went away from his village to chop wood . . . and he was never seen again." Haley writes:

My blood seemed to have congealed. This man . . . had no way in the world to know that he had just echoed what I had heard all through my boyhood years.

Through a similar oral process, the life and teaching of Jesus were preserved by the apostles.

5. LESSON INTERACTION

Exercise ❶ **Clarify** The floor shells correspond to the life stage of the Gospels: what the disciples experienced (what Jesus said and did). The beach shells correspond to the oral stage of the Gospel: what the apostles chose to preach to the people. Finally, the vase shells correspond to the written stage: the special things Jesus said or did that the evangelists wrote down in books. Point out that John ended his Gospel, saying:

There are many other things that Jesus did.
If they were all written down . . .
the whole world could not hold the books
that would be written. John 21:25

► **Notebook** We may sum up the comparison of the shells to the three gospel stages this way:

Stages	Floor shells	What disciples experienced
	Beach shells	What apostles preached
	Vase shells	What evangelists recorded

Exercise ❷ **Discuss** You might have the students answer this question privately on a sheet of paper before discussing it. This will "commit" them to one position and result in a more animated discussion.

Exercise ❸ **Clarify** Guided by the Holy Spirit, each of the four evangelists chose the final option. Each opted for a faith presentation of Jesus' words and works. Their reasons: they wanted not only to *inform* people of Jesus but also to *invite* them to believe in him. John writes:

These have been written in order that you may believe
that Jesus is the Messiah, the Son of God,
and that through your faith in him
you may have life. John 20:31

Exercise ❹ **Clarify** The four evangelists all chose the invitational approach.

To dramatize the purpose of the Scriptures the following story is often told. Repeat it to the class and ask the students what point the rabbi is making.

An old rabbi met a member of his congregation who began to boast: "I have been through our Torah many times." Rather than praise him, the rabbi said gently, "The important thing is not how often you have been through the Torah, but how often the Torah has been through you."

(The purpose of the four Gospels is not to re-create the words and works of Jesus, but to let them re-create us.)

Miniposter **Clarify** Ask: How is the miniposter on page 112 related to the Gospels? (It illustrates the point that the Holy Spirit illuminated Jesus' life so that the disciples saw it in a whole new way. It is this view of Jesus' life and teaching that we find in the Gospels. Recall that the video version of Jesus' life would be deprived of this illumination.)

Have the students attempt to solve the miniposter riddle in private, before opening it up to the entire class. The solution is as follows:

```
  888
   88
    8
    8
    8
-----
1,000
```

Photo **Clarify** Refer the students to the gospel fragment on page 112. Have them read the interlinear translation into English to get an idea of how the Greek language flows.

Four Gospel Perspectives

LESSON 54

1. LESSON BACKGROUND

▶ *Catechism of the Catholic Church,* 514–515.

2. LESSON QUIZ

Perfect score = 14 points

1. List and briefly explain the three approaches open to the evangelists when they sat down to record the Gospel. *(Lesson 53 review—6 points)*
2. List four events in the Gospel that relate to the Eucharist, or Lord's Supper, in a special way. *(Lesson 53 notebook review—4 points)*
3. Explain the four approaches by which tourists can arrive in New York City. *(Lesson 54 preview—4 points)*

3. LESSON HOMEWORK

▶ **Return** Lesson 53 review questions (page 113).

▶ **Collect** Lesson 54 review questions (page 115).

▶ **Read** Lesson 55 ("Mark's Gospel," pages 116–17).

▶ **Write** Lesson 55 review questions (page 117).

▶ **Appoint** Three students to mark their Bibles at the following places for ready references and reading for the next class (lesson 55).

1. Mark 14:51–52, 1 Peter 5:13, Colossians 4:10, Acts 12:12
2. Mark 8:29, 15:39
3. Mark 7:3, 14:12, 15:43, 3:17, 5:38–41, 7:9–13

4. LESSON PRESENTATION

Point ① **Read** Have student volunteers alternate reading aloud the core content of lesson 54.

▶ **Notebook** Have students enter the following diagram in their notebooks.

Synoptic ("similar") Gospels — Matthew / Mark / Luke

Point ② **Notebook** Jesus' teaching impacted his hearers at three personal levels: information (mind), formation (heart), transformation (soul). We may sum up these levels as follows:

Information	Mind taught	Truth understood
Formation	Heart moved	Truth valued
Transformation	Soul touched	Truth believed

▶ **Clarify** These three levels are illustrated in the life of Paul Stookey, who won fame with the singing group "Peter, Paul, and Mary."

In spite of Paul's fame, he was very unhappy and felt a deep "spiritual void" in his life.

The following report of Paul's efforts to fill that void is compiled from interviews with journalist Bob Combs and disc jockey Scott Ross. The report appeared in *Campus Life* magazine (May 1972) in an article entitled "Peter, Me, and Mary."

Before reading the report to the students, instruct them to identify the parts in the report that refer to the three levels where:

- Paul's mind was taught — Information level
- Paul's heart was moved — Formation level
- Paul's soul was touched — Transformation level

The report reads as follows:

If anybody
knew about man's spiritual nature back then
it was Bob Dylan. . . .
I thought he might give me some answers. . . .
So I told him about all the thinking I'd been doing. . . .
And it went like that for an hour and a half,
till I ended up leaving his house
with nothing but my own answers.

But he did say two things to me.
One was: "Go back to your high school.
Get a sense of what it is you are, from where you came."
The other thing he said was to read the Scriptures. . . .

I started reading the New Testament. Dylan was right,
because I began discovering that all the truths I sought
were contained in the life of this man
who was being described in the New Testament.

It was fantastic. . . . He set a good example . . .
but it never occurred to me
that he could really be the Son of God.

I started carrying the Scriptures around with me. . . .
It was almost like having a brother with you. . . .

Then I was backstage
during a concert in Austin, Tex., once,
walking along click clack, click clack
across the hall . . .
and there was this cat standing there
in a Navajo jacket. . . .
And he said, "Could I talk to you?" . . .

I sorta walked close to him and said,
"What is it you'd like to talk to me about?"
I wanted to be sort of a father to him.
And he said,
"I want to talk to you about the Lord!"
WHACK! . . . Somehow this guy
made all the reading in Scripture make sense. . . .
He explained to me [that Jesus] . . . says
in the Scriptures, "Behold I knock; if any man asks me
to enter I come and dwell with him."
And I said, "What does that mean . . . ?"
And he said,
"You ask him to come in and live in your life."

So, wow, I started to pray with him,
and I asked Jesus
to come in and take over my life.
And I started to cry and he started to cry. . . .

When you say, "All right, Lord . . .
point out where you want me to go" . . . even then
you are continually being called back
into this world. . . . There is a slipping.
But once you've seen the Light . . .
you just keep coming back to it.

The three parts of the report that refer to the three levels are as follows:

- **Information level:** *All the truths I sought were contained in the life of this man who was being described in the New Testament.*
- **Formation level:** *It was fantastic. . . . He set a good example.*
- **Transformation level:** *Somehow this guy made all the reading in Scripture make sense . . . [and he explained how Jesus said] . . . "Behold I knock; if any man asks me to enter I come and dwell with him." . . . So, wow, I started to pray with him, and I asked Jesus to come in and take over my life. And I started to cry and he started to cry.*

Ask: What does Paul mean when he says that even after accepting Jesus, "You are continually being called back into the world. . . . But once you've seen the Light . . . you just keep coming back to it"?

Point ❸ **Clarify** Self-help people have an expression: "Name it, claim it, and make it your own!"

How does this expression apply to people in need of help? Take alcoholics. When they finally admit they are alcoholic, they *name* their problem, *claim* it, and *make it their own.* As a result, the alcohol no longer controls them; they control it.

It is the same with ourselves and reading the events of Jesus' life in the Gospel. We must *name* them, *claim* them, and *make them our own.*

In other words, we do not just read the miracles of Jesus and theorize about them. We name them, claim them, and make them our own.

Ask: How can we go about naming, claiming, and making gospel events our own?

(Perhaps the best way to name, claim, and make the gospel events our own is through prayer. Recall Paul Stookey's prayer with his friend.)

5. LESSON INTERACTION

Exercise ❶ **Clarify** Ask: What is there about your relationship with each of these people that would make them describe you in different ways?

Exercise ❷ **Clarify** Two other explanations might be (1) that all three used a single common witness (either Peter, James, or John) and reported a story in a slightly different way, or (2) that each used a different witness (Peter, James, or John) and reported as that witness reported it.

Exercise ❸ **Clarify** Experts say that when people adapt the story of another, they often add details of the story that they have obtained from other sources. Thus experts say that the simplest-told story is probably the original one (Mark).

Exercise ❹ **Clarify** Mark omits "face," "pray," or "brothers." Luke adds "face," "pray," "hill," and "week." Matthew adds "brothers," "face," and "sun." Assuming two evangelists adapted a third one, the original account probably belonged to Mark. On the other hand, Luke's account is noticeably different. Perhaps Matthew and Mark followed one source, and Luke a different one. Or perhaps each evangelist adapted the same account to fit his unique purpose in writing for his specific audience.

CHAPTER TEN: Good News (pages 116–17)

Mark's Gospel

LESSON **55**

1. LESSON BACKGROUND

▶ *Catechism of the Catholic Church*, 464–483.

2. LESSON QUIZ

Perfect score = 14 points

1. List the probable times and the probable primary audience for which each of the four evangelists wrote his Gospel. *(Lesson 54 review—8 points)*
2. List the three synoptic Gospels and explain briefly why we give them this name. *(Lesson 54 notebook review—4 points)*
3. List the two main points into which Mark divides his Gospel. *(Lesson 55 preview—2 points)*

3. LESSON HOMEWORK

▶ **Return** Lesson 54 review questions (page 115).

▶ **Collect** Lesson 55 review questions (page 117).

▶ **Read** Lesson 56 ("Matthew's Gospel," pages 118–19).

▶ **Write** Lesson 56 review questions (page 119).

▶ **Appoint** Two students to mark their Bibles at the following places for ready references and reading for the next class (lesson 56).

1. "When Jesus finished . . .": Matthew 7:28, 11:1, 13:53, 19:1, 26:1
2. Matching Jesus' life with biblical prophecies: Matthew 1:23; 2:6, 15, 18, 23

4. LESSON PRESENTATION

Point 1 **Read** Have student volunteers alternate reading aloud the core content of lesson 55.

▶ **Notebook** Develop the following diagrams interactively with the students for entry in their notebooks. Have the appointed students read the passages from the Bible.

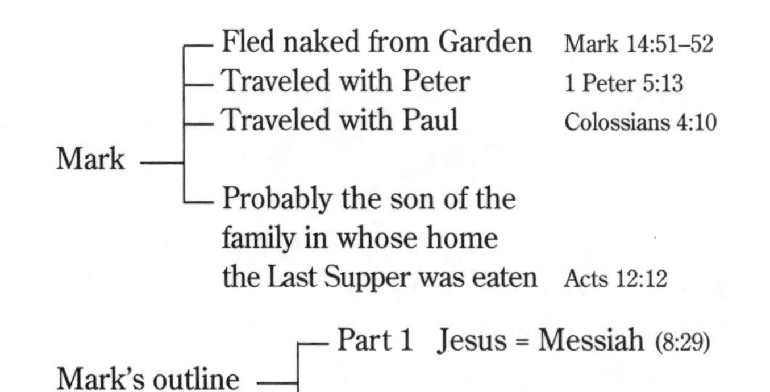

Mark's outline
- Part 1 Jesus = Messiah (8:29)
- Part 2 Jesus = God's Son (15:39)

▶ **Notebook** Develop the following diagram interactively for entry in student notebooks.

It lists the clues that tell us that the audience for whom Mark wrote primarily (Christians being persecuted in Rome) was made up largely of Gentiles (non-Jews). Mark takes special pains to explain Jewish customs and Jewish words for them.

Have the appointed student read the passages aloud to illustrate the point being made.

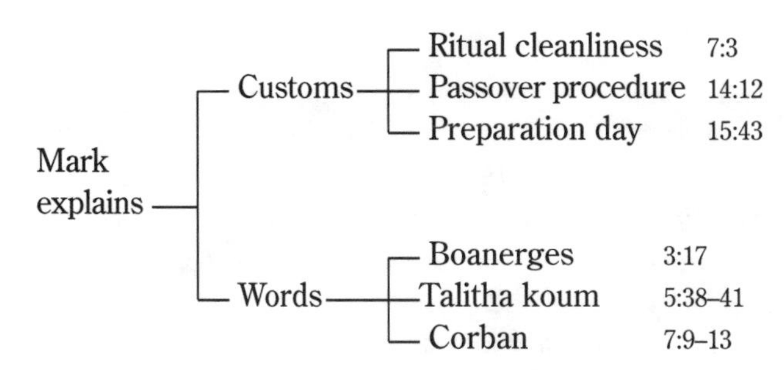

▶ **Clarify** Other words that Mark explains are *ephphatha* (7:34), *Golgotha* (15:22), *Eloi* (15:34). You might have students check these, also. Modern students are like the Roman Gentiles, unfamiliar with the meaning of Jewish words.

5. LESSON INTERACTION

Exercise 1 **Clarify** Describing Christianity's origin, Tacitus says it took its name from Christ, "who was executed during Tiberius's reign by sentence of Pontius Pilate."

Have the students turn to the photo on page 163, where the names of Tiberius Caesar and Pontius Pilate appear on a dedication stone, found in 1961 at Caesarea.

Have students check Caesarea's location on the map on page 107 of their textbooks.

Tacitus gives this dramatic description of the persecution of Christians in his *Annals:*

First, known members of the sect were seized. Then, on their information, crowds were seized, not so much on arson charges as out of hate. . . .

Unusual brutality attended their execution; they were dressed in animal skins and torn to pieces by enraged dogs; they were put on crosses and, at nighttime, burned as torches to light up the darkness.

Nero sponsored the exhibitions in his Gardens. He also held performances in his Circus [racetrack], mixing with the crowds and dressed in the garb of a charioteer. . . .

Although the sect deserved some punishment, a feeling of pity developed for them. For it seemed clear to many that they were executed not for the state's sake, but because of the madness of one man.

Exercise ❷ **Read** You might share with the students this moving prayer, written by a student. It will help them get started on writing their own prayers. (You might take the time to have them do this right in class. Then collect the prayers and read the better ones at the next class.)

Jesus, I'm only fifteen years old. My parents and two younger brothers became Christians about five years ago.

From the beginning it was hard to live as you taught, especially when many of my friends ridicule your teachings, like "turn the other cheek." But with your help, my parents and one of my brothers have persevered in following you.

My other brother has stopped following you, because he says it doesn't make sense to die for something that he finds it hard to believe in. This pains my parents, but they are very patient with him. I pray for him.

I will go to my death praying the Lord's Prayer, as you taught. I will also be offering my life for my brother's conversion back to you.

I am proud to die as you did. And like you I now say, "I forgive my persecutors. They do not know what they are doing."

I hope to see you face-to-face in paradise two hours from now.

Exercise ❸ **Clarify** Mark's style of having bystanders ask a question and leaving it unanswered facilitates the invitational approach. Recall that its purpose is to invite the reader to answer the same important question that the disciples did: "Who is this man?"

Exercise ❹ **Clarify** *Desert lion* symbol: Isaiah says that John will come out of the desert like a lion, crying out and startling the people.

Sacrificial bull symbol: The first scene of Luke's Gospel is that of Zechariah offering sacrifice in the Temple.

Man symbol: Matthew opens his Gospel with the family tree of Jesus, who enters the world as a human being like ourselves.

High-flying eagle symbol: From a literary point of view, John's Gospel opens in a "lofty" or "soaring" way.

Some students are incapable of connecting the text and the symbols. But this doesn't mean we should not try to stretch their minds in an aesthetic way.

Miniposter **Clarify** Refer the students to the miniposter on page 116. Ask: How does the saying on this poster relate to the content of this lesson? (Mark's portrait of Jesus stresses the "Suffering Messiah." It reminds the Christians of Rome that their Lord and God suffered, and they, too, can expect to suffer if they want to follow him into glory.)

Photo **Clarify** Refer the students to the photo of the Colosseum of Rome on page 116.

Built around 80 C.E., it is four tiers high and resembles a modern football stadium. The arched openings once housed statues of Roman heroes.

The Colosseum was frequently flooded for water spectacles, including sea battles in which hundreds of slaves met death. It is reported that the water turned red from the blood.

The Colosseum also witnessed gladiatorial combats. Begun in 264 B.C.E., these violent affairs continued until 400 C.E., when they were outlawed. To celebrate Rome's thousandth birthday, two thousand gladiators were billed to die.

For comic relief, contests were staged between cripples, dwarfs, and women fighting with wooden swords. These sickening bouts served as "appetizers" for the main event.

George Bernard Shaw used the Colosseum as the backdrop for his mock heroic play, *Androcles and the Lion.*

Based on a first-century legend, the play involved a Christian who had befriended a lion. Later, the Christian was condemned to die in the arena. His would-be executioner turned out to be the same lion, who remembered Androcles' kindness. When the lion refused to harm Androcles, the emperor granted Androcles' freedom.

Matthew's Gospel

LESSON **56**

1. LESSON BACKGROUND

▶ *Catechism of the Catholic Church,* 542–546.

2. LESSON QUIZ

Perfect score = 6 points

1. For whom did Mark write his Gospel, primarily, and what portrait of Jesus does he stress? *(Lesson 55 review—2 points)*
2. Why does Mark take special pains to explain Jewish customs and words, and with what two people did he frequently travel in preaching the Gospel? *(Lesson 55 notebook review—3 points)*
3. Why does Matthew take special pains to match up Jesus' life with Old Testament prophecies? *(Lesson 56 preview—1 point)*

3. LESSON HOMEWORK

▶ **Return** Lesson 55 review questions (page 117).

▶ **Collect** Lesson 56 review questions (page 119).

▶ **Read** Lesson 57 ("Luke's Gospel," pages 120–21).

▶ **Write** Lesson 57 review questions (page 121).

▶ **Appoint** Two students to prepare Bible readings:
1. Luke 7:11–17, 8:1–3, 15:8–10, 18:1–18 (lesson 57, exercise 3)
2. Luke 18:9–14, 19:1–9 (lesson 57, exercise 4)

4. LESSON PRESENTATION

Point ❶ **Read** Have student volunteers alternate reading aloud the core content of lesson 56.

▶ **Notebook** Develop the following diagram interactively for entry in student notebooks. It illustrates the orderly approach that Matthew takes in his Gospel.

Matthew's structure		
	Prologue	Jesus' early years
	Body	Jesus' kingdom teaching
	Epilogue	Jesus' death and rising

Point ❷ **Clarify** Matthew's love of order appears, also, in his prologue and his epilogue. Matthew matches his prologue reference to Jesus' "birth" (2:1) with his epilogue reference to Jesus' "rebirth," or resurrection (28:1).

Likewise, Matthew matches Jesus' Jordan "baptism" (3:16) with his cross "baptism" (20:22) ("cup of suffering," which Mark calls a baptism [Mark 10:38]). Finally, he matches Jesus' desert "temptation" (4:3) with Jesus' cross "temptation" (27:40).

▶ **Notebook** Develop the following schematic of Matthew's Gospel for entry in student notebooks. It shows the "chiasmic" pattern and the five-part "Torah-like" structure of the "body" of Matthew's Gospel.

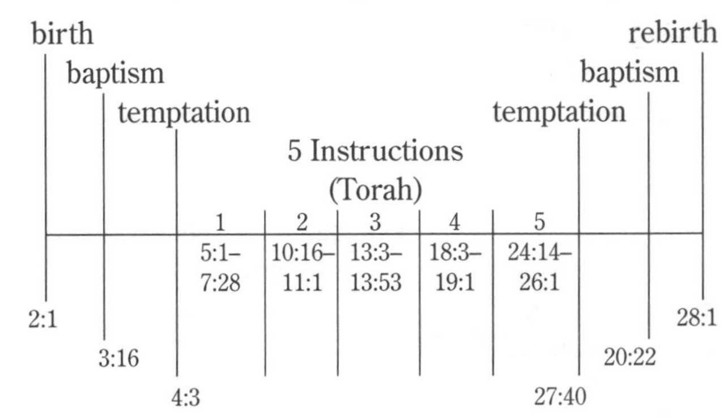

Another example of a "chiasmic" pattern is this quotation of Jesus from Isaiah:

Sluggish indeed is this people's heart.
They have scarcely heard with their ears,
they have firmly closed their eyes,
otherwise they might see with their eyes,
and hear with their ears,
and understand with their hearts.

Adapted from Matthew 13:15

The end words of the phrases form a chiasmic pattern:
heart, ears, eyes ———— eyes, ears, heart.

▶ **Clarify** Matthew begins his Gospel with a family tree of Jesus' ancestors. He ends the passage, saying:

So then, there were fourteen generations
from Abraham to David, and fourteen
from David to the exile in Babylon, and fourteen
from then to the birth of the Messiah. Matthew 1:17

This ending highlights the three great eras and figures of Jewish history: Abraham, David, and Jesus.

5. LESSON INTERACTION

Exercise 1 **Clarify** The phrase "according to" leaves open the possibility that a "disciple of Matthew" could have written Matthew's Gospel. In other words, it simply states that this is the Gospel that Matthew preached "orally" for many years.

The media frequently say something like this: "According to the president's press secretary, the president had no knowledge of this or that particular statement or episode." In other words, the press secretary acts as the president's official spokesperson.

Exercise 2 **Discuss** Matthew traces Jesus' family tree back to Abraham. Luke traces it back to Adam.

Matthew writes for Jews, who focus on Abraham as their "father," while Luke writes for Gentiles, who focus on Adam as their "father." In other words, Matthew focuses on Jesus as the "savior of the Jews," while Luke focuses on Jesus as the "savior of all people."

Exercise 3 **Clarify (a, b)** The pain that Matthew takes to show that Jesus fulfills the Old Testament prophecies is a clue that he is writing, primarily, for Jews, who would be very concerned about this.

Also, the pain he takes to match the events of Jesus' life with the Old Testament prophecies is intended to demonstrate and document that Jesus is the "long-awaited, promised Messiah."

► **Clarify** Matthew's reference to Mary's virginity might be taken up at this point. Matthew says that Mary and Joseph were engaged to be married when Joseph discovered Mary was already with child. This caused Joseph deep anguish, until he learned that Mary had conceived by the Holy Spirit.

The engagement of Mary and Joseph is of special interest. Unlike modern engagements, ancient engagements had the force of marriage. Many times the two young people did not know each other, because the marriage was arranged by their parents—sometimes even before they were born.

One of the purposes of the engagement, or "betrothal," was to give the young people a chance to get to know each other before coming together as husband and wife.

Significantly, if the young man died during the engagement period, the young woman was his legal widow.

In *Beyond East and West,* John Wu says that he and his wife never saw each other before their wedding. They were engaged when they were "barely six years of age." Wu writes:

To the Western reader, the old Chinese marriage system must appear inconceivable. I remember when I told my dear friend . . . about it, he simply could not believe it. . . . On my part, I was amazed by his amazement and amused by his amusement. I said to him . . . "Did you choose your parents, your brothers and your sisters? And yet you love them all the same."

► **Discuss** In India today there are two ways of getting a marriage partner. The first is sometimes called the "love" way. This means that the partners seek each other out, date, and make their own choice. The second way is sometimes called the "family" way. This means the two families decide. Interestingly, the "family" way has proved more stable (fewer divorces). Ask: How do you account for this? (Family support, etc.)

► **Discuss** Another way of getting a marriage partner in modern times is the "computer" way. Data on possible partners is fed into a computer, and it does the selection. Here are some questions taken from an actual computer-dating application:

1. How much formal education have you had?
2. What music do you enjoy most?
3. How religious are you?
4. What is your favorite leisure-time activity?
5. What is the financial status you are accustomed to?

Have the students evaluate the three ways of picking a marriage partner (love, family, computer).

Miniposter **Clarify** The "decoded reading" of the poster on page 118 is as follows:

"A *backward glance*
at the prophecies
enabled me to say,
'I understand.'"

Ask: How is the poster related to this lesson?

Photo **Clarify** Jesus' point in the photo caption on page 119 seems to be this: Allow no one to set limits on your service to another. It should not be governed by law, but by love and your own free will.

Luke's Gospel

LESSON **57**

1. LESSON BACKGROUND

▶ *Catechism of the Catholic Church,* 2419–2449.

2. LESSON QUIZ

Perfect score = 10 points

1. Why is the phrase "The Gospel *according to* Matthew" significant, and what portrait of Jesus does Matthew stress? *(Lesson 56 review—2 points)*
2. List and explain the threefold structure that Matthew gives to his Gospel. *(Lesson 56 notebook review—6 points)*
3. What clue do we find in Luke's Acts of the Apostles that tells us that Luke frequently traveled with Paul, and what portrait of Jesus does Luke paint for us in his Gospel? *(Lesson 57 preview—2 points)*

3. LESSON HOMEWORK

▶ **Return** Lesson 56 review questions (page 119).

▶ **Collect** Lesson 57 review questions (page 121).

▶ **Read** Lesson 58 ("John's Gospel," pages 122–23).

▶ **Write** Lesson 58 review questions (page 123).

▶ **Appoint** Four students to prepare Bible readings:
1. John 13:21–26, 19:25–27
2. John 2:1–11, 3:1–5, 5:1–14
3. John 6:1–52
4. John 7:37–39, 9:1–7, 17:9–19

4. LESSON PRESENTATION

Point 1 **Read** Have student volunteers alternate reading aloud the core content of lesson 57.

▶ **Notebook** Develop the following diagrams interactively for entry in student notebooks.

They summarize four key points: Luke's identity, Luke's Gospel structure, Luke's audience, and Luke's portrait of Jesus.

Luke
- Paul's coworker — 2 Timothy 4:11
- Gentile — Colossians 4:11, 14
- Physician — Colossians 4:14

Luke's Gospel
- Prologue (preministry) — 1:5–4:13
- Galilean ministry — 4:14–9:50
- Journey to Jerusalem — 9:51–19:27
- Jerusalem ministry — 19:28–21:38
- Epilogue (death-res.) — 22:1–24:53

Luke's audience (non-Jewish)
- Locates towns — Capernaum 4:31; Emmaus 24:13
- Explains customs — Passover 22:1

Luke's portrait (compassion)
- Happy the poor — 6:20
- Happy the hungry — 6:21
- Happy the sorrowful — 6:21

Point 2 **Clarify** Luke's prologue deals with the birth and preministry of Jesus. Of special interest is the message of the angel to Mary, concerning Jesus' birth. The angel says:

ANGEL *You will become pregnant and give birth*
to a son, and you will name him Jesus. . . .
The Lord God will make him a king,
as his ancestor David was, and . . .
his kingdom will never end!

MARY *I am a virgin. How, then, can this be?*

ANGEL *The Holy Spirit will come on you,*
and God's power will rest upon you.
For this reason the holy child will be called
the Son of God. . . .

MARY *I am the Lord's servant;*
may it happen to me as you have said.

Luke 1:31–38

Two remarkable things stand out in this passage.

First, the angel identifies Jesus with the promise to David concerning a Messiah (2 Samuel 7:16).

Second, the angel explains how Mary will conceive ("The Holy Spirit will come on you, and God's power will rest upon you").

The Hebrew word that is translated "rest upon" is rarely found in the Bible. One place it is found, however, is in the Book of Exodus.

There it is used to describe a mysterious cloud that "covered" ("rested upon") the "Tent" in which was housed the ark of the covenant (containing the stone tablets on which the Ten Commandments were written). At the moment the cloud covered ("rested upon") the meeting tent, "the dazzling light of the LORD's presence filled it" (Exodus 40:34).

Luke compares Mary's body to the meeting tent and the Holy Spirit to the cloud that "rested upon" it. Mary's body is then filled with the LORD's presence (infant Jesus), just as the meeting tent was.

Point ❸ **Clarify** Jesus showed special concern for the poor. For example, on one occasion Jesus said: "Happy are you poor; the Kingdom of God is yours!"

Jesus does not present poverty as something good in itself. Absolutely not!

Rather, poverty is good "as a means to an end." "Happy are you poor, because your poverty has made you turn to God and put all your trust in God. As a result, you have turned your plight into a 'means' to salvation. How happy you are because of that. The Kingdom of God is yours."

Point ❹ **Clarify** Some students may inquire about the concluding reference to the Statue of Liberty.

The statue stands on Liberty Island in New York Harbor. Towering 150 feet (half a football field) into the air, it was given to the United States in 1884 by France as a gesture of friendship.

The artist, Gustav Eiffel (of Eiffel Tower fame), cast it in copper (hence the greenish color). The symbols may be of interest.

Symbols		
	Right hand	Torch of freedom
	Left arm	Tablet with date 1776
	Feet	Shackles
	Head	Sunburst of new day (spikes)

The inscription (quoted in the textbook) is part of a poem, "The New Colossus," by Emma Lazarus. It was placed at its base in 1903.

5. LESSON INTERACTION

Exercise ❶ **Discuss** Luke's reference to "sweating blood" and the correct Greek word for "convulsions" supports Paul's reference to Luke as "our dear doctor."

Paul suffered from a "painful physical ailment" (2 Corinthians 12:7), and this may have been one of the reasons why Luke was traveling with him.

Exercise ❷ **Discuss** By its nature, the medical profession has always attracted service-minded people, which Luke appears to have been.

An example of a "lively social conscience" appeared in *Maryknoll* magazine some years back. It was written by the mother of a South Korean poet whose name was Kim Chi Ha. She told how her son had just been sentenced to life in prison in South Korea. What crime did he commit?

It was this. In a number of poems he had recently written he protested the government's treatment of the poor and oppressed. Kim Chi Ha's mother backed her son's position totally. She said:

Kim Chi Ha has said on many occasions . . . Jesus was always for the poor. . . . We, too, if we are followers of his, must be for the poor and the oppressed. . . . Society puts these people down, but the gospel tells us they are important. . . . We must take this world we live in seriously.

Kim Chi Ha never lost his deep-down joy and sense of humor throughout his ordeal. For example, when an angry judge added another seven years to his life sentence, Kim Chi Ha joked to his mother, "I must stay in prison seven years after I die!"

Kim Chi Ha's mother ended her article, saying that she was proud of her son. She said that she was going to continue his work of speaking out in behalf of the poor and the oppressed.

Exercise ❸ **Discuss** The common thread that runs through the four references in this exercise is that each deals with women, who were often treated as second-class citizens in Jesus' time.

Luke's inclusion of these episodes in his Gospel jibes with the portrait of the "compassionate Messiah" that he wished to paint.

Have the appointed student read the four episodes aloud for further discussion.

Exercise ❹ **Discuss** The tax collectors were also regarded as traitors to their Jewish brothers and sisters, by going to work for pagan Rome.

Have the appointed student read the two episodes aloud for further discussion.

Miniposter **Clarify** Ask: How does the miniposter on page 120 relate to the gospel portrait of Jesus that Luke paints?

John's Gospel

1. LESSON BACKGROUND

▶ *Catechism of the Catholic Church,* 1024–1029.

2. LESSON QUIZ

Perfect score = 6 points

1. Luke locates Jewish towns and describes Jewish customs. What does this say about the audience for which he wrote? *(Lesson 57 review—1 point)*
2. Who is the person who refers to Luke as "our dear doctor"? *(Lesson 57 notebook review—1 point)*
3. List four ways John's Gospel differs from the synoptic Gospels. *(Lesson 58 preview—4 points)*

3. LESSON HOMEWORK

▶ **Return** Lesson 57 review questions (page 121).

▶ **Collect** Lesson 58 review questions (page 123).

▶ **Read** Lesson 59 ("Birth," pages 124–25).

▶ **Write** Lesson 59 review questions (page 125).

4. LESSON PRESENTATION

Point ❶ **Read** Have student volunteers alternate reading aloud the core content of lesson 58.

▶ **Clarify** Have the appointed student read aloud the two passages that refer to John as the disciple Jesus loved: 13:21–26 and 19:25–27.

Point out that the second passage (John 19:25–27) portrays Jesus commending Mary to John's care. This raises two questions.

First, what about the claim that Mary had other children besides Jesus? Christians who support this claim cite Mark 6:3, which speaks of Jesus' brothers and sisters. In response to this citation, we need to keep in mind that ancient peoples often spoke of relatives and friends as "brothers and sisters." For example, Paul does this often. (See Philemon 1, 7, 16, and 20, to mention only a few.)

The second question is this: If Mary had other children besides Jesus, why would Jesus ask John to take care of his mother after his death? Wouldn't the "other children" do this?

Point ❷ **Discuss** Ask: To whom does "Word" refer in John's prologue (quoted in the textbook)? ("Word" refers to Jesus.) We sometimes hear the expression that "God has spoken to us in three words: cosmic word, prophetic word, and incarnate (flesh) word.

The cosmos is often referred to as God's "cosmic word" to humankind. It is the "first word" God spoke: "'Let there be light'—and light appeared."

Just as a song reflects a songwriter's personality, and a house's furnishings an owner's personality, so the cosmos reflects something of God's personality: God's power, intelligence, love, majesty. In this sense it is a "word" that tells us something about God. Paul has this cosmic word in mind when he says:

Since God created the world, his invisible qualities,
both his eternal power and his divine nature,
have been clearly seen; they are perceived
in the things that God has made. Romans 1:20

The "second word" God spoke was the prophetic word. Hebrews refers to it when it says:

In the past God spoke to our ancestors many times
and in many ways through the prophets. Hebrews 1:1

It is this prophetic word that is recorded for us in the books of the Old Testament.

The "third word" God spoke to us is the incarnate word. Hebrews continues:

In these last days
[God] has spoken to us through his Son. . . .
He reflects the brightness of God's glory and
is the exact likeness of God's own being. Hebrews 1:2–3

Thus Jesus says to Philip, "Whoever has seen me has seen the Father" (John 14:9).

And so Jesus is the "Word" in the sense that he reveals to us what God is like.

But Jesus is the "Word" in still another sense. Besides revealing to us what God is like, Jesus also reveals to us what we should be like. Jesus is the perfect picture of what we should strive to become. He is the perfect image of imperfect humans.

Point ③ **Notebook** Develop the following two diagrams for entry in student notebooks.

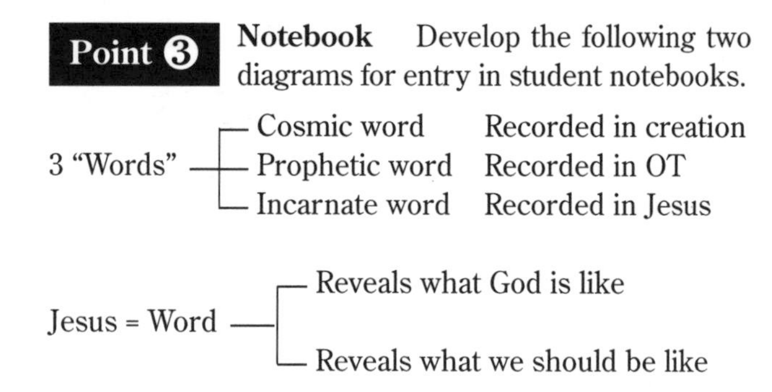

► **Notebook** John's Gospel may be structured this way:

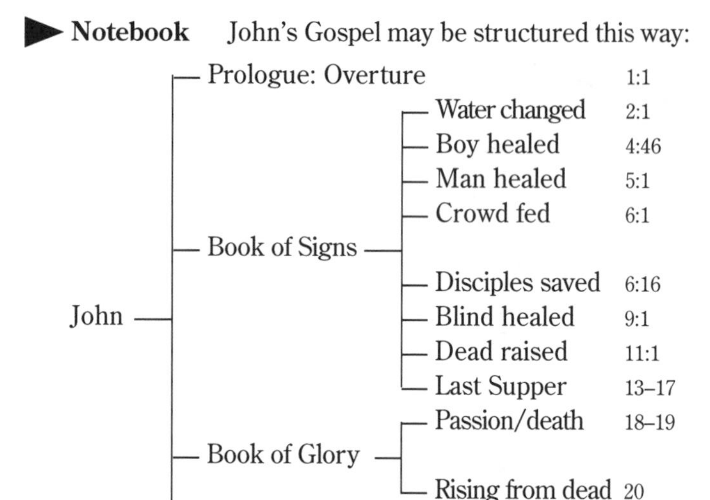

► **Clarify** The "Book of Signs" gets its name from the fact that John refers to Jesus' miracles as "signs" (in the original Greek): 2:11, 4:54, 6:14, 6:26, 11:47.

The "Book of Glory" gets its name from Jesus' words to his Father at the Last Supper:

"Father, the hour has come. Give glory to your Son,
so that the Son may give glory to you. . . .
I have shown your glory on earth; . . .
Father! Give me glory in your presence now,
the same glory I had with you
before the world was made." John 17:1, 4–5

Point ④ **Clarify** When God appeared to Moses in the burning bush and told him to lead the Israelites out of Egypt, Moses asked God:

"When I go to the Israelites and say to them,
'The God of your ancestors sent me to you,'
they will ask me, 'What is his name?'
So what can I tell them?"
God said, "I am who I am.
You must tell them: 'The one who is called I AM
has sent me to you.' " Exodus 3:13–14

It is against this background that we must read Jesus' words, where he repeatedly identifies himself with God's sacred name. For example, he says, "I am":

"the bread of life"	6:35
"the light of the world"	8:12
"the good shepherd"	10:11
"the resurrection and the life"	11:25
"the way, the truth, and the life"	14:6

5. LESSON INTERACTION

Exercise ① **Review** This exercise is a review of some key ideas that have been presented in the past four lessons.

Mark: Writing mainly for Roman Christians who were suffering greatly (persecution), Mark wanted to stress that Jesus also suffered greatly.

Matthew: Writing mainly for Jews who were schooled in the teachings of Moses and the prophets, Matthew wanted to stress that Jesus brought these teachings to completion.

Luke: Writing mainly for lower-class Greek Gentiles, Luke wanted to stress Jesus' concern for the second-class citizens of society.

John: Writing at a later date for all Christians, John wanted to stress that Jesus came to give us eternal life. Jesus said, "I have come in order that you might have life—life in all its fullness" (John 10:10).

► **Review** **(b)** That Luke's primary audience was unfamiliar with Jewish geography and customs is clear from the fact that Luke informs his readers that:

Capernaum is "a town in Galilee" 4:31
Festival of Unleavened Bread
is called "the Passover" 22:1

► **Review** **(c)** John's Gospel differs from the synoptics in four ways. John (1) rarely uses story format, (2) identifies Jesus by God's name "I AM," (3) identifies Jesus immediately as the Messiah, (4) uses the concept "Eternal Life" in place of "God's kingdom."

Exercise ② **Activity** This exercise is self-explanatory. Have the appointed student read several or all of the passages aloud, in preparation for showing the link between the episodes narrated and the sacraments of the Church.

Exercise ③ **Activity** Take time out in class to have the students compose their own "three-minute replay" prayer. Have volunteers read their prayers aloud. Or you might collect the prayers, read them before the next class, and share the best ones with the students.

Miniposter **Clarify** Ask: How does the saying on the miniposter on page 122 relate to this lesson on John's Gospel?

CHAPTER ELEVEN: Preministry (pages 124–25)

Birth

LESSON **59**

1. LESSON BACKGROUND

▶ *Catechism of the Catholic Church,* 456–463.

2. LESSON QUIZ

Perfect score = 10 points

1. How does John begin his Gospel, and what does it tip us off to about his approach to Jesus? *(Lesson 58 review—2 points)*
2. List and describe the three "words" by which God has spoken to us. *(Lesson 58 notebook review—6 points)*
3. Explain how the angel's announcement of Jesus' birth, made to the shepherds, previews Jesus' identity and mission. *(Lesson 59 preview—2 points)*

3. LESSON HOMEWORK

▶ **Return** Lesson 58 review questions (page 123).

▶ **Collect** Lesson 59 review questions (page 125).

▶ **Read** Lesson 60 ("Presentation," pages 126–27).

▶ **Write** Lesson 60 review questions (page 127).

4. LESSON PRESENTATION

Point ❶ **Read** Have student volunteers alternate reading aloud the core content of lesson 59.

▶ **Clarify** Stress two facts about Luke's description of the angel's announcement made to the shepherds regarding Jesus' birth.

First, stress that Jesus was born near Bethlehem.

Ask: What was the fate of lambs born near Bethlehem? (Most were sacrificed in nearby Jerusalem.)

Second, stress the fact that the angel appeared to the shepherds at night in a field near Bethlehem.

Ask: How does the fact that the shepherds had their flocks in a field at night, rather than in a pen or a cave, suggest the time of year when Jesus was born? (He was probably born in the spring during lambing season.)

▶ **Clarify** Stress that the above two facts (that Jesus was born in Bethlehem and that the shepherds had their flocks in a field at night) act as a poetic preview to Jesus' own *identity* and *mission.* He is the "lamb of God" destined to be "sacrificed" in nearby Jerusalem.

▶ **Clarify** Stress the fact that Jesus was born in a stable and placed in a feed box.

Ask: How does this serve as a poetic preview to Jesus' future *lifestyle?*

Point ❷ **Clarify** Locate Christianity within the context of other prominent world religions. All dates below (except for Islam, which is C.E.) are B.C.E. and approximate.

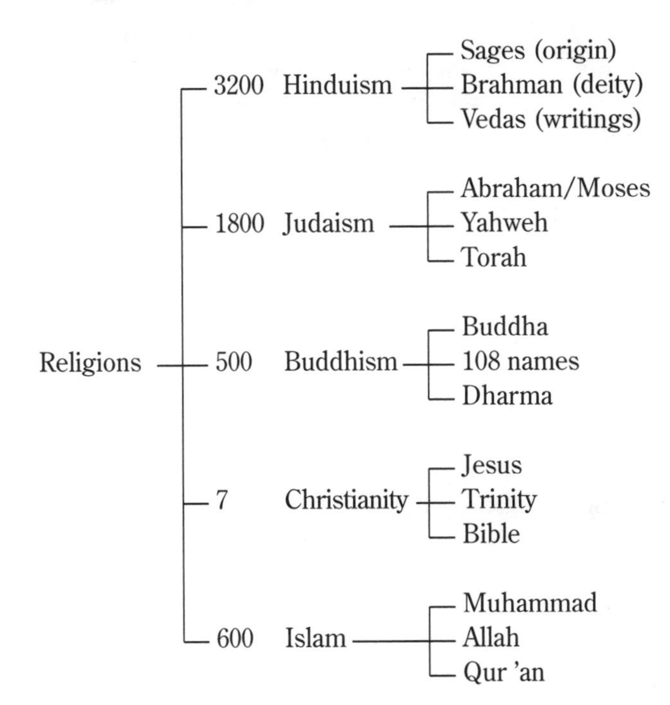

Point ❸ **Clarify** Writing around the year 100 C.E., the Jewish historian Josephus says Herod died four years before the beginning of the Christian era. He says Herod's death took place right after an eclipse. Astronomers have verified that an eclipse took place in March in 4 B.C.E.

Using the slaughter of the innocents as a reference, Jesus was apparently born two or three years before Herod's death. This would put Jesus' birth in 6 or 7 B.C.E.

▶ **Clarify** The present date for Christmas, December 25, was chosen by Roman Christians around 350 C.E.

December 25 was listed on ancient Roman calendars as a great pagan feast day: *Dies Natalis Invicti Sol* ("Birthday of the Unconquerable Sun").

December 25 is the day when the sun begins to reassert its power over darkness. The days prior to the 25th grow shorter and shorter. On the 25th they begin to lengthen. (Winter solstice—*sol* ["sun"] + *sistere* ["to stop"], i.e., the sun stops and reverses itself—occurs when the earth is farthest from the celestial equator.)

Christians saw Jesus as the true "unconquerable sun," the "light of the world." His birthday was the reassertion of the "power of light" over the "power of darkness."

Point ❹ **Clarify** Luke begins his narrative of the birth of Jesus in Bethlehem, saying:

At that time Emperor Augustus ordered a census
to be taken throughout the Roman Empire. . . .
Everyone . . . went to register himself,
each to his own hometown. Luke 2:1, 3

Returning to one's hometown for a census registration was once questioned by some historians. There is no question about it now, however. An Egyptian papyrus, discovered by archaeologists, testifies that a similar practice was followed in Egypt. Henri Daniel-Rops writes in *Jesus and His Time:*

> *In* A.D. *103 the prefect of Egypt, Gaius Vibras Maximus, ordered all those who were not living in the country whence their families originated to go back for registration; the papyrus recording this order may be seen in London.*

Some Bible readers also interpreted Luke's reference (2:7) to Jesus as Mary's "first son" ("firstborn son" in the ancient text) to imply that she had other children.

But scholars point out that the word *firstborn* was a legal title for the first male (Exodus 13:13). The "firstborn" was entitled to special rights and a double share of the family inheritance (Deuteronomy 21:17).

► **Notebook** The expression "body of Christ" can have multiple meanings. We may list them as follows:

Body of Christ	Physical	Born on Christmas
	Eucharistic	Born at Last Supper
	Mystical (Church)	Born on Pentecost

► **Clarify** For references to the Church as the body of Christ, see 1 Corinthians 12:12–31, Romans 12:4–8, Ephesians 2:20–22. Theologians sometimes refer to the Church as Christ's "mystical" body (to distinguish it from Christ's physical or eucharistic body).

Students sometimes ask, "How and why is Christ present in different ways?" It might help to clarify the idea of "presence." We can be present to another person in a number of ways: in person, by television, by telephone, by letter, by tape, in a photograph, through memory. The same is true of Jesus. He can be—and is—present in a number of ways.

5. LESSON INTERACTION

Exercise ❶ **Discuss** **(a)** The "explosive power" contained in the nativity set is the "reality" that in Jesus, the God of heaven and earth entered human history and lived among us.

An example will help to illustrate the significance of that event.

The book *Night Flight* deals with the early years of aviation. It describes the adventures of aviators who used to fly at night, without radar or radio. The book is not only a gripping story about the early years of aviation but also an instructive parable about the human situation before Jesus' coming.

Life was a mystery. We didn't know where we came from or where we were going. We were like night fliers lost in darkness and fog. Then Jesus came into the world. Jesus did not take away the fog and the night. He did something more incredible. He got into the plane with us. We are no longer flying blind through night and fog. We have a copilot sitting beside us.

(b) The only way to detect the presence of Jesus in our world is through our lives of love for one another. Jesus said, "If you have love for one another, then everyone will know that you are my disciples" (John 13:35).

Exercise ❷ **Discuss** Kelsey speaks for every Christian who has ever tried to follow Jesus. His statement is in perfect keeping with the Christmas spirit. (This is why Jesus came into the world: because we all are sinners and need redemption.)

Nor is Kelsey's statement a negative view. It is a realistic view. If we don't see ourselves as sinners, then we have no need of Jesus.

Exercise ❸ **Activity** This is a fun project. You might have the students work in teams and let the class vote on the top three creative approaches.

Exercise ❹ **Discuss** You might have the students comment on these three quotes in writing first, and then have them share and discuss their comments.

Miniposter **Discuss** Have students explain the meaning of the miniposter on page 124, phrase by phrase. In other words, in what sense may Christmas be described as:

1. Eternity shut in a span,
2. Summer in Winter,
3. Day in Night,
4. Heaven in earth,
5. God in man?

Chapter Eleven: Preministry (pages 126–27)

Presentation

LESSON **60**

1. LESSON BACKGROUND

▶ *Catechism of the Catholic Church,* 422–507.

2. LESSON QUIZ

Perfect score = 10 points

1. Luke describes Jesus being born in a cave and placed in a feed box. What does this detail preview concerning the future lifestyle Jesus will adopt? *(Lesson 59 review—1 point)*
2. The expression "body of Christ" may be applied to three different forms of Jesus' presence among us. List these three forms and the day on which each "body of Christ" was born. *(Lesson 59 notebook review—6 points)*
3. List the names of the three rites that took place when Mary and Joseph took the infant Jesus to the Temple. *(Lesson 60 preview—3 points)*

3. LESSON HOMEWORK

▶ **Return** Lesson 59 review questions (page 125).

▶ **Collect** Lesson 60 review questions (page 127).

▶ **Read** Lesson 61 ("Magi," pages 128–29).

▶ **Write** Lesson 61 review questions (page 129).

▶ **Appoint** One student to prepare the Luke 2:41–51 reading (lesson 61, exercise 2).

4. LESSON PRESENTATION

Point ❶ **Read** Have student volunteers alternate reading aloud the core content of lesson 60.

▶ **Notebook** Develop the following diagrams interactively with the students for entry in their notebooks.

Rites	Circumcision	Initiates into God's people
	Presentation	Consecrates to God
	Purification	Welcomes back mother

▶ **Clarify** The child was given the name *Jesus* ("God saves"). In biblical times, names of people were believed to do more than identify a person with an arbitrary tag. Some ancients even felt that the name affected the child's character and future.

▶ **Clarify** Presentation of a child in the Temple consisted of consecrating the firstborn male to God, in a spirit of thanksgiving for God's protection of Israel's firstborn in Egypt at the time of the final plague. Presentation recalls the tradition among ancients that a child was never given to parents by God, but only lent to them.

▶ **Clarify** A change in a person's name indicated an important change in the person. Recall how *Abram* was changed to *Abraham* after God called him.

Name changing continues in modern times. For example, Christians take new names upon being baptized, being confirmed, or entering a religious order.

Point ❷ **Clarify** Jesus' presentation occasions the prophetic witness of two aged Jews: Simeon and Anna. They are an idealized portrait of faithful Jews waiting for the Messiah. Seeing in Jesus the fulfillment of this dream, Simeon prays:

"You may let your servant go in peace.
With my own eyes I have seen your salvation,
which you have prepared in the presence of all peoples:
A light to reveal your will to the Gentiles
and bring glory to your people Israel." Luke 2:29–32

Turning to Mary, Simeon prophesied:

"This child is chosen by God
for the destruction and the salvation of many in Israel.
He will be a sign from God
which many people will speak against
and so reveal their secret thoughts.
And sorrow, like a sharp sword,
will break your own heart." Luke 2:34–35

▶ **Notebook** Develop the following two diagrams on the chalkboard interactively with the students for entry in their notebooks.

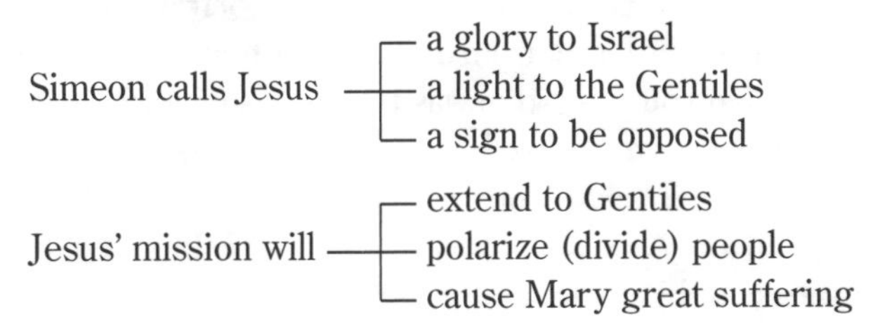

Point ❸ **Clarify** The "Superman" cartoon was created by two teens. They tried to sell it to editors. All rejected it, saying it was too far-fetched. The teenagers finally gave up on the idea and sold their rights to it for $130.

The first Superman strip appeared in 1939 with a story line that went something like this.

Just before the doomed planet of Kyrpton explodes, a scientist places his son on an experimental rocket ship and launches it toward planet Earth. It arrives unnoticed and is found by an elderly man and his wife, named Mary.

As the child grows, his foster parents discover that he is special. For example, his body is like steel and his strength is amazing. They tell him not to reveal his "specialness" to others, saying that when he gets older he should use it to help the oppressed and the needy.

Finally, the day comes when the young man, named Clark, decides to begin his life of service to others. It is at this point that "Superman" is born.

▶ **Discuss** Ask: What true story resembles that of Superman? List some similarities between the two stories.

(Jesus was also sent to earth by his Father; was raised by foster parents, one named Mary; was special, but kept it secret until adulthood; used his "specialness" to help the oppressed and the needy.)

Ask: Do you think Mary and Joseph were fully aware, from the beginning, of how special Jesus really was? Have students consult Luke 1:26–35 and 2:19, 33, 51 before drawing a conclusion.

(Many Bible readers regard these passages as an indication that Jesus' parents were not fully aware of Jesus' true identity. They knew he was special, but were not sure how special. This is a debated point, however. Present it as such.)

▶ **Discuss** Ask: Do you think Jesus was always fully aware of how special he was? Or do you think he discovered this as did Clark Kent—gradually?

(Some Bible readers agree with theologian William Barclay who theorizes in his book *The Gospel of Luke:*

At some time Jesus must have discovered his own unique relationship to God. He cannot have known it when he was . . . a baby at his mother's breast or he would be a monstrosity. As the years went on . . . there came a sudden blaze of realization of the consciousness that he was in a unique sense the Son of God.)

▶ **Discuss** The authors of "Superman" portray him as having a body different from that of other human beings.

Ask: Do you think this was true of Jesus also? How vulnerable do you think his body really was to pain, fatigue, sickness? Explain.

(John 4:6–7 speaks of Jesus' fatigue and thirst. Luke 4:2 speaks of his hunger.)

▶ **Notebook** Theorizing about Jesus' body spawned two early heresies: *Gnostic* (Greek meaning "knowledge") and *Docetist* (Greek meaning "to appear").

Risking gross simplification, we might say Gnostics held that since Jesus was really God's Son, his body had to be spiritual. Gnostics believed matter to be evil. It would be totally inappropriate for the divine to take on a material body.

Again risking gross simplification, we might say Docetists held that since Jesus was really God's Son, his body was spiritual, not physical. As a result, Jesus only appeared to suffer and die.

Summarize for entry into student notebooks.

Heresies	Gnostic	Since Jesus was really God's Son, it wasn't fitting for him to be clothed in "evil" matter.
	Docetist	Since Jesus was really God's Son, his body was really spiritual. He only appeared to suffer.

5. LESSON INTERACTION

Exercise ❶ **Discuss** **(a, b)** The poem captures the reason for honoring Mary. Inner beauty is spiritual (vs. physical).

▶ **Discuss** **(c, d, e)** This part of exercise 1 is self-explanatory and can be handled in a number of ways.

You might consider having the students break into small groups to discuss these three questions. The groups could then report back to the entire class.

Or you might consider having the students write out their responses and then read them to the class.

Exercise ❷ **Activity** This exercise is self-explanatory.

Exercise ❸ **Activity** This might be given as a homework assignment. Students could then report back to the group.

Exercise ❹ **Discuss** Again, you might consider having students write out their responses before sharing them with the group.

Photo **Discuss** Note the photo of the Marian sculpture on page 126. Ask: Can you identify and explain its symbols? (The dove symbolizes the Holy Spirit. "[Jesus] saw the Spirit of God coming down like a dove and lighting on him" (Matthew 3:16). The hand symbolizes the Father. There are numerous references to God's hand in Scripture. For example, the psalmist speaks of "the right hand of the Most High" (Psalm 77:11 [NAB]).)

Magi

LESSON 61

1. LESSON BACKGROUND

► *Catechism of the Catholic Church*, 527–534.

2. LESSON QUIZ

Perfect score = 14 points

1. What prophecy does Simeon make concerning Jesus? Concerning Mary? *(Lesson 60 review—2 points)*
2. List and explain briefly the three rites that took place when Mary and Joseph took the infant Jesus to the Temple. *(Lesson 60 notebook review—6 points)*
3. List the three gifts the magi gave the infant Jesus, and explain what facts about Jesus that each one pointed to. *(Lesson 61 preview—6 points)*

3. LESSON HOMEWORK

► **Return** Lesson 60 review questions (page 127).

► **Collect** Lesson 61 review questions (page 129).

► **Read** Lesson 62 ("Baptism," pages 130–31).

► **Write** Lesson 62 review questions (page 131).

4. LESSON PRESENTATION

Point ❶ **Read** Have student volunteers read aloud the core content of lesson 61.

► **Notebook** We may summarize the key ideas of the core content as follows for entry in student notebooks.

Threads	History	Remembered events
	Prophecy	Biblical prophecies
	Inspiration	Divine guidance
Gifts	Gold	Kingship
	Frankincense	Divinity
	Myrrh	Humanity
Preview	Jews	Many will reject Jesus
	Gentiles	Many will accept Jesus

Point ❷ **Clarify** Herod the Great was enraged when the magi left without telling him where Jesus was. So he ordered a massacre of "all the boys in Bethlehem and its neighborhood who were two years old and younger" (Matthew 2:16). Jesus escaped, however, because Joseph had taken him to Egypt (Matthew 2:13–14).

The massacre was the act of a sick man. An ancient historian, Josephus, tells us that not long after this order Herod attempted suicide. Rumors of the attempt caused loud wailing throughout his palace. When Herod's son (jailed by his father) heard the cries, he mistook them to mean that his father was dead. So he tried to bribe his jailers to release him. When Herod heard about this, he executed his son.

Now Herod's depression grew deeper. His own death was close, and he knew It. What pained him was the thought that his death would cause joy in Judea. To forestall this, he devised an incredible plan. Josephus says:

Having assembled the most distinguished men from every village from one end of Judea to the other, he ordered them to be locked in the hippodrome in Jericho.

Herod then gave the order that they be executed at the moment he himself died. His sick mind reasoned that their death would dispel any joy in Judea over his own death. The order was never carried out.

► **Clarify** In spite of his pathological character, Herod was a remarkable man. For example, he was a great patron of athletics. In his book *Biblical Archaeology*, G. Ernest Wright says:

Herod himself offered the largest prizes at the 192nd Olympiad, evidently held there [in Caesarea, map page 107] in his stadium. Indeed, he is said to have endowed the whole Olympiad institution when it faltered for lack of money.

Josephus informs us, also, that Herod himself was quite an athlete and was especially skilled in the javelin and bow (*Jewish Wars* 1, 21, 13). Josephus adds that it was Herod, in the 192nd Olympiad, who began the practice of giving second- and third-place awards.

Remind the students that the Olympic games were already ancient in Herod's day. They were begun in 765 B.C.E. in Greece, about the time Amos the prophet was preaching in Israel.

Clarify The date of Herod's death is given as 4 B.C.E. This looks as though he died before Jesus' birth. Actually, Jesus was born before 1 C.E.

Recall that our present B.C.E/C.E. (B.C./A.D.) calendar was designed in the sixth century by Dionysius Exiguus. He erred in his calculations by five to seven years. This means Jesus was probably born sometime between 7 and 5 B.C.E. Since it would be too troublesome to correct all the wrong dates, they are kept as they are.

Clarify Herod was buried in the Herodium (shown on page 128 of the textbook). This artificially shaped minimountain is located not far from Bethlehem. It was one of several fortress-palaces built by Herod the Great. Living quarters and fortifications were located inside the craterlike top.

Clarify One final point. Herod the Great is to be distinguished from Herod Antipas, his son, and from Herod Agrippa, his grandson. Herod Antipas is the "Herod" who beheaded John the Baptist (Mark 6:21–28) and the "Herod" who questioned Jesus before his crucifixion (Luke 23:7). Herod Agrippa is the "Herod" who jailed Peter and died a wretched death shortly afterward (Acts 12:1–5,20–23).

Notebook The following summary may be entered in student notebooks for reference. It shows the Herod and the Caesar families.

Herod the Great (infant Jesus)	Augustus Caesar (27 B.C.E.–14 C.E.)
Herod Antipas (adult Jesus)	Tiberius Caesar (14–37 C.E.)
Herod Agrippa I (jailed Peter, Acts 12)	Claudius Caesar (41–54 C.E.)
Herod Agrippa II (tried Paul, Acts 26)	Nero Caesar (54–68 C.E.)

Clarify When Joseph learned that Herod was dead, he took Jesus and Mary and returned to Israel. Matthew portrays Joseph as intending to return to Judea—in the Bethlehem area. Instead, because of a warning received in a dream, Joseph went to the region of Galilee.

5. LESSON INTERACTION

Exercise 1 **Discuss** **(a, b)** Matthew and Luke are the only evangelists who treat Jesus' infancy. Portraying events that took place in Jesus' infancy posed a much greater problem than portraying events that took place in Jesus' adulthood. Ask: Why?

Notebook Develop the reasons interactively with the students for entry in their notebooks.

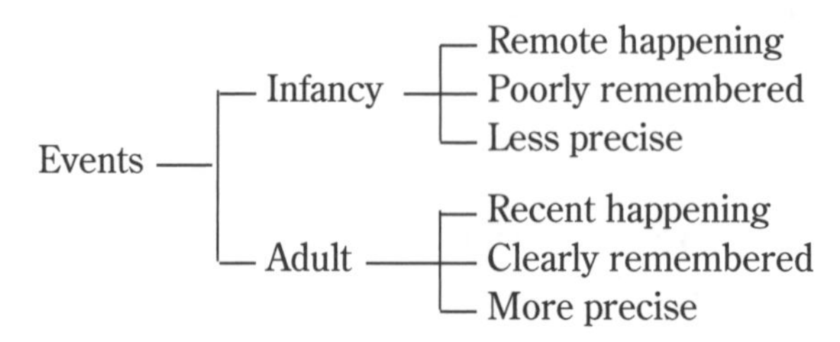

Exercise 2 **Read** **(a, b)** Have the student who prepared Luke 2:41–51 read it aloud to the class.

Note that when Jesus turned up missing, his parents looked for him "among their relatives and friends" (Luke 2:44). This suggests that Jesus was an only child.

Discuss **(c)** Jesus' response to Mary suggests that Jesus was growing in his awareness of his own identity and mission. Recall the words of theologian William Barclay cited under "Point 3" in the previous lesson.

Exercise 3 **Activity** **(a, b)** If there are no Jewish people in your area, have the students focus on part *a* of this exercise.

Photo **Clarify** Refer students to the photo on page 129. This boy prepares to read a selection from the prophets and the Pentateuch as part of his Bar Mitzvah service. The yarmulke is a reminder of God's presence.

Bar Mitzvah means "son of the Law." *Bar* means "son"—as in *Bartholomew* ("son of Tolmai"), *Barabbas* ("son of the father"), and *Barnabas* ("son of prophecy"). The Bar Mitzvah rite (as we know it today) is comparatively recent in Jewish history, about six hundred years old. Many Jewish communities now celebrate Bat Mitzvah ("daughter of the Law") as well.

Baptism

1. LESSON BACKGROUND

▶ *Catechism of the Catholic Church,* 535–537.

2. LESSON QUIZ

Perfect score = 12 points

1. List and explain the three "threads" Matthew used to weave the magi story. *(Lesson 61 review—6 points)*
2. How does the reaction of the magi to the infant Jesus preview the way Gentiles will react to the adult Jesus? How does Herod's reaction preview how many Jews will react? *(Lesson 61 notebook review—2 points)*
3. Explain how John's baptism differs from Christian baptism. *(Lesson 62 preview—4 points)*

3. LESSON HOMEWORK

▶ **Return** Lesson 61 review questions (page 129).

▶ **Collect** Lesson 62 review questions (page 131).

▶ **Read** Lesson 63 ("Temptations," pages 132–33).

▶ **Write** Lesson 63 review questions (page 133).

4. LESSON PRESENTATION

Point ① **Read** Have student volunteers alternate reading aloud the core content of lesson 62.

▶ **Clarify** The book *Night Flight* is a true story by Elie Wiesel. Elie was only fifteen years old when he was imprisoned in a Nazi concentration camp during World War II.

The people of Elie's hometown in Hungary had no idea what was going on in these camps. Their first indication that something horrible might be taking place came from a happy-go-lucky little Jew named Moche.

Moche used to live in the town, but he had been arrested and taken away by the Nazis because he was not a native Hungarian. Then, one night, Moche showed up again. But now, he was no longer happy-go-lucky. He was sad and depressed.

Moche said that he had been taken with other Jews to a prison camp in Poland. There they were put to work digging a big pit. When the pit was finished, the prisoners were machine-gunned and buried in the hole they had dug. Moche had miraculously survived.

Over and over Moche told his story, but the people didn't believe him. Finally Moche stopped telling his story. "They think I am crazy in the head," he said.

Many people in biblical times reacted to John the same way Moche's neighbors reacted to him.

▶ **Clarify** Stress the symbolism of the events following Jesus' baptism:

Sky opens: This image recalls Isaiah's prayer to God: "Why don't you tear the sky open and come down?" (Isaiah 64:1). The image of the sky opening signals the start of a "new era" on earth: God in the person of Jesus is entering the world.

Dove descends: This image of the dove hovering over the waters at Jesus' baptism recalls the "Spirit of God" hovering over the waters at the dawn of creation. Ancient rabbis compared God's Spirit to a dove hovering over its newborn. The image of the dove signals the dawn of a "new creation."

Voice speaks: Finally, a voice is heard to say, "You are my own dear Son." The image of the voice signals the appearance of the "new Adam."

▶ **Notebook** Develop the following diagram on the chalkboard for entry in student notebooks.

Baptism symbolism		
	Sky opens	New era
	Spirit descends	New creation
	Voice speaks	New Adam

5. LESSON INTERACTION

Exercise ① **Discuss** Tally the results (correct and incorrect responses) on the chalkboard. Have the students evaluate and then discuss the results of their survey.

Exercise ② **Clarify** (This is an extremely important exercise.) John told the people, "Turn away from your sins and be baptized and God will forgive your sins" (Mark 1:4).

John stressed that his baptism was a *sign* of repentance. It is incomplete in itself. John expressed it this way:

"I baptize you with water to show that you have repented, but the one who will come after me will baptize you with the Holy Spirit and fire. He is much greater than I am; and I am not good enough even to carry his sandals." Matthew 3:11

In other words, John stresses that his baptism is a "baptism of *repentance*," rejecting one's old life of sin, while Jesus' baptism will be a "baptism of *rebirth*," receiving a new life.

Notebook Develop the following diagram interactively with the students for entry in their notebooks.

Baptisms			
	John's	repentance	Rejection (old life)
	Jesus'	rebirth	Reception (new life)

Commenting on the difference between the baptisms, John L. McKenzie says in his *Dictionary of the Bible:*

The baptism of John is called in the Gospels (Mark 1:4) *the baptism of repentance, in contrast to the baptism of Jesus, which was the baptism of the Holy Spirit* (Acts 19:1–17). . . . *Baptism is the Christian's experience of the passion, death, and resurrection of Jesus in himself* (Romans 6:3 f.; Colossians 1:12). . . .

Baptism symbolizes and effects not only the incorporation of the Christian into Christ (Galatians 3:27) *but also his union with his fellow Christians as members of the one body of Christ* (1 Corinthians 12:13).

To better appreciate Paul's image of baptism, we should keep in mind that Christians of his time were baptized by submersion. This explains why the baptistry in early churches were sunk into the floor, with three steps leading down to the water. The person being baptized was submerged completely under the waters to symbolize Jesus' three-day burial in the tomb.

Thus, the baptistry had a twofold symbolism. It acted as a *tomb* into which the person descended and was buried, and a *womb* out of which the person emerged, reborn in Christ. Paul explains the meaning of baptism this way in a letter to the Christians of Rome:

When we were baptized into union with Christ Jesus,
we were baptized into union with his death.
By our baptism, then, we were buried with him
and shared his death, in order that,
just as Christ was raised from death . . .
so also we might live a new life. Romans 6:3–4

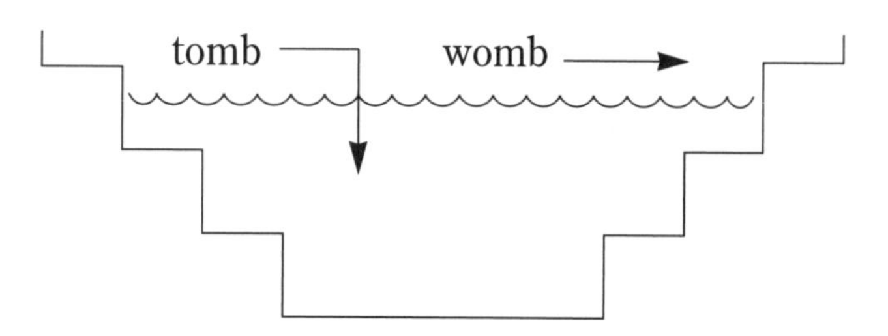

Clarify Three types of baptism are currently followed by Christian churches: immersion, sprinkling, and pouring.

The *Didache* (*"Teaching of the Apostles"*) is the work of an unknown Christian writer. Its date is uncertain, but all experts date it before 100 C.E. Concerning the procedure for baptizing a person, it says:

Baptize in the name of the Father and of the Son and of the Holy Spirit in living [running] water. But if running water is not available, baptize in still water. . . . If neither is available, then pour water three times on the head in the name of the Father and of the Son and of the Holy Spirit.

Exercise ③ **Discuss** The old organ must be removed before the new is implanted. This is also true of baptism. Our "old life of sin" must be removed before our "new life in Christ" can be implanted.

Exercise ④ **Discuss** Similarly, we must take special care that our sinful nature (that we retain) not reject our "new life in Christ" (as the human body tends to reject a new organ).

Exercise ⑤ **Discuss** Jesus is baptized because he identifies himself totally with sinful humanity. He cannot stand apart from it. He will carry the sins of humanity to the cross, die for them, and rise to new life.

Exercise ⑥ **Clarify** **(a)** The fall of the first Adam ended the "age of the creation." The rise of the second Adam begins the "age of re-creation."

(b) Baptism commits us to preaching the Gospel to others. How can a young person today do this effectively?

(c) Baptism unites us not only to the risen Christ but to one another.

Photos **Discuss** Cagliari's *Baptism of Jesus* (page 130) includes the "invisible" side of Jesus' baptism (angels). Angels are portrayed with wings to symbolize that they were, above all, "messengers of God."

Cagliari's painting contrasts with the painting by a British artist for a baptistry in a boys' school in Britain (page 131). The artist was obviously trying to put Jesus' baptism in an everyday setting so that the boys of the school could relate to it better.

Temptations

LESSON 63

1. LESSON BACKGROUND

► *Catechism of the Catholic Church,* 538–540.

2. LESSON QUIZ

Perfect score = 11 Points

1. List the three images that accompanied Jesus' baptism by John and tell what they signaled. *(Lesson 62 review—6 points)*
2. List and explain the twofold symbolism of the baptistry. *(Lesson 62 notebook review—4 points)*
3. What does Jesus' refusal to leap off the Temple and be rescued by angels preview concerning his future lifestyle? *(Lesson 63 preview—1 point)*

3. LESSON HOMEWORK

► **Return** Lesson 62 review questions (page 131).
► **Collect** Lesson 63 review questions (page 133).
► **Read** Lesson 64 ("Inauguration," pages 134–35).
► **Write** Lesson 64 review questions (page 135).

4. LESSON PRESENTATION

Point ① **Read** Have student volunteers alternate reading aloud the core content of lesson 64.

► **Notebook** Recall that the Bible uses the number 40 in a symbolic sense, much as we use certain numbers. For example, an exasperated mother tells her child, "I told you a thousand times not to slam the door." (She told her child many times.) Or a person says of a heavy object, "That thing must weigh a ton." (It is very heavy.) Or a person says, "I wouldn't do that even if you gave me a million dollars."

The number 40 means the lapse of a significant number of days or years, as seen in the following examples from the Bible. Have students record them in their notebooks.

Flood lasts 40 days	Genesis 7:12
Israel in the desert 40 years	Numbers 32:13
Moses on Mt. Sinai 40 days	Deuteronomy 9:9
Jesus fasted 40 days	Matthew 4:2

Point ② **Clarify** The nature of Jesus' encounter with the Devil is often discussed. For example, how did the Devil (Satan) manifest himself to Jesus?

Medieval artists portrayed the Devil in a starkly literal way (like the gargoyle in the miniposter on page 132). A British television team on assignment in Israel to film Jesus' life used "a black shadow" on the ground.

Ask: Which portrayal do you prefer and why?

Ask: How else might you portray the Devil and why?

Ask: What does Scripture suggest about what the Devil and evil spirits or demons are really like?

Point ③ **Clarify** Christian tradition holds that after the angels were created by God, they underwent a "test," as Adam and Eve did. Like Adam and Eve, a vast number failed. Christian tradition identifies Satan and the "fallen angels" with the angels who failed the test given them by God (Revelation 12:9–10).

Point ④ **Clarify** During their journey in the desert the Israelites fell into three major temptations:

- Sensuality — "Not bread alone" — Deuteronomy 8:3
- Idolatry — "Worship God only" — Deuteronomy 6:13
- Presumption — "Don't test God" — Deuteronomy 6:16

Jesus relived Israel's experience and underwent the same temptations Israel did. After each temptation, he cites the key words of Israel's temptations in the Book of Deuteronomy.

- "Not bread alone" — Matthew 4:4
- "Worship God only" — Matthew 4:10
- "Don't test God" — Matthew 4:7

Jesus succeeds where the Israelites failed. Jesus is the "new" Israel, firstborn of God's "new" people.

Point ⑤ **Notebook** Develop these preview summaries interactively for entry in student notebooks.

Identity		
	Tempted	Human: "Son of Man"
	Stands firm	Divine: "Son of God"

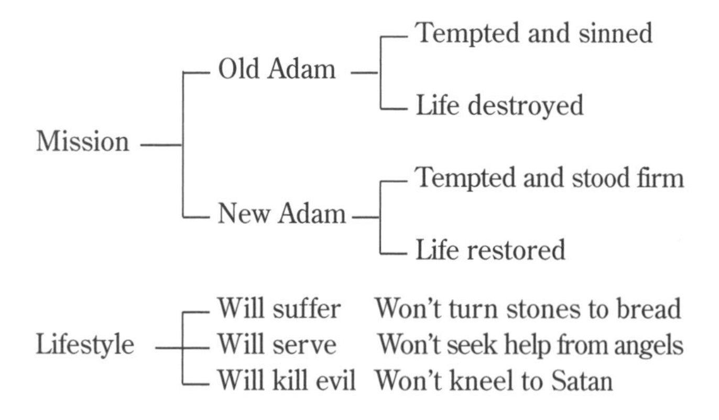

Point 6 Read or reproduce and distribute the following:

> *Sports Illustrated* writer Jerry Cowle described his initiation into a scout honor group. He was given only a blanket and moccasins, and was blindfolded, taken to a remote area, and left all alone. He was told not to stand, sleep, speak, or drink for twenty-four hours.
>
> Soon it was pitch dark. Suddenly Jerry heard a thumping noise, like the approach of a bear. He stayed deathly still, and it passed.
>
> Next Jerry heard a voice. It was his friend, Frank, carrying a sandwich for him. "How's it going?" Frank asked. Jerry didn't speak or accept the sandwich. Frank shouted, "You stupid fool! Do you think I'd squeal on you?" With that he threw the sandwich in Jerry's face and stomped off. Jerry remained silent and ignored the sandwich, even though he was famished.
>
> Hours passed and Jerry's eyes grew heavy. Only with the greatest willpower did he stay awake. Just as the sun was coming up, a farmer showed up, saw Jerry clothed only in a blanket, and said, "Get the hell off my property." When Jerry didn't move, the farmer left, saying he was returning with the police. They never came. That afternoon, twenty-four hours later, Frank and the others showed up, saying, "Shake, you made it!"

Notebook Have the students develop interactively the following "Table of Jerry's Temptations" on the chalkboard for entry in their notebooks.

Temptation	Source	Concern (fear)
Move	Bear	Injury
Speak	Frank	Rejection
Eat	Sandwich	Hunger
Sleep	Body	Weariness
Speak	Farmer	Embarrassment

Discuss Ask: Which of the above temptations would you have found most difficult and why?

Ask: Do you see any parallel between Jerry's initiation experience and Jesus' desert experience? Explain.

Discuss Ask: What point does the following quotation by J. W. Chapman make concerning temptation?

> *Temptation is the tempter looking through the keyhole into the room where you are living; sin is drawing back the bolt and making it possible for him to enter.*

(It makes the point that yielding to a temptation is something you do voluntarily. No one can force you to do something. At times, it is true the external pressure can become so great that it cuts into one's freedom.)

5. LESSON INTERACTION

Exercise 1 **Activity** Consider having the students take time out to do this exercise right in class. You might collect the responses, choose the best ones, and share them with the group in the next class.

It's surprising how future written exercises improve when the better ones are selected and read aloud in class.

Exercise 2 **Activity** Again, consider having the students take time out to do this exercise right in class. Select the better ones and read them aloud to the group in the next class.

Exercise 3 **Clarify** Egyptians fasted to stay healthy and look young. Ancient Greeks fasted to stay mentally sharp. American Indians fasted to demonstrate courage. Russian icon artists fasted to paint better. Ancient Hebrews fasted to seek God's help in important undertakings (Esther 4:16). Early Christians fasted to imitate Jesus' fast in the desert.

All of these facts, and many more, are reported in Dr. Allan Cott's provocative book, *Fasting: The Ultimate Diet*. Dr. Cott quotes Mohandus Gandhi, India's great leader, as saying:

> *Fasting, if it is a spiritual act, is an intense prayer or preparation for it. It is a yearning of the soul to merge in the divine essence. . . . How far I am in tune with the Infinite, I do not know. But I do know that the fast has made the passion for such a state intenser.*

Contrary to popular belief, fasting, even for prolonged periods of time, does not harm adult health. On the contrary, Dr. Cott cites these examples:

> *Japanese . . . soldiers who came out of the jungles of the Philippines and Guam after hiding for as long as 30 years were in better shape than their countrymen back home, many of whom had grown fat in affluence. . . .*
>
> *During World War II the British, whose food supplies were stringently rationed, remained remarkably fit. When the food shortages ceased, there was a decline in national health and an increasing incidence of ailments that had been almost nonexistent during the siege.*

Clarify Jesus presupposed his followers would fast after he left them (Matthew 9:14–15). He warned them not to make a great show of it (Matthew 6:16–18). Early Christians joined fasting to prayer, especially before important events (Acts 13:1–3, 14:23).

Inauguration

1. LESSON BACKGROUND

▶ *Catechism of the Catholic Church,* 541–543.

2. LESSON QUIZ

Perfect score = 10 points

1. List and explain the three things Jesus' victory over Satan previews about Jesus. *(Lesson 63 review—6 points)*
2. Explain how the number 40 is frequently used in Scripture. *(Lesson 63 notebook review—1 point)*
3. List and explain two episodes from Jesus' infancy that the Nazareth episode recalls. *(Lesson 64 preview—3 points)*

3. LESSON HOMEWORK

▶ **Return** Lesson 63 review questions (page 133).

▶ **Collect** Lesson 64 review questions (page 135).

▶ **Read** Lesson 65 ("Signs," pages 136–37).

▶ **Write** Lesson 65 review questions (page 137).

4. LESSON PRESENTATION

Point 1 **Read** Have student volunteers alternate reading aloud the core content of lesson 64.

▶ **Review** Refer the students to the photo of the Isaiah scroll (textbook page 82). This is the same scroll that the fifteen-year-old Bedouin boy (named Muhammad the Wolf) and his cousin found in a jar in the cave at Qumran.

Recall for the students that during its life a living substance absorbs radioactive carbon. When it dies, it releases the carbon back to the atmosphere at a constant rate. This allows scientists to calculate when the substance died.

Dr. Willard Libby of the University of Chicago used this method to date the Isaiah scroll. Remarkably, it was at least a hundred years older than Jesus. He could actually have read from it in the synagogue at Nazareth.

▶ **Review** Also refer the students to the photos on page 4 (jar and caves) and page 5 (Qumran "monastery" excavations). Among the excavated ruins archaeologists found a large room containing a long writing table and inkpots. Conceivably, in this very scriptorium and on this table, Essene "monks" copied the Isaiah scroll.

▶ **Review** Use this occasion as an opportunity to review the discovery of the Dead Sea Scrolls.

What was found	800 documents (mostly fragments; 200 biblical)
When found	Between 1947 and 1956
Where found	Eleven caves at Qumran near the Dead Sea
Why important	They are closer to the originals by 1,000 years and thus give us a clearer picture of biblical times.

Point 2 **Clarify** Refer the students to the photo (and caption) of the synagogue on page 136. Recall that the word *synagogue* comes from the Greek, meaning "assembly."

Dating from the Babylonian exile (587–537 B.C.E.), the synagogue substituted for the destroyed Temple to preserve Jewish unity and faith. Unlike the Temple, a place of sacrifice, the synagogue was a place of instruction.

Services were held in the synagogue on each Sabbath and on feast days. They began with the congregation reciting the *Shema Israel.* It reads:

"Israel, remember this!
The LORD—and the LORD alone—is our God.
Love the LORD your God
with all your heart, with all your soul,
and with all your strength." Deuteronomy 6:4–5

In *Man's Search for Meaning,* Viktor Frankl (a doctor interred in the Auschwitz Nazi concentration camp) writes:

I had to surrender my clothes and in turn inherited the worn-out rags of an inmate who had been sent to the gas chamber immediately after his arrival at the Auschwitz railway station. . . . I found in a pocket of the newly acquired coat a single page torn out of a Hebrew prayer book. [It contained the *Shema Israel.*]

▶ **Clarify** The *Shema Israel* is the first prayer a Jewish child learns and the last prayer a dying Jew utters. Jesus prayed it often.

The synagogue recitation of the *Shema Israel* was followed by prayer, readings from Scripture, a "homily," and a blessing.

Synagogue services in Jesus' time were conducted by members of the congregation or by invited guests. Acts 13:13–16 describes how Paul and Barnabas were invited to speak in a local synagogue.

Mark 5:22 identifies Jairus (whose daughter Jesus cured) as "an official of the local synagogue."

Luke 12:11 alludes to the fact that the local synagogue also served as a kind of local courtroom. Apparently, even punishments were meted out there (Matthew 10:17).

Finally, to be expelled from a synagogue was a serious thing and a grave punishment (John 9:22).

▶ **Clarify** Luke says:

Jesus rolled up the scroll,
gave it back to the attendant, and sat down.
All the people . . . had their eyes fixed on him,
as he said to them, "This passage of scripture
has come true today,
as you heard it being read." Luke 4:20–21

Point out that in Jesus' time, the "homilist" gave his "homily" while sitting. The chair became known as the *cathedra,* from which we get our word *cathedral.* Sitting was the ordinary position of a teacher.

Today, we speak of university teachers as occupying the "Chair of Theology" or the "Chair of Philosophy."

Finally, the synagogue scroll was kept in an "ark" in the front of the synagogue. An "eternal light" *(Ner Tamid)* burns continually before it (see photo on page 92 of textbook).

Point ❸ **Clarify** The full reading from Isaiah 61:1–2, quoted by Luke, reads:

"The Spirit of the Lord is upon me,
because he has chosen me to bring good news to the poor.
He has sent me to proclaim liberty to the captives
and recovery of sight to the blind, to set free the oppressed
and announce that the time has come
when the Lord will save his people." Luke 4:18–19

▶ **Notebook** The above reading cites four groups: poor, blind, prisoners, and captives. These groups represent evils from which people suffered and needed salvation.

Four evils		
	Poor	Economic
	Blind	Physical
	Prisoners	Political
	Captives	Moral

▶ **Clarify** Many people in Jesus' time were "prisoners" for political reasons. Others were held "captive" by their own vices and weaknesses.

Point ❹ **Clarify** For centuries, people had prayed for the coming of God's kingdom. Jesus proclaims this is now happening. The old world order, the "kingdom of Satan," is about to be challenged by the "kingdom of God." An old era is dying; a new era is being born.

Suddenly, the full impact of Jesus' teaching struck the synagogue congregation. A wave of whispering broke out, probably saying: "Is this not Joseph's son, a poor villager of Nazareth? Is he now pretending to be a prophet? What has come over him? What credentials has he to prove that he is God-appointed and not self-appointed?" Jesus motioned for silence and then said:

"I am sure that you will quote this proverb to me,
'Doctor, heal yourself.'
You will also tell me to do here in my hometown
the same things you heard were done in Capernaum.
I tell you this," Jesus added,
"prophets are never welcomed in their hometown. . . ."
When the people in the synagogue heard this,
they were filled with anger.
They rose up, dragged Jesus out of town,
and took him to the top of the hill. Luke 4:23–24, 28–29

▶ **Clarify** The violent reaction to Jesus was typical of Jewish responses to religious teachings that seemed to depart from orthodoxy. For example, see the responses to Stephen (Acts 7:54–8:1), Paul (Acts 22:22–23), and Paul and Silas (Acts 16:21–24).

Jesus' "miraculous" escape at Nazareth was repeated on other occasions during his ministry; see, for example, John 7:30, 7:44, 8:59.

5. LESSON INTERACTION

Exercises ❶ ❷ ❸ **Activity** Take time off right in class to have students respond in writing to these exercises. Collect the responses, pick out the best ones, and share them (with the students' permission) with the group.

Exercise ❹ **Clarify** Father Taban returned to Sudan in 1972. Two years after his return, people loved him with the deepest affection. In 1980, Pope John Paul II made him a bishop.

Exercise ❺ **Clarify** **(a)** Petty things often keep us from seeing the bigger picture in life. **(b)** The people in Nazareth were "defending" an erroneous principle they held, namely, that no one who grew up among them could be a prophet. They thought they were "fighting" for a principle: orthodoxy. **(c)** Just because we don't *understand* something is no *reason* to oppose it.

LESSON 65

1. LESSON BACKGROUND

▶ *Catechism of the Catholic Church*, 547–550.

2. LESSON QUIZ

Perfect score = 10 points

1. In what city and when did the synagogue have its origin? *(Lesson 64 review—2 points)*
2. List the four groups, mentioned in the Book of Isaiah that Jesus read from in Nazareth, that he came to help. *(Lesson 64 notebook review—4 points)*
3. List and explain the primary, twofold purpose of Jesus' miracles. *(Lesson 65 preview—4 points)*

3. LESSON HOMEWORK

▶ **Return** Lesson 64 review questions (page 135).

▶ **Collect** Lesson 65 review questions (page 137).

▶ **Read** Lesson 66 ("Proclamations," pages 138–39).

▶ **Write** Lesson 66 review questions (page 139).

▶ **Appoint** Student to prepare Luke 4:40, 8:41–48 (lesson 66, exercise 1).

4. LESSON PRESENTATION

Point ① **Read** Have student volunteers alternate reading aloud the core content of lesson 65.

▶ **Clarify** Acquaint the students with Capernaum, where Jesus made his residence (Matthew 4:13) during his ministry in Galilee.

Have students locate Capernaum on the minimap on page 136.

Have students take note again of the photo and caption on page 136. This excavated synagogue dates from a few centuries after Jesus' time. Because of ancient building customs, it was probably built on the site of the destroyed synagogue where Jesus taught.

Some stone carvings in the excavated synagogue may be from Jesus' synagogue. Ancients often reused sculptured pieces. Two carvings, especially, stir the imagination: an emblem of the Tenth Roman Legion and a manna bowl. Take the Roman army emblem. People ask: "Could it be linked with the Roman army officer who sent elders to ask Jesus to heal his servant?" Recall that the elders told Jesus:

"This man really deserves your help.
He loves our people
and he himself built a synagogue for us." Luke 7:4–5

Finally, have students take special note of the photo (and caption) of the fishing wharfs on the Sea of Galilee today (page 137). The Bible also refers to the Sea of Galilee as Lake Gennesaret (Luke 5:1) and Lake Tiberias (John 6:1). It is thirteen miles long, eight miles deep, and about seven hundred feet below sea level. (It is one of the lowest points on earth.)

Ask students: What is the lowest point on earth? (It is the Dead Sea, into which the Sea of Galilee flows by way of the Jordan River.)

The Sea of Galilee is one of modern Israel's primary sources of water for irrigating its new farmlands.

In Jesus' day, about 200,000 people (largely Gentiles) lived in the many towns along the shore of the Sea of Galilee. It was a fisherman's paradise then and remains so today.

Point ② **Notebook** Stress that the Gospels use three Greek words to refer to Jesus' miracles: *dynamis* (power), *teras* (marvel), and *semion* (sign). Develop the following diagram interactively on the chalkboard for entry in student notebooks.

Word/Meaning	Primary Stress of Miracles
Dynamis (power)	Show people Jesus' godlike power
Teras (marvel)	Make people wonder
Semion (sign)	Make people ask, "What's this mean?"

▶ **Notebook** Stress that Jesus' miracles are like a flashing red light. The important thing is not the flashing red light itself, but what it means.

The same is true of Jesus' miracles. The important thing is not the miracle itself, but its meaning (what Jesus was saying by his miracle).

Thus, we sometimes speak of the "sense level" and the "sign level" of miracles. We may summarize these two levels for entry in student notebooks.

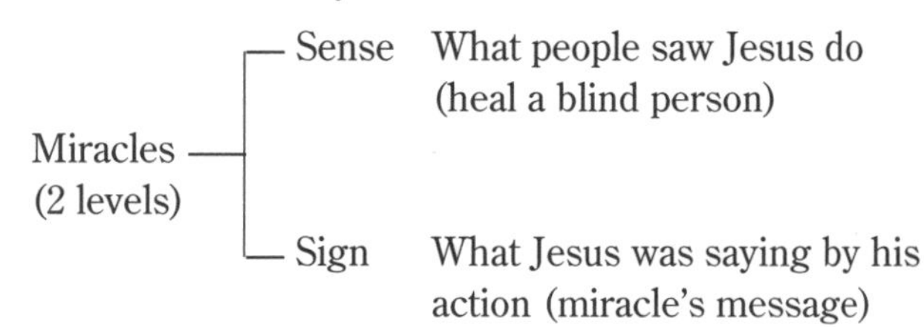

Notebook We may summarize the sign level of miracles this way for entry in student notebooks.

Miracles (sign level)
- *Proclaim* Jesus to be the Messiah (come to inaugurate God's kingdom)
- *Invite* people to open their hearts (to Jesus and his message)

Clarify Understanding the "message" of events is still a problem. Commenting on this, astronaut Ed Aldrin wrote after his return from the moon:

It is difficult for me to articulate my thoughts about the significance of this flight. On the surface it was three people on a voyage, but it was more than that. It was more than a team of people and government and industry working together. . . .

It is my hope that people will keep this whole event in their minds and see beyond minor details and technical achievements to the deeper meaning behind it all: challenge, a quest, the human need to do these things, and the need to recognize that we are all one mankind under God.

Activity What is true of "miracles" in gospel times and "great events" in modern times is also true of "personal actions" in our own lives. We all experience moments when we see beyond our "personal actions" (sense level) to the direction these actions are giving our lives (sign level).

For example, we find ourselves lying, cheating, and being tempted more and more to experiment with alcohol and drugs.

These actions are like indicators on a dial. They are like flashing red lights. They are warnings that something serious is taking shape in our lives.

Once we become aware of these warnings, we can refuse to "heed their message"—as some people failed to "heed the message" of Jesus' miracles—or we can do something about them.

Ask students: On an unsigned sheet of paper, list two things: (1) some warning signs in your life right now, and (2) what they might mean.

Collect the papers, shuffle them, and read them to the class.

5. LESSON INTERACTION

Exercise 1 **Discuss** The photograph corresponds to the sense level of an event. (You see only the "outer surface" of a thing.) The X ray corresponds to the sign level. (It takes you below the "outer surface.") The sign level probes the "inner meaning" of the event.

Exercise 2 **Discuss** To open our hearts is to let Jesus take over our lives and do with them whatever he wills. ("Thy will be done.") We fear to do this. But if we do it, we will discover a happiness that people rarely experience. Consider the following. It was found in the pocket of a dead Confederate soldier.

I asked for health,
that I might do greater things;
I was given infirmity,
that I might do better things. . . .
I asked for riches, that I might be happy;
I was given poverty, that I might be wise.
I asked for power,
that I might have the praise of men;
I was given weakness,
that I might feel the need of God. . . .
I got nothing I asked for,
but everything I hoped for.
Almost despite myself,
my unspoken prayers were answered.
I am among all men most richly blessed.

Exercise 3 **Discuss** Jesus is telling the people that they failed to go beyond the sense level of his miracle to the sign level. They have come for bread that will perish, not bread that will lead to eternal life.

Exercise 4 **Discuss** The blessing Evely refers to is this: If we share what we have, there will be enough for all.

Evely's explanation is beautiful, but it's not the "intended meaning" the Gospel has in mind.

The "intended meaning" is that Jesus is the promised Messiah, come into the world to give something greater than material bread. Jesus is the "living bread that came down from heaven. If you eat this bread, you will live forever" (John 6:51).

Exercise 5 **Discuss** Lewis misses the main point of Jesus' miracles. Surely Jesus worked them out of compassion. But Jesus' main point was to "proclaim" that he is the promised one, come to inaugurate God's kingdom and to "invite" people to open their hearts to him and his teaching.

Proclamations

1. LESSON BACKGROUND

▶ *Catechism of the Catholic Church*, 543–544.

2. LESSON QUIZ

Perfect score =12 points

1. List and explain the three Greek words the Gospels use to refer to Jesus' miracles. *(Lesson 65 review—6 points)*
2. List and explain the two levels of Jesus' miracles. *(Lesson 65 notebook review—4 points)*
3. What twofold coming do Jesus' miracles proclaim? *(Lesson 66 preview—2 points)*

3. LESSON HOMEWORK

▶ **Return** Lesson 65 review questions (page 137).

▶ **Collect** Lesson 66 review questions (page 139).

▶ **Read** Lesson 67 ("Invitations," pages 140–41).

▶ **Write** Lesson 67 review questions (page 141).

▶ **Appoint** Two students to prepare Luke 7:11–17 (lesson 67, exercise 1) and Matthew 19:16–30 (lesson 67, exercise 5).

4. LESSON PRESENTATION

Point 1 **Read** Have student volunteers alternate reading aloud the core content of lesson 66.

▶ **Clarify** Recall the *Exorcist* plot. Regan, a twelve-year-old girl, is seized by spasms. Her tongue flicks like a serpent; her voice grows husky; she yells obscenities; she throws a man to his death. Stymied, doctors suggest exorcism. The task falls to an old, holy priest, Father Merrin. On the verge of success, he dies of a heart attack.

In a dramatic gesture, young Father Karras, who has been working with Merrin, challenges the demon to take him and spare the girl. The demon obliges.

Karras is hurtled through an upstairs window to his death. The girl awakes from her ordeal with no memories of it.

▶ **Clarify** The *Rituale Romanum* is a book of rites giving the procedure for church rituals (baptisms, marriages, funerals, exorcisms, and so on).

According to the *Rituale Romanum,* exorcisms may be performed only after all medical and psychiatric remedies have proved ineffective. Moreover, the victim must demonstrate extraordinary signs, such as:

- speaking strange languages,
- knowing things that could not normally be known,
- suffering from unexplainable causes,
- possessing unusual physical powers, like strength.

Unlike many psychiatrists, the Church admits the possibility of ESP and other extraordinary psychic powers as natural phenomena—and, therefore, not as a sufficient basis for performing an exorcism.

▶ **Notebook** Develop the following diagram interactively with the students for entry in their notebooks.

Jesus "power" signals
- Demise of Satan's kingdom
- Rise of God's kingdom

Point 2 **Clarify** Some people contend that Jesus never worked miracles the way the Bible describes them. For example, they say that he didn't exorcise demons. He merely cured epileptics (who appeared to have demons). Or they say he didn't raise the widow's son, because the boy was not really dead. (He only appeared to be.)

The question of whether the widow's son was actually dead or not introduces us to the "leptic" twins (as the author tells his students). They are "Epi" and "Cata."

First, consider *epileptics.* They are people whose body movements are convulsive. Some Bible readers suggest this was the boy's situation in Luke 9:37–43. Recall the episode.

A large crowd met Jesus.
A man shouted from the crowd, "Teacher!
I beg you, look at my son—my only son!
A spirit attacks him with a sudden shout and
throws him into a fit, so that he foams at the mouth;
it keeps on hurting him and will hardly let him go!
I begged your disciples to drive it out, but they couldn't."

Jesus answered . . . , "Bring your son here."
As the boy was coming, the demon knocked him
to the ground and threw him into a fit.
Jesus gave a command to the evil spirit, healed the boy,
and gave him back to his father.
All the people were amazed at the mighty power of God.

Recall that Luke was a doctor. Wouldn't Luke know the difference between an epileptic fit and the above episode: hearing "a sudden shout" (from an invisible source) and seeing the boy knocked down and thrown "into a fit" (presumably by the same invisible source)?

Second, consider *cataleptics.* They are people whose body movements are suspended. Some say this was the case of the widow's son in Luke 7:12–16. This case will be discussed in lesson 67, exercise 1.

Clarify Commenting on the various attempts to rationalize Jesus' miracles, two of the greatest Scripture scholars of our time, David Stanley and Raymond Brown, had this to say:

To start with the presupposition that miracles are impossible . . . is to forget the unique character of the divine intervention in history of Jesus.

The whole Gospel conviction is that the kingdom (or dominion) of God was making its presence felt in an extraordinary way in the ministry of Jesus; and any attempt to set boundaries as to what was possible at this unique moment on the basis of our ordinary experience is very risky.

Point 3 **Discuss** Ask: Why didn't Jesus come right out and say he was the Messiah, rather than conceal it?

For example, after healing a deaf-mute, Jesus ordered him not to tell anyone (Mark 7:36). And after Peter professed faith in Jesus as the Messiah, Jesus said, "Do not tell anyone about me" (Mark 8:30).

Jesus concealed his identity for two reasons. First, many Jews expected the Messiah to be a great warrior king and wear a crown of gold. The reality was that Jesus would be a *servant* king and wear a crown of *thorns.* Jesus had to root out the false ideas before he could teach the true ones. This would take time. Second, it was God's plan that the Messiah would be able to be recognized only by faith, a gift from God (offered to all people). This explains why Jesus said to Peter (after Peter affirmed that Jesus was the promised Messiah):

"This truth did not come to you from any human being,
but it was given to you directly
by my Father in heaven." Matthew 16:17

Notebook Develop the following diagram on the chalkboard for entry in student notebooks.

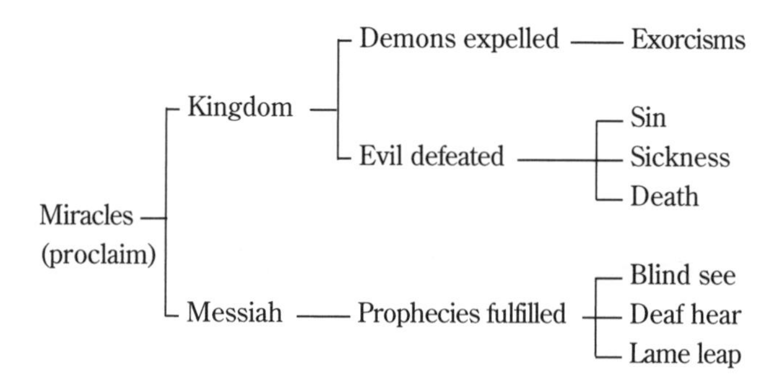

5. LESSON INTERACTION

Exercise 1 **Discuss** Ask: Why wouldn't speaking to the soldier produce the same effect as touching him? Have the student appointed to prepare readings of Luke 4:40 and 8:41–48 read how Jesus used touch to heal people.

Exercise 2 **Discuss** This exercise is self-explanatory. You might have students take time out to record their thoughts in writing and privately before sharing them. This often leads to better discussions.

Exercise 3 **Discuss** **(a)** Joni Eareckson, who is a quadriplegic, touched on this point when she said:

Wouldn't it be exciting if right now . . . I could be miraculously healed . . . ? More exciting and wonderful in the long run would be the miracle of your salvation—the healing of your own soul. You see, that's more exciting because that's something that will last forever. If my body were . . . miraculously healed, I'd be on my feet another thirty or forty years; then my body dies. But a soul lives for eternity. From the standpoint of eternity, my body is only a flicker in the time-span of forever.

(b, c) Responses should be written out privately, screened, and then shared (if the students give permission).

Invitations

LESSON 67

1. LESSON BACKGROUND

▶ *Catechism of the Catholic Church*, 545–546.

2. LESSON QUIZ

Perfect score = 8 points

1. What happened at Lourdes, and who was Dr. Alexis Carrel? *(Lesson 66 review—2 points)*
2. List three ways that Jesus fulfilled Isaiah's prophecies about how miracles would proclaim the Messiah's coming. *(Lesson 66 notebook review—3 points)*
3. Explain in what sense the following three miracles acted as invitations to people: healing blind, healing deaf, raising dead. *(Lesson 67 preview—3 points)*

3. LESSON HOMEWORK

▶ **Return** Lesson 66 review questions (page 139).

▶ **Collect** Lesson 67 review questions (page 141).

▶ **Read** Lesson 68 ("Responses," pages 142–43).

▶ **Write** Lesson 68 review questions (page 143).

4. LESSON PRESENTATION

Point 1 **Read** Have student volunteers alternate reading aloud the core content of lesson 67.

▶ **Notebook** The deeper meaning of Jesus' miracles may be summarized as follows for entry in student notebooks.

Invitations to people
- To open their eyes to what Jesus does
- To open their ears to what Jesus says
- To open their hearts to Jesus and God's kingdom

▶ **Notebook** Summarize the three groups of Jesus' followers for entry in student notebooks.

Followers
- The unnumbered crowd
- The seventy-two disciples
- The twelve apostles

▶ **Clarify** Referring to the unnumbered crowd, Matthew writes in his Gospel:

When Jesus came down from the hill
[Sermon on the Mount],
large crowds followed him. Matthew 8:1

Referring to the seventy-two disciples, Luke writes:

The Lord chose another seventy-two men
and sent them out two by two,
to go head of him to every town and place
where he himself was about to go [saying] . . .
"Whenever you go into a town and are made welcome . . .
heal the sick in that town, and say to the people there,
'The Kingdom of God
has come near you.' " Luke 10:1, 8–9

Referring to the twelve apostles, Luke writes:

[Jesus] called his disciples to him
and chose twelve of them, whom he named apostles:
Simon (whom he named Peter) and his brother Andrew;
James and John, Philip and Bartholomew,
Matthew and Thomas, James son of Alphaeus,
and Simon (who was called the Patriot),
Judas son of James, and Judas Iscariot,
who became the traitor. Luke 6:13–16

▶ **Clarify** Peter's name heads every list of the apostles, just as Judas's name ends every list (Matthew 10:2–4, Mark 3:16–19, Luke 6:14–16).

Peter's name occurs 115 times in the New Testament, compared to second-place John, whose name appears only 34 times.

Peter is closely linked with Jesus: paying the tax for Jesus (Matthew 17:27), walking on the water (Matthew 14:29), strengthening the brothers (Luke 22:32).

▶ **Notebook** The biblical themes of "rock," "key," and "shepherd" are linked in a special way to Peter. We may summarize them as follows for entry in student notebooks.

Rock theme
- God = rock — Isaiah 26:4 (NAB)
- Jesus = rock — 1 Corinthians 10:4
- Peter = rock — Matthew 16:18

Clarify The term *rock* is applied 41 times to God (Yahweh) in the Old Testament. Some Bible translations render the word *protector* instead of *rock*. The famous English hymn "Rock of Ages" derives from this title (Isaiah 26:4 [NAB]).

Notebook Develop the following diagrams on the chalkboard for entry in student notebooks.

Key theme
- God holds key — Isaiah 22:22
- Jesus holds key — Revelation 3:7
- Peter holds key — Matthew 16:19

Note that the one holding the key to a house or car controls the contents or the use of these objects. This person is either the owner or the owner's representative.

Shepherd theme
- God = shepherd — Psalm 23
- Jesus = shepherd — John 10:14
- Peter = shepherd — John 21:16

5. LESSON INTERACTION

Exercise 1 **Read** Have the student appointed to prepare this passage read it to the class.

Barclay suggests that the widow's son was in a cataleptic trance and in danger of being buried alive. Burials in Jesus' day took place the same day as death and, frequently, without embalmment of any kind.

Premature burial was a big fear as recent as the 1800s. The American writer Edgar Allan Poe was a cataleptic and had a fear of being buried alive. One of his short stories was called "The Premature Burial."

Michael Crichton touches on the same point in his book *The Great Train Robbery.* He said that some people devised incredible devices to guard against being buried alive. The wealthy used to insert a pipe into the coffin and have it protrude from the ground. "A trusted family servant would be required to remain at the cemetery, day and night, for a month or more, on the chance that the deceased would suddenly awake and call for help."

There are a number of other biblical stories of people being restored to life after apparent death, for example, Luke 8:49–56 (Jairus's daughter), John 11:32–44 (Lazarus), Acts 9:36–42 (Peter restores Dorcas).

Exercise 2 **Discuss** Ask: Isn't God calling young people today, or do young people hear the call and turn it down, as does the rich young man in Matthew 19:16–22?

Activity Have students copy this chart in their notebooks.

First choice	Evaluation
Second choice	

Instruct students: After "First choice" and "Second choice," list an occupation that you have seriously thought about doing as your life's work.

After the students have filled in their choices, instruct them to list below each choice the best reason they can think of for both choosing this life's work and for not choosing it.

After the students have written their reasons, have them do an evaluation of their reasons, using these norms:

A = altruistic (basically service-centered),
NA = nonaltruistic (basically self-centered).

Clarify Jesus portrays a Christian's vocation as being primarily a service-centered calling, saying to his disciples:

"I, your Lord and Teacher, have just washed your feet.
You, then, should wash one another's feet.
I have set an example for you, so that you will do
just what I have done for you." John 13:14–15

In choosing a vocation, therefore, a Christian should consider the following three factors in a special way:

- Gospel invitation — Jesus invites us to a life of loving service (God and neighbor).
- Social needs — What are the contemporary needs of the human family (society) and the faith family (Church)?
- Personal talents — How might we be "gifted" to serve the needs of these two families? Which family is in greater need?

Exercise 3 **Discuss** This is a fun exercise. You might have students break into pairs and do this exercise privately before sharing their conclusions with the entire class.

Exercise 4 **Activity** This is another fun exercise. You might assign it as a homework project, exhibit the ads, and have the class choose the best three ads.

Exercise 5 **Discuss** Have the student assigned to prepare this passage read it to the class. Then give the students a few minutes of quiet time to write out their responses privately before sharing them with the group.

Responses

LESSON 68

1. LESSON BACKGROUND

▶ *Catechism of the Catholic Church*, 1427–1429.

2. LESSON QUIZ

Perfect score = 8 points

1. List one way miracles proclaim Jesus to be the promised Messiah. *(Lesson 67 review—1 point)*
2. List the three groups into which tradition divides Jesus' followers. *(Lesson 67 notebook review—3 points)*
3. List the four seedbeds into which the farmer's seed falls in Jesus' parable of the sower (farmer). *(Lesson 68 preview—4 points)*

3. LESSON HOMEWORK

▶ **Return** Lesson 67 review questions (page 141).

▶ **Collect** Lesson 68 review questions (page 143).

▶ **Read** Lesson 69 ("Love As I Love," pages 144–45).

▶ **Write** Lesson 69 review questions (page 145).

▶ **Appoint** Student to prepare Luke 7:11–15, Mark 11:1–3, Luke 2:46–47, Luke 8:50–56 (lesson 69, exercise 3).

4. LESSON PRESENTATION

Point ① **Read** Have student volunteers alternate reading aloud the core content of lesson 68.

▶ **Activity** Before beginning this section, write the following equation on a sheet of paper large enough for all the students to see.

XI + I = X

Have a student come up and hold the sheet so that all can see the equation.

Next, ask the students: Is this equation correct or incorrect? Why? (Incorrect, because XI = 11 and I = 1. The solution should read XII.) While the student is still holding the equation, ask: Do you *believe* it is possible to make this equation correct without altering its letters in any way?

Be sure you word the question exactly as it is written above. Then give the students time to study the equation.

After letting the students study it, ask those students who do *not believe* it can be made correct to raise their hands. Then ask those who *believe* it can be made correct to explain how.

If no one comes up with an acceptable answer, have the student holding the sheet turn his or her back to the class, turn the sheet upside down, and turn back to the class. The equation now reads correctly:

X = I + IX

▶ **Discuss** Ask: How might this experiment give us an insight into why some people refuse to believe in miracles?

▶ **Clarify** A number of years ago an American newspaper reporter showed Asian peasants a photograph of the New York City skyline. They refused to believe such a place existed.

Belief implies something cannot be known by reason. If something is so contrary to our everyday experience that we cannot even imagine it, we tend not to believe.

It is the same way with "miracles." They are so contrary to human experience that many people cannot accept them.

▶ **Clarify** Recall the quotation by David Stanley and Raymond Brown in lesson 66 of this manual (point 2):

To start with the presupposition that miracles are impossible . . . is to forget the unique character of the divine intervention in history of Jesus.

The whole Gospel conviction is that the kingdom (or dominion) of God was making its presence felt in an extraordinary way in the ministry of Jesus; and any attempt to set boundaries as to what was possible at this unique moment on the basis of our ordinary experience is very risky.

What Stanley and Brown say is especially true of people in modern times.

People have been so conditioned by science that we think everything can be explained. By definition we tend to rule out the *mysterious* and the *miraculous*.

This is tragic because it makes the human intellect the final judge of what is or is not true. The norm: Can I understand it? This is a poor norm, as we saw when we studied the Book of Job. Recall its point:

Human wisdom falls so short of God's wisdom that it is folly for us to challenge God. For example, even at a human, everyday level there are so many things we don't understand, so why should we refuse to believe something at a divine level because we cannot understand it?

Recall that when Job finally got this through his head, he was transformed from being a sage (wise person) to being a saint (holy person). He was transformed from a person who walked by the *light of reason* to a person who walked also by the *light of faith*.

► **Clarify** A second reason why some people don't believe in Jesus' miracles is because they *don't want* to believe in them. For example, if they really believed, then they would have to reform and start living as Jesus taught. So they deny the reality of Jesus and miracles.

► **Clarify** A third reason why people refuse to believe is skepticism. Recall that when Neil Armstrong walked on the moon, 20 percent of inner-city residents doubted that it really happened. They thought the whole thing might have been staged in a television studio.

We have something similar when it comes to religion today. The cover of *Time* magazine (April 10, 1995) carried a painting of Jesus. Across it was this sentence: "Can We Still Believe in Miracles?"

In the same issue of *Time,* an article by Nancy Gibbs tells how people report "miraculous" sightings of Jesus or Mary everywhere, even on the "fender of a Dodge Dart." It goes on to quote Father John Meier, Bible professor at Catholic University of America in Washington, D.C. He says in Volume 2 of his book *A Marginal Jew: Rethinking the Historical Jesus* (Doubleday, 1991) that no one is more skeptical of accepting these sightings at face value than the Catholic Church.

Fanaticism has a way of giving all of religion a bad name and in making people skeptical about true religion and belief.

In spite of all the skepticism about religion, a *Time* magazine poll revealed that nearly 70 percent of people today "believe" in miracles.

► **Discuss** Have students explain the following quotes from the *Time* magazine article on miracles.

- *For the truly faithful, no miracle is necessary; for those who must doubt, no miracle is sufficient.*
- *When reports spread of statues weeping or crosses bleeding . . . the [Catholic] church is often slow to respond, fearful that the search for a sign will distract from the hard work of faith.*
- *Christ was either liar, lunatic, or Lord.* Thomas Aquinas

Point ❷ **Notebook** To clarify Jesus' parable of the sower, develop the following interactively with the students for entry in their notebooks.

Seeds' Bed	Seeds' Fate	Application of Seeds' Fate to My Life
Path	Stolen	I don't heed word (ignore).
Rock	Withers	I heed and fall (temptation).
Thorns	Chokes	I heed and forget (too busy).
Soil	Grows	I heed and grow (bear fruit).

► **Notebook** Develop the following interactively for entry in student notebooks to show the link between the plot and the point of Jesus' parable of the sower.

Plot	Comparison	Point
Seeds' growth depends on seedbed	Seed to word	Word's growth depends on heart

5. LESSON INTERACTION

Exercise ❶ **Discuss** The four stories illustrate the four seedbeds as follows: *path* (Kenneth Clark), *thorns* (girl), *rock* (Jordan brothers—Clarence told Robert, "You're not a *follower* of Jesus; you're just a *fan* of his"), *soil* (man in *Finding God* by Savary and O'Connor).

Exercise ❷ **Activity** Have students do this exercise in class in writing and in private. Collect the responses, pick out the best four or five, and read them in the next class (get student permission and keep responses anonymous).

Exercise ❸ **Activity** This makes an excellent homework assignment. Read the best four or five to the class.

Miniposter **Discuss** Ask: How does the quotation in the miniposter on page 142 apply to believing in Jesus and to living out his teachings?

Love As I Love

LESSON 69

1. LESSON BACKGROUND

▶ *Catechism of the Catholic Church*, 1965–1974.

2. LESSON QUIZ

Perfect score = 10 points

1. Explain what happened to (the fate of) the seeds that fell on the following four seedbeds: path, rock, thorns, soil. *(Lesson 68 review—4 points)*
2. Explain how the "seeds' fate" in each "seedbed" applies to a person's life. *(Lesson 68 notebook review—4 points)*
3. Explain in what sense Jesus made love the "sign" and the "power" of God's kingdom. *(Lesson 69 preview—2 points)*

3. LESSON HOMEWORK

▶ **Return** Lesson 68 review questions (page 143).

▶ **Collect** Lesson 69 review questions (page 145).

▶ **Read** Lesson 70 ("Forgive As I Forgive," pages 146–47).

▶ **Write** Lesson 70 review questions (page 147).

▶ **Appoint** Three students to each pick a song and plan how to communicate its title to the class without using words (lesson 70, exercise 1b).

4. LESSON PRESENTATION

Point ❶ **Read** Have student volunteers alternate reading aloud the core content of lesson 69.

▶ **Clarify** Reggie Williams was partially deaf. Try to give the students an appreciation of the plight of the deaf. The following might help.

Many people wake up each morning to the whir of a vibrator under their pillow. These people are deaf. Helen Keller, who was both deaf and blind, considered her deafness a greater handicap than her blindness. For deaf people, turning on a radio is useless, and watching TV is bland. The deaf cannot understand people around them. They soon begin to feel abandoned and lonely.

▶ **Notebook** Luke's Gospel begins "Dear Theophilus." *Theophilus* derives from two Greek words: *theo* ("God") and *philus* ("loved"). Thus, *Theophilus* means "loved by God." Interestingly, there are four words for "love" in Greek. Have students list the four words and their English equivalents in their notebooks.

Love (4 words)		
	Storge	Family love
	Eros	Sexual love
	Philia	Friendship love
	Agape	Christian love

Agape is often translated into English as "charity," rather than "love," to stress its special quality. This explains the expression "faith, hope, and charity."

▶ **Notebook** Jesus made *agape* ("Christian love") not only the *sign* to indicate the presence of God's kingdom on earth, but also the *power* by which the kingdom spreads. Have students copy this summary diagram in their notebooks.

Love		
	Sign	Shows God's kingdom
	Power	Spreads God's kingdom

Point ❷ **Clarify** Love is like sunlight, and flowers are like people. When warmed by sunlight (loved), flowers "open" and bloom; when deprived of sunlight (not loved), flowers "close."

When flowers are nipped by the frost, they become "hurt and disfigured." When people are nipped by the "frost of unlove," they too become "hurt and disfigured."

Worse yet, people put on masks to hide their hurt and disfigurement. This can lead to tragedy, as the following moving letter illustrates.

Written to the students of a Catholic high school in a southern city, it is dated Sunday, February 14, 1982, and was written by a boy's parents. It is reproduced in "sense lines" to facilitate your reading it to the class.

We buried our son Thursday.
He got into bed Tuesday
and very deliberately put a gun to his temple
and shot a bullet straight through his brain,
very bloodlessly so we would suffer less.
Mike was bright, handsome, witty, shy,
and with ease did well in school.
His phone rang constantly, and his friends
were in and out of the house all of the time.
The coroner's report showed no drugs.

In reality he had lots of friends.
Each individual, however,
has his own perception of reality—his reality.
Sunday night, Mike got drunk
and we had a long talk,
and for the first time we realized
our rosy perception of the state of his life
wasn't his.
He was very sad.
He felt his friends didn't care about him—
even though we know they DID.

We believe you all can help God
make this world a happier place to live.

Somewhere between the ages 20 and 35,
people begin to feel secure enough
to tell their friends "I love you"
or "I'm glad you're my friend."
Please be brave, because at your age
it is a scary, chancy thing to say,
but please tell your friends
that they are your friends and you do care.
This is most important
because a person can feel most alone
when he is surrounded by people.

There are also some in your school
who truly have no friends.
Their phone never rings
and friends never come over.
Please make friends with them.
They are really lonely.
If Mike felt such despair when he had friends,
just imagine the sadness and loneliness
those boys and girls must feel and endure.

God put each of us on earth
to do good and to bring joy.
Please help and make Mike's death
bring love and joy to the world
in a concrete manner.

Growing up is very hard
and there is so much each of you
must sort out for yourself.
Your parents and family are there,
but your peers are so important too.
Please, please open your hearts
and tell your friends that you love them.

Ask: What struck you most in this letter and why?

Ask: What were some thoughts that went through your mind as you listened to this letter?

Ask: What are some reasons why students are not kinder to one another?

5. LESSON INTERACTION

Exercise ❶ **Discuss** Many people don't help others in dangerous situations for fear of risking their own life.

Ask: How do you feel about this reason?

Ask: Can you name a situation in which you would risk your life to come to the aid of someone in this situation?

Copy the following on the chalkboard. It presents Augustine's allegory in the form of a matching quiz.

1. _____ Jerusalem	*a.* prophets
2. _____ Jericho	*b.* Jesus' second coming
3. _____ robbers	*c.* heaven
4. _____ wounded man	*d.* world
5. _____ priest	*e.* Torah
6. _____ Levite	*f.* Satan and bad angels
7. _____ Samaritan	*g.* the Church
8. _____ inn	*h.* Adam (human race)
9. _____ Samaritan's return	*i.* Jesus

The answers are as follows:

1. c	4. h	7. i
2. d	5. e	8. g
3. f	6. a	9. b

▶ **Activity** You might make this a class project. Have the students do a written report answering these questions:

- What was your random act of senseless kindness?
- What impact did it have on you? On the recipient?

Exercise ❷ **Activity** This exercise generates a lot of interest. Be sure to have the students respond to the questions at the end of the exercise. Reflection on this exercise is as important as the exercise itself.

Exercise ❸ **Activity** This exercise can be a lot of fun—and should be. Have the appointed student read the four Scripture passages. Some episodes that lend themselves to creative items are to be found in Mark 1:1–3:35 and Luke 18:1–19:48.

Photo **Discuss** Ask: What point does the Indian poet Tagore make in the quotation in the photo caption on page 145 of the textbook?

Forgive As I Forgive

LESSON 70

1. LESSON BACKGROUND

► *Catechism of the Catholic Church*, 976–983, 1439.

2. LESSON QUIZ

Perfect score = 8 points

1. In what sense was the setting of the parable of the Good Samaritan based on a real situation? *(Lesson 69 review—1 point)*
2. The Greeks had four words for love: *storge, eros, philia, agape.* To what love does each refer? *(Lesson 69 notebook review—4 points)*
3. Explain the meaning of the following images in the parable of the Prodigal Son: giving the son (a) a hug, (b) shoes, (c) a ring. *(Lesson 70 preview—3 points)*

3. LESSON HOMEWORK

► **Return** Lesson 69 review questions (page 145).

► **Collect** Lesson 70 review questions (page 147).

► **Read** Lesson 71 ("Pray As I Pray," pages 148–49).

► **Write** Lesson 71 review questions (page 149).

4. LESSON PRESENTATION

Point 1 **Read** Have student volunteers alternate reading aloud the core content of lesson 70.

► **Activity** Have the students think of someone who has hurt them intentionally, not just by accident.

Next, have the students write down in their notebooks why they found (perhaps still find) it hard to forgive that person as fully as Jesus forgives us.

Then, ask for volunteers to share (1) how someone hurt them intentionally and (2) why they found (perhaps still find) it hard to forgive that person.

Finally, ask for volunteers (who have forgiven someone fully) to share what helped them most to forgive someone who hurt them intentionally.

► **Clarify** One way Jesus suggested we go about trying to forgive those who have hurt us is to "pray for those who mistreat you" (Luke 6:28).

Ask: Why do you think this would help us forgive someone who hurt us intentionally?

An example of "praying for those who mistreat you" is this prayer found in the Ravensbruck concentration camp. Mary Craig quotes it in her article "Take Up Your Cross" in *The Way* (January 1973). It reads:

O Lord, remember not only the men and women of goodwill, but also those of ill will.

Do not remember all the suffering they have inflicted on us; remember the fruits we have bought, thanks to this suffering—our comradeship, our loyalty, our humility, our courage, our generosity, the greatness of heart which has grown out of all this, and when they come to judgment let all the fruits that they have borne be their forgiveness.

After reading this passage to the students, have them name the six fruits the prisoners "bought, thanks to their suffering." List them on the chalkboard and ask how the concentration camp experience produced them.

comradeship	humility	generosity
loyalty	courage	greatness of heart

Ask the students to explain how the concentration camp may have produced these six "fruits."

Point 2 **Reread** Have a student reread the portion of the parable of the Prodigal Son that is quoted in the textbook.

► **Clarify** Recall that the younger son's "share" of the inheritance was less than his brother's share. Ask: Why? (Deuteronomy 21:17 says that the father will give his firstborn son "a double share of his possession.")

► **Clarify** Point out that it was a cruel act for the younger son to ask for his share of the inheritance in advance. Ask: Why? (The father might need it because of sickness in his old age. Sirach 33:22–23 cautions a father against giving his inheritance beforehand, saying:

Keep control over all that you do. . . .
Wait until the last moment of your life,
when you are breathing your last,
and then divide your property among your heirs.)

► **Clarify** The pivotal point in the parable is the son's admission of sin and his decision to return home.

The first step in any conversion process is the admission of one's sinfulness. Today, there is a growing tendency to "whitewash" evil. This led Louis Evely to write the following in the book *In His Presence.* Read it to the students.

The worst evil lies not in committing evil, but in committing evil while pretending it is good. . . . Woe to him who does evil and lies to himself. It is better to commit a sin than to corrupt a principle. It is better to sin with sincerity than to lie to oneself in order to stay virtuous. . . . If you are weak enough to sin, do not be too proud to recognize the fact.

▶ **Clarify** Stress the father's response to the sight of his son returning home. It illustrates one of Jesus' main points in telling his parable. Recall the context that led Jesus to tell this parable.

One day when many tax collectors and other outcasts
came to listen to Jesus,
the Pharisees and the teachers of the Law [scribes]
started grumbling,
"This man welcomes outcasts
and even eats with them!"
So Jesus told them this parable. Luke 15:1–3

Jesus' point comes down to this: Your heavenly Father is like the father of the wayward boy. He is forgiving. We should forgive others as he forgives us.

Placing a robe on the boy's body and a ring on the boy's finger recalls a similar scene in 1 Maccabees 6:14–15. Aware that he is dying, Antiochus IV summons a friend, Philip, places a crown on his head, a robe on his body, and a ring on his finger. He transfers to him his authority and power.

▶ **Notebook** The key points of the father's response to his son may be summarized for entry in student notebooks.

Father's response	Embrace	Total welcome
	Shoes	Total forgiveness
	Ring	Total restoration

Point ❸ **Discuss** Stress that the parable has two parts. The first deals with the younger son, who repents. The second deals with the elder son, who resents the father's forgiveness so much that he won't celebrate.

Ask: How do the two parts reflect the audience to whom Jesus tells the parable? (Sinners and outcasts = younger son; Pharisees and scribes = elder son.)

▶ **Discuss** Stress that Jesus does not tell us how the parable ends. Ask: Why? (The Pharisees and scribes must write their own ending to the parable. After all, it is directed to them, saying in effect: "Will you imitate the father (who stands for your heavenly Father) and rejoice and celebrate with him, as I am doing?"

5. LESSON INTERACTION

Exercise ❶ **Discuss** **(a)** Jesus' parable of the Prodigal Son serves as a "window" through which people look and get a glimpse of God's eagerness to forgive us.

▶ **Activity** **(b)** Have the three appointed students mime their songs. Hopefully they will illustrate the problem Jesus faced in teaching about God and God's kingdom.

Exercise ❷ **Notebook** **(a)** We may sum up how the parable of the Prodigal Son acts as both a *window* and a *mirror* for entry in student notebooks.

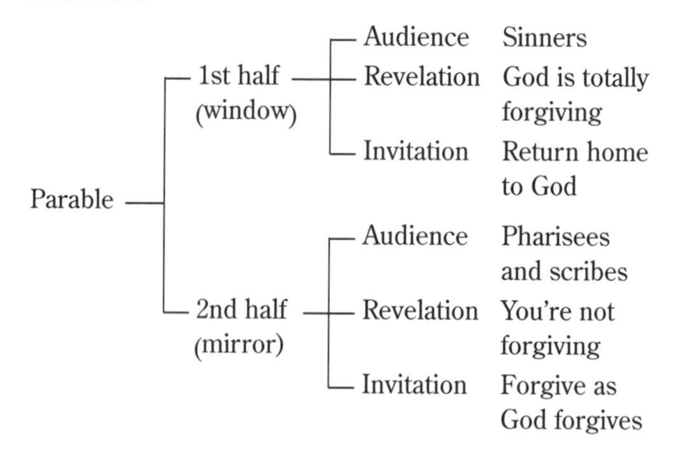

▶ **Discuss** **(b)** Mirror parables were ideal because they invited the leaders to "see" themselves as they really were: open or closed to truth. And they did this in a nonthreatening way, not by accusing them, but by inviting them to respond to what they "see." Other mirror parables in Luke include:

Lost sheep (15:1–7)	Am I concerned about the wayward as God is?
Samaritan (10:25–37)	Am I concerned about the needy as the Samaritan was?
Sower (8:4–15)	Which of the four seedbeds is my heart like?

Exercise ❸ **Discuss** **(a)** This quote recalls Jesus' forgiveness of humanity. The "fragrance" he left on our heels was eternal salvation.

(b) We should forgive as God forgives us: forever and forever. Recall that John said, "God is love" (1 John 4:8). Also, God is forgiveness.

Exercise ❹ **Activity** You might want to collect the reflections, sift through them, and read the better ones to the class.

Pray As I Pray

LESSON 71

1. LESSON BACKGROUND

▶ *Catechism of the Catholic Church*, 2598, 2621.

2. LESSON QUIZ

Perfect score = 7 points

1. Explain how the parable of the Prodigal Son acts as both a revelation and an invitation. *(Lesson 70 review—2 points)*
2. To whom (audience) is the first half of the parable of the Prodigal Son addressed, primarily? The second half? *(Lesson 70 notebook review—2 points)*
3. List the three different settings in which Jesus prayed. *(Lesson 71 preview—3 points)*

3. LESSON HOMEWORK

▶ **Return** Lesson 70 review questions (page 147).

▶ **Collect** Lesson 71 review questions (page 149).

▶ **Read** Lesson 72 ("Be Ready Always," pages 150–51).

▶ **Write** Lesson 72 review questions (page 151).

▶ **Appoint** Student to prepare Matthew 13:36–43 (lesson 72, exercise 1).

4. LESSON PRESENTATION

Point ① **Read** Have student volunteers alternate reading aloud the core content of lesson 71.

▶ **Clarify** Dr. Martin Luther King Jr. relates the Montgomery episode in his book *Stride toward Freedom.* Ask: Is prayer a "crutch"—something we grab for in an emergency situation such as King describes? (Prayer is no more a crutch than food and drink are. As food and drink are necessary to sustain our *physical* life, so prayer is necessary to sustain our *spiritual* life.)

Shortly before he died in Thailand, Thomas Merton, the Trappist priest-author, defined prayer in terms of our humanity. He said in a sermon in Darjeeling, India:

Prayer is an expression of who we are. . . . We are living incompleteness. We are gap, an emptiness that calls for fulfillment from someone else, and the very nature of our being as creatures implies this sense of need to be completed by him from whom we come.

Point ② **Notebook** Stress that Jesus prayed often. Besides the seven times a day that pious Jews prayed (Psalm 119:164), Luke's Gospel presents Jesus as praying at all the key moments of his life. Have students list a few representative examples in their notebooks.

Jesus prayed
- At his baptism 3:21
- Often during his ministry 5:16
- Before teaching disciples 11:1
- In Gethsemane 22:41
- On the cross 23:34

▶ **Notebook** Also stress that Jesus prayed in three settings. Have students list them in their notebooks.

Jesus prayed
- Alone Mark 1:35
- In small group Luke 9:28
- With community Luke 4:16

▶ **Discuss** Stress that more and more Christians are gathering in small groups to pray and share their faith.

Ask: Why? (Just as AA's say they could not achieve sobriety on their own, so many Christians are beginning to realize that they cannot live in our modern world without the support of other Christians.)

Consider one example. In 1991, the author began meeting weekly in early-morning faith-sharing sessions with seven Chicago business executives. Out of that experience grew the Vision 2000 Program, an invitation to Christians to pray *daily* (alone) and meet *weekly* (in a small group for support and faith-sharing). The executives have since incorporated into a nonprofit organization for the sole purpose of spreading this practice. Currently, over 700,000 of the program's books are in print.

School faculty members may obtain a complimentary copy of *Spirit 2000* by calling, writing, or faxing:

Victory 2000 Inc., Box 515,
Winnetka, IL 60093–0515
Telephone 708–501–3357
Fax 708–501–3377

The booklet is ideal for students. It contains seven weeks of daily meditations and instructions on conducting faith-sharing sessions. Here is a typical meditation.

The Word . . . brought light to people.
The light shines in the darkness,
and the darkness has never put it out. John 1:5–6

An artist painted a picture
of a single person rowing a boat
across a vast sea at night.
Off in the distant sky is a single star.
The impression you get
as you look at the single person and
the single star is this:
If the person in that boat
ever loses sight of that star in the sky,
the person will be utterly lost.
What the painting says of that person
can be said of me:
If I ever lose sight of Jesus in my life,
I will be utterly lost.

What was the closest I ever came
to losing sight of Jesus in my life?
What kept Jesus in my sight then?

Jesus, be a bright star before me.
Be a silent wake behind me.
Be a rolling path beneath me.
Be a ray of light within me.
Be all these things now and forever. Anonymous

Clarify Stress that Jesus prayed with freedom. Outwardly, he prayed in different bodily postures; inwardly, he used different prayer forms.

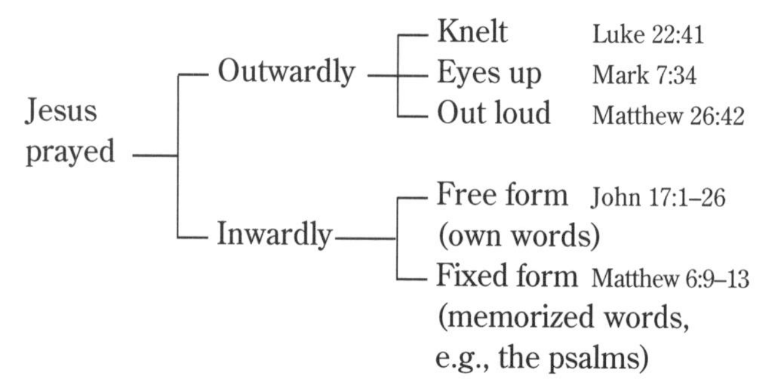

5. LESSON INTERACTION

Exercise ① **Activity** This exercise is important. It will give you a good idea of where your students are in their prayer. Item *f* of the exercise ("Explain your answer to *e*") is especially important to note.

Exercise ② **Notebook** Have the students list and explain the four forms in their notebooks.

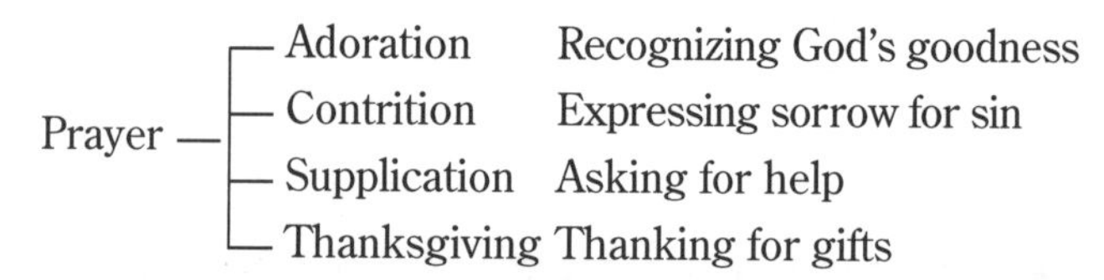

Exercise ③ **Notebook** Develop the following diagram of the "your" petitions and the "our" petitions for entry in student notebooks.

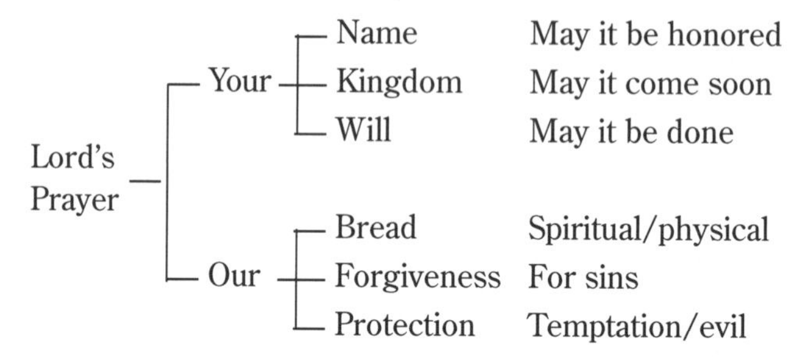

Clarify The *Catechism of the Catholic Church* subdivides the Lord's Prayer into seven petitions. For clarity and simplicity, however, the final two (closely linked in reality) have been combined in the schematic diagram above.

Discuss Jesus said, "The Kingdom of God is within you" (Luke 17:21). Ask: Why pray for God's kingdom to come if it is already here? (God's kingdom has come, but not yet in its fullness. Like a growing plant, it is growing but not yet fully grown.)

The current status of God's kingdom is not at all unique. Consider the following illustration by W. D. Davies.

One Sunday during World War II, I was walking home from church when a friend accosted me and said, "Have you heard the news?" I said, "What news?" And he replied, "Hitler has invaded Russia." And at once I answered, "Then the Allies have won the war."

This was in 1943, and the war went on till 1945. But I knew—as did all who knew the history of Napoleon—that, once Hitler had engaged a war on two fronts, West and East, his defeat was certain, however long the war continued. The turning point of World War II was the invasion of Russia.

In a similar way, Jesus' coming into human history was the turning point in another war—the war between good and evil. The kingdom of God was now assured of victory, even though the fighting would continue for an unspecified period of time.

Be Ready Always

LESSON 72

1. LESSON BACKGROUND

▶ *Catechism of the Catholic Church,* 668–679.

2. LESSON QUIZ

Perfect score =15 points

1. List and explain the four forms prayer can take. *(Lesson 71 review—8 points)*
2. List and explain the three "your" petitions of the Lord's Prayer. *(Lesson 71 notebook review—6 points)*
3. List one of the high points of ancient weddings. *(Lesson 72 preview—1 point)*

3. LESSON HOMEWORK

▶ **Return** Lesson 71 review questions (page 149).

▶ **Collect** Lesson 72 review questions (page 151).

▶ **Read** Lesson 73 ("Storm Clouds," pages 152–53).

▶ **Write** Lesson 73 review questions (page 153).

▶ **Appoint** Student to prepare Matthew 23:1–27 (lesson 73, exercise 4).

4. LESSON PRESENTATION

Point ❶ **Read** Have student volunteers alternate reading aloud the core content of lesson 72.

▶ **Clarify** You might introduce this lesson by sharing the following "fantasy story" with the students. It will help them get a better appreciation of why Jesus used parables to try to teach the people.

> One day an adventuresome fish wandered off from "Fishland." Suddenly he stumbled upon submarines, divers, and underwater cameras invading the sea world. Excited and alarmed, the adventuresome fish returned to "Fishland" to spread the news about the weird invaders from outerwater.
>
> When the inhabitants from "Fishland" asked the adventuresome fish to describe these invaders, he found it impossible, because the inhabitants had no experience of what a submarine or a camera looked like. So the inhabitants ended up ridiculing the adventuresome fish and not believing him.

▶ **Discuss** Ask students: When it came to teaching people about God's kingdom, how was Jesus' situation like that of the adventuresome fish? (Most of the ideas about God's kingdom were far beyond the experience level of the uneducated people of Jesus' time. At best, Jesus could give only a vague idea of what it was like. This Jesus did by using parables.)

A parable has been described as "an earthly story with a heavenly meaning." That is, it uses earthly images to teach people about spiritual ideas.

Point ❷ **Clarify** Two ideas that Jesus had to teach the people about God's kingdom were the following:

First, when it "reached its completion," Jesus himself would return to judge people on how they had lived their lives and used the talents that God had given them.

Second, the "hour of his return" would catch many people by surprise. They would not be prepared for it.

To teach these two ideas, Jesus made up an earthly story about a situation with which the people were all familiar. It has been called the parable of the young women.

▶ **Notebook** Develop the following diagram interactively with the students for entry in their notebooks.

Begin by having them identify the images in Jesus' parable of the young women (in the order that they appear in the parable). List them as follows:

Parable Images

1. Groom
2. Wise young women
3. Foolish young women
4. Oil in lamps
5. Groom's coming
6. Wedding feast

Next, have the students explain the parable images. (Who/What do they refer to in real life?) List them in the right-hand column opposite the parable image.

Parable Images	***Real life***
1. Groom	Jesus
2. Wise young women	Prepared Christians
3. Foolish young women	Unprepared Christians
4. Oil in lamps	Good works
5. Groom's coming	Jesus' second coming
6. Wedding feast	Heaven

Clarify The oil in the lamps needs clarification. Elsewhere in the Bible, oil is a symbol of "good works." For example, Jesus says in his Sermon on the Mount:

"No one lights a lamp and puts it under a bowl;
instead it is put on the lampstand,
where it gives light for everyone in the house.
In the same way your light must shine before people,
so that they will see the good things you do
and praise your Father in heaven." Matthew 5:15–16

Ask: How does this parable illustrate the fourth great teaching of Jesus? (It warns us to be prepared for Jesus' coming at the end of the world or at the end of our personal lives—whichever event comes first.)

5. LESSON INTERACTION

Exercise 1 **Discuss** Another parable that deals with the kingdom of God is the parable of the weeds and wheat.

Have the students identify the images. Have a "class secretary" list the images on the chalkboard.

Parable Images

a. Sower (farmer)
b. Field
c. Good seed (wheat)
d. Weeds
e. Enemy
f. Harvest
g. Harvest workers
h. Destroying weeds
i. Saving wheat

After the students have listed the images, have them list who or what each image refers to in real life.

When they have finished, have the students compare their answers to Jesus' own explanation to his disciples. Have the appointed student read Matthew 13:36–43.

Parable Images	***Real life***
a. Sower (farmer)	Son of Man (Jesus)
b. Field	World
c. Good seed (wheat)	Good people (kingdom)
d. Weeds	Bad people
e. Enemy	Devil/Evil One
f. Harvest	End of world
g. Harvest workers	Angels
h. Destroying weeds	Hell
i. Saving wheat	Heaven

Exercise 2 **Discuss** The Lord is merely saying what Jesus says in the above parable. The final "welcome home" will come when Jesus greets us in the final judgment.

Clarify Many scientists are now saying that everything we have ever done has been recorded in our brains and can be recalled.

Reporting on this remarkable fact, *Time* magazine (April 19, 1971) cited the work of Dr. Wilder Penfield, director of the Montreal Neurological Institute at that time.

While operating on a woman under local anesthesia, Dr. Penfield discovered that when he touched certain brain sites, the woman relived the experience of having her baby.

Similar experimentation on other patients produced the same results. *Time* magazine concludes:

Penfield's findings have led some scientists to believe that the brain has indelibly recorded every sensation it has ever received and to ask how the recording was made and preserved.

Exercise 3 **Discuss** Markham's point is a hard one for people to implement in their lives. We forget what Joni Eareckson said earlier in this manual (lesson 66, exercise 3).

Wouldn't it be exciting if right now . . . I could be miraculously healed . . . ? More exciting and wonderful in the long run would be the miracle of your salvation—the healing of your own soul. You see, that's more exciting because that's something that will last forever. If my body were . . . miraculously healed, I'd be on my feet another thirty or forty years; then my body dies. But a soul lives for eternity. From the standpoint of eternity, my body is only a flicker in the time-span of forever.

Exercise 4 **Activity** You might have the students do this exercise right in class or as a homework assignment. Select the better responses and share them with the class.

Storm Clouds

LESSON 73

1. LESSON BACKGROUND

▶ *Catechism of the Catholic Church*, 577–582.

2. LESSON QUIZ

Perfect score = 8 points

1. Retell Jesus' parable of the young women, and explain how it illustrates Jesus' fourth great teaching. *(Lesson 72 review—2 points)*
2. In Jesus' parable of the weeds and wheat, who or what do the following images stand for in real life: (a) sower or farmer, (b) field, (c) wheat, (d) weeds, (e) harvest? *(Lesson 72 notebook review—5 points)*
3. Explain how Caiaphas's words to the Jewish leaders were a prophecy in disguise. *(Lesson 73 preview—1 point)*

3. LESSON HOMEWORK

▶ **Return** Lesson 72 review questions (page 151).

▶ **Collect** Lesson 73 review questions (page 153).

▶ **Read** Lesson 74 ("Moment of Truth," pages 154–55).

▶ **Write** Lesson 74 review questions (page 155).

▶ **Appoint** Two students to prepare:
1. Matthew 21:33–46 (vineyard parable); see lesson 74, exercise 1.
2. Luke 6:46–49 (house builders parable), Luke 13:18–19 (mustard seed parable), Luke 15:8–10 (lost coin parable); see lesson 74, exercise 2c.

4. LESSON PRESENTATION

Point 1 **Read** Have student volunteers alternate reading aloud the core content of lesson 73.

▶ **Clarify** Read or explain the following to the class.

Jesus . . . asked his disciples,
"Who do people say the Son of Man is?"
"Some say John the Baptist," they answered.
"Others say Elijah, while others say
Jeremiah or some other prophet."
"What about you?" he asked them.
"Who do you say I am?"
Simon Peter answered,
"You are the Messiah, the Son of the living God." . . .

Then Jesus ordered his disciples
not to tell anyone that he was the Messiah.
From that time on
Jesus began to say plainly to his disciples,
"I must go to Jerusalem and
suffer much from the elders,
the chief priests, and the teachers of the Law.
I will be put to death,
but three days later I will be raised to life."

Peter took him aside and began to rebuke him.
"God forbid it, Lord!" he said.
"That must never happen to you!"

Jesus turned around and said to Peter,
"Get away from me, Satan!
You are an obstacle in my way,
because these thoughts of yours don't come from God,
but from human nature."

Then Jesus said to his disciples,
"If any of you want to come with me, you must
forget yourself, carry your cross, and follow me.
For if you want to save your own life, you will lose it;
but if you lose your life for my sake, you will find it.
Will you gain anything if you win the whole world
but lose your life?" Matthew 16:13–16, 20–26

▶ **Clarify** Point out that when Jesus invited people to follow him, he realized what he was asking of them. For some, the choice was like the one Chava had to make in *Fiddler on the Roof.*

The play, set in Russia around 1905, centers around a man named Tevye. The father of a poor Orthodox Jewish family, he has five daughters and no sons.

As the play develops, Tevye's eldest daughter, Tzeitel, marries a poor tailor, Motel, who was not chosen for her by the traditional matchmaker. Tevye accepts her marriage, but only after a conscience struggle.

Tevye's second daughter, Hodel, marries Perchik, a young student who has broken with many Jewish traditions. Again, Tevye accepts the marriage, but only after a conscience struggle.

Finally, Tevye's third daughter, Chava, marries a Gentile, a young Russian soldier. When Tevye learns what Chava has done (effectively abandoning Judaism for the man she loves), he tells his wife, "Chava is dead to us! We will forget her."

It was like this for many Jews who followed Jesus in the early days of the Church.

Point ❷ **Discuss** Ask: Why would Peter's confession of faith serve as a turning point in Jesus' ministry? (It marks the end of Jesus' teaching ministry in Galilee; the goal of the Galilean ministry [Jesus is the Messiah] is now complete. Recall the two divisions of Mark's Gospel, culminating in Peter's confession of Jesus' *messiahship* and the centurion's confession of Jesus' *divinity.*)

▶ **Discuss** After Peter's confession, Jesus begins his "journey" to Jerusalem, where the final act of the drama of salvation will be enacted.

Ask students: Why didn't the followers of Jesus understand his teaching about his death and rising? Why were they afraid to question him further?

(The answers to these two questions are not clear. Some think the disciples did not understand the part about being "handed over" and killed. Others think that the disciples were afraid to question Jesus further because of their concern about who would "hand over" Jesus. Would it be one of them?)

▶ **Notebook** The following confrontation episodes (there are more) between Jesus and the religious leaders might be entered in student notebooks for reference. Some quotes are adapted to facilitate entry.

Confrontations

Paralytic	"Your sins are forgiven."	Mark 2:5
Demons	"Satan gives him power."	Matthew 12:24
Washings	"Why don't they wash?"	Mark 7:5
Pharisees	"You hypocrites!"	Matthew 23:23
Lazarus	"What shall we do?"	John 11:47
Sellers	"Temple a thieves' den"	Matthew 21:13

5. LESSON INTERACTION

Exercise ❶ **Clarify** In Jesus' day there was not too much of a middle class. People, in general, were divided into two groups: the very rich and the very poor. The gap between them stands out dramatically in Jesus' parable of Lazarus and the rich man.

The rich man is covered with linen, while poor Lazarus is "covered with sores."

The rich man feasts splendidly, while poor Lazarus longs for scraps.

The rich man lives in disregard of Leviticus 25:23, which reminds wealthy landowners that the land "belongs to God, and you are like foreigners who are allowed to make use of it." Thus, rich landowners were expected to pay to God a kind of "rent":

"Share your food with the hungry
and open your homes to the homeless poor.
Give clothes to those
who have nothing to wear." Isaiah 58:7

The death of the two men reverse their situations totally. Lazarus rests in the bosom of Abraham, a symbol of ultimate contentment and intimacy. The rich man, on the other hand, is now licked by flames in contrast to Lazarus, who was once licked by dogs.

When the rich man asks to return to earth to warn his brothers to reform their lives, Abraham refuses:

"If they will not listen to Moses and the prophets,
they will not be convinced
even if someone were to rise from death." Luke 16:31

Abraham was right. Later, a man did rise from the dead. Ironically, his name was Lazarus, also; and many people were unconvinced (John 12).

Interestingly, Albert Schweitzer said it was this parable that made him decide to pass up a brilliant career in music in Europe to become a missionary doctor in Africa. He reasoned that he was the rich man and that his African brother was Lazarus. "How can I enjoy applause while Lazarus endures pain?" he reasoned.

Schweitzer was voted the "Man of the Century" for his work among Africa's poor. He said in an interview:

As I look back upon my youth I realize how important for me were the help, understanding and courage . . . so many people gave me. These men and women entered my life and became powers within me.

On another occasion he said:

The only ones among you who will be really happy are those who have sought and found a way to serve.

Exercises ❷ & ❸ **Discuss** Both of these exercises are self-explanatory.

Exercise ❹ **Discuss** Have the appointed student read Matthew 23:1–27 before discussing this passage. The discussion questions admit of a variety of replies. You may wish to have the students record them before sharing them.

Moment of Truth

LESSON 74

1. LESSON BACKGROUND

▶ *Catechism of the Catholic Church*, 583–586.

2. LESSON QUIZ

Perfect score = 4 points

1. Explain the reason for the hostility between Jesus and the Jewish leaders. *(Lesson 73 review—1 point)*
2. Where did the confrontation between Jesus and the sellers (money changers) take place? *(Lesson 73 notebook review—1 point)*
3. Why were people wondering whether Jesus would show up in Jerusalem for the Passover, and what shocked Jesus when he got to the Temple? *(Lesson 74 preview—2 points)*

3. LESSON HOMEWORK

▶ **Return** Lesson 73 review questions (page 153).

▶ **Collect** Lesson 74 review questions (page 155).

▶ **Read** Lesson 75 ("Passover Supper," pages 156–57).

▶ **Write** Lesson 75 review questions (page 157).

4. LESSON PRESENTATION

Point 1 **Read** Have student volunteers alternate reading aloud the core content of lesson 74.

▶ **Review** Ask: What great event in Jewish history did the Passover commemorate? (Israel's escape from Egypt after four hundred years of slavery under the Egyptians)

Ask: In round numbers, how many centuries before Jesus did that event take place? (Roughly thirteen centuries)

▶ **Clarify** Stress Jesus' courage in coming to Jerusalem even though Jesus knew there was a price on his head. Acquaint the students with General MacArthur's quote to the Filipino Air Force on July 31, 1941: "Only those are fit to live who are not afraid to die." Ask: What did the general mean?

Also share with the students the remark of President Lyndon Johnson to U.S. secret service agents on the occasion of John F. Kennedy's funeral. When they argued that it would be safer for him to ride in the funeral procession rather than to walk in it, he said, "I'd rather give my life than be afraid to give it."

Point 2 **Clarify** As Jesus neared a village a short distance from Jerusalem, he sent two of his disciples ahead to the village with these instructions: "You will find a colt tied up that has never been ridden. Untie it and bring it here" (Mark 11:2). They brought the colt to Jesus, who sat on it and continued his ride to Jerusalem.

Many people spread their cloaks on the road,
while others cut branches. . . .
The people who were in front
and those who followed behind began to shout,
"Praise God! God bless him
who comes in the name of the Lord!
God bless the coming kingdom of King David, our father!
Praise be to God!" Mark 11:8–10

▶ **Clarify** Carpeting the road with garments was not unusual in the East. *The Arabian Nights* mentions it several times. Likewise, the Jews honored Jehu this way when he was anointed king (2 Kings 9:13).

Matthew and John tied the enthusiastic reception of Jesus to Zechariah's prophecy concerning the Messiah:

Shout for joy, you people of Jerusalem!
Look, your king is coming!
He comes triumphant and victorious,
but humble and riding on a donkey. Zechariah 9:9

Luke concludes his Palm Sunday account, saying:

Pharisees in the crowd spoke to Jesus.
"Teacher," they said,
"command your disciples to be quiet!"
Jesus answered, "I tell you that if they keep quiet,
the stones themselves
will start shouting." Luke 19:39–40

Matthew adds:

When Jesus entered Jerusalem,
the whole city was thrown into an uproar.
"Who is he?" the people asked.
"This is the prophet Jesus, from Nazareth in Galilee,"
the crowds answered. Matthew 21:10–11

▶ **Clarify** Point out the photo on page 154 in the textbook. It captures the excitement and spirit of Jesus' entry into Jerusalem on the first Palm Sunday. Also point out the photo and plan of the Temple on page 155 and the artist's aerial view on page 178. The five main areas of the Temple are listed below. You may want to review with the students some of biblical references that relate to these areas.

Notebook Develop the following for entry in student notebooks.

1. HOLY OF HOLIES
   High priest alone enters — Hebrews 9:7
   Curtain torn — Mark 15:38
2. COURT OF PRIESTS
   Zechariah murdered — Matthew 23:35
3. COURT OF ISRAEL (MEN)
   Boy Jesus — Luke 2:46
   Two men went to pray — Luke 18:10
4. COURT OF WOMEN
   Mary purified — Luke 2:22
   Widow's mite — Luke 21:1–4
5. COURT OF GENTILES
   Jesus expels merchants — Matthew 21:12

Clarify A barrier separated the Court of Gentiles from the other courts. Archaeologists have discovered two signs on this barrier. A photo of one sign (and its chilling inscription) is found on page 201 of the textbook. Be sure to have the students check it.

Clarify Herod the Great was responsible for the remodeled Temple of Jesus' time. It was a massive undertaking.

Herod is said to have engaged ten thousand workers and to have trained a thousand priests in crafts to work in the sacred parts of the Temple, where laymen were not permitted. Decorative work in the Temple continued until 64 C.E. The Pharisees reminded Jesus, "It has taken forty-six years to build this Temple!" (John 2:20).

Clarify Money changers and sellers of animals and doves for sacrifice in the Temple were restricted to the Court of Gentiles. Commenting on Jesus' anger at what he saw in the Court of Gentiles, William Barclay writes:

There were times when a pair of doves cost as little as five new pence outside the Temple and as much as seventy-five new pence inside it. . . .

The stalls where the sacrificial victims were sold turned the Temple Court into a marketplace. What should have been a place of prayer had become a place of noisy bargaining.

Point 3 **Clarify** The parable of the vineyard tenants was inspired by Isaiah's "Song of the Vineyard" (Isaiah 5:1–7).

Clarify Ancient Jews divided the Bible into three groups of books: law, writings, and the prophets (early and later). The *early* prophetic books include Joshua, Judges, Samuel, and Kings. The *later* prophetic books include Isaiah, Jeremiah, Ezekiel, and so on.

Clarify The prophet Ezekiel attacked the leaders of Israel in his parable of the shepherds (34:1–16). It makes good reading. We could substitute "senators" for "shepherds" and apply it to our own times.

Notebook The three important truths that grow out of the parable of the tenants may be summarized this way:

Vineyard tenants (3 truths)
- Leadership passes to apostles
- Jewish leaders judged themselves
- Jesus is God's (owner's) Son

5. LESSON INTERACTION

Exercise 1 **Activity** Have the students do the matchup privately before sharing and discussing their responses.

Before they begin, have the appointed student who prepared Matthew 21:33–46 read the parable aloud. Instruct the students to listen carefully.

The correct matchup is as follows:

a. 4	*c.* 6	*e.* 3	*g.* 2	*i.* 1
b. 5	*d.* 9	*f.* 8	*h.* 7	

Exercise 2 **Notebook** **(a, b)** For a review of the window and mirror parables, see lesson 70, exercises 1 and 2.

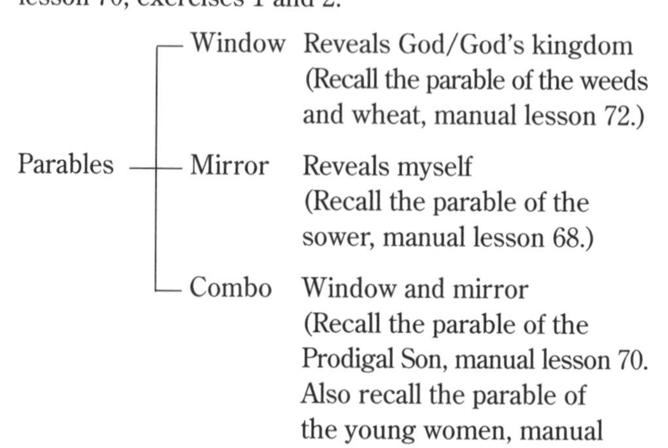

Activity **(c)** Have the appointed student who prepared the reading of the three parables read them one at a time. Have the class discuss them one at a time.

- House builders — Mirror: Which builder am I like?
- Mustard seed — Window: God's kingdom is like . . .
- Lost coin (combo) — Window: God's concern for me, when I'm lost (sin), and God's joy when I'm found (return). Mirror: Am I as concerned for wayward brothers and sisters as God is for me? Do I reach out to them or pray for them?

Passover Supper

LESSON 75

1. LESSON BACKGROUND

▶ *Catechism of the Catholic Church*, 610.

2. LESSON QUIZ

Perfect score = 15 points

1. What do the following images in the parable of the vineyard tenants stand for in real life: (a) vineyard owner, (b) vineyard, (c) owner's son, (d) first tenants, (e) first renting, (f) slaves, (g) second renting, (h) other tenants? *(Lesson 74 review—8 points)*
2. List the five main areas into which the Temple was divided. *(Lesson 74 notebook review—5 points)*
3. What two events would the drinking of red wine have recalled at the Passover supper? *(Lesson 75 preview—2 points)*

3. LESSON HOMEWORK

▶ **Return** Lesson 74 review questions (page 155).

▶ **Collect** Lesson 75 review questions (page 157).

▶ **Read** Lesson 76 ("Invitation to Remember," pages 158–59).

▶ **Write** Lesson 76 review questions (page 159).

4. LESSON PRESENTATION

Point 1 **Read** Have student volunteers alternate reading aloud the core content of lesson 75.

▶ **Notebook** The difference between the ordinary, or popular, idea of remembering and the biblical idea is important. It may be summarized for entry in student notebooks as follows:

Remember		
	Popular	Recall an event mentally
	Biblical	Recall an event *sacra*mentally (bring it into the present by faith, relive it, and share in its original power and blessing)

Point 2 **Clarify** Jesus sent Peter and John off with the following instructions to prepare for the Passover meal.

"Go and get the Passover meal ready for us to eat. . . .
As you go into the city,
a man carrying a jar of water will meet you.
Follow him into the house that he enters,
and say to the owner of the house:
'The Teacher says to you, Where is the room
where my disciples and I will eat the Passover meal?'
He will show you a large furnished room upstairs,
where you will get everything ready."
They went off and found everything
just as Jesus had told them. Luke 22:8–13

The secrecy of all this may have stemmed from a concern that an attempt may be made to arrest Jesus.

Point 3 **Clarify** Normally, Jews ate two meals daily: one about 10 A.M., the other late in the afternoon. The Passover meal, however, was eaten at night, after the appearance of the first stars. Thus, everyone celebrated the meal at the same time as one family.

As Jesus and his disciples awaited the first stars, they would have seen Passover fires blazing throughout the city. Once the stars appeared, Jesus, acting as father, began the Passover ceremonies. Instead of sitting, as at ordinary meals, Jews reclined at the Passover in the fashion of Greeks and Romans at banquets.

Point 4 **Clarify** Possibly after the disciples had all reclined, Jesus rose from the table, "poured some water into a washbasin and began to wash the disciples' feet" (John 13:5). Richard Foster writes:

The disciples [knew] . . . that someone needed to wash the others' feet. The problem was that the only people who washed feet were the least. So there they sat, feet caked with dirt. It was such a sore point that they were not even going to talk about it. Then Jesus took a towel and basin and redefined greatness.

Ask: In what sense did Jesus redefine greatness? (Jesus had said earlier (Matthew 23:11–12):

"The greatest one among you must be your servant.
Whoever makes himself great will be humbled,
and whoever humbles himself will be made great.")

Jesus underscored his action, saying to his disciples:

"I, your Lord and Teacher,
have just washed your feet. . . .
I have set an example for you,
so that you will do
just what I have done for you." John 13:14–15

▶ **Discuss** A group of Chinese Christians invited an American biblical scholar to come to China to give a workshop on Scripture. In the course of the workshop, the scholar asked the participants to select the episode in the Gospel that impressed them most.

To his surprise, the Chinese Christians did not pick the Sermon on the Mount, the crucifixion of Jesus, or the resurrection of Jesus. Rather, they picked Jesus' washing of his disciples' feet.

▶ **Discuss** Donald Hankey's book *The Beloved Captain* tells how the captain cared for his men's feet. After long marches he would go into the barracks of his men to inspect their feet. He would get down on his hands and knees to take a good look at the worst cases. If a blister needed lancing, he would lance it himself. Hankey says about the captain's concern for his men's feet, "There was no affectation about this."

Ask students: What did Hankey mean by saying "There was no affectation about this"?

Charles Colson had an office next to President Nixon. He was convicted in the Watergate scandal and sentenced to prison. There, he underwent a conversion to Christianity. One of his jobs in prison was to work in the laundry, sorting the dirty socks of prisoners and washing them. Colson said he tried to do this job in the "spirit of Jesus," who washed the feet of his disciples.

▶ **Clarify** The red wine that was used at Passover meals would have recalled two events, especially: (1) the blood-marked doorposts in Egypt and (2) the covenant blood at Mount Sinai.

Jesus drank from the cup and passed it. Drinking from the same cup symbolized and dramatized the close bond that united those gathered for the Passover meal.

5. LESSON INTERACTION

Exercise ① **Discuss** **(a)** This exercise is important in that it dramatizes the difference between the popular and the biblical idea of remembering.

(b) Every time we celebrate the Eucharist ("Do this in memory of me") we do more than recall what Jesus did at the Last Supper. By faith we bring it into the present, relive it, and share in its original power and blessing.

(c) This is a fun exercise. You might have the students write it out first, before sharing it. They could then do a "show-and-tell" for the group.

Exercise ② **Discuss** At Cana Jesus changed water into wine. At the Last Supper Jesus changed wine into his own body and blood.

Exercise ③ **Discuss** **(a)** Jesus says:

"Your ancestors ate manna in the desert,
but they died. . . .
I am the living bread that came down from heaven.
If you eat this bread, you will live forever." John 6:49–51

(b) Referring to the Last Supper, Jesus says:

"The bread that I will give you is my flesh,
which I give so that the world may live." John 6:51

Exercise ④ **Activity** This exercise should be recorded. Select the better interviews and share them with the class.

Photo **Activity** The tabernacle door in the photo on page 157 is a remarkable summary of the Eucharist. Have the students identify the four gospel events portrayed.

(The *first* panel depicts six water jugs, symbols of the miracle of Cana, where Jesus changed water into wine.

The *second* panel depicts five loaves and two fish, symbols of the miracle near Capernaum, where Jesus multiplied bread and fish to feed a hungry crowd.

The *third* shows Jesus and eleven disciples (Judas is omitted) at a table, symbolizing the Last Supper, where Jesus gave bread to his disciples, saying, "This is my body. . . . Do this in memory of me" (Luke 22:19).

The *fourth* shows three people around a table, symbolizing the Emmaus supper on Easter night.)

▶ **Clarify** The door is a beautiful summary of the key teachings of the Bible concerning the Eucharist. It was

- prefigured (pointed) at Cana,
- promised on the hillside at Capernaum,
- instituted at the Last Supper in Jerusalem,
- celebrated for the first time at Emmaus.

▶ **Notebook** Develop the following summary for entry in student notebooks.

CANA	CAPERNAUM
(John 2:3–10)	(John 6:51–56)
Eucharist prefigured	Eucharist promised
JERUSALEM	EMMAUS
(Luke 22:14–20)	(Luke 24:13–35)
Eucharist instituted	Eucharist celebrated

CHAPTER FOURTEEN: Last Supper (pages 158–59)

Invitation to Remember

LESSON 76

1. LESSON BACKGROUND

▶ *Catechism of the Catholic Church,* 611.

2. LESSON QUIZ

Perfect score = 10 points

1. What was the surprising way in which Jesus began the Passover meal of the Last Supper? *(Lesson 75 review—1 point)*
2. Identify and explain the four biblical events that sum up the key teachings of the Bible concerning the Eucharist. *(Lesson 75 notebook review—8 points)*
3. What do Jesus' Last Supper words "God's new covenant" recall? *(Lesson 76 preview—1 point)*

3. LESSON HOMEWORK

▶ **Return** Lesson 75 review questions (page 157).

▶ **Collect** Lesson 76 review questions (page 159).

▶ **Read** Lesson 77 ("Agony & Arrest," pages 160–61).

▶ **Write** Lesson 77 review questions (page 161).

▶ **Appoint** Student to prepare Mark 14:12–16 and Acts 12:12 (lesson 77, exercise 4).

4. LESSON PRESENTATION

Point 1 **Read** Have student volunteers alternate reading aloud the core content of lesson 76.

▶ **Notebook** Normally, Jewish meals began with the breaking of bread. The Passover meal, however, began with the passing of herbs and sauce. This cued the youngest to ask, "Why is tonight's meal different?" In obedience to Exodus 12:26, the father then explained the meaning of the Passover foods. The meaning of the foods may be developed interactively for entry in student notebooks.

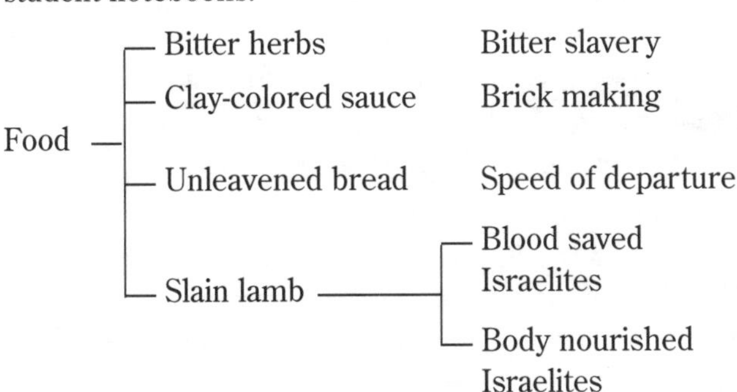

▶ **Discuss** Ask: Which of these foods are sometimes referred to as "freedom foods"? As "slavery foods"?

Point 2 **Clarify** It was during the eating of the herbs and sauce that Jesus spoke these shocking words:

"One of you will betray me—
one who is eating with me." Mark 14:18

Shortly afterward, Judas left. This bothered some of the apostles, until they remembered that Judas kept the purse. Perhaps Jesus had instructed him to go out and make an offering to the poor. It was customary to help the poor on this night (John 13:29).

▶ **Discuss** An old ballad by Robert Buchanan tells the story of Judas after he committed suicide (Matthew 27:3–9). It is paraphrased here in sense lines to facilitate reading to the students for discussion.

When the body of Judas was dead,
his soul tried to dispose of it,
but without success.
Earth refused to swallow it.
The sun refused to shine on it.
Even hell refused to let it in.

Desperately, the soul of Judas kept searching.
Then, one night, in a faraway region,
the soul of Judas saw a vast banquet hall.
Candlelight shone from within.
And at the head of an enormous table
sat a beautiful bridegroom, all in white.

Occasionally, the bridegroom glanced out
through the banquet hall windows,
as if looking for someone.
Suddenly, during one of these glances,
the bridegroom saw the soul of Judas
peering through one of the windows.

The bridegroom got up,
walked to the door, opened it, smiled,
and said softly to the soul of Judas:

"The Holy Supper is spread within,
And the many candles shine,
And I have waited long for thee
Before I poured the wine."

▶ **Discuss** After reading the poem, have the students write answers to these two questions:

- What do you think is the poet's point?
- To what extent do you agree/disagree with it?

After the students finish, ask for volunteers to share and discuss their responses.

Point ❸ **Clarify** The old covenant Passover meal involved the sacrifice of a lamb (Luke 22:7) and commemorated Israel's salvation from physical slavery and death (Exodus 12:21–27). The new covenant involves the sacrifice of the lamb of God and commemorates the salvation of all people from spiritual slavery (sin) and death.

Notebook Develop the following diagram on the chalkboard for entry in student notebooks. It sums up some striking parallels between the old Passover meal and the new Passover meal.

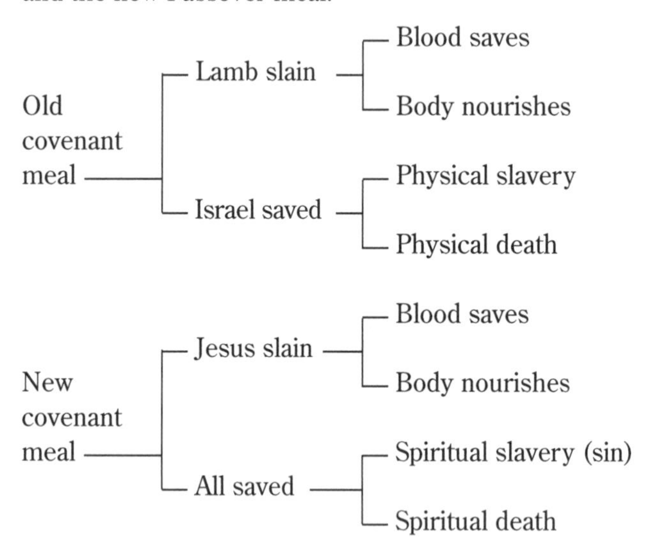

Point ❹ **Notebook** Compare what the celebrant does at the Mass to what Jesus did at the Last Supper.

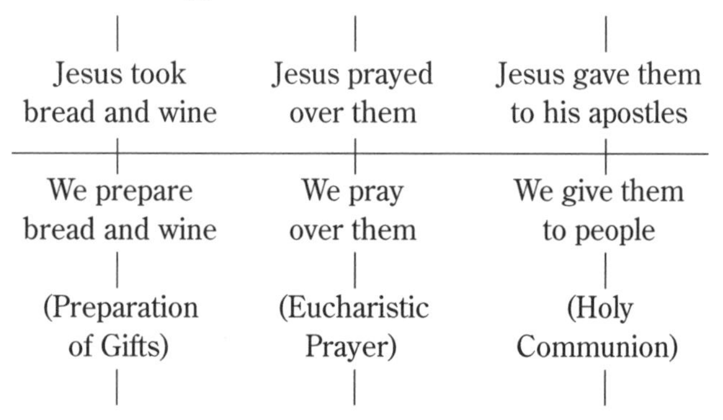

5. LESSON INTERACTION

Exercise ❶ **Discuss** Two "sorrow-shadowed things" that Jesus said during the course of the meal were that (1) his "body" would be "given [over]" and (2) his "blood" would be "poured out."

Exercise ❷ **Clarify** Some people say that Jesus meant the words "This is my body" metaphorically, just as when he said, "I am the vine, and you are the branches" (John 15:5). But this position is hard to hold—if not impossible—in the light of the following words of Jesus:

"The bread that I will give you is my flesh. . . ."
This started an angry argument among them.
"How can this man give us his flesh to eat?" they asked.
Jesus said to them, " . . . my flesh is the real food;
my blood is the real drink.
Those who eat my flesh and drink my blood
live in me, and I live in them. . . ."

Many of his followers heard this and said,
"This teaching is too hard. Who can listen to it?" . . .
Because of this, many of Jesus' followers
turned back and would not go with him any more.

John 6: 51–53, 55–56, 60, 66

Jesus' words have had a completely different effect on other people. For example, Emilie Griffin was a New York advertising executive who converted to Catholicism because of the Eucharist. In her book *Turning,* she writes:

A growing devotion to the Eucharist—and to belief in the Real Presence—drew me to Roman Catholic churches. . . .

As my devotion to the Eucharist grew, so did my attraction to Roman Catholicism.

Exercise ❸ **Clarify** The Eucharist involves "satisfaction and feasting," insofar as God's kingdom is begun and Christ is in our midst. It also involves "longing and fasting," insofar as God's kingdom is still incomplete and Christ is not with us in the fullness of glory.

A funeral involves a similar paradox: rejoicing and mourning. As Christians, we rejoice in a person's "birthday" into eternal life; as humans, we mourn the loss of a loved one from this life.

Exercise ❹ **Discuss** Have the students respond in writing and in private before sharing their responses.

The purpose of eating ordinary foods is to change them into us. The purpose of eating the Eucharist is to change us into it: the Body of Christ.

Exercise ❺ **Activity** You might read this "Prayer of Thanksgiving after Communion" to get the students thinking:

Jesus, you couldn't have found a better way to say to me, "I want to be one with you," than by coming to me as food. And, Jesus, I can't think of a better way to say to you, "I want to be one with you," than by receiving you as food. Thank you for such a beautiful expression of love.

CHAPTER FIFTEEN: Death & Rising (pages 160–61)

Agony & Arrest

LESSON **77**

1. LESSON BACKGROUND

▶ *Catechism of the Catholic Church*, 599–612.

2. LESSON QUIZ

Perfect score = 12 points

1. After the Last Supper, where did Jesus and the apostles go? *(Lesson 76 review—1 point)*
2. List the four ceremonial foods used at the Passover meal and what each recalled. *(Lesson 76 notebook review—10 points)*
3. What did the guards do in the garden when Jesus identified himself to them? *(Lesson 77 preview—1 point)*

3. LESSON HOMEWORK

▶ **Return** Lesson 76 review questions (page 159).

▶ **Collect** Lesson 77 review questions (page 161).

▶ **Read** Lesson 78 ("Trial & Suffering," pages 162–63).

▶ **Write** Lesson 78 review questions (page 163).

▶ **Appoint** Two students to prepare Mark 15:22–39 and Psalm 22:1–7, 15–18 and work out ahead of time (together) the parallels listed in exercise 1 of lesson 78.

4. LESSON PRESENTATION

Point ❶ **Read** Have student volunteers alternate reading aloud the core content of lesson 77.

▶ **Clarify** The Garden of Gethsemane was located at the base of the Mount of Olives, opposite Jerusalem's east wall. (See minimap on page 160 of the textbook.) A grove of eight ancient olive trees still grows there.

Pliny, the ancient Roman historian, says that olive trees never die. He probably refers to the fact that new shoots often emerge from old olive trunks. The shoots produce a new growth that matures and yields fruit long after the parent tree has died and decayed. And so the eight olive trees probably mark the exact spot where Jesus' passion began.

The name *Gethsemane* means "olive press," suggesting that the place contained a press for extracting oil from olives. The apparatus was probably housed in a cave—perhaps one of those still visible at the base of the Mount of Olives.

Since Jesus was a frequent visitor to Gethsemane, the plot may have belonged to a follower, possibly a family of means. Wealthy families frequently operated orchards or farms outside the city walls.

Point ❷ **Clarify** Recall that Jesus began his teaching ministry with prayer. Now he begins his suffering ministry the same way.

Jesus took Peter, James, and John apart from the others. They were the same three apostles who witnessed his transfiguration (Matthew 17:1). Refer the students to the photo and caption on page 161.

▶ **Notebook** Develop the following summary on the chalkboard for entry in student notebooks.

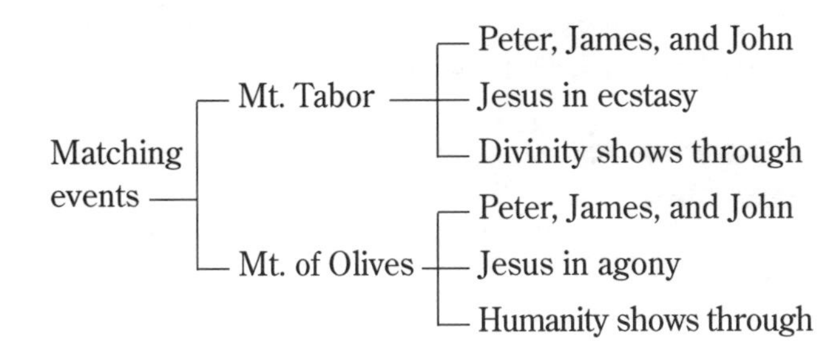

Point ❸ **Clarify** Jesus' prayer follows the basic spirit of the Lord's Prayer ("Our Father"), which he taught his disciples earlier (Matthew 6:9): "Father . . . not my will but yours be done" (Luke 22:42 [NAB]).

The kiss of Judas was not an unusual gesture. Orientals often greeted each other this way.

Commenting on the scuffle that follows Judas' kiss of Jesus, Mark reports that one of the disciples drew a knife and cut off the ear of the High Priest's slave.

Luke, the physician, notes that Jesus healed the ear. John adds the name of the slave, saying it was Malchus.

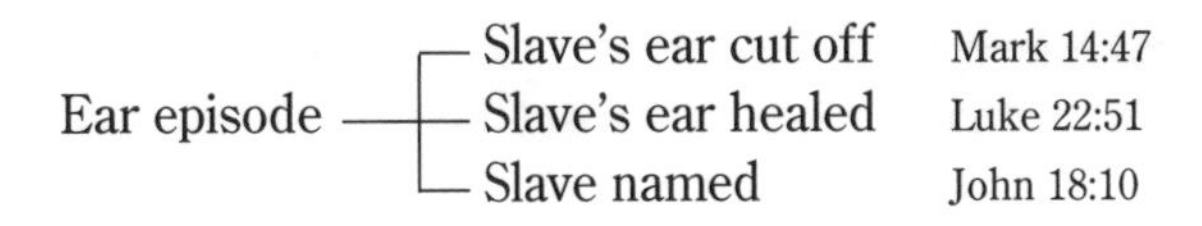

Ask: Why would these details be added by Luke and John, who wrote after Mark? (Perhaps skeptics questioned the episode. In effect, Luke says, "Not only was the slave's ear cut off, but Jesus healed it." And John says, "And if you still have any questions, ask Malchus. He's the one it happened to.)

Point ④ **Clarify** Another detail (only in John) takes place when Jesus identifies himself to the soldiers. "They moved back and fell to the ground" (John 18:6).

Many people have been intrigued by this report; they noted that the Romans Mark Antony and Marius reputedly had a similar impact on their assassins:

The sound of their voices was sufficient to strike terror into men sent to murder them but the latter were only individual assassins in circumstances quite different.
Guiseppe Ricciotti, *The Life of Christ*

The "moral" power radiated by a person's presence (effect of Jesus' presence on the soldiers) is unquestioned. The Duke of Wellington reportedly said that Napoleon's presence on the battlefield was equal to an additional several thousand soldiers. Napoleon himself told one of his generals:

I do indeed possess the secret of this magical power which lifts the soul, but I could never impart it to anyone. None of my generals ever learned it.

Ask students: Is this something that can be imparted or learned? If not, how do you explain it?

Point ⑤ **Clarify** Mark was the first evangelist to record Peter's denial.

Ask: Why would Mark do this? Why not keep Peter on a pedestal? Why open old wounds?

(Mark may have done it for pastoral purposes. He wanted to warn Roman Christians, who were suffering persecution, against the dangers of apostasy. If this happened to Peter, it could happen to them. Mark also wanted to remind them that if they did betray Jesus [some did], they could be forgiven as Peter was.)

▶ **Notebook** Summarize this important lesson for entry in student notebooks.

Lesson		
	Roman Christians	Danger of apostasy
	Christian apostate	Assurance of forgiveness

5. LESSON INTERACTION

Exercise ① **Activity** You may wish to give the students time to do this exercise in class. Collect the responses, sift out the better ones, and read them at the next class.

Exercise ② **Activity** Again, this could be done in class or as a homework assignment.

Exercises ③ & ④ **Clarify** Many believe that young Mark was the naked youth who fled from Gethsemane in Mark 14:51. (He included it as a personal signature.)

Some also believe Mark's family was wealthy. (Only the wealthy had a large upper room to spare.) Some also believe that Mark was the mysterious jar-carrying male who led Peter and John (Luke 22:10–12) to the upper room where they got everything ready for the Last Supper. Later the Last Supper room became a meeting place for Christians:

- Easter night gathering John 20:19
- Pentecost gathering Acts 2:1
- Prayer gathering Acts 12:12

▶ **Discuss** Have the appointed student read Mark 14:12–16 and Acts 12:12. Invite discussion of these passages.

▶ **Clarify** How did Mark get in the garden? He was probably in his early teens and in bed when the Last Supper ended. He possibly heard the apostles sing the Hallel at the end of it and leave for Gethsemane. This would explain the single linen sheet he was wearing. (Ancient wealthy people wore a single linen wrap to bed; the poor usually slept in their clothes.)

▶ **Notebook** Develop the following conjectures on the chalkboard for entry in student notebooks.

Male with a jar	Mark
Last Supper room	Mark's house
Gethsemane	Mark's family orchard
Naked youth	Mark
John Mark of Acts	Mark

Exercise ⑤ **Discuss** Other leaders would possibly be more angry than heartbroken had they been in Jesus' situation.

Photo **Clarify** Direct the students' attention to El Greco's famous painting on page 160. Luke says in his account of Jesus' agony: "An angel from heaven appeared to him and strengthened him" (Luke 22:43).

El Greco painted around 1600. A gifted portrait painter, he was recognized as a genius in his own day. But for some reason he was forgotten for a long period. Rediscovered in the twentieth century, he is now regarded as one of the greatest painters of all time.

Other El Greco paintings are found on pages 179 and 206.

Trial & Suffering

LESSON 78

1. LESSON BACKGROUND

▶ *Catechism of the Catholic Church*, 595–598.

2. LESSON QUIZ

Perfect score = 8 points

1. Which "nature" of Jesus is highlighted on Mount Tabor? On the Mount of Olives? *(Lesson 77 review—2 points)*
2. List the three disciples who were with Jesus both on Mount Tabor and on the Mount of Olives. *(Lesson 77 notebook review—3 points)*
3. Identify Sanhedrin, Gabbatha, Pilate stone. *(Lesson 78 preview—3 points)*

3. LESSON HOMEWORK

▶ **Return** Lesson 77 review questions (page 161).

▶ **Collect** Lesson 78 review questions (page 163).

▶ **Read** Lesson 79 ("Crucifixion," pages 164–65).

▶ **Write** Lesson 79 review questions (page 165).

▶ **Appoint** Student to prepare readings of Ephesians 1:23, 2:21 and Hebrews 10:9 (lesson 79, core content).

4. LESSON PRESENTATION

Point 1 **Read** Have volunteers read aloud the core content of lesson 78.

▶ **Discuss** Ask students: What is blasphemy?

[Blasphemy is] abusive or contemptuous language directed toward God or sacred things. . . . Blasphemy was punished by stoning (Leviticus 24:16).

John L. McKenzie, *Dictionary of the Bible*

Jesus was charged with blasphemy on several occasions during his ministry. For example, once Jesus told a paralyzed man that his sins were forgiven. Some teachers of the Law and some Pharisees heard him say this, grew angry, and said to themselves:

"Who is this man who speaks such blasphemy!
God is the only one who can forgive sins!" Luke 5:21

On another occasion when Jesus said, "The Father and I are one," the people interpreted it as blasphemy and "picked up stones to throw at him" (John 10:30–31).

Point 2 **Clarify** Note the shift of emphasis in the charges against Jesus when he is brought before Pilate. They went from religious ones to political ones.

▶ **Notebook** With the interactive help of the students, develop the following diagram on the chalkboard for entry in student notebooks.

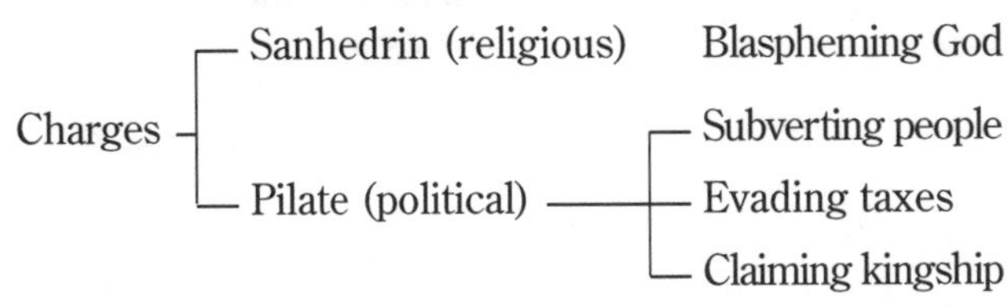

▶ **Clarify** Jewish historians Josephus and Philo give Pilate low marks as a governor. Josephus says Pilate used Temple funds (a cardinal sin for Jews) to build an aqueduct.

When Jews organized a mass protest, Pilate infiltrated the rally with plain-clothes soldiers. Then, upon a preset signal, they turned on the protesters, killing scores of them.

▶ **Clarify** The TV classic *Jesus of Nazareth* depicts Zealots taking the initiative to obtain Barabbas's release over Jesus. This fits the gospel comment that Barabbas was an insurrectionist (Zealot). (See John 18:40.)

▶ **Review** Recall that Zealots were one of five major groups at the time the Old Testament period came to an end. (See textbook page 105.)

▶ **Notebook** With the interactive help of students, develop the following diagram on the chalkboard for entry in student notebooks.

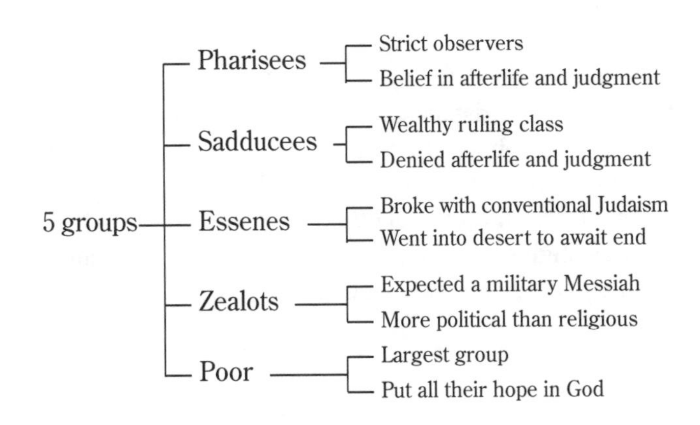

Discuss Ask: Why did the TV producers emphasize Zealot plotting rather than that of Jewish religious leaders? (Probably to offset the centuries-old practice of making Jews the scapegoat for Jesus' death)

Ask: Who really was to blame for the death of Jesus? (Everyone who has sinned! You and me!)

Notebook With the interactive help of students, develop the following diagram on the chalkboard for entry in student notebooks.

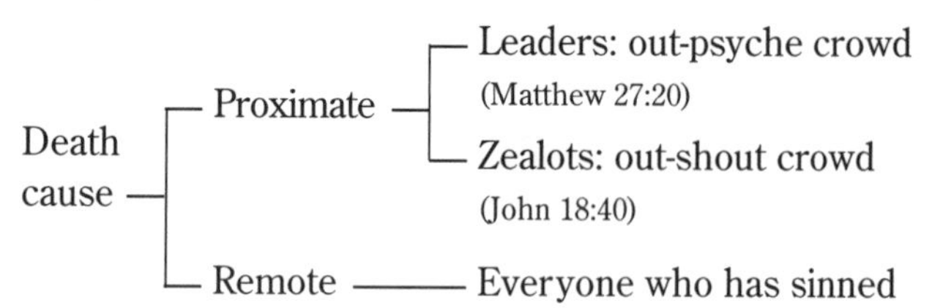

Activity On the minimap on page 160, have students trace the route of Jesus from the eating of the Last Supper to his crucifixion. (Pilate's headquarters is not marked on the map but was probably located in the square enclosure at the upper left corner of the Temple area.)

Clarify During Holy Week of 1986, *USA Today* carried a story about Jesus' crucifixion. It was based on an article by a doctor in the *New England Journal of Medicine.*

The doctor said Christians tend to romanticize the death of Jesus. In reality, it was brutal beyond belief. Ancient writers tell us that whippings often preceded the crucifixion and that victims sometimes died before the whipping was over. They also tell us that crucifixion victims sometimes went insane.

One writer says that after the fall of Jerusalem in 70 C.E., Jewish freedom fighters waged guerrilla warfare against the Romans. The leader of a guerrilla group was captured. When the Romans threatened to crucify him if the others refused to surrender, they surrendered rather than see their leader suffer such a horrible execution.

Discuss Christian spiritual writers, since Saint Paul (Colossians 1:24), have always taught that we can offer our own sufferings in union with Jesus' sufferings on the cross for the "salvation of others."

Ask students: Have you ever offered your sufferings in union with Jesus' sufferings on the cross? Explain.

5. LESSON INTERACTION

Exercise ❶ **Activity** Have students copy in their notebooks the two columns to be filled out. Then have the appointed students read Mark 15:22–39 and Psalm 22:1–7, 15–18 (including the verse numbers), pausing when appropriate to allow students to fill in the proper references.

	Mark 15	Psalm 22
Stripped	24	17
Divided clothes	24	18
Diced for robe	24	18
Crucified (nails)	24	16
Jeered	31	7
Thirsted	36	15
Forsaken	34	1

Exercise ❷ Responses to the four sufferings are as follows:

Agonized	Mental
Felt crushed	Mental
Accused falsely	Emotional
Experienced betrayal	Emotional
Experienced whipping	Physical
Felt abandoned by God	Spiritual

Clarify An example of mental suffering is anticipating a dentist appointment. Jesus suffered this way in the garden, when he anticipated his crucifixion.

An example of emotional suffering is being rejected by someone. Jesus suffered this way when his disciples fled him and Peter denied him.

An example of physical suffering is bodily pain. Jesus suffered this way when he was whipped.

An example of spiritual suffering is the feeling of abandonment by God. Jesus seems to have suffered like this on the cross.

Exercise ❸ **Discuss** **(a)** One of O'Connor's main points is that Parker's effort to please Ruth was far more spiritual than Ruth's self-righteous approach to religion.

O'Connor's description of welts and cuts appearing on the tattooed face of Jesus seems to say that what we do to our brothers and sister we do to him (Matthew 25:35–46).

(b) This exercise is self-explanatory.

Photos **Read** The captions explain how archaeology is helping us in our understanding and appreciation of Scripture.

CHAPTER FIFTEEN: Death & Rising (pages 164–65)

Crucifixion

LESSON **79**

1. LESSON BACKGROUND

▶ *Catechism of the Catholic Church*, 599–609.

2. LESSON QUIZ

Perfect score = 5 points

1. Why did Pilate finally relent and agree to crucify Jesus? *(Lesson 78 review—1 point)*
2. What three political charges were made against Jesus when he was brought before Pilate? *(Lesson 78 notebook review—3 points)*
3. What prophecy by Jesus was fulfilled when the soldier said of him, "This man was really the Son of God"? *(Lesson 79 preview—1 point)*

3. LESSON HOMEWORK

▶ **Return** Lesson 78 review questions (page 163).

▶ **Collect** Lesson 79 review questions (page 165).

▶ **Read** Lesson 80 ("Resurrection," pages 166–67).

▶ **Write** Lesson 80 review questions (page 167).

4. LESSON PRESENTATION

Point ❶ **Read** Have volunteers read aloud the core content of lesson 79.

▶ **Clarify** A bulldozer was clearing a Jerusalem hillside. Suddenly, it struck an ancient ossuary (small stone coffin housing human bones). On the side of the ossuary, the name *Yehohanan* (Hebrew for *John*) appeared in faded letters. When opened, it revealed a young man's heel bones pinned together by a seven-inch-long nail. Working with this and other data found, Nicu Haas of Jerusalem's Hebrew University reconstructed a picture of Yehohanan. He was probably a young Jewish resistance fighter, captured and crucified by the Romans around the time of Jesus.

The nail was apparently preserved by a freak accident. It was wedged into a knot of olive wood and could not be pulled out. The part of the cross to which the feet were nailed was removed and buried with the body.

Experts think the discovery sheds new light on Jesus' crucifixion. They have always felt uneasy about the way that artists portrayed Jesus' crucifixion: erect body, supported by nailed hands and feet. Nailed hands would not support a buckling body. Moreover, a sagging body would eventually arrest breathing and cause rapid death.

Haas believes the new evidence points to a truer picture: seated body, supported by nailed forearms, and legs twisted under the body and nailed from the side—as shown

▶ **Notebook** Have an art student reproduce a line drawing of Haas's sketch on the chalkboard, which students can reproduce in their notebooks. Finally, with the interactive help of the students develop an approximate "passion flow chart" for entry in notebooks.

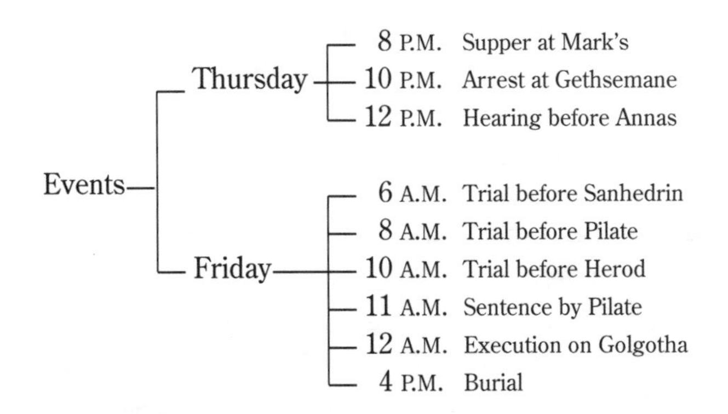

Point ❷ **Clarify** Mark says of the journey to Golgotha:

On the way they met a man named Simon,
who was coming into the city from the country,
and the soldiers forced him to carry Jesus' cross.
(Simon was from Cyrene and was the father
of Alexander and Rufus.) Mark 15:21

Roman soldiers were empowered to commandeer a Jew for a job, just as modern law-enforcement officers are empowered to commandeer a civilian's car.

Clarify Did the identification of Simon as "the father of Alexander and Rufus" have a special meaning for Christians in Rome, for whom Mark wrote?

A clue may lie in Paul's letter to the Romans. He says, "Greetings to Rufus . . . and to his mother" (Romans 16:13).

Some speculate that Simon became a Christian after his experience of carrying Jesus' cross. His son Rufus and his mother were now living in Rome. (Cyrene was in North Africa, not far from Rome.)

Point ❸ **Clarify** A painting by the sixteenth-century German painter Albrecht Durer portrays Jesus being taken down from the cross. A moving detail of the painting shows a disciple holding the crown of thorns that has just been removed from Jesus' head. He is pressing his finger against one of the thorns to get an idea of the pain Jesus felt when the crown was on his head.

Activity Catholics have always been devoted to Jesus in his passion (suffering and death). One form their devotion takes is a prayer model called the Way of the Cross. It involves journeying in spirit with Jesus to Calvary and contains the following fourteen stations. Some are referred to in Scripture; others have come down to us through tradition. The stations are:

1. Jesus is condemned.	Mark 15:6–15
2. Jesus carries his cross.	Mark 15:20
3. Jesus falls the first time.	Tradition
4. Jesus meets his mother.	Tradition (John 19:25)
5. Jesus is helped by Simon.	Mark 15:21
6. Veronica wipes Jesus' face.	Tradition
7. Jesus falls a second time.	Tradition
8. Jesus speaks to the women.	Luke 23:27–31
9. Jesus falls a third time.	Tradition
10. Jesus is stripped.	Luke 23:32–34
11. Jesus is nailed to the cross.	Luke 23:32–34
12. Jesus dies.	Mark 15:33–39
13. Jesus is taken down.	Mark 15:42–47
14. Jesus is laid in the tomb.	Mark 15:42–47

The procedure for reflecting on each station involves the following three steps:

Meditation	What are my thoughts about Jesus' suffering in this particular station?
Conversation	What might I say to Jesus about it?
Contemplation	What might Jesus say back to me?

Notebook Have students copy in their notebooks the fourteen stations and the three-step procedure for reflecting on them.

Next, have students pick a station (make sure all the stations are covered) and write out a meditation on it, following the three-step procedure. (Instruct them to begin their reflection with a sentence identifying the station. This will facilitate the activity that follows.)

Activity Give students about ten minutes to compose their reflection. When all are ready, ask fourteen volunteers (one per station) to come to the front of the class in three groups, as listed in the above summary of the Way of the Cross.

Clarify Stress the two points that stand out in Mark's description of Jesus' crucifixion. First, "early Christians interpreted the tearing of the curtain as a sign pointing to the end of the Old Testament *Temple* and of the Old Testament *sacrifice*" (text page 164). Have the appointed student read Ephesians 1:23 and 2:21 (Temple = Jesus' body) and Hebrews 10:9 (sacrifice = Jesus' death).

The second point that stands out in Mark's description is the officer's act of faith. Stress that "the Roman officer becomes the first person in an endless parade of people who look at Jesus on the cross, believe in him, and win eternal life."

5. LESSON INTERACTION

Exercise ❶ **Discuss** **(a, b)** Have students record their responses before sharing them with the class.

Exercise ❷ **Clarify** **(a, b)** Again, have students record their responses before sharing them with the class.

Activity **(c)** This is sometimes an enlightening activity. Ask three or four volunteers to share with the class an object or card they carry and to explain why they carry it.

Exercise ❸ **Discuss** The two questions might be answered together in writing—or orally.

Photo **Discuss** The figures in the photo on page 164 may be identified as follows: (1) Jesus, (2) thief one, (3) thief two, (4) soldier one (back of cross) throwing dice, (5) soldier two (back of cross) watching dice throw, (6) John kneeling before cross, (7) army officer who said, "This man was really the Son of God!"

Photo **Clarify** Goya's *Dead Jesus* on page 165 is a good example of this Spanish painter's intense realism. Goya (1746–1828) once wrote that he had three teachers: nature, Velazquez (Spanish painter who lived about two hundred years before him), and Rembrandt, the seventeenth-century Dutch master.

Resurrection

LESSON 80

1. LESSON BACKGROUND

▶ *Catechism of the Catholic Church*, 988–1009.

2. LESSON QUIZ

Perfect score = 10 points

1. What "new Temple" and what "new sacrifice" were born on the cross when Jesus was crucified? *(Lesson 79 review—2 points)*
2. List and explain the three steps Christians often follow in meditating on the fourteen stations of the Way of the Cross. *(Lesson 79 notebook review—6 points)*
3. Describe what happened to the two disciples on the road to Emmaus on Easter Sunday night. *(Lesson 80 preview—2 points)*

3. LESSON HOMEWORK

▶ **Return** Lesson 79 review questions (page 165).

▶ **Collect** Lesson 80 review questions (page 167).

▶ **Read** Lesson 81 ("Two Commissions," pages 168–69).

▶ **Write** Lesson 81 review questions (page 169).

▶ **Appoint** Three students to prepare readings from 1 Corinthians 15:1–12, 1 Corinthians 15:35–58, and Mark 12:18–27. (All three readings relate to lesson 81, exercise 5.)

4. LESSON PRESENTATION

Point ① **Read** Have volunteers read aloud the core content of lesson 80.

▶ **Clarify** An old movie concerns archaeologists who claimed to have found the tomb of Jesus. To their horror, they also found the mummified body of Jesus.

And so, according to the movie, the Gospel's claim that Jesus had been raised was a lie. The news crushed the Christian world. Some people were so angered that they looted churches and burned Bibles.

Years later, one of the archaeologists confessed on his deathbed that the finding of the tomb and the body had been fraudulently choreographed.

Whatever the merit of the film, it has this value. It makes us realize that nothing is more important than a knowledge of what happened in Jerusalem on the first Sunday after Jesus' crucifixion.

▶ **Clarify** If you compare the four resurrection accounts, you will notice slight variations in some details.

- Matthew An angel was seen seated outside tomb.
- John Two angels were seen inside.
- Mark One young man was seen seated inside.
- Luke Two men were seen standing inside.

▶ **Discuss** Ask: Don't these variations raise questions about the truthfulness of the resurrection account?

Rather than be concerned about these variations, many scholars regard them as indirect evidence that what they report is true. For example, Heinz Zahrnt reports in *The Historical Jesus:*

Any historian knows that if he comes across several similar-sounding accounts of one event he must use extreme caution, because he has to count on the possibility that one writer has copied from another.

If on the other hand the accounts differ and diverge, this can be taken as direct evidence that they are independent of each other and indirect evidence of the reality of what they report.

Lawyers, who are expert in evaluating eyewitness reports, draw the same conclusion. Paul E. Little writes in *Know What You Believe:*

Frank Morison was convinced that the Resurrection was a mere tissue of fable. . . . As a lawyer, he felt he had the critical faculties to rigidly sift evidence and to admit nothing as evidence which did not meet the stiff criteria for admission into a law court today.

However, while he was doing his research . . . he became persuaded, against his will, of the fact of the bodily resurrection.

Another lawyer, Edward Clarke, wrote to Rev. E. L. Macassey:

To me the evidence is conclusive, and over and over again in the High Court I have secured the verdict on evidence not nearly so compelling. Inference follows on evidence, and a truthful witness is always artless and disdains effect. . . . As a lawyer I accept it unreservedly as the testimony of truthful men to facts they were able to substantiate.

Point ❷ **Discuss** Matthew ends his account of Easter Sunday with this comment:

The chief priests . . . gave a large sum of money
to the soldiers and said, "You are to say
that his disciples came during the night
and stole his body while you were asleep. . . .
The guards took the money
and did what they were told to do.
And so that is the report spread around by the Jews
to this very day. Matthew 28:12–13, 15

Ask: What is the significance of the last four words of Matthew's account: "to this very day"? (It gives evidence of the oral stage of the Gospel. A considerable time lapsed between the life stage (event) and the written stage (recording of it).

► **Clarify** Tomb robbing was not unusual in Jesus' day. Evidence of this was found in 1878 in Nazareth.

It is a marble slab (now in the Louvre in Paris) containing a Roman decree stating that anyone who has "extracted the buried, or has maliciously transferred them" is to be "sentenced to capital punishment."

Solid scholarship identifies it as a decree of Claudius (41–54 C.E.). This puts it in the realm of possible "secular evidence" confirming the empty tomb of Jesus.

► **Discuss** Ask: What convinces you most that Jesus' body was raised by God, not stolen by the disciples?

5. LESSON INTERACTION

Exercise ❶ **Notebook** The man described in the episode was Cecil B. DeMille, the famous Hollywood director of such films as *The Ten Commandments*.

List on the chalkboard the four things that happened to the water beetle. With the interactive help of the students, develop, for entry in notebooks, the similarities to Jesus.

Water Beetle	Jesus
1. Died fastened to canoe.	______________
2. Body was transformed.	______________
3. Body has new powers.	______________
4. Others don't recognize.	______________

Answers:

1. Jesus died fastened to cross.
2. Jesus' body was transformed after three days.
3. Jesus' new body had new powers (John 20:19).
4. Jesus was not recognized by friends (John 20:14–15).

Exercise ❷ **Clarify** **(a)** Jesus' words on the road correspond to the Liturgy of the Word ("Jesus explained to them what was said about himself in all the Scriptures" [Luke 24:27]).

(b) Jesus' action at the table corresponds to the Liturgy of the Eucharist ("[Jesus] took the bread and said the blessing; then he broke the bread and gave it to them" [Luke 27:30]).

► **Review** Have the students check their notebooks for the relationship of the Emmaus episode to the Eucharist (lesson 75, exercise 4).

Exercise ❸ **Clarify** The story of the Emmaus disciples is similar to the story of many Christians. As children they hear the story of Jesus and it excites them. But as they pass out of childhood into adolescence, Jesus often passes out of their lives also. Like the Emmaus disciples, they leave Jesus behind in some unmarked tomb. All they have left are memories. Later, hopefully, they will rediscover Jesus in a new and more remarkable way.

Exercise ❹ **Clarify** **(a)** Had the resurrection not taken place, the Gospels ("Good News") would never have been written. There would be no "Good News."

(b) The risen body of Jesus was totally different from the body that was buried in the tomb. It was not a *resuscitated* body (one that had returned to the same life it had before). It was a *resurrected* body (one that had made a quantum leap forward into a higher life).

In other words, the body of Jesus was not a revived or *resuscitated* body, like the body of Lazarus. It was a *resurrected* body. It was glorified: totally different from his previous body. This explains why the apostles had trouble recognizing Jesus after his resurrection.

(c) Miller's story illustrates that some people must go through a Good Friday themselves before they can recognize the Risen Christ of Easter Sunday.

► **Notebook** The following diagram pinpoints the difference between resuscitation and resurrection. Have students enter it in their notebooks.

Body
- Resuscitated — Return to former life
- Resurrected — Quantum leap forward into infinitely higher life

Miniposter **Discuss** Ask: How does the miniposter on page 166 (section of a stained-glass window) say resurrection?

Two Commissions

LESSON 81

1. LESSON BACKGROUND

▶ *Catechism of the Catholic Church*, 551–553.

2. LESSON QUIZ

Perfect score = 5 points

1. Describe what happened in the house of the two disciples from Emmaus on Easter Sunday night. *(Lesson 80 review—1 point)*
2. Explain the difference between the resurrection of Jesus' body and the resuscitation of Lazarus' body. *(Lesson 80 notebook review—2 points)*
3. What gift did Jesus give his disciple on Easter Sunday night, and why was it the perfect gift? *(Lesson 81 preview—2 points)*

3. LESSON HOMEWORK

▶ **Return**	Lesson 80 review questions (page 167).
▶ **Collect**	Lesson 81 review questions (page 169).
▶ **Read**	Lesson 82 ("Ascension," pages 172–73).
▶ **Write**	Lesson 82 review questions (page 173).

4. LESSON PRESENTATION

Point ❶ **Read** Have volunteers read aloud the core content of lesson 81.

▶ **Discuss** Ask: Why might some people find it unusual that Jesus picked Easter Sunday night to give his disciples the power to forgive sins? (Some people seem to look upon anything connected with sin as being negative. They forget what a beautiful and fitting Easter gift the forgiveness of sin is. It sums up the reason for Jesus' death and resurrection. Paul writes:

By his blood
we are now put right with God. Romans 5:9

Jesus' gift of the power to forgive sin is the perfect Easter gift. It empowers the disciples (and their successors) to communicate personally to people yet unborn the gift that Jesus won for them by his death and resurrection.

▶ **Discuss** Greek Orthodox Christians celebrate the sacrament of Reconciliation with the priest and the penitent *both* facing an icon of the risen Jesus.

Ask: Why do they face the icon rather than each other? (It stresses that the sacrament takes place in Jesus' presence and by his power.)

▶ **Notebook** Summarize for entry in student notebooks the idea of facing the icon.

Facing icon stresses —
- Jesus' presence
- Jesus' power

▶ **Discuss** New York advertising executive Emilie Griffin was having problems with the sacrament of Reconciliation before her conversion to Catholicism. This situation changed dramatically after her conversion. She explains why in her book *Turning:*

I had begun to see priests . . . not as men but as Christ himself; and I remembered with what tenderness he dealt with the tax collector and the adulteress.

Ask: Why face an icon of the risen Jesus rather than an icon of the crucified Jesus? (The icon of the risen Jesus stresses that the Christians' ultimate victory over sin and death is assured because they share in Jesus' Easter victory over sin and death. It is Jesus' resurrection that makes it all possible.)

Point ❷ **Clarify** John caps off Jesus' sunrise appearance to his disciples on the beach in these words:

When [the disciples] stepped ashore,
they saw a charcoal fire there
with fish on it and some bread. . . .
Jesus said to them, "Come and eat." John 21:9, 12

It was after this breakfast that Jesus took Peter aside and commissioned him to "shepherd" his followers. To understand the significance of Jesus' action, we must voyage back to the Old Testament.

Ancient Hebrews looked upon God as their shepherd: "The LORD is my shepherd" (Psalm 23:1). And since Old Testament religious leaders were God's representatives, ancient Hebrews regarded them as shepherds too.

But the leaders were not always "good" shepherds. The prophet Ezekiel says, "You are doomed, you shepherds of Israel! You take care of yourselves, but never tend the sheep" (34:2).

When the religious leaders grew worse, God promised through Ezekiel, "I will rescue my sheep. . . . I will give them a king like my servant David to be their one shepherd" (34:22). It is within this context that Jesus says:

"I am the good shepherd,
who is willing to die for the sheep. . . .
They will become one flock with one shepherd."
John 10:11, 16

This, then, is the context for Jesus' words to Peter on the Galilee seashore: "Feed my lambs . . . tend my sheep." Jesus' words commission Peter to shepherd the community of Jesus' earthly followers.

Notebook Develop the following diagram summary of Jesus' two Easter commissions.

Commissions		
	Disciples	"Receive the Holy Spirit. . . . Forgive people's sins."
	Peter	"Take care of my lambs. . . . Take care of my sheep."

5. LESSON INTERACTION

Exercise 1 **Review** A significant feature of Jesus' Easter appearances is the consistent inability of his disciples to recognize him.

Review the important fact (lesson 80) that resurrection is not resuscitation (restoration of one's life). Rather, it is a quantum leap forward into an infinitely higher life. It is something that no human being had ever experienced prior to Jesus' own resurrection. Recall that Jesus said during his ministry:

"I have come in order that you might have life—
life in all its fullness." John 10:10

The body of Jesus that rose on Easter was infinitely different from the body that was buried on Good Friday. No wonder the disciples had difficulty recognizing Jesus.

Exercise 2 **Review** Paul's quote from 1 Corinthians puts the idea concretely. Even more concrete is this example.

A little boy came running up to his kindergarten teacher. "She's dead! I tell you she's really dead! They put her in the ground and everything. My sister is dead!"

The teacher put her arm around the sobbing five-year-old. Slowly, she walked him to the window. There on the sill was a plant box. Several days before, the little boy had excitedly planted a seed in it.

Taking her finger, the teacher dug into the dirt and found the seed. It was beginning to sprout. Pointing to the seed, the teacher said:

"See, something is happening to our seed. It is decaying. But at the same time, something *new* is happening—something *wonderful!*

"The seed is changing its form of living. It is changing from being a *seed* to being a *plant*. That's what the seed was made to be—a plant, not a seed."

Then the teacher turned to the little boy and said, "Something like that is happening to your sister. She was made for something more than our limited life in this world."

Clarify When you think about it, the idea of resurrection is not as incredible as it may first seem. Ancient Christians illustrated the point this way:

Some people find the idea of the resurrection incredible. Yet a baby is born and they don't find that incredible. But isn't it more incredible for something to begin to live for the very first time than to continue life in a higher way?
Anonymous

Exercise 3 **Clarify** Stress the final verse of the Pauline quotation. (Obviously there would be a great difference between the two bodies.)

Exercise 4 **Clarify** Just as the old tulip body dies and a lovely new tulip body emerges from the bulb, so the old human body dies and a lovely new body emerges from the soul.

Exercise 5 **Discuss** As time permits, have the appointed students read the prepared passages. Pause after each reading to let the students respond as indicated in the exercise.

CHAPTER SIXTEEN: Spirit's Coming (pages 172–73)

Ascension

1. LESSON BACKGROUND

▶ *Catechism of the Catholic Church,* 659–664, 670–673.

2. LESSON QUIZ

Perfect score = 7 points

1. To whom did Jesus give what commission on Easter night? Later on the shore of the Sea of Galilee? *(Lesson 81 review—4 points)*
2. Explain the two reasons why Greek Orthodox Christians (priest and penitent) celebrate the sacrament of Reconciliation facing an icon of Jesus rather than facing each other. *(Lesson 81 notebook review—2 points)*
3. What revelation did the "two men dressed in white" make to the disciples just after Jesus' ascension? *(Lesson 82 preview—1 point)*

3. LESSON HOMEWORK

▶ **Return** Lesson 81 review questions (page 169).

▶ **Collect** Lesson 82 review questions (page 173).

▶ **Read** Lesson 83 ("Pentecost," pages 174–75).

▶ **Write** Lesson 83 review questions (page 175).

4. LESSON PRESENTATION

Point 1 **Read** Have volunteers read aloud the core content of lesson 82.

▶ **Discuss** Legend says that when Jesus returned to heaven, the angel Gabriel asked him if all people knew of his love for them.

"Oh, no!" said Jesus. "Only a handful do."

Gabriel was shocked and asked, "How will the rest learn?"

Jesus replied, "The *handful* will tell them."

"But," said Gabriel, "what if they don't? What if they grow discouraged? Don't you have a back-up plan?"

"No," said Jesus, "I'm counting on my followers and their successors not to let me down."

Ask students: How confident are you that Jesus' followers and their successors won't let Jesus down? Explain.

Point 2 **Clarify** The ascension of Jesus introduces us to the Acts of the Apostles.

Ancient writers used the word *Acts* of "books" that list and describe the accomplishments of great leaders. Thus we have such books as the Acts of Hannibal and the Acts of Alexander. The Acts of the Apostles models itself after these books. It lists some accomplishments of some of the "apostles" (not just the twelve apostles).

▶ **Discuss** The first thing to notice about the Acts of the Apostles is the first sentence. Have the students compare it to the first sentence of Luke's Gospel.

Ask: Who wrote Acts, and what does it treat?

▶ **Notebook** Develop the following two diagrams on the chalkboard for entry in student notebooks.

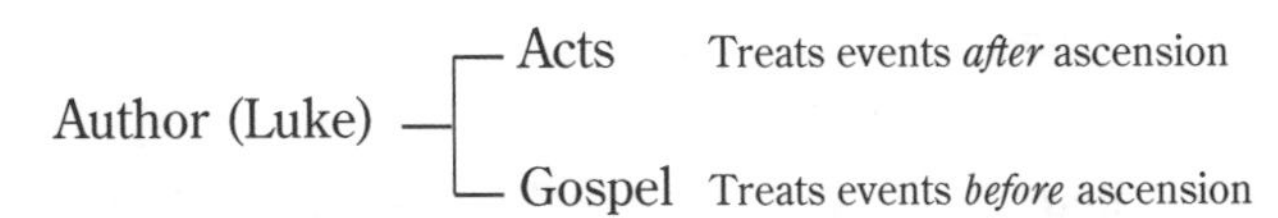

The names of the apostles and the chapters they dominate in Acts may be listed as follows:

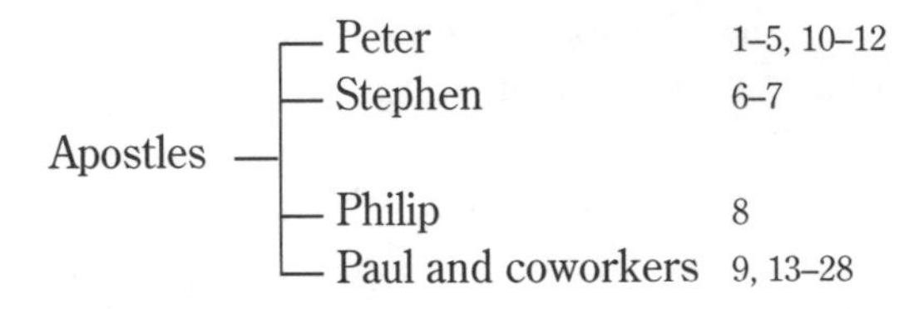

Point 3 **Clarify** Stress that the number "forty" (Acts 1:3) is used symbolically, not numerically. It designates an important transition from one significant period or event to another.

▶ **Notebook** Review some other forty-day/night examples and have students enter them in their notebooks.

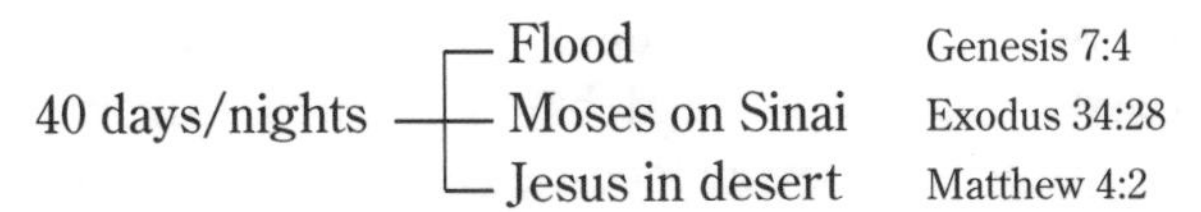

▶ **Clarify** Stress Jesus' final words to his disciples: "You will be witnesses for me in Jerusalem, in all of Judea and Samaria, and to the ends of the earth" (Acts 1:8). This sentence previews the "witness structure" of Acts.

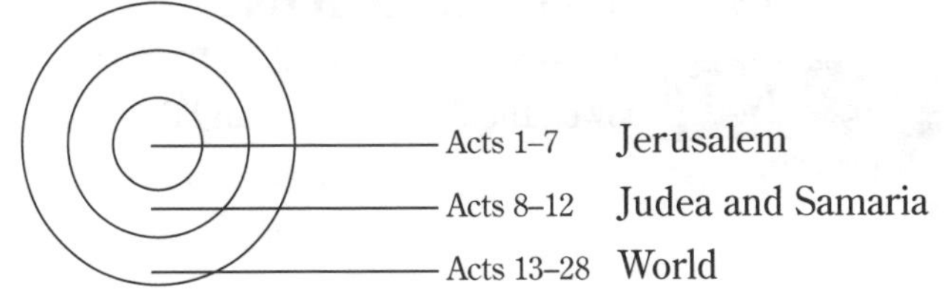

Point ④ **Clarify** Make sure that the students understand that the Holy Spirit did not begin to exist on Pentecost any more than electricity began to exist the day scientists discovered it.

▶ **Clarify** Acts 1:5 reads: "In a few days you will be baptized with the Holy Spirit."

Point out that just as the ministry of Jesus began with Jesus' baptism and the coming of the Holy Spirit upon him in the Jordan (Luke 3:21–22), so the ministry of Jesus' followers began with their baptism in Jerusalem and the coming of the Holy Spirit upon them (Acts 2:1–4).

▶ **Notebook** Develop the following diagram on the chalkboard for entry in student notebooks.

Ministries (begin)	Jesus	Baptism and Spirit's coming
	Followers	Baptism and Spirit's coming

Point ⑤ **Clarify** After Jesus ascended, "two men dressed in white" appeared and said:

"This Jesus, who was taken from you into heaven,
will come back in the same way
that you saw him go to heaven." Acts 1:11

This reiterates the prophecy of Jesus to his disciples concerning his "second coming."

"The Son of Man will come
like the lightning which flashes across the whole sky
from the east to the west." Matthew 24:27

▶ **Clarify** The followers of Jesus saw themselves living in the eye of a hurricane. To help students get an idea of this image, have them picture a Frisbee ten inches in diameter with a dime-sized hole cut in its center. (You might draw this image on the chalkboard.)

Tell the students: Expand the Frisbee to about one hundred miles in diameter, so that the hole expands to about fifteen miles. Now, spin the Frisbee at the rate of one hundred miles per hour and you have a hurricane.

The leading edge of the hurricane precedes the eye. The eye is followed by the trailing edge (note that the winds are reversed at this edge). The eye is often characterized by little or no wind, blue skies, and a shining sun. This was how the apostles viewed their own lifetimes. They were in the "eye of the hurricane" between Jesus' "first coming" and his "second coming."

5. LESSON INTERACTION

Exercise ① **Discuss** **(a)** The disciples (1) "narrowed the field" to two candidates and (2) prayed.

(b) We do *what we can* and let God do *what we can't.*

(c) Many answers are possible here.

(d) If your decision brings you "inner peace" (versus "inner agitation"), it is reasonable to conclude that the choice is God's will.

Exercise ② **Discuss** This exercise is a concrete application of what was discussed in exercise 1. An example will illustrate.

Years ago, Penn State football coach Joe Paterno was offered a $1-million contract to coach the New England Patriots. He accepted and agreed to ink the contract the next morning in New York.

That night Paterno could not sleep. He got up no less than half-a-dozen times. Finally, at 6:30 A.M., he phoned the Patriot owner, Billy Sullivan, and called off the New York meeting. Sportswriter Skip Myslenski quoted Paterno as explaining his decision this way:

"I've always hoped . . . that I could be a little more than just a football coach. That's what Penn State has allowed me to be. [I] . . . have had the opportunity to work with young people and have an influence on their lives. I think that was an overriding factor in my decision."

Chicago Tribune (12/29/78)

Paterno's decision brought him "inner peace" and was applauded by sportswriters and students alike. The Phi Beta Kappas at Penn State invited him to speak at their annual banquet, and the school seniors chose him to be their commencement speaker.

Photo **Notebook** Have students check the caption of the photo on page 173.

Ask: How is Pentecost like the passing of the baton in a race? In other words, who passes what to whom?

Baton	What	Spreading God's kingdom
	From whom	Jesus
	To whom	Jesus' followers

Exercise ③ **Discuss** **(a)** The spirit of both prayers is doing God's will. Also recall Jesus' Gethsemane prayer: "Father . . . take this cup of suffering away from me. Not my will, however, but your will be done" (Luke 22:42).

(b) An alternative would be to begin each class with the prayer. Have the students copy it and recite it.

Miniposter **Discuss** Have students read the quotation on the miniposter on page 172.

Ask: Why would people tend to think of Jesus' ascension as "removing" him from earth?

Ask: In what sense does Jesus' resurrection and ascension free Jesus from "space and time"?

LESSON 83

1. LESSON BACKGROUND

▶ *Catechism of the Catholic Church*, 691–701, 1076.

2. LESSON QUIZ

Perfect score = 9 points

1. Where did the disciples go, and what did they do to prepare for the Spirit's coming? *(Lesson 82 review—2 points)*
2. What two biblical books did Luke write, and how are the events in each related to Jesus' ascension? *(Lesson 82 notebook review—4 points)*
3. How many days after Passover did the Jewish celebration of Pentecost occur, and for what two events did Jews give thanks to God on this day? *(Lesson 83 preview—3 points)*

3. LESSON HOMEWORK

▶ **Return** Lesson 82 review questions (page 173).

▶ **Collect** Lesson 83 review questions (page 175).

▶ **Read** Lesson 84 ("Day of the Lord," pages 176–77).

▶ **Write** Lesson 84 review questions (page 177).

▶ **Appoint** Two students to prepare readings from Acts 16:10–17 and Acts 20:6–15. (Both readings relate to lesson 84, exercise 3.)

4. LESSON PRESENTATION

Point 1 **Read** Have volunteers alternate reading aloud the core content of lesson 83.

▶ **Discuss** Stress the images of wind and fire in the fourth paragraph. Ask: Which of these images signals the "Spirit's coming," and which signals the "Spirit's descent" and why?

▶ **Clarify** First, consider the wind image. The creation story uses the image of wind to portray God's coming to begin creation: "A mighty wind swept over the waters" (Genesis 1:2 [NAB]). And Jesus uses the image of wind to describe the Spirit's coming into the lives of the baptized (John 3:8).

▶ **Discuss** Second, consider the fire image and how the Bible uses it to portray the presence of God.

Ask students: Can you recall an episode where fire is used to symbolize God's presence in the Bible? (The "burning bush" [Exodus 3:2], the "pillar of fire" [Exodus 13:21], God's descent on Mount Sinai "in fire" [Exodus 19:18])

▶ **Notebook** Develop the following diagram on the chalkboard for entry in student notebooks.

Spirit images —
- Wind — Spirit comes
- Fire — Spirit descends on disciples

Point 2 **Clarify** Stress that the "gift of tongues," which enabled even foreigners to understand the disciples, reverses the "confusion of tongues" at Babylon.

▶ **Clarify** The "gift of tongues" given to the disciples on Pentecost is different from the "gift of tongues" that Paul talks about to the Corinthians:

Those who speak in strange tongues
do not speak to others but to God,
because no one understands them.
They . . . help only themselves,
but those who proclaim God's message
help the whole church.

I would like for all of you to speak in strange tongues;
but I would rather
that you had the gift of proclaiming God's message. . . .

If, then, the whole church . . .
starts speaking in strange tongues—
and if some ordinary people or unbelievers come in,
won't they say that you are all crazy?
But if everyone is proclaiming God's message . . .
they will . . . worship God, confessing,
"Truly God is here among you!" 1 Corinthians 14:2–5, 23–25

The "gift of tongues" that Paul speaks about is sometimes referred to as *glossolalia.* It was common in the community of the early Christians and seems to have served as a sign or confirmation of the Spirit's presence in their midst.

Unlike the Pentecost "gift of tongues," *glossolalia* took the form of an "unintelligible," ecstatic, vocal prayer.

We might think of it as a vocal expression of an intense exaltation of the *human spirit* in the presence of the *Holy Spirit.*

On a purely natural level, people often stammer "unintelligibly" when overwhelmed by some intense experience. So it is not too surprising that we find a parallel experience on the supernatural level.

On the other hand, the Pentecost "gift of tongues" is "intelligible." It enabled the disciples to be understood, even by foreigners who did not speak the same language that the disciples did.

▶ **Notebook** Develop the following diagram on the chalkboard for entry in student notebooks.

Gift of tongues (two types)	A gift enabling one to preach to all people
	A gift enabling one to pray in a special way

Point ❸ **Clarify** The greatest gift of Pentecost, however, is the one that empowered the apostles "to proclaim God's message with boldness" in the face of great opposition (Acts 4:31).

Peter (and the other apostles) were transformed by the Spirit's coming on Pentecost. Prior to it they lacked understanding (John 12:12–16) and courage (John 20:19). Now they have both.

Point ❹ **Clarify** Because Jesus rose on Sunday and because the Holy Spirit descended on Sunday, Christians observed Sunday as the "new Sabbath." This stressed the beginning of a new era (New Testament) and the end of an old era (Old Testament).

Ironically, Sunday has witnessed a number of important historical events. Consider just a sprinkling.

October 1871	Great Chicago fire started.
April 1912	Titanic sunk.
September 1939	World War II starts (Poland invaded).
June 1941	Nazis invade Russia.
December 1941	Japanese bomb Pearl Harbor.
August 1945	A-bomb dropped on Hiroshima.
September 1945	Japan surrenders officially.

5. LESSON INTERACTION

Exercise ❶ **Discuss** The boy's question is a key one: "What is God like?" It recalls these word of Jules Renard: "God does not believe in our God."

Ask students: What did Renard have in mind? (One of the biggest obstacles to faith in God is people's "false images" of God. When someone rejects God, often they reject not the "true God," but a "false God." One thinks of Tolstoy's classic comment:

When a savage ceases to believe in his wooden God,
this does not mean that there is no God,
but only that the true God is not of wood.

▶ **Clarify** When one person speaks to another about God, it is like one blind person speaking to another blind person about color. Neither has seen color. Even if they had, it would be impossible to give the other an accurate idea of color. The same is true in speaking of God. Augustine was right. We know God more by what God is not than by what God is. Ultimately, Christians turn to Jesus for their idea of God. Jesus said, "Whoever has seen me has seen the Father" (John 14:9).

(a, b, c) The three questions of this exercise review and extend the content treated under point 1 above.

Exercise ❷ **Notebook** **(a)** Pentecost's point is that God (through the Spirit) is "re-creating" the world that sin "de-created" at Babel. We may sum it up this way:

Meaning	Babel	Sin divides people (symbolized by "confusion of tongues")
	Pentecost	Spirit unites people (symbolized by "gift of tongues")
	Point	God (through Spirit) re-creates the world that sin de-created

(b) Jesus gave us (his followers) the "gift of the Spirit" to complete the work of re-creating the world. The baton has been passed to us and Jesus is counting on us to finish his work of re-creation.

Exercise ❸ **Activity** This is an important exercise. You might consider having the students begin it in writing and in private in class. You might screen the better responses and share them in the next class.

Exercise ❹ **Discuss** **(a, b)** The message is that we need the help of the Spirit to complete the work of re-creating our world. The key to completing the re-creation of the world is to open our hearts to the power and insight that only the Holy Spirit can give us.

(c) Select from the various poems the better lines. Combine them on the chalkboard into a "class poem."

CHAPTER SIXTEEN: Spirit's Coming (pages 176–77)

Day of the Lord

LESSON **84**

1. LESSON BACKGROUND

▶ *Catechism of the Catholic Church*, 668–679.

2. LESSON QUIZ

Perfect score = 8 points

1. Explain the link between Pentecost and the Tower of Babel event. *(Lesson 83 review—2 points)*
2. List and explain the two images of the Spirit that are portrayed in the Pentecost event. *(Lesson 83 notebook review—4 points)*
3. Explain how Peter interpreted the "Day of the Lord." *(Lesson 84 preview—2 points)*

3. LESSON HOMEWORK

▶ **Return** Lesson 83 review questions (page 175).

▶ **Collect** Lesson 84 review questions (page 177).

▶ **Read** Lesson 85 ("Peter & John," pages 178–79).

▶ **Write** Lesson 85 review questions (page 179).

▶ **Appoint** Three students to prepare readings from Acts 4:1–21, Acts 5:1–11, and Acts 5:12–16 (lesson 85, exercise 4).

4. LESSON PRESENTATION

Point 1 **Read** Have volunteers read aloud the core content of lesson 84.

▶ **Clarify** After the Spirit's descent, Peter called out:

"Listen to these words, fellow Israelites!
Jesus of Nazareth . . . whom you crucified is the one
that God has made Lord and Messiah!" Acts 2:22, 36

The apostles' conviction that Jesus is "Lord" came from the Holy Spirit, not from their own reasoning powers. Paul stresses this in his First Letter to the Corinthians:

No one can confess "Jesus is Lord,"
without being guided by the Holy Spirit. 1 Corinthians 12:3

To confess "Jesus is Lord" is to affirm Jesus' divinity. Avery Dulles says in *Apologetics and the Biblical Christ:*

In terms of the theological vocabulary
available to Jewish Christians
at the moment the Church was born,
we could scarcely hope for, or even conceive,
a more forceful affirmation of Christ's divinity. . . .
Since the apostles had not learned Jesus' divinity
through sheerly external evidences,
they did not seek to convince others by strict proofs.

They took the same approach as Paul, who said:

My teaching and message
were not delivered with skillful words of human wisdom,
but with convincing proof of the power of God's Spirit.
Your faith, then, does not rest on human wisdom
but on God's power. 1 Corinthians 2:4–5

▶ **Notebook** Develop the following diagrams on the chalkboard. The first diagram makes the point that the foundation of our faith is not human wisdom but God's power.

Faith rests —
- Not on human wisdom
- But on God's power

The second diagram makes the point that faith is never so clear as to remove all questions and never so obscure as to mislead the sincere searcher. Faith satisfies both possibilities.

Faith affords —
- Enough light to find the truth
- Enough darkness to hide from it

The final diagram makes the point that the goal of the Gospel is not to prove but to proclaim.

Gospel's goal —
- Not to prove Jesus = "Lord"
- But to proclaim Jesus = "Lord"

Point 2 **Clarify** As the Spirit led the apostles to identify Jesus as the "Lord," so the Spirit led them to identify Pentecost as the "Day of the Lord" (Acts 2:16, 20).

Few ideas influenced Israel's history as much as did the "Day of the Lord." By this phrase Jews meant that great moment in history when God would intervene on their behalf and be manifested to all people. Peter's point (Acts 1:15–17) may be paraphrased as follows:

What you see today is the start of the Day of the Lord.
It will end with Jesus' return at the end of time.

Touching on this point, Scripture scholar Neal Flanagan writes in *The Acts of the Apostles:*

Joel saw the beginning and the end
of the messianic era . . . without strict time sequence
and spoke of them as such.

▶ **Notebook** Develop the following diagram on the chalkboard for entry in student notebooks.

Day of the Lord — Starts with Pentecost
Day of the Lord — Ends with Jesus' return

5. LESSON INTERACTION

Exercise 1 **Discuss** Salvation is a joint enterprise between God's grace and our effort. We work at it as if everything depends on us, but pray as if everything depends on God.

Exercise 2 **Discuss** This exercise sets up the one that follows. Luke probably did what all ancient historians did; he reconstructed the speeches. In *Dictionary of the Bible* John L. McKenzie says of these speeches:

Their historical value lies in their faithful preservation
of the themes of the primitive preaching,
rather than in their exact agreement with the situation.

Exercise 3 **Discuss** Have the appointed students read the passages from Acts. Luke had an immense advantage over ancient historians, because he was writing under the inspiration and guidance of the Holy Spirit.

Exercise 4 **Discuss** This exercise is an effort to show that the important thing is the *message itself,* not the *exact words* that communicate it.

Photo **Clarify** Direct the students to the photo on page 176. Early Christians compared water to the Spirit. Water produces different results in different plants for the good of all: wood for building, cotton for weaving, and fruit for eating. So, too, the Spirit produces different results in different people "for the good of all" (1 Corinthians 12:7).

▶ **Activity** Leonard LeSourd said that he had known five different "Christs" in his life. Read the following summary of his explanation to prepare the students to write a brief description of their own relationship with Jesus.

The *first* Christ was the *fanciful* Christ.
This was the Jesus of LeSourd's childhood.
This Christ fell in the category of Santa Claus,
Easter Bunny, and the tooth fairy.
But this Christ was the "seed" of faith
out of which the "plant" of LeSourd's faith
would eventually grow.

The *second* Christ was the *historical* Christ.
He was a great person in history,
like Helen Keller or Abraham Lincoln.
This Christ might be likened to
the "stem" that emerges from a seed

The *third* Christ was the *teacher* Christ.
It was the Jesus who taught truths
that are as valid today
as they were two thousand years ago.
This Christ might be likened to
the "bud" that emerges from a stem.

The *fourth* Christ was the *savior* Christ.
This was the Christ who died for us.
This Christ might be likened to
the "flower" that emerges from a bud.

The *fifth* Christ was the *indwelling* Christ.
This was the risen Jesus, who said:

"I stand at the door and knock;
if any hear my voice and open the door,
I will come into their house
and eat with them and they will eat with me."
Revelation 3:20

This Christ might be likened to the "fruit" that emerges from a flower.

▶ **Notebook** With the help of the students, develop the following summary of LeSourd's five "Christs" on the chalkboard for entry in student notebooks.

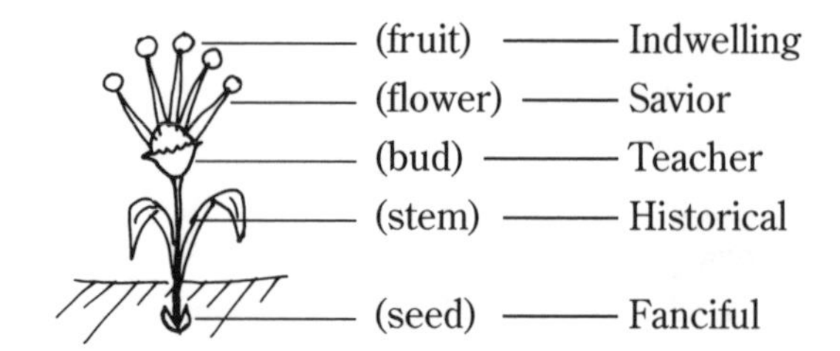

Peter & John

LESSON 85

1. LESSON BACKGROUND

► *Catechism of the Catholic Church,* 1506–1509.

2. LESSON QUIZ

Perfect score = 6 points

1. How did Peter interpret the "Day of the Lord"? *(Lesson 84 review—2 points)*
2. Explain (a) the purpose of the Gospel and (b) the source of our faith in the Gospel. *(Lesson 84 notebook review—2 points)*
3. Briefly explain Gamaliel's advice to the Jewish council. *(Lesson 85 preview—2 points)*

3. LESSON HOMEWORK

► **Return** Lesson 84 review questions (page 177).

► **Collect** Lesson 85 review questions (page 179).

► **Read** Lesson 86 ("Stephen," pages 180–81).

► **Write** Lesson 86 review questions (page 181).

4. LESSON PRESENTATION

Point ① **Read** Have student volunteers read aloud the core content of lesson 85.

► **Discuss** Peter's healing of the lame beggar raises the question of faith healing in general.

Many classical Pentecostals intimate that God wants to heal everyone right now. And so they urge everyone to present themselves for healing.

Francis MacNutt says in *The Power to Heal:* "The classical Pentecostal position fails ultimately because it doesn't pass the test of reality. Many people who present themselves for healing are, in fact, not healed."

Ask students: Why do you think this is the case? (Ultimately, this answer is known only to God. But three answers are commonly proposed. Consider each one.)

1. The one who wants to be healed does not have enough faith. Thus Luke says of Jesus' visit to Nazareth:

   [Jesus] was not able to perform any miracles there,
   except that he placed his hands on a few sick people
   and healed them. He was greatly surprised,
   because the people did not have faith. Mark 6:5–6

2. The healer does not have enough faith. Thus Matthew 17:16 describes a father bringing his possessed son to Jesus, saying, "I brought him to your disciples, but they could not heal him." Later the disciples ask Jesus, "Why couldn't we drive the demon out?" Jesus responds, "You do not have enough faith" (17:19–20).
3. God prefers to use the *physical* illness or defect to accomplish a deeper *spiritual* healing in the person.

Those who opt for the third reason cite the example of Eugene O'Neill.

Recall O'Neill's case. At the age of twenty-five he was rootless with no direction in his life. Then he came down with a serious illness. It gave him the time and the motivation to ask himself some serious questions. The result? It was from his hospital bed that he began to write the plays that revolutionized American drama.

Recall, also, Franklin D. Roosevelt's case. In 1921, he contracted infantile paralysis, which left him unable to walk. All of his biographers agree that this experience was the real educative process of his life. It mobilized his resources and turned him into the remarkable man who, in 1932, was elected to the first of four consecutive terms as president of the United States.

Ask: Why do you think sickness or tragedy is a stepping-stone for some people and a stumbling block for others?

► **Notebook** Develop the following summary on why physical healing does not always take place. Have students enter it in their notebooks.

Failed healing (physical)
- Sick person lacks faith
- Healer lacks faith
- God wants to use sickness to effect a deeper healing in person

Point ② **Clarify** Recall Jesus' warning to his disciples that they will be arrested and taken to court.

"When you are arrested and taken to court,
do not worry ahead of time
about what you are going to say;
when the time comes, say whatever is then given to you.
For the words you speak will not be yours;
they will come from the Holy Spirit." Mark 13:11

A good example of such a person is Joan of Arc. As was customary in the fifteenth century, girls rarely learned to read or write. By means of visions and voices, Joan felt herself being called to liberate France from British oppression. For this reason, she sought an audience with Charles VII (the Dauphin). Remarkably, he granted it.

When Joan arrived at the palace, Charles tested her by switching places with a courtier. Joan not only located him in the crowd but also told him what he had been doing earlier that day in the privacy of the chapel.

To make a long story short, Joan got her army and defeated the British in four consecutive battles. Later, she marched the French army to Rheims. There Charles VII (as yet uncrowned because the British controlled the area) was officially installed as king of France.

Sometime after this, Joan was captured by the British and cross-examined with tricky theological questions. The purpose was to catch her in heresy.

For example, one of her judges asked her if she were in the state of grace. (Theologians, at that time, held that we can never know this for certain.) Reminiscent of Jesus' promise that the Holy Spirit would guide his followers in what to say, Joan responded simply, "If I am, I pray God will keep me there; if not, I pray he will put me there."

Eventually Joan was tried, condemned as a witch, and burned to death in Rouen on May 30, 1431 (about sixty years before the discovery of the new world). She was retried posthumously in 1456 and acquitted. She was canonized a saint in 1920.

5. LESSON INTERACTION

Exercise ❶ **Discuss** **(a)** Review the three common sources of poverty treated earlier in lesson 40, "Israel Says 'No.' "

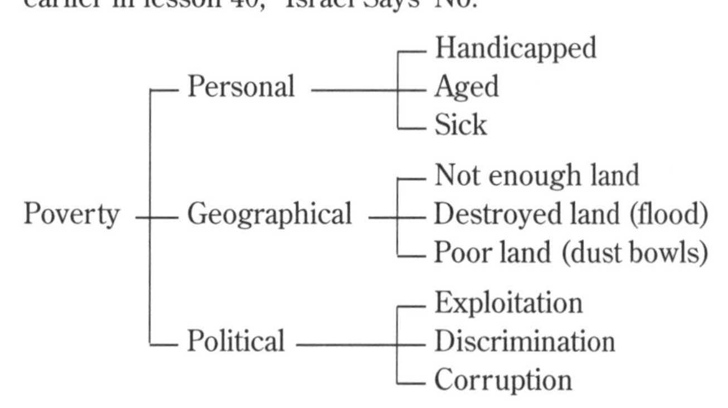

(b, c) These question admit of a variety of responses.

(d) This question sets up exercise 2.

Exercise ❷ **Discuss** **(a, b)** These two questions are important. Perhaps you might want the students to respond in writing before they share their responses. This procedure often improves the quality of sharing.

(c) This question has to do with getting involved and not praying or waiting around for God to act. Prayer is a marvelous gift, but God never intended it to be a substitute for hard work.

Recall the story about a woman who saw a little girl in the street. The child was poorly dressed, ill-nourished, and playing in the gutter with filthy trash. The woman became angry and said to God, "Why do you let a thing like that happen in the world you created? Why don't you do something about it?" God replied, "I did do something about it; I created you."

Exercise ❸ **Discuss** One thing that has confounded the critics of Christianity throughout history is its ability to survive persecution, internal strife, and human corruption among both its members and its leaders. As one critic put it, "The only explanation for Christianity's survival that makes sense is that it is, indeed, from God and not of human origin."

Exercise ❹ **Activity** Have the appointed students read aloud the indicated passages. Pause after each reading to give the students a chance to record their response to each of the three questions. Have the students share their responses before going on to the next reading.

Miniposter **Discuss** Ask: What point does the miniposter on page 178 make?

Photo **Clarify** Direct students' attention to the El Greco painting on page 179. Saint Martin of Tours lived in the fourth century. He became an extremely popular saint among the ordinary people, largely from the famous story of how one cold night he shared his cloak with a beggar. Recall what was said about El Greco in lesson 77 (see painting on page 160 of the textbook).

Drawing **Discuss** Direct students' attention to the Temple drawing on page 178. Review the Temple courts and what was said about them in lesson 74 (see lesson 74 of this manual).

CHAPTER SEVENTEEN: Local Witness (pages 180–81)

Stephen

LESSON 86

1. LESSON BACKGROUND

▶ *Catechism of the Catholic Church,* 101–104, 131–133.

2. LESSON QUIZ

Perfect score = 10 points

1. Briefly describe the response of Peter to (a) the Temple beggar and (b) the Jewish Council. *(Lesson 85 review—2 points)*
2. List three sources of poverty and one example of each. *(Lesson 85 notebook review—6 points)*
3. What happened to Christians in Jerusalem after Stephen's death, and how did this spread the Gospel? *(Lesson 86 preview—2 points)*

3. LESSON HOMEWORK

▶ **Return** Lesson 85 review questions (page 179).

▶ **Collect** Lesson 86 review questions (page 181).

▶ **Read** Lesson 87 ("Samaritan Pentecost," pages 182–83).

▶ **Write** Lesson 87 review questions (page 183).

▶ **Appoint** Three students to prepare 1 Corinthians 12:1–11, Galatians 5:16–26, Romans 8:1–17 (lesson 87, exercise 4).

4. LESSON PRESENTATION

Point ❶ **Read** Have volunteers read aloud the core content of lesson 86.

▶ **Clarify** Read aloud Acts 6:1–4:

There was a quarrel between the Greek-speaking Jews
and the native Jews. The Greek-speaking Jews
claimed that their widows were being neglected. . . .
[The] apostles . . . said, "It is not right for us to neglect
the preaching of God's word . . . to handle finances. . . .
Choose seven men among you who are known
to be full of the Holy Spirit and wisdom,
and we will put them in charge of this matter.
We ourselves, then, will give our full time
to prayer and . . . preaching."

▶ **Clarify** This inspired passage in the Bible makes it clear that the Church in apostolic times had its problems, just as the Church does in modern times.

▶ **Notebook** Ask: What similarities do you see between Jesus and Stephen? (Both were accused by false witnesses, made reference to the "Son of Man," were executed outside the city, commended their spirits to God, forgave their assailants.) Summarize for entry in student notebooks:

	Jesus	Stephen
False witnesses	Mark 14:56–59	Acts 6:11–13
Son of Man	Luke 22:69	Acts 7:56
Died outside city	Mark 15:20–22	Acts 7:58
Commend spirit	Luke 23:46	Acts 7:59
Forgive assailants	Luke 23:34	Acts 7:60

5. LESSON INTERACTION

Exercise ❶ **Discuss** The French writer Blaise Pascal said, "I really believe those stories whose writers get their throat cut." His point is that one of the strongest witnesses people can give is to die for their faith. When others see this, they stop and think.

Exercise ❷ **Clarify** On June 2, 1995, Captain Scott O'Grady's F-16 was shot down by Bosnian Serbs. For six days they stalked him as hunters stalk a prey. Sometimes they came within a few yards of him. He survived on grass, ants, and rain water squeezed from a sponge. He said:

For the most part my face was in the dirt,
and I was just praying they wouldn't see me or hear me.
I was a scared little bunny rabbit,
just trying to hide, just trying to survive.

▶ **Discuss** On July 8, at 2 A.M., with his radio batteries dying, Scott made voice contact with an F-16. He was rescued four and a half hours later by helicopters. O'Grady's courage and personality turned him into a hero—an "endangered species" in modern times.

Ask: How did heroes become an "endangered species"? (Three reasons are skepticism, disillusionment, and erosion. First, when we learned some heroes were "manufactured" during the Korean war for "morale purposes," we became skeptical. Second, when we learned some heroes had "clay feet," we became disillusioned. We expected them to be perfect. Third, when TV talk shows began placing "bogus heroes" [sex symbols] on a par with "true heroes" [missionaries], the image of the "true hero" became eroded.)

▶ **Notebook** Summarize the three reasons for vanishing heroes for entry in student notebooks.

Hero decline		
	Skepticism	"Manufactured"
	Disillusionment	"Clay feet"
	Erosion	"Bogus heroes"

▶ **Discuss** Ask: Do you think the decline of the hero has had an effect on people's attitudes toward Jesus and the saints (Stephen), who have traditionally been held up as heroes for our imitation?

▶ **Discuss** **(a)** The list of savior-heroes should include Socrates, Jesus, Stephen, Joan of Arc, Helen Keller, Mother Teresa, Martin Luther King Jr.—not to mention countless martyred saints.

Exercise ③ **Discuss** **(a, b)** The second question is the key one. List student responses on the chalkboard before opening up the discussion.

Exercise ④ **Activity** Have the students take a few minutes to meditate and write out their reflections right in class. Collect, screen, and share the better responses.

Miniposter **Discuss** Direct students' attention to the miniposter at the top of page 180. Ask: How do you explain the saying on the poster?

(Radio is like the Old Testament.
You hear God's word.
TV is like the New Testament.
You see God's word.)

Ask: In what sense do you only "hear" God's word in the Old Testament, while in the New Testament you also "see" God's word? (Jesus does not just tell us about God and God's word, as the Old Testament prophets and writers did. Jesus is the *Incarnate Word* ["Word made flesh"], who walked among us.)

In other words, Jesus is called the Incarnate Word because he communicates not only by what he says but also by what he is. Charles Schulz, author of the "Peanuts" cartoon, said of Jesus:

What Jesus means to me is this:
In him we are able to see God
and to understand his feeling toward us.

The Letter to the Hebrews sums up Jesus, the Incarnate Word, this way:

He reflects the brightness of God's glory
and is the exact likeness of God's own being. 1:3

▶ **Discuss** Just as Jesus is God's *Incarnate Word,* so the universe is God's *cosmic word.*

This is because the cosmos, or universe, gives us a vague glimmering of what God is like. In other words, creation reflects the creator, just as a song reflects something of the songwriter's personality. Saint Paul says in the Letter to the Romans:

Ever since God created the world,
his invisible qualities, both his eternal power
and his divine nature,
have been clearly seen; they are perceived
in the things that God has made. 1:20

Ask: How does a song tell us something about the songwriter? (It gives us an insight into what the songwriter's values and view on life are.)

▶ **Discuss** Finally, as Jesus is God's *Incarnate Word* and as the universe is God's *cosmic word,* so the Hebrew Scriptures are God's *prophetic word.* They are God's word as revealed to us through the Old Testament prophets and writers.

Ask: In what order did God speak these three words? (Pre-Testament times: cosmic word, Old Testament times: prophetic word, New Testament times: Incarnate Word)

Notebook Sum up the "three words" on the chalkboard for entry in student notebooks.

God's three words		
	Pre-Testament	Cosmic word
	Old Testament	Prophetic word
	New Testament	Incarnate Word

Samaritan Pentecost

LESSON 87

1. LESSON BACKGROUND

▶ *Catechism of the Catholic Church,* 1286–1288, 1306–1308.

2. LESSON QUIZ

Perfect score = 10 points

1. Who was the Church's first martyr, and what position did he hold? *(Lesson 86 review—2 points)*
2. List and briefly describe the "word" God spoke to us in Pre-Testament, Old Testament, and New Testament times. *(Lesson 86 notebook review—6 points)*
3. Who was Philip, and what missionary outreach did he spearhead? *(Lesson 87 preview—2 points)*

3. LESSON HOMEWORK

▶ **Return** Lesson 86 review questions (page 181).

▶ **Collect** Lesson 87 review questions (page 183).

▶ **Read** Lesson 88 ("Philip in Judea," pages 184–85).

▶ **Write** Lesson 88 review questions (page 185).

4. LESSON PRESENTATION

Point 1 **Read** Have volunteers read aloud the core content of lesson 87.

▶ **Clarify** Stress the idea that many great discoveries, like the laser beam, came by chance rather than by human design. For example, Columbus "discovered" America by accident. He was really trying to find a water route to India.

Someone said there is no such thing as coincidence or chance. Both of these are simply miracles in which God chooses to remain anonymous.

▶ **Notebook** Develop this diagram on the chalkboard for entry in student notebooks. It puts the "Samaritan Pentecost" in context.

Holy Spirit	Promised	Ascension (Acts 1:4–5)
	Comes	Pentecost (Acts 2:4)
	Communicated	Samaritans (Acts 8:17)

5. LESSON INTERACTION

Exercise 1 **Discuss** The second cup was filled with water (symbol of the Holy Spirit). It was the water that kept it from burning up. Jesus said in John 7:38–39:

"Whoever believes in me should drink.
As the scripture says,
'Streams of life-giving water will pour out from his side.'"
Jesus said this about the Spirit,
which those who believed in him were going to receive.

Saint Cyril of Jerusalem (fourth century) used this water metaphor to illustrate how the Holy Spirit acts in our lives: Water falls from the sky as rain and is always the same in itself. Yet it produces different results in different plants.

For example, it causes a tree to produce wood, a wheat stalk to produce grain, and a cotton plant to produce cotton fiber. In a similar way, the Holy Spirit produces different results in different people.

Exercise 2 **Discuss** There are a variety of theological opinions concerning the age at which a person should be confirmed. Some say the age of reason; others say young adulthood is better because confirmation involves an adult commitment (witnessing to Jesus and continuing his work). See *Catechism of the Catholic Church,* 1306–1308. Currently, a variety of approaches are followed.

▶ **Clarify** The liturgy ("sacred ritual") of the sacrament of Confirmation involves three central actions:

- laying on of hands,
- anointing the candidate's forehead,
- saying over the candidate, "Be sealed with the Gift of the Holy Spirit."

The laying on of hands has its origin in the Old Testament. For example, when God picked Joshua to succeed Moses, he told Moses:

"Place your hands on his head.
Have him stand in front of . . .
the priest and the whole community, and
there before them all proclaim him as your successor.
Give him some of your own authority. . . ."
Moses did as the LORD had commanded him.

Numbers 27:18–20, 22

And so the rite of placing hands on a person's head symbolized the calling and the empowering of that person to perform some special service in and for the community.

▶ **Clarify** Anointing the candidate's forehead with oil also has its origin in the Old Testament.

- Moses anointed Aaron a priest (Exodus 29:1–7).
- Samuel anointed David a king (1 Samuel 16:1–13).
- Elijah anointed Elisah a prophet (1 Kings 19:16).

And so the rite of anointing the forehead symbolized the calling and empowering of that person to serve as a prophet, priest, or king to the community.

▶ **Clarify** Finally, there are the words "Be sealed with the Gift of the Holy Spirit."

Ancient kings tattooed the hand of their soldiers with a "seal." Referring to this practice, an early writing addresses new Christians in these words:

The soldier chosen for service . . .
receives on his hand the seal
showing what king he will serve.
So with you.
You were chosen for the king of heaven,
and will henceforth bear his seal.

And another ancient writing addresses new Christians in these words:

Come near and receive the sacramental seal
so that you may be recognized by the Master.

These examples help us understand the words "Be sealed with the Gift of the Holy Spirit." Paul refers to the "sealing" this way in Ephesians 1:13:

God put his stamp ["seal"] of ownership on you
by giving you the Holy Spirit he had promised.

▶ **Clarify** And so the sacrament of Confirmation may be described this way:

It is a tangible encounter with the Risen Christ
in which we are sealed
with the fullness of the Gift of the Spirit
and called and empowered to witness to Jesus
and to continue his work.

▶ **Clarify** Being "sealed with the Gift of the Holy Spirit" does not automatically make us witnesses of Jesus any more than ancient Roman tattoos ("seals") made ancient men loyal soldiers of the king.

Rather, the presence ("sealing") of the Spirit calls and empowers us to witness. It does not take away our freedom. Ultimately, we decide if we will respond to the call and the power. Consider the example of someone who did not respond at first.

Napoleon Bonaparte was a great world leader until the British defeated him at Waterloo in 1815. After his defeat, he was exiled to the barren island of Saint Helena in the South Atlantic. There he died of cancer six years later. While on Saint Helena, he confessed to a friend:

Upon the throne surrounded by my generals . . .
I did not dare say aloud, "I am a believer." . . .
But now that I am at Saint Helena,
why should I conceal
that which I believe at the bottom of my heart? . . .
I will go to the Mass.

The History of Napoleon Bonaparte (vol. II, p. 611)

▶ **Notebook** Develop the following summary of the liturgy of Confirmation on the chalkboard for entry in student notebooks.

Liturgy
- Laying on of hands
- Anointing forehead with oil
- Sealing of person ("Be sealed . . .")

Exercise 3 **Discuss** **(a)** It would be helpful if you, personally, could give an example from your own life of a time

1. when you went from a state of fear or panic to a state of calm or peace, as Kathryn did, or
2. when you felt the presence of the Holy Spirit guiding you or helping you in some situation, as Kathryn did.

(b) Jesus said, "Every tree is known by the fruit it bears" (Luke 6:44). The fruit of Kathryn's experience was "a very real knowledge that I had a source of strength." In other words, what she felt is one of the reasons why Jesus gave the Holy Spirit to his followers.

Exercise 4 **Discuss** Have the appointed students present the three readings. The exercise is self-explanatory.

CHAPTER SEVENTEEN: Local Witness (pages 184–85)

Philip in Judea

LESSON

1. LESSON BACKGROUND

▶ *Catechism of the Catholic Church,* 1426–1428.

2. LESSON QUIZ

Perfect score = 10 points

1. In what sense did the Church's first missionary outreach take place more by accident than by design, and what deacon spearheaded the outreach? *(Lesson 87 review—2 points)*
2. List the three central actions of the Confirmation liturgy as it is practiced today. *(Lesson 87 notebook review—3 points)*
3. The Acts of the Apostles speaks of "God-fearers." Explain (a) what a "God-fearer" was, (b) the names of two such God-fearers, and (c) the two Christians who played a key role in their lives. *(Lesson 88 preview—5 points)*

3. LESSON HOMEWORK

▶ **Return**	Lesson 87 review questions (page 183).
▶ **Collect**	Lesson 88 review questions (page 185).
▶ **Read**	Lesson 89 ("Gentile Pentecost," pages 186–87).
▶ **Write**	Lesson 89 review questions (page 187).
▶ **Appoint**	Three students to prepare Acts 8:4–25, Acts 10:1–8, Acts 11:1–18 (lesson 89, exercise 3).

4. LESSON PRESENTATION

Point ❶ **Read** Have volunteers read aloud the core content of lesson 88.

▶ **Notebook** Recall Jesus' commission to his apostles in Acts 1:8: "Be witnesses for me in Jerusalem, in all of Judea and Samaria, and to the ends of the earth."

Review how Luke uses this commission as the outline for Acts. Develop the following diagram on the chalkboard again for entry in student notebooks.

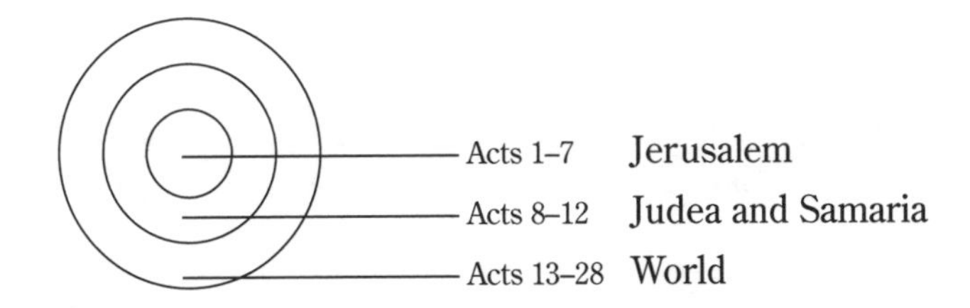

▶ **Notebook** Develop the following diagram for entry in student notebooks. It sums up the two kinds of Gentiles who aligned themselves with Judaism.

Gentiles	God-fearers	Accepted Judaism partly
	Proselytes	Accepted Judaism totally

▶ **Notebook** Develop the following diagram on the chalkboard for entry in student notebooks. It lists two prominent God-fearers in Acts of the Apostles and the two men who evangelized and baptized them as Christians.

God-fearers	Ethiopian	Philip evangelized/baptized
	Cornelius	Peter evangelized/baptized

5. LESSON INTERACTION

Exercise ❶ **Discuss** **(a)** The Holy Father ended World Youth Day in Denver by issuing two challenges to the young people of the world: (1) to lead the way for the rest of the world in undergoing a personal conversion to Jesus, and (2) to lead the way for the rest of the world in developing a personal relationship with Jesus.

When we think of personal conversion to Jesus, we usually think of going from "nonbelief to belief" in Jesus. This is one kind of conversion. But there are two more: (1) going from being a "fan" of Jesus to being a "follower" and (2) going from being a "follower" to being an "apostle" of Jesus.

▶ **Notebook** Develop this diagram on the chalkboard for entry in student notebooks.

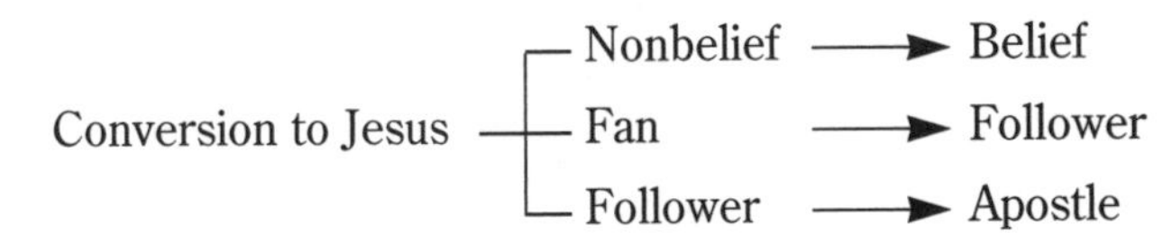

Discuss Ask: What is the difference between a fan, a follower, and an apostle?

(A *fan* is someone who admires another person but does not necessarily seek to imitate that person.

A *follower* is someone who not only admires another person but also seeks to live by the vision and values that person lives by.

An *apostle* is someone who not only admires another person and seeks to live by that person's vision and values but also wants to introduce others to that person.)

Clarify An example of a person who went through all three conversions is a friend of the author. You might want to share with your students excerpts from a letter he wrote to the author. (The friend gave this permission.) The letter will not only illustrate the above points but also help the students (a) identify a graced moment in their lives and (b) compose a prayer celebrating it.

My father left home [when I was eleven]. . . .
My whole family was broke [up].
The tears flowed for weeks, except mine. . . .
I began to hate my father,
especially for hurting my dear mother. . . .

I started into crime and drugs. At the age of twelve
I was picked up for the car thefts (accomplice).
Later, I was picked up for shoplifting . . .
and more under-age drinking fines
than I care to remember paying.
But this is just what I got caught doing.

Now my mother is a Christian.
She hounded me to go on this COR [retreat].
I knew nothing about it and
only registered to get her off my back. . . .

During one of the large group talks,
I began daydreaming about God.
Then I visualized myself on my knees
before Jesus as he hung on the cross.
An enormous weight of guilt was upon me. . . .
I . . . wept for forgiveness.
As I wept, God forgave me. . . .
He loved me in all my filth. . . .

I came off that COR . . . high for the first time
without smoking, dropping or drinking. . . .
I didn't want anything to keep me
from getting closer to Jesus,
and so I called my dad.

That night I went to his apartment. . . .
When I arrived, we sat down and talked about nothing.
Finally, he asked,
"So, what did you come here for?"
I was relieved he asked me,
because I didn't know how to lead into it.

So I explained how on the weekend I learned
how I cannot judge any person for anything,
no matter what.
Then, I asked for his forgiveness for hating him . . .
and judging him. . . .
He left the room and came back with a folder. . . .
Then he pulled out a slip of paper. . . .
[It was a note I had written him years before.
It went like this:]

"Bill. Who do you think you are,
and what are you doing? I hate you and
I don't ever want anything from you
ever again in my life. Your x-son."

I was aware of all the pain
he must have gone through
having carried that all those years. . . .
I threw my arms around him
and tears of forgiveness and love flowed. . . .

We talked a little longer, and then I kissed him . . .
and was on my way. . . .
I took a cab most of the way home that night.
Joy overflowed in me—as my walk turned into a jog
and a fast run. With arms outstretched,
I screamed, "I love you, God!"
He blessed me greatly that night.

The author's friend has since become a real apostle of Jesus and is sharing with others "his newfound friend," who changed his life so dramatically.

Exercise 2 **Discuss** **(a)** Conversion is an ongoing process. It is not a one-time event. It ends with death.

(b) Conversion is a lot like rowing a canoe upstream. If we don't keep "rowing," we're through.

(c) Nobody likes to change. The key to change is to be like the baby. We must be so discontented with our present situation that we want to change.

(d) The first step in changing the world is to change ourselves.

(e) The best defense against external pressures (recreational sex, drugs, etc.) is to build up an internal conviction (put on slippers) to be committed to Jesus and to living and loving as he did.

(f) See the answer to *c*.

(g) Unless we open our hearts to Jesus, as the friend who wrote the letter above did, God can't enter in and help us do what we could never do ourselves.

Exercise 3 **Activity** This exercise is self-explanatory.

Gentile Pentecost

1. LESSON BACKGROUND

▶ *Catechism of the Catholic Church*, 880–887.

2. LESSON QUIZ

Perfect score = 8 points

1. Why did some Gentiles in Philip's time turn to Judaism to satisfy their spiritual hunger? *(Lesson 88 review—1 point)*
2. List and briefly explain the two kinds of Gentiles who aligned themselves with Judaism in Philip's time. *(Lesson 88 notebook review—4 points)*
3. Name the group of people upon whom the Holy Spirit descended in (a) Jerusalem, (b) Caesarea, (c) Samaria. *(Lesson 89 preview—3 points)*

3. LESSON HOMEWORK

▶ **Return** Lesson 88 review questions (page 185).

▶ **Collect** Lesson 89 review questions (page 187).

▶ **Read** Lesson 90 ("Peter's Departure," pages 188–89).

▶ **Write** Lesson 90 review questions (page 189).

▶ **Appoint** Student to prepare Acts 6:1–4 and Acts 15:36–41 (lesson 90, exercise 3).

4. LESSON PRESENTATION

Point ❶ **Read** Have volunteers read aloud the core content of lesson 89.

▶ **Clarify** While Peter was speaking to Cornelius and the Gentiles gathered at his house, "the Holy Spirit came down on all those who were listening" and they began "speaking in strange tongues and praising God's greatness" (Acts 10:44, 46).

▶ **Review** Speaking in tongues may be viewed as a verbal outpouring resulting from an intense exaltation of the human spirit by the Holy Spirit. On a purely natural level, people often stammer incoherently when overwhelmed by some intense experience. It is not surprising to find a parallel to this on the supernatural level.

Paul discusses the question of speaking in tongues in 1 Corinthians 14:2–5, 23–25.

Point ❷ **Clarify** Stress that the outpouring of the Holy Spirit in the house of Cornelius is often referred to as the "Gentile Pentecost"— just as the outpouring of the Holy Spirit upon the Samaritans is often referred to as the "Samaritan Pentecost."

▶ **Notebook** Develop the following summary on the chalkboard for entry in student notebooks.

Spirit descends (3 "Pentecosts")
- On Jews in Jerusalem (Acts 2:4)
- On half-Jews in Samaria (Acts 8:17)
- On Gentiles in Caesarea (Acts 10:44)

Point ❸ **Clarify** Stress that the Jerusalem meeting (first Church council) resolved the question of whether Gentiles must become Jews (that is, be circumcised) preliminary to becoming Christians (Acts 15:1–35).

5. LESSON INTERACTION

Exercise ❶ **Discuss** **(a, b, c)** Expand the students' idea of a "turning point." It could be a car accident, failure in school, a death in the family, meeting someone who became a close friend, and so on. Give students time to reflect and to write out their responses privately before volunteering to share.

Exercise ❷ **Clarify** **(a, b, c)** Jesus clearly has in mind some form of "organized" religion, saying to Peter:

"You are a rock, and on this rock foundation
I will build my church. . . .
I will give you the keys of the Kingdom of heaven;
what you prohibit on earth will be prohibited in heaven,
and what you permit on earth
will be permitted in heaven." Matthew 16:18–19

Exercise ❸ **Clarify** **(a, b)** Have the appointed students read the passages from Scripture listed. Read and discuss them one by one. Students are particularly interested in the first reading, "The magician."

Magazine stands carry a wide variety of journals about such things as astrology, fortune-telling, and horoscopes. These journals claim that Hitler consulted the stars before planning certain important war strategies and that an astrologer warned Kennedy about going to Dallas (where he was assassinated).

Ironically, years later, the *Dallas Morning News* (May 4, 1988) carried an article by Owen Ullmann, denying that President Reagan "has made presidential decisions based on the advice Nancy Reagan got from a California astrologer."

A White House spokesperson admitted, however, that since the attempted assassination of her husband (March 30, 1981), Nancy has had "an interest in astrology," saying, "She was very concerned for her husband's welfare, and astrology has been part of her concern in terms of activities."

▶ **Clarify** The zodiac provides the basis for many astrological charts and forecasts. The word *zodiac* comes from a Greek word meaning "circle of animals." It is an imaginary path followed by the moon and the planets.

The path divides into twelve thirty-degree arcs, corresponding to the twelve divisions of the calendar year. Each arc contains a star pattern (sign), from which it takes its name: Taurus, Leo, Gemini, and so on.

As the earth circles the sun, the sun appears to go from one arc to the next. A person born when the sun occupies a given arc is supposedly influenced by its star pattern.

▶ **Clarify** The book *Astrology Disproved* by Lawrence E. Jerome contains a statement that was signed by 192 leading scientists, including 19 Nobel prize winners.

The statement protests the "uncritical dissemination of astrological charts, forecasts, and horoscopes by the media and by otherwise reputable newspapers, magazines, and book publishers."

The statement goes on to say, "We believe the time has come to challenge directly and forcefully the pretentious claims of astrological charlatans."

▶ **Notebook** The following diagram sums up areas involving the occult that are prohibited under the First Commandment.

Occult practices	Superstition	Attributing godlike powers to ordinary things
	Divination	Seeking to learn the future from horoscopes, etc.
	Spiritism	Seeking to communicate with the dead through mediums and seances

▶ **Clarify** Dabbling in the occult was also present in biblical times. Both the Old Testament (Deuteronomy 18:10–11) and the New Testament (Acts 16:16) forbade it.

This brings us back to Simon the magician. He was a popular occult figure in Samaria. Acts 8:11–13 says:

They paid this attention to him because . . .
he had astonished them with his magic.
But when they believed Philip's message
about the good news . . . ,
they were baptized, both men and women.
Simon himself also believed; and after being baptized,
he stayed close to Philip and was astounded
when he saw the great wonders and miracles
that were being performed.

When Peter and John conferred the Holy Spirit upon the Samaritans, Simon slipped back to his old ways.

He offered money to Peter and John,
and said, "Give this power to me too. . . ."

But Peter answered him,
"May you and your money go to hell,
for thinking that you can buy God's gift. . . .
Your heart is not right in God's sight.
Repent . . . and pray to the Lord
that he will forgive you." Acts 8:18–22

We are not told what happened to Simon. But to this day, the sin of trying to buy spiritual gifts gets its name from him—*simony.*

Exercise 4 **Discuss** See exercise 2 above. It refers to Peter's special status in the Church (given him by Jesus), which explains why he should preside over each of the three "Pentecosts."

Minimap **Discuss** Direct students' attention to the minimap on page 186. Have them locate Caesarea.

The photo on the same page gives an aerial view of the famous amphitheater that was excavated at Caesarea and has been restored.

Refer students to the photo (page 163) of the "Pilate Inscription," found during excavations of Caesarea.

Caesarea is sometimes called Caesarea-on-the-Sea to distinguish it from Caesarea Philippi, where Peter professed his faith in Jesus and was given the "keys of the Kingdom."

CHAPTER SEVENTEEN: Local Witness (pages 188–89)

Peter's Departure

LESSON **90**

1. LESSON BACKGROUND

▶ *Catechism of the Catholic Church*, 552–553, 862.

2. LESSON QUIZ

Perfect score = 10 points

1. What problem was the first Church council in history called to settle, and how did the council settle it? *(Lesson 89 review—2 points)*
2. List and briefly describe three occult practices prohibited by the First Commandment. *(Lesson 89 notebook review—6 points)*
3. Who assumed leadership of the Jerusalem church after whose departure? *(Lesson 90 preview—2 point)*

3. LESSON HOMEWORK

▶ **Return**	Lesson 89 review questions (page 187).
▶ **Collect**	Lesson 90 review questions (page 189).
▶ **Read**	Lesson 91 ("Paul's Conversion," pages 190–91).
▶ **Write**	Lesson 91 review questions (page 191).
▶ **Appoint**	Student to prepare 1 Corinthians 12:12–27 (lesson 91, exercise 2).

4. LESSON PRESENTATION

Point ❶ **Read** Have volunteers read aloud the core content of lesson 90.

▶ **Clarify** The Herod mentioned here is not Herod Antipas, Herod the Great's son, but Herod Agrippa I, grandson of Herod the Great.

Herod the Great was a paradox. He built many beautiful buildings in Judah, was a good athlete, and supported the Olympic movement. He gave the order to slaughter the children (to do away with the child Jesus) and even murdered his own son. He also gave the order to murder the leaders of the country when he died, to insure a flow of tears throughout the country. That order was never carried out.

Herod Antipas ruled during Jesus' adulthood. He interrogated Jesus just before Pilate sentenced him to death (Luke 23:7).

Herod Agrippa was raised in Rome and was a close friend of the emperor Caligula. It was Caligula who gave Agrippa the title *king*.

▶ **Clarify** The ancient Jewish historian Josephus, who wrote about the time John wrote his Gospel, says Agrippa died suddenly and strangely in 44 C.E. Acts says:

On a chosen day Herod put on his royal robes,
sat on his throne,
and made a speech to the people.
"It isn't a man speaking, but a god!" they shouted.
At once the angel of the Lord struck Herod down,
because he did not give honor to God.
He was eaten by worms and died. Acts 12:21–23

Josephus adds to the mystery of Herod's death, saying that the superstitious king believed an owl would trumpet his demise. (Even to this day some cultures hold the owl to be a sign of impending death. Recall the movies *I Heard the Owl Call My Name* and *My Family*.)

While basking in the applause of the crowd, Agrippa spotted an owl perched on an awning. Josephus adds that immediately the king got stomach cramps and died within days of a "loathsome" disease.

▶ **Notebook** Develop the following diagram summary of the "Herods" on the chalkboard for entry in notebooks.

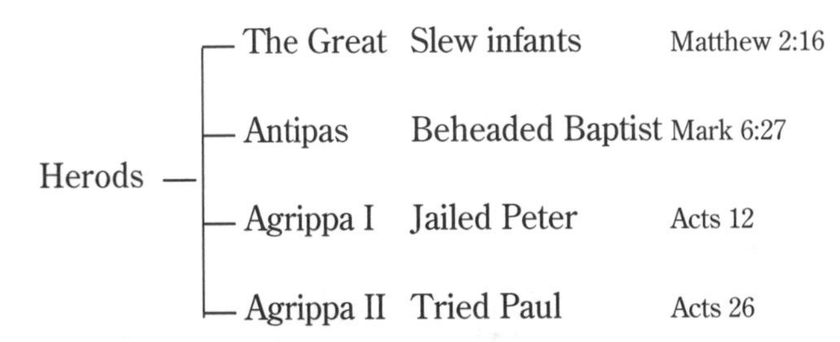

Point ❷ **Clarify** The James who succeeds Peter is not James the brother of John. Paul mentions him in two letters (1 Corinthians 15:7 and Galatians 1:19, 2:9).

Point ❸ **Clarify** The story of Peter's dramatic escape from jail ends with this short statement:

When morning came, there was
a tremendous confusion among the guards—
what had happened to Peter?
Herod gave orders to search for him,
but they could not find him.
So he had the guards questioned
and ordered them put to death. Acts 12:18–19

These guards suffered the fate that was not uncommon in the ancient world: those responsible for the prisoner's escape received the prisoner's punishment.

5. LESSON INTERACTION

Exercise 1 **Notebook** **(a, b, c)** Like everything in life, faith grows and develops by stages. Develop these three main "faith stages" on the chalkboard for entry in student notebooks.

Faith stages	Childhood	Faith by birth
	Adolescent	Faith in transition
	Adult	Faith by choice

Clarify Of these three stages, the adolescent stage is normally the most critical and the most painful. It is the most critical stage because at this time in our lives we begin the important transition from being a Christian by culture (physical birth) to being a Christian by conviction (personal choice).

Likewise, the adolescent stage is the most painful stage because during this stage our childhood faith must die in order that our adult faith can be born. The dying of our childhood faith is what causes the pain.

John Kirvan's book *The Restless Believers* contains a moving description of how the death of our childhood faith affects us. He quotes a young person as saying:

I don't know what's gone wrong,
but I just don't believe like I used to.
When I was in grade school
and for the first couple of years of high school
I was real religious,
and now I just don't seem to care.

The death of our childhood faith makes us feel sick of heart—even guilty. This is unfortunate, for our faith is simply going through an important growth stage. It is changing from being a cultural faith to being a convictional faith.

The transition from being a Christian by culture (birth) to being a Christian by conviction (choice) is a gradual process that is never fully complete. It goes on all our lives.

Discuss **(d)** Read John 4:39–42 (see below). It is a great example of moving from a cultural faith (basing my faith on what another says) to a convictional faith (basing my faith on my own discovery of Jesus). It deals with the Samaritan woman at the well.

Many of the Samaritans in that town
believed in Jesus because the woman had said,
"He told me everything I have ever done."
So when the Samaritans came to him,
they begged him to stay with them,
and Jesus stayed there two days.
Many more believed because of his message,
and they told the woman,
"We believe now, not because of what you said,
but because we ourselves have heard him,
and we know that he really is the Savior of the world."

Exercise 2 **Discuss** **(a)** There is nothing like the example of a good person. It is the most eloquent sermon most of us ever hear.

(b) This quotation builds on the first. A truly good person becomes a conduit through which the light of Christ shines and makes Christ visible to us.

(c) This final quotation builds on the second. When we let Jesus shine through us, we lose nothing. Witness to Christ is like love. The more we give it, the more there is to give. Someone said it is like a mother's milk. If it is not given, it dries up.

Exercise 3 **Discuss** **(a, b, c)** Have the appointed student read these passages aloud. By including these "warts" Luke makes what he says about the early Church more credible. He does not whitewash problems.

Paul's Conversion

LESSON 91

1. LESSON BACKGROUND

▶ *Catechism of the Catholic Church,* 787–795.

2. LESSON QUIZ

Perfect score = 10 points

1. How did Peter end up in prison, and how did he get out of prison? *(Lesson 90 review—2 points)*
2. List and briefly describe the three stages of faith that people go through. *(Lesson 90 notebook review—6 points)*
3. In what city were believers first called Christians, and what kind of city was it spiritually? *(Lesson 91 preview—2 points)*

3. LESSON HOMEWORK

▶ **Return** Lesson 90 review questions (page 189).

▶ **Collect** Lesson 91 review questions (page 191).

▶ **Read** Lesson 92 ("First Missionary Trip," pages 192–93).

▶ **Write** Lesson 92 review questions (page 193).

4. LESSON PRESENTATION

Point ❶ **Read** Have volunteers read aloud the core content of lesson 91.

▶ **Clarify** Few experiences are more discussed than Paul's conversion experience on the road to Damascus. People ask, "What happened? Did he have a vision? Did he see Jesus?"

Paul describes the experience as both a "vision" from heaven (Acts 26:19) and an "appearance" of Jesus (1 Corinthians 15:8). Paul himself seems hard pressed to know what actually happened. Speaking of himself in the third person, he says:

I know a certain Christian man
who fourteen years ago
was snatched up to the highest heaven
(I do not know whether this actually happened
or whether he had a vision—only God knows).

2 Corinthians 12:2

Regardless of what happened, Paul was instantly and dramatically transformed by the experience. He would never again be the same.

Point ❷ **Clarify** After Paul's sight returned, he began to preach in the synagogues of Damascus. Acts 9:21–25 says:

All who heard him were amazed and asked,
"Isn't he the one who in Jerusalem was killing those
who worship that man Jesus? . . .

Saul's preaching became even more powerful,
and his proofs that Jesus was the Messiah
were so convincing that the Jews who lived in Damascus
could not answer him.

After many days had gone by,
the Jews met together and made plans to kill Saul,
but he was told of their plan.
Day and night they watched the city gates
in order to kill him.
But one night Saul's followers took him
and let him down through an opening in the wall,
lowering him in a basket.

▶ **Clarify** The names *Saul* and *Paul* are different versions of the same name (*Saul* is Jewish; *Paul* is Greco-Roman). The switch in names takes place when Paul begins to travel and preach in the Greco-Roman world (Acts 13:9).

Point ❸ **Clarify** After escaping from Damascus, the sequence of events is not too clear.

Combining the data of Acts 9 and Galatians 1, it appears that he first went to Arabia for three years. . . . Paul himself gives no reason for this interval; it must be understood as a retirement to the desert like the retirements of Moses, Elijah, and Jesus himself.

John L. McKenzie, *Dictionary of the Bible*

Edgar J. Goodspeed is probably right when he says in his book *Paul:*

To some retreat . . . Paul must have gone,
to begin a tremendous reconstruction
of his religious thinking.
For he had not just lightly added Jesus
to his Jewish theology, as the Messiah
foretold by the prophets. . . .
The cornerstones of his theology and practice
must be rigorously reexamined,

in the light of his new religious experience.
How drastically and honestly this was done
his letters will show.

Point ④ **Clarify** After his extended retreat in Arabia, Paul returned to Damascus and eventually Jerusalem (Galatians 1:18). There he began preaching again. When his old allies (now his enemies) tried to kill him, he fled.

As Paul left Jerusalem under cover of darkness, he must have wondered about the strange turn of events. He had made a tremendous conversion, but the very people he wanted to share his good fortune with refused to listen to him.

Perhaps as Paul looked up at the stars, he felt a strange new kinship with his master and Lord, Jesus, who "came to his own country, but his own people did not receive him" (John 1:11). He might also have felt a strange new kinship with his father in the faith, Abraham. God had called him, too, and had him leave his familiar surroundings without telling him why—or even where he should go (Genesis 12:1).

► **Clarify** Paul returned to the area of his birthplace, Tarsus, where he remained for an extended period, probably preaching the "good news."

In any event, Paul eventually teamed up with Barnabas to preach and teach in Antioch. It was the prelude to one of the greatest missionary undertakings in the history of Christianity.

Point ⑤ **Notebook** Develop the following diagram for entry in student notebooks. It summarizes the key events in Paul's life up to this point. (Note: The exact dates are difficult to reconstruct but are probable.)

Paul	Birth in Tarsus	10 C.E.
	Conversion in Damascus	34
	Ministry in Antioch	43–44

5. LESSON INTERACTION

Exercise ① **Activity** This exercise can be a lot of fun if you get the right students to present it. Much hinges on how well they prepare the answers to the questions and how well they try to assimilate a TV situation with "call-in" questions.

Exercise ② **Discuss** **(a)** Have the students write out their responses in private before sharing them with the class.

► **Clarify** Chris says, "I don't need the Church. I have my own way of relating to Christ." Chris ignores the fundamental point of Paul's vision. A voice asked Paul, "Why do you persecute me?" Paul asked immediately, "Who are you, Lord?" The voice said, "I am Jesus, whom you persecute" (Acts 9:4–5). Then it dawned on Paul: Jesus and his followers formed one body. "[Christ] is the head of his body, the church" (Colossians 1:18).

To try to separate Jesus from his Church and relate to him apart from the Church is contrary to the revelation of Scripture. There is only one Christ and that is the Risen Christ who forms one body with his Church.

► **Discuss** **(b)** Have the appointed student read 1 Corinthians 12:12–27. The operative lines are:

Christ is like a single body . . .
made up of different parts. . . .
God put every different part in the body
just as he wanted it to be. . . .
So then, the eye cannot say to the hand,
"I don't need you!" . . . All of you are Christ's body,
and each one is a part of it. 1 Corinthians 12:12, 18, 21, 27

Exercise ③ **Discuss** **(a, b)** Refer the students to the caption of the photo on page 231. The caption quotes Jesus as saying, "Because you are lukewarm, neither hot nor cold, I am going to spit you out" (Revelation 3:16).

Ask: How does this quote shed light on why the people of Antioch were so "hot" and "ready" to hear Jesus' message? (They had lived it up but came up dry. So they were ready to listen to Jesus' followers, who seemed to have it all together.)

Exercises ④ & ⑤ **Discuss** These exercises are straightforward and should pose no problem.

Minimap **Activity** Direct attention to the minimap on page 190. Have the students locate Tarsus.

Photo **Clarify** Direct students' attention to the photo below the minimap. It shows an archway that leads into Tarsus, Paul's birthplace. Greek geographer Strabo says that at one time Tarsus even surpassed Athens as a center of culture and learning. No wonder Paul was proud of his birthplace (Acts 22:25–29). Ancient celebrities who visited Tarsus include both Julius Caesar and Augustus Caesar. They also include Mark Anthony and Cleopatra.

Like all Jewish boys, Paul grew up in Tarsus learning a trade. In his case it was "tent making," although the original Greek word could be translated as "leather working." Paul worked at this trade even in his missionary days (Acts 18:3).

First Missionary Trip

LESSON 92

1. LESSON BACKGROUND

▶ *Catechism of the Catholic Church*, 854–856.

2. LESSON QUIZ

Perfect score = 5 points

1. What new view of Jesus' followers did Paul's conversion experience on the road to Damascus give him? *(Lesson 91 review—1 point)*
2. List the approximate dates of the following events in Paul's life: (a) birth in Tarsus, (b) conversion in Damascus, (c) ministry in Antioch. *(Lesson 91 notebook review—3 points)*
3. What prompted Paul and Barnabas to make their first missionary journey? *(Lesson 92 preview—1 point)*

3. LESSON HOMEWORK

▶ **Return** Lesson 91 review questions (page 191).

▶ **Collect** Lesson 92 review questions (page 193).

▶ **Read** Lesson 93 ("Second Missionary Trip," pages 194–95).

▶ **Write** Lesson 93 review questions (page 195).

4. LESSON PRESENTATION

Point ❶ **Read** Have volunteers read aloud the core content of lesson 92.

▶ **Clarify** Every major movement in history has had its champion. Organized labor had Samuel Gompers. Women's suffrage had Susan B. Anthony. Civil rights had Martin Luther King Jr. Ecumenism had Pope John XXIII. Christianity had Paul of Tarsus.

▶ **Discuss** From this point on (Saul's missionary call by the Holy Spirit), the "Acts of the Apostles" could be called the "Acts of Paul." For he dominates the rest of Acts like sun dominates summer.

From this point on, also, Paul drops his Jewish name, Saul, in favor of its Greco-Roman counterpart. It is possibly a sign of his calling to preach the Good News to the Gentiles.

Ask: How is Paul's name change in keeping with the purpose of name changes in the Bible? What are some earlier name changes in the Bible? (A change of name was the sign of a new calling. Some examples include *Abram* to *Abraham*, *Sarai* to *Sarah*, *Jacob* to *Israel*, *Simon* to *Peter*.)

Point ❷ **Discuss** Who was Barnabas? Acts 4:36 identifies him as a Levite who was born in Cyprus—and whose name was originally Joseph. The apostles gave him the name Barnabas.

Ask: Where did we run across the term *Levite* before, and who were the Levites? (A Levite passed by the injured man in Jesus' parable of the Good Samaritan [Luke 10:32]. Levites were members of the tribe of Levi, one of the twelve tribes of Israel. 1 Chronicles 23:32 says: "They were given the responsibility of taking care of . . . the Temple, and of assisting . . . the priests . . . in the Temple worship." At the risk of oversimplification, we could compare them to modern lay deacons.)

The fact that Barnabas was born in Cyprus could explain why the first port of call for Paul and Barnabas was Cyprus.

Point ❸ **Activity** Direct students' attention to the minimap on page 192. As a kind of review of the highlights of the first missionary trip of Paul and Barnabas, have the students locate and explain the significance of the key cities on the map.

▶ **Notebook** By way of summary, develop this chart on the chalkboard for entry in student notebooks.

City	Highlight Event
Tarsus	Paul was born here.
Antioch	Paul and Barnabas set out from here.
Cyprus	Paul and Barnabas preach to governor here. Paul causes a magician to be temporarily blind here.
Lystra	Paul healed cripple here. Paul and Barnabas were hailed as gods here. Paul was stoned here.

Point ❹ **Clarify** The ancient story of Zeus and Hermes' visit to Lystra is preserved in *Metamorphoses* by Ovid, a first-century Roman poet. Have the students turn to page 219 of the student text for a photograph of a coin from Lystra that Paul or Barnabas could have handled during their visit there.

5. LESSON INTERACTION

Exercise ❶ **Discuss** It was not unusual in Paul's time for those in political power and influence to have private astrologers. Possibly, Elymas was employed by Governor Sergius for this purpose.

► **Discuss** **(a)** For people who do not love or have not yet found the "God of love," fear can play an immense role. Even for people who do love and have found the "God of love," fear can play an important role. Saint Ignatius of Loyola, a practical spiritual guide, acknowledges that when love cools (as it does on certain occasions), fear may have to "kick in" to keep us from sin.

(b) Recall what was said earlier about motivation. It is like a cable—made up of a variety of strands. For example, love of God and neighbor may make up 40 percent of it; fear of punishment, 30 percent; hope of reward, 30 percent.

Exercise ❷ **Clarify** The early Church fasted, prayed, and imposed hands on Barnabas and Paul. Fasting has a long history.

► **Notebook** Here are some of the reasons why people have fasted. Develop the chart on the chalkboard for entry in student notebooks.

People	Reason for Fasting
Egyptians	To look better (thinner)
Greeks	To keep sharp and alert
Native Americans	To demonstrate courage
Russian icon artists	To paint better
Jews	To seek God's help

► **Discuss** Jews frequently combined fasting with prayer. For example, David fasted and prayed for the recovery of his son (2 Samuel 12:16–17); the nation of Israel fasted and prayed for guidance in time of national danger (2 Chronicles 20:3); Daniel prayed and fasted for sinners (Daniel 9:1–4).

Ask: Why combine fasting with prayer? What does fasting add to prayer? (It adds action to words.)

► **Clarify** Imposing hands on someone is a way of ritualizing (giving external, symbolic expression) to an internal state or intention. A secular example is a handshake or hug.

Exercise ❸ **Discuss** **(a)** A sensitive soul is someone who is capable of deep perception and feeling. Actors can "sense" the mood of an audience. Artists can detect beauty where other people see nothing. Recall the line from the poem "Reading Gaol":

Two men looked out from prison bars—
one saw mud, the other stars.

(b, c) Sensitive people feel rebukes and rejection deeply. They are said to have a "thin skin." On the other hand, they experience "highs" and "ecstasies" that nonsensitive people never can feel. Sensitive people pay a price for their sensitivity, but they also reap great rewards from it.

Exercise ❹ **Activity** This exercise will give you an insight into how sensitive some of your students are.

Give the students three or four minutes to reflect silently on the prayer model, with a view to either doing a completely different one or rephrasing the second half of each paragraph of the model prayer given.

Photo **Activity** Direct students' attention to the photo below the minimap. For a better close-up of Hermes, have the students turn back to page 170. The sculpture is magnificently executed and remarkably preserved.

Have the students also check the map on page 171. The first city in Cyprus that Paul and Barnabas evangelized was Salamis. The encounter with Elymas took place in Paphos, on the opposite side of the island.

Some students may be familiar with Aphrodite, the goddess of love. Legend says she emerged from the sea off the coast of Cyprus.

Photo **Discuss** Direct students' attention to the photo on page 193. Ask: What symbols can you identify in the photo, and what meaning do we attach to them?

Fish	(inflated balloons)	Jesus
Cross	(yellow banner)	Jesus' crucifixion
Butterfly	(purple banner)	Jesus' resurrection
Fire tongues	(white banner)	Descent of Spirit

Ask: Why is the butterfly a resurrection symbol? (It emerges from a caterpillar upon the latter's death.)

Second Missionary Trip

LESSON 93

1. LESSON BACKGROUND

▶ *Catechism of the Catholic Church*, 711–713.

2. LESSON QUIZ

Perfect score = 6 points

1. Where did Paul and Barnabas begin their preaching, and where did they go next? *(Lesson 92 review—2 points)*
2. List two events that took place in Lystra and one in Cyprus. *(Lesson 92 notebook review—3 points)*
3. Who was the Jerusalem Christian who accompanied Paul on his second missionary trip? *(Lesson 93 preview—1 point)*

3. LESSON HOMEWORK

▶ **Return** Lesson 92 review questions (page 193).

▶ **Collect** Lesson 93 review questions (page 195).

▶ **Read** Lesson 94 ("Paul in Corinth," pages 196–97).

▶ **Write** Lesson 94 review questions (page 197).

4. LESSON PRESENTATION

Point ① **Read** Have volunteers read aloud the core content of lesson 93.

▶ **Notebook** Develop the following summary of key events that took place on Paul's second missionary trip.

Events (2nd trip)
- Lystra — Timothy joins Paul and Silas in preaching the Gospel.
- Troas — Vision sends Paul to Macedonia (European mainland).
- Philippi — Paul and Silas imprisoned for expelling demon from slave girl.
- Thessalonica — Enemies threaten lives of Paul and Silas.
- Berea — Paul and Silas take refuge here after leaving Thessalonica.

5. LESSON INTERACTION

Exercise ① **Discuss** **(a)** Give the students time to reflect on the first response before recording and sharing it.

(b, c) Saint Patrick makes the point that at privileged moments in life our heart is filled with an unexplainable love for God, for one another, and for our world.

Ask: Can you recall such a moment in your life?

Exercise ② **Clarify** Epicurus taught in Athens three hundred years before Jesus' birth. His disciples were called Epicureans. Paul knew he would have trouble preaching to them on certain concepts. Let us consider three of them: (1) the origin of life, (2) life after death, and (3) judgment after death.

Today, few people think the universe originated by chance. It is too much of a "statistical monstrosity." Professor Conklin, formerly of Princeton, used this example to show how monstrous it is: It would be akin to saying that the unabridged dictionary is the product of an explosion in a printing factory. All the type floated down letter by letter, page by page, and definition by definition—just as they appear in the dictionary.

▶ **Discuss** A. Cressy Morrison uses a somewhat similar example in his book *Man Does Not Stand Alone.*

Take ten pennies and mark them 1 to 10. Put them in a hat and give them a good shake. Now try to draw them out in sequence, putting each coin back in the hat after each draw. Your chances of drawing 1 is 1 in 10. Your chances of drawing 1 and 2 in succession are 1 in 100. Your chances of drawing 1, 2, and 3 in succession are 1 in 1,000.

Ask: What are the chances of drawing 1 to 10 in succession? (It skyrockets to 1 in 10 billion. And remember, we are talking about only ten items. The universe contains trillions and trillions of items.)

▶ **Discuss** This brings us to the question of life after death. Epicureans considered the idea of life after death to be nonsense. They believed death was simply a breakup of atoms. It was the end of things. Paul held just the opposite. Death was the beginning of things.

Life after death is no longer dismissed so casually in modern times. One modern advocate of life after death was the great scientist Wernher von Braun.

Ask: Who was von Braun? (He designed the *Saturn 5* rocket that carried the *Apollo 11* astronauts to the moon.) Von Braun approached life after death from a scientific perspective, saying:

Science, for instance, tells us that nothing in nature, not even the tiniest particle, can disappear without a trace. Nature does not know extinction. All it knows is transformation.

Now, if God applies this fundamental principle to the most minute and insignificant parts of His universe, doesn't it make sense to assume that He applies it also to the human soul? I think it does. And everything science has taught me—and continues to teach me—strengthens my belief in the continuity of our spiritual existence after death.

▶ **Clarify** This brings us to the third and final question: judgment after death. Some years ago, *Time* magazine (April 19, 1971) filed this provocative report:

Montreal surgeon Wilder Penfield . . . while performing operations under local anesthesia, by chance found brain sites that when stimulated electrically led one patient to hear an old tune, another to recall an exciting childhood experience in vivid detail, and still another to relive the experience of bearing her baby.

In a report to the Smithsonian Institute, Dr. Penfield summed up his findings this way:

Your brain contains a permanent record of your past that is like a single continuous strip of movie complete with soundtrack. This film library records your whole waking life, from childhood on.

Penfield goes on to say that in reliving this record, you feel again the same emotion that the first event produced in you. And you are aware of the "same interpretations, true or false, that you gave the experience in the first place." An example will illustrate.

Suppose you stole something as a child. At the time, you felt it was wrong, but you did it anyway. This is exactly what you would feel now, if your brain were stimulated electrically at the proper place.

Finally, Dr. Elisabeth Kubler-Ross, former University of Chicago authority on death and dying, made these comments after interviewing hundreds of people who had been revived after having been declared legally dead:

Patients commonly report that they experience an instantaneous reviewing of their lives, "like you have all your memory at once including all the things you have forgotten." . . . When you come to this point, you see there are only two things that are relevant: the service you render others, and love. All those things we think are important, like fame, money, prestige, and power, are insignificant.

The ramifications of all this, of course, are mind-boggling. They provide a physiological basis for the theological teaching of a personal judgment after death.

Exercise ③ **Clarify** Paul was very familiar with Stoic thought. Tarsus, his birthplace, was a center of Stoic learning. Stoicism traced its origin to a penniless Cypriot named Zeno, who came to Athens about three hundred years before Jesus. Because he was poor, he used the stoa (covered walkways) as his classroom. Hence his students were called Stoics.

Paul's own writing style reflects a Stoic influence. For example, he skillfully uses the diatribe. Basically, it consists in a conversational style of argumentation with a fictitious opponent. Take this excerpt from Romans:

What about you? You call yourself a Jew. . . .
You teach others—why don't you teach yourself?
You preach, "Do not steal"—
but do you yourself steal? . . .
You boast about having God's law—
but do you bring shame on God
by breaking his law? Romans 2:17, 21, 23

▶ **Discuss** **(a)** The Stoic image of creation being like a spark coming from and returning to a "divine origin" is more in harmony with Christian thought than is Epicurean atomism.

(b) The idea that God lacks feeling and, therefore, cannot love is an example of how we tend to impose human concepts and limitations on divine beings. It is like someone looking at a bicycle and saying, "Why doesn't it bark?" (It doesn't bark because it is totally different from a dog!) Similarly, God is totally different from us.

(c) The saying about learning "to want what you get" has merit. It is a matter of record that "handicapped" people learn to see great value in their "handicap," which they would never have chosen had they been given the choice.

▶ **Notebook** Summarize for entry in student notebooks the objections that Epicureans and Stoics had to Paul's teaching.

Objections		
	Epicureans	No life after death (death = atom breakup)
	Stoics	No loving God (God can't have feelings)

Paul in Corinth

LESSON 94

1. LESSON BACKGROUND

▶ *Catechism of the Catholic Church,* 1226–1228.

2. LESSON QUIZ

Perfect score = 10 points

1. What happened in these towns: (a) Lystra, (b) Troas, (c) Philippi? *(Lesson 93 review—3 points)*
2. List and briefly describe the objection that (a) the Epicureans and (b) the Stoics had to Paul's teaching. *(Lesson 93 notebook review—4 points)*
3. Who brought Paul before what Roman governor and why? *(Lesson 94 preview—3 points)*

3. LESSON HOMEWORK

▶ **Return** Lesson 93 review questions (page 195).

▶ **Collect** Lesson 94 review questions (page 197).

▶ **Read** Lesson 95 ("Third Missionary Trip," pages 198–99).

▶ **Write** Lesson 95 review questions (page 199).

▶ **Appoint** Five students to prepare (1) Acts 17:22–34 (lesson 95, exercise 2), (2) Acts 19:11–20, (3) Acts 19:21–41, (4) Acts 20:7–12, (5) Acts 20:17–38 (lesson 95, exercise 3).

4. LESSON PRESENTATION

Point ① **Read** Have volunteers read aloud the core content of lesson 94.

▶ **Clarify** Corinth was a commercial "hub" of ancient times. But it paid a high price for its popularity and prosperity, attracting a parade of unsavory characters: con artists, fortune hunters, and deviates. As a result, it developed a scandalous reputation that is still remembered today.

But Paul preferred preaching to the *outwardly sinful* Corinthians over the *inwardly proud* Athenians.

▶ **Notebook** Develop on the chalkboard the key difference between the Athenians and the Corinthians.

Difference		
	Athenians	Inwardly proud
	Corinthians	Outwardly sinful

Point ② **Discuss** Ask: How might you explain Paul's preference for the "outwardly sinful" Corinthians?

▶ **Clarify** Psychologists talk about the *persona.* It is that part of ourselves that we like. The persona is that part of ourselves that we show to others. It is sometimes called our *social self.*

The underside of the persona is the *shadow.* It is that part of ourselves that we do not like and try to hide from others. We might call it our *secret self.* It is a character weakness that we try to sweep under the rug and forget about.

But the shadow never forgets about us. It lives in our subconscious. Periodically, it pops up uninvited. For example, we might have a "jealous streak" that we try to keep hidden from others. Then one day it rears its ugly head in conversation to embarrass us.

The way to control a shadow—and we all have one—is to become aware of it and admit it. When we "name" it, it ceases to control us; and we start to control it. Consider the example of a top aide to President Nixon: Charles Colson, convicted in the Watergate scandal.

Colson's *persona* was his ability to get things done. His *shadow* was his pride of achievement, which blinded him to everything, including God. The thing that finally led him to admit his shadow and control it was a passage from C. S. Lewis's book *Mere Christianity.* Lewis writes:

Pride leads to every other vice:
it is the complete anti-God state of mind. . . .
As long as you are proud, you cannot know God.
A proud man is always looking down;
you cannot see something above you.

▶ **Discuss** Have the students take time to list (anonymously) on a half sheet of paper their *persona* and their *shadow.* Collect the papers and select five responses at random to share with the class. (Explain what you plan to do so that if some students do not want to participate, they can write "Don't read!" across their response.)

▶ **Notebook** Develop on the chalkboard for entry in student notebooks the distinction between the *persona* and the *shadow.*

Two sides — Persona: Social self (part we like)
Two sides — Shadow: Secret self (part we dislike)

5. LESSON INTERACTION

Exercise ❶ **Clarify** Pioneers of new ventures are a lot like the Old Testament prophets. Recall that Amos (text, page 84) and Jeremiah (text, page 90) were ridiculed. Visionaries are never popular with people who lack vision.

▶ **Discuss** Ask: Why would Western Union be interested in ridiculing the telephone? (They undoubtedly saw it as a potential rival and would have had a vested interest in trying to "put down" the idea.)

Admiral Leahy was a naval man, and his reaction may have been influenced by the fact that the atom bomb would give the Air Force a leg up in the rivalry between the services.

It is a sad fact that personal interests often compete with the common good.

Exercise ❷ **Discuss** **(a, b)** Have the students take a few minutes to do this exercise in private. Have volunteers share their responses with the class. You might want to make a list of the "discouraging things" on the chalkboard and have the students vote on the top three.

Exercise ❸ **Discuss** **(a)** The best illustration of God's words ("my power is greatest when you are weak") are members of Alcoholics Anonymous. Their first and most important step toward sobriety is to admit that they are powerless over their addiction. In other words, they are strongest when they are weakest—when they realize that they must turn their lives over to God. The reason? At this moment they open themselves humbly to the greatest power in all the world: God's grace.

(b) An example might illustrate this question. A man found the cocoon of an emperor moth. He brought it into his house to study how it emerges from its furry little prison. After days of watching it struggle, he decided to help the moth out by putting a slight slit in the cocoon. The moth emerged but was still scrawny and undeveloped. It died. Upon inquiry, the man was told that he had caused the moth's death. Nature so designed moths that they develop by struggling to break the cocoon. When they are strong enough to break out, that means they are strong enough to fly.

Exercise ❹ **Discuss** **(a, b)** A recent example of an athlete overcoming a handicap is Jim Abbott. Pitching for the New York Yankees against the Cleveland Indians on September 4, 1993, Jim Abbott did what every pitcher dreams of. He pitched a 4–0 no-hitter.

Ask: What was even more remarkable about Abbott's feat? (He was born with only a stump of a right forearm. With amazing dexterity he learned to flip his baseball glove from stump to left hand and back again—while juggling the ball into throwing position. People applauded Jim when he became an All-American at the University of Michigan. They cheered when he starred on the 1988 U.S. Olympic team. But when he pitched a no-hitter in the major leagues, they stood up and cheered and cheered.

An editorial on Abbott's no-hitter (*Chicago Tribune,* September 5, 1993) ended:

The odds
against any pitcher doing this are enormous.
The odds against a one-handed pitcher—
of even making the big leagues—are incalculable.
But don't tell Jim Abbott.

Minimap **Activity** Direct attention to the minimap on page 196. Have the students locate Athens and Corinth.

▶ **Notebook** By way of review, have the students retrace key cities in Paul's second missionary trip, give one significant event that took place in each city, and copy this diagram in their notebooks.

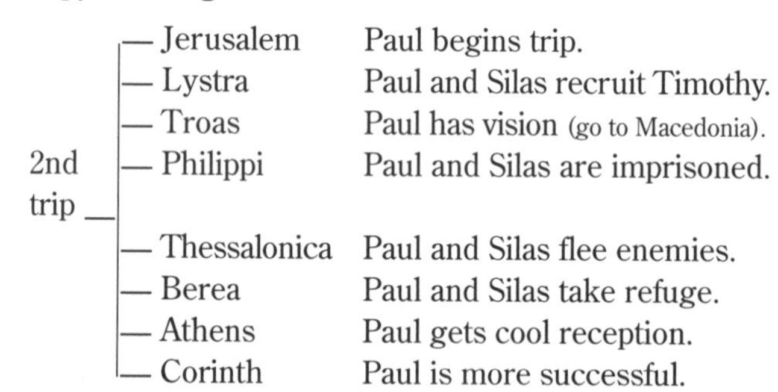

Photo **Clarify** Direct students' attention to the photo on page 196. These fragments, found Delphi in Greece, reproduce (for public reading) a letter of Tiberius Claudius Caesar (name partially visible, upper left). From this Roman document we learn that Gallio was proconsul of Achaia after Emperor Claudius's twenty-sixth acclamation. This allows us to date Paul's arrival in Corinth. From related sources we know that Claudius's acclamation took place in 52 B.C.E. This means Paul arrived in Corinth about 50 B.C.E., which fits the biblical account perfectly.

Third Missionary Trip

LESSON **95**

1. LESSON BACKGROUND

▶ *Catechism of the Catholic Church,* 2700–2719.

2. LESSON QUIZ

Perfect score = 10 points

1. How did the Athenians and the Corinthians differ dramatically. *(Lesson 94 review—2 points)*
2. List and briefly describe the two sides of our personality that psychologists talk about. *(Lesson 94 notebook review—4 points)*
3. Briefly explain (a) Paul's link to Artemis and to Eutychus and (b) what exciting events took place in Ephesus and Troas on Paul's third missionary trip. *(Lesson 95 preview—4 points)*

3. LESSON HOMEWORK

▶ **Return** Lesson 94 review questions (page 197).

▶ **Collect** Lesson 95 review questions (page 199).

▶ **Read** Lesson 96 ("Paul in Custody," pages 200–201).

▶ **Write** Lesson 96 review questions (page 201).

▶ **Appoint** Two gifted students to read Acts 21:27–23:11 and prepare a radio or TV report on the near-riot situation involving Paul in Jerusalem (lesson 96, exercise 5).

4. LESSON PRESENTATION

Point ➊ **Read** Have volunteers read aloud the core content of lesson 95.

▶ **Clarify** Paul's first stop on his third trip was in Galatia, where he revisited the Christian communities of Derbe, Lystra, and Iconium. Apparently, Paul was pleased with what he saw, since Luke says nothing else about the visit.

The same is true of Paul's second stop. It included the neighboring communities of Colossae, Laodicea, and Hierapolis. (Recall how Laodicea was connected by aqueduct to the water springs of Hierapolis. See the photo and photo caption on page 231 of the text.)

Point ➋ **Clarify** The real excitement of Paul's third missionary trip took place in the famous ancient city of Ephesus (modern Turkey). Ephesus was the site of the temple of Artemis and the center of the religious cult of Artemis. The temple was listed among the Seven Wonders of the Ancient World. (Refer the students to the magnificent and well-preserved statue from the temple on page 192.)

Point ➌ **Discuss** The miracles that accompanied Paul's preaching led people to touch Paul's body with various items. They would then use these items to try to heal the sick and expel evil spirits. This introduces us to the fascinating subject of relics.

Collecting relics is not only a religious phenomenon but a human one as well. Shakespeare portrays the Romans dipping handkerchiefs in the blood of Caesar after his assassination.

In the so-called "age of faith," it became customary to append a tiny shred of cloth to a card. Below the cloth was written: "This cloth touched the body of [some holy person]."

The practice became so widespread—and out of control—that the Council of Trent (1545–1563) laid down penalties for abuses linked with relics.

Ask: Why do people collect memorabilia—especially of athletes and rock stars?

Ask: Does anyone in this class have any memorabilia of this kind? If so, what?

Point ➍ **Clarify** Luke and Timothy joined Paul in Troas, "where we [indicating Luke's presence with Paul] spent a week" (Acts 20:6). It was long enough for Luke to record one of the most delightful episodes in Acts.

The Christians of Troas had gathered on Saturday evening for a fellowship meal. Paul got carried away instructing them. A tired young man named Eutychus happened to be sitting on a window ledge. Suddenly, he nodded, fell asleep, and toppled three floors to the ground.

When they picked him up, he was dead.
But Paul went down and threw himself on him
and hugged him.
"Don't worry," he said, "he is still alive!"

Then he went back upstairs, broke bread, and ate.

After talking with them for a long time,
even until sunrise, Paul left.

They took the young man home alive
and were greatly comforted. Acts 20:9–12

▶ **Clarify** Early Christians followed the ancient Jewish practice of using sunset to divide their days. In other words, the Lord's Day began at sunset on Saturday.

▶ **Clarify** Stress that early Christians celebrated the Lord's Supper (Mass) within the framework of a weekly fellowship gathering and common meal together. In the case of the Corinthians, these gatherings sometimes turned into settings unfit for celebrating the Lord's Supper. And so Paul rebukes them strongly for this in 1 Corinthians 11:17. (Recall that Corinthian Christians were, for the most part, of low social standing. Paul refers to this in 1 Corinthians 1:26, saying:

From the human point of view few of you were wise
or powerful or of high social standing.)

5. LESSON INTERACTION

Exercises ❶ & ❷ **Clarify** The reference that introduces exercise 1 is from Martin Kelsey's book *Dreams*. In one part of it he tells of a missionary friend who preached the Christian message on the island of Bali. His friend said that the easiest person to convert was the witch doctor, because he already possessed a "spiritual mentality."

Exercise ❷ **Discuss** **(a)** Have the appointed student read Acts 17:22–34, which relates Paul's presentation to the Athenians.

(b) One reason Paul's usual approach was less successful in Athens was the pride of the Athenians. Another was their lack of a "spiritual mentality." Recall that Epicureans held that life originated from a chance coming together of atoms and that death was the breakup of these atoms.

Exercise ❸ **Read** **(a)** Have the appointed student read Acts 19:11–20, the Sceva scandal.

▶ **Clarify** Roving exorcists were common in Ephesus in Paul's day. Archaeologists have found a number of papyrus scrolls that contain rites of exorcism.

Ask: What is a papyrus? (Refer the students to the photo on page 6 of the text. It shows Egyptians making papyrus scrolls.)

Note that the seven brothers identified themselves as sons of a Jewish High Priest named Sceva. No high priest by that name is known. Possibly, the identification was so outlandish that Luke repeats it for humor's sake.

One ancient Jewish formula for exorcism is reminiscent of the one that prompted the evil spirit to say, "I know Jesus, and I know about Paul; but you—who are you?" (Acts 19:15). Read it to the students:

Invocation to be uttered over the head
[of the possessed one].
Place before him branches of olive,
and standing behind him say:
"Hail, spirit of Abraham, Isaac, and Jacob;
Jesus Christ the holy one. . . .
I adjure thee, O demon, whoever thou art. . . .
Come forth . . . and depart. . . .
I give you over to black chaos. Greek Papyrus 47

▶ **Discuss** **(b, c, d)** Have the appointed students read the Bible passages. Invite volunteers to present their reports.

Exercise ❹ **Discuss** The three prayer forms in the young person's prayer experience line up as follows:

- meditation "I relaxed and began to think."
- contemplation "I marveled at what God. . . ."
- conversation "God and I sort of communed."

▶ **Notebook** Summarize the three forms prayer usually takes for entry in student notebooks.

3 prayer forms
- Meditation — Thinking about God
- Contemplation — Marveling at God
- Conversation — Communing with God

Minimap **Clarify** Direct attention to the minimap on page 198 (blowup on page 171). Have the students locate Ephesus.

Photo **Clarify** Direct students to the photo on page 198. This amphitheater was the site of a recent outdoor concert that attracted a capacity crowd of 24,000 people. The theater's diameter is about two football fields in length.

▶ **Notebook** Develop this diagram on the chalkboard for entry in student notebooks.

Ephesus
- City where tradition says John brought Mary to live after Jesus' ascension
- City in which Council of Ephesus (431 C.E.) met and gave Mary the title of "Mother of God"

CHAPTER NINETEEN: Ongoing Witness (pages 200–201)

Paul in Custody

LESSON **96**

1. LESSON BACKGROUND

▶ *Catechism of the Catholic Church*, 2471–2474.

2. LESSON QUIZ

Perfect score = 10 points

1. How does tradition say Mary got to Ephesus, and what group in 431 C.E. gave Mary what title? *(Lesson 95 review—3 points)*
2. List and briefly describe the three forms that prayer usually takes. *(Lesson 95 notebook review—6 points)*
3. Why was Paul attacked outside the Temple? *(Lesson 96 preview—1 point)*

3. LESSON HOMEWORK

▶ **Return** Lesson 95 review questions (page 199).

▶ **Collect** Lesson 96 review questions (page 201).

▶ **Read** Lesson 97 ("Paul in Rome," pages 202–3).

▶ **Write** Lesson 97 review questions (page 203).

▶ **Appoint** Three students do prepare "The Storm": Acts 27:13–20, 21–32, 33–44 (lesson 97, exercise 2).

4. LESSON PRESENTATION

Point ① **Read** Have volunteers read aloud the core content of lesson 96.

▶ **Clarify** The Roman security force that rescued Paul from the mob was housed in the fortress of Antonia, almost adjacent to the Temple. (See the sketch of it, with its four towers, to the right of the Temple on text page 178.) After rescuing Paul, the Romans took him inside it.

The Roman commander ordered his men . . .
to whip him in order to find out
why the Jews were screaming like this against him.
But when they had tied him up to be whipped,
Paul said to the officer standing there,
"Is it lawful for you to whip a Roman citizen
who hasn't even been tried for any crime?" Acts 22:24–25

Paul was on solid ground in making this statement. The ancient Romans Livy and Cicero state clearly that the *Lex Porcia* protected Roman citizens from being flogged, a common punishment in ancient times—even in modern times (as we saw in lesson 5 of this Resource Manual).

When the Roman commander heard Paul was a Roman citizen, he ordered him untied and kept in custody for the night. The Jewish High Council (Sanhedrin) would review Paul's case the next morning.

▶ **Discuss** The morning meeting before the Sanhedrin got so violent that the Romans had to rescue Paul a second time. The violence was sparked by Paul himself. In a desperate effort to defend himself against this body (which was hostile to Christianity), Paul took a calculated risk. He accused the Sadducee members of the Sanhedrin of opposing him because of his belief in the resurrection of the body. Luke writes:

As soon as he [Paul] said this, the Pharisees
and Sadducees started to quarrel. Acts 23:7

Ask: Why would Paul's remark trigger a quarrel between the two groups? (Pharisees believed in the resurrection; Sadducees did not. Recall the pun: That's why they were "*sad you see.*")

▶ **Notebook** Develop on the chalkboard for entry in student notebooks this schedule of events from Paul's arrival back into Jerusalem to his being sent to Caesarea.

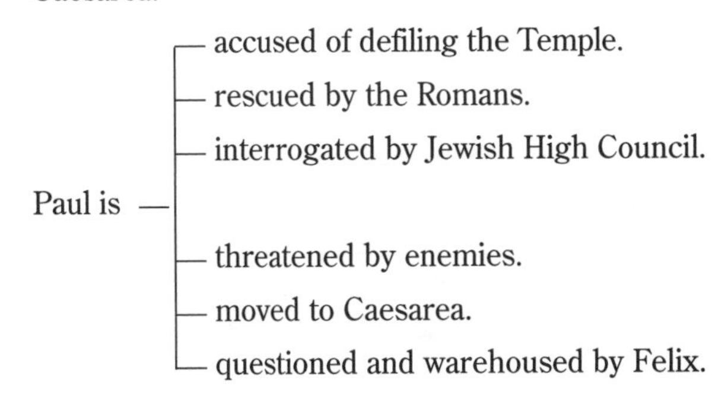

5. LESSON INTERACTION

Exercise ① **Clarify** Felix ruled in Caesarea from 52 C.E. to 57 C.E. Historians describe him as being grossly insensitive to the Jews. Besides taking bribes, he fomented unrest among groups, so that he could execute whomever he wished and confiscate their property for his use. Many historians blame him for the final rebellion of Jews against Rome, leading to the destruction of the Temple in 70 C.E.

People have always wrestled with the problem of evil. Ultimately it is a mystery, as the Book of Job asserts. About his own personal suffering, Paul wrote:

I have learned this secret,
so that anywhere, at any time . . .
I have the strength to face all conditions
by the power that Christ gives me. Philippians 4:12–13

And to the Romans, he wrote:

What we suffer at this present time
cannot be compared at all with the glory
that is going to be revealed to us. Romans 8:18

Exercise ❷ **Discuss** Have the students respond to this question in writing before sharing their response with the class. The purpose of the question is to set up the next exercise.

Exercise ❸ **Discuss** **(a)** The Lewis Cass quote challenges those who would advocate that Paul play Felix's game. Paul preached truth and goodness; playing Felix's game would contradict that preaching.

(b) G. B. Shaw's quote pushes the above point a step further. It is not what we say but what we do that reveals what we believe.

(c) E. C. McKenzie's quote pushes the point to the final step. When young people hear us say one thing and we do another, our action tends to destroy not only our own credibility but also the credibility of the faith we profess.

Exercise ❹ **Clarify** Fyodor Dostoevski (1821–1881) turned out to be a tragic figure. Share the story of his life with the students.

Dostoevski began as a young novelist. His first novel, *Poor Folk,* was a hit with critics and the public. Success went straight to his head. He drank, partied, and criticized the government recklessly. (You didn't do that then.) He was arrested and sentenced to die. At the last minute Emperor Nicholas I commuted his sentence to ten years of hard labor in a Siberian prison camp.

In Siberia, Dostoevski was permitted only one book, the New Testament. Reading it turned his life around.

After his return from Siberia, Dostoevski reeled off a series of literary masterpieces, including the novels *Crime and Punishment* and *The Brothers Karamazov.* Both became Hollywood movies.

Then things fell apart for Dostoevski. His Christian commitment stagnated. He began to drink, gamble, and dissipate his life away. After receiving a "second chance" from God, he dropped the ball. He died penniless and wasted.

Exercise ❺ Have the appointed team make their presentation. Its purpose is twofold: (1) to drive home an important chapter in Paul's story and (2) to bring a certain note of realism to it.

Minimap **Activity** Direct attention to the minimap on page 200. Have the students locate Caesarea. Refer them to the photo of the famous amphitheater that was excavated there (photo on page 186).

▶ **Discuss** Ask: What famous dedication stone did archaeologists find during the excavation? (See photo of the "Pilate stone" on page 163.)

Photo **Notebook** Direct students' attention to the photo and photo caption of the Western Wall of the Temple plaza (page 200). Summarize these key events in the Temple's history for entry in student notebooks.

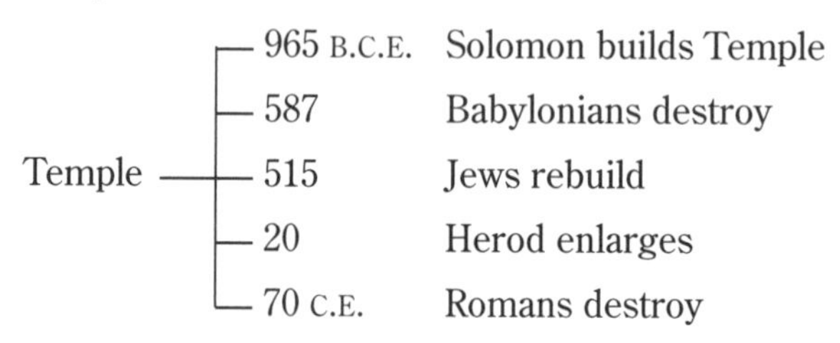

Photo **Clarify** Direct students' attention to the photo and photo caption on page 201. The sign was found in 1936. Traces of red paint can still be seen on the Greek letters.

▶ **Discuss** Refer the students to the Temple sketch on page 178. The "warning signs" were posted on the small barrier shown between the Temple structure and the outer wall that surrounded the Court of the Gentiles.

Ask: What were the names of the five main Temple areas? (Holy of Holies, Court of Priests, Court of Men, Court of Women, Court of Gentiles. See photo of Temple model and floor plan on page 155.)

CHAPTER NINETEEN: Ongoing Witness (pages 202–3)

Paul to Rome

LESSON 97

1. LESSON BACKGROUND

▶ *Catechism of the Catholic Church*, 2465–2470.

2. LESSON QUIZ

Perfect score = 9 points

1. To what city did Jerusalem authorities transport Paul, and who was the Roman governor in that city? *(Lesson 96 review—2 points)*
2. Match the approximate dates in column two with the correct Temple event in column one. *(Lesson 96 notebook review—5 points)*

___ Jews rebuild Temple	a. 587 B.C.E.
___ Babylonians destroy	b. 20 B.C.E.
___ Solomon builds	c. 70 C.E.
___ Romans destroy	d. 965 B.C.E.
___ Herod enlarges	e. 515 B.C.E.

3. Name one of the two people who accompanied Paul to Rome, and tell how he probably got permission to travel with Paul. *(Lesson 97 preview—2 points)*

3. LESSON HOMEWORK

▶ **Return** Lesson 96 review questions (page 201).

▶ **Collect** Lesson 97 review questions (page 203).

▶ **Read** Lesson 98 ("Shipwrecked," pages 204–5).

▶ **Write** Lesson 98 review questions (page 205).

4. LESSON PRESENTATION

Point ① **Read** Have volunteers read aloud the core content of lesson 97.

▶ **Clarify** Dietrich Bonhoeffer was executed shortly before Easter in 1945. Read to the students a prison doctor's description of how Bonhoeffer met his death:

I saw Pastor Bonhoeffer . . . kneeling on the floor,
praying fervently. . . . I was most deeply moved
by the way this lovable man prayed,
so devout and so certain that God heard his prayer.
At the place of execution, he . . . climbed the steps
to the gallows, brave and composed.
His death ensued after a few seconds.
In the almost fifty years . . . as a doctor,
I have hardly ever seen a man
die so entirely submissive to the will of God.

Eberhard Bethge, *Dietrich Bonhoeffer*

▶ **Discuss** Before Christmas 1943, Bonhoeffer penned these words in his prison journal:

Life in a prison reminds me a great deal of Advent.
One waits and hopes and putters around.
But in the end what we do is of little consequence.
The door is shut,
and it can only be opened from the outside.

Ask: How is Bonhoeffer's prison entry a good description of the human race before the coming of Jesus on the first Christmas? (The human race was imprisoned by sin. The door to its salvation was shut and could not be opened, except from the outside. That is what Jesus did; he opened the door.)

▶ **Notebook** Develop on the chalkboard the following schedule of events that occurred when Festus replaced Felix as Roman governor of Palestine.

Paul —
- Ordered to Jerusalem for trial
- Granted trial in Rome
- Accompanied by Luke
- Endangered by storm

5. LESSON INTERACTION

Exercise ① **Clarify** On January 17, 1912, five explorers leaped and shouted for joy as they reached the South Pole. It was a remarkable human achievement. But their joy was short-lived.

On their eight-hundred-mile trek back to civilization, two men met death. The three remaining men collapsed seventeen miles short of safety. When their bodies were found, the diaries of the explorers were still intact and readable. The excerpt from the journal of Edward Wilson (quoted in this exercise) sounds like something Paul might have written as he set out from Caesarea for Rome.

▶ **Discuss** Wilson's words may sound fatalistic to some people. But to believers who understand true surrender to God, they are not the words of a "fatalistic" person, but of a "faith-filled" person.

Clarify Compare Wilson's words to the following two passages in Paul's letters:

I have thrown everything away; I consider it all
as mere garbage, so that I may gain Christ
and be completely united with him. . . . All I want
is to know Christ and . . . share in his sufferings
and become like him in his death, in the hope
that I myself will be raised from death to life.
Philippians 3:8–11

The hour has come for me to be sacrificed
[apparent reference to Paul's death sentence];
the time is here for me to leave this life.
I have done my best in the race,
I have run the full distance, and I have kept the faith.
And now there is waiting for me
the victory prize of being put right with God,
which the Lord, the righteous Judge,
will give me on that Day—and not only to me,
but to all those who wait with love for him to appear.
2 Timothy 4:6–8

Photo

Clarify Direct students' attention to the photo and caption of the discus thrower on page 211. Paul uses several athletic images in his letters, suggesting his own interest and that of his readers in athletics.

Exercise ②

Clarify Have the three appointed readers come to the front of the room together, so that there will be no disturbance between readings.

If one of your students is fairly skilled in sketching, you might have that student do a quick sketch of the route Paul would follow to Rome. Then the readers can indicate the places along the route as they occur in the readings.

This account of Paul's sea voyages is regarded as an excellent documentary of ancient sea voyages.

Exercise ③

Discuss It is surprising to see how frequently the Bible speaks of fear. An actual account turns up roughly four hundred references. Consider three biblical references to fear:

"Do not be afraid or discouraged,
for I, the LORD your God,
am with you wherever you go." Joshua 1:9

The LORD says . . .
"I am the LORD who created you;
from the time you were born,
I have helped you.
Do not be afraid." Isaiah 44:1–2

[Jesus said,]
"Aren't five sparrows sold for two pennies?
Yet not one sparrow is forgotten by God.
Even the hairs of your head have all been counted.
So do not be afraid; you are worth
much more than many sparrows!" Luke 12:6–7

Ask: Why do you think the Bible deals so frequently with the question of fear?

Ask: What is Jesus' point when it comes to fear?

Discuss **(a)** Have a student copy the six fears on the chalkboard while the other students copy them on a sheet of paper.

After the students have graded their fears (1–6), have a "class secretary" list the results (show of hands) on the chalkboard.

(b) Ask for volunteers to share the reason for their "number one" fear.

(c) Have a "class secretary" list the fears that students expressed, other than the six listed. Screen the written explanations and have students discuss the results.

(d) Ask for volunteers to say what gives them hope in the midst of their fears, for example, God's love for us. (Recall the sparrow example above.)

Exercise ④

Discuss **(a)** Have a student copy the six responses on the chalkboard while the other students copy them on a sheet of paper (remaining anonymous).

After the students have graded their parents, collect the papers and shuffle them (to assure anonymity).

Then pass the papers out again, at random, and have a "class secretary" list the results (show of hands) on the chalkboard.

(b) Next, record eight or ten of the "suggestions for parents" on the chalkboard for discussion.

Photo

Clarify Direct students' attention to the caption and the photo of the aqueduct on the coast of Caesarea (page 202). The fragile water pipe carried along the top of the aqueduct was the jugular vein of ancient cities in Asia Minor.

Once the fragile pipe was smashed and the water supply cut off, it was just a matter of time before the city perished.

LESSON 98

Shipwrecked

1. LESSON BACKGROUND

▶ *Catechism of the Catholic Church,* 2465–2470.

2. LESSON QUIZ

Perfect score = 7 points

1. What architectural structure still visible in Caesarea was there in Paul's time? *(Lesson 97 review—1 point)*
2. Briefly answer: (a) Where was Paul first ordered to stand trial? (b) To what city was Paul's trial changed? (c) Who accompanied Paul on his journey to this city? (d) What frightening event happened on the way to the city? *(Lesson 97 notebook review—4 points)*
3. Describe Paul's prison situation in Rome and how he spent his time awaiting his trial. *(Lesson 98 preview—2 points)*

3. LESSON HOMEWORK

▶ **Return** Lesson 97 review questions (page 203).

▶ **Collect** Lesson 98 review questions (page 205).

▶ **Read** Lesson 99 ("Paul in Rome," pages 206–7).

▶ **Write** Lesson 99 review questions (page 207).

4. LESSON PRESENTATION

Point 1 **Read** Have volunteers read aloud the core content of lesson 98.

▶ **Discuss** Half-naked sailors swimming vigorously, armed soldiers dog-paddling behind planks, prisoners clinging to wreckage—this was the amazing sight that greeted the island dwellers of Malta as they ran excitedly to the beach.

The shipwrecked crew was fortunate to have landed on friendly Malta. There were other shores where they would have been attacked—and even killed. Luke continues his story, saying:

It had started to rain and was cold,
so they built a fire and made us all welcome.
Paul gathered up a bundle of sticks
and was putting them on the fire
when a snake came out on account of the heat
and fastened itself to his hand.
The natives saw the snake hanging
on Paul's hand. Acts 28:2–4

Ask: How do you think the natives reacted to this sight and why?

Luke describes the reaction of the natives to the snake hanging on Paul's hand, saying to one another:

"This man must be a murderer,
but Fate will not let him live,
even though he escaped from the sea."

But Paul shook the snake off into the fire
without being harmed at all.
They were waiting for him to swell up
or suddenly fall down dead.
But after waiting for a long time
and not seeing anything unusual
happening to him, they . . . said . . . Acts 28:4–6

Ask: What do you think the natives said now?

They changed their minds and said,
"He is a god!"

Not far from that place were some fields
that belonged to Publius,
the chief of the island.
He welcomed us kindly
and for three days we were his guests.

Publius' father was in bed,
sick with fever and dysentery.
Paul went into his room, prayed,
placed his hands on him, and healed him.
When this happened,
all the other sick people on the island came
and were healed.
They gave us many gifts,
and when we sailed, they put on board
what we needed for the voyage.

After three months we sailed away
on a ship . . . called "The Twin Gods." Acts 28:6–11

Point 2 **Clarify** *The Twin Gods* had "spent the winter" in Malta (Acts 28:11). It was named in honor of the pagan gods Castor and Pollux, protectors of sailors.

Ancient ships were remarkable. Lengths of 100–150 feet were ordinary. They had a single mast, which made steering awkward at best.

They did not have a hinged rudder as ships today have. Rather, they were steered with two great paddles, one in front and one in back.

Most ancient ships carried dinghies. (Luke describes how some sailors tried to escape in the dinghy when their ship was in danger of going down [Acts 27:30–32].) Normally the dinghy was towed in good weather and stored on deck in bad weather. It was not for emergency use, but for use in getting to and from the ship in the harbor.

Point ❸ **Clarify** *The Twin Gods* sailed from Malta to Syracuse, Rhegium, and Puteoli, an ancient port of entry for Rome. (See minimap on page 204.)

As the ship glided into Puteoli Bay around 61 C.E., Paul may have pointed an inquiring finger at Mount Vesuvius in the distance. Paul had no idea that he would feel the shock waves from an earthquake while in Rome, which would prove to be the harbinger of its explosion in 79 C.E.

Refer students to the remarkable photo of victims of Vesuvius on page 209 of the text.

Notebook Develop on the chalkboard the following schedule of events that marked Paul's voyage to Rome.

Paul
- Left Caesarea by ship
- Survived shipwreck of Malta
- Worked miracles on Malta
- Reached Rome via Puteoli
- Was placed under house arrest

5. LESSON INTERACTION

Exercise ❶ **Discuss** **(a, b)** In his book *Days Demanding Courage,* H. B. Walker writes, "When a Harvard University president was asked to name the fundamental quality of leadership, he replied, 'The capacity to inflict pain.'"

Ask: What do you think the Harvard president meant? (Walker went on to explain, "That is a blunt way of saying that leadership requires courage to speak the unvarnished truth, however unpopular it may be.")

In this same vein, Abraham Lincoln began his presidency, saying:

"I desire
so to conduct the affairs of this administration
that if at the end,
when I come to lay down the reins of power,
I have lost every other friend on earth,
I shall at least have one friend left,
and that friend shall be down inside me."

It was this kind of courage that made Paul a great leader. He spoke the truth, even when it cost him dearly. That is what made some people hate him and other people admire him.

Exercise ❷ **Discuss** This true story, told by one of the author's students who was present on the canoe trip, is a modern, real-life example of the episode described in the novel *The Apostle.* Everybody was discouraged. But one young person saw what the others saw, only in a totally different way.

In his book *God Can Make It Happen,* Russ Johnston shows what a difference a person's viewpoint can make.

When Goliath came against the Israelites,
the soldiers all thought,
"He's so big we can never kill him."
David looked at the same giant and thought,
"He's so big I can't miss him."

Stress that the same reality (from a different viewpoint) leads to a radically different perspective.

Ask: Do stairs go up, or do they go down?

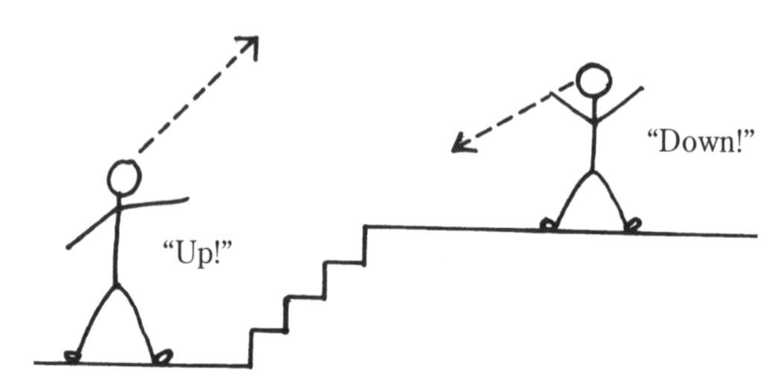

Ask: Does mortar hold bricks together or apart?

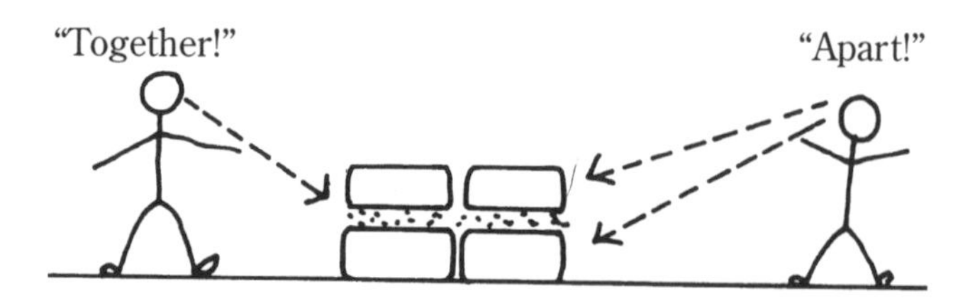

Ask: What are some other examples? (For example, is glass half full or half empty?)

Chapter Nineteen: Ongoing Witness (pages 206–7)

Paul in Rome

LESSON **99**

1. LESSON BACKGROUND

▶ *Catechism of the Catholic Church*, 1961–1964.

2. LESSON QUIZ

Perfect score = 6 points

1. On what island did the wreck of Paul's ship occur? *(Lesson 98 review—1 point)*
2. How did Paul spend much of his time on Malta, and what was his situation as he awaited trial in Rome? *(Lesson 98 notebook review—2 points)*
3. When, where, and how does tradition say that Paul's life ended? *(Lesson 99 preview—3 points)*

3. LESSON HOMEWORK

▶ **Return** Lesson 98 review questions (page 205).

▶ **Collect** Lesson 99 review questions (page 207).

▶ **Read** Lesson 100 ("1–2 Thessalonians," pages 208–9).

▶ **Write** Lesson 100 review questions (page 209).

▶ **Appoint** Student to prepare 1 Thessalonians 4:13–18 (lesson 100, exercise 4).

4. LESSON PRESENTATION

Point ❶ **Read** Have volunteers read aloud the core content of lesson 99.

▶ **Clarify** Rome was magnificent in Paul's day. Yet there was also much about it that was shocking.

First of all, there was a total absence of sanitation. Dung heaps and cesspools lay at intervals, and human wastes were carried to them and dumped. Unfortunately, however, many people did not bother to do this. They simply threw their refuse out into the street.

Second, there was "noise pollution." The ancient writer Seneca said the noise was unbearable at times. By day, priests of Isis and Cybelle paraded through the streets with their followers, singing exotic chants to the loud crash of cymbals. By night, heavy wagons with metal wheels clanked along the narrow cobblestone streets, waking everyone within earshot.

It was to this city of paradoxes that Paul brought the message of Jesus.

▶ **Notebook** Develop the following concluding summary of Paul's life and ministry for entry in student notebooks. (The dates are approximate and probable.)

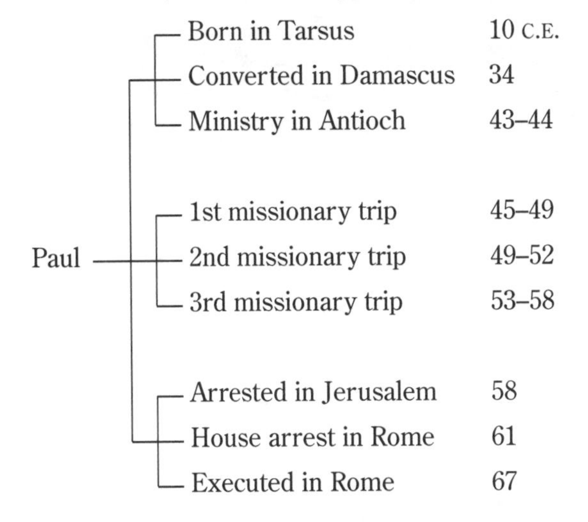

5. LESSON INTERACTION

Exercise ❶ **Clarify** Muggeridge and a British television crew went to Calcutta to film Mother Teresa and her nuns at work in the Home for the Dying. When the camera crew saw the low level of lighting available, they said it would be impossible to film. They were persuaded to try anyway. To their enormous surprise, the footage was spectacular. It was bathed in a mysterious warm light.

Muggeridge, who was not Catholic at the time (though he become so later), is "absolutely convinced" the light came from the loving people in the home, saying:

This love is luminous, like the haloes artists have seen and made visible round the heads of the saints.
I find it not at all surprising that the luminosity should register on a photographic film. . . .
I am personally persuaded that Ken [cameraman] recorded the first authentic photographic miracle.

Discuss **(a)** The quality that enables Mother Teresa to impact audiences so deeply is her personal holiness, which allows God to use her as a channel of grace.

(b) The message to me, personally, is that my power for good will be in direct proportion to my own personal holiness.

Exercise ❷ **Discuss** **(a)** Paul's point reinforces the point made in exercise 1: The power to impact people comes not from the eloquence of the speaker but from the openness of the speaker to the Holy Spirit.

(b) Have the students be as concrete as possible in answering this question.

Exercise ❸ **Discuss** **(a)** Cleansing sin from our lives is the first step. Opening ourselves to the Holy Spirit—through such things as daily prayer and reaching out to others, especially those in need—is the second.

Miniposter **Activity** Direct students' attention to the miniposter on page 206. Before doing so, instruct them not to call out their answer. Give the others a chance to exercise their ingenuity. When they have the solution, instruct them to write it in their notebook. The answer is:

$99^{99}/_{99}$

Clarify Stress the point of the above exercise. Paul tried to help the Jewish leaders of Rome see the writings of Moses and the prophets in a new light. Unfortunately, Paul could not demonstrate his point as clearly as the solution to the miniposter puzzle can be demonstrated.

Photo **Discuss** Direct students' attention to El Greco's painting of Paul on page 206. El Greco was born in Crete. (See location on minimap, page 204.)

Ask: What two paintings by El Greco do you recall seeing previously in the textbook? (*Agony in the Garden of Gethsemane*, page 160, and rendering of Saint Martin and the beggar, page 179)

Discuss Have the students check these two previous paintings and see if they can see a common trait that El Greco follows in painting the human figure. (He elongates the figures. This applies to Paul's face on page 206, but it is not as evident as the elongation in the previous paintings.)

Ask: Why elongate the figures? (It gives them a nobler appearance and makes them look more heroic.)

Ask: Isn't this being a bit dishonest—elongating figures to make them appear more heroic? (Most artists do not see themselves as "photographers"; they see themselves as poets. In other words, they are interested in symbolic representation, not literal representation.)

Photo **Clarify** Direct attention to the photo on page 207. Share with the students the terrible fate of Jerusalem at the hands of Titus and his Roman army. Titus stationed his army on the Mount of Olives, where all in the city could see how formidable it was.

Titus's next step was to seal off the city, preventing anyone from entering or leaving it. In *Jewish Wars,* the ancient historian Josephus describes the terrible impact the blockade had on its Jewish defenders. Read it to your students.

The alleys were piled high with the bodies of the aged.
Children and young people, swollen from hunger,
wandered about like ghosts until they dropped.
Those who survived were so far spent
that they couldn't bury anyone, and if they tried,
they fell dead upon the corpses themselves.

The misery was indescribable.
And as soon as
even the shadow of something edible
appeared anywhere, a fight began over it,
and the best of friends fought each other.

Some people in Jerusalem tried to steal out of the city under cover of darkness. Their fate is described by Henri Daniel-Rops in *Daily Life in the Time of Jesus:*

Those who tried to escape the city
went straight into the arms of the Romans . . .
who sent them back with their hands cut off
if they were women,
or crucified them in full view of the city
if they were men. . . .

The agony was endured for a hundred days. . . .
Titus hesitated to use fire. . . .
But in the end,
he was forced to resort to it. . . .
Titus and his staff tried to limit the disaster. . . .
But the soldiers, exasperated by the resistance,
paid no heed.

Jerusalem was transformed into a sea of fire. All that remained of it was a vast graveyard of charred bodies and buildings.

CHAPTER TWENTY: Paul's Letters (pages 208–9)

1-2 Thessalonians

LESSON 100

1. LESSON BACKGROUND

▶ *Catechism of the Catholic Church*, 673–677.

2. LESSON QUIZ

Perfect score = 15 points

1. When, where, and how does tradition say Paul's life ended? *(Lesson 99 review—3 points)*
2. What event in Paul's life took place (a) in 34 C.E. in what place, and (b) in 67 C.E. in what place? *(Lesson 99 notebook review—4 points)*
3. List the four groups into which Paul's letters are usually divided and one letter that is found in each group. *(Lesson 100 preview—8 points)*

3. LESSON HOMEWORK

▶ **Return** Lesson 99 review questions (page 207).

▶ **Collect** Lesson 100 review questions (page 209).

▶ **Read** Lesson 101 ("1–2 Corinthians," pages 210–11).

▶ **Write** Lesson 101 review questions (page 211).

▶ **Appoint** Student to prepare 1 Corinthians 1:18–31 (lesson 101, exercise 2).

4. LESSON PRESENTATION

Point 1 **Read** Have volunteers read aloud the core content of lesson 100.

▶ **Notebook** Develop the following diagram showing groups and approximate dates of Paul's letters for entry in student notebooks.

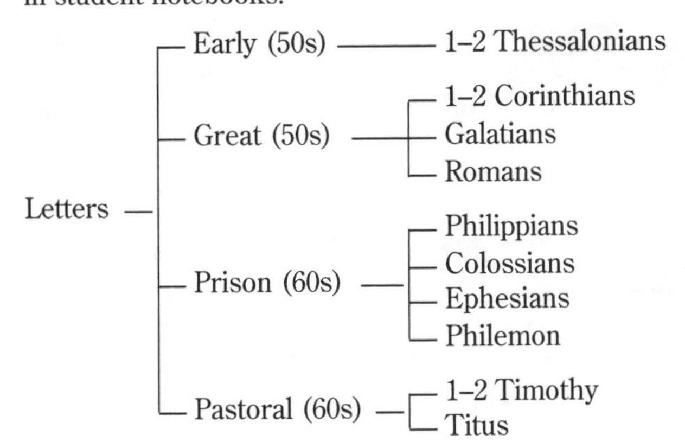

Point 2 **Discuss** There were two ways to write letters in Paul's day: (1) write them yourself or (2) dictate them to a scribe. 2 Thessalonians 3:17 reads:

With my own hand I write this: Greetings from Paul.
This is the way I sign every letter; this is how I write.

Ask: What conclusion do we draw concerning the way Paul wrote this letter? Explain. (The words "my own hand" imply that the rest of the letter was not in Paul's own hand.)

Romans 16:22 makes it even clearer that Paul used a scribe for that letter. It begins: "From Paul" and ends with the scribe identifying himself: "I, Tertius, the writer of this letter, send you Christian greetings."

Point 3 **Clarify** The two questions that Paul takes up in his two letters to the Thessalonians are:

1. What about those who die before Jesus' second coming? (They have nothing to worry about. The Father will take care of them.)
2. When will Jesus' second coming take place? (Nobody knows. This much is certain: It will be preceded by a major confrontation between the forces of good and evil.)

Point 4 **Notebook** Develop the following diagram interactively with the students. It illustrates the general format that Paul used in his letters.

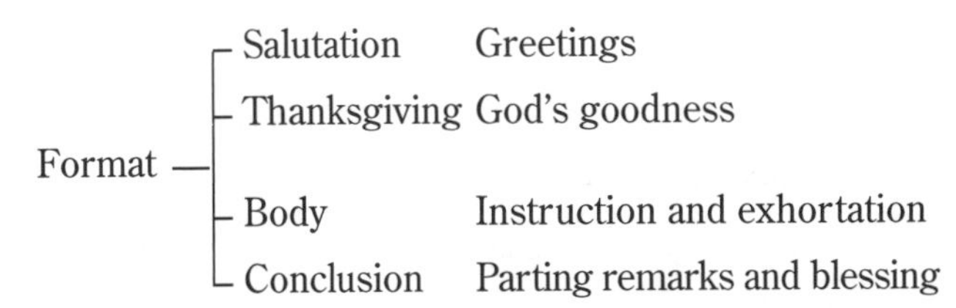

5. LESSON INTERACTION

Exercise 1 **Clarify** **(a)** Stress the difference between "proving" (reason) and "being sure" (faith). For example, I cannot "prove" that my best friend will stay loyal in a crisis, but I can "be sure" (have faith) that this will be the case. The love and the trust that bond us make me "sure" (have faith).

(b) The philosopher says, "You can't love anything you don't know." The theologian says, "You can't know anything you don't love."

Ask: What is the point that each is making?

The theologian's point is especially important: Love is productive of insight. Albert Schweitzer stresses this point in *Reverence for Life,* saying:

Do you really want to believe in Jesus?
Then you must do something for him.
In this age of doubt, there is no other way to him.
And if for Jesus' sake . . . [you do for your neighbor]
those smallest acts of kindness which he promised
to bless as though they were done to him . . .
then he will come to you as one who is alive.

Exercise ❷ **Clarify** **(a, b)** The poet's point is that she may die "in darkness" (about God and afterlife), but the "stars" (God's love and mercy) remove all fear of dying in the dark.

Exercise ❸ **Clarify** Archaeologists are still "digging" at Pompeii. What they continue to find is amazing: carbonized loaves of bread, fruit still retaining its flavor, and olives still swimming in their oil.

► **Clarify** **(a)** The Second Coming will come without warning, as Vesuvius erupted without warning.

► **Discuss** **(b)** Help the students get in touch with their feelings about Jesus' coming by guiding them through this meditation. Begin, saying:

Take a comfortable position.
Lie on the floor, if you wish. [Give them time to settle.]
Now close your eyes and follow my instructions:

Relax your jaw [pause three seconds],
your shoulders [pause three seconds],
your stomach [pause three seconds].
Now monitor your breathing. Don't change it;
just monitor it. [Pause ten seconds.]

For the next thirty seconds, count the number of times
that you inhale. [Pause thirty seconds.]

Now imagine all tension and worry
flowing out of your body.
Feel it flow out the tips of your fingers and toes,
like water through an open faucet. [Pause ten seconds.]

Now imagine the following:

You are vacationing alone in a mountain cabin.
You have no telephone, but you do have a TV set.
It is about midnight and you are watching a movie.
Suddenly it is interrupted by a special news bulletin.
[Pause ten seconds.]

Astronomers have spotted a mysterious object
of immense magnitude streaking toward earth
at an incredible, accelerating speed.
They estimate that it will collide with earth
in less than an hour.
They predict the collision will cause an explosion
that will disintegrate earth.
Finally, they say that
as the object approaches earth's atmosphere,
it will disrupt all TV communication,
leaving all screens blank and all sets silent.
[Pause ten seconds.]

After the announcement, a TV camera cuts away
to the mysterious object, streaking toward earth,
getting brighter and brighter.
[Pause ten seconds.]

As you watch, these words come from the set:
"The president of the United States
would like to make a brief statement.
Then in an emotional voice, you hear the president say,
"My fellow Americans, I urge you . . ."
But before he can say another word,
the TV screen goes blank and the set goes silent.
The object has entered earth's atmosphere.
[Pause ten seconds.]

Now for the next three minutes,
remain in your mountain cabin—
alone with your thoughts, awaiting the end.
[Pause three minutes.]

Now come back slowly.
When you are ready, open your eyes.

Adapted from *Prayer Paths* by Mark Link, S.J.
(Allen, Texas: Tabor Publishing, 1990), pp. 76-77.

Ask: Could you get into the meditation? What struck you most during it?

Exercise ❹ **Activity** Have the appointed student read the assigned passage. Give the students time to record their responses before sharing them.

Photo **Clarify** Direct attention to the photo and photo caption on page 208. The slab testifies to Luke's care and accuracy in documenting his narrative in Acts.

Miniposter **Discuss** Direct students' attention to the miniposter on page 208. Ask: How does it relate to the priest's response to the old woman in exercise 1? (The key to discovering God and soul is love of neighbor.)

1-2 Corinthians

LESSON 101

1. LESSON BACKGROUND

▶ *Catechism of the Catholic Church,* 787–796.

2. LESSON QUIZ

Perfect score = 10 points

1. List the name of one letter that Paul wrote while in prison. *(Lesson 100 review—1 point)*
2. List the four main groups into which Paul's letters fall and the approximate date of each group. *(Lesson 100 notebook review—8 points)*
3. What link is there between the Corinth canal and Jesus' prophecy about Jerusalem? *(Lesson 101 preview—1 point)*

3. LESSON HOMEWORK

▶ **Return** Lesson 100 review questions (page 209).

▶ **Collect** Lesson 101 review questions (page 211).

▶ **Read** Lesson 102 ("Galatians & Romans," pages 212–13).

▶ **Write** Lesson 102 review questions (page 213).

4. LESSON PRESENTATION

Point ① **Read** Have volunteers read aloud the core content of lesson 101.

▶ **Notebook** Develop on the chalkboard the following diagram for entry in student notebooks. It lists three of the points Paul discusses in his letters to the Corinthians.

Three points
- Their moral lapses
- Their inner divisions
- His own weakness

Point ② **Discuss** Discussing their "moral lapses," Paul tells the Corinthians that God purposely chose them because they were weak. God did this to put to shame what the world thinks is "powerful" (1 Corinthians 1:27).

Ask students: Why would God act in this manner?

(God is not looking for human skill. God is looking for love and for openness to the divine will. God is looking for "conduits" or "instruments" by which divine love and divine power can flow into our world. Recall the Prayer of Saint Francis: "Make me an instrument of your peace.")

▶ **Clarify** God's choice of those who appeared "outwardly" to be unqualified is a recurring theme in Scripture. God sometimes follows that same pattern today. Recall Lincoln's observation about being chosen president:

God selects his own instruments,
and sometimes they are queer ones;
for instance, he chose me
to steer the ship through a great crisis.

▶ **Notebook** Develop on the chalkboard the following diagram for entry in student notebooks. It lists three examples of "outwardly" unqualified people chosen to do big jobs.

Unqualified
- Moses "poor speaker" Exodus 4:10
- Jeremiah "too young" Jeremiah 1:6
- Gideon "least important" Judges 6:15

▶ **Clarify** Discussing the Corinthians' moral lapses, Paul makes this statement: "You must remove the old yeast of sin" (1 Corinthians 5:7). This imagery is interesting.

In preparation for celebrating the Passover, ancient Jews followed an unusual ritual. They removed all yeast from their homes. Jewish housewives used yeast to leaven the bread that they made each day. They removed the yeast to comply with Exodus 12:19, which says that "for seven days no yeast must be found in your houses."

The unleavened bread that was eaten during these seven days recalled the Israelites' exodus from Egypt. They left so quickly that they did not even have time to let their bread leaven (rise). Many Jews still follow the practice of eating only unleavened bread (matzos) in celebrating the Passover.

And so Paul tells the Jewish Corinthian converts to Christianity to remove sin from their lives—just as their ancestors removed all yeast from their homes in preparation for celebrating the Passover.

Point ❸ **Clarify** This brings us to Paul's discussion of the "divisions" within the Corinthian community. Paul says they contradict the "inner reality" of things. Christians form one body in Christ. The parts of Christ's body are different and are to be used for the benefit of the whole body. He goes on to say:

And so there is no division in the body,
but all its different parts
have the same concern for one another.
If one part of the body suffers,
all the other parts suffer with it;
if one part is praised,
all the other parts share its happiness. 1 Corinthians 12:25–26

Discuss An example will illustrate how individual members of Christ's body have different gifts to be used for the benefit of the entire body—not just themselves.

An elderly woman, taking her daily stroll for her arthritis, was walking down the street on which a senior citizens' complex was located. Suddenly she spotted a five-dollar bill in the gutter of the street. But she couldn't bend down to pick it up because of her severe arthritic condition.

Just then, she spotted a blind man with a white cane approaching. She recognized him as a resident of the home and told him about her discovery. Then she put the tip of his cane on the bill. He followed down the cane with his hand and retrieved the five-dollar bill. The two of them then headed for a nearby ice-cream parlor.

Ask: How does this story of the senior citizens illustrate the point of the miniposter on page 210?

(If the woman had not spotted the five-dollar bill, or if the blind man had not helped her, both would have suffered because of it. It is the same with the body of Christ. When individual members fail to use the talents God gave them, the whole body suffers.)

Point ❹ **Discuss** This brings us to Paul's third point: his own personal weakness. Paul does not tell us what the weakness was. He simply tells us that God refused to remove it, saying, "My grace is all you need, for my power is greatest when you are weak" (2 Corinthians 12:9).

Ask: Why is it appropriate for Paul to conclude his letter with this reference to his own weakness—and to the way God helped him use it to grow spiritually?

(Having rebuked the Corinthians for their weaknesses, Paul lets them know that he too has weaknesses, and that God's grace is sufficient to help the Corinthians not only overcome their weaknesses but also use them to grow spiritually.)

Ask: How do you explain God's words to Paul: "My grace is all you need, for my power is greatest when you are weak"?

(An example from Alcoholics Anonymous will illustrate. An alcoholic is, indeed, strongest when weakest. For when the alcoholic admits "powerlessness" over alcohol and turns to God for help, the alcoholic discovers infinite strength.)

5. LESSON INTERACTION

Exercise ❶ **Discuss** **(a)** Anderson's remark is another way of saying "My power is greatest when you are weak."

(b) Have the students record their responses before sharing.

Exercise ❷ **Discuss** Have the appointed student read the assigned Scripture passage. Again, have the students record their responses in private right in class before sharing them.

Exercise ❸ **Discuss** **(a, b)** The nature of these two questions is such that they could be discussed directly (without having the students write them out first), although the quality of discussions is usually better if students write out their responses first.

Exercise ❹ **Discuss** **(a)** The story that introduces this exercise is from Robert Herhold's book *Moments of Grace* (Philadelphia: Fortress Press, 1981, p. 16).

An example that helps us understand Paul's words is, again, from Alcoholics Anonymous. A recovering alcoholic is directed to minister to other alcoholics, drawing upon the same grace he or she received from God.

(b) Give the students time to reflect on this question before recording and sharing it with the class.

Photo **Clarify** Direct students' attention to the photo on page 211. Paul frequently used athletic images to illustrate spiritual points. Commenting on this, Jerry Kramer, former all-pro Green Bay Packer, wrote in his best-seller *Instant Replay:*

Before the game [with Los Angeles], Coach Lombardi took his text from one of St. Paul's Epistles. I don't know which one. Maybe Vince was just using St. Paul's name to back up his own theories. . . . Vince has a knack for making all the saints sound like they would have been great football coaches.

Galatians & Romans

LESSON 102

1. LESSON BACKGROUND

▶ *Catechism of the Catholic Church*, 790–795.

2. LESSON QUIZ

Perfect score = 5 points

1. What weakness in his own life did Paul share with the Corinthians? *(Lesson 101 review—1 point)*
2. List three biblical examples to illustrate that God sometime chose "outwardly" unqualified people to do big jobs. *(Lesson 101 notebook review—3 points)*
3. What problem triggered Paul's letter to the Galatians? *(Lesson 102 preview—1 point)*

3. LESSON HOMEWORK

▶ **Return** Lesson 101 review questions (page 211).

▶ **Collect** Lesson 102 review questions (page 213).

▶ **Read** Lesson 103 ("Philippians & Colossians," pages 214–15).

▶ **Write** Lesson 103 review questions (page 215).

4. LESSON PRESENTATION

Point ① **Read** Have volunteers read aloud the core content of lesson 102.

▶ **Discuss** Galatia was the name of a Roman province that included such cities as Lystra and Iconium (see map on page 171).

Ask: With whom did Paul visit these cities on his first missionary trip? Who did the Lystrans think the two missionaries were in disguise? Why? (Barnabas accompanied Paul. When Paul healed a crippled man, the citizens thought the two missionaries might be Greek gods in disguise. See lesson 92.)

▶ **Discuss** Paul returned to these cities again on his second missionary trip.

Ask: Who joined Paul in Lystra on this second trip and, later on, became the recipient of two letters from Paul? (Timothy)

▶ **Clarify** Like some of Paul's other letters, his Letter to the Galatians was to be circulated among all the churches in that area. This practice is explicitly mentioned in Colossians 4:16. Paul writes: "After you read this letter, make sure that it is read also in the church at Laodicea. At the same time, you are to read the letter that the believers in Laodicea will send you."

Paul's Letter to the Galatians is packed with emotion. He even forgets the conventional "thanksgiving," starting right out: "I am surprised at you!" (1:6).

Why was Paul so upset? Hostile Jews were leading his Galatian converts astray by saying, among other things, that Jewish converts to Christianity had to be circumcised.

Ask: How was this question eventually resolved by the early Church? (Recall that the question led to the Jerusalem Council, the forerunner of later church councils. The Jerusalem Council marked the "official" rejection of the rigid view that Gentile converts were obliged to follow the Mosaic law in all its details.)

Point ② **Clarify** The question about circumcision raised a bigger question about the Mosaic law, which Paul phrases this way: "What, then, was the purpose of the Law?" (Galatians 3:19). His answer is twofold.

First, the Law shows how sinful we are and how badly we need redemption.

Second, it serves as a kind of spiritual "scaffolding." It prepares us for Christ. Once Christ comes, the Law has served its purpose. Paul puts it this way:

And so the Law was in charge of us until Christ came,
in order that we might then be put right with God
through faith.
Now that the time for faith is here,
the Law is no longer in charge of us. Galatians 3:24–25

▶ **Notebook** Develop the following diagram on the chalkboard for entry in student notebooks. It lists the twofold reason that Paul gives for the Law.

The Law —
- Convicts us of sin — Galatians 3:19
- Prepares us for Christ — Galatians 3:24

Point ③ **Clarify** The Letter to the Galatians contains one of Paul's most quoted passages. It reads:

I have been put to death with Christ on his cross,
so that it is no longer I who live,
but it is Christ who lives in me.
This life that I live now, I live by faith in the Son of God,
who loved me and gave his life for me. Galatians 2:19–20

▶ **Discuss** A beautiful modern example to illustrate what Paul is talking about is the famous Broadway musical *Man of La Mancha.* It was inspired by the life and work of Cervantes. Born and raised in cruel poverty, he became a soldier and was captured in the Battle of Lepanto.

Cervantes was sentenced to years of slavery in Africa. Broken in body, if not spirit, be died in 1616, after completing his major work, *Don Quixote.*

Near the end of the musical, Quixote is dying. At his side is Aldonza, a worthless woman whom he had idealized and called Dulcinea. Quixote loved her with a pure love, unlike anything she had previously experienced.

When Quixote breathes his last, Aldonza begins to sing "The Impossible Dream." As the last echo of the song dies away, someone shouts to her, "Aldonza." She responds, "My name is Dulcinea." With Quixote's death, Aldonza died, too, and Dulcinea began to live in her.

Ask: In what sense does this scene from *Man of La Mancha* illustrate Paul's famous passage in Galatians?

(Jesus showed us what we were capable of becoming, and when he died, he gave us both the inspiration and the power to become that image. The famous eighteenth-century German poet and philosopher Johann Wolfgang Goethe expressed the idea this way: "Treat people the way they ought to be, and you help them become what they are capable of being.")

Point ❹ **Discuss** In Corinth in 57 C.E., Paul often walked down to the harbor to look at ships. When he saw one from Rome, his thoughts winged westward not only to Rome but even to Spain (Romans 15:28). But visiting Rome was out of the question for the present. So Paul did the next best thing. He wrote a letter to the Christians there. It turned out to be an excellent summary of Christianity. Paul begins:

The Good News was promised long ago
by God through his prophets. . . .
It is about his Son, our Lord Jesus Christ. Romans 1:2–3
As the one sin condemned all people . . .
one righteous act sets all people free. Romans 5:18

Ask: Whose sin is Paul referring to? Whose act? (Paul spells this out beautifully below.)

The first Adam, made of earth, came from the earth;
the second Adam [Christ] came from heaven. . . .
Just as we wear the likeness of the man made of earth,
so we will wear the likeness of the Man from heaven.
1 Corinthians 15:47, 49

When we were baptized into union with Christ Jesus,
we were baptized into union with his death. . . .
We were buried with him and share his death,
in order that, just as Christ was raised . . .
so also we might live a new life.
For since we have become one with him in dying as he did,
in the same way we shall be one with him
by being raised to life as he was. Romans 6:3–5

Recall how the early Christians dramatized this Pauline statement. They built their baptisteries into the floor to resemble a tomb. They even had three steps going down into it to symbolize the three days Jesus was buried in the tomb. After baptism, the tomb was transformed, as it were, into a womb from which the newly baptized emerged a new creation (risen, as Christ was).

▶ **Notebook** Have students copy the following diagram in their notebooks as a review.

5. LESSON INTERACTION

Exercise ❶ **Discuss** **(a, b)** The burly security guard thought he was doing right, just as the Jews demanding circumcision thought they were doing right.

Exercise ❷ **Discuss** **(a)** Faith alone is not enough. Recall Paul's words in 1 Corinthians 13:2: "I may have all the faith needed to move mountains—but if I have no love, I am nothing."

(b) Discuss Sumner's point. If we let faith lie stagnant and do not act on it, it dies.

Exercise ❸ **Discuss** **(a, c, d)** These questions are self-explanatory.

▶ **Notebook** **(b)** Have the students enter the following diagram in their notebooks.

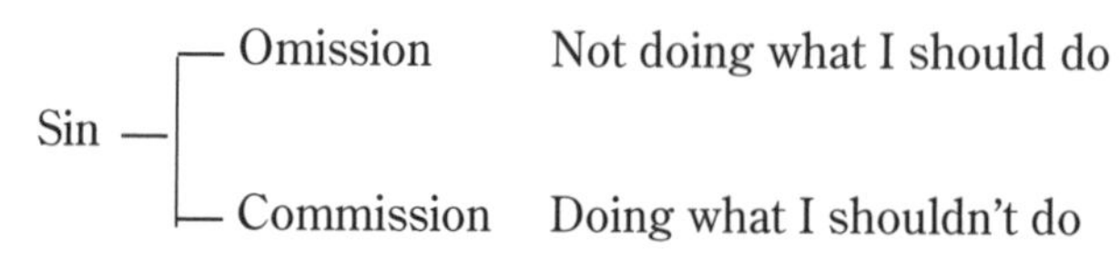

Philippians & Colossians

LESSON 103

1. LESSON BACKGROUND

▶ *Catechism of the Catholic Church,* 470–478.

2. LESSON QUIZ

Perfect score = 10 points

1. Explain how baptism changes (a) our relationship to Christ and (2) the impact that sin has on us. *(Lesson 102 review—2 points)*
2. Explain (a) the difference between sins of omission and sins of commission and (b) how a baptistery functions as both a tomb and a womb. *(Lesson 102 notebook review—4 points)*
3. List and briefly explain the twofold focus of Paul's meditation on Jesus, found in his Letter to the Philippians. *(Lesson 103 preview—4 points)*

3. LESSON HOMEWORK

▶ **Return** Lesson 102 review questions (page 213).

▶ **Collect** Lesson 103 review questions (page 215).

▶ **Read** Lesson 104 ("Philemon & Ephesians," pages 216–17).

▶ **Write** Lesson 104 review questions (page 217).

▶ **Appoint** Student to prepare Ephesians 2:11–22 (lessons 104, exercise 2).

4. LESSON PRESENTATION

Point ① **Read** Have volunteers read aloud the core content of lesson 103.

▶ **Review** Use the introduction to the prison letters as an opportunity for review. Invite student volunteers to diagram on the chalkboard

- four traditional groups into which the thirteen letters traditionally attributed to Paul are divided,
- the "ball park" dates of when Paul wrote each group of letters, and
- the names of the letters in each group.

▶ **Notebook** Have the students copy the completed review entry in their notebooks. It should look something like this:

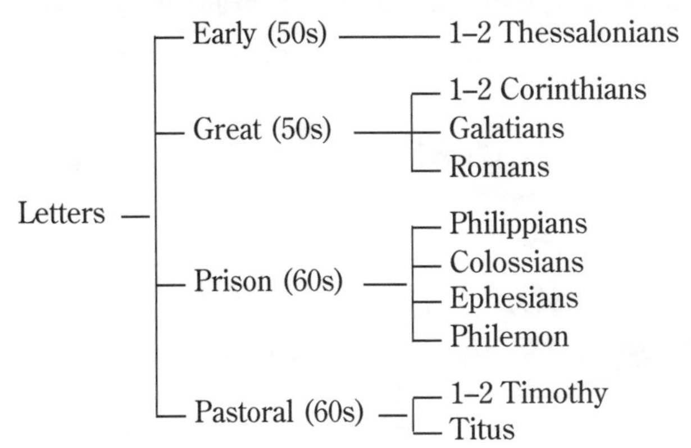

Point ② **Notebook** Develop the following diagram on the chalkboard. It gives Paul's references to being in prison. Use the conventional abbreviations of the letters to acquaint the students with them.

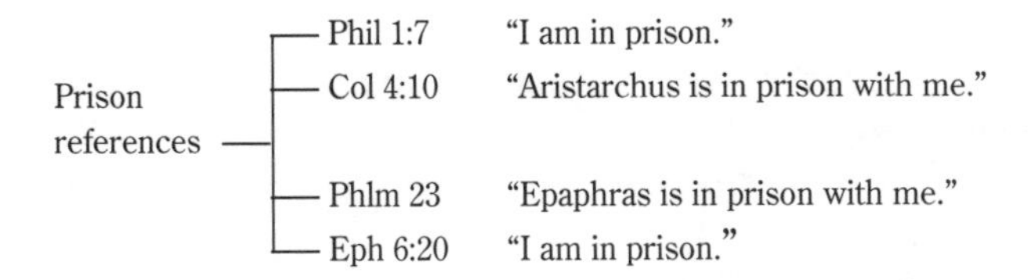

▶ **Clarify** From what prison did Paul write these letters? The question is debated. Two prisons where Paul spent a long stretch of time were in Caesarea and Rome. Tradition says he wrote the letters in Rome, but not all modern scholars agree.

Point ③ **Discuss** Paul's prison experience recalls that a number of great people have used prison to accomplish things they may not have accomplished otherwise.

For example, while in prison, John Bunyan wrote *Pilgrim's Progress,* Cervantes wrote *Don Quixote,* and Sir Walter Raleigh wrote his *History of the World.*

Point ④ **Notebook** Develop the following diagram on the chalkboard. It identifies the twofold focus of Paul's meditation on Jesus that Paul shared with the Christians of Philippi. (Locate Philippi on the map on page 171. Colossae is not shown on the map since Paul did not visit it. But it is roughly between Ephesus and Lystra.)

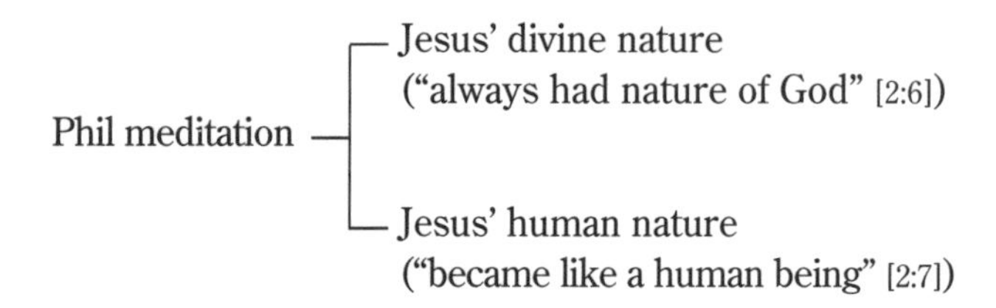

Notebook Develop the following diagram on the chalkboard. It identifies the twofold focus of Paul's meditation on Jesus' role in God's plan and the Church.

Jesus' role —
- God's plan — Head of creation (Col 1:20)
- Church — Head of Church (Col 1:18)

5. LESSON INTERACTION

Exercise 1 **Discuss** **(a, b)** John Dear's full letter appears in the *National Jesuit News* (February 1994). Share these additional excerpts from the letter with your students before discussing this exercise.

On the morning of December 7, 1993, Phil Berrigan, Bruce Friedrich, Lynn Fredriksson and I walked onto Seymour Johnson Air Force War Base near Goldsboro, North Carolina, right into the middle of military "war games" and took up again the cause of disarmament.

We approached one of the sixty F15 Eagle nuclear war machines [and] hammered on it several times. . . . We were arrested, denied bail, and jailed. A judge called us "a danger to society." We each could face up to ten years in prison for our witness to peace. . . .

We were pointing out that these weapons of mass destruction should not exist; that they are anti-property and anti-life; that they go against God's will and God's reign; and that they make possible the crucifixion of humanity. . . .

Trying to proclaim God's message and struggling to be faithful to this gentle God are worth whatever chains, jails, trials, persecutions, suffering and years of prison that lie ahead.

Exercise 2 **Discuss** **(a)** Muslims use "prayer beads" as part of their own spiritual life. The guards could identify with and relate to the action of making a rosary. Moreover, Father Jenko was doing something that they respected and approved of. It forged a common bond between them.

(b) The softened attitude shows that the guards had another side to them—a side that could appreciate and respect spiritual things.

(c) You might have to give the students a little time to reflect on this part of the exercise. If you can, share with them a time when you experienced something like this yourself.

Exercise 3 **Notebook** **(a, b, c)** Develop the following diagram on the chalkboard for entry in student notebooks. It sums up Donahue's three stages.

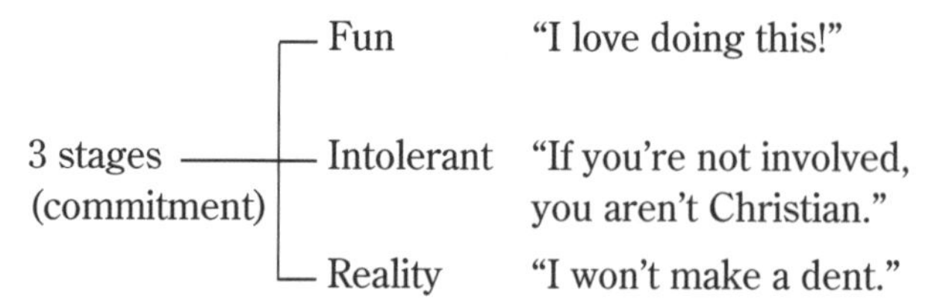

Miniposter **Discuss** Direct attention to the miniposter on page 214. Have the students reverse the drawing of the jail, *retaining its exact shape,* and jailing the jailor and freeing Paul.

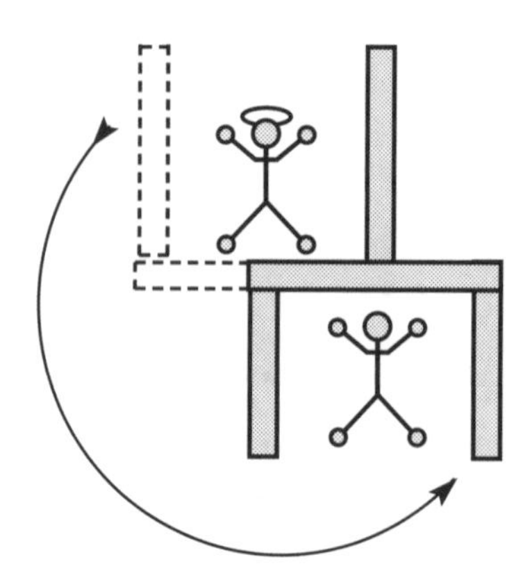

Photo **Clarify** Direct students' attention to the photo on page 214. Stress the idea that Paul used scribes. Be sure to point out the contrast in writing on the fragment.

Clarify Direct students' attention to the famous prize-winning photo on page 215. It shows four marines planting the flag on Iwo Jima's Mount Surabachi during World War II.

The photo was taken by Joe Rosenthal, a Jew with an interesting background. After becoming convinced that Jesus was indeed the promised Messiah, he became a staunch Catholic. In an interview with a journalist, he said, "The day before we went ashore on Iwo Jima, I attended Mass and received Holy Communion."

Philemon & Ephesians

1. LESSON BACKGROUND

► *Catechism of the Catholic Church*, 770–776.

2. LESSON QUIZ

Perfect score = 10 points

1. List and explain the three stages of Christian commitment as described by Phil Donahue. *(Lesson 103 review—6 points)*
2. List the names of two letters that Paul wrote in prison. *(Lesson 103 notebook review—2 points)*
3. Who was Onesimus, and what was his relationship with Paul? *(Lesson 104 preview—2 points)*

3. LESSON HOMEWORK

► **Return** Lesson 103 review questions (page 215).

► **Collect** Lesson 104 review questions (page 217).

► **Read** Lesson 105 ("1–2 Timothy & Titus," pages 218–19).

► **Write** Lesson 105 review questions (page 219).

► **Appoint** Student to prepare Mark 10:42–45 and John 13:12–15) (lessons 105, exercise 1).

4. LESSON PRESENTATION

Point ❶ **Read** Have volunteers real aloud the core content of lesson 104.

► **Discuss** Direct students' attention to the photo and photo caption on page 216. Note the first five letters of the second line on the slave tag: F-U-G-I-A.

Ask: What English word translates this word? Explain why. (The English word *escape* is used to translate it. The English word *fugitive* derives from F-U-G-I-A.)

► **Discuss** Also note the last six letters of the third line: D-O-M-N-U-M.

Ask: What English word translates this word? Explain why. (The English word *master* is used to translate it. The words *dominate* and *dominion* derive from D-O-M-N-U-M. Recall that God created human beings and gave them "dominion" ("mastery") over the rest of creation.

Point ❷ **Discuss** Paul's Letter to Philemon can be read in three or four minutes. It is filled with interesting things. Read the selected excerpts (below) to the students for discussion. The letter begins:

From Paul, a prisoner for the sake of Christ Jesus,
and from our brother Timothy—
To our friend and fellow worker Philemon,
and the church that meets in your house. 1–2

Ask: How do you explain the expression "the church that meets in your house"? What does it tell us about the place where early Christians first worshiped? (They met in someone's large home. Often it was slightly remodeled to function for this purpose.)

The remains of such a remodeled home were found in Dura-Europos on the Euphrates River in the 1930s. C. Ernest Wright describes it in *Biblical Archaeology:*

In plan it consisted of a series of rooms
around a paved open court. . . .
One of the rooms had been used as a chapel.
In a small neighboring room was the baptistry.
At one end of it was a niche and a receptacle or tub
for the water.
Above the latter a scene was painted on the wall,
showing Christ as the Good Shepherd.
Other wall paintings show Scriptural scenes,
such as . . . Peter attempting to walk on the water.

Point ❸ **Discuss** Continue the reading of Philemon with the following excerpt:

I hear of your love for all of God's people. 4

Ask: What title is usually given to the city of Philadelphia? ("City of Brotherly Love")

Ask: How is this a clue to the English translation of the Greek name *Philemon?* (It is translated as "loving." Paul uses a play on words by speaking of Philemon's "love.")

► **Clarify** The Greeks used three different words to designate love.

The first word is *eros*, indicating the "passion of sexual desire." The English word *erotic* derives from it. This word is not found in the New Testament.

The second word is *philia*, indicating, chiefly, "love of friendship." We get our words *Philadelphia* and *philanthropy* from it.

The third word is *agape*, indicating the "noblest form of love." Rarely used by Greeks, it was popularized by New Testament writers to designate "love of Christians" for God and for one another. It is sometimes translated "charity" to set it off from the popular notion of love.

▶ **Notebook** Develop the following diagram on the chalkboard for entry in student notebooks. It lists the three Greek words for love and shows how early Christians distinguished them (for the most part).

Love	Eros	"Passion of sexual desire"
	Philia	"Love of friendship"
	Agape	"Love of Christians"

Point ❹ **Discuss** Continue the reading of Philemon with the following excerpt:

Onesimus . . . is my own son in Christ;
for while in prison I have become his spiritual father.
At one time he was of no use to you,
but now he is useful both to you and to me. 10–11

▶ **Discuss** The Greek name *Onesimus* means "useful." Again, Paul plays on words: "of no use" and "useful."

Ask: Why do you think Paul uses these plays on words in his Letter to Philemon? (Possibly because he wanted to keep the letter light and not heavy. The request he is laying on Philemon is "heavy" enough.)

Point ❺ **Discuss** Conclude the reading of Philemon with the following well-constructed excerpt. Ask the students to listen carefully for the three plays on words that Paul uses.

Onesimus was away from you for a short time
so that you might have him back for all time. . . .
How much he means to me!
And how much more he will mean to you. . . .
Welcome him *back*
just as you would welcome me. 15–17

Ask: What is the point behind Paul's word plays? (He is spelling out the ramifications that, by baptism, "slave Onesimus" has become "brother Onesimus."

▶ **Clarify** Interestingly, a letter of Ignatius of Antioch (written around 110 C.E.) refers to Onesimus, bishop of Ephesus. Some scholars think this is the slave Onesimus.

Point ❻ **Clarify** The Letter to the Ephesians contains a concise overview of God's plan for all creation.

God's plan is to unite all of creation into one body, with Christ as its head.

God's procedure is to appoint leaders (apostles, prophets, evangelists) to prepare people for putting their talents at the service of building up Christ's body.

▶ **Notebook** Develop the following summary of God's plan on the chalkboard for entry in student notebooks.

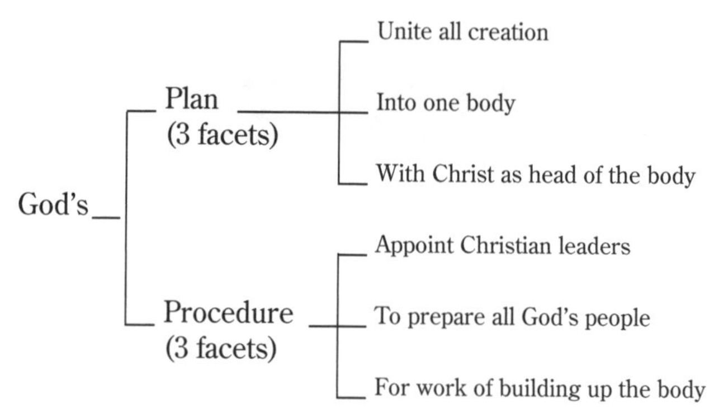

5. LESSON INTERACTION

Exercise ❶ **Discuss** **(a, b c)** Obviously, the big barrier was slaves like Onesimus becoming brothers of free people like Philemon. That barrier is akin to racial (black/white), social (employer/employee), and economic (rich/poor) barriers of our own time.

Exercise ❷ **Discuss** **(a, b)** Have the appointed student read the passage from Ephesians. The major barrier Paul refers to is Jew and Gentile. His approach is to show that by his death on the cross Christ destroyed the barrier. Paul returns to the "plan, which God will complete when the time is right . . . to bring all creation together . . . with Christ as head" (1:10).

Exercise ❸ **Notebook** **(a, b, c)** By way of review develop the following diagram, which spells out the general format Paul used in his letters.

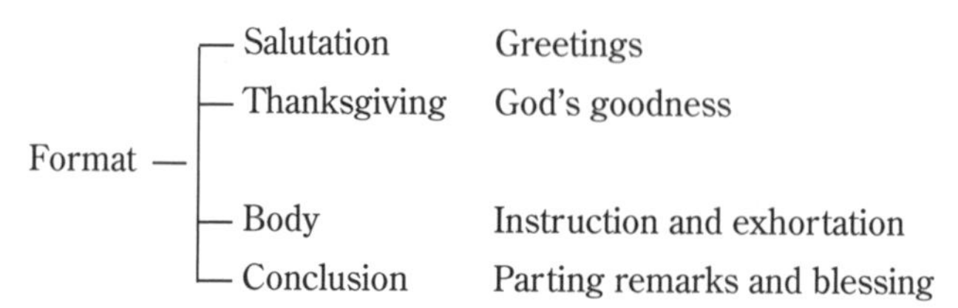

Exercise ❹ **Discuss** The quote suggests Paul knew the Colossians through Epaphras. There is no record of Paul's visiting them.

Miniposter **Activity** Be ready to duck when you give the students the answer to the riddle in the miniposter on page 216. It is the letter *e*.

CHAPTER TWENTY: Paul's Letters (pages 218–19)

1-2 Timothy & Titus

LESSON **105**

1. LESSON BACKGROUND

▶ *Catechism of the Catholic Church,* 880–887.

2. LESSON QUIZ

Perfect score = 10 points

1. To whom does Paul write concerning Onesimus and why? *(Lesson 104 review—2 points)*
2. List the three facets of (a) God's plan and (b) God's procedure for implementing the plan. *(Lesson 104 notebook review—6 points)*
3. What name do we give to Paul's letters to Timothy and Titus, and why do some scholars think they were written some years after Paul's death by a disciple of Paul? *(Lesson 105 preview—2 points)*

3. LESSON HOMEWORK

▶ **Return** Lesson 104 review questions (page 217).

▶ **Collect** Lesson 105 review questions (page 219).

▶ **Read** Lesson 106 ("James," pages 220–21).

▶ **Write** Lesson 106 review questions (page 221).

4. LESSON PRESENTATION

Point 1 **Read** Have volunteers read aloud the core content of lesson 105.

▶ **Notebook** By way of review and putting the "pastoral" letters in context, develop the following summary of Paul's life and ministry for entry in student notebooks. (Remind the students that the dates are approximate and probable.)

Paul's life		
	Birth in Tarsus	10 C.E.
	Conversion in Damascus	34
	Ministry in Antioch	43–44
	1st missionary trip	45–49
	2nd missionary trip	49–52
	3rd missionary trip	53–58
	Arrest in Jerusalem	58
	House confinement in Rome	61
	Execution in Rome	67

▶ **Clarify** The *traditional date* that is assigned to Paul's "pastoral" letters lies between his house confinement in Rome and his execution.

▶ **Notebook** By way of review, develop the following summary of the thirteen letters *traditionally* attributed to Paul and the four groups into which they are *traditionally* divided. (Use the conventional abbreviations of the letters, asking the students to identify them.)

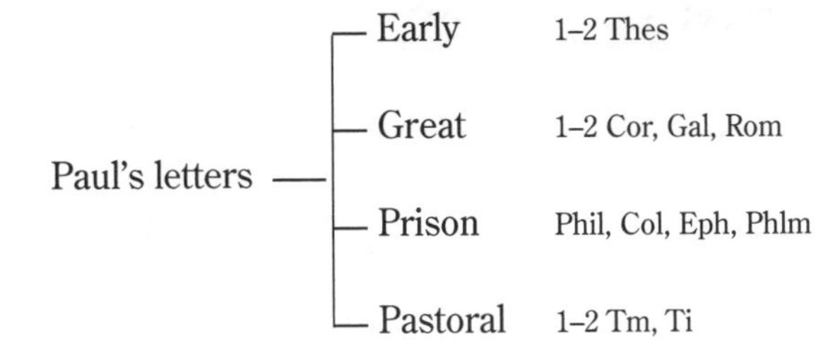

Point 2 **Review** 2 Timothy 3:16 contains a classic statement: "All Scripture is inspired by God."

▶ **Notebook** Three scripture passages, especially, refer to "inspiration." List them on the chalkboard for entry in student notebooks. (Again, use the abbreviations of the books to get students use to identifying them: Mark = Mk, Peter = 1 Pt and 2 Pt, Timothy = 1 Tm and 2 Tm.

Inspiration		
	Mk 12:36	David inspired by Spirit
	2 Pt 1:21	Prophets impelled by Spirit
	2 Tm 3:16	All Scripture inspired by God

▶ **Clarify** The important point about inspiration is *that* the human authors were inspired, not necessarily *how* they were inspired.

▶ **Discuss** Ask: Do you recall the three inspiration theories that have been proposed by Christians? (See below.)

▶ **Notebook** List the three theories on the chalkboard for entry in student notebooks.

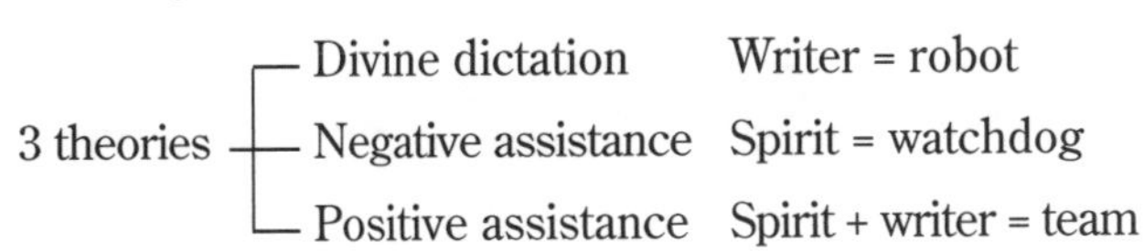

Clarify Have the students underline the positive assistance theory to indicate that it is the one Catholics and mainline Protestants hold. It may be stated as follows:

The Holy Spirit
worked in and through the human writers
in such a way that they were empowered
to use their own talents and words
to communicate
what God wanted them to communicate. Page 7 of textbook

Point ❸ **Discuss** The First Letter to Timothy opens "To Timothy, my true son in the faith."

Ask: Do you recall how Paul first met Timothy? (See photo and caption on page 219.)

Discuss 1 Timothy 1:15 states: "Christ Jesus came into the world to save sinners. I am the worst of them."

Ask: Is Paul, perhaps, exaggerating here? Explain.

Saints have made similar remarks. Consider David Brainerd, a missionary who worked among the native Americans in the Delaware territory.

In spite of a crippling pain, Brainerd rode from place to place on horseback, preached in the open, and slept in the open. His diary is filled with beautiful expressions of love. But alongside these expressions are contrary ones as well. John R. Stott says of Brainerd in *Basic Christianity:*

He complains
of his lack of prayer and love for Christ.
He calls himself "a poor worm," "a dead dog,"
and "an unspeakable wretch."
This is not because he had a morbid conscience.
He simply lived near Christ
and was painfully aware of his sinfulness.

An awareness of sin is related to a nearness to God. As nearness to God grows, so does awareness of sin. Distance from God, on the other hand, reduces the contrast we need in order to see ourselves as we really are. This is Kilian McDonnell's point in *Commonweal* magazine (August 31, 1970). He writes:

Many do not recognize Christ because
they do not recognize themselves as sinners.
If I am not a sinner, then I have no need for Christ.
No man will celebrate the mystery of Christ in joy
if he does not first recognize in sorrow
that he is a sinner who needs a savior.

Point ❹ **Clarify** Paul's Letter to Titus begins with an interesting memo. It reads:

I left you in Crete, so that you could put in order
the things that still needed doing
and appoint church elders in every town.
Remember my instructions:
an elder must be without fault. 1:5

Clarify The Acts of the Apostles makes no reference to Paul and Titus being in Crete. Paul's above memo to Titus leads some scholars to theorize that the two of them may have visited Crete *after* Paul's first Roman imprisonment. (Recall that it seems Paul was cleared after his first trial in Rome around 63 C.E. See the brief discussion of this point on page 206 of the student textbook.)

5. LESSON INTERACTION

Exercise ❶ **Discuss** **(a, b)** After reading the introduction to this exercise, have the students take a few minutes to tally their score and explain what keeps them from scoring higher.

(c) Have the appointed student read the two passages: Mark 10:42–45 ("The Son of man . . . came to serve and to give his life to redeem many people") and John 13:12–15 ("Wash one another's feet").

Exercise ❷ **Discuss** **(a, b)** Depending on the level of trust present among the students, you might have them do this exercise anonymously. You could then screen the responses for quality and share the better ones with the group at the next class meeting.

Exercise ❸ **Discuss** **(a, b)** One way to handle this exercise is to have the students indicate anonymously on a slip of paper which of the four entries comes closest to their situation: 1, 2, 3, or 4.

Have several students collect the slips and call them out orally for a "class secretary" to tally them on the chalkboard. This will provide a general profile on where the class stands on this question.

Once the general profile has been established, the discussion could begin.

CHAPTER TWENTY-ONE: Other Letters (pages 220–21)

James

LESSON 106

1. LESSON BACKGROUND

▶ *Catechism of the Catholic Church,* 120, 153–165.

2. LESSON QUIZ

Perfect score = 10 points

1. What is one way Paul's Letter to Titus reflects a community organizing itself? *(Lesson 105 review—1 point)*
2. List the four groups into which Paul's letters are traditionally divided and one letter that falls within each group. *(Lesson 105 notebook review—8 points)*
3. Explain James's point about the link between faith and works. *(Lesson 106 preview—1 point)*

3. LESSON BACKGROUND

▶ **Return** Lesson 105 review questions (page 219).

▶ **Collect** Lesson 106 review questions (page 221).

▶ **Read** Lesson 107 ("Peter," pages 222–23).

▶ **Write** Lesson 107 review questions (page 223).

4. LESSON PRESENTATION

Point 1 **Read** Have volunteers read aloud the core content of lesson 106.

▶ **Notebook** Develop on the chalkboard the following summary of the four major divisions into which the twenty-seven books of the New Testament are divided.

- New Testament divisions
  - Gospels (4)
  - Acts (1)
  - Letters (21)
  - Revelation (1)

Point 2 **Notebook** Develop the following summary of the twenty-one letters of the New Testament. It puts the seven "catholic" letters in context. They are called "catholic" because they are intended for all Christians—rather than a specific group (e.g., Romans) or a specific person (e.g., Timothy).

- Letters (21)
  - Pauline (13)
    - Early (2)
    - Great (4)
    - Prison (4)
    - Pastoral (3)
  - Non-Pauline (8)
    - Special (1) — Hebrews
    - Catholic (7)
      - James
      - 1–2 Peter
      - 1–2–3 John
      - Jude

Point 3 **Clarify** The seven "catholic" letters are also given the name *deuterocanonical,* because they were *not immediately* accepted as canonical (inspired) by all Christians. (The name *protocanonical* refers to New Testament books universally accepted immediately.)

Regarding the seven "catholic" letters, some sixteenth-century Protestant reformers rejected all seven letters. Other reformers rejected only some of them. In time, however, all reformers eventually accepted all seven. Today Protestants and Catholics are in full agreement on the New Testament canon.

Point 4 **Clarify** The late acceptance of deuterocanonical books (letters) raises a question. Who decides which books (letters) are canonical (inspired)?

Catholics believe that the same Spirit who inspired the writing of the books inspires and guides the Church in making this important decision.

History shows that the prayerful process of discerning which books were inspired began early. For example, already in 2 Peter 3:16 we find Paul's letters being revered as scriptural:

There are some difficult things in his [Paul's] letters
which ignorant and unstable people explain falsely,
as they do with other passages of the Scriptures.

In other words, Paul's letters were revered as Scripture from early on. Paul's letters are also mentioned with similar reverence in the writings of Ignatius of Antioch and Polycarp, around 115 C.E.

Around 250 C.E., Origen indicates that a consensus existed concerning the four Gospels, Paul's letters, 1 John, 1 Peter, and Revelation.

Finally, in 393 a church council approved as canonical (inspired) the present list of twenty-seven New Testament books.

Point ❺ **Clarify** The play *The Teahouse of the August Moon* opens with the spotlight focused on Sakini. He is a native interpreter for the American army on the island of Okinawa. Dressed in tattered clothes and GI shoes, several sizes too big, Sakini walks down to the footlights. Hands folded, as in prayer, he bows and introduces himself.

After describing how Okinawa has been conquered many times in its long history, Sakini notes that this has helped to educate his people. He then adds, reflectively:

Not easy to learn. Sometimes painful.
But pain makes man think.
Thought makes man wise.
Wisdom makes life endurable.

This same philosophical approach to life pervades the first of the "catholic" letters: the Letter from James. It takes the form of a series of guidelines for Christian living.

▶ **Notebook** Develop on the chalkboard the following summary of some of the topics addressed in James.

Topics	Avoiding discrimination	2:1–13
	Living the faith you profess	2:14–26
	Controlling the tongue	3:1–12
	Helping the poor	5:1–6
	Anointing the sick	5:14–15

▶ **Clarify** The following excerpt is from a personal letter to the author from a Vietnam veteran. It describes the veteran's experience of receiving the sacrament of the Anointing of the Sick, referred to in James 5:14–15.

From the split second I was hit, I was completely alone. I've heard it said, but never realized it—when you're dying there is no one but you. You're all alone. I was hurt bad, real bad; a 4.2 mortar landed about six feet behind me and took off my left leg, badly ripped up my left arm, hit me in the back, head, hip, and right heel and ankle. Shock was instantaneous, but I fought it—knowing that if I went out, I'd never wake up again.

There were three or four medics hovering over me, shook up, trying to help me; but all I could do was to try to pray. The trouble was I couldn't think. . . .

No one could tell me there wasn't a God at that moment. I knew I would die and fought desperately for ground, every inch, breath of life. . . .

Well, with a hell of a lot of stubbornness and luck (providence), I lived to make it to the chopper, two hours after being hit. When they carried me into the first-aid station, I felt four or five people scrubbing my body in different places. This brought me to open my eyes, and I could see about a foot in front of me. . . .

Anyway, someone bent over me. I wasn't sure who it was, but it looked like our battalion chaplain; his nose was practically on mine. After I saw him, I started to go out—I figured for the last time. When I talked I could only whisper, and this took all I had. As I was going out, my eyes closed, and I heard Father say, "Are you sorry for your sins?"

With my last breath and all I had, I whispered, "Hell, yes!" Then a split second before I went out, I felt oil on my forehead; and something happened which I'll never forget. Something which I never experienced before in my life! All of a sudden, I stopped gasping for every inch of life; I just burst with joy and thought I'm ready to die, please take me, I'm ready. . . .

I felt like I had just got a shot of a million cc's of morphine. I was on Cloud Nine. I felt free of body and mind. After this, I was conscious about three or four times during the next ten-day period; I never worried about dying; in fact I was waiting for it.

I hope you can decipher this. My permission is given for this statement to be placed in a published context.

5. LESSON INTERACTION

Exercise ❶ **Discuss** **(a)** Have the students respond in writing. Collect and screen the responses. Share the better ones with the group at the next class meeting.

(b) A variety of responses is possible.

Exercise ❷ **Discuss** **(a)** You might want to rephrase this question to fit your class. For example, rephrase it to read as follows: What advice would you give to a friend who is at a party and confides to you that he or she has been given some drugs and plans to try them for the first time that night?

(b, c) Have the students respond in writing to these questions. Collect and screen the responses. Share the better ones with the group at the next class.

Exercise ❸ **Discuss** **(a)** Evil thoughts come to our minds, but they are not sinful if we "prevent them from settling," to use John Collins's expression.

(b) The point of this question is important. For example, from previous experience, I learn that looking at something billed as pornographic on the computer "Internet" causes me problems. The Collins quote does not apply in this case. It is like removing the scarecrow from the seedplot and inviting the birds to settle in.

Peter

LESSON 107

1. LESSON BACKGROUND

▶ *Catechism of the Catholic Church,* 1503–1510.

2. LESSON QUIZ

Perfect score = 10 points

1. What makes some scholars think the Letter from James did not start out as a letter? *(Lesson 106 review—1 point)*
2. List the seven "catholic" letters. *(Lesson 106 notebook review—7 points)*
3. Identify (a) Alice Marble and (b) Father Brandsma. *(Lesson 107 preview—2 points)*

3. LESSON HOMEWORK

▶ **Return** Lesson 106 review questions (page 221).

▶ **Collect** Lesson 107 review questions (page 223).

▶ **Read** Lesson 108 ("John," pages 224–25).

▶ **Write** Lesson 108 review questions (page 225).

4. LESSON PRESENTATION

Point 1 **Read** Have volunteers read aloud the core content of lesson 107.

▶ **Discuss** The First Letter from Peter begins with this salutation:

To God's chosen people who live as refugees
scattered throughout the provinces
of Pontus, Galatia, Cappadocia, Asia, and Bithynia. 1:1

The province of Bithynia is of special interest. (See map on page 171. Bithynia is not labeled on it, but it lies between Galatia and the south shore of the Black Sea.) In 110 C.E., Bithynia was plagued with problems. Its "governor," Pliny, made Christians his scapegoat. He filed this report with the Roman emperor Trajan. Read it to the students.

I questioned them, personally,
asking them if they were Christian.
If they said they were . . . I ordered them punished.
Those who denied being Christian, I released—
but only after they acknowledged the gods,
honored your image, and defamed Christ. . . .

Some affirmed they had once been Christian,
but no longer were. . . .
They admitted meeting regularly at sunrise
on a stated day to pray to Christ as to a god. . . .
After their sunrise meeting, they broke up,
but gathered again later the same day
to share together in a harmless meal.

I now want your personal advice on this matter,
because of the growing number of offenders. . . .
This contagious superstition has infected
not only the cities, but also the towns and countryside.
But I am confident we can still contain it.

Ask: Can you identify three Christian beliefs/practices referred to in Pliny's report?

▶ **Notebook** The three beliefs/practices that Pliny refers to may be summarized as follows for entry in student notebooks.

3 points		
	Lord's Day	meet on "stated day"
	Lord's divinity	"pray to Christ as to a god"
	Lord's Supper	"share . . . in a harmless meal"

▶ **Clarify** Trajan's reply to Pliny is interesting.

My dear Pliny,
You have followed the right course. . . .
These people must be hunted out.
If they are brought before you
and the charge against them is proven,
they must be punished.

Point 2 **Clarify** Besides being threatened "from without" (Roman persecution), Bithynian Christians were being threatened "from within" (false teachers). Referring to these false teachers, who were distorting the Gospel, Peter says:

They have left the straight path
and have lost their way. . . .
It would have been much better for them
never to have known the way of righteousness
than to know it and then turn away from [it].
2 Peter 2:15, 21

One part of the Gospel that the false teachers were distorting concerned the Second Coming. Early Christians expected Jesus to come quickly. When this did not happen, they became vulnerable to false teachers. Addressing himself to this problem, Peter writes:

My dear friends!
There is no difference in the Lord's sight
between one day and a thousand years;
to him the two are the same.
The Lord is not slow to do what he has promised,
as some think. Instead, he is patient with you,
because he . . . wants all to turn away from their sins.
2 Peter 3:8–9

Notebook Develop the following diagram on the chalkboard for entry in student notebooks. It sums up the dangers "from without" and "from within" that Christians were facing.

Two dangers	Without	Roman persecution
	Within	False teachers

Point ❸ **Clarify** One final point concerning the Second Letter of Peter. Recall that it said of Paul's letters:

There are some difficult things in his letters
which ignorant and unstable people explain falsely,
as they do with other passages of the Scriptures.
2 Peter 3:16

This reference is significant for two reasons. First, it indicates that Paul's letters are not only well-known but also referred to frequently. Second, it implies that Paul's letters were esteemed as having the status of Scripture itself.

Some scholars think that these two facts, along with others in Peter's second letter, demand that we date this letter well after Peter's death (ca. 67). In other words, they suggest the letter may have been written by a later hand and attributed to Peter. Defending this possibility, scholar John L. McKenzie writes in his *Dictionary of the Bible:*

The attribution to Peter may indicate
that the author had been a disciple of Peter
who attempted to answer the question
of the delay of the Parousia [Second Coming]
in terms which he remembered as those of Peter.

Such an attribution would not have been frowned upon in the ancient world.

5. LESSON INTERACTION

Exercise ❶ **Discuss** **(a)** Motivation plays a major role in giving people courage and strength to endure pain in striving for something. Recall the discussion of the two kinds of courage (and the threshold of pain) in lesson 29 (point 4) of this Resource Manual.

(b) Review the discussion of the four kinds of pain in lesson 78 (exercise 2) of the textbook.

(c) God permits pain to teach us or help us grow spiritually. Touching on this point, Dr. Louis Bisch writes:

Suffering may teach you something valuable,
something that you could not have learned otherwise.
Possibly it may change for the better
the entire course of your life.

Bisch cites the example of Nobel and Pulitzer prize winner Eugene O'Neill, who revolutionized American drama. Recall his story, which was discussed earlier.

At the age of twenty-five, O'Neill was a drifter. He contracted a serious illness and was bedfast for an extended period. During this time he reflected on his situation and changed it, becoming a great playwright.

Recall, also, Edna Ferber's novel *So Big.* In the story, Dirk DeJong (a young architect who has never struggled in his life) wants to marry Dallas O'Meara (a young artist). She turns down his proposal, saying that she wants to marry someone who has struggled and suffered. She explains that such experience has a way of mellowing a person. She concludes, "You're all smooth; I like 'em bumpy."

Discuss **(d, e)** When the author was a boy, his mother taught him, his brothers, and his sisters to offer their sufferings (mental and physical) with Jesus' suffering on the cross for the salvation of the world. This practice transformed their suffering into prayer and grace. It also deepened their faith.

Exercise ❷ **Activity** **(a, b, c)** You might have the students write out these three responses in private. Collect, screen, and share the better responses with the group at the next class meeting.

Photo **Discuss** Refer the students to the photo and the caption on page 222. The photo is foggy, but a reading of Luke 9:28–33 will make it clear who the five figures are (upper level: Moses and Elijah; lower level: Peter, James, and John).

John

1. LESSON BACKGROUND

▶ *Catechism of the Catholic Church,* 675–677.

2. LESSON QUIZ

Perfect score = 10 points

1. What vexing question did Peter address in his second letter? *(Lesson 107 review—1 point)*
2. List and explain the three Christian beliefs/practices that Pliny refers to in his letter to the Roman emperor Trajan. *(Lesson 107 notebook review—6 points)*
3. Identify (a) apostasy, (b) Parousia, (c) eschatological. *(Lesson 108 preview—3 points)*

3. LESSON HOMEWORK

▶ **Return** Lesson 107 review questions (page 223).

▶ **Collect** Lesson 108 review questions (page 225).

▶ **Read** Lesson 109 ("Jude," page 226–27).

▶ **Write** Lesson 109 review questions (page 227).

4. LESSON PRESENTATION

Point ① **Read** Have volunteers read aloud the core content of lesson 108.

▶ **Clarify** Tradition attributes the First Letter of John to the author of John's Gospel, who is the disciple "whom Jesus loved" in a special way. Recall that this affectionate reference occurs

- at the Last Supper, John 13:23
- under the cross, John 19:26
- at the tomb, John 20:2
- on the seashore. John 21:7

Tradition says that John was the son of Zebedee and the brother of James. Mark says that Jesus tagged the brothers with "the name Boanerges, which means 'Men of Thunder' " (Mark 3:17). The name may have been triggered by the brothers' explosive response to Samaritans when they barred Jesus from their town (Luke 9:54).

John, along with James and Peter, was selected by Jesus to be with him on several special occasions:

- raising of Jairus' daughter, Luke 8:51
- ecstasy on Mount Tabor, Luke 9:28
- agony on Mount of Olives. Mark 14:33

▶ **Review** Recall that Jesus' ecstasy (Mount Tabor) and agony (Mount of Olives) are complementary events. The first spotlights Jesus' divinity; the second, his humanity. It is significant that the same three disciples are present at both events.

▶ **Notebook** Develop the following review summary on the chalkboard for entry in student notebooks.

Parallel events	Mt. Tabor	Ecstasy spotlights Jesus' divinity
	Mt. of Olives	Agony spotlights Jesus' humanity

Point ② **Clarify** The First Letter of John is of special value to us because it gives a powerful affirmation of the humanity and divinity of Jesus. It does this in the process of refuting the two sets of false teachers (Gnostic and Docetist) who were spreading two sets of false teaching (*dogmatic* and *moral*).

Gnostics took their name from the Greek word *gnosis,* meaning "knowledge." Gnosticism took various twists and defies simple definition. This much might be said: Gnostics taught (1) matter was evil, (2) only certain people were destined for salvation, (3) salvation came through "secret knowledge" that enabled the "destined people" to detach themselves at death from the material world and escape into the spiritual world.

As a result Gnostics (1) fell into the *dogmatic* error of teaching that Jesus was *not divine,* because divinity could never attach itself to evil, and (2) fell into the *moral* error of denying the *reality* of sin, explaining that since the body was material and inherently evil, only the spirit (soul) was relevant. Therefore, bodily behavior was of no consequence, and there was no link between Christian belief and bodily behavior. This would explain John's stress on the *reality* of sin (1 John 1:8–10).

Point ③ **Clarify** Docetists took their name from the Greek word *dokeo,* meaning "to appear." They followed the Gnostic view that matter was inherently evil and that divinity would never attach itself to evil.

But, contrary to the Gnostics, Docetists taught that Jesus was *indeed divine.* Therefore, they denied Jesus' humanity, saying that Jesus merely "appeared" to have a human body. This explains John's great stress on his own personal, physical contact with Jesus (1 John 1:1–4).

As a result Docetists fell into the *dogmatic* error of teaching that Jesus was *not human.*

Notebook Develop the following diagram on the chalkboard for entry in student notebooks.

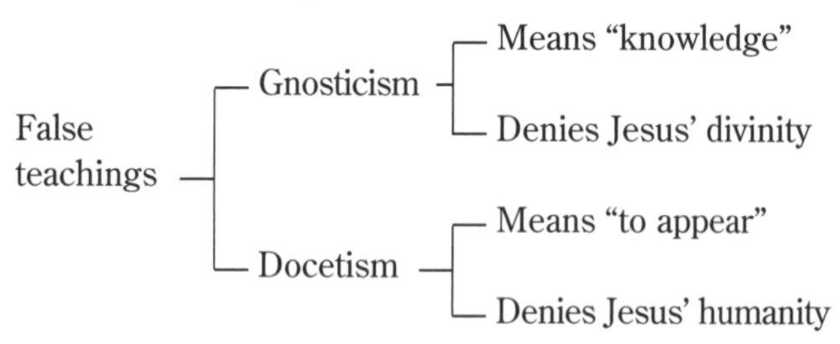

Point 4 **Clarify** One of the most famous passages of the First Letter of John is:

If we say we love God, but hate others,
we are liars. For we cannot love God,
whom we have not seen, if we do not love others,
whom we have seen. 1 John 4:20

1 John 3:18 says that our love of others should show itself in actions. Saint Paul lists twelve of these actions in his First Letter to the Corinthians:

Love is patient and kind; it is not jealous or conceited
or proud; love is not ill-mannered or selfish or irritable;
love does not keep a record of wrongs;
love is not happy with evil, but is happy with the truth.
Love never gives up. 1 Corinthians 13:4–7

Activity Have the students list the numbers 1 through 12 vertically in their notebooks. To the right of each number have them write the appropriate word or phrase (for example, *1. Patient, 9. Keep a record of wrongs*). To the right of each word or phrase have them write the numbers 1 through 5 with some space between the numbers. The first entry should look something like this:

1. Patient 1 2 3 4 5

Next, read the twelve entries below. Pause after each entry to let the students grade themselves on a scale of 1 (regularly) to 5 (rarely) by circling the appropriate number. When they are finished, have them total their score.

1. **Am I patient?** Do I tend to let the failures or mistakes of others get on my nerves?
2. **Am I kind?** Do I tend to ignore others, make fun of them, or treat them coldly?
3. **Am I jealous?** Do I tend to get upset when others are preferred to me?
4. **Am I conceited?** Do I tend to act superior or think I'm better than others?
5. **Am I proud?** Do I tend to brag about myself or my achievements?
6. **Am I selfish?** Do I tend to be possessive of things or friends?
7. **Am I ill-mannered?** Do I tend to act or speak rudely to others?
8. **Am I irritable?** Do I tend to be hard to deal with when I'm not in a good mood?
9. **Do I keep a record of wrongs?** Do I tend to hold grudges and not forgive and forget?
10. **Am I happy with evil?** Do I delight in another's bad luck, especially when it benefits me?
11. **Am I happy with truth?** Do I accept the truth, even when it hurts me personally?
12. **Do I give up?** Do I tend to let failure or rejection discourage me or cause me to quit?

0–24 = "I'm a drag!" 37–48 = "I'm a joy!"
25–36 = "I'm average!" 49–60 = "I'm a dream!"

Discuss Do a class profile. Have a "class secretary" list numbers 1 to 12 on the chalkboard. Then ask: How many scored a *2* or lower on item 1 (continue down through 12). Next, add up the figures to find out which of the twelve "love items" the class did poorest on. Ask: Why is this such a difficult item for young people?

5. LESSON INTERACTION

Exercise 1 **Notebook** List the following definitions for entry in student notebooks.

Wicked One	Claims to be God
Antichrist	Enemy of Christ
Parousia	Final (Second) Coming of Christ
Eschatological	Pertains to end time (world's end)
Apostasy	Defection from Christianity
Personification	Treat something as a person

Discuss **(a, b)** Given the above definitions, the students should be able to handle the questions posed.

Exercise 2 **Discuss** Evely's statements are both appeals to personal honesty and integrity. In essence they say, "If you are weak enough to sin, be humble enough to admit it."

Jude

LESSON 109

1. LESSON BACKGROUND

▶ *Catechism of the Catholic Church,* 144–159.

2. LESSON QUIZ

Perfect score = 10 points

1. List three truths about Jesus that false teachers were denying. *(Lesson 108 review—3 points)*
2. Match the left-hand column with the correct answer in the right-hand column.

__ Wicked One	a. Pertains to end time
__ Antichrist	b. Second Coming of Christ
__ Parousia	c. Claims to be God
__ Eschatological	d. Treat something as a person
__ Apostasy	e. Enemy of Christ
__ Personification	f. Defection from Christianity

(Lesson 108 notebook review—6 points)

3. Explain how the Letter from Jude addresses a situation much like the one Jesus describes in one of his parables. *(Lesson 109 preview—1 point)*

3. LESSON HOMEWORK

▶ **Return** Lesson 108 review questions (page 225).

▶ **Collect** Lesson 109 review questions (page 227).

▶ **Read** Lesson 110 ("Hebrews," pages 228–29).

▶ **Write** Lesson 110 review questions (page 229).

4. LESSON PRESENTATION

Point ❶ **Read** Have volunteers read aloud the core content of lesson 109.

▶ **Discuss** Jesus' parable of the weeds and the wheat, which introduces this lesson, has been called a mini-Gospel.

Ask: Why? (It is a capsule summary of the gospel message.)

▶ **Notebook** Have the students identify the parable's "cast of characters" (left-hand column). List these on the chalkboard for entry in student notebooks. The completed "cast of characters" should look like this:

Cast of Characters	
Parable	**Real Life**
Farmer	Jesus
Enemy	Satan
Field	Human race
Wheat	Jesus' followers
Weed	Satan's followers
Harvesttime	End of world
Harvesters	Angels

Point ❷ **Clarify** Jude's point about the clash between belief and behavior is important, especially in helping us understand "faith problems." When a clash occurs, we begin living a "conflicting" life: *believing* one way and *behaving* another. When this happens, we frequently try to resolve the "conflict" by changing our behavior so that it conforms with our belief. If we can't change, we sometimes question our belief. This questioning proceeds either constructively or destructively.

Constructive questioning means we want to *know* what is really true so that we can do *what is right.*

Destructive questioning means we want to *prove* our belief false so that we can do *what we want.*

For example, we suddenly find ourselves *believing* one thing (it is wrong to steal) and *behaving* just the opposite (stealing). Since living this way turns us into a Dr. Jekyll and Mr. Hyde, which is agonizing, we question our faith *destructively.* That is, we try to prove it is false so that we can continue our behavior—and be at peace with ourselves. For example, we may try to convince ourselves that Jesus' teaching is out of date and no longer relevant.

▶ **Notebook** Summarize the difference between constructive and destructive faith questioning for entry in student notebooks.

Faith questioning —	Constructive	Search for truth (so I can do what is right)
	Destructive	Desire to prove false (so I can do what I want)

What should we do if we discover ourselves questioning our faith *destructively?*

First, we should be honest and admit our destructive questioning. Once we admit it, it ceases to control us and we control it.

Second, we should understand that because we are human, faith and behavior will always be in conflict to some extent. This is why Jesus came into the world. We need redemption. We need forgiveness for our sins and we need the grace to do what is right. This is the purpose of the sacrament of Reconciliation.

Point ❸ **Clarify** Behavior that is contrary to belief is a common phenomenon. It is a human situation. In other words, a great sinner may still be a person of deep faith. Recall Hamlet.

The young prince's father was killed by his uncle. Hamlet swears revenge. One day he comes upon his uncle, who is alone, unarmed, and trying to pray. Hamlet says:

Now might I do it pat, now he is praying . . .
and am I then revenged
To take him in the purging of his soul,
When he is fit and seasoned for his passage?
No! Up sword; and know a more horrid hent:
when he is drunk asleep, or in his rage . . .
Or about some other act
That has no relish of salvation in it. Act 3, Scene 2

Ask: Why does Hamlet decide to wait? How does this episode reflect both *sin* and *faith* on Hamlet's part?

(Hamlet waits because if he kills his uncle now, his uncle will be saved, because he is repenting: "praying" and "purging his soul." Hamlet's action reflects *faith*, because it shows that he believes in reward and punishment in an afterlife. It also reflects *sin*, because it shows that his desire for revenge is so great that he refuses to conform his *behavior* to his *belief*.)

Point ❹ **Discuss** Just as bad behavior can have a negative impact on belief, so good behavior can have a positive impact on belief. In other words, instead of diminishing belief or faith, good behavior nourishes it.

An episode in Dostoevski's *The Brothers Karamazov* illustrates this point.

Ask: Where did we meet Dostoevski previously, and what do you recall about him? (Lesson 96, exercise 4)

At the last minute his sentence of death (for opposing the government) is commuted to ten years of hard labor in Siberia. In Siberia, Dostoevski undergoes a conversion to Jesus. He returns home and reels off a series of literary masterpieces, including *The Brothers Karamazov.* Then things fall apart. His Christian commitment stagnates; he starts to drink and throws his life away. He dies penniless.

Ask: Where did we previously read about *The Brothers Karamazov?* (Lesson 100, exercise 1)

In the episode described there, Dostoevski describes an old woman having doubts about the existence of God and the existence of life after death. She asks an old priest, Father Zossima, how these things can be proved.

Ask: Do you recall what the priest told her? (He says, "You can't prove these things, but you can become sure of them." He goes on to say, "Love your neighbor from the heart. As your love grows so will sureness of God's existence and life after death.")

Ask: What is the old priest's point? (Faith does not admit of "intellectual proof." If it did, it would cease to be faith. Faith, however, does admit of "certitude." For example, I am "certain" my best friend would not hurt me deliberately, because of our mutual love and trust.)

Ask: How does the priest's answer fit in with what we have just been saying about faith? (A loving behavior tends to have a positive impact on faith. It is a matter of experience that when we live the Gospel, our doubts tend to diminish. Similarly, an unloving behavior tends to have a negative impact on faith. It tends to feed our doubts and make them grow.

▶ **Notebook** Summarize the interplay between behavior and belief for entry in student notebooks.

Behavior impacts faith	Bad	Nourishes doubt
	Good	Diminishes doubt

5. LESSON INTERACTION

Exercise ❶ **Discuss** Review what was said under point 2 above. If this does not help your friend, suggest that your friend consult a believing adult, like a parent or a priest.

Exercise ❷ **Discuss** This question usually makes for some excellent discussion. Give the students time to think about and write out their responses privately before sharing them.

Exercise ❸ **Discuss** Again, this question usually generates some great discussion.

Exercise ❹ **Discuss** **(a)** Jesus' sufferings point to Jesus' love: Why would anyone do this for another? Jesus' miracles point to something beyond themselves: Why does Jesus do these things, and where does he get the power to do them?

(b) Pompeii was destroyed in 79 C.E., when Christianity was an outlaw religion. Everything had to be underground.

(c) The "dark and contrary rumors" refer to rumors that Christians did terrible things in their rituals.

CHAPTER TWENTY-ONE: Other Letters (pages 228–29)

Hebrews

LESSON **110**

1. LESSON BACKGROUND

▶ *Catechism of the Catholic Church,* 160–165.

2. LESSON QUIZ

Perfect score = 7 points

1. Explain Jude's point that a conflict in belief and behavior can turn us into a kind of Dr. Jekyll and Mr. Hyde. *(Lesson 109 review—1 point)*
2. List and briefly explain the ways we can question our belief or behavior. *(Lesson 109 notebook review—4 points)*
3. What is one proposal about who the "Hebrews" (in the Letter to the Hebrews) were and why they were suffering. *(Lesson 110 preview—2 points)*

3. LESSON HOMEWORK

▶ **Return** Lesson 109 review questions (page 227).

▶ **Collect** Lesson 110 review questions (page 229).

▶ **Read** Lesson 111 ("Seven Messages," pages 230–31).

▶ **Write** Lesson 111 review questions (page 231).

▶ **Appoint** Student to prepare Revelation 2:1–7 (lesson 111, exercise 4).

4. LESSON PRESENTATION

Point ❶ **Read** Have volunteers read aloud the core content of lesson 110.

▶ **Discuss** Ask: In what sense is the way the author of Hebrews approached his readers similar to the way the skipper approached young Joseph Conrad? (He expressed trust in his readers and encouraged them to stand firm and hold to their course.)

Point ❷ **Clarify** Stress that the Letter to the Hebrews falls into a special category of its own. For example, it is the only New Testament letter (First Letter of John excepted) that contains no introductory greeting or the sender's name.

Scholars gave it the name "Letter to the Hebrews" because of its content, which seems directed to a group of Jewish priests who converted to Christianity and were being persecuted for their action.

Scholars suggest that the letter was written shortly before the destruction of the Jerusalem Temple by the Romans in 70 C.E.

▶ **Notebook** The following diagram shows how the letter fits into the context with the other New Testament letters. Have students enter it in their notebooks.

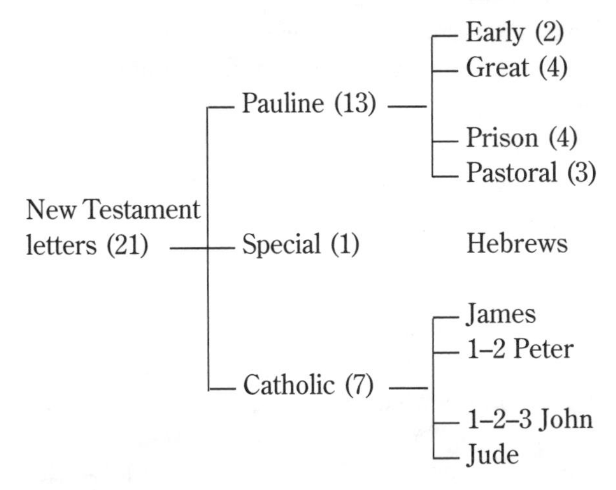

Point ❸ **Clarify** Scholars outline the content of the Letter to the Hebrews differently. One way is to divide it into two major parts: (1) *exposition* (Christ's person, high priesthood, covenant, and sacrifice) and (2) *exhortation* (encouraging the persecuted priests).

▶ **Notebook** Develop the following diagram for entry in student notebooks.

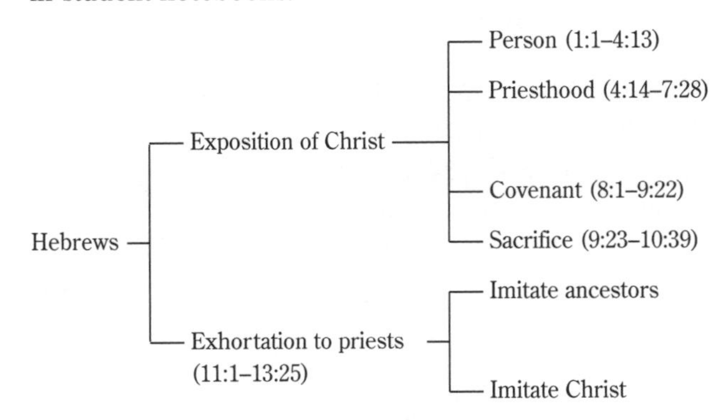

The exhortation section of the letter is riddled with repetitious expressions:

"So let us"	10:22	"It was faith"	11:4
"Let us"	10:23	"It was faith"	11:5
"Let us"	10:24	"It was faith"	11:7
"Let us"	10:25a	"It was faith"	11:8
"Instead, let us"	10:25b	"It was faith"	11:11

This repetitious style, along with the letter's use of the Old Testament (1:4–4:11), prompts some scholars to suggest that Hebrews was originally a homily. They also suggest that the ending, more in the style of a letter, was added later as a kind of personal note by the author.

Point ❹ **Clarify** Scholars engage in a guessing game concerning the author of Hebrews. Candidates range from Paul himself to Jude to Barnabas. (The argument against Pauline authorship is that it is totally different from other Pauline letters in terms of style, tone, and content.)

Use this guessing game as an opportunity to review an important point about the authorship of New Testament books.

An apostle's name attached to a book
may indicate no more than
that he gave it his approval, or simply
that it is the written form of his personal teaching.
Roderick A. F. MacKenzie, *Introduction to the New Testament*

A modern example illustrates. The president of the United States rarely writes his own official documents. He simply approves what someone else wrote under his direction. So, too, the pope and other leaders do the same thing. Concerning this point, John L. McKenzie reminds us that New Testament letters were almost always penned by a scribe. He says:

It appears
that word-for-word dictation was extremely rare;
the scribe was given instructions
and perhaps an outline.
The part of the scribe in the composition
of the New Testament epistles [letters]
was thus considerable, since the literary formulation
was principally his work.

Point ❺ **Clarify** Hebrews concludes with an exhortation to the Hebrews to imitate the faith of their ancestors. Use this as an opportunity to remind the students that faith does not preclude questioning. Recall the two kinds of faith questioning:

Faith questioning		
	Constructive	Search for truth
	Destructive	Desire to prove false

Stress that faith questioning, if done constructively, is healthy and leads to faith maturity. How so?

First, it *produces faith clarity.* For example, we may have had immature ideas about God. After questioning, we see God in a much more mature way.

Second, it *purifies faith motives.* Take the case of God, again. Before our questioning, we may have motivated to pray because our parents told us to. After questioning, we do so because *we* want to.

Third, it *deepens faith commitment.* Take the case of God, once again. Before questioning, we may have prayed in a "mechanical way"—out of habit. After questioning, we pray in a "personal way"—out of love.

Finally, it *widens faith horizons.* Before questioning, we may have thought that evolution contradicted what the Bible said. After questioning, we discover that it does not.

► **Notebook** Develop the following summary of how constructive questioning can lead to a more mature faith.

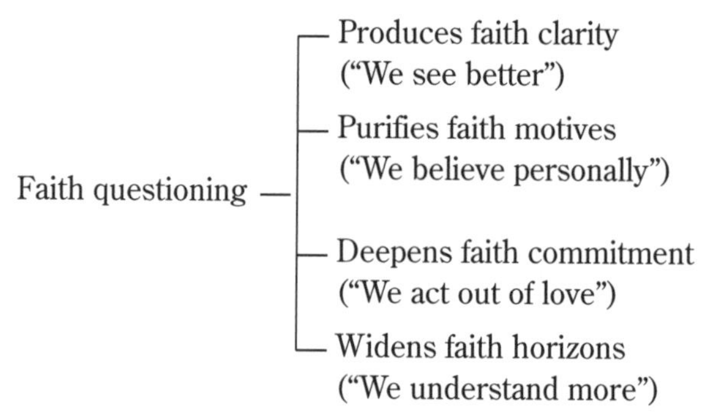

Like a fractured arm, a fractured faith can grow back even stronger after a period of constructive faith questioning.

5. LESSON INTERACTION

Exercise ❶ **Discuss** This exercise focuses on temptation, such as that experienced by the recipients of the Letter to the Hebrews as a result of being persecuted. Temptation goes with the territory of being human.

Exercise ❷ **Discuss** This exercise takes up two questions that many students experience but frequently do not face up to. Be understanding and gentle.

Exercise ❸ **Discuss** Hebrews quotes God as saying of God's people, "The days are coming" when "I will forgive their sins and will no longer remember their wrongs" (8:8, 12). In this day of divided homes and child abuse, students need to discuss forgiveness of their parents.

Miniposter **Discuss** Direct students' attention to the poster quote. Ask: What point does it make? (It focuses on lack of faith and trust. To some extent we all lack faith and trust in God. We need a "push" from God—in the form of some tragedy or crisis, which gives us no other option but to trust.)

Seven Messages

LESSON **111**

1. LESSON BACKGROUND

► *Catechism of the Catholic Church,* 1427–1433.

2. LESSON QUIZ

Perfect score = 12 points

1. What two specific recommendations did the Letter to the Hebrews make to its recipients? *(Lesson 110 review—2 points)*
2. List and briefly explain four ways that constructive faith questioning leads to a more mature faith. *(Lesson 110 notebook review—8 points)*
3. Briefly explain the twofold format that each of the messages to the seven churches followed. *(Lesson 111 preview—2 points)*

3. LESSON HOMEWORK

► **Return** Lesson 110 review questions (page 229).

► **Collect** Lesson 111 review questions (page 231).

► **Read** Lesson 112 ("Preview Visions," pages 232–33).

► **Write** Lesson 112 review questions (page 233).

► **Appoint** Student to prepare Revelation 21:12–14 (lesson 112, exercise 1).

4. LESSON PRESENTATION

Point 1 **Read** Have volunteers read aloud the core content of lesson 111.

► **Notebook** The following diagram summarizes the key points about the "prologue" vision that sets the stage for the panorama of visions that are to follow. Have the students enter the diagram in their notebooks.

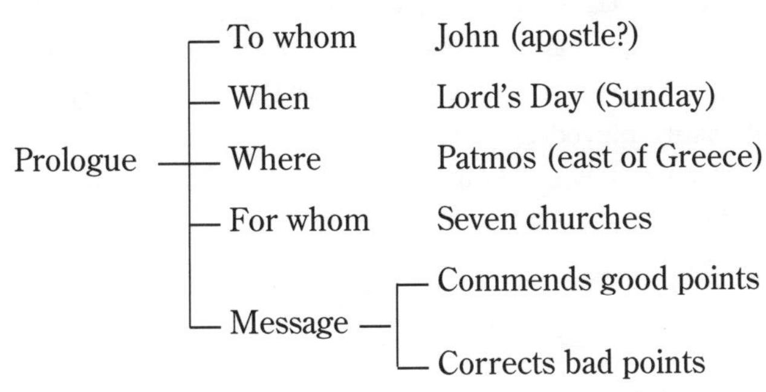

► **Discuss** Call special attention to the excerpt from the message to the church in Smyrna. It is an excellent summary of the overriding theme of the Book of Revelation:

"Be faithful to me . . . and I will give you life."

Ask: Why does God permit Satan to "test" us? (Read 1 Peter 1:6–7: "Be glad . . . of the many kinds of trials you suffer. Their purpose is to prove that your faith is genuine. Even gold, which can be destroyed, is tested by fire; and so your faith, which is much more precious than gold, must also be tested, so that it may endure."

Ask: How do you explain Peter's words? (Trials and temptations reveal our weaknesses. The awareness of weakness invites us to open ourselves more to God's grace. For only by God's grace can trials and temptations be overcome.)

Ralph Waldo Emerson offers another reason why God permits us to be tempted:

As the Sandwich Islander believes
that the strength and the valor of the enemy he kills
passes into himself, so we gain strength
from the temptations we resist.

Point 2 **Notebook** The following diagram summarizes the general format or outline of the Book of Revelation. Have the students enter it in their notebooks.

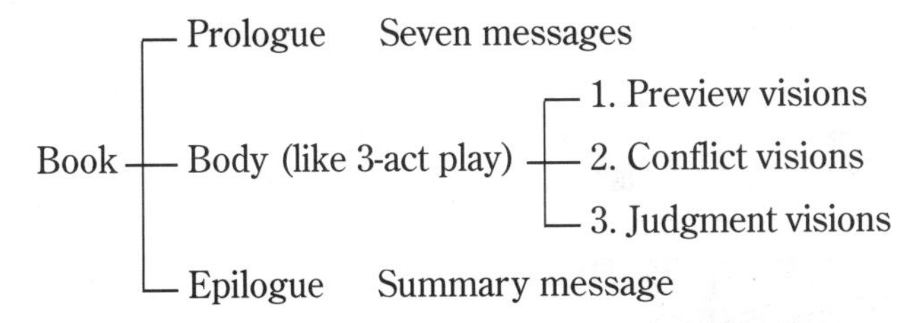

Point 3 **Clarify** Strictly speaking, the Book of Revelation contains no new revelation. It spotlights and dramatizes well-known revelations, including:

- unity of Christ with his Church and
- reward and punishment after death.

► **Notebook** One revelation is Christ's unity with his Church. This is illustrated in a variety of ways. Have the students list them in their notebooks.

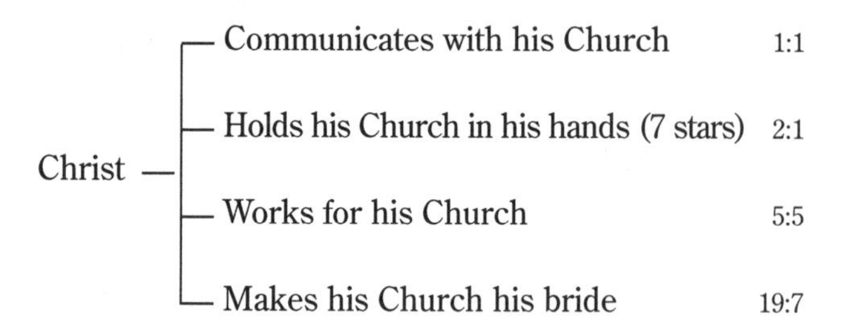

▶ **Notebook** A second revelation that is spotlighted is the final judgment, involving reward and punishment. Have the students enter the diagram in their notebooks.

Final judgment —
- Punishment for evil 20:11–15
- Reward for good 21:1–4

5. LESSON INTERACTION

Exercise 1 **Discuss** **(a)** Lewis's remark stresses his "freedom" to do whatever he wished.

(b, c) Lewis stresses that there was no "pressure" put upon him in any way, positively or negatively. He was in total, unpressured control.

(d) Lewis's remark that to open the door meant the "incalculable" is evidence that he was well aware that if he opened the door, his whole life could change in ways he had never dreamed of.

Exercise 2 **Discuss** **(a, b, c)** A good way to begin this exercise is to have a "class secretary" list on the chalkboard suggestions from the students concerning doors that they might be keeping shut (forgiving someone, stopping smoking, studying harder, and so on).

After a list has been compiled, have the students pick out one item and respond to questions *b* and *c* in writing. Have volunteers share their responses and engage in a discussion of them with the class.

Exercise 3 **Discuss** This exercise is self-explanatory.

Exercise 4 **Discuss** **(a)** Have the appointed student read aloud Revelation 2:1–7.

Compliments: You have (1) worked hard, (2) suffered patiently, (3) refused to tolerate evil, (4) guarded against false teachers, (5) persevered in the faith and not given up, (6) hated what the Nicolaitans do (it is not clear what is meant here; some suggest they distort the Gospel to their own ends).

Criticisms: You have (1) cooled in your love, (2) failed to turn away from sin.

(b) *Warning:* If you do not repent, your community of faith will cease. *Promise:* If you repent, you will receive eternal life ("fruit of the tree of life").

(c) Instruct the students to be as realistic and honest as they can be in their letter to their parish. If it seems more appropriate, they could write the letter to the student body of the school. They should follow the format of the "seven messages": (1) introduction, (2) commendations, (3) criticisms, (4) warning, (5) promise.

▶ **Clarify** You might wish to share the following letter of a student to her parish.

This is the message from one who has lived in St. Anne's parish all her life. I feel guilty writing this letter, because I have not been involved that deeply in parish activities. Hopefully, this letter will motivate me to take steps to correct this failure.

I want to commend our parish for its programs to help the poor. I also want to commend those who lector, sing in the choir, usher, or serve as eucharistic ministers.

I do have some suggestions. I think the eucharistic ministers could smile slightly when giving out the Body and Blood of Christ. They look so severe. I also wish the choir sang songs we all know. Choirs are supposed to lead us in song, not perform for us. Finally, I'd like for our parish to develop more projects for young people—like going with the eucharistic ministers to retirement homes and prisons. Also, we could use more lock-ins and things like that.

I promise you that if our parish works at these things, it will attract more young people like myself. I warn you, however, that if we don't, the work of Jesus will be hurt.

Forgive me for being so bold, but I do want to be a part of something that is helping to change our world.

Collect, screen, and share the better letters.

Photo **Discuss** Direct attention to Dali's painting on page 230. Ask: Why do you think Dali (1904–1989) titled his painting as he did? (The watches, limp with age, and the bizarre objects probably played a part. The painting reminds us of a dream vaguely remembered.)

Ask: Does such a dream persist in your memory?

CHAPTER TWENTY-TWO: Revelation (pages 232–33)

Preview Visions

LESSON **112**

1. LESSON BACKGROUND

▶ *Catechism of the Catholic Church,* 1373–1381.

2. LESSON QUIZ

Perfect score = 5 points

1. The Book of Revelation begins with a vision of Jesus dictating seven messages to seven churches. What suffering did each of the churches have in common? *(Lesson 111 review—1 point)*
2. The main visions of the Book of Revelation may be thought of as a stage play made up of three acts. List the name we give to the visions in each of these three acts. *(Lesson 111 notebook review—3 points)*
3. Who is found worthy to break the seven seals? *(Lesson 112 preview—1 point)*

3. LESSON HOMEWORK

▶ **Return** Lesson 111 review questions (page 231).

▶ **Collect** Lesson 112 review questions (page 233).

▶ **Read** Lesson 113 ("Conflict Visions," pages 234–35).

▶ **Write** Lesson 113 review questions (page 235).

▶ **Appoint** Two students to prepare Exodus 2:1–10 and Matthew 2:13–15 (lesson 113, exercise 1).

4. LESSON PRESENTATION

Point 1 **Read** Have volunteers read aloud the core content of lesson 112.

▶ **Discuss** Ask: What number appears to be very popular with the author of the Book of Revelation? (Seven—it is the biblical number for "fullness," or "completeness." The number is also popular outside the Bible.)

Ask: What are some examples of things that occur in sevens? (Seven continents, seven seas, seven sacraments, seven days of the week, seven wonders of the world, seven dwarfs [Snow White])

▶ **Notebook** Have the students enter in their notebooks this expanded outline of the Book of Revelation.

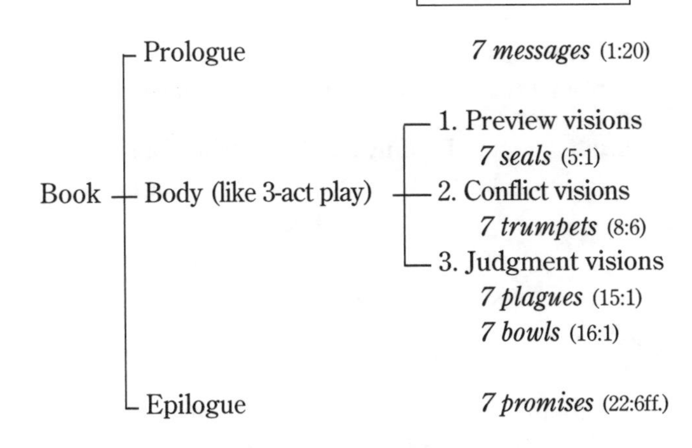

▶ **Clarify** Some Bible readers see the Epilogue of Revelation (22:6–21) as being made up of "seven promises." Though these "promises" are not stated explicitly as such in the book, some readers see them present as follows: verses 7 (two), 12 (two), 14 (one), 17 (one), 20 (one). In any event, they do make a fitting epilogue to the book.

Point 2 **Discuss** John's reference to "a Lamb standing in the center of the throne" is the first of nearly thirty "Lamb" references in the Book of Revelation.

Direct students' attention to the photograph of the mosaic (small chunks of marble mortared together to form a painting) on page 232. Have them answer the question posed in the caption: Why is the Lamb an ideal eucharistic symbol?

▶ **Notebook** Review the following diagram (from lesson 76) summarizing the similarity between the old Passover meal and the new Passover meal (Eucharist).

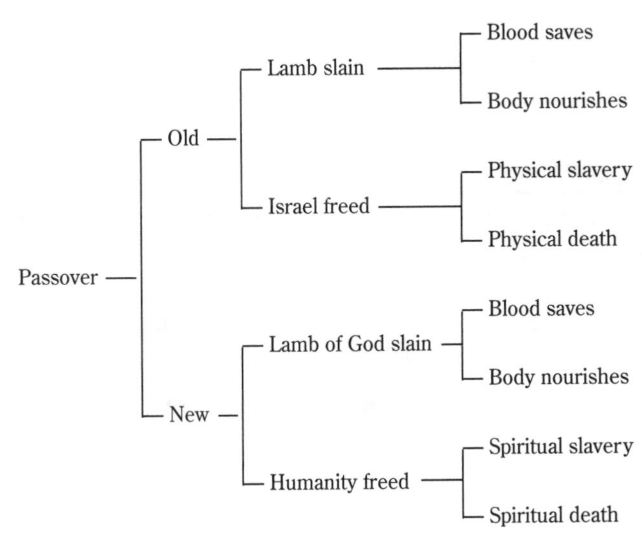

Discuss Recall that John the Baptist identified Jesus as "the Lamb of God, who takes away the sin of the world!" (John 1:29). Ask: Where is that phrase used in the Liturgy of the Eucharist? (Just before Communion)

The symbol of the blood flowing from the lamb into a cup (mosaic) is spelled out by Paul in 1 Corinthians 10:16: "The cup we use in the Lord's Supper . . . when we drink from it, we are sharing in the blood of Christ."

Discuss Ask: Identify and explain four other eucharistic symbols in the mosaic. (They are as follows:)

1. *Loaves and fishes.* Recall John 6:9, where Jesus took "five loaves of barley bread and two fish" and fed five thousand people. The next day, Jesus said to the people who came looking for him:

   "You are looking for me
   because you ate the bread and had all you wanted,
   not because you understood my miracles. . . .
   I am the living bread that came down from heaven.
   If you eat this bread, you will live forever.
   The bread that I will give you is my flesh. . . ."
   This started an angry argument among them.
   "How can this man give us his flesh to eat?" . . .
   Jesus said to them, "I am telling you the truth:
   if you do not eat the flesh of the Son of Man
   and drink his blood, you will not have life."
   John 6:26, 51–53

2. *Six water jars.* Recall the marriage feast in Cana, where the "stone water jars" (John 2:6) were filled with water that was transformed into wine. This miracle prefigured the Eucharist, where Jesus would transform wine into his own blood (1 Corinthians 11:25–27).
3. *Wheat and grapes.* Just as wheat is planted and "multiplies," so vines are planted, draw water from the soil, and turn the grapes into eucharistic wine.
4. *Pelican* (bottom center). Medieval folklore held that the pelican fed its young with its own blood. This explains how it came to symbolize Jesus and the Eucharist. (See the miniposter on page 156. Also see the photo and caption on page 157 for a biblical overview of the Eucharist *prefigured* at Cana, *promised* in Capernaum, *instituted* at the Last Supper, and *celebrated* at Emmaus.)

Point ❸ **Notebook** Develop the following diagram on the chalkboard. It summarizes the revelations of the first four seals, "preview visions" of what is to come. Ask: How do the riders and colors symbolize victory, and so on?

4 horsemen	Wearing crown, white horse	Victory
	Carrying sword, red horse	Conflict
	Carrying scale, black horse	Judgment
	Named death, greenish horse	Evil's fate

Discuss Some of your sports buffs might bring up the four horsemen of Notre Dame of 1925. They were Knute Rochne's famous backfield: Stuhldreher, Miller, Crowley, Layden.

5. LESSON INTERACTION

Exercise ❶ **Discuss** Have the students write out the four responses to this exercise privately. Then have volunteers give their responses and explanations.

The probable answers are **(a)** Christ, **(b)** God the Father, **(c)** the four evangelists (see lesson 55, exercise 4, and photo on page 117). **(d)** Have the appointed student read Revelation 21:12–14 to provide the clue for this response, which is the twelve sons of Jacob ("twelve tribes of the people of Israel") and the "twelve apostles of the Lamb [Jesus]."

Exercises ❷ & ❸ **Discuss** These two exercises are self-explanatory.

Photo **Discuss** Direct attention to the photo and caption on page 233. Take time to introduce the students to one of the greatest pieces of architecture of its kind.

Chartres is about a thirty-minute ride southwest of Paris. The cathedral, built over seven hundred fifty years ago, is nearly a hundred feet longer than a football field and rises the same distance into the air.

Remarkably, the cathedral contains over eighteen hundred stone statues. Called a "poor man's Bible" in stone, it depicts the entire biblical story. In the days before radio and television, families packed a lunch and spent Sunday afternoon walking around it and reliving every significant event from Genesis to Revelation.

The artists used a regular code for identifying the biblical characters. For example, God, Jesus, and the apostles are always shown without shoes or sandals. Peter always has a crop of fuzzy hair. Paul is always bald with a long beard.

The cathedral also contains two hundred magnificent stained-glass windows. During World War II, the people of Chartres removed the priceless windows, piece by piece, numbering them, packing them carefully in crates, and burying them until the bombing was over.

After the war, the people dug the windows up, uncrated them, and put them back in the exact pattern and place they originally had. To see what a task this was, see the stained-glass window in the miniposter on page 174. (The window is not from Chartres, but it gives an idea of the work involved.) Each window contained hundreds, even thousands of small chunks of glass, leaded together.

Chapter Twenty-two: Revelation (pages 234–35)

Conflict Visions

LESSON 113

1. LESSON BACKGROUND

▶ *Catechism of the Catholic Church*, 391–395.

2. LESSON QUIZ

Perfect score = 10 points

1. List the three things that set the stage for the conflict visions. *(Lesson 112 review—3 points)*
2. Match the left-hand column with the correct answer in the right-hand column.
   __ conflict *a.* black horse + scale
   __ victory *b.* red horse + sword
   __ judgment *c.* white horse + crowned rider
   __ fate of evil *d.* pale green horse + rider named Death and Hades
   (Lesson 112 notebook review—4 points)
3. List (a) one suggestion about whom "666" stands for and (b) two suggestions about the identity of the "mysterious woman dressed in the sun." *(Lesson 113 preview—3 points)*

3. LESSON HOMEWORK

▶ **Return** Lesson 112 review questions (page 233).

▶ **Collect** Lesson 113 review questions (page 235).

▶ **Read** Lesson 114 ("Judgment Visions," pages 236–37).

▶ **Write** Lesson 114 review questions (page 237).

4. LESSON PRESENTATION

Point ① **Read** Have volunteers read aloud the core content of lesson 113.

▶ **Clarify** Be sure the students see the parallel between the series of catastrophes described here and the plagues of ancient Egypt. Both are signs of God's intervention to save God's people. They also serve as instruments to try to get evil people to reform their ways, but the evil people remain obstinate.

▶ **Clarify** Stress the point, also, that just as the infant Moses was saved from the Egyptians and the infant Jesus was saved from Herod, so the infant Church is saved from the dragon, who seeks to destroy it.

Point ② **Clarify** Read the reference to Emperor Nero in Revelation 13:15–18:

The second beast was allowed
to breathe life into the image of the first beast,
so that the image could talk and put to death
all those who would not worship it.

The beast forced all the people,
small and great, rich and poor, slave and free,
to have a mark placed on their right hands
or on their foreheads.
No one could buy or sell without this mark,
that is, the beast's name
or the number that stands for the name.

This calls for wisdom.
Whoever is intelligent can figure out
the meaning of the number of the beast,
because the number
stands for the name of someone.
Its number is 666.

The key to understanding this passage is to realize that ancients attached numerical values to their letters.

Ask: What is the numerical value of the following Romans numerals: I, V, X, L, C? (I = 1, V = 5, X = 10, L = 50, C = 100)

Ask: Where do Roman numerals appear on a dollar bill? (Reverse side, base of pyramid)

▶ **Clarify** Ancient Jews also had a numbering system that involved the use of letters. The number 666 derives from the ancient Jewish numbering system. Jean-Louis D'Aragon explains 666 this way:

The most widely accepted theory identifies 666 with Nero Caesar, written nrwn qsr *in Hebrew (= 50 + 200 + 6 + 50 + 100 + 60 + 200). . . . Nero fits the context, for he was the first emperor to persecute the Christians; he embodied all the worst characteristics of the Beast.*

Point ③ **Discuss** Review the persecution of the Christians under Nero in 64 C.E. Tacitus (ca. 110) informs his readers that the Christians took their name from Christ, "who was executed during Tiberius's reign by sentence of Pontius Pilate." He continues (read to the students):

First, known members of the sect were seized.
Then, on their information, crowds were seized,
not so much on arson charges as out of hate. . . .

Although the sect deserved some punishment,
a feeling of pity developed for them.
For it seemed clear to many
that they were executed not for the state's sake,
but because of the madness of one man.

▶ **Clarify** We sometimes hear the expression, "Nero fiddled while Rome burned." There is some basis, at least, for the expression.

Nero was a musician of sorts. He left Rome in 68 C.E. to sing at some Greek festivals. When he returned, the political situation in Rome was in shambles. This, along with other problems, prompted Nero to commit suicide at the age of thirty-one.

Violence was nothing new to Nero. He was responsible for having his ex-wife and his stepson executed earlier in his reign.

Nero became emperor when he was quite young, hence his fourteen-year reign in spite of his early death. He was the "last of the Caesars" to rule Rome.

▶ **Notebook** For ready reference have the students work up the following diagram for entry in their notebooks. The diagram gives the dates of the reign of each Roman emperor, along with biblical references to the emperors (Augustus, Tiberius, and Claudius are mentioned directly; Nero, indirectly—"666"; Caligula is omitted). The diagram also lists key events that took place within the reign of each emperor.

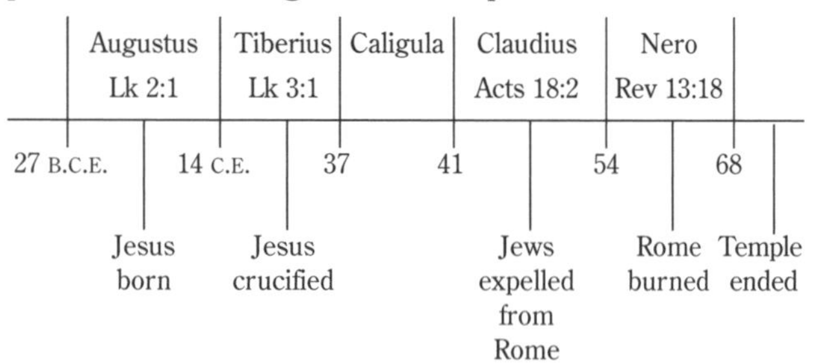

▶ **Clarify** The following Roman emperors followed Nero: Vespasian (69–79), Titus (79–81), Domitian (81–96), Nerva (96–98), and Trajan (98–117).

5. LESSON INTERACTION

Exercise ❶ **Discuss** **(a)** Have the appointed students read Exodus 2:1–10 (how Moses is saved from the Egyptians) and Matthew 2:13–15 (how Jesus is saved from the Romans).

(b) The infant son of the "mysterious woman dressed in the sun" is saved from an early, violent death, as were the infant Moses and the infant Jesus. Assuming the woman symbolizes Israel, the "infant son" is the "infant church." Revelation 12:5–9 reads:

Then she gave birth to a son. . . . But the child was
snatched away and taken to God and his throne.
The woman fled to the desert. . . .
Then war broke out in heaven.
Michael and his angels fought against the dragon,
who fought back with his angels;
but the dragon was defeated, and he and his angels
were not allowed to stay in heaven any longer.
The huge dragon was thrown out—
that ancient serpent, named the Devil, or Satan,
that deceived the whole world.
He was thrown down to earth,
and all his angels with him.

Exercise ❷ **Clarify** Recall the explanation of 666 and review the background on Nero, as appropriate, in preparation for the discussion questions.

The students should not have a great deal of difficulty discussing these questions. Questions *a, b,* and *c* set up the final question, which is the "hot button" in the discussion: "Why do/don't you think such atrocities are possible in our own country today?"

The Branch Davidian episode in 1993, the Oklahoma City bombing in 1995, and the "militia movement" should come up in the discussion.

Exercise ❸ **Discuss** This exercise may be a bit difficult for students. You may simply pick out one example and read the passages cited. Take the "seven eyes" example.

Revelation 5:6 says: "The Lamb appeared to have been killed. It had seven horns and seven eyes" ["fullness" of power (horns) and knowledge (eyes)].

Zechariah 4:10 says: "The angel said to me, 'The seven lamps are the seven eyes of the LORD, which see all over the earth.'"

Photo **Notebook** Direct attention to the photo and caption on page 234. Have the students develop this diagram summary of the painting symbolism.

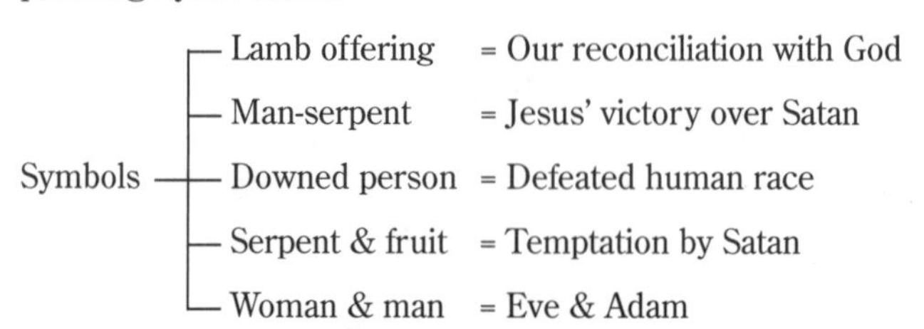

Judgment Visions

LESSON 114

1. LESSON BACKGROUND

▶ *Catechism of the Catholic Church*, 675–679.

2. LESSON QUIZ

Perfect score = 10 points

1. Describe how the start of the "conflict visions" parallels the start of Israel's flight to freedom in Egypt. *(Lesson 113 review—1 point)*
2. Name (a) three Roman emperors and (b) a key event that took place during the reign of each one. *(Lesson 113 notebook review—6 points)*
3. Explain the meaning of (a) the dragon, (b) seven horns, (c) seven eyes. *(Lesson 114 preview—3 points)*

3. LESSON HOMEWORK

▶ **Return** Lesson 113 review questions (page 235).

▶ **Collect** Lesson 114 review questions (page 237).

▶ **Read** Lesson 115 ("Interpreting Revelation," pages 238–39).

▶ **Write** Lesson 115 review questions (page 239).

4. LESSON PRESENTATION

Point 1 **Read** Have volunteers read aloud the core content of lesson 114.

▶ **Clarify** *Armageddon* means "Mount Megiddo." Megiddo was the scene of several decisive biblical battles (for example, Judges 5:19). It is symbolically portrayed as being the site of the decisive battle between "the kings of the earth" and the "king of kings" (Revelation 19:19).

The battle ends swiftly. Then an angel appears from heaven, seizes the dragon (Satan), and confines him for a "thousand years."

Finally, the souls of the just, who had suffered the "first death" (bodily death), are *raised from the dead* to rule with Christ for the millennium. "The rest of the dead did not come to life until the thousand years were over" (20:5). John comments:

This is the first raising of the dead. . . .
The second death [eternal death]
has no power over them. 20:5–6

After the thousand years are over, Satan is freed from his confinement and leads a final assault against the forces of good. He is defeated and thrown into the lake of fire ("second death").

▶ **Notebook** Develop the following diagram of the sequence of events for entry in student notebooks.

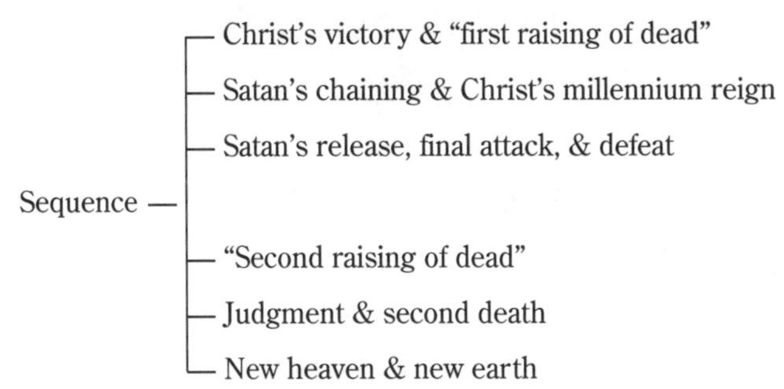

5. LESSON INTERACTION

Exercise 1 **Review** Have the students turn to lesson 49 and read aloud the introductory matter to exercise 3 (page 103). It explains and illustrates the difference between the two types of "symbol writing" found in the Bible: *apocalyptic* and *prophetic*.

▶ **Notebook** Summarize the main differences between prophetic and apocalyptic writing for entry in student notebooks.

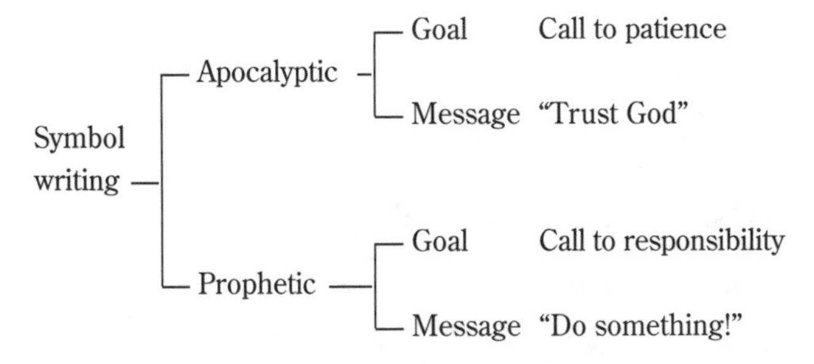

▶ **Clarify** *Newsweek* magazine (November 23, 1992) carried this chilling headline: "How the World Might End."

It reported that a mountain-sized object, called Swift-Tuttle (named for the two astronomers who first spotted it in the 1800s) was streaking toward Earth with blinding speed. It could hit in the twenty-first century with a speed one hundred times that of a bullet and with a heat that would vaporize rock and wipe out all human life.

A half-mile asteroid missed Earth in 1989. "No one saw it coming; if it had arrived a mere six hours later," said *Newsweek*, "it would have wiped out all civilization." The magazine went on to say that "space is filled with objects that threaten Earth." For example, it noted:

Thousands of meteorites the size of a lump of coal
fall every year, usually harmlessly.
But one smashed through a garage roof
in Illinois in 1938, and another totaled a car
in a New York City suburb last month.

▶ **Clarify** For a discussion of Jesus' teaching about the end of the world, refer the students to lesson 72. The parable of the ten young women embodies the heart of Jesus' teaching.

The parable describes ten young women. Five are wise and have a full supply of oil. Five are foolish and have only a small supply of oil. When the bridegroom delays in coming, the young women fall asleep. At midnight, they are awakened by the shout, "Here is the bridegroom!"

The foolish women discover, to their dismay, that their oil is used up. Since the supply of the wise women is low, the foolish women are forced to go off to get more oil. While they are gone, the groom arrives.

The five who were ready
went in with him to the wedding feast,
and the door was closed. Matthew 25:10

▶ **Notebook** Review the imagery and point of this important parable. Begin by having the students list the following images from the parable in their notebooks.

Parable Images

1. Groom
2. Wise young women
3. Foolish young women
4. Oil in the lamps
5. Groom's coming
6. Wedding feast

Next, have the students explain the parable images. (Who/what do they refer to in real life?) List them in the right-hand column opposite the parable image.

Parable Images	Real Life
1. Groom	Jesus
2. Wise young women	Prepared Christians
3. Foolish young women	Unprepared Christians
4. Groom's coming	Jesus' Second Coming
5. Oil in lamps	Good works
6. Wedding feast	Heaven

▶ **Clarify** The "oil in the lamps" needs clarification. Elsewhere in the Bible, oil is a symbol of good works. For example, Jesus says in his Sermon on the Mount:

"No one lights a lamp and puts it under a bowl;
instead it is put on the lampstand,
where it gives light for everyone in the house.
In the same way your light must shine before people,
so that they will see the good things you do
and praise your Father in heaven." Matthew 5:15–16

▶ **Clarify** The point of the parable is this: We must be prepared for Jesus' coming at the end of the world or at the end of our personal lives—whichever event comes first.

Exercise ❷ **Clarify** Early Christians did not have to puzzle out the symbolism used in the Book of Revelation. They came by it gradually from hearing the Scriptures read, especially the books of the prophets. In other words, they learned the symbolism almost like a second language.

▶ **Discuss** (a) Refer the students to the excerpt of the message to the church in Smyrna (page 230). It is a good statement of the *general* message of Revelation:

"This is the message from the one . . .
who died and lived again. . . .
The devil will put you to the test. . . .
Be faithful to me . . . and I will give you life
as your prize of victory." Revelation 2:8, 10

Photo **Discuss** Direct attention to the photo and caption on page 237. Have the students answer the question posed in the caption. The responses are:

3:4	Those clothed in white who walk with Jesus
5:1	Scroll with seven seals
7:1	Four angels at earth's four corners
5:6	Lamb that appeared to have been killed
11:15	Angel blowing seventh trumpet
14:14	Gold crown on one seated on cloud
14:3	The 144,000 people

3:4	5:6	11:15
5:1		
7:1	14:14	14:3

CHAPTER TWENTY-TWO: Revelation (pages 238–39)

Interpreting Revelation

LESSON **115**

1. LESSON BACKGROUND

▶ *Catechism of the Catholic Church,* 1038–1050.

2. LESSON QUIZ

Perfect score = 10 points

1. Explain the meaning of (a) Armageddon and (b) the book of life. *(Lesson 114 review—2 points)*
2. List the goals of apocalyptic and prophetic writing. *(Lesson 114 notebook review—2 points)*
3. List and briefly explain the three approaches to interpreting the Book of Revelation that have emerged over the centuries. *(Lesson 115 preview—6 points)*

3. LESSON HOMEWORK

▶ **Return** Lesson 114 review questions (page 237).

▶ **Collect** Lesson 115 review questions (page 239).

4. LESSON PRESENTATION

Point 1 **Read** Have volunteers read aloud the core content of lesson 115.

▶ **Notebook** Develop the following diagram on the chalkboard for entry in student notebooks. It summarizes the three different interpretations given to the Book of Revelations over the years.

- 3 approaches
  - Early history
    - Guide to Christians of early times
    - Stay faithful! Christ won; so will you.
  - Sweep of history
    - Guide to Christians of all times
    - Persevere! God's plan is on track.
  - End of history
    - Guide to Christians of end times
    - Behold the Son of Man! Your salvation is near.

▶ **Clarify** Stress the final sentence of the section: "Perhaps the best approach is to realize that the Book of Revelation, as the inspired word of God, has a message for every Christian—regardless of time or place."

▶ **Review** Recall the "five Christs" in lesson 84 of the Resource Manual (fanciful, historical, teacher, savior, indwelling). Recall how we compared these "five Christs" to the five growth stages of a plant (seed, stem, bud, flower, fruit).

▶ **Activity** List on the chalkboard the two columns below. Have the students match the five stages in God's plan of salvation (right column) with the appropriate growth stages of a plant (left column).

1. __ Fruit	*a.* Jesus (Promised Messiah)
2. __ Bloom	*b.* Jesus' followers (Church)
3. __ Bud	*c.* Abraham
4. __ Stem	*d.* God's kingdom (heaven))
5. __ Seed	*e.* Jews (Chosen people)

Answers: 1 = d, 2 = b, 3 = a, 4 = e, 5 = c

▶ **Notebook** Develop the following diagram on the chalkboard for entry in student notebooks.

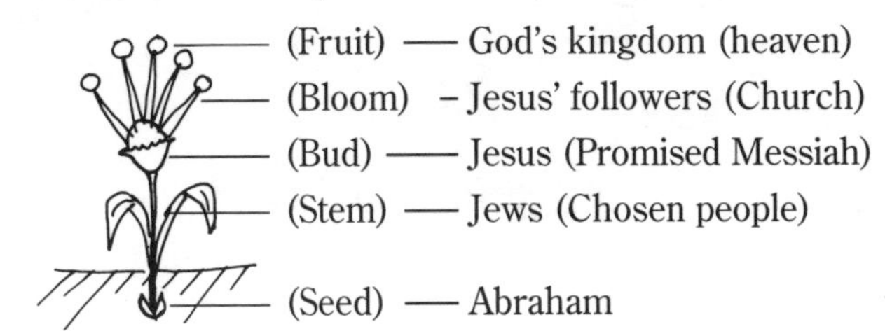

5. LESSON INTERACTION

Exercise 1 **Discuss** **(a)** Like the early Christians, the black slaves of early America were hanging on to hope solely on the basis of their faith in Jesus and his promises—especially in the Book of Revelation. The key paragraph to stress is the following:

Only because they knew
that Christ was present with them
and that his presence included
the divine promise to come again
and to take them to the New Jerusalem.

A parallel example to that of the black slaves is an episode that occurred during World War II.

The film *The Bridge over the River Kwai* immortalized the Kwa Noi River in Thailand. Along its banks, twelve thousand POWs died of disease, starvation, and brutality while building a railroad during World War II.

Working in heat that sometimes hit 120 degrees, husky men became walking skeletons in weeks. Morale hit zero. Something had to be done about the Kwa Noi situation. And something was done.

Two prisoners organized Bible study groups. Reading the Bible and sharing their faith transformed the camp beyond belief. Ernest Gordon recalls this transformation in his book *Through the Valley of the Kwai.*

I was hobbling back to my shack
after a rather late discussion session.
Passing one of the huts . . . I heard
the sound of men . . . singing "Jerusalem the Golden." . . .
The words of the grand old hymn . . .
made the darkness seem friendly. . . .
The difference between this joyful sound
and the joyless stillness of months past
was the difference between life and death. . . .
The resurgence of life increased.
It grew and leavened the whole camp.

It was the author's good fortune to meet a British soldier who was in the camp during the time of transformation. He said the transformation of that camp was the most amazing thing he ever witnessed.

Ask: Do you think the situation in our world could be transformed if small groups of people would begin to do what the prisoners of the camp did? Explain.

Discuss **(b)** During the 1984 presidential debates, at the height of the Cold War between Russia and the United States, NBC's Marvin Kalb asked Ronald Reagan if he thought the world might be heading toward a "nuclear Armageddon." Reagan said yes, he had entertained such thoughts.

Many people were shocked to think that a president had given serious consideration to a biblical position that reputable biblical scholars universally reject. Espoused by certain fringe TV evangelists, it holds that the Book of Revelation should be interpreted as referring specifically to the two nuclear powers of the '80s: the United States and the Soviet Union.

The Reagan-Kalb exchange brought a storm of protests from the wider Christian community. Among other reasons, it created the climate for a nuclear arms race (leading to a final showdown at Armageddon between two nuclear giants).

A typical scenario of these fringe evangelists begins with "the rapture," which they base on 1 Thessalonians 4:16–18. There Paul responds to Thessalonian converts who thought Jesus' Second Coming was just around the corner. When their loved ones died, therefore, these converts grew concerned the dead would be deprived of being with Christ forever. Paul uses colorful imagery (that they can understand) to assure them this is not the case.

The Lord himself will come down from heaven.
Those who have died believing in Christ
will rise to life first;
then we who are living at that time
will be gathered up along with them in the clouds
to meet the Lord in the air.

The words "gathered up" translate the Latin word *rapiemur,* which literally means "to snatch up." The English phrase "the rapture" is derived from this Latin word. It is then combined with Luke 17:34 ("There will be two people sleeping in the same bed; one will be taken away, the other will be left behind") to give rise to the concept of "the rapture" as preached by many TV preachers.

According to these preachers, the rapture will be followed by a period of worldwide tribulation. Emerging from this period will be the Antichrist. Then Christ and his army of "raptured saints" will return to earth to battle the Antichrist and his army. The final battle will take place at Armageddon. The victory of Christ and the raptured saints will usher in a thousand years of peace (Revelation 20:1–10). This millennium will be followed by the Last Judgment.

These evangelists fed the arms race of the '80s by advocating that the United States arm itself to the full to protect "true Christians" until they are "raptured out of danger" by Christ.

The Catholic view of the end of the world is summed up in Jesus' words: "No one knows, however, when that day and hour will come . . . ; the Father alone knows" (Matthew 24:36).

Nor do Catholics pretend to know how the end will take place. They interpret descriptions of it ("the sun will grow dark, the moon will no longer shine" [Matthew 24:29]) as following the traditional practice of Old Testament prophets, who described catastrophic events in apocalyptic terms, as we have seen.

Exercise 2

Discuss **(a)** The poet's point is that life on earth is a preparation for a more important life to come.

Activity **(b)** The prayer should include the idea that if we are faithful now, we will be victorious later.

REFERENCE NOTES

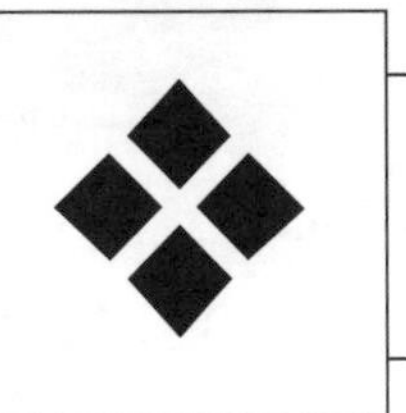

Lesson 4

Louis F. Hartman, *Encyclopedic Dictionary of the Bible* (New York: McGraw-Hill Book Co., 1963), p. 2166.

Lesson 7

John A. Hardon, *The Protestant Churches of America* (Westminster, Md.: Newman Press, 1957), pp. 227–28.

Lesson 8

Ted Howard and Jeremy Rifkin, *Who Should Play God?* (New York: Delacorte Press, 1977), pp. 117–18.

Lesson 9

Robert Jastrow, *God and the Astronomers* (New York: W. W. Norton, 1978).

Lesson 10

John L. McKenzie, *Dictionary of the Bible* (New York: Macmillan, 1965), pp. 935–36.

Richard P. McBrien, *Catholicism* (San Francisco: Harper & Row, 1981).

Lee Salk, *My Father, My Son* (New York: G. P. Putnam's Sons, 1982).

Lesson 13

John R. Connery, "Sin, Sickness and Psychiatry," *America* (January 23, 1960).

Thomas Merton, *The Seven Storey Mountain* (New York: Harcourt Brace & Co., 1948).

Lesson 15

David Ritz, *Divided Soul* (New York: McGraw-Hill, 1985).

Doris Donnelly, *Putting Forgiveness into Practice* (Allen, Texas: Argus Communications [Tabor Publishing], 1982), pp. 83–84.

Lesson 19

Carlo Carretto, *Letters from the Desert,* trans. by Rose Mary Hancock (New York: Pillar Books, 1976).

Lesson 23

Jim Bishop, *The Day Lincoln Was Shot* (New York: Harper & Row, 1955).

Lesson 24

Erich Von Daniken, *Gods from Outer Space* (New York: Bantam Books, 1972), p. 54.

Lesson 26

John A. Wilson, "The World of Moses," in *Everyday Life in Bible Times* (Washington, D.C.: National Geographic Society, 1967).

C. W. Ceram, *Gods, Graves, and Scholars,* 2nd rev. ed. (New York: Alfred A. Knopf, 1967), pp. 205–7.

Lesson 31

Jim Irwin, "Apollo 15: Three Views of the Moon," *Reader's Digest* (November 1971).

Keith Miller, *A Taste of New Wine* (Waco, Texas: Word Books, 1965), p. 39.

Lesson 34

Robert Wallace, "Kingly Glory and Ordeal," *Life* (December 25, 1964), p. 63.

Lesson 38

Stuart E. Rosenberg, *Judaism* (New York: Paulist Press, 1966), pp. 147–49.

Lesson 41

Janice Rothschild, "I Met a Samaritan," *The Atlanta Journal-Constitution* (September 20, 1970).

Lesson 53

Alex Haley, *Roots* (New York: Doubleday & Co., 1976), pp. 547, 578.

Lesson 56

John Wu, *Beyond East and West* (Beaverton, Ore.: International Scholarly Book Services, 1980).

Lesson 57

Chong Kum Song, "I Want to Follow My Son," *Maryknoll* (March 1978), pp. 27–30.

Lesson 60

William Barclay, *The Gospel of Luke* (Philadelphia: Westminster Press, 1957), p. 30.

Lesson 61

G. Ernest Wright, *Biblical Archaeology* (Philadelphia: Westminster Press, 1963).

Lesson 62

John L. McKenzie, *Dictionary of the Bible*, p. 80.

Lesson 63

Allan Cott, *Fasting: The Ultimate Diet* (reference data not available).

Lesson 64

Viktor Frankl, *Man's Search for Meaning* (Boston: Beacon Press, 1963).

Lesson 65

Ed Aldren, *Life* magazine (July 20, 1969).

Lesson 66

David Stanley and Raymond Brown, "Aspects of New Testament Thought," in *The Jerome Biblical Commentary*, ed. by Brown, Fitzmyer, and Murphy (Englewood Cliffs, N.J.: Prentice-Hall, 1968), pp. 786–87.

Joni Eareckson, with Joe Musser, *Joni* (Grand Rapids: Zondervan Publishing House, 1976).

Lesson 67

Michael Crichton, *The Great Train Robbery* (New York: Alfred A. Knopf, 1975).

Lesson 68

Nancy Gibbs, "The Message of Miracles," *Time* (April 10, 1995), pp. 65–73.

Lesson 70

Louis Evely, *In His Presence* (New York: Seabury Press, 1970), pp. 53–54.

Lesson 71

W. D. Davies, *Invitation to the New Testament* (New York: Doubleday & Co., 1966).

Lesson 74

William Barclay, *Jesus of Nazareth* (Cleveland, Ohio: William Collins & World Publishing Co., 1977), pp. 81–82.

Lesson 75

Donald Hankey, *The Beloved Captain* (reference data not available).

Lesson 76

Emilie Griffin, *Turning* (New York: Doubleday & Co., 1980), p. 112.

Lesson 77

Guiseppe Ricciotti, *The Life of Christ* (Westminster, Md.: Christian Classics, 1952), p. 592.

The History of Napoleon Bonaparte by J. S. C. Abbot, 1895, p. 617.

Lesson 78

John L. McKenzie, *Dictionary of the Bible*, p. 97.

Lesson 80

Heinz Zahrnt, *The Historial Jesus* (reference data not available).

Paul E. Little, *Know What You Believe* (Wheaton, Ill.: Scripture Press Publications, 1970).

Lesson 81

Emilie Griffin, *Turning*, p. 112.

Lesson 84

Avery Dulles, *Apologetics and the Biblical Christ* (New York: Paulist-Newman Press, 1963), pp. 68–69.

Neal Flanagan, *The Acts of the Apostles*, New Testament Reading Guide Series (Collegeville, Minn.: Liturgical Press, 1960), p. 13.

John L. McKenzie, *Dictionary of the Bible*, pp. 10–11.

Lesson 85

Francis MacNutt, *The Power to Heal* (Notre Dame, Ind.: Ave Maria Press, 1977).

Lesson 90

John Kirvan, *The Restless Believers* (Mahway, N.J.: Paulist Press, 1966).

Lesson 91

John L. McKenzie, *Dictionary of the Bible*, p. 649.

Edgar J. Goodspeed, *Paul* (Nashville: Abingdon Press, 1947), p. 21.

Lesson 93

Wernher von Braun, "Points to Ponder," *Reader's Digest* (June 1960).

Elisabeth Kubler-Ross, reported in "Doctor Tells of Visit from Dead" by James Pearre, *Chicago Tribune* (November 7, 1976).

Lesson 97

Eberhard Bethge, *Dietrich Bonhoeffer* (New York: Harper & Row, 1970).

Lesson 98

Russ Johnston, *God Can Make It Happen* (Wheaton, Ill.: Victor Books, 1976).

Lesson 99

Malcolm Muggeridge, *Something Beautiful for God* (New York: Harper & Row, 1971), pp. 32–33.

Henri Daniel-Rops, *Daily Life in the Time of Jesus* (New York: Hawthorn Books, 1962), pp. 453–54.

Lesson 101

Jerry Kramer, *Instant Replay: The Green Bay Diary of Jerry Kramer,* ed. by Dick Schaap (New York: World Publishing, 1968), p. 233.

Lesson 103

John Dear, S.J., "Reflections from Prison," *National Jesuit News* (February 1994), p. 6.

Lesson 104

C. Ernest Wright, *Biblical Archaeology*, p. 252.

Lesson 105

John R. Stott, *Basic Christianity* (Downers Grove, Ill.: Inter-Varsity Press, 1958), p. 39.

Lesson 106

John Patrick, *The Teahouse of the August Moon*, adapted from a novel by Vern Sneider (New York: G. P. Putnam's, 1952).

Lesson 107

John L. McKenzie, *Dictionary of the Bible,* p. 11.

Louis Bisch, *Reader's Digest* (November 1973).

Lesson 110

Roderick A. F. MacKenzie, *Introduction to the New Testament,* New Testament Reading Guide Series (Collegeville, Minn.: Liturgical Press, 1960), p. 20.

John L. McKenzie, *Dictionary of the Bible*, p. 243.

Lesson 115

Ernest Gordon, *Through the Valley of the Kwai* (New York: Harper & Row, 1962), p. 145.

QUIZZES

Prepared by Michael H. Cheney, M.A.
Loyola High School
Los Angeles, California

Matching

1. ______ canon
2. ______ Septuagint
3. ______ Saint Jerome
4. ______ Dead Sea Scrolls

a. the Greek translation of the Bible
b. oldest copies of biblical books
c. translated the Septuagint into Latin
d. list of inspired books of the Bible

True/False

1. ______ Like the stories of "Snow White" and "Rapunzel," the Scriptures were passed down orally before being written down.

2. ______ The original biblical writers divided their writings into verses.

3. ______ Catholics accept the Septuagint listing of the Bible.

4. ______ The Church believes that the Holy Spirit dictated God's word to the human authors, much as an executive dictates to a secretary.

5. ______ Catholics believe the Bible is free from religious error, that is, errors in matters related to salvation.

6. ______ The Bible contains no scientific or historical errors.

7. ______ The Holy Spirit acted as a "watchdog" so that the inspired authors would not make any errors in the Bible.

8. ______ The Dead Sea Scrolls contain some biblical manuscripts that are closer to the originals by one thousand years.

9. ______ The Dead Sea Scrolls were found in caves between 1947 and 1956.

10. ______ Catholics and Protestants agree fully on the Old Testament canon.

Fill In the Blanks

1. The three stages by which Scripture reached its final form are:
   (a) ______________________
   (b) ______________________
   (c) ______________________

2. Give the approximate dates when the Bible was translated into:
   (a) Greek ______________________
   (b) Latin ______________________
   (c) English ______________________

Bonus

What name is given to those who copied biblical manuscripts by hand? ______________

Matching

1. ______ Darwin
2. ______ Darrow
3. ______ Scopes
4. ______ nontheists
5. ______ polytheism
6. ______ theists

a. belief in many gods
b. deny existence of God
c. wrote *Origin of the Species*
d. lawyer for Civil Liberties Union
e biology teacher
f. affirm belief in God

True/False

1. ______ Literalists believe you must take into account both the text and the context when you interpret the Bible.

2. ______ Contextualists believe you need to take into account only the text in interpreting the Bible.

3. ______ When the Bible portrays the man as naming the animals, this is a sign that God is giving humans dominion or power over them.

4. ______ By portraying God as creating the first woman from man's rib, the Bible indicates that women are slightly inferior to men.

5. ______ The second creation story indicates that the only purpose of marriage is to have children.

6. ______ All literalist interpreters of the Bible agree that one day of creation is equivalent to a twenty-four-hour day.

7. ______ All believers of evolution reject the existence of God.

8. ______ Literalist interpreters of the Bible accept the theory of evolution.

9. ______ The second creation story says that God created people last.

10. ______ The creation stories teach that there is an intimate union between God and humans.

Fill In the Blanks

List the four truths that the creation stories teach us.

1. ______________________________

2. ______________________________

3. ______________________________

4. ______________________________

Bonus

What nickname was given to the Dayton, Tennessee, trial involving Darrow and Bryan?

____

Matching

1. ______	eating forbidden fruit	**a.**	tower mountain
2. ______	cherubim	**b.**	stumbling block to immortality
3. ______	ziggurat	**c.**	sign that sin is increasing
4. ______	declining life spans	**d.**	symbol of immortality
5. ______	tree of life	**e.**	experience of evil

True/False

1. ______ Sin (moral evil) opens the door to suffering and death (physical evil).
2. ______ Contextualists take the sin stories of Genesis as symbolic teachings of what went wrong with God's good creation.
3. ______ Chapters 3–11 of Genesis teach us that God is responsible for the origin of evil in our world.
4. ______ The first couple's awareness of their nakedness symbolizes alienation from themselves.
5. ______ Family trees in the Book of Genesis act as a literary bridge (rapid passage of time) between Adam and Noah.
6. ______ The tragic effect of the sin of the first couple is called the state of original sin.
7. ______ Chapters 3–11 of Genesis describe a chain of sin stories that leads to the destruction of ourselves and our world.
8. ______ The Cain and Abel story teaches that alienation of nation from nation is one of the effects of sin.
9. ______ Literal interpreters of the Bible believe that the flood story is factual-symbolic.
10. ______ The first couple learned about evil by experience, not by reason or by having someone tell them about it.

Fill In the Blanks

Name the five tragic effects of sin.

1. ____
2. ____
3. ____
4. ____
5. ____

Bonus

What is the name of the non-Jewish flood story (epic) that is similar to the one found in Genesis? ____

Name ______________________________

Matching

1. ______	Ur	**a.**	Sarai's maid
2. ______	Haran	**b.**	son of Hagar and Abram
3. ______	Sarah	**c.**	Abram's birthplace
4. ______	Ishmael	**d.**	city to which Abram's family moved
5. ______	Isaac	**e.**	son of Abraham and Sarah
6. ______	Hagar	**f.**	Abraham's wife

True/False

1. ______ The word *re-creation* refers to God's action to reverse the spread of sin.

2. ______ Prehistory is narrated in symbol stories.

3. ______ "Cutting a covenant" means breaking an oral agreement.

4. ______ Abram's new name, Abraham, was a sign of his new vocation to be the "father of many."

5. ______ Abram's mark of circumcision was an outward sign of God's covenant with him and his ancestors.

6. ______ Faith is a one-time decision; once you "get the faith," your struggle with faith is over.

7. ______ To this day, the Arab nations trace their ancestry back to Abraham through his son Ishmael.

8. ______ A name change in the Bible is generally a sign that God is displeased with the person.

9. ______ An Old Testament person or event that points to a New Testament person or event is called a "type."

Fill In the Blanks

1. This twofold promise was made to Abram when God covenanted with him:

(a) ______________________________

(b) ______________________________

2. God's test of Abraham's faith teaches us that faith involves:

(a) ______________________________

(b) ______________________________

(c) ______________________________

Bonus

What do Muslims commemorate on the holy day of *Id al-Adha*?

____

Name ____________________

Matching

1. ______ Rebecca
2. ______ Joseph
3. ______ Esau
4. ______ Jacob
5. ______ Jacob's sons
6. ______ Israel
7. ______ YHWH
8. ______ Potiphar
9. ______ plagues
10. ______ Passover

a. involves eating a sacrificial lamb
b. Hebrew spelling of God's name
c. terrible happenings in Egypt
d. younger son of Isaac
e. firstborn of Isaac
f. Isaac's wife
g. Egyptian officer
h. new name of Jacob
i. forerunners of the twelve tribes of Israel
j. known for interpreting dreams

True/False

1. ______ Jacob sold his birthright to his brother.
2. ______ Out of jealousy, Joseph's brothers sold him as a slave to traders who took him to Egypt.
3. ______ The stories of Abraham, Isaac, and Jacob are examples of prehistory.
4. ______ The stories of Isaac and Jacob illustrate that God programmed people of the Bible to be saints.
5. ______ The Book of Exodus begins with the coming into power of a new Egyptian king who helped the Israelites grow powerful and wealthy.
6. ______ Moses fled to Midian after accidently killing a Hebrew slave.
7. ______ Moses encountered God in a burning bush in the desert.
8. ______ God's name in Hebrew is spelled WWWH.
9. ______ After the tenth plague struck, Pharaoh ordered the Hebrews to leave Egypt.
10. ______ After fleeing Egypt, the Israelites crossed *yam suph*, which can be translated "Reed Sea."

Fill In the Blanks

1. What two points are illustrated by the story of Esau's getting the blessing of the firstborn's birthright? (a) ________________________________
(b) ________________________________
2. The number of sons Jacob had was (a) ____________________. They were the forerunners of the (b) ____________________.
3. *El* is one of several words used to refer to ____________________.

Bonus

How did Joseph end up in an Egyptian prison? ________________________________

____

Name ______________________________

Matching

1. ______	Ark of the Covenant	a.	God's priestly people
2. ______	Sinai covenant	b.	housed tablets of Ten Commandments
3. ______	Israel's identity	c.	food Israel ate in the desert
4. ______	manna	d.	God's sacred agreement with Israel
5. ______	Yom Kippur	e.	God's Chosen People
6. ______	Israel's destiny	f.	Day of Atonement
7. ______	Moab	g.	land where Moses died
8. ______	Passover	h.	ram's horn used to sound the call to worship
9. ______	shofar	i.	housed Ark of the Covenant
10. ______	sacred Tent	j.	celebration of God's freeing Israel from slavery in Egypt

True/False

1. ______ The Bible says the Israelites wandered about in the desert for twenty years.
2. ______ God's covenant with the Israelites at Mount Sinai was modeled after the treaty format of that day (pacts between a powerful king and a weak king).
3. ______ God promised on Mount Sinai that Israel would be God's "Chosen People" and "priestly people" by which God will re-create the world.
4. ______ During Yom Kippur the Israelites confessed their sins over a goat and drove it into the desert.
5. ______ Moses entered the Promised Land before he died.
6. ______ The Israelites never gave up hope in Moses during their time in the desert.
7. ______ The Torah is another name for the first five books of the Old Testament
8. ______ The Israelites saw the Ten Commandments as freeing them "for" a life of love and service.
9. ______ The Book of Deuteronomy ends with the death of Isaac.
10. ______ The Promised Land was made up of stretches of sand and expanses of rock.

Fill In the Blanks

1. What are three ways the Israelites experienced God's help in the desert?
   (a) ______________________________
   (b) ______________________________
   (c) ______________________________
2. God's covenant with the Israelites at Mount Sinai introduced them to two revolutionary changes in their life: (a) ______________________________
   (b) ______________________________

Bonus

What event concludes the Torah? ______________________________

Matching

1. ______	Joshua	**a.**	son of David
2. ______	Deborah	**b.**	credited with writing the Psalms
3. ______	David	**c.**	anointed one
4. ______	Samuel	**d.**	mass killing
5. ______	Saul	**e.**	Israel's first king
6. ______	Goliath	**f.**	gifted natural leaders who led Israel back to God
7. ______	"the ban"	**g.**	anointed Israel's first king
8. ______	Solomon	**h.**	a famous Israelite judge
9. ______	messiah	**i.**	led Israelites after Moses died
10. ______	judges of Israel	**j.**	Philistine warrior

True/False

1. ______ The Red (Reed) Sea crossing and the Jordan River crossing are closely related, like two sides of the same coin.

2. ______ Some experts suggest that an earthquake may have toppled the walls of Jericho.

3. ______ Samson anointed the first king of Israel.

4. ______ David made Jerusalem the religious and political capital of Israel.

5. ______ Solomon built the Temple of Jerusalem.

6. ______ Royal psalms frequently begin with "Happy are those."

7. ______ There are 150 psalms in the Book of Psalms.

8. ______ God's promise that David's kingly line would last forever begins a series of "messianic" prophecies.

9. ______ The Song of Songs is a love poem with no spiritual or religious significance.

Fill In the Blanks

1. The Book of Psalms was Israel's (a) ______________________________ and (b) ______________________________.

2. Solomon is credited with authoring which three wisdom books?

(a) ______________________________

(b) ______________________________

(c) ______________________________

3. The purpose of the Book of Proverbs is ______________________________

______________________________.

Bonus

What are the approximate dates of the Era of the Judges? ______________________________

Name ______________________________

Matching

1. ______	Bethel	**a.**	weds an unfaithful wife
2. ______	Rehoboam	**b.**	first writing prophet to Israel
3. ______	Jeroboam	**c.**	pagan wife of Ahab
4. ______	Jezebel	**d.**	continued Elijah's ministry
5. ______	Elijah	**e.**	led revolt against southern tribes
6. ______	Elisha	**f.**	a religious center in the North
7. ______	Amos	**g.**	defeated 450 pagan prophets
8. ______	Hosea	**h.**	succeeded Solomon as king
9. ______	Isaiah	**i.**	prophet of God's holiness
10. ______	Manasseh	**j.**	young reformer king
11. ______	Josiah	**k.**	persecuted prophet of Israel
12. ______	Jeremiah	**l.**	one of Judah's worst kings

True/False

1. ______ The ten northern tribes tried to settle their grievance peacefully before revolting.
2. ______ The revolt split the people into two kingdoms, Israel in the north and Judah in the south.
3. ______ The northern tribes continued to worship in Jerusalem.
4. ______ Israel was conquered by the Assyrians in 722 B.C.E.
5. ______ The fall of Israel shocked Judah into instant reform.
6. ______ Hosea is described as departing this life in a chariot of fire pulled by horses of fire.
7. ______ Amos spoke out against the way the wealthy people of Israel exploited that nation's poor people.
8. ______ Jews who intermarried with the Assyrians were called Samaritans.
9. ______ The prophet Jeremiah worked with Josiah to reform Judah.
10. ______ Jeremiah remodeled the Temple and found an old book of the law.

Fill In the Blanks

1. The writing prophets are sometimes divided into two groups:
   (a) four ____________________ prophets and (b) twelve ____________________ prophets.
2. No prophet, apart from Elijah, is more highly regarded in Judaism than ____________________.

Bonus

What pagan god did some people in the north begin to worship? ____________________________

Matching

1. ______	Antiochus IV	**a.**	writer of the Book of Consolation
2. ______	Cyrus	**b.**	Jewish freedom fighters
3. ______	587 B.C.E.	**c.**	young Jewish hero
4. ______	Ezekiel	**d.**	king of Judah
5. ______	Second Isaiah	**e.**	prophet to the returned exiles
6. ______	Jonah	**f.**	freed Jewish exiles
7. ______	Herod the Great	**g.**	preached the "universal" God
8. ______	Haggai	**h.**	first prophet of the Babylonian exile
9. ______	Hasmoneans	**i.**	fall of the Temple and Jerusalem
10. ______	Maccabees	**j.**	reflection on the presence of evil
11. ______	Book of Job	**k.**	Greek-minded tyrant
12. ______	Daniel	**l.**	used office of high priest for political purposes

True/False

1. ______ The Babylonians attacked Jerusalem two times, destroying the city and the Temple after the second attack.

2. ______ The Jewish synagogue first came into existence before the Babylonian exile.

3. ______ Scribes began to record the oral portions of God's word during the Babylonian exile.

4. ______ Ezekiel played the role of "comforter" during the first period of his ministry.

5. ______ An ancient record called the Cyrus Cylinder says that Cyrus entered Babylon as a friend when he conquered it.

6. ______ When the people returned from Babylon, all of Judah's neighbors rallied to help rebuild the Temple and Jerusalem.

7. ______ The Book of Daniel refers to a mysterious "Son of Man," a title that Jesus used to refer to himself.

8. ______ The Book of Ecclesiastes lets us glimpse the heart of a Jew awaiting further revelation.

9. ______ Job describes in detail the rebuilding of the Temple and Jerusalem.

Fill In the Blanks

Identify the four religious groups that made up Judah at the close of the Old Testament period.

1. ______________________________________ hoped for a military messiah.

2. ______________________________ believed in the after-life, angels, and a final judgment.

3. ______________________________________ went into the desert to prepare for the end.

4. ____________________________ were made up of wealthy people and many chief priests.

Bonus

Who wrote the "Suffering Servant" prophecies? ______________________________________

Matching

1. ______	New Testament	**a.**	wrote for Christians of all backgrounds
2. ______	Old Testament	**b.**	wrote for Christians of Jewish background
3. ______	suffering Messiah	**c.**	Luke's portrait of Jesus
4. ______	teaching Messiah	**d.**	John's portrait of Jesus
5. ______	life-giving Messiah	**e.**	wrote for Christians of Greek background
6. ______	compassionate Messiah	**f.**	Matthew's portrait of Jesus
7. ______	Matthew	**g.**	Hebrew Scriptures
8. ______	Mark	**h.**	wrote for persecuted Christians in Rome
9. ______	Luke	**i**	Christian Scriptures
10. ______	John	**j.**	Mark's portrait of Jesus

True/False

1. ______ The early Christians believed that the Lord would come back in their own lifetime as long as the Gospels were preached to all nations.

2. ______ The initial reaction of disciples to the coming of the Spirit on Pentecost was to immediately sit down and record the Gospels.

3. ______ Matthew divides his Gospel into "five instructions" to symbolically parallel the five books of Moses (the Torah).

4. ______ Mark's Gospel has two parts: (1) Jesus is the Christ, and (2) Jesus is the Son of God.

5. ______ The Gospels of Matthew, Mark, and Luke are synoptic Gospels.

6. ______ The New Testament replaces the Old Testament.

7. ______ The Gospel of Luke and the Acts of the Apostles were written by the same author.

8. ______ John's Gospel identifies Jesus by God's name "I AM."

Fill In the Blanks

1. The four sections into which the books of the New Testament are divided are:

(a) ____

(b) ____

(c) ____

(d) ____

2. The three stages by which the Gospels developed into the form they now have are:

(a) ________________________ stage, (b) ________________________ stage,

(c) ________________________ stage.

Bonus

Which Gospel was addressed to "Dear Theophilus"? ______________________

Name ______________________________

Matching

1. ______ gold
2. ______ frankincense
3. ______ myrrh

a. symbol of Jesus' divinity
b. symbol of Jesus' humanity
c. symbol of Jesus' kingship

True/False

1. ______ Circumcision initiated the child into the community of God's people.
2. ______ Purification welcomed Mary back into full participation in the worshiping community after Jesus' birth.
3. ______ Anna prophesied that Mary would suffer great sorrow.
4. ______ The magi's visit acts as a preview that many Gentiles will accept Jesus.
5. ______ The story of the magi interweaves history, prophecy, and inspiration to reveal Jesus' identity and his acceptance by others.
6. ______ Jesus' temptations show that he was not truly God.
7. ______ Jesus' temptations preview the answer to the question "Who is Jesus?"
8. ______ Jesus' temptations show that his mission is to be the new Adam who is to right the wrong of the first Adam.
9. ______ Jesus experienced the temptations in the desert before he was baptized by John the Baptist.
10. ______ Jesus' birth during lambing season and in Bethlehem points to his identity and mission.
11. ______ Herod's hostile reaction, opposed to the magi's positive reaction, previews how people will react to Jesus.

Fill In the Blanks

1. The ______________________________ at Jesus' baptism is a sign that a new era is dawning in human history.
2. The ______________________________ at Jesus' baptism is a sign that a new creation is taking place.
3. The ____________________ at Jesus' baptism is a sign that Jesus is the new Adam.
4. Jesus' refusal to ______________________________ previews that his lifestyle will be to destroy evil, not barter with it.
5. Jesus' refusal to ______________________________ previews that his lifestyle will be to serve, not to be served.
6. Jesus' refusal to ______________________________ previews that his lifestyle will be to suffer, not to avoid suffering.

Bonus

What is the name of the Jewish rite that consecrated the firstborn male to God?

____

Matching

1. ______	nature miracle	**a.**	driving out the demons
2. ______	healing miracle	**b.**	word doesn't take root in them
3. ______	expulsion miracle	**c.**	Greek word for "marvel"
4. ______	teras	**d.**	word bears much fruit in them
5. ______	dynamis	**e.**	calming the storm
6. ______	semeion	**f.**	Greek word for "sign"
7. ______	thorn people	**g.**	word choked by their worries
8. ______	path people	**h.**	giving sight to the blind
9. ______	soil people	**i.**	Greek word for "power"
10. ______	rock people	**j.**	word burned up by their trials

True/False

1. ______ Jesus was enthusiastically received when he preached for the first time in his hometown.

2. ______ Jesus worked miracles mainly out of pity for people.

3. ______ Jesus' miracles were signs inviting people to believe in him and his message.

4. ______ The Bible portrays Adam's sin as having destroyed the harmony that once existed between people and nature.

5. ______ Jesus' raising of the dead was a sign inviting people to be reborn and become "new creations" in God's kingdom.

6. ______ Miracles had two levels, a sense level (what was seen) and a sign level (what was signified).

Fill In the Blanks

1. The people of the town of ____________________ rejected Jesus and threatened his life.

2. List three ways in which tradition divides those who opened their hearts to Jesus' teaching and the kingdom of God.

(a) ____

(b) ____

(c) ____

Bonus

Which book of the Old Testament did Jesus read from in the synagogue at Nazareth?

____

Matching

1.	______	father	**a.**	stands for sinners and outcasts
2.	______	younger son	**b.**	sign of total restoration
3.	______	elder son	**c.**	sign of total welcome
4.	______	hug	**d.**	stands for God
5.	______	shoes	**e.**	sign of total forgiveness
6.	______	ring	**f.**	stands for Jewish religious leaders

True/False

1. ______ Love is the sign of God's kingdom, and the power that spreads it.

2. ______ Jesus' parables are both a revelation and an invitation.

3. ______ The parable of the wise and foolish bridesmaids deals with the Second Coming of Christ.

4. ______ Jesus revealed the exact timing of the Second Coming to his disciples.

Fill In the Blanks

1. List the three settings in which Jesus prayed.

(a) ______________________________

(b) ______________________________

(c) ______________________________

2. List the three "your" petitions of the Lord's Prayer.

(a) ______________________________

(b) ______________________________

(c) ______________________________

3. List and briefly explain the four kinds of prayer found in the Gospels.

(a) ______________________________

____

(b) ______________________________

____

(c) ______________________________

____

(d) ______________________________

____

Bonus

Who said "Boys, if you ever pray, pray for me now"?

____

Matching

1.	______	landowner	**a.**	apostles
2.	______	vineyard	**b.**	Jesus
3.	______	first renting	**c.**	early prophets
4.	______	first tenants	**d.**	God
5.	______	slaves	**e.**	Israel
6.	______	other slaves	**f.**	old covenant
7.	______	owner's son	**g.**	new covenant
8.	______	second renting	**h.**	later prophets
9.	______	other tenants	**i.**	Jewish leaders

True/False

1. ______ The Jewish leaders understood and approved Jesus' healing a man on the Sabbath.

2. ______ Jesus began the Last Supper as any Passover meal began, by washing the disciples' feet.

3. ______ For Jews, washing feet was humiliating.

4. ______ The unleavened bread at the Last Supper recalls Israel's hasty departure from Egypt.

5. ______ The bitter herbs at the Last Supper recall Israel's slavery in Egypt.

Fill In the Blanks

1. What was Jesus teaching his apostles through the washing of their feet?

____

2. What two events would the drinking of red wine have recalled at the Passover supper?

(a) ____

(b) ____

3. What events in the life of the Hebrews were symbolized by the following foods at the Passover meal?

(a) bitter herbs ____

(b) clay-colored sauce ____

(c) unleavened bread ____

Bonus

Identify one miracle that foreshadowed what Jesus did at the Last Supper.

____

Name ______________________________

Matching

1. _______ Sanhedrin
2. _______ Judas
3. _______ Pilate
4. _______ Golgotha

a. betrayed Jesus
b. place of crucifixion
c. dedicated an amphitheater to Tiberius
d. council of chief priests and leaders

True/False

1. _______ Three times Peter vehemently denied he was a disciple of Jesus.
2. _______ Jesus was brought before Pilate because Jesus was mainly guilty of a religious crime, namely, blasphemy.
3. _______ All four resurrection accounts found in the Gospels agree perfectly in every detail of the resurrection.
4. _______ Early Christians interpreted the tearing of the Temple curtain as a sign of God's anger over Jesus' crucifixion.
5. _______ A Roman soldier recognized and believed in Jesus as he looked at Jesus on the cross.
6. _______ The disciples' first reaction upon hearing of Jesus' resurrection was not to believe.
7. _______ The term *resurrection* designates a return to one's former life.
8. _______ In spite of Jesus' bodily change after the resurrection, his disciples were always able to recognize him at once.
9. _______ On Easter night the Risen Lord commissioned and empowered his disciples to forgive sins.
10. _______ Pilate's original intention was to try to keep from executing Jesus.

Fill In the Blanks

1. Jesus' words on the road to Emmaus and his action around the table resemble what two parts of the Mass? (a) ______________________________
(b) ______________________________
2. ______________________________ was the man who arranged Jesus' burial.
3. (a) ______________________ and (b) ______________________ were the two women who Matthew says found Jesus' tomb empty.
4. What gift did Jesus give his disciples on Easter Sunday night?
____

Bonus

What is the name of the place where Jesus and his disciples went after the Last Supper?

____

Name ______________________

Matching

1. ______ Ascension
2. ______ Pentecost
3. ______ Day of the Lord
4. ______ Peter
5. ______ Mary

- **a.** preached to crowd at Pentecost
- **b.** gathered with disciples to pray
- **c.** coming of the Spirit
- **d.** return of Jesus to heaven
- **e.** ends with Jesus' second coming

True/False

1. ______ The Acts of the Apostles tells the story of the thirty years that followed Jesus' ascension to his Father.
2. ______ Christianity grew so spectacularly that by Pentecost it was already established in far-off Rome.
3. ______ Two men in white told the apostles that Jesus would return "the same way that you saw him go to heaven."
4. ______ With the Spirit's coming, God's plan for re-creating the world takes a giant leap forward.
5. ______ The Spirit enabled Jesus' disciples to speak in different languages.
6. ______ Originally Pentecost was a time for thanking God for the year's harvest and for the Sinai covenant with Israel.
7. ______ The apostles prepared for the coming of the Holy Spirit by going into the desert.
8. ______ The first Christian Pentecost occurred in the city of Jerusalem.
9. ______ Wind is an image of God's spirit.
10. ______ Jews used fire as an image of God.
11. ______ Initially, the apostles were certain the Second Coming of Christ would take place centuries after they died.

Fill In the Blanks

1. ______________________ wrote the Acts of the Apostles.
2. ______________________ was chosen to succeed Judas.
3. ______________________ means "fiftieth."
4. ______________________ was the Old Testament event that was reversed by the Pentecost event.

Bonus

About how many were baptized on the first Christian Pentecost?

____

Matching

1. ______ Gamaliel
2. ______ Stephen
3. ______ Philip
4. ______ Cornelius
5. ______ God-fearer
6. ______ proselyte
7. ______ James
8. ______ Peter
9. ______ Herod

a. Roman centurion
b. slew John's brother, James
c. preached to the Samaritans
d. reportedly left Jerusalem for Rome
e. first Christian martyr
f. advised leaving the apostles alone
g. Gentile who attended the synagogue
h. Jerusalem leader after Peter
i. Gentile convert to Judaism

True/False

1. ______ The Jewish Council tried to prevent the apostles from preaching about Jesus.
2. ______ Stephen was a young deacon.
3. ______ A positive result of the persecution of Christians in Jerusalem was that many disciples fled to Judea and Samaria and began to preach the Good News there.
4. ______ The "Gentile Pentecost" took place in the house of a Roman officer named Philip.
5. ______ Peter and John refused to share the gift of the Holy Spirit with Samaritans.
6. ______ The first Church Council in history dealt with the question of whether Gentiles had to be circumcised before becoming Christians.
7. ______ James died a slow and painful death.
8. ______ The Acts of the Apostles states clearly that Peter left Jerusalem after his prison escape and went to Rome, where he was martyred years later.

Fill In the Blanks

Identify the three "Pentecosts" of the Acts of the Apostles.

1. ____
2. ____
3. ____

Bonus

In what city, built by Herod, did Cornelius live? ______________________

Matching

1. _______	Saul	**a.**	Roman governor in Corinth
2. _______	Ananias	**b.**	pagan goddess
3. _______	Tarsus	**c.**	joined Paul and Silas in Lystra
4. _______	Corinth	**d.**	a wild port city
5. _______	Timothy	**e.**	another name for Paul
6. _______	Silas	**f.**	Paul's birthplace
7. _______	Antioch	**g.**	imprisoned with Paul in Philippi
8. _______	Lystra	**h.**	healed Paul's blindness
9. _______	Gallio	**i.**	the word *Christian* originated here
10. _______	Artemis	**j.**	Paul was called Hermes here

True/False

1. _______ Paul was on his way to Tarsus when he had his conversion experience.

2. _______ Barnabas accompanied Paul on his first missionary trip.

3. _______ Paul changed his plans and went to Macedonia when the ruler of that country invited him to preach there.

4. _______ Everywhere that Paul went he was accepted with open arms.

5. _______ Paul got into trouble in Philippi for driving out an evil spirit of a slave girl.

6. _______ Paul converted a number of Philippians.

7. _______ Most of Corinth's citizens were refined, cultured, and highly educated.

8. _______ When Paul departed Corinth, he left behind a sizable Christian community.

9. _______ The religious devotion of the Ephesians who became Christians was originally to a pagan goddess.

10. _______ Eutychus was a young man whom Paul restored to health in Troas after he had fallen from an upstairs window.

Fill In the Blanks

1. What city was Paul going to when he fell down and was blinded?

____

2. What did a voice say to Paul as he lay there on the ground?

____

3. What three things did the early Christians do before sending Paul and Barnabas off on their first missionary journey?

(a) ______________ (b) ______________ (c) ______________

Bonus

To what city does tradition say John brought Mary after Jesus' ascension?

____

Matching

1. ______	Felix	**a.**	Paul was shipwrecked off this island
2. ______	Luke	**b.**	kept a journal of Paul's sea voyage
3. ______	Festus	**c.**	corrupt Roman governor
4. ______	Titus	**d.**	leveled the Jerusalem Temple
5. ______	Malta	**e.**	city to which Romans in Jerusalem moved Paul
6. ______	Aristarchus	**f.**	let Paul go to Rome for trial
7. ______	Caesarea	**g.**	accompanied Paul to Rome

True/False

1. ______ Some Jews accused Paul of speaking against the Law of Moses and defiling the Temple.

2. ______ The Romans transferred Paul to Caesarea because they feared his enemies might try to kill him.

3. ______ The Roman governor in Caesarea kept Paul in prison for two years.

4. ______ Paul was a Roman citizen.

5. ______ Paul's sea voyage to Rome was doubly difficult because he didn't know a soul on board the ship.

6. ______ Paul arrived in Rome around 61 C.E.

7. ______ Paul was thrown into a prison with thieves and murderers when he got to Rome.

8. ______ The Acts of the Apostles describes Paul's trial in Rome in detail.

9. ______ It is possible that Luke left the Acts of the Apostles unfinished to stress that the teaching of the Good News is not yet finished.

Fill In the Blanks

1. Under what form of arrest was Paul placed in Rome?

____

2. When, where, and how does tradition say that Paul was executed?

(a) when ______________________________ (b) where ______________________________

(c) how ______________________________

Bonus

What is the name of the Lutheran pastor who openly opposed the Nazis in Germany?

____

Matching

The following answers may be used more than once.

1. ______ 1 Thessalonians
2. ______ 1 Corinthians
3. ______ Philemon
4. ______ Galatians
5. ______ 2 Timothy
6. ______ Philippians
7. ______ Romans
8. ______ Ephesians
9. ______ Titus
10. ______ Colossians

a. pastoral letter
b. prison letter
c. early letter
d. great letter

True/False

1. ______ Paul's letters follow a fairly consistent format.
2. ______ Paul's letters, as a rule, contain an opening salutation that includes the sender's name, the receiver's name, and a greeting.
3. ______ Paul's pastoral letters reflect a pattern of little theological growth.
4. ______ Paul never signed his letters with his own name.
5. ______ Paul's first letter was to the Thessalonians.
6. ______ Some people suggest a disciple of Paul, not Paul, wrote the pastoral letters.
7. ______ Paul's Letter to the Ephesians highlights an overview of God's plan.
8. ______ 2 Timothy affirms the priority of teaching Scripture.
9. ______ The Letter to the Colossians deals with Jesus' human and divine natures.
10. ______ Paul's Letter to the Romans deals with the priority of faith over the law.

Fill In the Blanks

1. This letter is the shortest and the warmest that Paul ever wrote. ______________________
2. These letters deal mainly with Jesus' second coming. ______________________________
3. This letter was triggered by Jewish converts who told Paul's Gentile converts that they had to be circumcised.______________________________
4. These letters portray a community that is organizing itself.__________________________
5. This letter presents qualities of church elders.________________________________

Bonus

What is the approximate date of Paul's first letter?______________________________

Name ______________________________

Matching

1. ______	Hebrews	**a.**	warns about immoral, false teachers
2. ______	Jude	**b.**	classified as a "special" letter
3. ______	John	**c.**	discusses Jesus' second coming
4. ______	2 Peter	**d.**	reads more like a sermon than a letter
5. ______	James	**e.**	author of three "catholic" letters

True/False

1. ______ The "catholic" letters are so-called because only Catholics accept them as being inspired.

2. ______ The Letter to the Hebrews is addressed to people who seem to have been suffering because of their faith.

3. ______ 1 Peter was sent to suffering people who believed Jesus would return during their lifetime.

4. ______ The Letter from James teaches clearly that faith alone is enough to save.

5. ______ The "Antichrist" in 1 John refers to one who opposes or replaces Christ.

6. ______ The Gnostics taught that Jesus was neither the Son of God nor the Messiah because neither of them would be joined to evil matter.

7. ______ The Letter to the Hebrews makes two recommendations: the imitation of Christ and the imitation of ancestors.

8. ______ The Letter to Jude accuses "godless people" of distorting their beliefs to fit their behavior.

9. ______ The Docetists believed that Jesus only "appeared" to have a human body, and therefore was not really human.

10. ______ There are ten "catholic" letters.

Fill In the Blanks

1. The "false teachers" described by John denied Jesus to be:

(a) ______________________________ (b) ______________________________

(c) ______________________________

2. The Letter of Jude implies that we can become a Dr. Jekyll and Mr. Hyde when it comes to a clash between what we (a) ______________________________

and how we (b)______________________________.

Bonus

Many people think that Jesus' transfiguration took place on Mount ____________________.

Name ______________________________

Matching

1. ______	apocalyptic	**a.**	the new Israel
2. ______	white horse	**b.**	fate of evil forces
3. ______	red horse	**c.**	judgment
4. ______	black horse	**d.**	victory
5. ______	pale green horse	**e.**	conflict
6. ______	140,000 people	**f.**	writing style of crisis situations

True/False

1. ______ The immediate audience for which the Book of Revelation was written was first-century Christians being persecuted for their faith.
2. ______ The Book of Revelation contains a series of dreamlike images granted to a man named John.
3. ______ The Book of Revelation begins with twelve letters written by twelve apostles.
4. ______ The Lamb was given a scroll with twelve seals to be opened.
5. ______ After the Lamb broke the last seal, a great silence fell upon heaven, suggesting that the judgment of God was near.
6. ______ The blowing of the trumpets produced catastrophes on earth that remind us of the plagues in ancient Egypt.
7. ______ In the vision of the woman and the dragon, the woman stands for all the women of the world.
8. ______ In the vision of the two beasts, the beasts stand for two Roman emperors who persecuted Christians.
9. ______ The "thousand years" referred to in the Book of Revelation symbolize the reign of the Church from the end of the Roman persecution to the Last Judgment.
10. ______ The number 666 in the Book of Revelation probably refers to the emperor Domitian.
11. ______ The Book of Revelation ends with all eyes fixed on the Second Coming.

Fill In the Blanks

Three interpretations of the Book of Revelation have emerged over the centuries. What are the primary audiences of these three interpretations?

1. ____
2. ____
3. ____

Bonus

Identify the Roman emperor who persecuted Christians during 81–96 C.E.

____

ANSWER KEY

Chapter One: Scripture

Matching (4 x 5 = 20 points)

1. d
2. a
3. c
4. b

True/False (10 x 5 = 50 points)

1. T
2. F
3. T
4. F
5. T
6. F
7. F
8. T
9. T
10. F

Fill In the Blanks (6 x 5 = 30 points)

1. (a) life, (b) oral, (c) written
2. (a) 300 B.C.E. –150 B.C.E. (or 200 B.C.E.)
   (b) 400 C.E., (c) 14th century

Bonus scribes

Chapter Two: Creation

Matching (6 x 5 = 30 points)

1. c
2. d
3. e
4. b
5. a
6. f

True/False (10 x 5 = 50 points)

1. F
2. F
3. T
4. F
5. F
6. F
7. F
8. F
9. F
10. T

Fill In the Blanks (4 x 5 = 20 points)

1. God is one.
2. God created by plan.
3. God created everything good, not evil.
4. God made the Sabbath special.

Bonus the monkey trial

Chapter Three: De-creation

Matching (5 x 5 = 25 points)

1. e
2. b
3. a
4. c
5. d

True/False (10 x 5 = 50 points)

1. T
2. T
3. F
4. T
5. T
6. T
7. T
8. F
9. F
10. T

Fill In the Blanks (5 x 5 = 25 points)

1. alienation from self
2. alienation from God
3. alienation from nature
4. alienation from other people
5. alienation of nation from nation

Bonus Epic of Gilgamesh

Chapter Four: Re-creation

Matching (6 x 5 = 30 points)

1. c
2. d
3. f
4. b
5. e
6. a

True/False (9 x 5 = 45 points)

1. T
2. T
3. F
4. T
5. T
6. F
7. T
8. F
9. T

Fill In the Blanks (5 x 5 = 25 points)

1. (a) descendants, (b) land
2. (a) loving trust, (b) constant struggle,
   (c) times of darkness

Bonus
Abraham's readiness to sacrifice his son to God

Chapter Five: Peoplehood

Matching (10 x 4 = 40 points)

1. f	6. h
2. j	7. b
3. e	8. g
4. d	9. c
5. i	10. a

True/False (10 x 4 = 40 points)

1. F	6. T
2. T	7. T
3. F	8. F
4. F	9. T
5. F	10. T

Fill In the Blanks (5 x 4 = 20 points)

1. (a) God respects our free will, (b) the power of the spoken word
2. (a) twelve, (b) twelve tribes of Israel (or Israelites)
3. God

Bonus

Potiphar's wife falsely accused him of a crime.

Chapter Six: Covenant

Matching (10 x 4 = 40 points)

1. b	6. a
2. d	7. g
3. e	8. j
4. c	9. h
5. f	10. i

True/False (10 x 4 = 40 points)

1. F	6. F
2. T	7. T
3. T	8. T
4. T	9. F
5. F	10. F

Fill In the Blanks (5 x 4 = 20 points)

1. (a) pillars of cloud and fire,(b) quail, (c) manna
2. (a) new worship style, (b) new life style

Bonus death of Moses

Chapter Seven: Nationhood

Matching (10 x 4 = 40 points)

1. i	6. j
2. h	7. d
3. b	8. a
4. g	9. c
5. e	10. f

True/False (9 x 4 = 36 points)

1. T	6. F
2. T	7. T
3. F	8. T
4. T	9. F
5. T	

Fill In the Blanks (6 x 4 = 24 points)

1. (a) prayer book, (b) hymnbook
2. (a) Proverbs, (b) Song of Songs, (c) Ecclesiastes
3. to teach Jewish youth how to live

Bonus 1240 B.C.E.–1040 B.C.E.

Chapter Eight: Division

Matching (12 x 4 = 48 points)

1. f	7. b
2. h	8. a
3. e	9. i
4. c	10. l
5. g	11. j
6. d	12. k

True/False (10 x 4 = 40 points)

1. T	6. F
2. T	7. T
3. F	8. T
4. T	9. T
5. F	10. F

Fill In the Blanks (3 x 4 = 12 points)

1. (a) major, (b) minor
2. Isaiah

Bonus Baal

Chapter Nine: Rebirth

Matching (12 x 4 = 48 points)

1. k
2. f
3. i
4. h
5. a
6. g
7. d
8. e
9. l
10. b
11. j
12. c

True/False (9 x 4 = 36 points)

1. T
2. F
3. T
4. F
5. T
6. F
7. T
8. T
9. F

Fill In the Blanks (4 x 4 = 16 points)

1. Zealots
2. Pharisees
3. Essenes
4. Saddcees

Bonus Second Isaiah

Chapter Ten: Good News

Matching (10 x 4 = 40 points)

1. i
2. g
3. j
4. f
5. d
6. c
7. b
8. h
9. e
10. a

True/False (8 x 4 = 32 points)

1. T
2. F
3. T
4. T
5. T
6. F
7. T
8. T

Fill In the Blanks (7 x 4 = 28 points)

1. (a) Gospels, (b) Acts, (c) Letters, (d) Revelation
2. (a) life, (b) preaching (oral), (c) written

Bonus Luke

Chapter Eleven: Preministry

Matching (3 x 5 = 15 points)

1. c
2. a
3. b

True/False (11 x 5 = 55 points)

1. T
2. T
3. F
4. T
5. T
6. F
7. T
8. T
9. F
10. T
11. T

Fill In the Blanks (6 x 5 = 30 points)

1. heaven opening
2. dove descending
3. voice speaking
4. bow to Satan
5. leap off the Temple
6. turn stone into bread

Bonus presentation

Chapter Twelve: Miracle Ministry

Matching (10 x 5 = 50 points)

1. e
2. h
3. a
4. c
5. i
6. f
7. g
8. b
9. d
10. j

True/False (6 x 5 = 30 points)

1. F
2. F
3. T
4. T
5. T
6. T

Fill In the Blanks (4 x 5 = 20 points)

1. Nazareth
2. (a) the unnumbered crowd, (b) the 72 disciples, (c) the Twelve

Bonus Isaiah

Chapter Thirteen: Teaching Ministry

Matching (6 x 5 = 30 points)

1. d	4. c
2. a	5. e
3. f	6. b

True/False (4 x 5 = 20 points)

1. T	3. T
2. T	4. F

Fill In the Blanks (10 x 5 = 50 points)

1. (a) alone, (b) in small groups, (c) with the community
2. (a) your name be hallowed, (b) your kingdom come, (c) your will be done
3. (a) Adoration acknowledges God as God. (b) Contrition acknowledges our need for God's mercy. (c) Thanksgiving acknowledges God's many gifts to us. (d) Supplication acknowledges our need for God's help.

Bonus Harry Truman

Chapter Fourteen: Last Supper

Matching (9 x 5 = 45 points)

1. d	6. h
2. e	7. b
3. f	8. g
4. i	9. a
5. c	

True/False (5 x 5 = 25 points)

1. F	4. T
2. F	5. T
3. T	

Fill In the Blanks (6 x 5 = 30 points)

1. They were to serve others as Jesus did.
2. (a) the Passover blood smeared on Israel's houses, (b) the covenant blood sprinkled on the Israelite people
3. (a) bitter years of slavery, (b) making bricks under hot sun, (c) haste in fleeing Egypt

Bonus multiplication of the loaves or wedding at Cana

Chapter Fifteen: Death & Rising

Matching (4 x 5 = 20 points)

1. d	3. c
2. a	4. b

True/False (10 x 5 = 50 points)

1. T	6. T
2. T	7. F
3. F	8. F
4. F	9. T
5. T	10. T

Fill In the Blanks (6 x 5 = 30 points)

1. (a) the Liturgy of the Word, (b) the Liturgy of the Eucharist
2. Joseph of Arimathea
3. (a) Mary Magdalene, (b) Mary
4. power to forgive sins

Bonus Mount of Olives

Chapter Sixteen: Spirit's Coming

Matching (5 x 5 = 25 points)

1. d	4. a
2. c	5. b
3. e	

True/False (11 x 5 = 55 points)

1. T	7. F
2. F	8. T
3. T	9. T
4. T	10. T
5. T	11. F
6. T	

Fill In the Blanks (4 x 5 = 20 points)

1. Luke
2. Matthias
3. Pentecost
4. Babel

Bonus 3,000

Chapter Seventeen: Local Witness

Matching (9 x 5 = 45 points)

1. f
2. e
3. c
4. a
5. g
6. i
7. h
8. d
9. b

True/False (8 x 5 = 40 points)

1. T
2. T
3. T
4. F
5. F
6. T
7. F
8. F

Fill In the Blanks (3 x 5 = 15 points)

1. Jews in Jerusalem
2. half-Jews in Samaria
3. Gentiles in Caesarea

Bonus Caesarea

Chapter Eighteen: Global Witness

Matching (10 x 4 = 40 points)

1. e
2. h
3. f
4. d
5. c
6. g
7. i
8. j
9. a
10. b

True/False (10 x 4 = 40 points)

1. F
2. T
3. F
4. F
5. T
6. T
7. F
8. T
9. T
10. T

Fill In the Blanks (5 x 4 = 20 points)

1. Damascus
2. "Why do you persecute me?"
3. (a) fasted, (b) prayed, (c) laid hands on them

Bonus Ephesus

Chapter Nineteen: Ongoing Witness

Matching (7 x 5 = 35 points)

1. c
2. b
3. f
4. d
5. a
6. g
7. e

True/False (9 x 5 = 45 points)

1. T
2. T
3. T
4. T
5. F
6. T
7. F
8. F
9. T

Fill In the Blanks (4 x 5 = 20 points)

1. house arrest
2. (a) 67 C.E., (b) Rome, (c) beheaded

Bonus Bonhoeffer

Chapter Twenty: Paul's Letters

Matching (10 x 4 = 40 points)

1. c
2. d
3. b
4. d
5. a
6. b
7. d
8. b
9. a
10. b

True/False (10 x 4 = 40 points)

1. T
2. T
3. F
4. F
5. T
6. T
7. T
8. T
9. F
10. T

Fill In the Blanks (5 x 4 = 20 points)

1. Philemon
2. 1–2 Thessalonians
3. Galatians
4. 1–2 Timothy
5. Titus

Bonus 50 C.E.

Chapter Twenty-one: Other Letters

Matching (5 x 5 = 25 points)

1. b
2. a
3. e
4. c
5. d

True/False (10 x 5 = 50 points)

1. F
2. T
3. T
4. F
5. T
6. T
7. T
8. T
9. T
10. F

Fill In the Blanks (5 x 5 = 25 points)

1. (a) a human being, (b) the Messiah, (c) the Son of God
2. (a) believe, (b) behave

Bonus Tabor

Chapter Twenty-two: Revelation

Matching (6 x 5 = 30 points)

1. f
2. d
3. e
4. c
5. b
6. a

True/False (11 x 5 = 55 points)

1. T
2. T
3. F
4. F
5. T
6. T
7. F
8. T
9. T
10. F
11. T

Fill In the Blanks (3 x 5 = 15 points)

1. persecuted Christians of first century
2. Christians of all times
3. Christians living when the world ends

Bonus Domitian